EDVANTAGE INTERACTIVE

UTS M4 Chemistry

Development Team

Authors

Cheri Smith
Yale Secondary
School District 34 Abbotsford

Gary Davidson
School District 22 Vernon

Megan Ryan
Walnut Grove Secondary
School District 35 Langley

Chris Toth
St. Thomas More Collegiate
Burnaby, British Columbia

Program Consultant
Lionel Sandner
Edvantage Interactive

Customization by
Sarah Cescon
UTS, Toronto

Jennifer Pitt-Lainsbury
UTS, Toronto

COPIES OF THIS BOOK MAY BE OBTAINED BY CONTACTING:

Edvantage Interactive

E-MAIL:
info@edvantageinteractive.com

TOLL-FREE FAX:
866.275.0564

TOLL-FREE CALL:
866.422.7310

EDVANTAGE
INTERACTIVE

ISBN 978-1-77249-174-6
UTS M4 Chemistry

Vice-President of Marketing: *Don Franklin*
Director of Publishing: *Yvonne Van Ruskenveld*
Design and Production: *Donna Lindenberg*
Proofreading: *Eva van Emden*
Editorial Assistance: *Rhys Sandner*
Index: *Noeline Bridge*
Photos: *p. 33, K. Jung; p. 34, Bureau international des poids et mesures (BIPM)*

QR Code — What Is This?
The image to the right is called a QR code. It's similar to bar codes on various products and contains information that can be useful to you. Each QR code in this book provides you with online support to help you learn the course material. For example, find a question with a QR code beside it. If you scan that code, you'll see the answer to the question explained in a video created by an author of this book.
You can scan a QR code using an Internet-enabled mobile device. The program to scan QR codes is free and available at your phone's app store. Scanning the QR code above will give you a short overview of how to use the codes in the book to help you study.
Note: We recommend that you scan QR codes only when your phone is connected to a WiFi network. Depending on your mobile data plan, charges may apply if you access the information over the cellular network. If you are not sure how to do this, please contact your phone provider or us at info@edvantageinteractive.com

Contents

UTS M4 Chemistry

EDVANTAGE INTERACTIVE

1 Skills and Processes of Chemistry

By the end of this chapter, you should be able to do the following:

- Demonstrate appropriate safety techniques and proper use of protective equipment
- Demonstrate skills in measuring and in recording data
- Communicate results and data in clear and understandable forms

---

By the end of this chapter, you should know the meaning of these **key terms**:

- accuracy
- analysis
- interpretation
- observation
- precision
- SI unit
- significant figures
- unit

In this chapter, you'll learn about the range of tools, skills, and techniques you'll be using as you study chemistry.

1.1 Staying Safe Around Matter

Warm Up

- Examine each of the following pairs of equipment.
- Consider how the structure of each piece relates to its function.
- Circle the better piece of equipment for each task.

(a) Boiling a solution

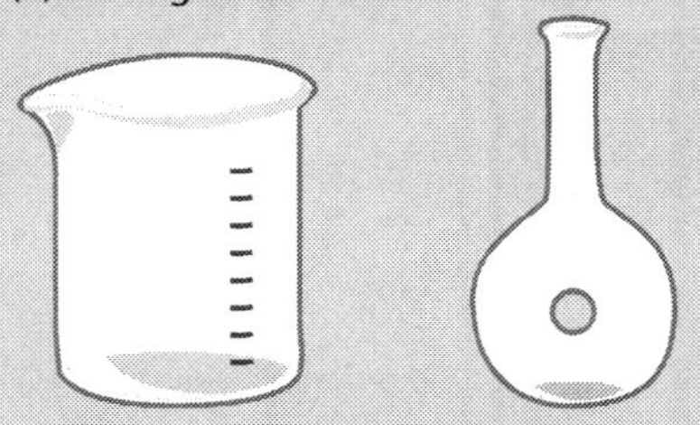

(b) Holding a hot test tube

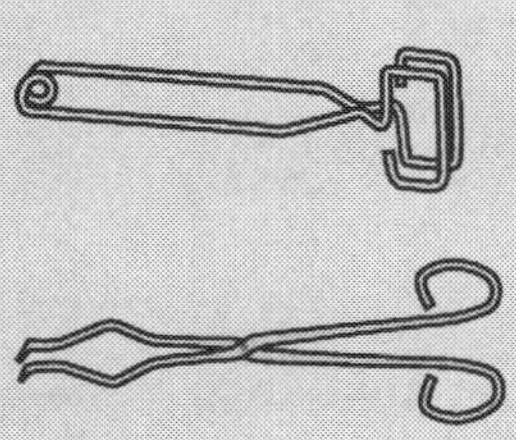

(c) Measuring a volume of liquid

(d) Evaporation over a hot flame

Chemistry Equipment and Its Uses

The equipment used for manipulating and measuring chemicals can be classified in a variety of ways. One of the most common methods of classification is based on the material it is made from. Table 1.1.1 and Table 1.1.2 divide equipment into glassware and hardware.

Most of the glassware found in the laboratory is made of a special type of glass with a low *coefficient of expansion*. This simply means the glass expands so slowly as it is heated that it is unlikely to break. Two common brand names for this type of glassware are Pyrex® and Kimax®. Some glassware is made of ceramic material. It may be heated to red-hot temperatures without breaking or melting. Hardware is made of various types of metal including wrought iron, stainless steel, aluminum, and brass.

Table 1.1.1 *Commonly Used Glassware in the Chemistry Lab*

Glassware	Name	Use
	beaker	Holding liquids • may be graduated (sometimes in two directions) • has a white spot for labeling • various sizes including 50, 150, 250, 450, 650, and 1000 mL
	Erlenmeyer flask	Holding liquids • shape avoids loss due to splashing • used for titration • common sizes include 125, 250, and 500 mL
	Florence flask	Heating liquids • shape allows even distribution of heat while boiling • never graduated • common sizes include 250 and 500 mL
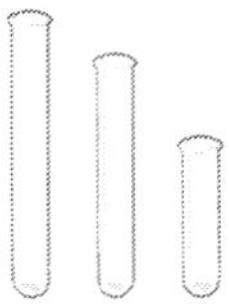	test tubes	Holding liquids or solids • can be heated directly or in a water bath • may be used to mix small quantities of chemicals • large variety of sizes
	fluted funnel	Funneling liquids • useful for pouring liquids through small openings • can contain filter paper for separating solids from suspensions by filtration
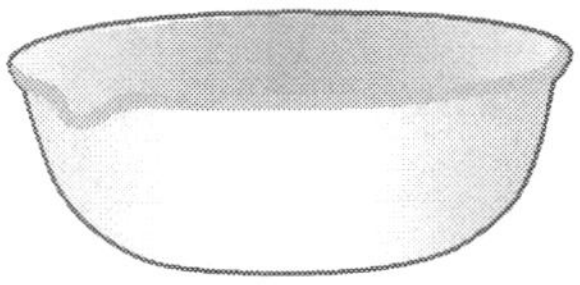	evaporating dish	Evaporating solvent • evaporation from a solution • can be used to dry a damp product • ceramic material allows direct heat to high temperatures
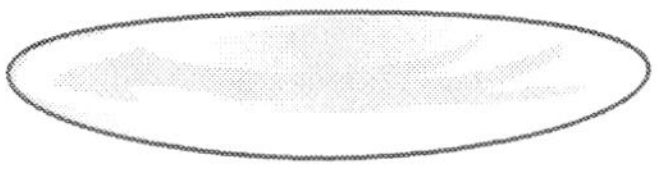	watch glass	Holding or covering • useful for holding a sample of chemical • may cover a beaker or flask to prevent evaporation • holds chemicals while drying
	crucible	Heating to high temperatures • heating covered or partially covered samples • ceramic material may be directly heated until red hot

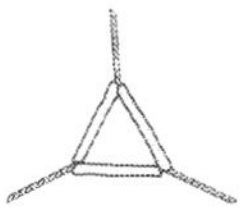	pipe stem triangle	Providing a base to hold a crucible • sits atop a wrought-iron ring • stems are made of ceramic material
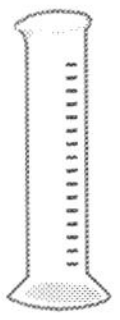	graduated cylinder	Measuring volumes of liquids • sizes vary • commonly 10, 25, 50, 100, and 250 mL
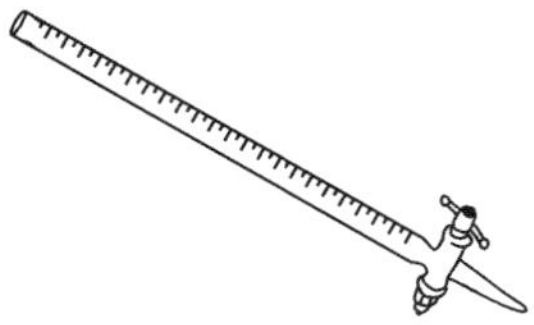	burette	Measuring volumes of liquids • delivers various volumes through a valve called a stop cock • more precise (exact) than the graduated cylinder
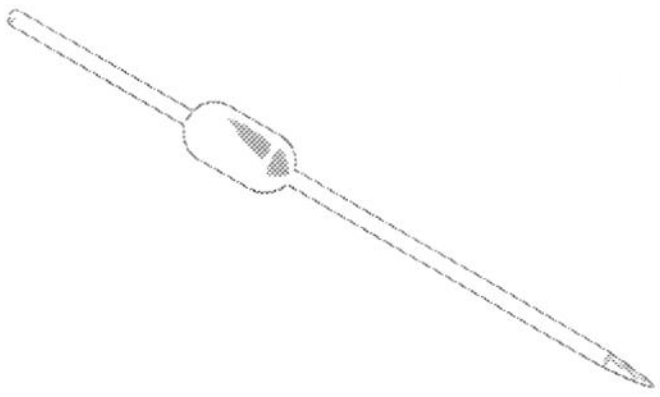	pipette	Measuring volumes of liquids • may be graduated • may be volumetric (designed to deliver one specific volume) • liquid is drawn up with a pipette bulb or suction device
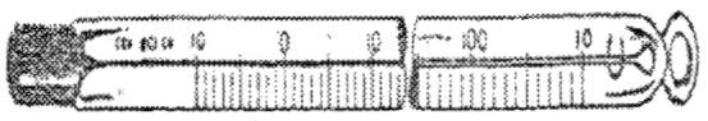	thermometer	Measuring temperatures • bulb should be submerged in the fluid being measured • temperature ranges vary • most contain dyed alcohol • more precise thermometers contain mercury • commonly measure temperature in degrees Celsius

Quick Check

Working with a partner, design a classification scheme and use it to put the glassware into groups according to common characteristics.

Compare your classification scheme with that of another pair of students.

Table 1.1.2 *Commonly Used Hardware in the Chemistry Lab*

Hardware	Name	Use
	ring stand	Providing a post to attach • ring clamps, burette clamps, extension clamps, etc. • also called a utility stand
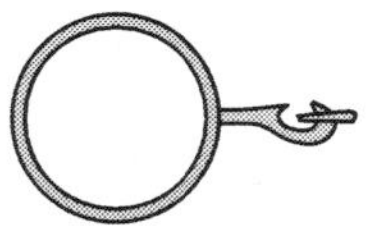	ring clamp	Attaching to a ring stand • supports a ceramic pad, a pipe stem triangle, or an evaporating dish • may surround a beaker as a safety ring
	burette clamp	Attaching to a ring stand • holds a burette • may hold a test tube in a stationary position • may support the neck of a flask
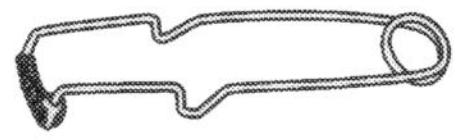	flint striker	Lighting a Bunsen burner • provides a spark by moving a flint across a file
	Bunsen burner	Providing heat • adjusts flame temperature by addition of air through the barrel • adjusts flame height by turning the regulator valve
	test tube holder	Holding hot test tubes • used for heating test tubes over flame • used for removing test tubes from water baths
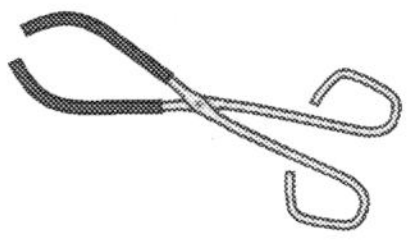	beaker tongs	Lifting hot beakers • rubber cover allows tongs to firmly grasp and move beakers of all sizes
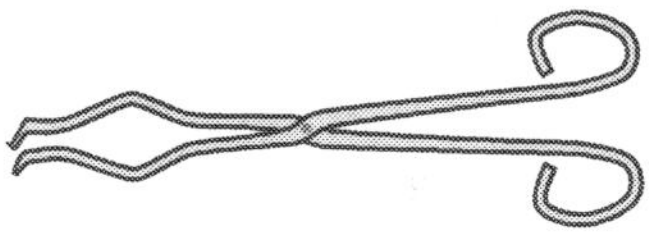	crucible tongs	Holding hot crucibles • may remove or adjust crucible lid • holds hot evaporating dishes • NOT designed for lifting beakers or test tubes
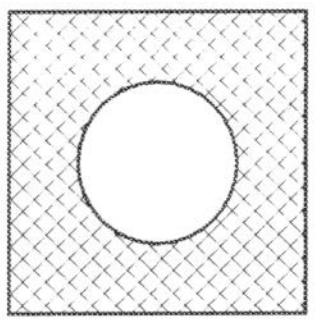	ceramic pad	Providing a base to hold glassware • sits atop a wrought-iron ring • provides a flat surface for beakers or flasks • sometimes called a wire gauze
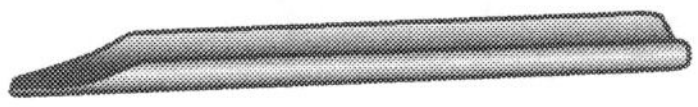	scoopula	Moving samples of solids • sometimes called a spatula • should NOT be used as a stirring rod (stirring rods should be glass)

Quick Check

Working with a partner, design a classification scheme and use it to put the hardware into groups according to common characteristics.

Compare your classification scheme with that of another pair of students.

Labelling Chemicals

Globally Harmonized System of Classification and Labelling of Chemicals

The **Globally Harmonized System of Classification and Labelling of Chemicals** (**GHS**) is the United Nations system for communicating information about the safety requirements for working with chemicals. The main components of GHS are:

- a labelling system consisting of eight specialized safety icons (see below)
- training programs for people who work with chemicals
- **Safety Data Sheets** (**SDS**) providing information about chemicals

oxidizers

flammable and combustible material

explosive material

acute toxicity

aquatic toxicity (non-mandatory)

corrosion

gas under pressure

carcinogen, toxic to humans

irritant or narcotic effects

People who work with chemicals are required to take GHS training with varying frequencies depending on their jobs. It is possible that you or some of your classmates may have taken GHS training for a part-time job. Your chemistry teacher has certainly had GHS training.

As a condition of sale, a Safety Data Sheet (SDS) must be provided with every chemical purchased. Your chemistry teacher has a binder full of these sheets containing hazard information and safety procedures associated with each and every chemical in your science stock rooms and elsewhere in the school.

Quick Check

An excerpt from an SDS for hydrochloric acid solution follows the questions below. This is only an excerpt. An actual SDS may contain more than 15 sections, each of which may be quite detailed. Read this abbreviated excerpt carefully and answer these questions.

1. What GHS labels would you expect to find on hydrochloric acid?

   ____

2. Give a synonym for hydrochloric acid.

   ____

3. What are the chemicals that make up hydrochloric acid?

   ____

4. What are the hazards of spilling hydrochloric acid on the skin?

   ____

5. How should you treat a person who has ingested hydrochloric acid?

   ____

SAFETY DATA SHEET

1. Product Identification
- Hydrochloric Acid
- Synonym: Muriatic Acid

2. Composition/Information on Ingredients
- Hydrogen Chloride 38% by weight
- Water 62% by weight

3. Hazards Identification
- Potential acute health effects
  - Skin Contact: Corrosive, irritant, permeation causing itching, reddening, scaling, or blistering
  - Eye Contact: Corrosive, irritant causing redness, watering, and itching
  - Inhalation: Irritation of respiratory tract, coughing, choking, or shortness of breath
- Potential chronic health effects
  - May be toxic to: kidneys, liver, mucous membranes, upper respiratory tract, skin, eyes, circulatory system, and teeth

4. First Aid Measures
- Eye contact: Remove contact lenses, rinse with cold water for 15 minutes, get medical attention immediately.
- Skin contact: Remove effected clothes, rinse with cold water for 15 minutes, get medical attention immediately.
- Inhalation: Remove to fresh air, if breathing is difficult; give oxygen, if not breathing; give artificial respiration.
- Ingestion: If swallowed, do not induce vomiting, loosen tight clothing, get medical attention immediately.

5. Handling and Storage
- Storage: Keep container tightly closed in a cool, well-ventilated area.

6. Stability and Reactivity Data
- Is highly reactive with metals.
- Reactive with oxidizing agents, organic materials, alkalis and water

Household Hazardous Products Labels

The Consumer Chemicals and Containers Regulations (CCCR) is another example of a labelling system that requires specific packaging and labelling of **household products**. There are only four different household labels. These labels may be bordered in two different ways. The border indicates whether the label refers to the *container* or the *contents* within the container. The octagonal border refers to the contents of the labelled container while the triangular border refers to the container itself. The latest household labels are as follows:

corrosive product

flammable product

poisonous product

explosive container

Quick Check

What household labels would you expect to find on a container of muriatic acid?

Safety in the Chemistry Lab

Safety Equipment

Every chemistry laboratory has a number of items "built in" to the facility for use in case of an accident or simply to ensure the safest laboratory operation possible. It is important to know the location and instructions for operation of each of these items. Table 1.1.3 summarizes important information on each of these important pieces of equipment.

If you think you might need to use any of the equipment in this table for an emergency, don't hesitate. Call out to inform others of the situation and immediately use the equipment as instructed. Note that any accident requiring the use of the eyewash station, safety shower, or fire blanket is likely serious enough that medical attention should be sought quickly after using the equipment.

Table 1.1.3 *Laboratory Safety Equipment*

Safety Equipment	Information Regarding Operation
Fume hood	• Enclosed area equipped with fans to draw vapors out of the hood and vent them outside • May contain gas jets, sinks, lights, and electrical outlet • Enclosed by a sliding safety glass window • May store chemicals emitting toxic fumes • Useful for venting odors, smoke, and toxic fumes
Eyewash station	• If a chemical is splashed or spilled into the eyes, they should be held open and rinsed continuously for 10 to 15 min. Contact lenses should be removed. • Eyewash stations may be operated by pushing on a hand bar and/or a foot pedal. • Some labs may use a squeeze bottle apparatus or a piece of rubber tubing attached to a sink.
Safety shower	• Spills over a large portion of the body require removal of clothing and washing of the entire region for 10 to 15 min under the safety shower. • Safety showers are operated by pulling on a ring that will begin the flow of some 200 L of water over a drained area of the lab.

Fire extinguisher	• Small fires such as those that occur in a beaker or a crucible usually may be smothered by placing a ceramic pad or cover on top.
	• If a larger fire occurs, pull the safety pin from the top of the extinguisher, point the hose at the base of the fire, and squeeze. Extinguishers operate by depriving the fire of oxygen and by lowering the temperature.
	  • There are five classes of fires:
	  • Type A: wood or paper
	  • Type B: oil or grease (most chemicals)
	  • Type C: electrical equipment
	  • Type D: metals (such as magnesium)
	  • Type E: radioactive materials
	• Most extinguishers contain carbon dioxide and are good for class A, B, and C fires.

Fire blanket	• A fire extinguisher should *never* be used on a person. • *STOP, DROP, and ROLL* is the best way to extinguish a fire involving a person. A fire blanket may be used in combination with this process to smother the fire. • Fire blankets may be enclosed in a box or a cylindrical container attached to a wall, or they may be upright. An upright blanket may be wrapped around the victim while he or she is standing.
Emergency gas shut off	• The emergency gas shut off valve allows *all* gas outlets in the laboratory to be shut off at once. • To use the shut off, turn a handle so it is perpendicular to the gas line or simply push a large red button. • At the end of the day, this valve should always be left in the off position.
Spill control station	• Spill control stations contain absorbent pillows to soak up spills, safety goggles and gloves, and chemicals to neutralize acid and base spills. • Some labs simply have the neutralizing chemicals stored in a dedicated area. • Acid spills should be neutralized with sodium bicarbonate or baking soda. • Base spills should be neutralized with acetic acid or vinegar. • Neutralization is only necessary for large spills of concentrated reagents. Smaller spills may simply be diluted with water and wiped up with paper towel.

First aid kit	• All labs should have access to a first aid kit. The kit may be stored in a common storage area adjacent to the lab so that all teachers have easy access. • Such a kit should contain an antibiotic cream or ointment and plenty of bandages. • Burns are the most common injury in the chemistry lab. While ice followed by cold water is generally enough, the kit may contain a topical anesthetic cream. It is critical to ensure a student has no anesthetic allergies before using such a product. • Avoid burns from hot glass or metal by bringing your hand near the object first to test for heat. • Small cuts closely follow burns on the list of chemistry lab injuries. These may be treated with the antibiotic cream and a bandage.
Glass disposal container	• Broken glass should never be placed in the garbage can as this presents a hazard to the custodian. • A plastic bucket or a specially designated recyclables box can be found on a counter or the floor for the disposal of broken glassware or glass tubing.
Chemical disposal	• Containers clearly marked "Chemical Disposal" should be used for disposing solutions or precipitates containing heavy metals or any other toxic chemicals. • Some organic waste may release toxic fumes. Such waste often warrants its own container, which may be covered and/or placed in the fume hood. • Some chemicals such as dilute solutions of acids and bases and non-toxic salts may be flushed down the sink with plenty of water. • The ultimate judge of correct chemical disposal is, of course, your lab instructor.
Fire alarm	• Though it may be in the hall outside of your lab, you must know where the fire alarm is located.

Quick Check

1. How would you deal with each of the following accidents should it occur during a lab you are performing this year?

   (a) While heating a small amount of alcohol in a beaker, it bursts into flame.

   (b) Your partner hands you a piece of hot glass they've just bent after heating over a Bunsen burner.

   (c) A test tube full of concentrated hydrochloric acid is dropped and broken on the floor.

2. How could you have prevented each accident from happening to begin with?

Safety Procedures

Any time you know you will be working in the laboratory, it is important to arrive fully prepared to perform all work as safely as possible. We call this *lab preparedness*. The following are some things you should always do *before* you begin doing a lab.

- Read the entire experiment carefully, paying close attention to any safety issues. Prepare any data tables that may be required. Your teacher may ask you to prepare an abstract (summary) or a flow chart before you arrive for lab.
- Clear all binders, backpacks, book bags, coats, etc. away from your work area.
- Always wear eye protection during the laboratory period.
- Wear lab aprons or lab coats if available.
- Tie back long hair to keep it away from flames or chemicals.
- Secure loose sleeves or jewellery to keep them away from flames or chemicals.
- Consider wearing clothing made of natural fibres such as cotton and wool, as those are the most fire resistant fibres.
- Do not wear open-toed shoes during laboratory work.
- Be sure all equipment is in good working order. Do not use chipped glassware or damaged electrical equipment.
- Never attempt laboratory procedures without your instructor's permission and direct instruction.

Laboratory Technique

There are several things that all good chemists know about using equipment and chemicals in the lab. We refer to these things as *proper laboratory technique*.

- Always approach lab work with a business-like attitude and keep voices kept to a reasonable volume.
- Do not consume food or drink or chew gum during laboratory period.
- Never touch or taste chemicals.
- Never inhale chemicals directly. Use your hand to sweep odors toward you.
- Bring your hand near metal or glass to test for heat. Handle hot equipment with appropriate tongs, test tube holders, or mitts.
- Never use open flames around flammable materials. Use a hot plate or mantle.
- Clamp test tubes near the top and hold at a 45° angle with constant motion and the end pointed away from everyone during heating.
- Never pipette liquids directly by mouth.
- Never leave heat sources unattended. Turn off Bunsen burners and hot plates when not in use.
- Read the labels on all chemicals at least twice. Always grasp bottles on the label side so that drips do not obscure the label.
- Always use an appropriate lubricant such as glycerin or saliva when inserting glass tubing or thermometers into rubber stoppers.
- When diluting chemicals, always begin with water. It is particularly important to add acid to water, never the other way around.

Laboratory Clean Up

Last, but not least, there are a number of things that relate to **laboratory clean up**. Some of these things may be related to accidents that occur in the lab. Others simply relate to leaving the lab in as good, or better, condition than you found it.

- Sweep broken glassware into a dustpan and place it in the proper disposal container. Always notify neighbors of any broken glass.
- Clean up spilled chemicals immediately as outlined in Table 1.1.3. Be sure to notify neighbors of any chemical spill.
- Never return unused chemical to the original stock bottle. Either share it with another student or properly dispose of any excess.
- Always wash glassware well with soap and a proper brush, then rinse it, and leave it to air dry.
- Rinse your hands well following the use of any chemicals. Wipe your lab bench with a damp paper towel when you have completed your lab.
- Clean up should begin with a reasonable amount of time to allow all equipment to be washed well and replaced in the appropriate spot.
- For experiments that run for more than one period, clearly label all materials and leave them in the appropriate place as instructed by your teacher.

1.1 Activity: Safety in the Laboratory

Question

Where is the safety equipment located in your chemistry laboratory?

Procedure

1. In the space below, draw an outline map of your chemistry laboratory, including every item in Table 1.1.3.

2. Add at least five more items that contribute to safety in your lab.

1.1 Review Questions

1. Where is the closest fire alarm to your chemistry laboratory?

2. Outline the route you should follow in case of a fire alarm while you are in chemistry class.

3. How many fire extinguishers are in your laboratory? What are their classifications?

4. Knowing you have lab on a particular school day, describe how you should dress.

5. Give the *name* and *use* of each of the following pieces of equipment:

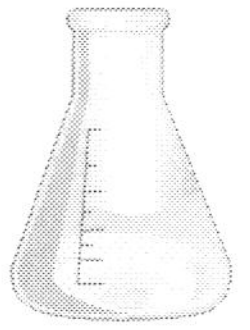

6. List three things you should do before beginning any chemistry experiment.

7. Give three uses for the fume hood.

8. What is the most common injury in the chemistry lab? How might you avoid this injury? How would you treat this injury?

9. How would you assist your lab partner in each of the following cases?
   (a) Partner has spilled a chemical into his or her eyes.

   (b) Partner's clothing has caught fire.

   (c) Partner has spilled concentrated acid onto the floor.

   (d) Partner took more chemical than required for the lab.

   (e) Partner has broken a test tube on the floor.

10. What is the meaning of each of the following labels?

11. Outline a three-step procedure for cleaning glassware at the end of the period.

12. Why should long hair always be secured back during lab?

13. Why do you suppose food and drink are not allowed during lab?

14. What do you think is safer: the laboratory or your kitchen? Explain why.

15. Give the name and use of each of the following pieces of equipment:

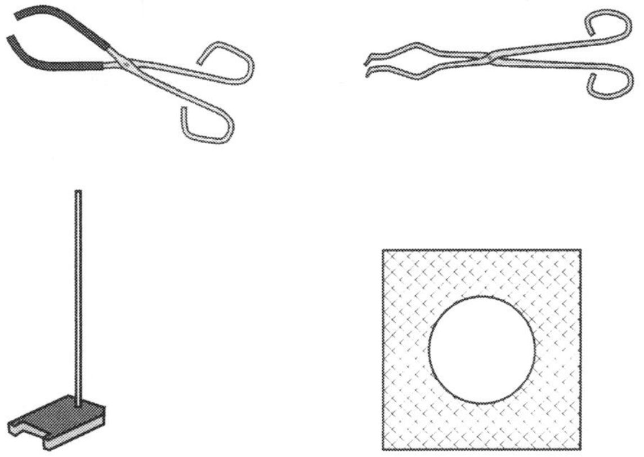

16. Where should binders, book bags, and backpacks be stored during the lab?

17. What is an SDS? Where might an SDS be found in your school?

18. Where would you dispose of each of the following?
(a) a few milliliters of excess dilute acid

(b) a sample of heavy metal precipitate

(c) an excess piece of glass tubing

(d) used litmus paper

(e) a few milliliters of excess acetone (nail polish remover)

19. Give four things to keep in mind while heating a test tube half-filled with liquid.

1.2 Laboratory and Reporting Skills

Warm Up

Classify the following observations as *quantitative* or *qualitative* by placing a checkmark in the correct column. Hint: Look at each syllable of those words: *quantitative* and *qualitative*. What do they seem to mean?

Observation	Quantitative	Qualitative
The melting point of paradichlorobenzene is 53.5°C.		
Mercury(II) oxide is a deep red powder.		
The density of scandium metal is 2.989 g/cm^3.		
Copper metal may be pulled into a wire. (It is ductile.)		
Silver metal forms a black layer of tarnish over time.		
Zinc has a specific heat capacity of 388 J/(kg·K).		
Oxygen gas supports combustion.		

The Scientific Method

How do you approach the problems you encounter in everyday life? Think about beginning a new class at the start of the school year, for example. The first few days you make observations and collect data. You might not think of it this way, but in fact, when you observe your classmates, the classroom and your instructor, you actually are making observations and collecting data. This process will inevitably lead you to make some decisions as you consider the best way to interact with this new environment. Who would you like for a partner in this class? Where do you want to sit? Are you likely to interact well with this particular teacher? You are drawing conclusions. This tried and true method of solving problems is called the **scientific method**.

Figure 1.2.1 *Robert Boyle*

Robert Boyle pioneered the use of the scientific method (Figure 1.2.1). He was born into a wealthy family in Ireland in 1627. He attended Eton College of England where he performed controlled experiments. He recorded his work with detailed explanations of the procedure and apparatus used and carefully wrote out tabular records of his observations. His records allowed him to repeat his experiments to test the theories he developed using his scientific method. In addition to receiving credit for pioneering the scientific method, Boyle is remembered for publishing a book called the *Sceptical Chymist*. The book put forth a new definition of the term, *element* and challenged the theories of alchemists such as Aristotle and Paracelsus.

Different groups of scientists outline the parts of the scientific method in different ways. Here is one example, illustrating its steps.

Steps of the Scientific Method

1. **Observation**: Involves collecting data. **Quantitative** has numbers or quantities associated with it. **Qualitative** data describes qualities or changes in the quality of matter including a substance's color, odor, or physical state. Observations may also be categorized as **physical**, related to the color, the temperature at which the substance changes state or the density. Or they may be **chemical**, related to the substance's chemical reactivity or its behavior during a chemical change.
2. **Statement of a hypothesis**: The formulation of a statement in an "if…then…" format that explains the observations.
3. **Experimentation**: After making a set of observations and formulating a hypothesis, scientists devise an experiment to determine whether the hypothesis accurately explains the observations. Depending on the results, the hypothesis may be adjusted and experiments repeated collecting new observations a multitude of times.
   Frequently the results of an experiment differ from what was expected. There are a variety of reasons this might happen. Things that contribute to such differences are called **sources of error**. Sources of error are different from mistakes. Rather, they are things we have *no control over*.
4. **Statement of a Theory**: Once enough information has been collected from a series of experiments, a coherent set of explanations called a theory may be deduced. This theory may lead to a **model** that helps us explain a collection of observations. (Sometimes the scientific method leads to a **law**, which is a general statement of *fact*, without an accompanied set of explanations.)

Quick Check

1. What is the difference between a law and a theory?

   ____

2. What are the fundamental steps of the scientific method?

   ____

   ____

   ____

   ____

3. Place a checkmark in the appropriate column to indicate whether each of the reasons for determining an incorrect mass is a mistake or a source of error.

Event	Mistake	Source of Error
The balance used to weigh the product was not zeroed.		
The product being weighed was damp.		
The balance used to weigh the product only reads to the nearest centigram.		
Your partner read the value for a mass incorrectly.		
You made a subtraction error when determining the mass.		

The Bunsen Burner

Introduction

Robert W. Bunsen was a German chemist who, with physicist Gustav Robert Kirchhoff, invented the spectroscope and discovered spectrum analysis. Their work with spectra led to the joint discovery of the elements cesium and rubidium, as atoms of these elements emit characteristic wavelengths of light when heated. Bunsen also popularized the device that is named after him, although credit for its design should go to the British chemist and physicist Michael Faraday.

The gas supply used is a mixture, but the primary component is methane, CH_4. The model of Bunsen burner used in high school chemistry labs is called a pre-mix burner as the methane and oxygen are mixed in the barrel of the Bunsen burner before combustion takes place.

Last year, you learned about 2 different types of combustion: complete combustion and incomplete combustion. In this lab you will be asked to differentiate between the two. When the methane in the Bunsen burner is undergoing complete combustion, the hottest part of the flame is the top of the inner cone. Whenever you are told to strongly heat a chemical you should always place it in the hottest part of the flame.

Prelab

For future labs, you will be required to complete a prelab before the actual lab day. For the purpose of quality control, we will be doing this prelab together in class. However, you should read through this lab before coming to class on Monday or Tuesday. The prelab work that we will do:

Prepare lab book (title, intro, purpose, materials and procedure reference)
Creation of a flow chart
Looking at Analysis Questions to determine if any can be answered ahead of time

Purpose

In this activity, you will learn how to properly operate a Bunsen burner and discover some of the properties of the flame produced.

Materials

- Bunsen burner with tubing
- Beaker with water
- Ring clamp
- Wire gauze
- Beaker Tongs
- Spark igniter
- Retort stand
- Copper wire

Safety

* Flames and hot objects can cause fires and burn. Keep flammable materials away from a Bunsen burner
* Make sure long hair and loose clothing is tucked in
* Know the location of the fire extinguisher and fire blanket, and how to use both of these safety devices.

Procedure

1. Connect your Bunsen burner to the gas outlet.
2. Close the air supply by turning the barrel of the Bunsen burner down.
3. Practice using the spark igniter. Make sure you can get a visible spark with the lighter. If your flint appears to be worn, inform your teacher. All lab partners must demonstrate that they can use the lighter.
4. Turn the gas control valve so it is just open. Do not turn the valve all of the way as this will allow too much gas to enter the barrel and a large flame will result. If a large flame

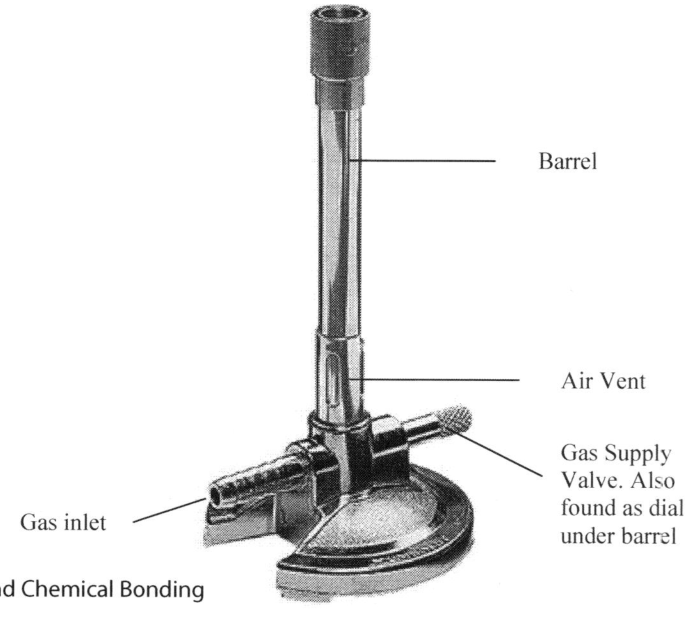

is produced, control its height with the gas control valve, and not the bench gas supply.

5. Turn on the gas supply at your bench. Ignite the gas as soon as possible. If you cannot light the gas within 10 seconds turn off the gas. Ensure that you are actually able to get a visible spark with the igniter then turn on the gas and try again. All lab partners must successfully demonstrate lighting the Bunsen burner.
6. Sketch and describe the appearance of the flame with the air supply closed.
7. Turn off the gas. Set up the apparatus as shown using a ring clamp, a wire heating pad and a 250 mL beaker containing 150 mL of water. For safety, make sure the ring clamp is no more than 4 cm above the top of the Bunsen Burner. Make sure the Bunsen Burner is off to the side when you light it. Never light the Bunsen burner while it is under the heating pad. Heat the beaker containing water over a flame with a closed air supply for about 2 minutes.
8. Turn off the gas. After a suitable cooling period, lift the beaker off of the heating pad using beaker tongs and place the beaker on your heating pad. Describe the appearance of the wire heating pad. Rinse the pad with water.

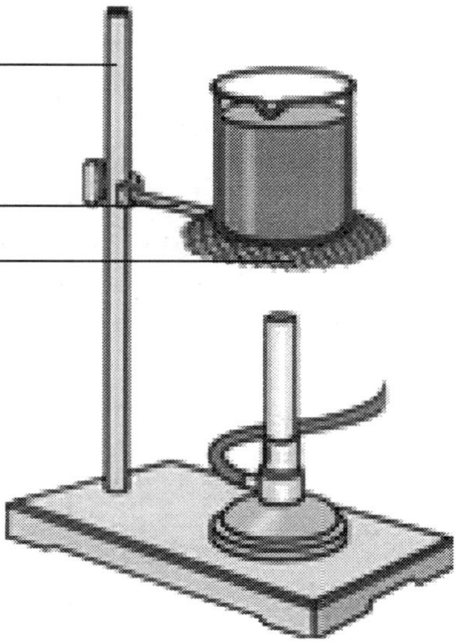

9. Remove the ring clamp and heating pad and pour the water down the sink.
10. Relight the Bunsen burner. Open the air inlet until you can clearly see an inner and an outer flame. Observe the colour and appearance of the flame. If the flame separates from the top of the barrel, decrease the air supply immediately. With too much air, the gas can burn inside of the barrel and the flame will disappear but you will hear a roaring sound. This is known as **flashback**; if it happens, turn off the Bunsen burner immediately. Handle the barrel carefully as it will be hot. Relight the burner after closing the air supply; open the air supply until you have an inner and outer flame visible again.
11. Cover the air vents with your fingers. Describe what happens.
12. Obtain a piece of copper wire. Using a pair of crucible tongs, hold the piece of wire at one end and place the other in the hottest part of the Bunsen burner flame. Record your observations

Analysis Questions

1. Write the balanced chemical reaction for the complete combustion of methane.
2. If complete combustion were to occur in the Bunsen burner, what type of observations would you expect to make as the flame heated the glassware? Explain your answer.
3. There are several possible equations of the incomplete combustion of methane. Provide one plausible chemical equation for the incomplete combustion of methane.
4. If incomplete combustion were to occur in the Bunsen burner, what type of observations would you expect to make as the flame heated the glassware (hint: look at your products for the incomplete combustion reaction)? Explain your answer.
5. Which type of combustion do you think is preferred when heating during chemical reactions? Why?
6. Sketch the Bunsen burner flame when the air vents are open and indicate the hottest point of the flame (you may need to do some research to figure this out).

Conclusion

Lab Performance

1.2 Review Questions

1. Complete the following table for the listed observations by checking the appropriate columns.

Property Observed	Qualitative	Quantitative
Freezes at 52.0°C		
Dissolves in ethylene glycol		
Fractures into cubic crystals		
5.4 mol dissolve in each liter		

2. Complete the following table for the listed observations by checking the appropriate columns.

Property Observed	Qualitative	Quantitative
Attracts to a magnet		
Changes to $Br_2(l)$ at –7.2°C		
Has a density of 4.71 g/mL		
Is a bright orange solid crystal		

1.3 The Periodic Table

Warm Up

1. Can you suggest the meaning of the word "periodic" in the term "periodic table"?
2. On what basis are the elements arranged in the modern periodic table?
3. What is true about chemical elements that appear in the same vertical column in the table?

Discovering an Elemental Order

Science in general and chemistry in particular exist because our human species has always had an insatiable desire to make sense of the world around us. We have relentlessly sought to explain nature's phenomena, to solve her mysteries, and to discover her order and logic by deciphering the events and objects we encounter.

One of the most important and successful examples of such efforts is the development of the periodic table of the elements. This single document is arguably more valuable to chemists, and perhaps even society itself, than any piece of equipment, wonder drug, or process ever invented.

The periodic table had its beginnings in the early part of the 1800s. By 1817, 52 elements had been discovered. Although some had been known since ancient times, many new elements were being discovered using the energy available from the electric battery invented by Volta in 1800. Researchers saw the need to organize those elements and the enormous amount of information gathered about them into some kind of meaningful form. German scientist Johann Dobereiner noticed similarities within several groups of three elements such as chlorine, bromine, and iodine, which he called "triads." These similarities gave chemists some evidence that an organizational scheme was at least possible.

In 1857, English chemist William Odling proposed that the elements could be divided into groups based on their chemical and physical properties. Many of those groups actually resemble the vertical columns in the periodic table today.

In 1862, French geologist Alexandre-Emile de Chancourtois arranged the elements by increasing atomic mass. He noted that elements with similar properties seemed to occur at regular intervals. He devised a spiral graph with the elements arranged onto a cylinder such that similar elements lined up vertically. When his paper was published, however, it was largely ignored by chemists. Unfortunately, de Chancourtois had left out the graph, which made the paper hard to understand. As well, he had written the paper from a geologist's rather than from a chemist's perspective.

In 1864, English chemist John Newlands noticed that similar properties seemed to repeat every eighth element in much the same way that the notes of a musical scale repeat every eighth tone. Newlands called this the "law of octaves" and it resulted in several similar elements being grouped together, but with limited success.

The Periodic Law

The most successful organization of the elements was arrived at independently and almost at the same time by the German chemist Julius Lothar Meyer and the Russian chemist Dmitri Ivanovich Mendeleev. The chemical community, however, ultimately awarded Mendeleev the majority of the credit.

In a paper submitted to the Russian Chemical Society in March 1869, Mendeleev arranged the elements into a **periodic table** and proposed the **periodic law**, which can be stated as follows:

If elements are arranged in order of increasing atomic mass, a pattern can be seen in which similar properties recur on a regular or *periodic* basis.

Notice that this is called a "law" rather than a "theory." Theories attempt to explain *why* relationships or phenomena exist, whereas laws simply identify *that* they exist. We will see if we can supply the "why" by the end of this section.

Dmitri Mendeleev received most of the credit for several reasons. First, Mendeleev's work was published a year before Meyer's. Second, Mendeleev chose to concentrate on the chemical properties of the elements, while Meyer focused mainly on physical properties. Third, and most importantly, Mendeleev chose to leave several blank spaces in his table where he predicted as-yet-undiscovered elements with specific properties would eventually be placed. Because he had arranged similar elements vertically in his table, the location of those blank spaces effectively identified the properties that those elements would have upon being discovered. When the elements were eventually discovered, the predictions turned out to be extremely accurate.

A version of Mendeleev's table, published in 1872 and showing 65 elements is shown in Table 1.1.1.

Reiben	Gruppo I. — R^2O	Gruppo II. — RO	Gruppo III. — R^2O^3	Gruppo IV. RH^4 RO^2	Gruppo V. RH^3 R^2O^3	Gruppo VI. RH^3 RO^3	Gruppo VII. RH R^2O^7	Gruppo VIII. — RO^4
1	H = 1							
2	Li = 7	Be = 9,4	B = 11	C = 12	N = 14	O = 16	F = 19	
3	Na = 23	Mg = 24	Al = 27,8	Si = 28	P = 31	S = 32	Cl = 35,5	
4	K = 39	Ca = 40	— = 44	Ti = 48	V = 51	Cr = 52	Mn = 55	Fo = 56, Co=59, Ni = 59, Cu=63.
5	(Cu = 63)	Zn = 65	— = 68	— = 72	As = 75	So = 78	Br = 80	
6	Rb = 86	Sr = 87	?Yt = 88	Zr = 90	Nb = 94	Mo = 96	— = 100	Ru = 104, Rh=104, Pd = 106, Ag=108.
7	(Au = 199)	Cd = 112	In = 113	Sn = 118	Sb = 122	To = 125	J = 127	
8	Cs = 133	Bs = 137	?Di = 138	?Ce = 140	—	—	—	— — — —
9	(—)	—	—	—	—	—	—	
10	—	—	?Er = 178	?La = 180	Ta = 182	W = 184	—	Os = 195, Ir=197, Pt = 198, Au=199.
11	(Ag = 108)	Hg = 200	Tl = 204	Pb = 207	Bi = 208	—	—	
12	—	—	—	Th = 231	—	U = 240	—	— — — —

Figure 1.3.1 *The blank spaces marked with lines for elements with atomic masses 44, 68, 72, and 100 represent Mendeleev's belief that those elements would eventually be discovered and fit in the spaces. The symbols at the top of the columns (e.g., R^2O and RH^2) are molecular formulas written in the style of the 1800s. The letter "R" represents any element in the family and the formulas represent the probable hydrogen and oxygen compounds.*

An example of the accuracy of one of Mendeleev's predictions (and thus support for his periodic table) can be seen in Table 1.3.1. The table displays the properties predicted in 1871 for the element with atomic mass 72, compared to the actual properties for that element, called germanium, which was discovered in 1886.

Table 1.3.1 *Predicted and Observed Properties of Germanium*

Properties of Germanium	Predicted Properties in 1871	Observed Properties in 1886
Atomic mass	72	72.3
Density	5.5 g/cm^3	5.47 g/cm^3
Melting point	very high	960ºC
Specific heat	0.31 J/g ºC	0.31 J/g ºC
Oxide formula	RO_2	GeO_2
Oxide density	4.7 g/cm^3	4.70 g/cm^3
Chloride formula	RCl_4	$GeCl_4$

Using the oxide formulas that he had proposed as a guide, Mendeleev also corrected the atomic masses of the elements beryllium, indium, and uranium.

Because of its obvious usefulness, Mendeleev's periodic table gained widespread acceptance among chemists. We should remember that the periodic table was constructed prior to any discoveries about the inner structure of the atom. The similarities of various elements were eventually explained based on the quantum mechanical description of their electron arrangements, but the table identified those regularities more than 50 years before they were understood!

Quick Check

1. Who was the first person to arrange the chemical elements into groups?

 ____

2. How did Newland's analogy to music apply to elemental properties?

 ____

3. How did blank spaces in Mendeleev's periodic table help it eventually gain acceptance?

 ____

 ____

The Modern Periodic Table — By the Numbers

Since its creation, the periodic table has undergone several changes. Many new elements have been discovered or synthesized since 1872, but the most significant modification occurred in 1913. Data gathered by the young British chemist Henry Moseley, combined with the discovery of isotopes, resulted in the elements of the periodic table being re-ordered according to their *atomic numbers* rather than their atomic masses.

If elements are arranged in order of increasing atomic number, a pattern can be seen in which similar properties recur on a regular or periodic basis.

The Modern Periodic Table

With the inclusion of element 117 in April 2010, the periodic table includes 118 elements, 92 of which occur naturally. Each element is assigned its own box in the table containing that element's one- or two-letter symbol, atomic number and sometimes, but not always, atomic mass. The boxes are arranged in order of increasing atomic number beginning at the top left with hydrogen and proceeding horizontally left-to-right. Because elements 113 to 118 have not yet been assigned permanent names, their temporary names simply reflect their atomic numbers. Figure 1.3.2 shows a simplified periodic table.

The horizontal rows in the periodic table are called **periods** and these are numbered beginning at the top from 1 down to 7. Each vertical column is called a **family** or **group** and these are labeled using one of two schemes. Many chemists prefer an older system, which assigns each column a number from 1 to 8 combined with either the letter A or B.

A newer system adopted by the international governing body of chemistry called IUPAC (International Union of Pure and Applied Chemistry) simply numbers each group from 1 through 18 and uses no letters. For ease of reference, we will use the IUPAC numbering system.

Because each element is a member of both a horizontal period and a vertical group, its position on the table can be specified in much the same way as a geographic location on a map can be identified using lines of longitude and latitude.

The two most important things to know about the periodic table are:

1. Elements in the same chemical family have similar chemical properties because they have similar outer electron configurations. (This is among the most important of all chemical concepts.)
2. As we move down a chemical family or across a period, there are regular changes in these properties called periodic trends.

Groups 1 and 2 on the left, and 13 through 18 on the right contain the **representative** or **main group elements**. Groups 3 through 12 are the **transition elements.** Within the transition elements are two horizontal series collectively called the **inner transition elements.** The first series, known as the **lanthanides**, fits between elements 56 and 72 in the 6th period and the second series, called the **actinides**, fits between elements 88 and 104 in the 7th period.

Representative Elements (Groups 1–2) | Transition Elements (Groups 3–12) | Representative Elements (Groups 13–18)

Group → / Period ↓	1	2	3	4	5	6	7	8	9	10	11	12	13	14	15	16	17	18
1	1 H																	2 He
2	3 Li	4 Be											5 B	6 C	7 N	8 O	9 F	10 Ne
3	11 Na	12 Mg											13 Al	14 Si	15 P	16 S	17 Cl	18 Ar
4	19 K	20 Ca	21 Sc	22 Ti	23 V	24 Cr	25 Mn	26 Fe	27 Co	28 Ni	29 Cu	30 Zn	31 Ga	32 Ge	33 As	34 Se	35 Br	36 Kr
5	37 Rb	38 Sr	39 Y	40 Zr	41 Nb	42 Mo	43 Tc	44 Ru	45 Rh	46 Pd	47 Ag	48 Cd	49 In	50 Sn	51 Sb	52 Te	53 I	54 Xe
6	55 Cs	56 Ba		72 Hf	73 Ta	74 W	75 Re	76 Os	77 Ir	78 Pt	79 Au	80 Hg	81 Tl	82 Pb	83 Bi	84 Po	85 At	86 Rn
7	87 Fr	88 Ra		104 Rf	105 Db	106 Sg	107 Bh	108 Hs	109 Mt	110 Ds	111 Rg	112 Cn	113 Uut	114 Uuq	115 Uup	116 Uuh	117 Uus	118 Uuo

Lanthanides	57 La	58 Ce	59 Pr	60 Nd	61 Pm	62 Sm	63 Eu	64 Gd	65 Tb	66 Dy	67 Ho	68 Er	69 Tm	70 Yb	71 Lu
Actinides	89 Ac	90 Th	91 Pa	92 U	93 Np	94 Pu	95 Am	96 Cm	97 Bk	98 Cf	99 Es	100 Fm	101 Md	102 No	103 Lr

Inner Transition Elements

Figure 1.3.2 *This periodic table shows only the element's symbols and their atomic numbers.*

Consider the periodic table in Figure 1.3.2. The first distinction among the elements relating to their properties that we will discuss is their classification as metals, non-metals, or metalloids. The "staircase" line descending from group 13 down to group 16 separates metals on the left side from non-metals on the right.

About three-quarters of the elements are metals, including some main group elements and all of the transition and inner transition elements. Properties of **metals** include:

- solids at room temperature, except for mercury, which is a liquid
- generally shiny or lustrous when freshly cut or polished
- good conductors of heat and electricity
- generally malleable, which means they can be rolled or hammered into thin sheets
- generally ductile, which means they can be rolled or stretched into wires
- generally flexible as thin sheets or wires
- during chemical changes, tending to give up electrons relatively easily to form cations

The **non-metals** are located in the upper right portion of the table. Properties of non-metals include:

- usually gases or brittle solids at room temperature, except for liquid bromine
- solid non-metals ranging in appearance from dull or lustrous and translucent to opaque
- poor conductors of heat and electricity
- during chemical changes, tending to gain electrons from metals to form anions or share electrons with other non-metals.

Along the staircase line are several **metalloids** (also called **semi-metals**), including the elements boron, silicon, germanium, arsenic, antimony, tellurium, and polonium. These solid elements are semiconductors, which mean they are poor electrical conductors at room temperature, but become better conductors at higher temperatures. This is opposite to how metal conductivity varies with temperature. Metals become less conductive as temperature increases.

As we move right-to-left across a period and down a chemical family, the elements become more metallic. These changes involve both physical and chemical properties, and those and other trends will be discussed in the next section.

Quick Check

1. Fill in the missing spaces in the table below:

Element Name	Element Symbol	Group Number	Period Number	Metal/Non-metal/ metalloid
	Si			
osmium				
		6	4	
	Mt			
antimony				metalloid
		17	5	

2. (a) Rearrange the following alphabetical list in order of least metallic to most metallic.
aluminum, cesium, chromium, fluorine, gallium, oxygen, sulfur, zirconium

____

(b) Based on your answer to (a) above, which of the eight elements would you expect to have the:

- greatest tendency to gain an electron? ____________________
- greatest tendency to lose an electron? ____________________

A Closer Look at the Periodic Table

It is the number and type of outermost electrons that are primarily responsible for an atom's chemistry. The members of a chemical family have similar numbers and types of outermost electrons. The outermost electrons that participate in chemical bonding are known as **valence electrons**. We will be discussing chemical bonding in more detail in a later section. For now, this section will introduce some families in the periodic table and the corresponding electron arrangements that will influence the bonding behavior of their elements.

Group 1 — The Alkali Metals

Table 1.3.2 *Alkali Metal Electron Configurations*

Alkali Metal	Core Notation Configuration
Li	[He] 2**s**^{1}
Na	[Ne] 3**s**^{1}
K	[Ar] 4**s**^{1}
Rb	[Kr] 5**s**^{1}
Cs	[Xe] 6**s**^{1}
Fr	[Rn] 7**s**^{1}

Alkali metals are located on the far left side of the periodic table. This group includes lithium, sodium, potassium, rubidium, cesium, and the rare and radioactive francium. Alkali metals are all soft, silvery solids and the most reactive of all metals. The name of the group is based on the fact that the oxide compounds of the alkali metals dissolve in water to produce strongly basic solutions. They all corrode rapidly in air to a dull gray appearance, react vigorously with water to produce hydrogen gas, and readily form compounds with non-metals.

Alkali metal atoms have one valence electron in the s sublevel with the general electron configuration [noble gas]ns^1 where "*n*" represents the outer energy level. In their chemical reactions, they readily lose that outer electron to form 1+ cations and so assume the electron configuration of the previous noble gas. Notice in Figure 1.2.1 that each of the alkali metals has the same number and type of valence electrons. Note also, that as we move down the group and the value of "*n*" increases, the outermost electron spends most of the time farther and farther from the nucleus so the atoms become larger.

Group 2 — The Alkaline Earth Metals

The **alkaline earth metals** are also silver-colored reactive metals. Although they are not as reactive as the alkali metals, they readily form compounds with non-metals. Their oxides are also alkaline but unlike alkali compounds, some group 2 compounds have a low solubility in water. They have two valence electrons and have the general electron configuration [noble gas]ns^2. They will readily form 2+ cations by losing those two valence electrons and so will achieve the identical electron configuration of the nearest noble gas. Chemists call this becoming **isoelectronic** with the noble gas.

Group 17 — The Halogens

The family of **halogens** contains the most reactive elements and is the only one in which all three states of matter are represented. At room temperature, fluorine and chlorine are gases, bromine is a liquid, and iodine and the very rare and radioactive astatine are solids.

The elemental halogens exist as diatomic molecules and readily form compounds with metals, and also hydrogen, carbon, and other non-metals. The halogens possess seven valence electrons with two electrons in the outer s sublevel and five electrons in the p sublevel. They therefore have the general ns^2np^5 outer electron configuration. In their reactions with metals, halogens will typically gain a single electron forming 1– anions and acquiring a noble gas electron configuration. When they react with non-metals, they will often share valence electrons.

Group 18 — The Noble Gases

As the name suggests, the family of **noble gases** is generally unreactive, although compounds of argon, krypton, xenon, and radon have been prepared.

All of the noble gases, except helium, have filled s and p sublevels. As the s and p sublevels are an atom's outermost orbitals, atoms of neon down to radon have eight electrons in their outer charge clouds with the ns^2np^6 configuration. They are said to possess "stable octets." This particularly stable electron configuration explains the low reactivity of the noble gases. It also explains the electron configuration achieved by many cations and anions. For example, consider Table 1.3.3, showing elements from four different families. Note that the stable ion of each element has the same electron configuration as the noble gas nearest to it in the periodic table.

Table 1.3.3 *Electron Configurations of Noble Gases and Nearby Elements*

Element	Electron Configuration for Atom	Nearest Noble Gas	Symbol and Electron Configuration for Stable Ion	
oxygen	$[He]2s^22p^4$	neon	O^{2-}	$[He]2s^22p^6$
calcium	$[Ar]4s^2$	argon	Ca^{2+}	$[Ne]3s^23p^6$
arsenic	$[Ar]4s^23d^{10}4p^3$	krypton	As^{3-}	$[Ar]4s^23d^{10}4p^6$
cesium	$[Xe]6s^1$	xenon	Cs^+	$[Kr]5s^24d^{10}5p^6$

Transition Elements

The **transition elements** include groups 3 through 12 in the periodic table. All are metals and most are hard solids with high melting and boiling points. An explanation of their chemical behavior is beyond the scope of this course, but it differs from the representative elements. For example, the transition elements show similarities within a given period as well as within a group. In addition, many transition elements form cations with multiple charges and those cations often form complex ions. A number of transition metal compounds have distinct and recognizable colors. The differences occur mainly because the last electrons added for transition metals are placed in inner d orbitals. Electrons in these orbitals are usually closer to the nucleus than in the outer s or p orbitals filled for the representative elements.

Quick Check

1. Identify the family number and name to which each of the following properties best apply:

Property	Family Number	Family Name
(a) reactive non-metals possessing seven valence electrons		
(b) reactive solids that form 2+ cations during reactions		
(c) invisible gases that are almost totally unreactive		
(d) soft, very reactive silvery solids with one valence electron		

2. Elements in the same family demonstrate similar chemical behavior. Consider the following chemical formulas: LiBr, K_2O, Sr_3N_2, AlF_3, CaO, H_2S. Write chemical formulas for:

   (a) sodium iodide ________________________
   (d) rubidium sulfide ________________________
   (b) barium sulfide ________________________
   (e) magnesium phosphide ________________________
   (c) gallium chloride ________________________
   (f) hydrogen selenide ________________________

3. Which two families contain the most reactive elements? Can you suggest a possible reason for this given their location on the periodic table?

   ____

   ____

1.3 Review Questions

1. What is the most important thing to know about the periodic table?

2. What significant modification to the periodic table occurred just before World War I?

3. Why do elements in the same chemical family have similar chemical properties?

4. (a) Where are the most metallic elements located on the periodic table?

   (b) Where are the most non-metallic elements located on the periodic table?

5. Consider the properties listed for eight different elements. Match each element on the left to its property on the right by writing the element's chemical symbol next to its property.

Element	Properties	Symbol
(a) chlorine	found in carbohydrates and an elemental gas in 21% of the atmosphere	
(b) silver	soft conductor that reacts explosively with water producing H_2 gas	
(c) neon	less than 30 g of this solid radioactive nonconductor exists on Earth	
(d) cesium	waxy yellow solid non-metal found in match heads, fertilizers, and detergents	
(e) oxygen	blue-gray metalloid used extensively in the computer industry	
(f) phosphorus	very reactive green gas used in the trenches in World War I	
(g) silicon	shiny solid that is the best conductor of heat and electricity	
(h) astatine	invisible unreactive gas used in lasers and some electric street signs	

6. Six different elemental properties are listed below corresponding to family numbers 1, 2, 6, 14, 17, and 18 in the periodic table. Write the appropriate family number next to each of the properties listed below. Each family number may be used only once.

Element Properties	Family Number
unreactive gas used in electric street signs and comprising 0.93% of the atmosphere	
shiny multivalent solid, good conductor, forms colored compounds	
soft silvery solid, good conductor, reacts vigorously with water	
gray-white metalloid predicted by Mendeleev and discovered in 1886	
reactive metal present in bones and teeth possessing two valence electrons	
yellow-green gaseous non-metal and the most reactive of all the elements	

7. State four properties of elements classified as metals.

8. State four properties of elements classified as non-metals.

9. State a general rule for predicting the ion charges of many of the representative or main group elements.

10. Use your answer to question 8 above and write the formulas for the stable ions of the following:

(a) Be ____________________

(b) Te ____________________

(c) Cs ____________________

(d) Ra ____________________

(e) Ga ____________________

(f) Se ____________________

(g) In ____________________

11. Identify three properties of the elements belonging to each of the following chemical families:

(a) alkali metals

(b) alkaline earth metals

(c) halogens

(d) noble gases

1.4 Atoms and Isotopes

Atomic Number, Mass Number, and Neutron Number

We can use the above table to discuss three important numbers associated with every element. The **atomic number (Z)** of an element equals the number of protons and the positive charge on the nucleus of each of its atoms. All of the atoms of a given element have the same atomic number, and each element's atomic number is different from that of any other element. For example, there are six protons in the nucleus of every carbon atom so Z = 6 for carbon. For nitrogen, Z = 7; for oxygen, Z = 8, and so on. This illustrates an extremely important point to remember: It is the number of protons that determines the identity of an atom. While the number of neutrons may vary in atoms of the same element, the number of protons always remains the same.

The presence of neutrons in the nucleus also contributes mass to an atom. The **mass number (A)** for each atom equals the sum of the number of protons and neutrons in the nucleus. A proton and a neutron each contribute one unit to an atom's mass number. For example, an atom of nitrogen with 7 protons and 7 neutrons has a mass number of 14, and an aluminum atom with 13 protons and 14 neutrons has a mass number of 27. Any particular atom can be represented using a notation that includes the element's symbol, mass number, and atomic number as shown in Figure 1.4.6.

$$\text{mass number } {}^{A}_{Z}X \text{ element symbol}$$

atomic number Z

Figure 1.4.6 *Notation for showing the mass number and the atomic number of the atom of an element*

Using this notation, we can see that the **neutron number (N)** can easily be calculated by the following: N (neutron number) = A (mass number) – Z (atomic number). For example,

${}^{14}_{7}\mathbf{N}$ represents a nitrogen atom with 7 neutrons (read as "nitrogen-14")

${}^{19}_{9}\mathbf{F}$ represents a fluorine atom with 10 neutrons (read as "fluorine-19")

An atom's mass is measured relative to an atomic standard. The modern standard is a carbon-12 atom whose mass is defined as exactly 12 atomic mass units. Therefore, one **atomic mass unit (amu)** is defined as exactly 1/12 the mass of a carbon-12 atom. **Atomic mass** is the average mass of an element's atoms.

Chemical changes never involve change to the nucleus but often involve electrons being added to or removed from neutral atoms that form ions. An **ion** is an electrically charged atom or group of atoms. For every electron an atom gains, it also gains that amount of excess negative charge and becomes a negative ion or **anion**. Each electron lost by an atom leaves that amount of excess positive charge on the resulting positive ion or **cation**. We can use the notation in Figure 1.4.6 to represent ions as well as neutral atoms. For example:

${}^{24}_{12}\mathbf{Mg}^{2+}$ shows a magnesium cation with 12 protons, 12 neutrons, and 10 electrons

${}^{31}_{15}\mathbf{P}^{3-}$ shows a phosphide anion with protons, 16 neutrons, and 18 electrons

Isotopes and Mass Spectrometry

Although all the nuclei of the atoms of a particular element have the same atomic number, they may not have the same atomic mass. Isotopes are different forms of the same element with different numbers of neutrons and therefore different mass values. For example, 98.89% of naturally occurring carbon atoms have 6 neutrons (carbon-12), 1.11% have 7 neutrons (carbon-13) and fewer than 0.01% have 8 neutrons (carbon-14).

Remember that the chemical behavior of a particular element is determined primarily by the number of electrons. The atomic number of any neutral element equals the number of electrons surrounding the nuclei of that atom, so all of the isotopes of a particular element have almost identical chemical properties.

Sample Problem — Atomic Number, Mass Number, and Neutron Number

1. Determine the number of protons, neutrons, and electrons present in a 4+ ion of Pb-207.
2. Write the symbol for this cation using the notation described above.

What to Think about

Question 1

1. A 4+ cation has 4 fewer electrons than protons. The atomic number of Pb is 82. Therefore there are 82 protons present, but only 78 electrons because of the 4+ charge.
2. The number of protons = the atomic number. The neutron number is determined by subtracting the atomic number from the mass number.

How to Do It

The number of neutrons is given by:
207 − 82 = 125 neutrons.

The correct notation is: $^{207}_{82}Pb^{4+}$

Practice Problems — Atomic Number, Mass Number, and Neutron Number

1. Determine the number of protons, neutrons and electrons present in each of the following:
   (a) $^{40}_{20}Ca^{2+}$ (b) $^{128}_{52}Te^{2-}$ (c) $^{52}_{24}Cr^{3+}$
   20p, 20n, 18e 52p, 76n, 54e 24p, 28n, 21e
2. Write atomic notation for neutral atoms of the following:
   (a) bromine-79 $^{79}_{35}Br$ (b) gold-197 $^{197}_{79}Au$ (c) thorium-232 $^{232}_{90}Th$
3. Complete the following table for atoms and ions:

Notation	Atomic Number	Mass Number	Number of Protons	Number of Neutrons	Number of Electrons
$^{95}_{42}Mo$	42	95	42	53	42
$^{79}_{34}Se^{2-}$	34	79	34	45	36
$^{109}_{47}Ag^{+}$	47	109	47	62	46
$^{232}_{90}Th^{4+}$	90	232	90	142	86
$^{209}_{83}Bi$	83	209	83	126	83

The number of naturally occurring isotopes of an element and their relative masses and abundances may be determined by a mass spectrometer, an instrument based on the same principles employed by J.J. Thomson to discover the electron (Figure 1.4.7).

Mass spectrometry uses the fact that charged particles moving through a magnetic field are deflected from their original path based on their charge-to-mass (e/m) ratio. The greater the ratio, the more deflection occurs. Consider the example of a beam of ionized neon (Ne^{1+}) containing the isotopes neon-20, neon-21, and neon-22. The beam enters the magnetic field chamber of a mass spectrometer, and the three isotopes separate on the basis of their e/m ratios. A detector in the spectrometer records the separations, the percent abundance, and the mass of each isotope. The mass number for neon that appears on the periodic table is the weighted average of those naturally occurring isotopes. The sample problem below shows how the calculation is done.

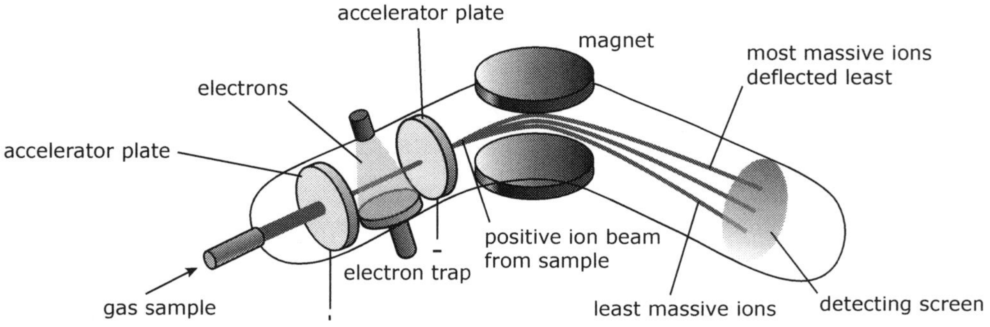

Figure 1.4.7 *Mass spectrometer*

Sample Problem — Calculating Atomic Mass

1. Use mass spectrometry data below to calculate the atomic mass of neon.

Isotope	Mass of Atom in amu (relative to ^{12}C = 12.0000)	Percent Abundance in Nature
neon-20	19.9924	90.48
neon-21	20.9938	0.27
neon-22	21.9914	9.25

What to Think about

1. The calculated atomic mass is the weighted average of the masses of each isotope.
   The sum of the three (mass) × (% abundance) products will therefore represent the atomic mass of neon.

How to Do It

(mass Ne-20) (% abundance) + (mass Ne-21) (% abundance) + (mass Ne-22) (% abundance)

(19.9924 amu) (90.48/100) + (20.9938 amu) (0.27/100) + (21.9914 amu) (9.25/100) = 20.18 amu

Sample Problem — Calculating Isotope Percent Abundance

1. Boron has two naturally occurring isotopes. Calculate the percent abundances of boron-10 and boron-11 using the following data:

Atomic mass of boron	10.81 amu
Isotopic mass of boron-10	10.0129 amu
Isotopic mass of boron-11	11.0093 amu

What to Think about

1. The weighted averages of the isotopes yield the atomic mass of 10.81 amu.
   The sum of the fractional abundances must be 1. So if x = abundance of boron-10, then the abundance of boron-11 must be $1 - x$.
   Use the method shown in the previous sample problem.
2. Solve for (x) and ($1 - x$) and then express those fractions as percentages to answer the question.

How to Do It

$(x)(10.0129 \text{ amu}) + (1 - x)(11.0093 \text{ amu}) = 10.81 \text{ amu}$

$11.0093x - 10.0129x = 11.0093 - 10.81$

$0.9964x = 0.1993$

$x = 0.2000$ and $1 - x = 0.8000$

Therefore % abundance boron-10 = 20.00%
and % abundance boron-11 = 80.00%

Practice Problems — Using Mass Spectrometry Data

1. Use the mass spectrometry data below to calculate the atomic mass of gallium.

Isotope	Mass of Atom in amu (relative to ^{12}C = 12.0000)	Percent Abundance in Nature
gallium-69	68.9256	60.11
gallium-71	70.9247	39.89

(68.9256)(0.6011) + (70.9247)(0.3989) = 69.7230 u

2. The following neon ions enter the magnetic field chamber of a mass spectrometer. Arrange them in order from the isotope that will be deflected most to the isotope deflected least.

$^{22}_{10}Ne^{1+}$ $^{21}_{10}Ne^{1+}$ $^{20}_{10}Ne^{1+}$

Most Deflection ⟶ Least Deflection		
$^{20}_{10}Ne^{+}$	$^{21}_{10}Ne^{+}$	$^{22}_{10}Ne^{+}$

3. Chlorine has two naturally occurring isotopes. Calculate the percent abundances of chlorine-35 and chlorine-37 using the following data:

Atomic mass of chlorine	35.453 amu
Isotopic mass of chlorine-35	34.9689 amu
Isotopic mass of chlorine-37	36.9659 amu

35 = 75.76%
37 = 24.24%

$34.9689x + 36.9659(1-x) = 35.453$

$-1.997x = -1.5129$ $x = 75.76\%$

1.4 Review Questions

1. Briefly describe the structure of the atom as proposed by each of the following:

   (a) John Dalton Big massy particle.

   (b) J.J. Thomson Plum pudding. Electrons floating around in positive charge.

   (c) Ernest Rutherford Small mass (+) in middle withelectrons outside.

2. What evidence led J.J. Thomson to propose that the mysterious negative particles he was studying were smaller than atoms?

   Shot atoms through cathode ray tubes. Mass to charge ratio

3. How did the discovery of radioactivity contribute to Ernest Rutherford's atomic model?

4. Why was Rutherford so surprised by the results of his gold foil experiment?

5. Complete the following table for neutral atoms.

Notation	Name	Atomic Number	Mass Number	Number of Protons	Number of Neutrons	Number of Electrons
					77	54
			210	84		
	neptunium-237					
		97			150	
			257			100

6. Write the notation for the following neutral atoms.

(a) An atom with 78 protons and 117 neutrons	
(b) An atom with a mass of 237 having 90 electrons	
(c) An atom with 69 electrons and 100 neutrons	

7. Write the notation for the following ions.

(a) A 3+ cation with 80 electrons and 127 neutrons	
(b) A 1– anion with 54 electrons and 78 neutrons	
(c) An ion with 66 electrons, 69 protons and 100 neutrons	

8. Use the following mass spectrometry data to calculate the atomic mass of magnesium.

Isotope	Mass of Atom in amu (relative to $^{12}C = 12.0000$)	Percent Abundance in Nature
magnesium-24	23.9850	78.99
magnesium-25	24.9858	10.00
magnesium-26	25.9826	11.01

9. An atom's volume is mostly empty space containing a cloud of negative electrons surrounding a very tiny positive nucleus. Therefore "solid matter" as we know it is really an illusion. Suggest a reason why all matter doesn't simply collapse.

10. Silver has two naturally occurring isotopes. Calculate the percent abundances of silver-107 and silver-109 using the following data:

Atomic mass of silver	107.87 amu
Isotopic mass of silver-107	106.9051 amu
Isotopic mass of silver-109	108.9045 amu

1.5 Lewis Structure Diagrams

Warm Up

1. Why do elements in the same chemical family display similar chemical behavior?
____
2. How can you determine the number of valence electrons in each of the representative or main group elements?
____
3. Define the term "stable octet."
____

Depicting Atoms, Ions, and Molecules in Two Dimensions

As you learned earlier, an atom's valence electrons are the outermost electrons. These are the electrons involved in chemical bonding. This means that, in chemical behavior, the valence electrons of an atom are really the only electrons that matter.

In 1916, the American chemist Gilbert N. Lewis devised a system of representing the atoms of the elements based on the number of valence electrons they possess. This notation system uses each element symbol to represent the nucleus and all of the inner electrons of an atom (Lewis called this the "kernel" of an atom). It then surrounds that symbol with a series of dots representing that atom's valence electrons. These **electron dot diagrams** are called **Lewis structures**.

The notation is a simple and useful way to represent atoms and serves as a foundation to help us understand and predict chemical behaviors and compound structures without the need for sophisticated bonding theories. Our discussion of Lewis structures and diagrams will be confined to the representative or main group elements in the periodic table, that is, groups 1, 2, 13, 14, 15, 16, 17, and 18.

We will begin by discussing Lewis structures for individual atoms and ions, and then expand that discussion to include Lewis diagrams for molecular compounds and polyatomic ions.

Lewis Structures for Atoms

To draw a Lewis structure for an atom, you need only determine the number of an atom's valence electrons. Recall from our discussion of the periodic table that this process is straightforward for the main group elements. For any period, beginning at the alkali metals, we see that atoms of this family have one valence electron. As we move across the period, each main group family has atoms with one additional valence electron up to the stable octet of four electron pairs present in each noble gas (except helium) (Table 1.5.1).

Table 1.5.1 *Valence Electrons in Main Group Atoms*

Main Group Number	1	2	13	14	15	16	17	18
Valence Electrons	1	2	3	4	5	6	7	8

To draw Lewis structures for the atoms, follow these steps:

1. Write the element symbol.
2. For hydrogen place a single dot next to the symbol. For helium place a pair of dots.
3. For 2nd period elements and beyond: for each valence electron present, place one dot around that symbol at one of the four positions of the compass: west, east, north, or south.
4. If more than four valence electrons are present, begin pairing the dots only after the four compass positions are filled.

The relative placement of the paired and unpaired dots isn't as important as how many of each is present. Figure 1.5.1 shows the Lewis structures for the main group elements of the first three periods.

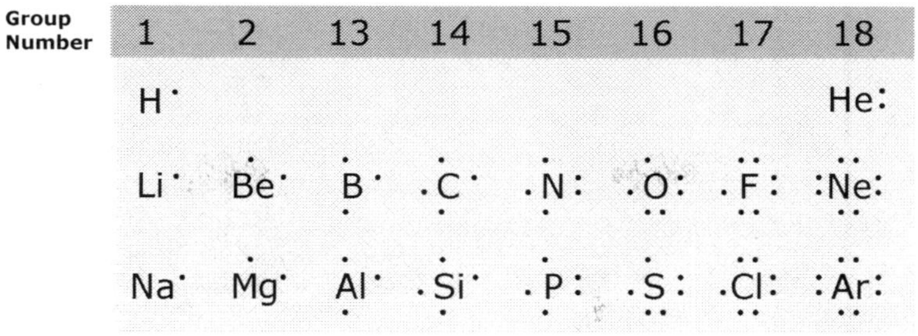

Figure 1.5.1 *Lewis structures for main group elements of the first three periods*

As you view Figure 1.5.1, consider the following important points:

1. As each element in a family has the same number of valence electrons, the Lewis structure for those elements has the same number of dots.
2. For the metals, the *total number of dots* represents the number of electrons that each atom loses when forming a cation.
3. In a correctly drawn Lewis structure for a non-metal, the number of *unpaired* dots shown represents either the number of electrons that atom *must gain* when forming an anion, or the number the electrons the atom *must share* to complete its octet when forming covalent bonds.

Lewis Structures for Monatomic Ions

From points 2 and 3 above, we can see that writing Lewis structures for monatomic ions is straightforward.

For the metals in groups 1, 2, and 13, the Lewis structure for their *stable ions* does not include any dots. The element symbol is usually enclosed in square brackets with the cation's charge written outside the brackets on the upper right. The magnitude of that positive charge simply equals the number of dots (which represent electrons) that were removed from the neutral atom's Lewis structure. Remember that because the number of protons in the nucleus has not changed, a loss of any number of electrons will result in that amount of positive charge on the cation.

For the non-metals in groups 15, 16, and 17, the Lewis structures for their anions all include four pairs of dots surrounding the element symbol enclosed in square brackets with the appropriate negative charge written outside the brackets on the upper right. The magnitude of the negative charge written outside the brackets equals the number of *unpaired* dots that were originally present in the parent atom's Lewis structure. This also equals how many electrons were required to generate the four pairs resulting in a stable octet.

The Lewis structures are shown for the sodium and chloride ions in Figure 1.5.2. Note that the chlorine atom originally had one unpaired dot. This required one electron for four pairs resulting in the charge of 1– on the anion. The sodium has had its one dot removed to form a 1+ cation.

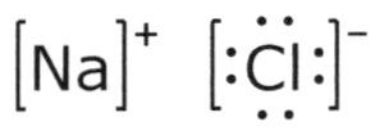

Figure 1.5.2 *Lewis structures for sodium ions and chloride ions*

Lewis Structures for Molecules

Each of the pages in this book is a flat surface and any diagrams or images that you see on these pages can only be two-dimensional representations of the real three-dimensional world. Of course, the ionic and molecular compounds that make up that world are also three-dimensional. Understanding their shapes is a very important part of explaining and predicting their behavior.

Quick Check

1. What do the "dots" in a Lewis structure for an atom or an ion represent?

   ____

2. What do the total number of dots present in the Lewis structures for the metals in groups 1, 2, and 13 tell us about the cations these atoms will form during a chemical change?

   ____

3. The Lewis structures for nitrogen, phosphorus, and antimony include one pair of dots and three unpaired dots. How many electrons do these atoms require to form a stable octet?

   ____

Sample Problem — Drawing Lewis Structures

Draw the Lewis structures for the representative elements belonging to period 4 of the periodic table.

What to Think about

1. Elements in the same chemical family have the same number of valence electrons.
2. Those electrons are represented by placing dots around each element symbol.
3. Consider Figure 6.4.1. Begin at group 1 and give potassium 1 valence electron. Continue to the right placing the same number of dots around each symbol in the same way that the dots appear for the other members of each group.

How to Do It

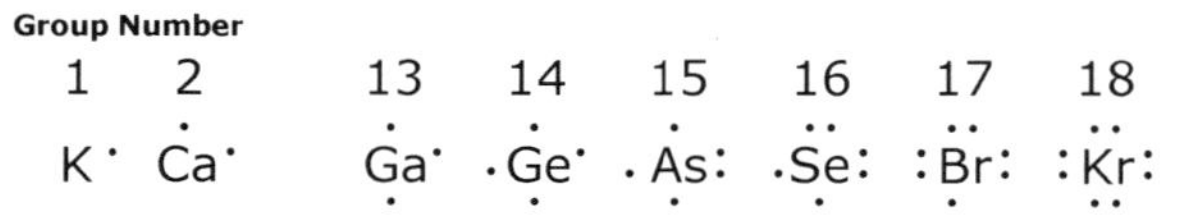

Practice Problems — Building Lewis Structures

1. Write the Lewis structures for the main group elements in period 5 of the periodic table.

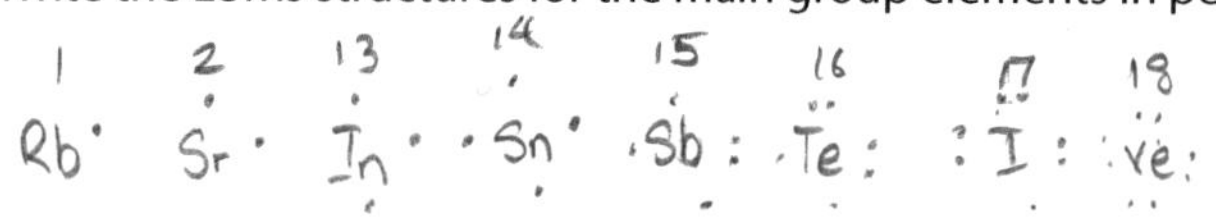

2. Write the Lewis structures for the following atoms and ions.

   (a) Ba (b) Al^{3+} (c) Bi (d) I^- (e) Te

3. Convert the following atomic symbols to the Lewis structures for the ions of those elements:

   (a) Ca (b) Se (c) Ga (d) As

Recall that ionic compounds normally exist as ordered, three-dimensional arrays of cations and anions called crystal lattices. The arrangement of ions in these crystals maximizes the attractions between the oppositely charged ions within the lattices and minimizes the repulsions between ions with the same charges. The diagram of an NaCl crystal lattice, Figure 6.4.2, helped with visualizing such a structure.

When molecules form, their three-dimensional shapes are also governed by the attractive and repulsive forces that exist within them. The first step toward visualizing the three-dimensional shape of a molecule is to convert its molecular formula into a two-dimensional Lewis structure.

One of the simplest examples of a Lewis structure is a diatomic halogen molecule such as Cl_2 (Figure 1.5.3). The single line between the atoms represents one pair of shared electrons. The other pairs of electrons are referred to as non-bonding or **lone pairs** of electrons. Note that all 14 of the valence electrons possessed by the 2 chlorine atoms are accounted for in the Lewis structure. Note also that each chlorine atom now has the benefit of an extra valence electron and thus has a stable octet.

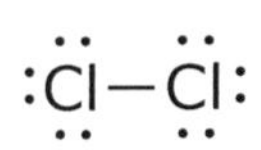

Figure 1.5.3 *Lewis structure of Cl_2*

As with any new procedure, learning to draw Lewis diagrams for molecules is easier if you follow a series of steps. Let's begin with a simple example: the Lewis structure for a molecule of nitrogen trichloride, NCl_3.

Step 1: Determine the total number of valence electrons in the molecule.

A correctly drawn Lewis structure must account for all of the valence electrons present. In this case, nitrogen has five valence electrons and each chlorine atom has seven. Therefore the total number of valence electrons is given by: $5 + (3 \times 7) = 26$.

Note that this is an even number, which will be true for all of the examples you will see. There are a few cases where odd numbers of electrons exist, but the vast majority of molecules (and polyatomic ions) possess even numbers of valence electrons. All bonding electrons exist in pairs.

Step 2: Construct the "skeleton" of the molecule using lines to indicate single covalent bonds between the atoms.

To generate the most likely skeleton of the molecule, the following set of guidelines will be of great help. The guidelines are based on numerous empirical observations and hold true for the vast majority of molecules. They also correspond to what we would expect given the electron configurations and electronegativities of the atoms involved. They may seem difficult to remember at first, but you won't need to use all of them for every molecule you draw. As with any new skill, the steps will become more familiar with practice.

Guidelines for Generating Molecule "Skeletons"

1. If the general formula for the compound is of the form "AX_n," then the central atom "A" will be the one with the lower group number, which also usually corresponds to the lower electronegativity. Obviously, if only two atoms exist in the molecule, then no central atom exists.
2. Hydrogen atoms form only one bond and so do not achieve an octet of electrons.
3. Fluorine atoms always form only one bond, and the other halogen atoms *usually* form only one bond. Exceptions to this occur if those halogens are central atoms and are bonded to other smaller halogens or to oxygen.
4. (a) Oxygen atoms normally form two bonds and don't often bond to each other in compounds with other elements. (An exception to this is hydrogen peroxide.)
   (b) Nitrogen atoms normally form three bonds.
   (c) Carbon atoms normally form four bonds.
5. Avoid creating rings or cyclic structures when you draw skeletons.

Using the above rules, we see that a central atom exists and that nitrogen is most likely that central atom. We can therefore sketch the molecular skeleton for NCl_3 shown in Figure 1.5.4. The relative orientation of each chlorine atom around the nitrogen atom isn't that important because Lewis structures do not depict shape or 3-D geometry. All the matters at this stage is that nitrogen is in the centre and each chlorine atom is a peripheral or surrounding atom.

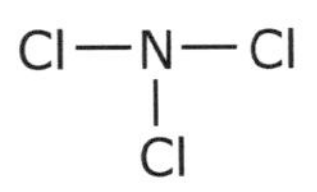

Figure 1.5.4 *Molecular skeleton for NCl_3*

Step 3: Subtract the number of valence electrons used to construct the skeleton from the total number of valence electrons available from step 1 to determine the number of valence electrons remaining.

Consider that each line drawn in the skeleton represents a pair of bonding valence electrons, so, in this case, the number of valence electrons remaining is:
$26 - (3 \times 2) = 20$.

Step 4: Assume that all of the atoms in the molecule obey the octet rule (except hydrogen). Determine the number of additional valence electrons required (beyond those already present as a result of the bonds drawn) to give all of those atoms the required eight valence electrons.

In this case, because each peripheral chlorine atom has one bond and is therefore associated with two valence electrons, each chlorine atom needs six more electrons to complete its octet. The central nitrogen has three bonds and so has the benefit of six valence electrons. This means that the nitrogen atom needs only two more valence electrons to complete its octet. The calculation to determine the total number of required valence electrons is: $(3 \times 6) + 2 = 20$

Step 5: Compare the number of valence electrons available (from step 3) to the number of valence electrons needed to complete the octets of the atoms (from step 4). If those two numbers match, pair up the electrons. Beginning with the peripheral atoms and ending with the central atom, place those electron pairs where they're needed to satisfy the octets. In this case, the two numbers do indeed match and so the resulting Lewis structure is shown in Figure 1.5.5. If the numbers don't match, there is a procedure we'll discuss later.

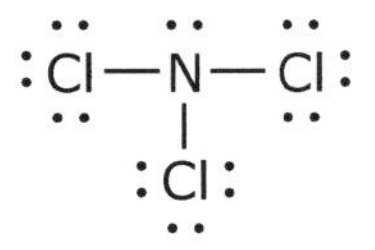

Figure 1.5.5 *Lewis structure for NCl_3*

At this point, consider the following:

Criteria Governing the Octet Rule in a Lewis Structure

(a) A peripheral or surrounding atom must not violate the octet rule in a Lewis structure. If an atom does violate the octet rule, then it must be a central atom in the molecule. This doesn't apply to hydrogen, which is associated with only two electrons in molecules.

(b) ***Exception (i)*** Atoms belonging to the second period in the periodic table will not have expanded octets in Lewis structures. An expanded octet (more than eight valence electrons) is only possible for elements belonging to the 3rd period or higher because only those atoms have access to d orbital electrons. These electrons are unavailable below the third energy level.
Exception (ii) The atoms Be, B, and Al will often have incomplete octets such that only two or three pairs of valence electrons will be associated with these central atoms in Lewis structures for molecules.

Step 6: If the numbers in step 5 above agree, then as a final step, check that the total number of valence electrons represented in the diagram matches the total number of valence electrons you began with in step 1.

In this example, the number of valence electrons in the diagram matches the number in the molecule.

We have seen that one pair of valence electrons shared between two adjacent nuclei constitutes a single covalent bond. There are also many cases where the covalent bonds between two atoms involve more than one pair of shared electrons. These are known as **multiple bonds**. If two pairs of electrons are shared between the same two atoms, the bond is called a double bond and if three pairs exist, the bond is a triple bond.

Quick Check

1. Suggest a reason why the elements Be, B, and Al are not able to achieve a valence octet when they form covalent compounds.

   ____

2. Hydrogen sulfide, H_2S, is a poisonous, foul-smelling, and flammable gas. Why is the molecular skeleton "S – H – H" incorrect for this molecule?

   ____

3. Determine the total number of valence electrons present in each of the following molecules:
   (a) H_2Se _____ (b) CCl_4 _____ (c) NF_3 _____ (d) PCl_5 _____ (e) SF_6 _____

Sample Problem — Drawing a Lewis Structure for a Molecule

Draw the Lewis structure for a molecule of water, H_2O.

What to Think about	How to Do It
1. Each hydrogen atom will form one bond and the oxygen will form two. The oxygen must therefore be the central atom even though it has a higher electronegativity than hydrogen. Oxygen has six valence electrons and hydrogen has one.	
2. Use the steps listed above:	
Step 1: Determine the total number of valence electrons in the molecule.	$6 + (2 \times 1) = 8$ valence electrons present in molecule
Step 2: Construct the "skeleton" of the molecule.	H – O – H
Step 3: Determine the number of valence electrons remaining.	Electrons available: 8 Electrons used in skeleton: 4 Electrons remaining: 8 – 4 = 4
Step 4: Assume that all of the atoms in the molecule obey the octet rule (except hydrogen).	
Step 5: Compare the number of valence electrons available to the number of valence electrons needed to complete the octets of the atoms. Pair up remaining electrons and place them where needed to satisfy oxygen's octet.	Electrons required to complete oxygen's octet: 4
Step 6: Available electrons match electrons in the diagram. Note that in the final structure, oxygen is associated with two bonding pairs and two non-bonding (or lone pairs).	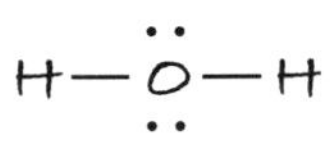

Practice Problems – Drawing Lewis Structures for Molecules

1. Construct the Lewis structure for a molecule of carbon tetrachloride, CCl_4.

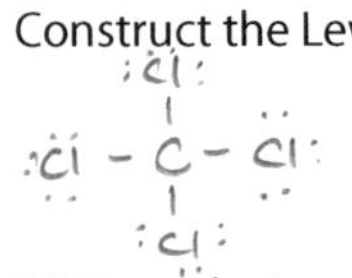

2. (a) Draw the Lewis structure for a molecule of ammonia, NH_3.

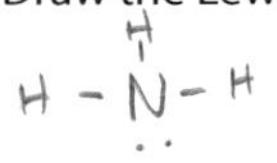

   (b) When you're finished drawing the structure, determine how many bonding pairs and how many lone pairs of electrons are associated with the central atom.

   3 bonding pairs. 1 lone pair

3. (a) Draw the Lewis structure for a molecule of boron trichloride, BCl_3.

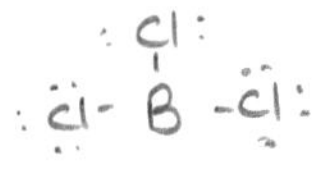

   (b) Consider the central atom in your structure. Does it possess a stable octet of eight electrons?

   No. Only 6 electrons

1.5 Review Questions

1. Consider the following list of elements. Place each in the appropriate column in the table below depending on whether it obeys the octet rule, likely has an incomplete octet, or could potentially have an expanded octet in a Lewis structure.

   H, Be, B, C, N, O, F, Al, Si, P, S, Cl

Incomplete Valence Octet	Valence Octet	Expanded Valence Octet

2. Helium and neon are in the same chemical family but yet have different numbers of dots in their Lewis structures. What is the reason for this? Explain why neither element ever forms chemical compounds.

3. Consider the following pairs of elements in the table below. If each pair was part of a molecule or polyatomic ion, which of the two would most likely be the central atom and which would be the peripheral or surrounding atom? Place each element of each pair in the appropriate column in the table.

Element Pair	Probable Central Atom	Probable Peripheral Atom
(a) phosphorus and chlorine		
(b) nitrogen and oxygen		
(c) carbon and sulfur		
(d) nitrogen and hydrogen		
(e) oxygen and fluorine		

5. Draw Lewis structures for each of the following molecules in the space provided.

   OF_2

   H_2S

   PCl_3

   CCl_2F_2

6. Draw Lewis structures for each of the polyatomic ions in the space provided.

   OH^-

   AlH_4^-

   CN^-

1.6 Describing Chemical Bonding

Warm Up

1. What term do we give to an atom's outer electrons that take part in chemical bonding?
   ____
2. Define electronegativity.
   ____
3. In which region of the periodic table are elements located that tend to
   (a) lose outer electrons most easily during chemical changes?
   ____
   (b) gain outer electrons most easily during chemical changes?
   ____

An Introduction to Chemical Bonding

All matter is composed of atoms, and those individual atoms are far too small to see. From that, it seems reasonable to conclude that matter must be made up of large numbers of atoms connected or bonded together. In this section, we will investigate the nature of the bonds between atoms and how those bonds determine important properties in compounds.

Atoms are electrical species with a negative cloud of electrons surrounding and attracted to a positive nucleus. As you have learned, the electrostatic forces of attraction and repulsion within atoms influence properties such as atomic size, ionization energy, and electronegativity. Those same forces and properties also play a role whenever atoms bond together.

When two atoms approach each other, all of the electrostatic interactions associated with equally and oppositely charged particles occur. The negative electron clouds of the atoms exert repulsive forces on each other, as do the positive nuclei of each atom. This repulsion slows the approaching atoms and converts some of their kinetic energy to potential energy. In addition, each nucleus also begins to attract the approaching atom's outer electron cloud. These attractive forces are most intense in the region of space where the electron clouds "overlap" between the adjacent nuclei. If the attractive forces between the atoms are stronger than the repulsive forces, the two atoms together are in a state of lower energy than when they were apart. Thus, a chemical bond forms between them.

Types of Chemical Bonds

The events described above apply to the formation of all chemical bonds. But recall that we have classified elements as metals and non-metals based on a number of physical and chemical properties that correlate to different positions on the periodic table. These properties and the three possible ways that these two varieties of elements can combine give rise to three different *types* of chemical bonds, which are listed in Table 1.6.1. In this course, we will cover ionic and covalent bonds.

Table 1.6.1 *Types of Chemical Bonds*

Atoms Involved in Chemical Bond	Type of Chemical Bond
1. metal bonded to non-metal	ionic bond
2. non-metal bonded to non-metal	covalent bond
3. metal bonded to metal	metallic bond

Table 1.6.1 is a simplified summary of chemical bonds because the bonds between atoms in most chemical compounds have varying proportions of both ionic and covalent characteristics. We will begin with clear examples of each type of bond to introduce the concepts involved.

Ionic Bonds

Ionic bonds form between two atoms with large differences in their ionization energies and electronegativities. Recall that such combinations typically occur when relatively large metal atoms located on the far left side of the periodic table in groups 1 or 2 combine with smaller non-metal atoms on the far right side of the table belonging to groups 16 or 17.

Look again at the table of electronegativities introduced in Figure 1.4.7. Imagine a "collision," for example, between an alkali metal atom such as sodium and a halogen atom such as chlorine. These elements are located at opposite ends of the 3rd period of the periodic table and therefore exhibit significant differences in size, ionization energy, and electronegativity.

Compared to an atom of sodium, a chlorine atom is smaller with a higher ionization energy and electronegativity. As a result, when the outer electron clouds of these two atoms encounter each other, sodium's lone valence electron will be closer to chlorine's nucleus than to its own. It will therefore feel a stronger attraction from chlorine's nucleus than from its own. In fact, because the difference in the electronegativities of these two elements is *greater than 1.7*, the probability of finding sodium's outer electron near chlorine's nucleus is so great that the sodium atom can be considered to *transfer* that valence electron to the chlorine atom. Electronegativity difference is often abbreviated as **Δ**EN.

The large sodium atom, having lost the only electron in its 3rd energy level, is now a much smaller positively charged sodium cation (Na^+). The relatively small chlorine atom, having gained an extra electron, becomes a larger negatively charged chloride anion (Cl^-). These two oppositely charged ions are now bound together by an electrostatic attraction called an **ionic bond**.

An **ionic bond** is the electrostatic attractive force between the oppositely charged ions produced when a metal atom transfers one or more electrons to a non-metal atom.

The electron transfer from sodium to chlorine and the resulting ionic bond is shown in Figure 1.6.1. These diagrams are **Bohr model** diagrams, showing the number of electrons in the shells surrounding the nuclei of the atoms and ions.

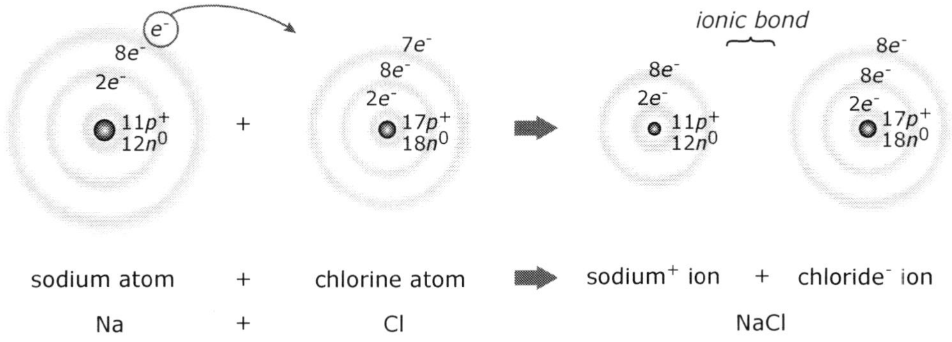

Figure 1.6.1 *An electron transfers from sodium atom to a chlorine atom, resulting in the formation of an ionic bond between the ions.*

The Ionic Crystal Lattice

Obviously, when any macroscopic sample of chlorine gas and sodium metal react together, countless atoms will transfer electrons to form countless oppositely charged ions. These oppositely charged species being produced in close proximity are drawn together into an ordered, solid, three-dimensional array of cations and anions called a **crystal lattice** (Figure 1.6.2). The smallest whole number cation-to-anion ratio in this structure represents the chemical formula for the ionic compound, in this case, NaCl.

Figure 1.6.2 *NaCl crystal lattice*

The vast number of interionic forces present in a crystal lattice locks all of the ions into place. This helps explain why all ionic compounds are solids with high melting temperatures (e.g., sodium chloride melts at 801°C.)

Ionic compounds form a number of different crystal structures depending on the relative sizes and ratios of their ions. Those ratios in turn depend on the charges on the ions in the compound.

Recall that the representative elements in groups 1, 2, 13, 15, 16, and 17 of the periodic table tend to form stable ions by losing or gaining sufficient electrons to become isoelectronic with the nearest noble gas. This results in the common ion charges shown in Table 1.6.2 for those groups.

Table 1.6.2 *Common Ion Charges in Groups 1, 2, 13, 15, 16, and 17*

Group Number	1	2	13	15	16	17
Most Common Ion Charge	1+	2+	3+	3-	2–	1–

We can think of ionic bond formation as a case of *extremely unequal electron sharing*. Both metal and non-metal nuclei attract the valence electrons between them when their atoms meet. However, the non-metal pulls those electrons so close to its own nucleus that it effectively captures the metal's valence electrons and forms the metal cation and non-metal anion. An accurate analogy might be a grossly mismatched tug-of-war, except that in this case, the smallest competitor wins.

Several important points should be mentioned when summarizing ionic bonding:

1. Ionic compounds form between metals and non-metals whose ΔEN exceed 1.7. They typically form when metals from groups 1 or 2 react with non-metals from groups 16 or 17 of the periodic table.
2. During the formation of an ionic bond, metal atoms will transfer one or more valence electrons to the more electronegative non-metal atoms. This occurs because of the metal's relatively low ionization energies and electronegativities. In the process, metal cations and non-metal anions form and are attracted to each other by ionic bonds.
3. Ionic compounds form structures known as crystal lattices. The vast number of attractive forces present in such lattices account for the high melting temperatures of ionic compounds.
4. The formulas for ionic compounds represent the smallest whole number ratios of cations-to-anions that are electrically neutral.

Quick Check

1. What event occurs when atoms of metals and non-metals react to become cations and anions?

____

2. Identify the three types of chemical bonds based on the different elements involved.

____

____

____

3. Which chemical families in the periodic table are typically associated with ionic bond formation?

____

Sample Problem — Ionic Bond Formation

Write formulas for the compounds formed when the following elements combine and justify that the bonds present are ionic by determining the ΔEN in each case.

(a) Ca and Br (b) Al and O (c) Be and O (d) Rb and N (e) Ba and Cl

What to Think about	How to Do It
1. Write the element symbols with their charges and criss-cross the numbers. 2. Reduce formulas to smallest whole number ratios 3. Determine ΔEN values using the table above. Values above 1.7 represent ionic bonds.	(a) Ca^{2+} Br^{1-} → $CaBr_2$ ΔEN = 1.8 (ionic bond) (b) Al^{3+} O^{2-} → Al_2O_3 ΔEN = 2.0 (ionic bond) (c) Be^{2+} O^{2-} → BeO ΔEN = 2.0 (ionic bond) (d) Rb^{1+} N^{3-} → Rb_3N ΔEN = 2.2 (ionic bond) (e) Ba^{2+} Cl^{1-} → $BaCl_2$ ΔEN = 2.1 (ionic bond)

Practice Problems — Ionic Compounds

1. Write formulas for the ionic compounds formed when the following elements combine:

(a) Ba and Br $BaBr_2$
(b) Be and O BeO
(c) Sr and N Sr_3N_2
(d) Mg and Cl $MgCl_2$
(e) Fr and F FrF

2. Justify that the bonds in the following compounds are ionic by calculating the ΔEN values for each.

(a) RbF 3.16 Ionic
(b) $RaCl_2$ 2.26 Ionic
(c) KBr 2.14 Ionic
(d) Na_2O 2.51 Ionic

3. Write formulas for the ionic compounds formed when the following elements combine. Using the ΔEN values, arrange the compounds in order of the increasing ionic character of the bonds in each compound.

(a) Na and N (b) Sr and Br (c) Li and Cl (d) Cs and F (e) Rb and O

Na_3N 2.11 $SrBr_2$ 2.01 LiCl 2.18 CsF 3.19 Rb_2O 2.62

$SrBr_2$ < Na_3N < LiCl < Rb_2O < CsF

Covalent Bonds

Now let's look at the formation of a bond between two atoms of the same non-metal element, such as hydrogen (Figure 1.6.3). Obviously, the electronegativities of these or any two identical atoms would be the same.

As mentioned above, bond formation begins with atoms "colliding." As the two hydrogen atoms approach each other, their kinetic energy increases as each electron cloud is attracted to the other's approaching positive nucleus. The two atoms continue moving together until the repulsive forces of the two negative electron clouds and the two positive nuclei slow the atoms and convert their kinetic energy into potential energy.

As the atoms get close to each other, their electron clouds may overlap enough to cause attractive forces to exceed repulsive ones. The two valence electrons will move into the region of space between the adjacent nuclei because this is where they experience the most attractive force from those two centres of positive charge. The two atoms will settle into a position next to each other with the pair of valence electrons in a cloud of negative charge between the two nuclei. As the electron clouds of each hydrogen atom overlap, the two valence electrons experience the maximum attractive force between the two adjacent nuclei. This force of attraction of a pair of valence electrons between two adjacent nuclei constitutes a single **covalent bond**. In our example, the result of this covalent bond is a molecule of hydrogen, H_2

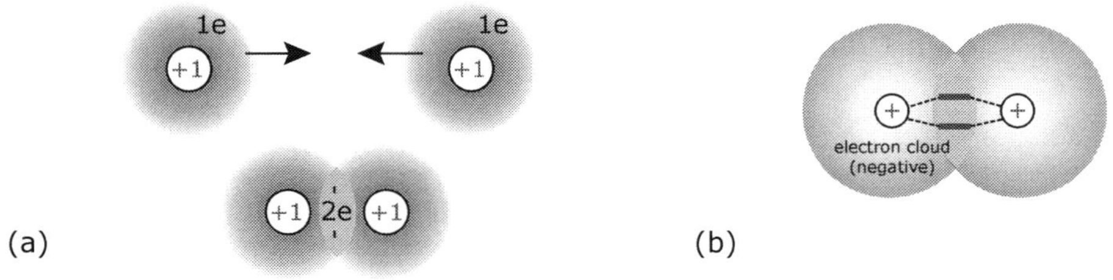

Figure 1.6.3 *(a) Two hydrogen atoms collide and two valence electrons move into the space between the nuclei. (b) The valence electrons experience a force of attraction from the two nuclei. This attraction holds the two atoms together to form* H_2.

Because this bond has formed between two atoms of hydrogen, the electronegativity difference associated with the atoms in the bond must be zero. This tells us that, on average, the pair of bonded electrons will spend the majority of their time equidistant between the two hydrogen nuclei. Stated another way, this means that the density of the electron charge cloud is greatest in the region of space halfway between the two adjacent nuclei. This is true whenever two atoms of the same element form covalent bonds. The "equal sharing" of valence electrons is sometimes referred to as a "pure covalent" or non-polar covalent bond.

Although both ionic and covalent bond formation involves only valence electrons, there are several important differences between the two events:

1. Covalent bonds typically form between two non-metal atoms rather than between metal atoms and non-metal atoms.
2. Because no electron transfer occurs and no ions form, all of the species prior to and following covalent bond formation between two atoms are electrically neutral.
3. The force of attraction in a covalent bond is between a pair of electrons and two adjacent positive nuclei, rather than between a cation and an anion as in an ionic bond. Electrons in covalent bonds are *always associated into pairs*.
4. Covalent compounds often exist as independent molecules rather than large crystal structures.

Polar Covalent Bonds

Table 1.6.3 *Relationship of ΔEN and Bond Designation*

ΔEN	Bond Designation
0	non-polar covalent
< 0.4	mostly covalent
0.4 – 1.7	polar covalent
> 1.7	ionic

We have discussed above the two extreme cases of bonding: complete electron transfer and completely equal electron sharing. Between these extremes are covalent bonds involving *unequal* electron sharing.

When atoms with different electronegativities form covalent bonds, those ΔEN values may be minimal or significant. If ΔEN is less than 0.4, the bonding electrons between the two atoms spend no more of their time nearer one nucleus than the other. Such bonds are designated as being mostly covalent because ΔEN appears to be insignificant. Another way to characterize this is to say that these bonds have very little "ionic character."

However, as ΔEN increases beyond 0.4, the pair of bonding electrons will be drawn closer and closer to the nucleus of the atom with the higher electronegativity. This unequal distribution of electron density will give that end of the bond a partially negative "pole" and the other a partially positive "pole." A bond "dipole" is said to exist and the bond itself is known as a **polar covalent bond**.

As the ΔEN increases and the bonds become more and more polar, we could say that the amount of ionic character in those bonds increases (Table 1.6.3).

Let's look at an example of a polar covalent bond. When a hydrogen atom having an electronegativity of 2.1 bonds to a chlorine atom with an electronegativity of 3.0, the ΔEN = 0.9. The electron density will be concentrated near chlorine giving that end of the bond a partial negative charge and leaving the hydrogen end with a partial positive charge. The bond dipole is said to be in the direction of chlorine and we can designate this polar covalent bond in several ways. Two are shown in Figure 1.6.4. The lower case Greek deltas (δ) indicate that there are slight or *partial* charges associated with each end of the HCl molecule. Note also that more electron density is associated with chlorine. Another depiction of this polar covalent bond simply shows the hydrogen chloride bond as a straight line between the element symbols. Beneath this is an arrow facing in the direction of the highest electron density or the negative end of the bond dipole.

Figure 1.6.4 *Polar covalent bond depictions. The bond dipole is in the direction of the chlorine.*

Atoms That Form More Than One Bond

So far we have considered the formation of only one bond per atom in two different molecules, namely H_2 and HCl. Notice that hydrogen and chlorine each require a single electron to become isoelectronic with their nearest noble gas. In hydrogen's case, one more electron will complete its first energy level. When chlorine acquires another electron it achieves a stable octet in its valence shell.

In each example, the sharing of a pair of valence electrons, whether equal or not, gives each atom in the bond the benefit of that extra electron in its valence shell. The bond also allows both atoms to have *all of their valence electrons paired,* which is a very stable configuration from a quantum mechanical perspective.

Of course, non-metals sometimes require more than one electron to achieve a stable outer electron shell and have all of their valence electrons paired. Consider several non-metals in groups 14, 15, and 16. To achieve a stable octet containing four electron pairs in each of their valence shells, carbon requires four electrons, nitrogen needs three, and oxygen needs two.

This tells us that the number of electrons required by an atom to achieve the stable outer electron configuration of the nearest noble gas also represents the number of covalent bonds that the atom must form.

We can use Table 1.6.4 to predict formulas for compounds formed between elements in these families. For example, when phosphorus and chlorine react together, phosphorus requires three electrons to complete its octet, while chlorine requires only one.

Table 1.6.4 *Electrons Needed to Achieve a Stable Octet for Non-metals*

Periodic Table Group Number	14	15	16	17
Electrons Needed to Achieve Stable Octet	4	3	2	1

The element with the lower electronegativity, in this case phosphorus, normally requires the most electrons and is written first in a chemical formula. Place the number of electrons it requires above its symbol on the right (similar to a charge without the sign). Then do the same for chlorine as follows: P^3 Cl^1 Now criss-cross those numbers to give the formula: PCl_3.

The process is similar to writing ionic formulas except no charges exist and you don't always reduce the formula to the smallest ratio of atoms. This is because a covalent formula does not represent a ratio. Rather, it tells us the actual number of atoms that exist in the molecule. Assume at this point, however, that you *can* reduce covalent formulas unless told otherwise by your teacher.

There are also numerous examples where more than one pair of electrons is shared between the same two atoms. Two pairs of shared valence electrons results in a double covalent bond and three pairs will produce a triple covalent bond. We will discuss multiple bonds in detail in the next section. For now, we will only mention that as the number of electron pairs shared between two adjacent nuclei increases, so does the strength of the covalent bond.

Sample Problem — Covalent Bond Formation

Predict the formulas for the compounds formed when the following elements combine and determine whether the bonds present are non-polar covalent or polar covalent.

(a) N and F (b) C and H (c) Si and N (d) C and S (e) O and O

What to Think about

1. Determine how many electrons each atom requires to complete its valence shell and write that number above the symbol.
2. Criss-cross those numbers and reduce ratios if possible (for now).
3. Determine the ΔEN for each and classify the bonds present.

How to Do It

(a) $N^3 F^1 \rightarrow NF_3$ $\Delta EN = 1.0$ (polar covalent)

(b) $C^4 H^1 \rightarrow CH_4$ $\Delta EN = 0.4$ (polar covalent)

(c) $Si^4 N^3 \rightarrow Si_3N_4$ $\Delta EN = 1.2$ (polar covalent)

(d) $C^4 S^2 \rightarrow CS_2$ $\Delta EN = 0$ (non-polar covalent)

(e) $O^2 O^2 \rightarrow O_2$ $\Delta EN = 0$ (non-polar covalent)

Practice Problems — Comparing Types of Chemical Bonds

1. Consider the ΔEN values and pair up the elements Al, Cl, N, and Na to write the formula for the types of compounds identified below. Justify each choice by showing the appropriate ΔEN value next to each formula.
   (a) A compound with an ionic bond

   NaCl 2.23

   (b) A compound with a polar covalent bond

   AlN 1.43

   (c) A compound with a non-polar covalent bond

   NCl_3 0.12

2. Calculate the ΔEN values for the bonds in the following compounds. Then arrange the compounds in order from those containing bonds in which the electrons are shared most equally to those in which the electrons are shared most unequally.
   (a) H_2O (b) PCl_3 (c) Cl_4 (d) SiO_2 (e) AlN
   1.24 0.97 0 1.54 1.43

   Cl_4, PCl_3, H_2O, AlN, SiO_2

3. Complete the following table:

Elements Present	Formula	ΔEN Value	Nature of Bonds	Atom Possessing Greater Electron Density
C and S	CS_2	0.03	NPC	S
B and Cl	BCl_3	1.12	PC	Cl
Al and O	Al_2O_3	1.83	I	O
N and I	NI_3	0.38	NPC	N
Ca and F	CaF_2	2.98	I	F

The Strength of Ionic vs. Covalent Bonds

Remember that ionic compounds are solids at room temperature and have high melting points. This results from the vast number of interionic forces locking all of the ions together in place in the crystal lattice. As mentioned earlier, the common ionic compound NaCl melts at 801°C.

Covalent compounds, however, usually exist as individual molecules and in any of the three states of matter: solid, liquid, or gas. We shouldn't conclude from this, however, that covalent bonds are any weaker than ionic bonds. Consider, for example, the molecule methane, CH_4, the main component of natural gas.

Although the melting point of methane (–182°C) is very low compared to sodium chloride, this physical property does not reflect the strength of the C – H bonds in methane or indicate that the bonds are weak compared to those in NaCl.

This is because no chemical bonds are broken when methane or any molecular covalent compound melts. Instead, weak intermolecular forces *between* the molecules are overcome. The result is that molecules are separated *from each other* rather than breaking the bonds between the atoms within those molecules.

The energy required to separate the bonded carbon and hydrogen atoms within the molecules from each other is far more than that required to simply pull the molecules apart. In the final section of this chapter, we will discuss the different forces that hold molecules together. Although some of those forces are stronger than others, *none are as strong as chemical bonds*.

Compelling evidence of the strength of covalent bonds can be seen by studying compounds called **network covalent solids**. Rather than consisting of individual molecules, these substances are held together by covalent bonds that extend throughout the entire sample. In the same way that melting an ionic solid requires overcoming all of the attractive forces between the oppositely charged ions in the crystal lattice, melting a network covalent solid involves breaking all of the covalent bonds within what is effectively a giant molecule literally as big as the sample.

Consider quartz, for example, which is a network covalent solid having the formula SiO_2 (Figure 1.6.5). The fact that no separate molecules exist in a quartz crystal means that the melting point is very high: 1550°C. The melting point does reflect the strength of the bonds in the compound. It shows us that covalent bonds can be as strong as ionic bonds.

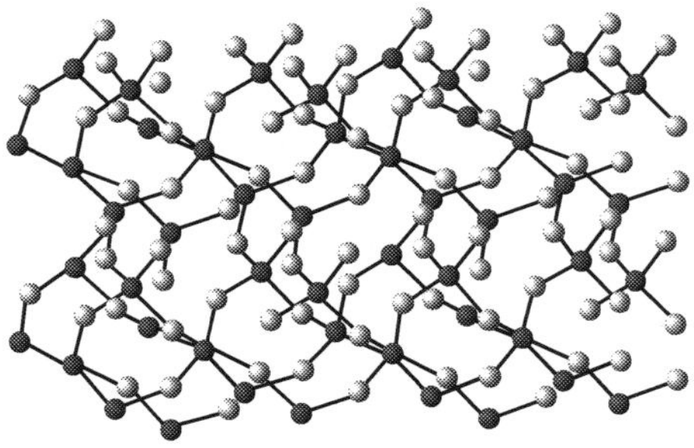

Figure 1.6.5 *A quartz crystal*

Metallic Bonding

Metals have low ionization energies and low electronegativities; therefore, they can lose electrons easily and do not have a tendency to gain them.

The model of metallic bonding stems from these two characteristics. If many atoms of one type of metallic element, say Mg, come together to form a strip of magnesium, we picture the metal atoms as positive ions, packed closely together, like a box of oranges packed in a box. The valence electrons are free to travel from ion to ion but spend little time with one particular ion. Electrons that are free to move about like this are called delocalized electrons. The electrons are said to form a "sea of negative charge" in which the positive ions are embedded. This model is successful in explaining many characteristics of metals, such as: i) conductivity of heat and electricity; ii) ductility and malleability; iii) metallic luster; and iv) hardness.

Draw a diagram of what a metal structure would look like with its delocalized electrons:

The mixing of different types of metal atoms results in a new metal called an <u>alloy</u>. An alloy is usually stronger, more durable and more resistant to oxidation. One very famous alloy is bronze, which is a mixture of copper, tin, and some zinc. It is famous because its discovery sparked a revolution in the production of superior weapons, tools, and everyday equipment. This discovery was so important to the people at that time an era carries its name, <u>The Bronze Age</u>.

Fig: The Composition of Some Common Alloys

Name	**% Composition**	**Properties**	**Uses**
Brass	Cu 70-85, Zn 15-30	Harder than Cu	Plumbing
Bronze	Cu 70-95, Sn 1-18, Zn 0-25	Harder than brass	Machinery statues
Gold 18-carat	Au 75, Ag 10-20, Cu 5-15	Harder than pure gold (24-carat)	Jewelry, electronics
Nickel coins	Ni 75, Cu 25	Corrosion resistant	Coinage
Steel	Fe 99, C 1	Hard, durable	Buildings, rail tracks
Steel, stainless	Fe 65-85, Cr 12-20, Ni 2-15, Mn 1-2, C 0.1-1, Si 0.5-1	Corrosion resistant, hard	Chemical equipment, tools, cutlery
Silver, sterling	Ag 92.5, Cu 7.5	Harder than pure silver, durable	Silverware, jewelry

Intermolecular Forces

Intermolecular Attractive Force

Intermolecular attractive forces are forces that causes otherwise independent atoms and molecules to attract each other. Intermolecular forces are forces between molecules. Explain why intermolecular forces must be overcome for phase changes (melting, boiling) to occur:

van der Waals Forces

In general, all intermolecular attractive forces are referred to as van der Waals forces which are named after Dutch physicist Johannes van der Waals. Van der Waals recognized attractive intermolecular forces cause gases to deviate from ideal behavior. Van de Waals Forces can be categorized

Dipole-Dipole Forces

Many covalent molecules have permanent dipoles because of the shape of the molecule and the electronegativity difference between the two atoms in the covalent bond.

- In the intramolecular covalent bond between two atoms, the atom with the lower electronegativity will have a partial positive charge and the atom with the greater electronegativity will have a partial negative charge. These partial charges arise because the two electrons in the intramolecular covalent bond reside closer to the more electronegative atom.
- The dipole-dipole intermolecular force occurs as the positive end of polar molecules are attracted to the negative end of other molecules.

Draw a picture to represent this process

- The ends with the same partial charges will repel each other.
- Although molecules are in constant motion, and their orientations keep changing, the polar molecules will be oriented, on average, such that oppositely charged ends are closer to each other than ends with like charges
- The strength of the dipole-dipole force increases with increasing polarity of the molecules involved

Practice: N_2 and CO are isoelectronic. Which substance should have a higher melting point? Why?

Hydrogen Bonding

When hydrogen forms an intramolecular covalent bond with nitrogen, oxygen or fluorine, the covalent bond is very polar and, because fluorine, nitrogen and oxygen are so electronegative, hydrogen has a larger partial positive charge than when it is bonded to other elements.

- The intermolecular forces **between** the molecule where the relatively strong partial positive charge of hydrogen attracts the negative partial charge of oxygen, fluorine or nitrogen in **neighbouring** molecules is called a hydrogen bond.

- Molecules that participate in H-bonding have higher melting and boiling points (H_2O, NH_3, HF) than would be expected based on periodic trends. Therefore, the H-bond is considered a relatively strong intermolecular force.

Draw a picture of a hydrogen bond:

- H-bonding helps to maintain the structure of ice, which causes it to be less dense than liquid water.
- In order for intermolecular hydrogen bonding to occur between two molecules, the molecules must have intramolecular covalent bonding between H-O, H-N or H-F within their structures.
- Hydrogen bonding occurs between molecules. It is an intermolecular force between the partial positive charge on a hydrogen atom of one molecule and the partial negative charge of N, F or O on another molecule.

Practice: Would you expect a significant degree of hydrogen bonding between the molecules of (a) NH_3, (b) CH_3OH, (c) HBr?

London Dispersion Forces

London Dispersion Forces occur between all molecules due to the temporary dipoles created by the electrons which are constantly moving within atoms. As they move, electrons have a very high probability of being unevenly distributed. Even in a non-polar molecule, a temporary partial negative charge occurs when more electrons than protons are on one side of the molecule. This temporary dipole within the molecule affect the molecules around it inducing other temporary dipoles and interacting with temporary dipoles that are already present. The interaction of temporary dipoles between molecules are the London Dispersion forces.

- Electrons in an atom or molecule are in constant motion.
- The motion of electrons produces a fluctuating charge distribution and a changing polarity that varies from instant to instant, resulting in an induced dipole, although the net result is 0.
- In general, large atoms and molecules are more easily polarized than smaller atoms, explain why.

Practice: Which element should have a higher melting point, O_2 or Cl_2?

Ion- dipole

- Ions attract the charged ends of polar molecules (e.g NaCl dissolves in water – the attraction of ions for water molecules is also known as **hydration**)

Ion-induced dipole

- Attractions that occur when ions distort electron clouds in neighbouring molecules (Br_2 liquid will dissolve in water)

Fig: Summary of Inter and Intramolecular forces

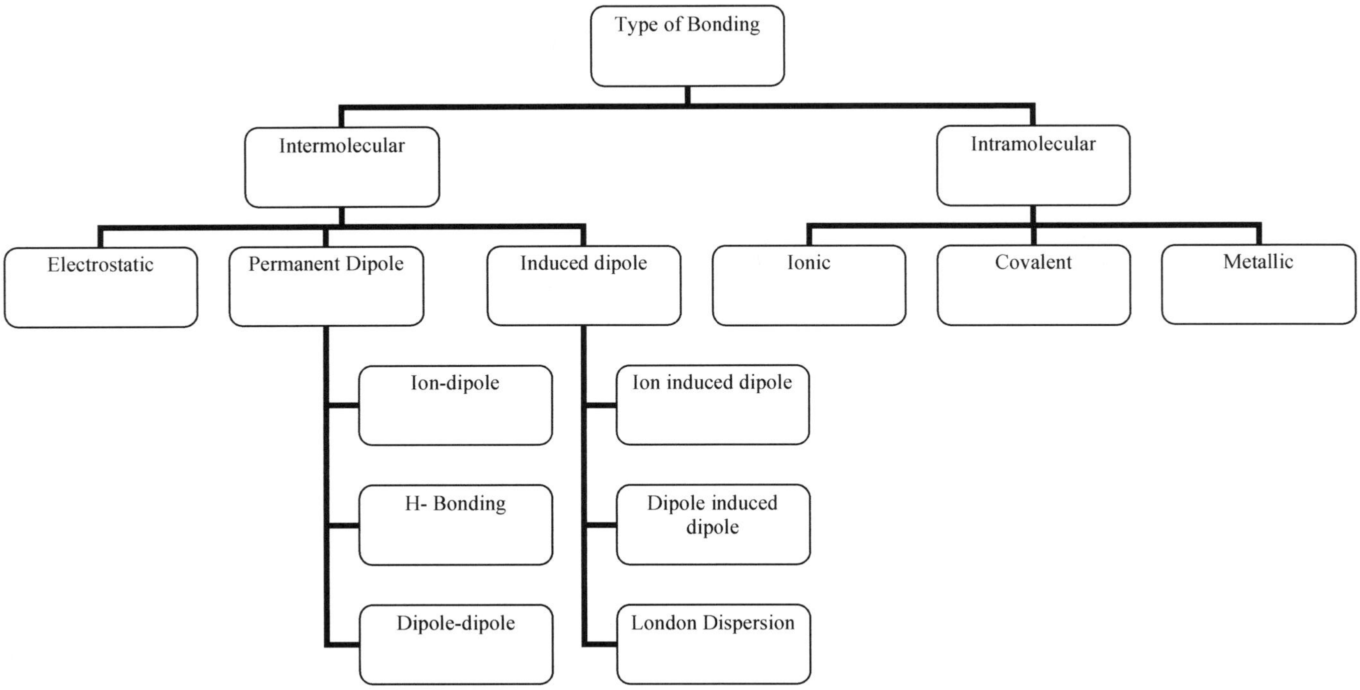

Practice: With diagrams explain why the chemical properties of a substance are based on the intramolecular bonding in the substance and the physical properties are based on the intermolecular bonding in the substance.

1.6 Review Questions

1. (a) For a chemical bond to form between two atoms, how must the energy associated with the bonded atoms compare to the energy when the atoms are apart?

   (b) What does this tell us about the attractive forces compared to the repulsive forces between them?

2. What is an ionic crystal lattice and how does it explain the high melting points of ionic compounds?

3. Use your answer to question 2 to explain why formulas for ionic compounds do not represent neutral independent molecules of those compounds.

4. Identify the attractive forces associated with
   (a) ionic bonds

   (b) covalent bonds

5. (a) Identify two similarities between ionic and covalent bonds.

   (b) Identify two differences between ionic and covalent bonds.

6. Complete the following table by writing in the formulas of the compounds formed from the pairs of elements. Determine the ΔEN value for each and then classify the bonds as non-polar covalent, polar covalent, or ionic.

Elements	Compound Formula	ΔEN Value	Nature of Bonds Present
(a) rubidium and oxygen			
(b) strontium and bromine			
(c) carbon and sulfur			
(d) silicon and chlorine			

7. Magnesium is a metal and sulfur is a non-metal. Compare the ΔEN value for these elements in the compound MgS to the ΔEN value for the non-metals hydrogen and oxygen in water, H_2O. Which of the two compounds possesses a greater amount of ionic character in its bonds?

8. Glucose is a covalent compound with the molecular formula $C_6H_{12}O_6$. This and many other covalent formulas aren't reduced to the smallest whole-number ratios of atoms in the compound. Why not?

9. Many covalent compounds have much lower melting points than ionic compounds. Why does this not mean that covalent bonds are weaker than ionic bonds?

10. Diamond is a form of pure carbon containing only covalent bonds. It is the hardest substance known and has a melting point of about 3550°C. What name do we give to this type of covalent substance? Suggest a reason for its very high melting point.

11. Consider the nature of the covalent bonds present in HCl and in N_2. Which substance would you expect to have the higher melting point? Give a reason for your answer.

2 Chemical Formulae and Nomenclature

By the end of this chapter, you should be able to do the following:

- Relate the observable properties and characteristics of elements, compounds, and mixtures to the concept of atoms and molecules
- Write the names and formulas for ionic and covalent compounds, given appropriate charts or data tables
- Differentiate between physical and chemical changes
- Select an appropriate way of separating the components of a mixture

By the end of this chapter, you should know the meaning of these **key terms**:

- acid
- atom
- base
- boiling point
- chemical change
- chemical property
- chemical reactivity
- chromatography
- compound
- distillation
- element
- evaporation
- filtration
- freezing point
- gas
- ion charge
- ion/ionic
- kinetic molecular theory
- liquid
- mass
- matter
- melting point
- metal
- mixture
- molecular formula
- molecule
- monatomic ions
- non-metal
- physical change
- physical property
- pure substance
- salt
- solid

Your cellphone, your food, your books, your school, you — everything is made up of matter. How matter can be combined into compounds that form all the different parts of your cellphone depends on physical and chemical properties and physical and chemical changes. In this chapter, you'll learn about the nature of matter and its properties.

2.1 Oxidation Numbers

Oxidation Numbers — A System for Tracking Electrons

The easiest way to determine whether electrons have been transferred between elements during a chemical reaction is to keep track of each atom's **oxidation number** (also referred to as the **oxidation state**). In junior science, you probably referred to the oxidation state as the combining capacity. Multivalent metals such as iron, for example, may combine with chlorine to form $FeCl_2$ or $FeCl_3$, depending on the oxidation state of the iron ion involved. The compound containing iron with an oxidation state of +2 has the formula $FeCl_2$ and is called iron(II) chloride. This distinguishes it from $FeCl_3$ or iron(III) chloride containing iron with an oxidation state of +3. Notice that the charge is indicated before the number in an oxidation state.

Oxidation numbers (oxidation states) actually extend beyond combining capacities as they may be assigned to any atom in any aggregation, whether atoms exist as elements, monatomic ions, or part of a polyatomic ion or compound. The easiest way to assign oxidation states to atoms is to follow the simple set of rules in Table 2.1.1.

Table 2.1.1 *Rules for Oxidation Numbers*

Rule	Statement Regarding the Oxidation Number	Examples
1.	Atoms in elemental form = 0	Na, O_2, P_4, As, Zn
2.	Monatomic ions = the ion's charge	K^{+1},Ca^{+2}, Fe^{+2}, Fe^{+3}, Cl^{-1}
3.	Oxygen always = –2 except in peroxides (O_2^{2-}) = –1 and OF_2 = +2	Na_2O_2 and OF_2
4.	Hydrogen always = +1 except in metal hydrides = –1	CaH_2, LiH
5.	Oxidation states in compounds must sum to zero.	CuCl, $CuCl_2$ contain copper(I) and copper(II)
6.	Oxidation states in polyatomic ions must sum to the ion charge.	ClO_4^{1-}, ClO_3^{1-} contain chlorine = +7 and +5
7.	Always assign the more electronegative element a negative oxidation number.	PF_5 contains F = –1 and thus P = +5
8.	In a compound or ion containing more than two elements, the element written farthest to the right takes its most common oxidation state.	SCN^- contains N = –3 (most common), S = –2 (negative value), thus C = +4.

If the species contains oxygen and/or hydrogen, it is often best to assign their oxidation states first. For a species containing multiple types of atoms, assign the more electronegative element first. If the more electronegative element has more than one oxidation state, use its most common oxidation state.

It is important to note that we always calculate the oxidation number of *one* atom of a particular element. The subscripts that may be assigned to a particular atom have *no effect* on the oxidation number of that atom.

Sample Problem — Assigning Oxidation States

Assign the oxidation state of each atom in the following species:

1. H_2CO_3
2. PO_4^{3-}
3. $Fe(NO_3)_2$

What to Think about	How to Do It
Species 1 1. For H_2CO_3 assign oxidation states to hydrogen and oxygen first, following the rules. Neither hydrogen nor oxygen is in elemental form. This is not an exception for oxygen (the compound is not a peroxide nor is it OF_2) or hydrogen (the compound is not a metal hydride). Consequently these two elements are assigned their usual oxidation states. Specifically, apply rule 3 for oxygen and rule 4 for hydrogen.	Hydrogen is +1 and oxygen is -2. For hydrogen, (2 × +1) = a total of +2 For oxygen, (3 × -2) = a total of -6
2. Apply rule 5 to calculate the oxidation state for the middle atom in the formula, in this case, carbon.	For carbon: (+2) + ( ) + (-6) = 0 so the oxidation state must be +4.
Species 2 1. For PO_4^{3-} assign the oxidation state of oxygen first, following rule 3. Oxygen is not in elemental form, nor is it in a peroxide or OF_2.	Oxygen is -2. For oxygen, (4 × -2) = a total of -8
2. Apply rule 6 to calculate the oxidation state for the phosphorus.	For phosphorus: ( ) + (-8) = -3 so the oxidation state must be +5.
Species 3 1. For $Fe(NO_3)_2$, begin by considering the nitrate ion NO_3^- as a group and following rule 5 to calculate the oxidation state of iron. As there are two NO_3^- groups, each with an overall charge of 1–, the oxidation state of the Fe must be **+2.**	Iron is +2. Oxygen is a -2. For oxygen, (3 × -2) = a total of -6
2. Remember that subscripts have no effect on oxidation states, so rules 3 and 6 can now be applied to complete the problem.	For nitrogen: ( ) + (-6) = -1 so the oxidation state must be +5.

Practice Problems — Assigning Oxidation States

Assign the oxidation state of each atom in the following species:

1. H_2O
2. Li_2O_2
3. $AgMnO_4$
4. $K_2Cr_2O_7$
5. AlH_3
6. NH_4^+
7. OF_2
8. $Ca(NO_3)_2$
9. ClO_3^-
10. $(N_2H_5)_2CO_3$

Quick Check

1. Write a balanced equation for the combination of magnesium metal with oxygen gas to synthesize a metal oxide.

2. Indicate the oxidation state of each element over top of its symbol.
3. Use arrows to indicate the direction of electron transfer between the reactants.

Oxidation and Reduction

When an atom gains electrons during a reaction, its oxidation number becomes more negative. This is logical as the electrons the atom gains are negative particles. The substance whose oxidation number becomes smaller is being reduced.

A *decrease in oxidation state* is called **reduction.**

On the other hand, when an atom loses electrons during a reaction, its oxidation number becomes more positive. This is because the number of protons (positive charges) does not change, but there are fewer electrons. Consequently, the atom now has more positive protons than negative electrons and so the net charge is greater. The substance whose oxidation state increases is being oxidized.

An *increase in oxidation state* is called **oxidation.**

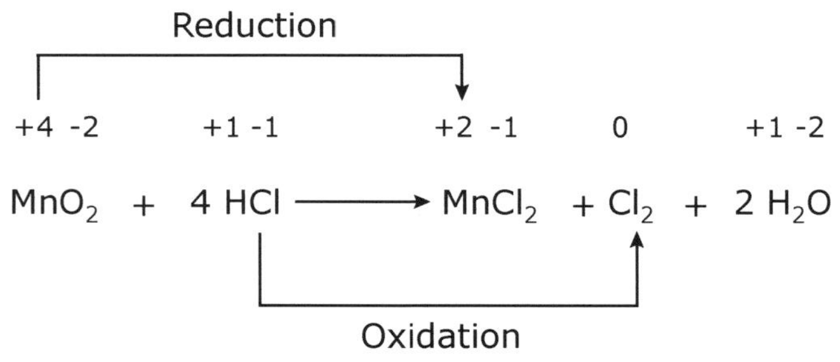

Figure 2.1.1 *Reduction and oxidation always occur together in a reaction.*

It is important to realize that reduction and oxidation always occur together in a reaction (Figure 2.1.1). If the oxidation number of one atom increases due to a loss of electrons, the oxidation number of another substance must decrease due to a gain of electrons. This is why reactions that involve electron transfer are called oxidation-reduction reactions or redox reactions for short. The oxidation number changes are entirely due to the transfer of electrons.

Remember that we always state the oxidation number for just *one* atom of a particular element, *no matter what subscript or coefficient* may be associated with the atom.

A *gain of electrons* is REDUCTION, while *a loss of electrons* is OXIDATION.

The following is a handy device to help remember what happens to electrons during the redox process:

LEO goes GER

lose electrons oxidation — gain electrons reduction

Quick Check

1. (a) How many electrons did each magnesium atom lose in the previous Quick Check? ____
   (b) How many electrons did each oxygen atom gain? _____
   (c) Which species was oxidized? __________
   Which was reduced? ___________
2. (a) In Figure 4.3.1, how many electrons did each manganese(IV) ion gain? _____
   (b) How many electrons did each chloride ion lose? _____
   Did all the chloride ions lose electrons? _____

Agents are the Cause of Electron Transfer

Examination of the two examples in the Quick Check above indicates that the number of electrons lost by the species being oxidized must always equal the number of electrons gained by the species being reduced.

So far we have examined electron transfer in terms of the species that lost or gained the electrons. Another approach is to view the reaction from the perspective of the species that cause the electron loss or gain. In this sense, the species that is oxidized causes another species to gain electrons and be reduced. Such a species may be called a reducing agent. A similar argument describes the chemical that is reduced as an oxidizing agent (Figure 2.1.2).

A substance that is reduced acts as an **oxidizing agent**, while a substance that is oxidized acts as a **reducing agent**.

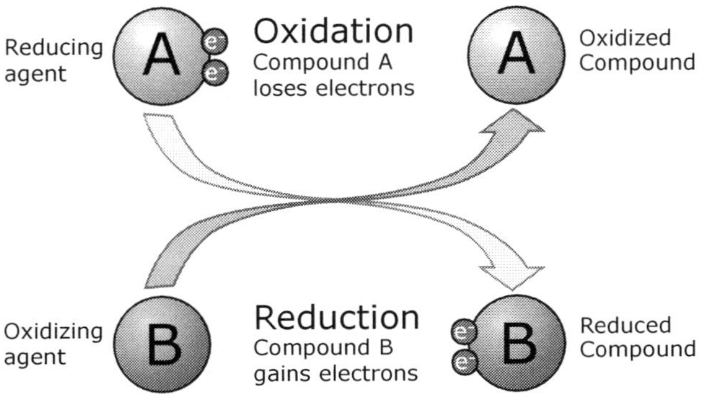

Figure 2.1.2 *Oxidizing agents and reducing agents*

Sample Problem — Recognizing Oxidizing and Reducing Agents

Indicate the oxidizing and reducing agent in each of the following reactions:

1. $Zn(s) + 2\ HCl(aq) \rightarrow ZnCl_2(aq) + H_2(g)$
2. $4\ NH_3(g) + 7\ O_2(g) \rightarrow 4\ NO_2(g) + 6\ H_2O(l)$

What to Think about

Reaction 1

1. Assign oxidation states to all elements in the equation.
2. Indicate the increase in oxidation state as an oxidation and the decrease in oxidation state as a reduction.
3. Identify the species that was oxidized as the reducing agent. Identify the one that was reduced as the oxidizing agent.

Notice that the Zn atom lost two electrons, while each H^+ ion gained one.

Reaction 2

1. The second example may appear not to fit any of the traditional five categories of classification from previous section. (It is the combustion of ammonia.) Often redox reactions do not fit our classic categories. You will encounter many more of these in future Chemistry courses.
2. Notice that even though hydrogen is written second in the formula for ammonia, this species is not a metal hydride so hydrogen is assigned its usual oxidation state.

NOTE: When the atom that is oxidized or reduced belongs to a covalent compound, we indicate the entire species as the agent.

How to Do It

Reaction 1

Zn: $0 \rightarrow +2$
H: $+1 \rightarrow 0$
Cl: $1 \rightarrow -1$
Zinc atom was oxidized.
Hydrogen ion was reduced.

Zinc atom is the reducing agent.
Hydrogen ion (H^+) is the oxidizing agent.

Reaction 2

H: $+1 \rightarrow +1$
O: $0 \rightarrow -2$ (in both products)
N: $-3 \rightarrow +4$

Oxygen gas was reduced.
N in ammonia was oxidized.

Oxygen gas is the oxidizing agent.
Ammonia is the reducing agent.

Practice Problems — Recognizing Oxidizing and Reducing Agents

Determine the oxidizing and reducing agent in each of the following reactions. Begin by clearly indicating the oxidation states of all elements in each equation.

1. $Si(s) + 2\ H_2(g) \rightarrow SiH_4(g)$
2. $3\ Ca(s) + 2\ AlBr_3(aq) \rightarrow 2\ Al(s) + 3\ CaBr_2(aq)$
3. $5\ CO(g) + I_2O_5(s) \rightarrow 5\ CO_2(g) + I_2(s)$
4. $2\ NH_3(g) \rightarrow N_2(g) + 3\ H_2(g)$
5. $Mg(s) + 2\ H_2O(l) \rightarrow Mg(OH)_2(s) + H_2(g)$

2.1 Activity: Building a Table of Reduction Strengths

Question

Can you build a table of reduction strengths?

Background

It is possible to separate out the reduction and oxidation portions of a redox reaction and to represent them as half reactions. For example, the sample reaction from the previous page: $Zn(s) + 2\ HCl(aq) \rightarrow ZnCl_2(aq) + H_2(g)$ may be broken into the following half reactions: $Zn \rightarrow Zn^{2+} + 2e^-$ (oxidation) and $2H^+ + 2e^- \rightarrow H_2$ (reduction). Notice that the chloride ion is not included in either reaction, as its oxidation state does not change.

An attempt to replace zinc with hydrogen in the following single replacement reaction: $H_2(g) + ZnCl_2(aq) \rightarrow 2HCl(aq) + Zn(s)$ is *unsuccessful* because H_2 gas is too weak as a reducing agent to be oxidized to H^+. Similarly Zn^{2+} is too weak as an oxidizing agent to be reduced to Zn. Comparing these two competing reactions shows us that H^+ ion is a stronger oxidizing agent than Zn^{2+}. Consider the following data:

Attempted Reaction	Result
1. A piece of zinc metal is placed in a solution of $CuCl_2$.	Brown coating results on the zinc.
2. A piece of copper metal is placed in a $ZnCl_2$ solution.	No reaction occurs.
3. Hydrogen gas is bubbled through a solution of $CuCl_2$.	Bits of brown metal form in an acid.
4. Copper metal is placed in a solution of HCl.	No reaction occurs.
5. Manganese metal is placed in a solution of $ZnCl_2$.	Black solid forms in pink $Mn^{2+}(aq)$.
6. Manganese metal is placed in a solution of $CaCl_2$.	No reaction occurs.
7. Calcium metal is placed in a solution of KCl.	No reaction occurs.
8. A coil of zinc wire is placed in a solution of HCl.	Bubbles form as the zinc breaks up.

Procedure

1. Work with a partner or by yourself to design a table of reduction half reactions. Your table should be organized with the strongest oxidizing agent (the species most likely to be reduced) at the top. See the Results and Discussion section below for more ideas.
2. Compare your completed table with those of other groups.

Results and Discussion

1. Write a balanced equation for each attempted reaction (successful and *unsuccessful*) in the space below.

2. Write a half reaction for the reduction process that would occur in each equation.

3. Use the result of each attempted reaction to help list the reductions from the most likely to the least likely to occur.

4. Label the species at the top of your list as the "strongest oxidizing agent."

5. What role do metals always play in these reactions (oxidizing or reducing agent)?

6. Where would the strongest reducing agent be located?

2.1 Review Questions

1. Give the oxidation state for the underlined element in each of the following species:
   (a) $\underline{Ca}Br_2$
   (b) $\underline{O}F_2$
   (c) $\underline{C}_6H_{12}O_6$
   (d) $K_2\underline{O}_2$
   (e) $\underline{S}_2O_3^{2-}$
   (f) $Ba\underline{H}_2$
   (g) $\underline{Cl}O^-$
   (h) $\underline{S}_8$

2. Complete and balance each of the following reactions. (States are not required.) Indicate which involve electron transfer.
   (a) $Ca + O_2 \rightarrow$
   (b) $CaO + H_2O \rightarrow$
   (c) $Ca + H_2O \rightarrow$
   (d) $Ca(OH)_2 + HCl \rightarrow$

3. (a) What is an oxidizing agent?

   (b) What is a reducing agent?

   (c) How would you expect electronegativity to be related to the strength of each?

4. For each of the following reactions, indicate the species being oxidized and reduced and show the oxidation states above their symbols.

   (a) $2\ KClO_3(s) \rightarrow 2\ KCl(s) + 3\ O_2(g)$

   (b) $Mg(s) + 2\ AgNO_3(aq) \rightarrow Mg(NO_3)_2(aq) + 2\ Ag(s)$

   (c) $P_4(s) + 5\ O_2(g) \rightarrow 2\ P_2O_5(g)$

   (d) $NH_4NO_3(s) \rightarrow N_2O(g) + 2\ H_2O(l)$

5. In which chemical family would you expect to find:
   (a) the most readily oxidized elements? Explain.

   (b) the most readily reduced elements? Explain.

6. Determine the oxidizing and reducing agent in each of the following reactions. Then indicate the number of electrons transferred by one atom of the reducing agent.

(a) $2\ Pb(s) + O_2(g) \rightarrow 2\ PbO(s)$ OA: RA: No. e^-:

(b) $Pb(s) + 2\ Br_2(l) \rightarrow PbBr_4(s)$ OA: RA: No. e^-:

(c) $2\ Al(s) + 6\ HCl(aq) \rightarrow 2\ AlCl_3(aq) + 3\ H_2(g)$ OA: RA: No. e^-:

(d) $C_3H_8(g) + 5\ O_2(g) \rightarrow 3\ CO_2(g) + 4\ H_2O(g)$ OA: RA: No. e^-:

7. Predict the products and write balanced equations for each of the following reactions. Include state indicators. Classify each equation according to one of the six reactions from the previous section. Then classify each again as redox or not.

(a) Sulfur dioxide gas reacts with solid calcium oxide.

(b) Solid potassium nitrate is heated to form solid potassium nitrite and a gas.

(c) Strontium hydroxide solution reacts with nitric acid.

(d) Aluminum hydroxide solid is decomposed.

(e) Chlorine gas is bubbled through a solution of cesium iodide.

(f) Tetraphosphorus decaoxide solid is reacted with water.

(g) Aluminum metal reacts with liquid bromine.

(h) Zinc metal is placed in a solution of nickel(III) choride.

8. Give an oxidation and a reduction half reaction for each of the following redox reactions:

(a) $Sn(s) + 2\ AgNO_3(aq) \rightarrow Sn(NO_3)_2(aq) + 2\ Ag(s)$

(b) $F_2(g) + 2\ NaCl(s) \rightarrow 2\ NaF(s) + Cl_2(g)$

Oxidation Number Worksheet

Format for presenting answers on oxidation number questions
Examples:

Oxidation number	**+1-2+1**		
	NaOH		
Oxidation number	**+1 x -2**	**Oxidation number**	**+1-7 -2**
	$KMnO_4$		**$KMnO_4$**
Total charge	**+1+ x + (-8) =0**		

1. Determine the Oxidation Numbers for the following compounds

a) H_2 b) FeO c) $BeCl_2$ d) CO_2

e) $K_2Cr_2O_7$ f) KNO_3 g) PO_4^{3-} h) CaH_2

i) H_2O_2 j) Rb k) MnO_2 l) CO_3^{2-}

m) P_2O_4 n) $KClO_4$ o) Fe_2O_3 p) OF_2

q) $Al(OH)_3$ r) H_2SO_4 s) $Cu(NO_3)_2$ t) AsO_3^{3-}

2.2 Names and Formulas of Inorganic Compounds

Warm Up

Ions are charged atoms or charged groups of atoms. Ions always associate (bond) together in the ratio that results in their charges cancelling to form neutral compounds. Complete the table by providing the formulas of the compounds formed by the ions specified.

	Br^-	O^{2-}	N^{3-}	OH^-	SO_4^{2-}	PO_4^{3-}
Na^+	NaBr		Na_3N			
Ca^{2+}						$Ca_3(PO_4)_2$
Al^{3+}				$Al(OH)_3$		
NH_4^+		$(NH_4)_2O$				
Sn^{4+}					$Sn(SO_4)_2$	

Binary Ionic Compounds

Recall that non-metals form molecular compounds with other non-metals but they form ionic compounds with metals. The names and formulas of these two types of compounds are handled differently.

A **binary compound** contains the atoms of only two elements, and binary ionic compounds contain only two types of **monatomic ions** (charged individual atoms).

The name of any ionic compound is simply the name of its constituent metal ion followed by the name of its constituent non-metal ion.

For example, a compound containing sodium ions and chloride ions is called sodium chloride.

The ratio of the ions formed when a particular metal and non-metal react can be predicted through the charge of their common ions, which can be found in the table of common ions at the back of this book. Positively charged ions are called **cations** (think of the letter 't" as a + sign). Negatively charged ions are called **anions.** Note that the sign of the ion charge (+ or –) is written after the numeral. For example, the aluminum ion is denoted as Al^{3+} rather than as Al^{+3}. Scientists felt that placing the plus or minus charge before the numeral might mislead people into believing that it meant greater than or less than zero. In fact, these plus and minus signs designate the type of electrical charge. The different types of electrical charge are called opposite charges because they have opposing effects. They can cancel each other. Note that there is a difference between cancelling two things and two things cancelling. Cancelling two things (e.g., magazine subscriptions) means eliminating them. By contrast, two things cancelling means they negate each other's effects. This is what happens with positive and negative ion charges. When particles with equal but opposite charges bond together, the charges cancel to yield a product with a net charge of zero.

The concept of a net property means that the property of the whole is equal to the sum of the still existing properties of its parts. Ions always associate together in a ratio that results in their charges cancelling to form neutral compounds. For example:

separate (over the reactants) — combined (over the product)

$$2Al^{3+}(aq) + 3S^{2-}(aq) \rightarrow Al_2S_3(s)$$

$$6+ \quad + \quad 6- \quad = \quad 0$$

> All compounds are neutral. There is no such thing as a charged compound.

The formula Al_2S_3 means that there are $2Al^{3+}$ ions for every $3S^{2-}$ ions. Chemists know the charges but don't show the charges in the formulas of ionic compounds. The ionic nature of the compound is implicit in the combination of a metal and a non-metal. The formula of an ionic compound shows that the compound as a whole is neutral even though it contains both positively and negatively charged ions. Remember that a neutral atom also contains positively and negatively charged particles (protons and electrons) that are not evident in its symbol.

Look at the formula of aluminum sulfide shown below on the left. The number of aluminum ions equals the numerical value of the sulfide ion's charge and vice versa. This simple shortcut for determining the formula of ionic compounds is sometimes called the cross-over method. The cross-over method matches up the opposite charges so that they cancel and will always work if you reduce the formula to its simplest ratio.

Al^{3+} S^{2-} Al_2S_3 $\qquad$ Pb^{4+} S^{2-} Pb_2S_4 which reduces to PbS_2

$2(3+) = 3(2-)$ $\qquad$ $2(4+) = 4(2-)$

Multivalent Ions

Some elements have two or more possible valence shell electron configurations (ways of arranging its electrons). These **multivalent** elements have more than one form of stable ion. Many of the transition metals (groups 3 to 12 in the periodic table) are multivalent. For example, iron has two stable ions, Fe^{2+} and Fe^{3+}. Rather than Fe^{2+} being called the iron two plus ion, it is simply called the iron two ion, but it is written as iron(II), bracketing the roman numeral for the numerical value of the ion's charge after the name. Likewise Fe^{3+} is called the iron(III) ion. The roman numerals only appear in the compound's name, never in its formula.

A different method for naming the ions of multivalent elements was used in the not too distant past, and you may encounter it occasionally. In that method, an *–ous* or *–ic* suffix was added to the root of the element's name from which the symbol was derived. The *–ous* suffix denoted the lesser ion charge and the *–ic* suffix denoted the greater ion charge. For example, the iron(II) ion, Fe^{2+}, was called the ferrous ion, and the iron(III) ion, Fe^{3+}, was called the ferric ion.

Sample Problem — Determining the Formula of a Binary Ionic Compound from Its Name

What is the formula of tin(IV) sulfide?

What to Think about	How to Do It
1. Write the symbols of the ions named. 2. Combine the ions in the simplest ratio that results in their charges cancelling.	Sn^{4+} S^{2-} $1\,Sn^{4+} + 2\,S^{2-} \rightarrow SnS_2$ $4+ \quad + \quad 4- \quad = \quad 0$

Sample Problem — Determining the Name of a Binary Ionic Compound from Its Formula

What is the name of Fe_2S_3?

What to Think about	How to Do It
1. Write the names of the two constituent ions. 2. Write the formulas of the possible compounds to see which one has the correct formula.	iron(II) or iron(III), sulfide iron(II) sulfide $Fe^{2+} + S^{2-} \rightarrow FeS$ ✗ iron(III) sulfide $2\,Fe^{3+} + 3\,S^{2-} \rightarrow Fe_2S_3$ ✓

Practice Problems — Determining the Names and Formulas of Binary Ionic Compounds

1. Write the formula of each of the following binary ionic compounds:
   (a) lithium sulfide
   (b) chromium(III) oxide
   (c) aluminum chloride
   (d) lead(II) sulfide
   (e) tin(II) iodide
   (f) zinc bromide

2. Name each of the following binary ionic compounds:
   (a) ZnO ______________________
   (b) $PbCl_4$ ______________________
   (c) $CuCl_2$ ______________________
   (d) NaI ______________________
   (e) K_2S ______________________
   (f) CrO ______________________

Nomenclature of Ionic Compounds with Transition Metals

Most transition metals can form more than one kind of ion. Metals that can have more than one valence, or oxidation state are classified as multivalent. The IUPAC name of compounds with multivalent ions is simple. The name of the multivalent metal includes the oxidation state of the metal in brackets

CuCl2 is named copper (II) chloride

CuCl is named copper (I) chloride

MnO2 is

FeS is

CrBr3

Ni2O3 is

This IUPAC naming system for multivalent metals is also known at the Stock system.

It is important to remember that metals which only have one valence state never used the stock system and their valence states should not be included in brackets

Al2O3

ZnCl2

Ag2O

CdO

In the past, another system of naming compounds with two valence states was also used. Although this method has several disadvantages, it is still fairly widely used today and you will commonly see labels that used these names. In this method called the classical method, the ending –ic is used to represent the higher valence state and the ending –ous is used to represent the lower valence state.

Metal	Compound	Stock method	Classical method
Copper	Cu_2O		Cuprous oxide
	CuO		Cupric oxide
Iron			Ferrous chloride
		Iron (III) chloride	
Tin	SnS		
			Stannic sulfide
Lead			Plumbous oxide
Antimony			Stibnous nitride
	Sb_3N_5		
Cobalt			Cobaltous bromide
		Cobalt (III) bromide	
Gold			Aurous phosphide
	AuP		
Mercury	HgI		
			Mercuric iodide

Common Chemical names

In addition to the IUPAC names for compounds there are also common names which are sometimes used more often than the IUPAC names e.g. water

IUPAC Name	Chemical Formula	Common name	Use of property
	Al_2O_3	Alumina, bauxite	Abrasive
	$CaCO_3$	Limestone, marble	Building, sculpting
	CaO	Lime, quicklime	Neutralizing acidified lakes
	HCl	Muriatic acid	Cleaning metal
	$Mg(OH)_2$	Milk of magnesia	Antacid
	N_2O	Laughing gas	Used in dentistry as an anaesthetic
	SiO_2	Quartz sand	Manufacture of glass
	Na_2CO_3	Washing soda	General cleaner
	$NaCl$	Table salt	Enhancing flavour
	$NaHCO_3$	Baking soda	Making baked goods rise
	$NaOH$	Lye	Neutralizing acids
Sodium thiosulfate	NaS_2O_3	Hypo	Fixer in photography
	$CaCl_2$	Road Salt	Lowers the melting point of water
	$NaNO_3$, KNO_3	Saltpetre	Gunpowder, fertilizer, production of nitric acid
	K_2CO_3	Potash	Animal feed, fertilizer
	NH_3	Ammonia	Cleaner, fertilizer
	PH_3	Phosphine	Catalyst, fertilizer
	AsH_3	Arsine	Doping gas for semiconductor preparation
	SbH_3	Stibnine	Electronics

Polyatomic Ions

Recall that a molecule is a *neutral* group of covalently bonded atoms. A **polyatomic ion** is a *charged* group of covalently bonded atoms so it's like a molecule except that it has a charge. Polyatomic ions play an extremely important role in the environment, the laboratory, and industry. They are relatively stable species that often remain intact in chemical reactions. Many polyatomic ions are **oxyanions**, consisting of an atom of a given element and some number of oxygen atoms. Typically the element forms polyatomic ions with different numbers of oxygen atoms. When the element forms two such ions, the one with the lesser number of oxygen atoms takes an *–ite* suffix, while the one with the greater number of oxygen atoms takes an *–ate* suffix. For example:

nitrite	NO_2^-	nitrate	NO_3^-
sulfite	SO_3^{2-}	sulfate	SO_4^{2-}

When there are more than two oxyanions in a series, the prefixes *hypo-* (less than) and *per-* (more than) are used to indicate polyatomic ions with still less or still more oxygen atoms. For example:

hypochlorite	ClO^-
chlorite	ClO_2^-
chlorate	ClO_3^-
perchlorate	ClO_4^-

The prefix bi- before the name of a polyatomic ion adds an H^+ to it. For example:

carbonate	CO_3^{2-}	hydrogen carbonate or bicarbonate	HCO_3^- $(H^+ + CO_3^{2-})$
sulfate	SO_4^{2-}	hydrogen sulfate or bisulfate	HSO_4^- $(H^+ + SO_4^{2-})$

Note that there are some exceptions to these naming conventions. The hydroxide ion is the only polyatomic ion to have an *–ide* suffix. The dichromate ion has the formula $Cr_2O_7^{2-}$ and despite its prefix does not refer to two chromate ions.

Because they are charged, polyatomic ions associate with oppositely charged ions to form ionic compounds. Polyatomic ions are bracketed in formulas. For example, the formula of calcium nitrate is $Ca(NO_3)_2$. This means that the atoms within the brackets are bonded covalently to each other and as a group they are bonded ionically to the atom or atoms outside the brackets. The brackets are necessary to show that the formula ratio applies to the entire polyatomic ion, not just to its last atom. For example, the formula of calcium hydroxide is $Ca(OH)_2$ meaning that there are two hydroxide (OH^-) ions for each calcium ion. If the brackets were omitted, the formula would look like this: $CaOH_2$. In that case, the subscript 2 would apply only to the hydrogen atom. By convention, chemists omit the brackets if no subscript is required. For example, Na(OH) is written as just NaOH.

The ionic compounds that you'll encounter in this course will each have only two types of ions unless otherwise specified. Therefore, the first element in the formula will represent the cation and the remainder will represent the anion. The one exception is in ammonium compounds; the only polyatomic cation you'll encounter is the ammonium ion, NH_4^+. For example:

$ZnCr_2O_7$ must consist of Zn^{2+} ions and $Cr_2O_7^{2-}$ ions (to cancel the 2+).

$Cr_2O_7^{2-}$ is the dichromate ion so this compound is called zinc dichromate.

$NaClO_2$ must consist of Na^+ ions and ClO_2^- ions (to cancel the 1+).

ClO_2^- is the chlorite ion so this compound is called sodium chlorite.

See page 436 for a list of common polyatomic ions.

Sample Problem — Determining the Formula of any Ionic Compound from Its Name

What is the formula of potassium sulfite?

What to Think about	How to Do It
1. Write the symbols of the ions named. 2. Combine the ions in the simplest ratio that results in their charges cancelling.	K^+ SO_3^{2-} $2\,K^+ + SO_3^{2-} \rightarrow K_2SO_3$ $2+ \quad + \; 2- \quad = \quad 0$

Sample Problem — Determining the Name of any Ionic Compound from Its Formula

What is the name of $Cr(HSO_4)_2$?

What to Think about	How to Do It
1. Write the names of the two constituent ions. 2. Write the formulas of the possible compounds to see which one has the correct formula.	chromium(II) or chromium(III), bisulfate chromium(II) bisulfate $Cr^{2+} + 2\,HSO_4^- \rightarrow Cr(HSO_4)_2$ ✓ chromium(III) bisulfate $Cr^{3+} + 3\,HSO_4^- \rightarrow Cr(HSO_4)_3$ ✗

Practice Problems — Determining the Names and Formulas of Ionic Compounds

1. Write the formula of each of the following ionic compounds:

   (a) barium sulfate
   (b) silver nitrate
   (c) mercury(II) bromide
   (d) tin(IV) oxalate
   (e) aluminum dichromate
   (f) potassium fluoride

2. Name each of the following ionic compounds:

   (a) $Zn(OH)_2$ ____________________
   (b) SnO ____________________
   (c) $Cu(ClO)_2$ ____________________
   (d) $NaCH_3COO$ ____________________
   (e) MgI_2 ____________________
   (f) $FeCr_2O_7$ ____________________

Polyatomic ions

The most common polyatomic **cation** is NH_4^+ which is called ______________________

Table of polyatomic anions

Valence = -1			
Ion	**Name**	**Ion**	**Name**
CN^-		$H_2PO_3^-$	
$C_2H_3O_2^-$		$H_2PO_4^-$	
ClO^-		MnO_4^-	
ClO_2^-		NO_2^-	
ClO_3^-		NO_3^-	
ClO_4^-		OCN^-	
HCO_3^-		$HC_2O_4^-$	
HSO_3^-		OH^-	
HSO_4^-		SCN^-	
BrO_3^-		IO_3^-	

Valence = -2			
Ion	**Name**	**Ion**	**Name**
CO_3^{2-}		O_2^{2-}	
$C_2O_4^{2-}$		SiO_3^{2-}	
CrO_4^{2-}		SO_3^{2-}	
$Cr_2O_7^{2-}$		SO_4^{2-}	
HPO_3^{2-}		$S_2O_3^{2-}$	
HPO_4^{2-}			

Valence = -3			
Ion	Name	Ion	Name
AsO_3^{3-}		PO_3^{3-}	
AsO_4^{3-}		PO_4^{3-}	
BO_3^{3-}			

Names and Formulas of Binary Molecular Compounds

Any cation and anion combine in a single ratio that is easily predictable from their charges. This is why ionic compounds' names do not need to explicitly contain their formulas. On the other hand, two non-metal atoms may share electrons and combine in several ratios. Therefore, the name of the molecular compound must reveal its formula to distinguish it from the other compounds of the same two elements. The name of a molecular compound uses a prefix code to provide its formula. The prefixes used are shown in Table 2.2.1.

Table 2.2.1 *Prefixes for Molecular Compounds*

Number	Prefix
1	mono-
2	di-
3	tri-
4	tetra-
5	penta-
6	hexa-
7	hepta-
8	octa-
9	nona-
10	deca-

The names of all binary compounds have an *–ide* suffix. N_2O_4 is therefore dinitrogen tetroxide. Note that the number of atoms comes before the *name* of the element but after the *symbol* of the element. The prefix *mono-* is understood for the first element named if no prefix is stated. For example, carbon dioxide is CO_2.

Sample Problem — Determining the Formula of a Molecular Compound from Its Name

What is the formula of xenon tetrafluoride?

What to Think about	How to Do It
1. Write the symbols of each element and the number of atoms of each.	1 Xe and 4 F
2. Rewrite this information as a formula.	XeF_4

Sample Problem — Determining the Name of a Molecular Compound from Its Formula

What is the name of P_4S_{10}?

What to Think about	How to Do It
1. Write the names of each element and the number of atoms of each.	4 phosphorus and 10 sulfur
2. Rewrite this information using the prefix code.	tetraphosphorus decasulfide

Practice Problems — Determining the Names and Formulas of Molecular Compounds

1. Write the formula of each of the following molecular compounds:

   (a) nitrogen monoxide

   (b) nitrogen dioxide

   (c) dinitrogen tetroxide

   (d) dinitrogen trioxide

2. Name each of the following molecular compounds:

   (a) PCl_5 ______________________

   (b) SO_2 ______________________

   (c) CO ______________________

   (d) P_2O_5 ______________________

Hydrates

When many salts crystallize out of aqueous solution they incorporate water molecules in a fixed ratio and pattern into their ionic crystal lattice. These salts are called **hydrates.** Many salts are supplied as hydrates. The water in the crystal doesn't usually present a problem as most salts are destined for aqueous solutions anyway. Water is an integral part of hydrates and thus must be accounted for in both their names and their formulas. The same prefixes used for naming molecules precede the term *-hydrate* to denote the number of water molecules in the formula. This tells you the ratio of water molecules to ions.

Gently warming a hydrated salt will usually remove the water from the crystal. The term "**anhydrous**" refers to the form of the salt without ("an") water ("hydrous"). Some anhydrous salts are *hygroscopic* which means that they can absorb water from the air to form hydrates. Hygroscopic salts that are being used to keep the air dry in a container are called **desiccants**. Pouches containing silicate salts are sometimes used as desiccants in boxes or cases containing binoculars, guitars, shoes, etc. Most labs have a special airtight glass container designed to store containers of hygroscopic salts. This container is called a **desiccator**. One of the salts is poured onto the bottom of the desiccator to keep its air dry so the others are not exposed to water vapor.

Sample Problem — Determining the Formula of a Hydrate from Its Name

What is the formula of copper(II) sulfate heptahydrate?

What to Think about	How to Do It
1. Write the symbols of the ions named.	Cu^{2+} SO_4^{2-}
2. Combine the ions in the simplest ratio that results in their charges cancelling.	$Cu^{2+} + SO_4^{2-} \rightarrow CuSO_4$
3. Tack on the appropriate number of water molecules to complete the formula.	heptahydrate means $7H_2O$ $CuSO_4 \cdot 7H_2O$

Sample Problem — Determining the Name of a Hydrate from its Formula

What is the name of $NaCH_3COO \cdot 3H_2O$?

What to Think about	How to Do It
1. Write the names of the two constituent ions.	sodium, acetate
2. Tack on the appropriate number of water molecules using the prefix code (–hydrate).	sodium acetate trihydrate

Practice Problems — Determining the Names and Formulas of Hydrates

1. Write the formula of each of the following hydrates:
   (a) barium chloride dihydrate
   (b) sodium carbonate monohydrate
   (c) iron(III) nitrate nonahydrate
   (d) barium hydroxide octahydrate

2. Name each of the following hydrates:
   (a) $CoCl_2 \cdot 6H_2O$ ____________________
   b) $FeCl_3 \cdot 4H_2O$ ____________________
   (c) $Na_2Cr_2O_7 \cdot 2H_2O$ ____________________
   (d) $MgSO_4 \cdot 7H_2O$ ____________________

NAMING ACIDS
Binary Acids

Binary acids are classically named by using the prefix *hydro-* with the stem of the name of the most electronegative element and the ending *–ic* and the word acid. This is the classical naming system. Acids are named using the classical system rather than the IUPAC system. Acids will always have the subscript (aq). The binary compound that does not have the (aq) subscript does not act like an acid and follows IUPAC nomenclature.

e.g. $HCl(aq)$ hydrochloric acid HCl (g) hydrogen chloride

$HF(aq)$

$HBr(aq)$

HI (aq)

$H_2S(aq)$

Acids with polyatomic acids

For polyatomic ions that end in *–ide* also use the classical naming system.

$HCN(aq)$

Oxyacids

Oxyacids are combinations of oxyanions with hydrogen. The names of oxyacids can be derived by referring to the IUPAC name of the oxyanion..

1. For anions that end in *–ate*, the suffix of the acid is *–ic*.
2. For anions that end in *–ite*, the suffix of the acid is *–ous*.
3. The prefix *hypo-* and *per-* remain as part of the acid.

Oxyanion	Formula of acid	Name
SO_5^{2-}	H_2SO_5	persulfuric acid
SO_4^{2-}		
SO_3^{2-}		
SO_2^{2-}		

2.2 Review Questions

1. In each case below, write out the chemical equation for the association of the ions that form the given binary ionic compound.
   Example: magnesium phosphide
   $3\ Mg^{2+} + 2\ P^{3-} \rightarrow Mg_3P_2$
   (a) sodium fluoride

   (b) iron(II) bromide

   (c) tin(IV) chloride

   (d) chromium(III) sulfide

2. Write the formulas of the following binary ionic compounds:
   (a) chromium(III) chloride

   (b) aluminum fluoride

   (c) magnesium iodide

   (d) tin(IV) oxide

3. Write the names of the following binary ionic compounds:
   (a) K_2O

   (b) $ZnBr_2$

   (c) PbO_2

   (d) $HgCl_2$

4. Write the name and formula of the binary ionic compound formed by:

   (a) potassium and chlorine

   (b) manganese(IV) and oxygen

   (c) iron(III) and sulfur

   (d) copper(II) and iodine

5. In each case below, write out the chemical equation for the association of the ions that form the given ionic compound,
   Example: magnesium nitrate
   $Mg^{2+} + 2\ NO_3^- \rightarrow Mg(NO_3)_2$
   (a) sodium nitrite

   (b) silver phosphate

   (c) lithium ethanoate (lithium acetate)

   (d) chromium(III) oxalate

6. Write the formulas of the following ionic compounds:

   (a) copper(I) perchlorate

   (b) calcium bisulfide

   (c) aluminum monohydrogen phosphate
   (d) magnesium hydroxide

7. Write the names of the following ionic compounds:

   (a) $Ba_3(PO_4)_2$

   (b) $Fe(HSO_3)_2$

   (c) $Pb(HC_2O_4)_4$

   (d) CuH_2PO_4

8. Many minerals contain three types of ions. You can mine several minerals of copper including two forms of copper(II) carbonate hydroxide.
   malachite
   $2\ Cu^{2+} + CO_3^{2-} + 2\ OH^- \rightarrow Cu_2(CO_3)(OH)_2$
   $4+ \quad + \quad 2- \quad + \quad 2- \quad = \quad 0$
   azurite
   $3\ Cu^{2+} + 2\ CO_3^{2-} + 2\ OH^- \rightarrow Cu_3(CO_3)_2(OH)_2$
   $6+ \quad + \quad 4- \quad + \quad 2- \quad = \quad 0$
   Notice that more than one ratio of the ions results in their charges cancelling. Thus there is more than one possible compound of three ion combinations. Write a possible formula for:
   (a) iron(III) sodium chromate

   (b) zinc sulfate nitrate

9. Write the formulas of the following molecular compounds:
(a) chlorine monoxide

(b) tetraphosphorus hexaoxide

(c) arsenic pentafluoride

(d) nitrogen tri-iodide

10. Write the names of the following molecular compounds:
(a) P_3Br_5

(b) B_2H_6

(c) SO_3

(d) CF_4

11. Write the formulas of the following hydrated salts:
(a) sodium sulfate decahydrate

(b) calcium chloride dihydrate

(c) copper(II) acetate monohydrate

(d) chromium(III) chloride hexahydrate

12. Write the names of the following hydrated salts:
(a) $Cd(NO_3)_2 \cdot 4H_2O$

(b) $Na_2HPO_4 \cdot 7H_2O$

(c) $CuSO_4 \cdot 5H_2O$

(d) $Fe(NO_3)_3 \cdot 9H_2O$

13. Why is a hydrate not a mixture of salt and water?

14. Suggest why hydrate formulas are written in the manner they are, rather than bracketing the number of water molecules in the formula (e.g., $SrCl_2 \cdot 6H_2O$ rather than $SrCl_2(H_2O)_6$).

15. Write the formulas of the following acids:
(a) hydrobromic acid

(b) chromic acid

(c) chloric acid

(d) hypochlorous acid

16. Write the names of the following acids:
(a) H_2S

(b) $HClO_4$

(c) HNO_2

(d) HSCN

17. Write the formulas of the following variety of compounds:
(a) potassium oxide

(b) permanganic acid

(c) sulfur dioxide

(d) ammonium carbonate

(e) iron(II) sulfate heptahydrate

(f) hydrocyanic acid

(g) sulfur hexafluoride

(h) calcium acetate monohydrate

(i) chromium(III) bisulfite

(j) magnesium hydroxide

More Nomenclature practice

No	Name	Formula	No	Name	Formula
1	calcium hypoiodite	$Ca(IO)_2$	26	Iron (III) sulfate	$Fe_2(SO_4)_3$
2	Carbon tetraiodide	CI_4	27	Manganese (II) chloride	$MnCl_2$
3	Antimony (V) cyanide	$Sb(CN)_5$	28	Aluminum nitrate	$Al(NO_3)_3$
4	Dichlorine pentoxide	Cl_2O_5	29	Copper (II) chlorate	$Cu(ClO_3)_2$
5	Manganese (IV) oxide	MnO_2	30	Barium bromite	$Ba(BrO_2)_2$
6	Barium perbromate	$Ba(BrO_4)_2$	31	Silicon carbide	
7	Sodium permanganate	$Na(MnO_4)$	32	Magnesium thiosulfate	MgS_2O_3
8	Silver (IV) hypoiodite	$AgIO_4$	33	Potassium iodite	$K(IO_2)$
9	Sulfur dioxide	SO_2	34	Mercury (II) hypochlorite	$Hg(ClO)_2$
10	Mercury (I) perchlorate	$HgClO_4$	35	Nitric acid	H_2NO_3
11	diphosphorus pentasulfide	P_2S_5	36	Arsenic (III) acetate	$As(C_2H_3O_2)_3$
12	Sulfur trioxide	SO_3	37	Zinc thiochromate	$Zn(SCrO_3)_2$
13	Tin (II) nitrite	$Sn(NO_2)_2$	38		Cu_3N
14	Ammonia phosphate	$(NH_4)_3PO_4$	39	Magnesium hypobromite	
15	Manganese (II) chlorite	$Mn(ClO_2)_2$	40		$PbSO_3$
16	Sulfuric acid	$H_2SO_{4\,(aq)}$	41	Antimony (V) sulfite	
17	Carbon monoxide	CO	42		$H_3PO_{4\,(aq)}$
18	Tin (II) permanganate	$Sn(MnO_4)_2$	43	Arsenic (III) hydride	
19	Antimony (III) acetate	$Sb(C_2H_3O_2)_3$	44		$Fe(SCN)_3$
20	Hydroiodic acid	$HI_{(aq)}$	45	Copper (I) arsenate	
21	Tin(II) bromate	$Sn(BrO_3)_2$	46		$AgClO_4$
22	Arsenic (III) cyanate	$As(OCN)_3$	47	dichlorine monoxide	
23	Sodium chlorite	$Na(ClO_2)$	48		$HgBrO_3$
24	Potassium fluoride	KF	49	Aluminum sulfate	
25	Copper (II) hydroxide	$Cu(OH)_2$	50		$Sn(NO_3)_4$

No	Name	Formula	No	Name	Formula
1	Aluminum nitrate		26		$Fe_2(CrO_4)_3$
2		$MnCl_2$	27	diarsenic pentasulfide	
3	Iron (III) sulfate		28		$Ca(CH_3COO)$
4		$Cu(ClO_3)_2$	29	Ammonium cyanate	
5	Barium bromite		30		$Al_2(HPO_3)_3$
6		SiC	31	Cobalt (III) hydrogen carbonate	
7	Magnesium thiosulfate		32		$K_2S_2O_2$
8		KIO_2	33	Nickel (II) chlorite	
9	Mercury (II) hypochlorite		34		$BeCO_3$
10		HNO_3	35	Strontium dichromate	
11	Arsenic (III) acetate		36		$Zn(ClO_4)_2$
12		$ZnSCrO_3$	37	Lead (II) phosphite	
13	Copper (I) nitride		38		NH_4CH_3COO
14		$Mg(BrO)_2$	39	Calcium thiosulfite	
15	Lead (II) sulfite		40		$Cu_2S_2O_3$
16		$Sb_2(SO_3)_5$	41	Hydrogen cyanide	
17	Phosphoric acid		42		$Sn(MnO_4)_2$
18		AsH_3	43	Acetic acid	
19	Iron (III) thiocyanate		44		$CuHPO_3$
20		Cu_3AsO_4	45	Hydrogen sulfide	
21	Silver perchlorate		46		$BaCrO_4$
22		ClO_2	47	Zinc dihydrogen phosphate	
23	Mercury (I) bromate		48		$Al_2(C_2O_4)_3$
24		$Al_2(SO_4)_3$	49	Magnesium thiosulfate	
25	Tin (IV) nitrate		50		H_2O_2

No	Name	Formula	No	Name	Formula
1	diphosphorus trisulfide		26		U_2O_5
2		$BaCl_2$	27	Potassium phosphide	
3	Cupric oxide		28		$B(MnO_4)_3$
4		$AlPO_4$	29	Sodium iodide	
5	Mercury (II) nitrate		30		XeF_6
6		SbH_3	31	Calcium sulfate	
7	Silver fluoride		32		$BaSO_3$
8		PCl_5	33	Antimony (V) periodate	
9	Ammonium carbonate		34		$CH_3COOH_{(aq)}$
10		TiO_2	35	Zinc hypobromite	
11	Carbon tetrachloride		36		$As_2(Cr_2O_7)_3$
12		K_2S	37	Magnesium silicate	
13	Nickel (II) bromate		38		$(NH_4)HS$
14		Sb_2S_5	39	Sodium hydrogen sulfite	
15	Zinc acetate		40		$CaSO_4 \cdot 2H_2O$
16		$Co(ClO_3)_3$	41	Potassium oxalate	
17	Magnesium sulfite		42		$Ag_2Cr_2O_7$
18		$H_2SO_{3\,(aq)}$	43	Tin (II) thiosulfite	
19	Iron (II) sulfide		44		$Mg(NO_2)_2$
20		$HF_{(aq)}$	45	Lead (II) chromate	
21	Aluminum nitride		46		HgS
22	AgH_2PO_3		47	Sodium hydrogen sulfate	
23	Lithium oxide		48		NH_4ClO_4
24		$Mg(SCN)_2$	49	Barium dihydrogen arsenate	
25	Gold (III) chloride		50		$NaNO_2$

No	Name	Formula	No	Name	Formula
1		Na_3PO_3	2	diphosphorus trisulfide	
3	Aluminum nitride		4		$BaCl_2$
5		$(NH_4)_2Cr_2O_7$	6	Cupric oxide	
7	Periodic acid		8		$AlPO_4$
9		OF_2	10	Mercury (II) nitrate	
11	Lead (II) oxalate		12		SbH_3
13		$KClO_3$	14	Silver fluoride	
15	Aluminum chromate		16		PCl_5
17		$Ca(OH)_2$	18	Ammonium carbonate	
19	Magnesium hydrogen hypophosphite		20		TiO_2
21		$HI_{(aq)}$	22	Carbon tetrachloride	
23	Nickel (II) thiocyanate		24		K_2S
25		$H_2SO_{3\,(aq)}$	26	Nickel (II) bromate	
27	Chloric acid		28		Sb_2S_5
29		Hg_2HPO_2	30	Zinc acetate	
31	Barium carbonate		32		$Co(ClO_3)_3$
33		$Fe(NO)_2$	34	Magnesium sulfite	
35	Gold (III)silicate		36		$H_2SO_{4\,(aq)}$
37		$Sr(CN)_2$	38	Iron (II) sulfide	
39	Ammonium hypoiodite		40		$HBr_{(aq)}$
41		SbH_3	42	Aluminum nitride	
43	Zinc manganate		44		AgH_2PO_2
45		$Ca(HSO_4)_2$	46	Lithium oxide	
47	Iron (III) cyanate		48		$Mg(SCN)_2$
49		$Ca(CH_3COO)_2$	50	Gold (III) chloride	

No	Name	Formula	No	Name	Formula
1	Sodium sulfate		26		Na_3PO_3
2		B_2O_3	27	Aluminum nitride	
3	Potassium dihydrogen phosphate		28		$NiCO_3$
4		$Cu(NO_2)_2$	29	Periodic acid	
5	Iron (III) nitrate		30		OF_2
6		$KMnO_4$	31	Lead (II) oxalate	
7	Manganese (II) hydroxide		32		$KClO_3$
8		$Co(ClO_4)_2$	33	Aluminum chromate	
9	Sodium sulfite		34		$Ca(OH)_2$
10		$CuSO_4 \cdot 5H_2O$	35	Magnesium hydrogen hypophosphite	
11	Hydrocyanic acid		36		$HI_{(aq)}$
12		$FeBr_3$	37	Nickel (II) thiocyanate	
13	Lithium peroxide		38		H_2SO_3
14		$ZnCO_3$	39	Chloric acid	
15	Ammonium dichromate		40		Hg_2HPO_2
16		$KClO$	41	Barium carbonate	
17	Hypobromous acid		42		$Fe(NO)_2$
18		$Pb(NO_3)_2$	43	Gold (III) silicate	
19	Magnesium sulfide		44		$Sr(CN)_2$
20		$Co_2(S_2O_3)_3$	45	Ammonium hypoiodite	
21	Mercury (I) oxide		46		SbH_3
22		N_2O_4	47	Zinc permanganate	
23	Potassium perbromate		48		$Ca(HSO_4)_2$
24		UF_5	49	Iron (III) cyanate	
25	Ammonium hydrogen carbonate		50		$Ca(CH_3COO)_2$

No	Name	Formula	No	Name	Formula
1	Iron (II) dichromate		26		$Ca(IO)_2$
2		$SbBr_3$	27	Carbon tetriodide	
3	Hydrosulfuric acid		28		$Sb(CN)_5$
4		$As_3(PO_4)_5$	29	dichlorine pentoxide	
5	Potassium arsenite		30		MnO_2
6		PbC_2O_4	31	Barium perbromate	
7	Antimony (V) carbonate		32		$NaMnO_4$
8		NH_3	33	Silver periodate	
9	Zinc chromate		34		SO_2
10		PF_3	35	Mercury (I) perchlorate	
11	Sodium peroxide		36		P_2S_5
12		NO_2	37	Sulfur trioxide	
13	Carbon dioxide		38		$Sn(NO_2)_2$
14		$Fe(BrO_3)_3$	39	Ammonium phosphate	
15	Manganese (II) iodate		40		$Mn(ClO_2)_2$
16		$CaCO_3$	41	Sulfuric acid	
17	Hydrofluoric acid		42		CO
18		$Si(IO_4)_4$	43	Tin (II) permanganate	
19	Hypoiodous acid		44		$Sb(C_2H_3O_2)_3$
20		$HCl_{(aq)}$	45	Hydroiodic acid	
21	Mercury (II) hyponitrite		46		
22		Cu_2SO_4	47	Arsenic (III) cyanate	
23	Barium nitride		48		$NaClO_2$
24		$Pb(ClO)_2$	49	Potassium fluoride	
25	Aluminum manganate		50		$Co(OH)_2$

No	Name	Formula	No	Name	Formula
1	Copper (I) bromide		26		NH_4Cl
2		$Be(HSO_4)_2$	27	Aluminum chlorite	
3	Iron (III) hydrogen hypophosphite		28		$B_2(SO_4)_3$
4		$ZnCrO_4$	29	Chromium (III) arsenate	
5	Cuprous acetate		30		$Cr_2(SeO_4)_3$
6		$Sn(ClO_4)_2$	31	Copper (II) dihydrogen phosphate	
7	Nickel (II) sulfide		32		$Fe(IO_2)_2$
8		$Al(OF)_3$	33	Arsenic (V) oxide	
9	Ammonium bromate		34		CsSCN
10		$FeAsO_4$	35	Silver sulfide	
11	Barium cyanide		36		$KMnO_4$
12		$Ca(SCN)_2$	37	Ammonium hydroxide	
13	Antimony (V) periodate		38		$Hg(BrO)_2$
14		$Pb(H_2PO_2)_4$	39	Nickel (III) hydrogen sulfide	
15	Fluoric acid		40		$SrCr_2O_7$
16		$FeSO_4$	41	Nitrous acid	
17	Chromium (III) perchlorate		42		$CaMnO_4$
18		RbOH	43	Magnesium oxalate	
19	Sodium hydrogen chromate		44		HCN
20		$ZnCr_2O_7$	45	Hydrofluoric acid	
21	Sodium nitride		46		$Zn(NO)_2$
22		$Mg(FO_3)_2$	47	Aluminum carbonate	
23	Ammonium phosphate		48		$HI_{(aq)}$
24		KOCN	49	Potassium acetate	
25	Lead (II) phosphide		50		$Pb(S_2O_2)_2$

3 Chemical Reactions

By the end of this chapter, you should be able to do the following:

- Explain chemical reactions in terms of the rearrangement of the atoms as bonds are broken and new bonds are formed
- Apply the law of conservation of mass to balance formula equations
- Devise balanced equations for various chemical reactions
- Describe reactions in terms of energy changes
- Perform stoichiometric calculations involving chemical reactions

---

By the end of this chapter, you should know the meaning of these key terms:

- acid-base neutralization
- chemical reactivity
- coefficient
- combustion reaction
- decomposition reaction
- double displacement reaction
- endothermic
- exothermic
- formula equation
- limiting reagent
- precipitate
- product
- reactant
- single displacement reaction
- stoichiometry
- synthesis reaction
- thermochemical equation

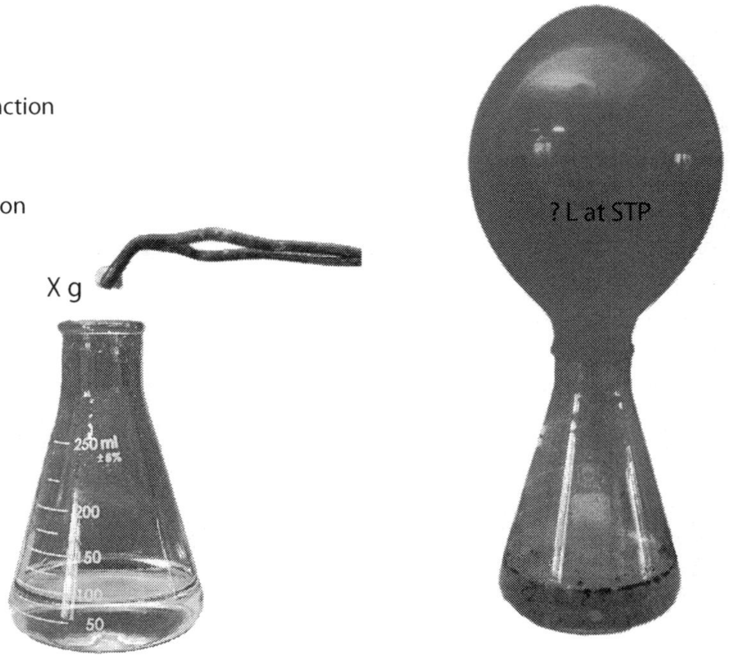

$$Zn(s) + 2HCl(aq) \rightarrow ZnCl_2(aq) + H_2(g)$$

Chemical reactions transform one set of chemicals (reactants) to completely different chemicals (products).

3.1 Writing and Balancing Chemical Equations

Warm Up

Water may be broken down into its component elements, oxygen and hydrogen, by the application of electric current. This process is called electrolysis.

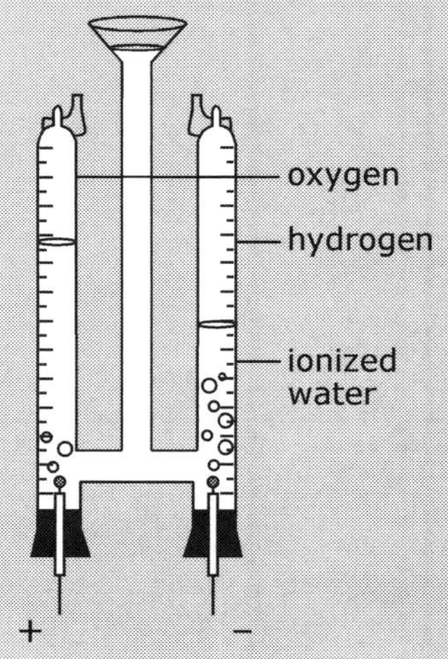

1. Use your knowledge of chemical nomenclature to write an equation showing the process occurring in the diagram. (Be sure to indicate hydrogen and oxygen as diatomic molecules.)
2. Count the total number of atoms of hydrogen and oxygen before and after the change. Make any necessary changes to ensure that these are equal.
3. Make any necessary changes to indicate the states of the substances in your equation.
4. Include anything else you feel is necessary to help your equation fully describe what is happening during this process.

Chemical Reactions Run Our World

Chemistry is the study of matter and its changes and you have already learned how physical and chemical changes differ. Chemical changes always produce new substances with new properties and their own unique chemical formulas. Such changes involve the breaking and forming of chemical bonds. They are referred to as chemical reactions. The processes of photosynthesis and aerobic cellular respiration, for example, involve a series of chemical reactions that produce and use oxygen. These reactions are taking place right now in our bodies and in most of the living things in our world.

Another series of oxygen-requiring chemical reactions are necessary to heat our homes and move our vehicles from place to place. Chemical reactions involving oxygen can also be a problem when the metal in many human-made objects spontaneously breaks down in a chemical process called corrosion. Most people take chemical reactions for granted as if they were magic. It is important to appreciate that every waking moment of our lives, the matter of our world is continually undergoing an endless series of chemical reactions.

The Use of Chemical Shorthand

When you email or text message your friends, you probably use abbreviations or "text-speak" that makes it easier to communicate quickly (and less expensively). In mathematics, equations are often used to communicate operations involving numbers. Chemists use chemical equations to condense a large amount of information into a short expression.

In 1774, Joseph Priestley performed a famous chemical reaction that led to the discovery of oxygen. His synthesis involved the heating of a deep red powder to produce a silver liquid and a clear odourless gas (Figure 3.1.1). This chemical reaction can be represented by two different types of chemical equations:

Word equation: mercury(II) oxide → mercury + oxygen
Formula equation: $HgO(s) \rightarrow Hg(l) + O_2(g)$

Formula equations may sometimes be referred to as molecular equations. Both of these equations indicate a starting substance or **reactant** forming new substances or **products.** Formula equations may include italicized letters to indicate the physical state of the reactants and products: solid (*s*), liquid (*l*), or gas (*g*). The symbol (*aq*) stands for aqueous, meaning the substance is dissolved in water.

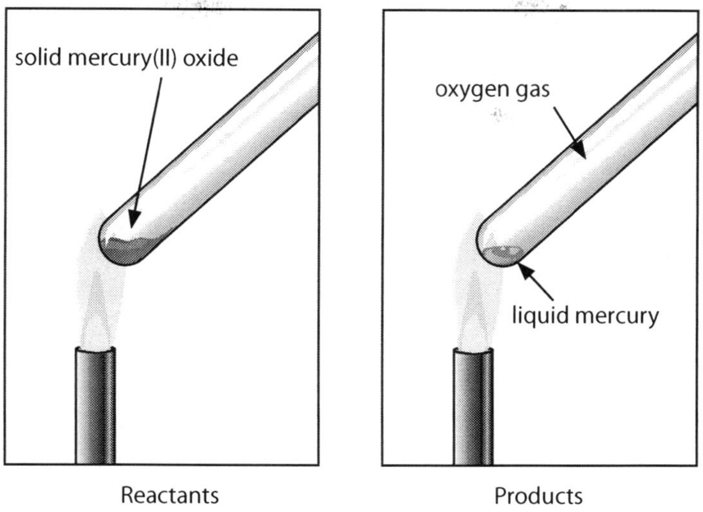

Figure 3.1.1 *Heating solid mercury(II) oxide results in the formation of liquid mercury and oxygen gas.*

You can tell that a chemical reaction has occurred by looking for evidence of chemical change. Some examples of such evidence include:

- noticeable absorption or release of heat (or sometimes light)
- a color change
- evolution of a gas (bubbles may be visible)

Quick Check

1. List three pieces of evidence of chemical change in the decomposition of mercury(II) oxide.

   ____

   ____

2. Convert the following from a word equation to a formula equation:
   Calcium oxide powder is combined with water to form calcium hydroxide solid.

   ____

   ____

3. Convert the following from a formula equation to a word equation: $H_2CO_3(aq) \rightarrow CO_2(g) + H_2O(l)$

   ____

- formation of a solid from two solutions. Such a solid is called a **precipitate**.

Balancing Chemical Equations

Historical evidence connects Joseph Priestley's experiments with oxygen with another famous chemist, Antoine Lavoisier. Lavoisier's experiments were more quantitative than those of Priestley. That is, Lavoisier liked to measure the volumes and masses of the chemicals he studied. Lavoisier is generally credited with formulating the **law of conservation of mass**. The law states that the mass before and after a chemical reaction occurs remains constant. Priestley and Lavoisier were both radical thinkers for the time they lived in. Englishman Priestley's support of the French Revolutionists led to his persecution, and he eventually had to flee from Europe altogether. He lived the last of his days in Pennsylvania in the United States. Lavoisier's problems were even more severe as he eventually lost his head to the guillotine at the height of the French Revolution.

A brief examination of the equation for the decomposition of mercury(II) oxide, $HgO(s) \rightarrow Hg(l) + O_2(g)$, shows that it does not obey the law of conservation of mass. The reactant, HgO contains one less oxygen atom than the products, Hg and O_2. If these atoms could somehow be placed on a balance, it would be evident that the reactant weighs less than the products (Figure 3.1.2). To show that the mass before and after a chemical reaction occurs remains constant, the formula equation has to be balanced.

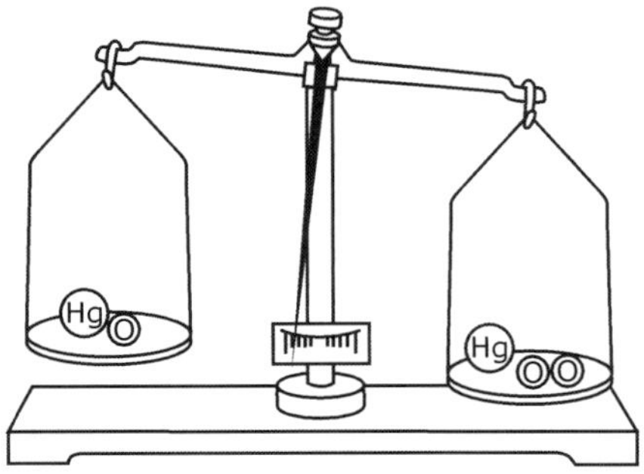

Figure 3.1.2 *The reactant in this reaction weighs less than the products.*

Balancing a chemical equation requires the placement of coefficients in front of reactant and/or product species. **Coefficients** are numbers that multiply the entire chemical species that follows them. These numbers ensure that the number of atoms of each kind on the reactant side is equal to those on the product side of the equation.

It is critical to remember balancing must always involve the placement of coefficients and never the changing of subscripts. Altering the subscripts will give an incorrect formula for a substance. Placing a coefficient 2 in front of the reactant HgO is a start, but the equation is still not balanced, $2\ HgO\ (s) \rightarrow Hg(l) + O_2(g)$. The balancing of the oxygen has resulted in an imbalance of the mercury (Figure 3.1.3).

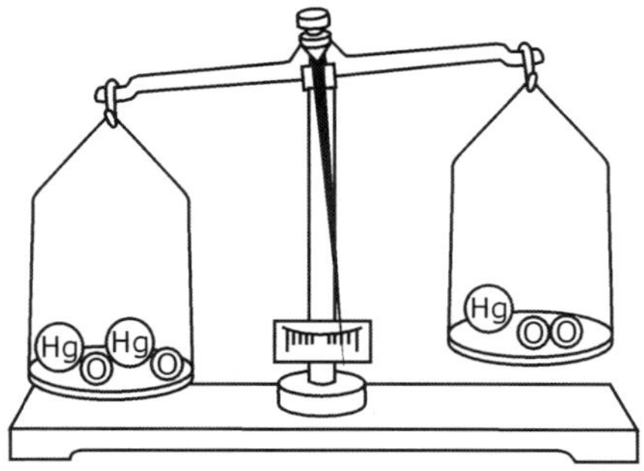

Figure 3.1.3 *Adding a coefficient to one side of the equation may not be enough to balance it.*

Placement of a coefficient 2 in front of the mercury will finally balance the entire equation, $2\ HgO(s) \rightarrow 2\ Hg(l) + O_2(g)$. By convention, a space is placed between the coefficient and the species it multiplies. It is always a good practice to check to make sure that you have accomplished your goal (Table 3.1.1).

Table 3.1.1 *Equation Balancing Check*

Atom	Reactant Side	Product Side
Hg	2	2
O	2	2

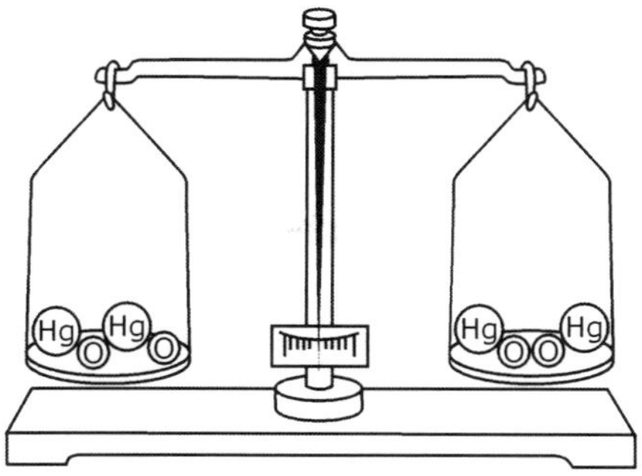

Figure 3.1.4 *This reaction required coefficients on both sides of the equation to balance it.*

Quick Check

Circle the letter of the properly balanced equations:

(a) $Na(s) + Cl_2(g) \rightarrow NaCl_2(s)$

(b) $AgNO_3(aq) + KBr(aq) \rightarrow AgBr(s) + KNO_3(aq)$

(c) $H_2O(l) + SiCl_4(l) \rightarrow SiO_2(s) + 4\ HCl(g)$

(d) $C_3H_8(g) + 5\ O_2(g) \rightarrow 3\ CO_2(g) + 4\ H_2O(l)$

(e) $3\ LiOH(aq) + Fe(IO_4)_3(aq) \rightarrow Fe(OH)_3(s) + 3\ LiIO_4(aq)$

Keeping Your Balance — Helpful Hints

Often students balance equations by simply attacking each atom in turn, moving back and forth with pencil and eraser until they accomplish their objective. Given enough time, most equations can eventually be balanced this way. However, the job can be made much easier if you follow a good plan of attack. Keep the following hints in mind when attempting to balance an equation:

- Begin by balancing atoms that appear in only one place on each side of the equation. Atoms that appear in too many places will be more difficult to balance and should always be left until last. Oxygen and hydrogen often appear in multiple places.
- Balance atoms that occur in *elemental form* last. This simply means atoms that are not grouped with any other type of atom. Examples include metals such as Zn, non-metals such as P_4 or diatomic gases such as H_2, O_2, N_2 or any halogen.
- Balance polyatomic ions such as nitrate or sulfate as a group whenever possible.
- Once a coefficient has been placed in front of a molecule or formula unit, finish balancing the rest of the atoms in that species before moving on. In other words, let your coefficients lead you through the equation.
- When balancing word equations, begin by making certain all formulas are correct. One formula error will cause a sequence of errors leading to disaster.
- It is always a good idea to perform a check such as the one shown in Table 3.1.1 above. This is particularly important with longer, more difficult equations.

Sample Problem — Balancing Formula Equations – Introductory

$Ba(s) + Al(NO_3)_3(aq) \rightarrow Ba(NO_3)_2(aq) + Al(s)$

What to Think about	How to Do It
1. Barium and aluminum must be left until last as both appear in elemental form.	
2. The nitrate ion may be balanced as a group as it is the only *aggregation* of nitrogen and oxygen in the equation. The way several atoms are combined in an equation is called their aggregation. Consider the lowest common multiple of nitrate's subscripts 3 and 2 to determine the first set of coefficients. That number is 6 so coefficients of 2 and 3 are required to make the number of reactant and product nitrate groups equal.	$Ba + 2\,Al(NO_3)_3 \rightarrow 3\,Ba(NO_3)_2 + Al$
3. Now it is simply a matter of balancing the elements. As the coefficient 2 is first, you could balance aluminum next.	$Ba + 2\,Al(NO_3)_3 \rightarrow 3\,Ba(NO_3)_2 + 2\,Al$
4. Complete the balance with the barium and replace the phase indicators if required.	$3\,Ba(s) + 2\,Al(NO_3)_3(aq) \rightarrow 3\,Ba(NO_3)_2(aq) + 2\,Al(s)$
5. Be sure to complete the process by checking the total number of barium, aluminum, nitrogen, and oxygen atoms on each side.	

Sample Problem — Balancing Formula Equations — Advanced

$NaOH(aq) + Cr_2O_3(s) + O_2(g) \rightarrow Na_2CrO_4(aq) + H_2O(l)$

What to Think about	How to Do It
1. Leave oxygen until last as it occurs in every species in the equation and appears in elemental form. You cannot balance hydroxide and chromate as groups because they each appear on only one side of the equation.	$2\,NaOH + Cr_2O_3 + O_2 \rightarrow Na_2CrO_4 + H_2O$
2. Begin with sodium, as it is the first atom that has not been left until last. There are two sodiums on the reactant side, so you need a coefficient of 2 on the product side.	

Continued

Sample Problem — *Continued*

What to Think about

3. The coefficient in front of sodium leads you to balance hydrogen next (remember, oxygen will be balanced last). As hydrogen is already balanced, you may proceed to chromium.
   The advantage of balancing in pencil becomes clear, as the sodium must now be rebalanced along with the hydrogen.

4. A careful count of the oxygen atoms indicates there are 9 on the reactant side and 10 in the products. The balance can be finished easily by placing a coefficient of 3/2 or 1.5 in front of the elemental oxygen molecule. Eliminate the fraction by multiplying all coefficients by a common value.

5. Always perform balancing using the smallest values of whole number coefficients, so everything must be doubled to complete the balance. If required, include the phase indicators.

How to Do It

$2\ NaOH + Cr_2O_3 + O_2 \rightarrow 2\ Na_2CrO_4 + H_2O$

$4\ NaOH + Cr_2O_3 + O_2 \rightarrow 2\ Na_2CrO_4 + 2\ H_2O$

$4\ NaOH + Cr_2O_3 + 1.5\ O_2 \rightarrow 2\ Na_2CrO_4 + 2\ H_2O$

$8\ NaOH(aq) + 2\ Cr_2O_3(s) + 3\ O_2(g) \rightarrow 4\ Na_2CrO_4(aq) + 4\ H_2O(l)$

Practice Problems — Balancing Formula Equations

1. Complete the following table to check the balancing of the sample equation above.

Atom	Reactant Side	Product Side
Na		
O		
H		
Cr		

2. Balance each of the following using the smallest possible whole number coefficients.
   (a) $Al(s) + H_2SO_4(aq) \rightarrow Al_2(SO_4)_3(aq) + H_2(g)$
   (b) $Mg_3N_2(s) + H_2O(l) \rightarrow Mg(OH)_2(s) + NH_3(g)$
   (c) $NH_3(g) + O_2(g) \rightarrow H_2O(l) + NO(g)$

Sample Problem — Writing Balanced Formula Equations from Word Equations

Butane gas burns in oxygen to produce carbon dioxide and water vapour.

What to Think about

1. Make sure the formulas are correct.
2. Leave oxygen until last as it appears twice on the product side and is in elemental form on the reactant side. Balance carbon first, followed by hydrogen.
3. Don't forget that oxygen is diatomic. Use a fraction initially for oxygen as there are 13 oxygen atoms on the product side. Insert 13/2 or 6.5 for the oxygen gas.
4. Butane is a four-carbon hydrocarbon whose formula might best be determined by drawing its bonding arrangement.
5. Multiply the equation by 2 and add the appropriate phase indicators to complete the balance.
6. Once the balance is complete, be sure to perform a check.

How to Do It

$C_4H_{10} + O_2 \rightarrow CO_2 + H_2O$

$C_4H_{10} + O_2 \rightarrow 4\,CO_2 + 5\,H_2O$

$C_4H_{10} + 6.5\,O_2 \rightarrow 4\,CO_2 + 5\,H_2O$

$2\,C_4H_{10}(g) + 13\,O_2(g) \rightarrow 8\,CO_2(g) + 10\,H_2O(g)$

Atom	Reactant Side	Product Side
C	8	8
H	20	20
O	26	26

Practice Problems — Writing Balanced Formula Equations from Word Equations

Write balanced equations for each of the following, using the smallest possible whole number coefficients. Include appropriate phase indicators.

1. Solid iron and chlorine gas combine to form iron(III) chloride.
2. Aqueous solutions of ammonium phosphide and lead(II) bromate react to give a precipitate of lead(II) phosphide and aqueous ammonium bromate.
3. Calcium metal reacts in an aqueous solution of nickel(III) sulfate to form calcium sulfate solution and nickel metal.

3.1 Activity: Building a Balanced Equation

Question

How can you represent the chemical reaction between nitrogen dioxide gas and water to form nitric acid and nitrogen monoxide?

Materials

You may use any of the following materials:

- a series of coins of different sizes representing nitrogen, oxygen, and hydrogen atoms
- modelling clay in different colors and sizes representing the required atoms
- a chemical model kit
- a series of drawings using different colors and sizes of images to represent the required atoms

Procedure

1. Use the materials you've selected to build a model of the balanced equation that represents the reaction in the question.
2. Compare your model with models done by one or more of your classmates.

Results and Discussion

1. Sketch your model in the space provided:

2. Make a table to check the balancing in your model equation:

3. How many chemical bonds were broken during your reaction? Describe each of these bonds.

4. How many chemical bonds were formed during your reaction? Describe each.

5. Were more bonds formed or broken? What might this mean for your reaction?

3.1 Review Questions

1. State two examples of chemical change from everyday life. What evidence indicates that these are chemical changes?

2. What chemical law requires us to balance chemical equations?

   Who was responsible for formulating this law?

3. Write a word equation for each formula equation below:

   (a) $C(s) + O_2(g) \rightarrow CO_2(g)$

   (b) $CH_4(g) + 2\ O_2(g) \rightarrow CO_2(g) +\ 2\ H_2O(g)$

   (c) $Cl_2(g) + 2\ KI(s) \rightarrow I_2(s) + 2\ KCl(s)$

   (d) $HCl(aq) + NaOH(s) \rightarrow NaCl(aq) + H_2O(l)$

   (e) $KF(s) \rightarrow K(s) + F_2(g)$

4. Balance each of the following equations. (State indicators are not required.)

   (a) $CdF_2 + NaBr \rightarrow CdBr_2 + NaF$

   (b) $Cr + F_2 \rightarrow CrF_3$

   (c) $Ca + H_2O \rightarrow Ca(OH)_2 + H_2$

   (d) $Bi(NO_3)_3 + Na_2S \rightarrow Bi_2S_3 + NaNO_3$

   (e) $C_2H_5OH + O_2 \rightarrow CO_2 + H_2O$

   (f) $V + S_8 \rightarrow V_2S_5$

   (g) $LiNO_3 + Li \rightarrow Li_2O + N_2$

   (h) $Ca_3(PO_4)_2 + H_2SO_4 \rightarrow CaSO_4 + H_3PO_4$

   (i) $PH_3 + O_2 \rightarrow P_2O_5 + H_2O$

   (j) $Ba + Ag_3PO_4 \rightarrow Ba_3(PO_4)_2 + Ag$

   (k) $Ca(ClO_3)_2 \rightarrow CaCl_2 + O_2$

   (l) $C_{12}H_{22}O_{11} + O_2 \rightarrow CO_2 + H_2O$

   (m) $Ca_2C + H_2O \rightarrow Ca(OH)_2 + CH_4$

   (n) $NH_4Br + BaO \rightarrow NH_3 + BaBr_2 + H_2O$

   (o) $LiAlH_4 + BF_3 \rightarrow LiF + AlF_3 + B_2H_6$

5. Write a balanced formula equation for each of the following (phase indicators should be included if possible):

(a) Titanium metal reacts with selenium to produce crystals of titanium(III) selenide.

(b) Phosphoric acid is neutralized with barium hydroxide to produce a precipitate of barium phosphate in water.

(c) Nitrogen gas reacts with lead(II) oxide powder to yield lead(II) nitride and oxygen gas.

(d) Xenon hexafluoride crystals react with water to produce xenon trioxide powder and hydrofluoric acid.

(e) Aluminum carbide is reacted with water in the synthesis of methane gas. Aluminum hydroxide precipitate is also formed.

(f) Plants produce the simple sugar $C_6H_{12}O_6$ and oxygen gas from carbon dioxide and water during photosynthesis.

(g) Ammonia gas (NH_3) is formed along with a precipitate of magnesium hydroxide from the reaction of magnesium nitride powder with water.

(h) Strong heating of copper(II) nitrate trihydrate produces copper(II) oxide, nitrogen dioxide, oxygen gas, and water.

6. Balancing Bonkers: Some equations are extremely difficult to balance even with the application of the balancing hints! Later on in your chemistry career, you will learn to balance some equations using the concepts of oxidation and reduction. This will be a major stress reducer when it comes to balancing. In the meantime, try to balance a few of these exhauster equations:

(a) $Ag + HNO_3 \rightarrow NO + AgNO_3 + H_2O$

(b) $Al + NaOH + H_2O \rightarrow NaAl(OH)_4 + H_2$

(c) $HNO_3 + Zn \rightarrow Zn(NO_3)_2 + H_2O + NH_4NO_3$

(d) $H_2O + As + HClO_3 \rightarrow H_3AsO_3 + HClO$

(e) $H_2SO_4 + H_2O_2 + KMnO_4 \rightarrow MnSO_4 + O_2 + H_2O + K_2SO_4$

3.2 Endothermic and Exothermic Reactions

Warm Up

Complete the following table by placing a checkmark in the appropriate energy-change column for each of the classifications of chemical change listed.

Reaction Type	Energy is Released	Energy is Absorbed
Most Synthesis (Combination) Reactions		
Most Decomposition Reactions		
Neutralization Reactions		
Combustion Reactions		

Sources of Energy

Fuels such as natural gas, wood, coal, and gasoline provide us with energy. Did you ever wonder where this energy comes from? Most of it is stored as chemical potential energy that can be converted into heat. The amount of potential energy available depends on the position of the subatomic particles making up a chemical sample and the composition of the sample. While the absolute potential energy content of a system is not really important, a change in potential energy content often is. We use changes in chemical energy to other energy forms to heat our homes and move our vehicles. Because chemical energy is most commonly converted to heat, we use the symbol ΔH to symbolize a change in energy available as heat. The symbol is sometimes read as delta *H* or an **enthalpy** change. Enthalpy is defined as potential energy that may be evolved or absorbed as heat.

All sorts of processes, both physical and chemical, have an enthalpy change associated with them. While a general change in enthalpy is symbolized as ΔH, specific types of enthalpy changes may be symbolized by a subscripted explanation attached to this symbol. Some examples include:

$$KOH(s) \rightarrow K^+(aq) + OH^-(aq) \qquad \Delta H_{solution} = -57.8 \text{ kJ/mol}$$

$$C_3H_8(g) + 5\,O_2(g) \rightarrow 3\,CO_2(g) + 4\,H_2O(l) \qquad \Delta H_{combustion} = -2221 \text{ kJ/mol}$$

$$H_2O(s) \rightarrow H_2O(l) \qquad \Delta H_{fusion} = 6.0 \text{ kJ/mol}$$

$$Fe_2O_3(s) + 2\,Al(s) \rightarrow Al_2O_3(s) + 2\,Fe(s) \qquad \Delta H_{reaction} = -852 \text{ kJ/mol}$$

$$Ca(s) + O_2(g) + H_2(g) \rightarrow Ca(OH)_2(s) \qquad \Delta H_{formation} = -986 \text{ kJ/mol}$$

What is it that causes the enthalpy stored in reactants to differ from that in the products of a physical or chemical change? What exactly is responsible for producing a ΔH value? The answer is the chemical bonds.

Quick Check

Examine each of the equations listed on the previous page. Consider the sign of the ΔH value and determine whether the reactants or products have more stored energy in each case. Put a checkmark under the side with more enthalpy.

Reaction	Reactants	Products
Dissolving potassium hydroxide		
Combustion of propane		
Melting ice		
Displacement of iron by aluminum		
Formation of calcium hydroxide		

The Energy of Chemical Bonds

Suppose your work text has fallen off your desk to the floor. When you lift it back to the desktop, you give the text potential energy because of its position above the floor. The gravitational potential energy your text now has could easily be converted into mechanical, as well as sound energy, should it happen to fall again.

In a similar way, the electrons in the atoms of the molecules of any substance have potential energy. Think of the negative electrons as being pulled away from the positive nucleus of their atom. If it were not for their high velocity, they would certainly rush toward and smash directly into the nucleus of their atom, much like your work text falling to the floor. By virtue of the position of the negative electrons in an atom relative to the positive nucleus and the other nuclei nearby in a molecule, the electrons (and the protons in the nuclei for that matter) have potential energy. This is the chemical potential energy called **bond energy.**

The bond energy just mentioned is the energy of **intramolecular bonds**. These are bonds that are formed *between atoms within a molecule.* Weaker bonds exist *between molecules* in a sample of solid, liquid, and even gaseous matter. These weak bonds hold the molecules of a solid or liquid together. These weak interactions between molecules are called **intermolecular forces.** The details of intermolecular forces relate to the polarity or lack of polarity of a molecule. The difference between the potential bond energy of reactants and products before and after a chemical or physical change is known as the enthalpy change or ΔH value.

Bond breaking requires *energy input* while *bond forming* results in *energy release.*

It's fairly intuitive to most of us that breaking something requires energy. For a karate master to break a board, he must apply energy. Similarly breaking chemical bonds requires energy. This energy is used to overcome the electrostatic forces that bind atoms or ions together. It follows from this that bond formation must result in a more stable situation in which energy is released.

If more energy is absorbed as bonds break than is released as bonds form during a chemical change, there is a net absorption of energy. As energy is required to break bonds there will be a gain in enthalpy. Reactions such as these have a positive ΔH value and are called endothermic reactions. Such a reaction may be shown graphically in an energy profile, sometimes called a *potential energy diagram* (Figure 3.2.1).

Potential Energy vs. Reaction Proceeding

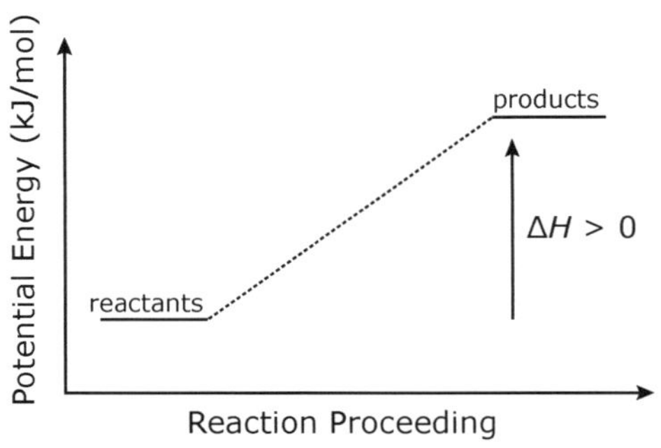

Figure 3.2.1 *Potential energy diagram for an endothermic reaction*

> The energy absorbed to break bonds is greater than the energy released during bond formation in an *endothermic* reaction so they have positive ΔH values.

If, on the other hand, more energy is released as bonds are formed than is absorbed as they are broken during a chemical change, there is a net release of energy and so a decrease in enthalpy content occurs. Reactions such as these will have a negative ΔH value and may be called exothermic. Such a reaction may be represented graphically as shown in Figure 3.2.2.

Potential Energy vs. Reaction Proceeding

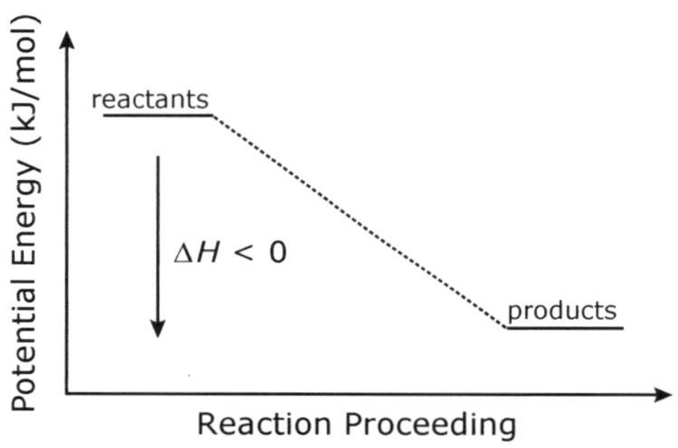

Figure 3.2.2 *Potential energy diagram for an exothermic reaction*

More energy is released during bond formation than is absorbed during bond breaking in an *exothermic* reaction so they have negative ΔH values.

Quick Check

Complete the right column in the following table by labelling each of the introductory reactions in this section as endothermic or exothermic.

Reaction	Endothermic or Exothermic
Dissolving potassium hydroxide	
Combustion of propane	
Melting ice	
Displacement of iron by aluminum	
Formation of calcium hydroxide	

Potential Energy Diagrams

Potential Energy Diagrams summarize the energy changes during the course of a reaction and provide us with a way of visualizing the progress of a chemical reaction from reactants to products.

Explanation of terms

Reaction Coordinate: The extent to which the reactants have changed into products, also called the progress of the reaction or reaction pathway.

Potential Energy of Reactants: The chemical potential energy, measured in kilojoules (kJ) in the intramolecular bonds of the reactants. This is also known as the Bond Energy (you can look these up) and is a measure of the amount of energy that must be put into the chemical system to break the intramolecular bonds.

Potential Energy of Products: The chemical potential energy measured in kilojoules (kJ) in the intramolecular bonds of the products. The is a measure of the energy released when intramolecular bonds form in the products.

Enthalpy of a Reaction (ΔH) : The difference between the potential energy of the products and the potential energy of the reactants, measured in kJ. If this value is positive (the products have a greater chemical potential energy than the reactants), the overall reaction is ENDOTHERMIC and more energy is be absorbed from the surroundings to break the reactant bonds than energy released in the formation of product bonds. If this value is negative (the products have less chemical potential energy than reactants), then the overall reaction is EXOTHERMIC.

Activation Energy (E_a): The threshold kinetic energy that colliding reactant molecules must have to produce products (not all collisions with the Ea are successful).

Transition state: The brief moment during a successful collision when reactant bonds are partially broken and product bonds are partially formed. This corresponds to the high point on a potential energy diagram.

Activated complex: The chemical species that is formed in the transition state.

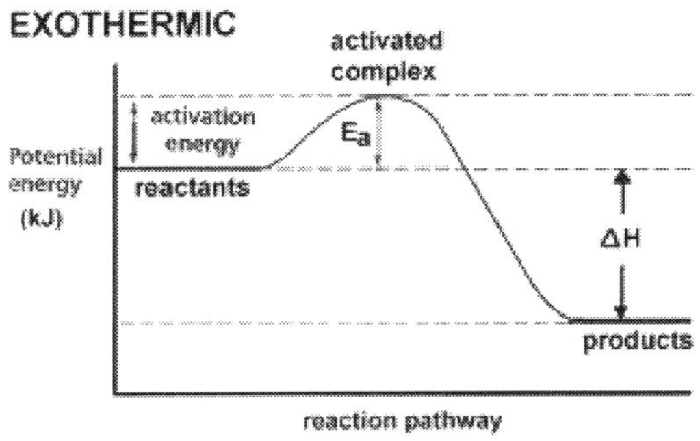

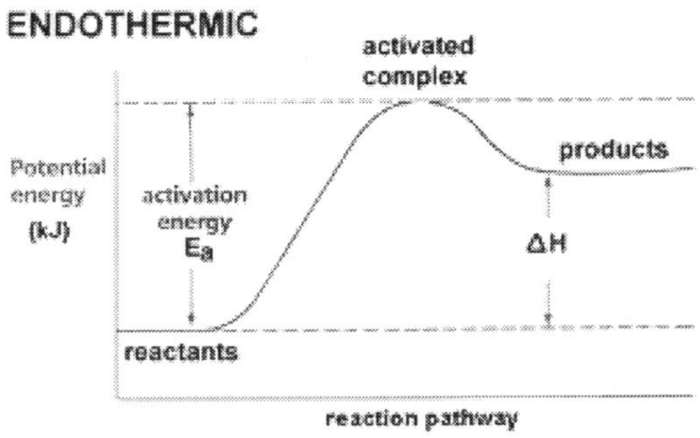

Here is a good video to visualize the chemical reaction process:
http://www.youtube.com/watch?feature=player_embedded&v=VbIaK6PLrRM

Worksheet on Potential Energy Diagrams

1) Complete the diagram below with the correct labels (include all of the things defined not just the letters) and a proper title.

Fig 1:

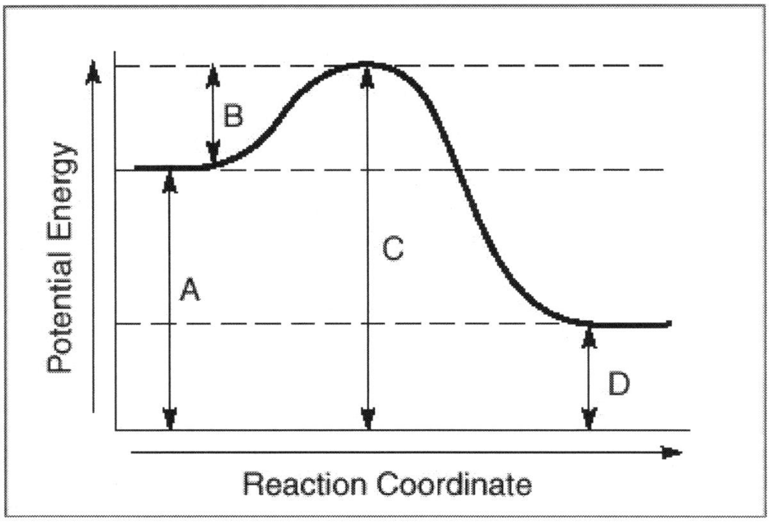

2) Sketch a potential energy diagram for and endothermic reaction with an activation energy of 250 kJ and an enthalpy of 170 kJ. Label all parts of your diagram.

3) The activation energy of an endothermic reaction is always (smaller, greater) ______________ than or equal to the enthalpy of the reaction.
4) The larger the Ea the ______________ (slower, faster) the reaction
5) For an exothermic reaction what kind of inference can you make about the activation energy based on the magnitude of the enthalpy? Explain.

6) Is the activated complex stable? Explain.

7) Give an everyday example of a fast reaction and a slow reaction. What would the potential energy diagrams of these look like?

3.2 Review Questions

1. Indicate whether each of the following changes is endothermic or exothermic:
   (a) Barbecuing a steak

   (b) Freezing a tray full of water to make ice

   (c) Neutralizing an acid spill with baking soda

   (d) Making a grilled cheese sandwich

   (e) Lighting a barbecue igniter

   (f) Condensing water on a mirror

2. Convert the following ΔH notation equations into thermochemical equations using the smallest whole number coefficients possible:
   (a) $\frac{1}{2}\ C_3H_8(g) \rightarrow \frac{1}{2}\ C_3H_8(l)$ $\Delta H = -175$ kJ/mol

   (b) $Li(s) + \frac{1}{2}\ CaCl_2(aq) \rightarrow LiCl(aq) + \frac{1}{2}\ Ca(s)$ $\Delta H = -362$ kJ/mol

   (c) $2\ B(s) + 3\ H_2O(g) \rightarrow B_2H_6(g) + 3/2\ O_2(g)$ $\Delta H = 762$ kJ/mol

   (d) $\frac{1}{2}\ P_4(s) + 3\ Cl_2(g) \rightarrow 2\ PCl_3(s)$ $\Delta H = -613$ kJ/mol

   (e) $NH_3(g) + 3/2\ N_2O(g) \rightarrow 2\ N_2(g) + 3/2\ H_2O(l)$ $\Delta H = -505$ kJ/mol

   (f) $\frac{1}{2}\ Fe_3O_4(s) + \frac{1}{2}\ CO(g) \rightarrow 3/2\ FeO(s) + \frac{1}{2}\ CO_2(g)$ $\Delta H = 9$ kJ/mol

3. Convert the following thermochemical equations into ΔH notation using the smallest whole number coefficients possible.
   (a) $C(s) + 2\ H_2(g) + \frac{1}{2}\ O_2(g) \rightarrow CH_3OH(l) + 201$ kJ/mol

   (b) $\frac{1}{2}\ Cu(s) + \frac{1}{2}\ H_2(g) + \frac{1}{2}\ O_2(g) \rightarrow \frac{1}{2}\ Cu(OH)_2(s) + 225$ kJ/mol

   (c) 389 kJ/mol $+ \frac{1}{2}\ Sb_4O_6(s) + 3\ C(s) \rightarrow 2\ Sb(s) + 3\ CO(g)$

   (d) 56 kJ/mol $+ NO_2(g) \rightarrow NO(g) + \frac{1}{2}\ O_2(g)$

   (e) $PCl_3(g) + \frac{1}{2}\ O_2\ (g) \rightarrow Cl_3PO(g) + 286$ kJ/mol

   (f) $F_2(s) + \frac{1}{2}\ O_2(g) \rightarrow OF_2(g) + 22$ kJ/mol

4. Use the equations in question 3 to answer the following questions:
(a) How much energy would be released during the formation of 4 mol of methanol?

(b) How many moles of nitrogen dioxide could be decomposed through the use of 168 kJ of energy?

(c) Is more energy absorbed or released during the formation of Cl_3PO gas from PCl_3 and O_2 gas?

(d) What is the ΔH value for the decomposition of OF_2 gas into its elements?

(e) How much energy is required to decompose 1 mol of copper(II) hydroxide?

5. Does the following potential energy diagram represent an endothermic or an exothermic reaction? What is ΔH for this reaction?

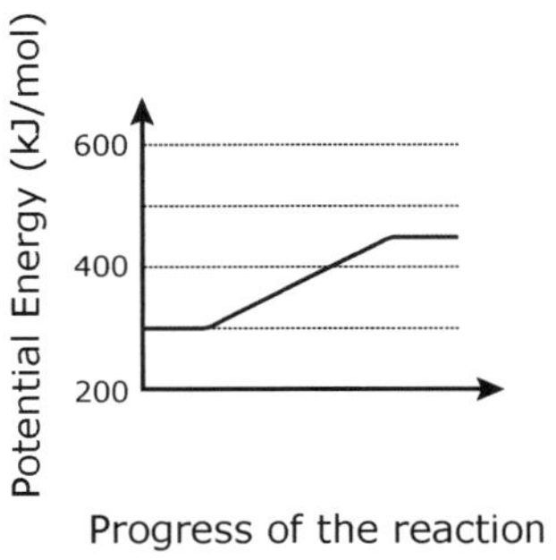

6. What is ΔH for this reaction?

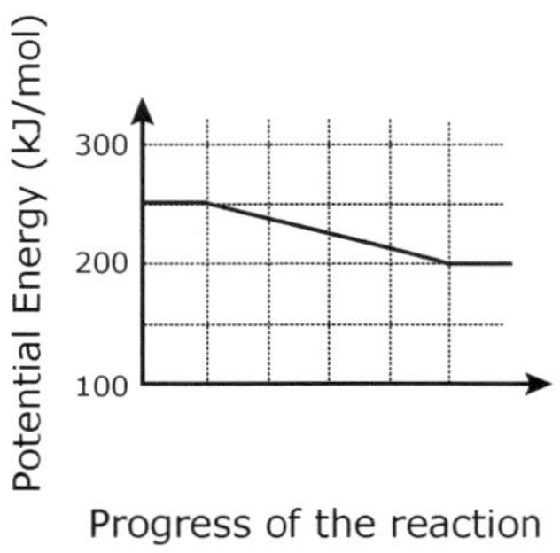

3.3 Classifying Chemical Changes and Predicting Products

Warm Up

Reaction Type	Reactants	Products
Synthesis (combination)	two substances	one substance
Decomposition	one substance	two substances
Single displacement	element + compound	new element + compound
Double displacement	two compounds	two new compounds
Neutralization	acid + base	salt + water
Combustion	organic compound + oxygen	carbon dioxide + water

Balance the following equations. Then use the table above to classify each as one of the major reaction types listed:

1. $Na(s) + H_2O(l) \rightarrow NaOH(aq) + H_2(g)$
2. $Li_2O(s) + H_2O(l) \rightarrow LiOH(aq)$
3. $C_6H_{14}(l) + O_2(g) \rightarrow CO_2(g) + H_2O(g)$
4. $HCl(aq) + Sr(OH)_2(aq) \rightarrow SrCl_2(aq) + H_2O(l)$
5. $AlBr_3(s) \rightarrow Al(s) + Br_2(l)$

Classification of Chemical Reactions

Reactions, much like elements and compounds, can be classified according to type. The ability to recognize and classify reactions can help us predict the products of those chemical changes. Classification can also help us predict whether a reaction is likely to occur or not.

It is not always easy to classify a reaction. Most reactions, however, can be classified according to the six major categories described in the warm up table above.

Synthesis (Combination) Reactions

A **synthesis** (or combination) reaction involves two or more simple substances (elements or compounds) combining to form one more complex substance.

Usually synthesis reactions are accompanied by the release of a significant amount of energy in the form of heat and/or light. That is they are **exothermic**. The prefix "exo" means outside, while "thermo" refers to heat. It should be noted, however, that synthesis reactions sometimes require a small amount of "start-up" energy to begin. This start-up energy is known as activation energy.

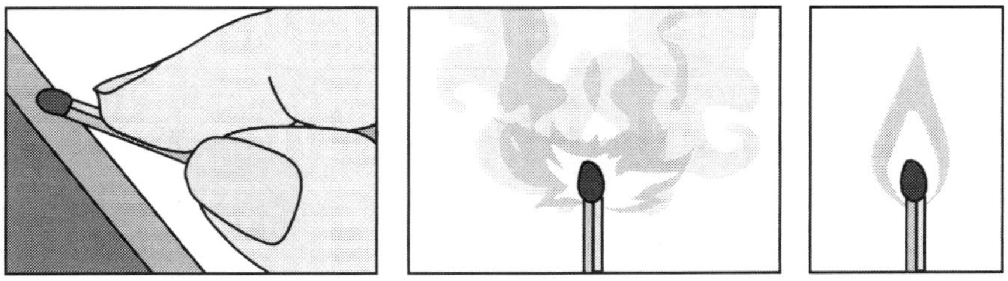

Figure 3.3.1 *Activation energy is required for both lighting and burning the match.*

An example of activation energy is shown in Figure 3.3.1. The friction in striking a match against a rough surface provides activation energy for the very exothermic reaction between the red phosphorus on the match head and the oxygen gas in the air around it. The product of this match-lighting reaction is the poof of a white gaseous oxide of phosphorus. The reaction is:

$P_4(s) + 5\ O_2(g) \rightarrow 2\ P_2O_5(g)$ + energy. This exothermic reaction in turn provides the activation energy for a second reaction involving the combustion of the wood or paper of the match stick. The combustion reaction is, of course, also exothermic.

Synthesis reactions may involve the combination of two elements to form a simple binary compound. Halides and oxides are formed in this way.

Halide example: $Ba(s) + Cl_2(g) \rightarrow BaCl_2(s)$
Oxide example: $2\ Sn(s) + O_2(g) \rightarrow 2\ SnO(s)$

Some synthesis reactions involve the combination of two compounds to form a more complex compound. The most common reactions of this type involve oxides of metals or non-metals and water. When a non-metal oxide combines with water, the product is always an acid. This type of reaction occurs in the atmosphere and is responsible for the formation of acid precipitation. The non-metal oxide is sometimes called an acidic oxide or an acid anhydride. Sulfur trioxide from factory exhaust reacts with water in the atmosphere to form sulfuric acid as follows:

$$SO_3(g) + H_2O(l) \rightarrow H_2SO_4(aq)$$

This then falls to Earth's surface in the form of acid precipitation, which is harmful to the natural environment and to objects with marble and metal surfaces in our built environment.

Metal oxides react with water to form bases. The metal oxide is sometimes called a basic oxide or a basic anhydride. When a metal oxide reacts with a non-metal oxide, the product is a complex or ternary salt. Examples of these two reaction types are:

Example of a metal oxide reacting with water: $K_2O(s) + H_2O(l) \rightarrow 2\ KOH(aq)$
Example of a metal oxide reacting with a non-metal oxide: $CaO(s) + CO_2(g) \rightarrow CaCO_3(s)$

Decomposition Reactions

A **decomposition** reaction involves a complex compound being broken down or decomposed into two or more simpler substances (elements or compounds).

Decomposition reactions are really just the opposite of synthesis reactions. Most decomposition reactions require a continuous source of energy. This energy is used to break the bonds between the elements of the starting material. Reactions that absorb more energy to break bonds than they release during bond formation are said to be **endothermic**. The prefix "endo" means inside and "thermo" is from the Greek for heat.

Decomposition reactions are commonly used in the mining industry to separate metals from their ores. For example, aluminum production occurs when electric current is passed through molten aluminum oxide or bauxite ore:
$2\ Al_2O_3(l) \rightarrow 4\ Al(s) + 3\ O_2(g)$. Charles Martin Hall developed this electrolysis process in 1886. Hall was a 21-year-old university student at the time. Before the development of the Hall cell, pure aluminum was very rare and it was worth nearly $100 000 a pound.

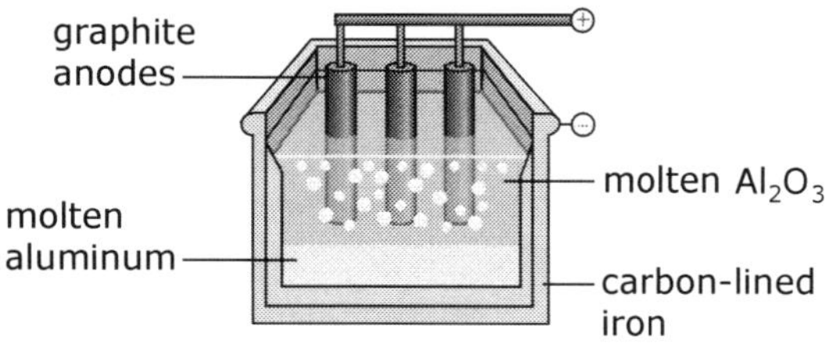

Figure 3.3.2 *The Hall cell produces aluminum metal and oxygen gas from melted bauxite ore.*

Some decomposition reactions form simple compounds instead of elements. These reactions generally involve one of the following reactions:

- acids decomposing to form water and non-metal oxides
- bases decomposing to form metal oxides and water
- ternary salts decomposing to form oxides of metals and non-metals

Examples of each of these types of reaction include:

Acid decomposition: $H_2SO_3(aq) \rightarrow H_2O(l) + SO_2(g)$
Base decomposition: $Ba(OH)_2(s) \rightarrow BaO(s) + H_2O(l)$
Salt decomposition: $Fe_2(SO_4)_3(s) \rightarrow Fe_2O_3(s) + 3\ SO_3(g)$

The relationship between various types of synthesis and decomposition reactions are summarized in Table 3.3.1.

Table 3.3.1 *Relationships between Synthesis and Decomposition Reactions*

	Reaction Direction	
Non-metal Oxide + Water	Synthesis → ← Decomposition	Acid
Metal Oxide + Water	Synthesis → ← Decomposition	Base
Non-metal Oxide + Metal Oxide	Synthesis → ← Decomposition	Complex (Ternary) Salt
Metal and Non-metal Elements	Synthesis → ← Decomposition	Simple (Binary) Salt

Combustion Reactions

A **combustion** reaction involves the reaction of a hydrocarbon (a compound made up of hydrogen and carbon) or a carbohydrate (a compound made up of hydrogen, carbon and oxygen) with oxygen gas to produce carbon dioxide gas and water.

Combustion reactions are exothermic and release a significant amount of energy in the form of heat, sometimes light, and even sound, depending on the conditions. Generally the combustion is rapid and involves the burning of an organic compound in atmospheric oxygen. Under these conditions, water will be released as vapour. The combustion of a variety of hydrocarbons such as propane, fuel oil, and natural gas provides most of the energy for our homes. The following combustion of octane in gasoline provides the energy to move most of our vehicles:

$$2\ C_8H_{18}(l) + 25\ O_2(g) \rightarrow 16\ CO_2(g) + 18\ H_2O(g)$$

Slow combustion, sometimes referred to simply as oxidation, occurs in the cells of our body to produce energy. One of the most common examples is this reaction of the simple sugar glucose with oxygen:

$$C_6H_{12}O_6(s) + 6\ O_2(g) \rightarrow 6\ CO_2(g) + 6\ H_2O(l)$$

Quick Check

Balance each of the following reactions and classify them as synthesis, decomposition or combustion.

1. $P_2O_5(g) + H_2O(l) \rightarrow H_3PO_4(aq)$ ______________________________

2. $CH_4(g) + O_2(g) \rightarrow CO_2(g) + H_2O(g)$ ______________________________

3. $H_2CO_3(aq) \rightarrow H_2O(l) + CO_2(g)$ ______________________________

Sample Problem — Predicting Products of Combination, Decomposition, and Combustion Reactions

Predict the products of the following reactions:

1. $CH_3OH(l) + O_2(g) \rightarrow$
2. $B_2O_3(s) + H_2O(l) \rightarrow$
3. $Sc(OH)_3(s) \rightarrow$

What to Think about	How to Do It
Reaction 1	
1. Classify the reaction based on the reactants provided. A carbohydrate reacts with oxygen, so this must be a combustion reaction. All combustion reactions form CO_2 and water.	$CH_3OH(l) + O_2(g) \rightarrow CO_2(g) + H_2O(l)$
2. Once the products have been determined, balance the equation.	$2\,CH_3OH(l) + 3\,O_2(g) \rightarrow 2\,CO_2(g) + 4\,H_2O(l)$
Reaction 2	
1. Reaction 2 is combining a non-metal oxide with water. This must be a combination reaction to form an acid.	
2. Determine the correct formula for the acid by combining the H^+ ion with an oxyanion of boron. To determine the oxyanion of boron, calculate the **oxidation number** (charge) on boron in the B_2O_3. As oxide is –2, boron must be +3. This indicates that borate, BO_3^{3-}, is the oxyanion in the acid.	$B_2O_3(s) + H_2O(l) \rightarrow H_3BO_3(aq)$
3. Balance the equation.	$B_2O_3(s) + 3\,H_2O(l) \rightarrow 2\,H_3BO_3(aq)$
Reaction 3	
1. Reaction 3 has only one reactant so it must be a decomposition reaction.	
2. As the reactant is a base, it must decompose to form a metal oxide and water. The metal oxide has to be an oxide of the metal in the base. As this is scandium, the products have to be scandium oxide and water	$Sc(OH)_3(s) \rightarrow Sc_2O_3(s) + H_2O(l)$
3. Balance the equation.	$2\,Sc(OH)_3(s) \rightarrow Sc_2O_3(s) + 3\,H_2O(l)$

Practice Problems — Predicting Products of Reactions

First classify the equations, then determine the products and write a balanced formula equation for each of the following:

1. $Fe_2O_3(s) \rightarrow$ Class: ________________

2. $C_3H_7OH(l) + O_2(g) \rightarrow$ Class: ________________

3. $Ag_2O(s) + H_2O(l) \rightarrow$ Class: ________________

4. $Pb(OH)_4(s) \rightarrow$ Class: ________________

Single Displacement Reactions

A **single displacement** reaction involves a reaction between a compound and an element so that the element replaces an element of the same type in the compound. The result is a new compound and a new element.

During a single displacement reaction, a free, uncombined element "kicks out" a combined element and takes its place. It is important to remember that a metal element always bonds with a non-metal element. Hence metals replace metals, while non-metals replace non-metals. Active metals may also replace hydrogen, kicking out hydrogen gas, from either water (family I and II metals) or acids (family I and II and several transition elements). For example:

- metal displacement: $2\ K(s) + Cu(NO_3)_2(aq) \rightarrow 2\ KNO_3(aq) + Cu(s)$
- hydrogen displacement: $2\ Na(s) + 2\ HOH(l) \rightarrow 2\ NaOH(aq) + H_2(g)$
- non-metal displacement: $Br_2(l) + 2\ NaI(aq) \rightarrow 2\ NaBr(aq) + I_2(s)$

Notice that, when hydrogen is being replaced in water, it is a good idea to think of the water's formula as HOH. This makes it evident that the product is a hydroxide of the metal (or a base), rather than an oxide. Although water is a covalent compound, thinking of it as being composed of hydrogen and hydroxide ions, rather than hydrogen and oxide ions will help simplify these equations.

To determine whether a single displacement reaction will proceed or not, we must compare the **chemical reactivity** of the element to that of the element it will replace in the compound Table 3.3.2. Chemical reactivity is the tendency of a substance to undergo chemical change. A more reactive element will kick off a less reactive one. Periodic properties and trends such as electronegativity and ionization energy to be discussed in future sections are certainly useful in predicting the reactivity of chemical elements. Interestingly, however, when an element replaces another element from an aqueous solution of a compound, the series of energy changes that occur result in a somewhat different reactivity series than we might predict based on the trends we will study later.

Table 3.3.2 *Series of Chemical Reactivity*

Two Activity Series		
Metals	Decreasing Activity	Halogens
lithium		flourine
potassium		chlorine
calcium		bromine
sodium		iodine
magnesium		
aluminum		
zinc		
chromium		
iron		
nickel		
tin		
lead		
HYDROGEN*		
copper		
mercury		
silver		
platinum		
gold		

* Hydrogen may be displaced from most acids by all metals above it in the series. However, it may only be displaced from water (at room temperature) by those above magnesium.

Quick Check

Use the series of chemical reactivity in Table 3.3.2 to determine whether each of the following single displacement reactions would proceed. Predict the products for those that do proceed and balance the equations.

1. $Na(s) + AlCl_3(aq) \rightarrow$

2. $Cu(s) + KBr(aq) \rightarrow$

3. $F_2(g) + LiI(aq) \rightarrow$

4. $Ca(s) + HOH(l) \rightarrow$

Double Displacement Reactions

A **double displacement** reaction is a chemical reaction between two compounds that trade cations (or anions) with one another.

It is important to remember that an ionic compound is made up of a positively charged ion called a **cation** bonded to a negatively charged ion called an **anion**. When these ions trade positions in their compounds, a new set of compounds is formed. As is usual in an ionic compound, the cations' and anions' charges must balance. The cation's formula will be listed first. There are three categories of double displacement reactions: precipitation, neutralization, and gas formation.

In a precipitation reaction, two freely soluble salts are combined in solution. When their ions "trade partners," two new salts are formed, at least one of which is not very soluble. This low solubility salt gives immediate evidence of chemical change as it forms a solid suspended in solution called a precipitate.

Predicting which product salt will precipitate requires information about the relative solubilities of the products. A future chapter will provide more information on solubility, but for now, keep in mind that compounds containing family I ions (alkali metal ions) and/or nitrate are always soluble. The precipitate is always indicated by a symbol (*s*), which indicates that a solid has been formed. The equation for the precipitation reaction in Figure 3.3.3 is:

$$NaCl(aq) + AgNO_3(aq) \rightarrow AgCl(s) + NaNO_3(aq)$$

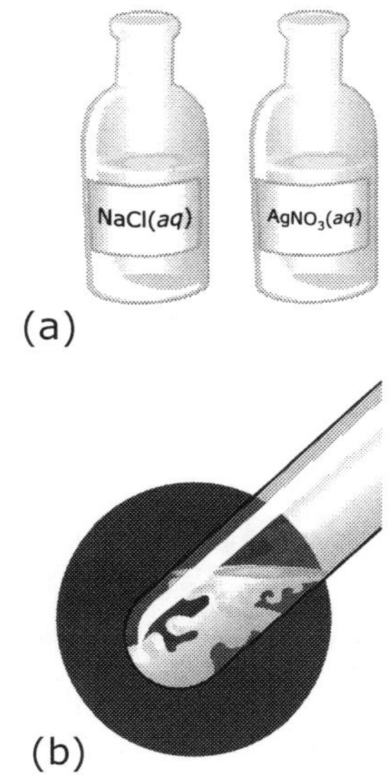

Figure 3.3.3 (a) *Solutions of sodium chloride and silver nitrate; (b) Precipitate of silver chloride suspended in a solution of sodium nitrate*

A **neutralization** reaction always occurs between an acid and a base. The products are always water and a salt.

The salt is composed of the cation from the base and the anion from the acid. The hydrogen ion from the acid and the hydroxide ion from the base combine to form the water. Evidence of chemical change is less obvious during a neutralization reaction, although detectable heat is released:

$$H_2SO_4(aq) + 2\ KOH(aq) \rightarrow K_2SO_4(aq) + 2\ H_2O(l) + \text{heat}$$

A few products of double displacement reactions are not very stable and spontaneously decompose to form water and a gas. The two most common ones are:

- carbonic acid, which decomposes to form carbon dioxide and water, and
- ammonium hydroxide, which decomposes to form ammonia gas and water

At first glance, the full equation of a neutralization reaction may not appear to represent a double displacement reaction as two compounds form three new compounds. Watch for reactions such as:

$$K_2CO_3(aq) + 2\ HCl(aq) \rightarrow 2\ KCl(aq) + H_2O(l) + CO_2(g)$$

or $$NH_4Br(aq) + NaOH(aq) \rightarrow NaBr(aq) + H_2O(l) + NH_3(g)$$

The evolution of CO_2 gas following addition of an acid to a compound is a good indication that the compound contains the carbonate anion. Similarly, the evolution of ammonia gas, with its characteristic odour, following addition of a base to a compound is indicative of the presence of the ammonium cation in the compound.

More on Precipitation

Different compounds have different degrees of solubility in water. In order to talk about solubility we need to understand what solutes and solvents are. Solvents are substances in which compounds are ______________ (e.g. ______________). Solutes are substances which are ______________ (e.g. ______________).

We can classify ionic compounds, in three categories according to the degree to which they dissolve in the solvent, water. These three categories are __________________ if its solubility is greater than 10 g/L, ____________________ if its solubility is between 1 to 10 g/L and ______________________ if its solubility is less than 1 g/L. These designations are arbitrary and NOTHING is completely insoluble.

If we mix an aqueous solution of sodium chloride with silver nitrate and a double displacement reaction occurs what will the reaction look like (include the subscripts to indicate the state of the reactants and the products)?

A chemical reaction in which one or more solids is produced as the result of mixing two aqueous solutions of ionic compounds is known as a _______________________________. The process of forming a solid is called _______________ and the solid that is formed is called a ______________________. What is the precipitate in the example reaction?

A precipitate forms if one of the product compounds is insoluble.

The Solubility Rules for Ionic Compounds in Water

Soluble Compounds	Exceptions
Nitrates	None
Chlorates	Except Ca^{2+}
Na^+, K^+, NH_4^+ compounds	None
Halides	Except Ag^+, Hg_2^{2+}, Cu^+, Pb^{2+}
Sulfates	Except Ca^{2+}, Sr^{2+}, Ba^{2+}, Pb^{2+}, Hg_2^{2+}, Ag^+
Acetates	Except Ag^+
Insoluble Compounds	**Exceptions**
Sulfides (S^{2-})	Except NH_4^+, Group I and II ions
Carbonates	Except NH_4^+, Group I ions
Phosphates	Except NH_4^+, Group I ions
Hydroxides	Except NH_4^+, Group I ions, Ba^{2+}

Practice: Predict whether the following reaction would give a precipitate. Indicate which compound would be the precipitate.

a) $Fe(NO_3)_3$ (aq) + NaOH (aq) →
b) Na_3PO_4(aq) + $AgNO_3$(aq) →
c) $Pb(NO_3)_2$ (aq) + KI (aq) →
d) NH_4OH(aq) + $Ba_3(PO_4)_2$ (s) →
e) $AgNO_3$(aq) + NaBr (aq) →
f) Na_2CO_3 (aq) + K_3PO_4 (aq) →

Sample Problem — Predicting Products of Displacement Reactions

Predict the products of the following displacement reactions:

1. $Br_2(aq) + KI(aq) \rightarrow$
2. $Li_2SO_3(aq) + Ca(NO_3)_2(aq) \rightarrow$
3. $Na_2CO_3(aq) + HBr(aq) \rightarrow$

What to Think about	How to Do It
Reaction 1	
1. Classify the reaction based on the reactants provided. Reaction 1 has an element and a compound and so must be a single displacement.	
2. As bromine is a non-metal, it must replace the non-metal iodine in the salt. A check of the reactivities of bromine and iodine indicates this is possible. Recall that iodine is diatomic.	$Br_2 + KI \rightarrow KBr + I_2$
3. Balance the completed equation and include phase subscripts if required.	$Br_2(aq) + 2\,KI(aq) \rightarrow 2\,KBr(aq) + I_2(s)$
Reaction 2	
1. Two reactant compounds indicate reaction 2 must be a double displacement reaction.	
2. Consider ion charges and be sure to write correct formulas. Show the results of the exchange of cations.	$Li_2SO_3 + Ca(NO_3)_2 \rightarrow LiNO_3 + CaSO_3$
3. Balance the completed equation.	
4. As the reactants are not acids and bases and neither of the products that decompose is formed, there must be precipitation. As the first product contains a family IA cation and is a nitrate, it must be soluble, so you can label $CaSO_3$ with an (*s*) if phase indicators are added.	$Li_2SO_3(aq) + Ca(NO_3)_2(aq) \rightarrow 2\,LiNO_3(aq) + CaSO_3(s)$
Reaction 3	
1. Reaction 3 appears to be a double displacement also.	$Na_2CO_3 + HBr \rightarrow NaBr + H_2CO_3$
2. Show the results of the exchange of cations.	
3. The formation of H_2CO_3 should remind you that this particular acid spontaneously decomposes into its non-metal oxide and water.	$Na_2CO_3 + HBr \rightarrow NaBr + CO_2 + H_2O$
4. Balance the equation and include phases.	$Na_2CO_3(aq) + 2\,HBr(aq) \rightarrow 2\,NaBr(aq) + CO_2(g) + H_2O(l)$

Practice Problems — Predicting Products of Displacement Reactions

First classify the equations, then determine the products and write a balanced formula equation for each of the following:

1. $HCl(aq) + Fe(OH)_3(s) \rightarrow$ Class:________________
2. $Zn(s) + AgClO_3(aq) \rightarrow$ Class:________________
3. $(NH_4)_2S(aq) + CsOH(aq) \rightarrow$ Class:________________
4. $Cl_2(g) + Li_2S(aq) \rightarrow$ Class:________________

3.2 Activity: Identifying an Unknown Substance

Question

Can you identify an unknown substance based on its chemical reactions?

Procedure

1. Working with a partner or by yourself, use the information in the table below to determine the identity of each of the four unknown substances.

Possible Identities	Added	Observation
1) $Cl_2(aq)$ or $I_2(aq)$? An unknown halogen dissolved in water contained in an opaque dropper	$NaBr(aq)$ — colorless solution	An orange-brown solution results.
2) $MgCO_3(s)$ or $Mg(OH)_2(s)$? An unknown white powder	$HNO_3(aq)$ —colorless acid solution	Bubbles of gas form as powder dissolves. Heat is released.
3) $Pb(NO_3)_2(aq)$ or $KNO_3(aq)$? An unknown compound dissolved to form a colorless solution	$NaI(aq)$ — colorless solution	Bright yellow precipitate forms.
4) $CaCl_2(aq)$ or $ZnCl_2(aq)$? An unknown compound dissolved to form a colorless solution	$Al(s)$ — freshly sanded strip of metal.	Dark grey coating forms on the shiny metal. Metal slowly disintegrates and falls apart.
5)		

Continued →

Results and Discussion

1. Use the table below to record all information and answer the questions below.

Identity of Unknown	Balanced Equation	Explanation
1)		
2)		
3)		
4)		
5)		

2. Write a balanced chemical equation, including phase indicators for each of the confirming tests performed.

3. Explain why you decided on the unknown in each equation.

4. Design a test to distinguish between a fifth pair of unknown substances. Give the substances, the test and the expected observations in the provided spaces in the table above. Complete row #5 for your identified substance in the second table above.

3.3 Review Questions

1. Balance each of the following reactions:

   (a) $CdF_2 + NaBr \rightarrow CdBr_2 + NaF$

   (b) $Na_2SO_4 + Cu \rightarrow Cu_2SO_4 + Na$

   (c) $Cr + F_2 \rightarrow CrF_3$

   (d) $Fe(OH)_3 \rightarrow Fe_2O_3 + H_2O$

   (e) $Ca + H_2O \rightarrow Ca(OH)_2 + H_2$

   (f) $Bi(NO_3)_3 + Na_2S \rightarrow Bi_2S_3 + NaNO_3$

   (g) $C_{25}H_{52} + O_2 \rightarrow CO_2 + H_2O$

   (h) $Al + H_2SO_4 \rightarrow Al_2(SO_4)_3 + H_2$

   (i) $LiClO_3 \rightarrow LiCl + O_2$

   (j) $K + Cl_2 \rightarrow KCl$

   (k) $Au + H_2S \rightarrow Au_2S_3 + H_2$

   (l) $Nb + S_8 \rightarrow Nb_2S_5$

   (m) $P_4O_{10} + H_2O \rightarrow H_3PO_4$

   (n) $HClO \rightarrow Cl_2O + H_2O$

   o) $H_3PO_4 + KOH \rightarrow K_3PO_4 + H_2O$

   (p) $Rb + Sc_2(CrO_4)_3 \rightarrow Rb_2CrO_4 + Sc$

   (q) $V(OH)_5 \rightarrow V_2O_5 + H_2O$

   (r) $Ba_3P_2 \rightarrow Ba + P_4$

   (s) $K_2C_2O_4 + Ca(NO_3)_2 \rightarrow CaC_2O_4 + KNO_3$

   (t) $BaCO_3 + HCl \rightarrow BaCl_2 + CO_2 + H_2O$

2. (a) Classify each of the reactions in question 1 as synthesis, decomposition, combustion, single displacement, double displacement, or neutralization.

   (b) Which of the single displacement reactions would *not* proceed spontaneously?

   (c) Which of the double displacement reactions involve precipitate formation?

   (d) Indicate the precipitates with an (*s*).

3. Classify each of the following reactions, using the following key: **S** = Synthesis, **D** = Decomposition, **C** = Combustion, **SR** = Single Displacement, **DR** = Double Displacement, **N** = Neutralization. Complete the equations and balance them. Indicate any precipitates that form with an (*s*).

   ___(a) $Rb + ZnF_2 \rightarrow$

   ___(b) $Sc_2O_3 + H_2O \rightarrow$

   ___(c) $Pb(NO_3)_2 + NaCl \rightarrow$

   ___(d) $H_2CO_3 \rightarrow$

   ___(e) $GeO_2 + SO_2 \rightarrow$

   ___(f) $SrCO_3 + H_2S \rightarrow$

   ___(g) $C_2H_6 + O_2 \rightarrow$

   ___(h) $Cs + NiCl_2 \rightarrow$

___(i) $Zr(OH)_4$ →

___(j) Br_2 + InI_3 →

___(k) H_3PO_4 + $Ba(OH)_2$ →

___(l) $AgNO_3$ + $Ca(CH_3COO)_2$ →

___(m) C_3H_5OH + O_2 →

___(n) N_2O_5 + H_2O →

___(o) $AlCl_3$ + Na_2CO_3 →

___(p) NH_4F + $LiOH$ →

___(q) HNO_3 + $Sr(OH)_2$ →

___(r) F_2 + K_2S →

___(s) $Mg(OH)_2$ →

___(t) Na + N_2 →

4. Classify each of the following chemical changes using the key from question 3. Write balanced formula equations for each, including state indicators.

___(a) A piece of magnesium ribbon on a stock shelf reacts over time with nitrogen gas in the air to form a black coating.

___(b) Phosphoric acid solution removes iron(III) hydroxide stains from an old bath tub.

___(c) Butane gas is combusted in a disposable lighter.

___(d) A zinc strip placed in a solution of copper (II) sulfate becomes coated with brownish solid.

___(e) Sulfur dioxide emitted from industrial plants combines with water vapour to form acid rain.

___(f) Calcium carbonate in marble structures is eroded over time by nitric acid in acid rain.

___(g) Nickel(III) hydroxide reacts with a cadmium anode in a prototype rechargeable battery.

___(h) Solutions of gold(III) nitrate and sodium carbonate are combined.

___(i) Potassium chromate solution indicates the endpoint in a potato chip analysis with a standard silver nitrate solution.

___(j) Methanol (CH_3OH) is combusted in race car engines.

___(k) Baking soda (sodium hydrogen carbonate) is used to neutralize a spill of hydrochloric acid.

___(l) A bright yellow pigment once used in paints is formed from the reaction of lead(II) nitrate and sodium iodide solutions.

___(m) Iron(III) oxide and water combine to form a basic compound often called rust.

___(n) Dark silver sulfide tarnish may be removed from knives and forks by placing them in contact with a piece of aluminum foil in a dilute ionic solution.

___(o) A precipitate of barium oxalate forms in a solution of sodium nitrate following the combination of two solutions.

___(p) A precipitate of barium sulfate and hydrogen gas are formed from the combination of a metal and an acid.

___(q) Diphosphorus pentoxide gas and water are produced from the decomposition of an acid.

4 The Structure of the Atom

By the end of this chapter, you should be able to do the following:

- Describe the development of the model of the atom
- Describe the subatomic structures of atoms, ions, and isotopes, using calculations where appropriate

By the end of this chapter, you should know the meaning of the following key terms:

- atom
- atomic mass
- atomic number
- Bohr model
- electron
- isotope
- neutron
- particle charge
- proton
- relative atomic mass

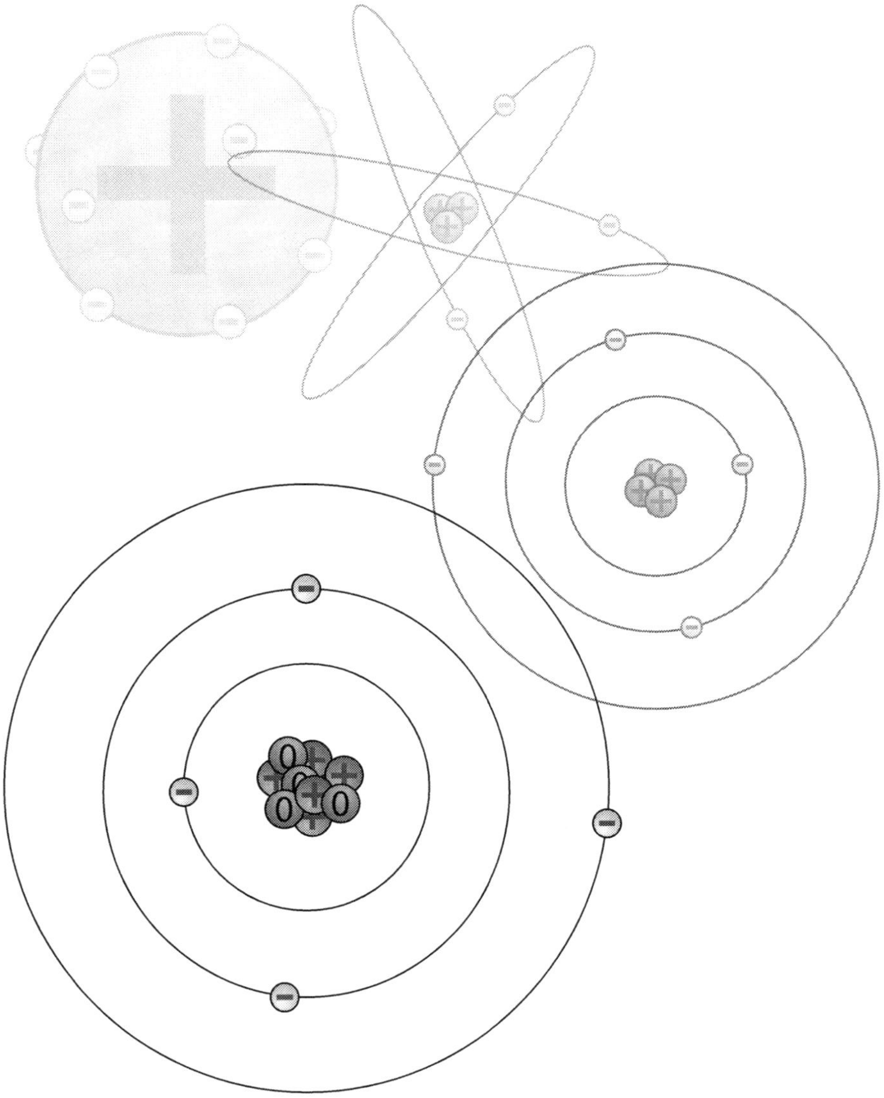

Models of the atom have gradually developed as our understanding of the composition of the atom has increased.

4.1 Periodic Trends

Warm Up

1. What attractive force is responsible for holding the cloud of electrons in place in atoms?

____

2. What effect would a strengthening of that force have on the sizes of atoms?

____

3. What might cause a strengthening of that force?

____

4. What might contribute to a weakening of that force?

____

Periodic Trends

All of the chemical and physical behavior of the elements is really a result of their electron configurations. In the last section, we discussed how similar outer-electron configurations explained the similar properties of elements within the chemical families of the periodic table. We will now concentrate on a second key concept associated with the organization of the elements in the table.

As we move across a period or down a chemical family, there are regular changes in elemental properties.

These consistent and predictable changes in elemental properties are known as **periodic trends.** Identifying and explaining them can be a great benefit when describing chemical interactions between atoms.

Periodic Trends in Atomic Size

In the quantum mechanical model, the outer boundaries of an atom depend on the size of a charge cloud in which electrons spend approximately 90% of their time. This means that the sizes of individual atoms cannot be determined in the same way as we might, for example, measure the size of objects such as marbles or grapefruits. In these cases, the object's boundaries are hard and definite, unlike those of atoms.

However, we can estimate the sizes of atoms based on how close they get to one another when bonds form between them. This can be done by measuring the distance between the nuclei of identical adjacent atoms in an element sample and dividing that distance by two.

The two common definitions of atomic size stem from the classification of elements into metals and non-metals. Non-metal elements commonly occur as diatomic molecules. For these elements, atomic size is defined as the **covalent radius**, which represents one half the distance between the two identical nuclei in the molecule.

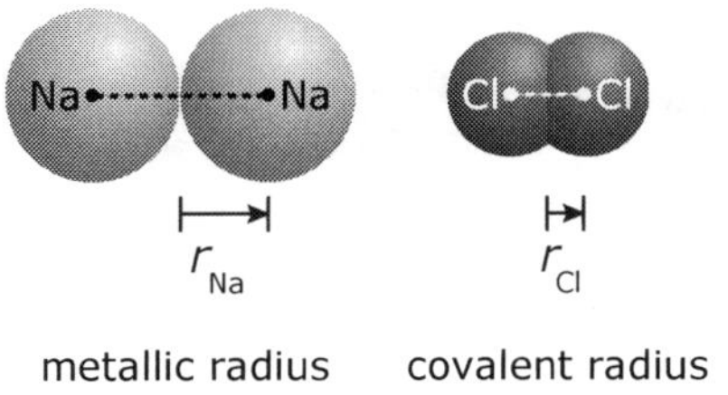

Figure 4.2.1 *Estimating atomic size involves determining bond length.*

Although the nature of bonding between metal atoms is beyond the scope of this course, the process of estimating their atomic size is very similar to that for non-metals. Metal atoms pack together in the solid state to form a crystal lattice much like ions in a salt. In a sample of a metal element, half the distance between the identical nuclei of adjacent metal atoms in the crystal is defined as the **metallic radius**.

Both of the above techniques for estimating atomic size involve determining half the bond length between identical atoms in element samples as shown in Figure 4.2.1.

Factors Influencing Atomic and Ionic Size

Let's consider for a moment what might influence the size of an atom. Because an atom's volume is really the result of a cloud of electrons, this question is really the same as asking: What affects the size of an atom's electron cloud? Seen from that perspective, it makes sense that two opposing factors influence atomic size:

1. The number of energy levels present. As the number of energy levels (n) increases, the probability that outer electrons will spend more time further from the nucleus increases and so the atoms become larger.
2. The amount of nuclear charge "felt" or "seen" by the outer electrons. As this effective nuclear charge increases, the outer electron cloud is pulled closer to the nucleus and the atom becomes smaller. Chemists use the symbol "Z_{eff}" to refer to the effective nuclear charge.

Of these two opposing factors, the one that predominates as we move across a period or down a chemical family will most influence how the sizes of those atoms change.

Consider Figure 4.2.2, showing the relative atomic radii of the elements. The **atomic radius** of an atom is the distance from the nucleus to the boundary of the surrounding cloud of electrons. The actual sizes range from the smallest, helium, at 31 pm to the largest, cesium, at 270 pm. How those sizes change across periods and down families shows a clear pattern.

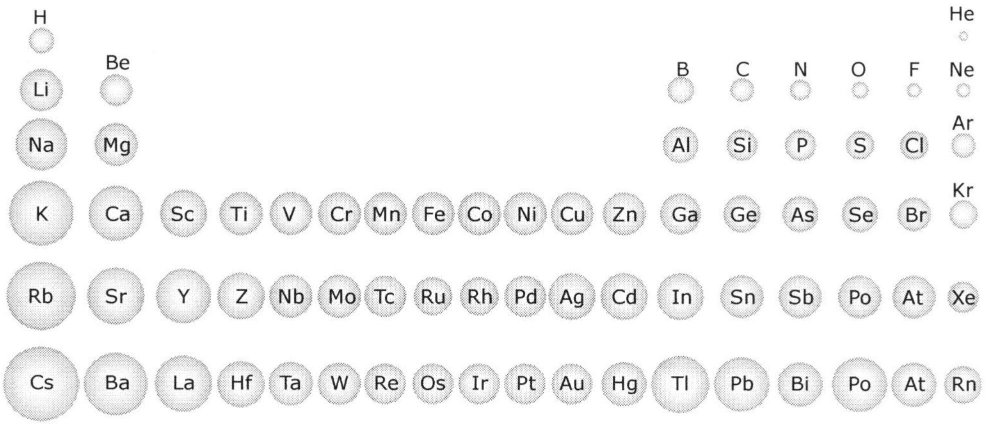

Figure 4.2.2 *Periodic table showing atomic radii*

Two definite periodic trends are evident:

As we move down a family or group, the sizes of the atoms generally increase.
As we move across a period, the sizes of the atoms generally decrease.

As we move down a chemical family and the value of *n* increases for each new element, a new inner electron level is added between the nucleus and the atom's outer electron cloud. Even though the positive charge on the nucleus is increasing, each additional inner level of electrons *effectively shields* the outer cloud from the attractive force of that nucleus, and the electron cloud increases in size. The additional inner electron clouds also repel each other, which further contributes to the increasing size of atoms in the group as we move lower in the table. This clearly shows that as the number of energy levels present in the atom increases, the size of the atom also increases.

As we move left-to-right across a period, the electrons are being added to the same outer level. This means that the level of shielding by the inner electrons remains the same. It also means that the added electrons are *ineffective at shielding each other* from the increasing positive charge on the nucleus. The result is that Z_{eff} on those outer electrons increases and the charge cloud is pulled closer and closer to the nucleus so the size of the atom decreases.

Consider Figure 4.2.3, which shows the periodic changes in atomic radii as we move from period 1 through period 6. The alkali metals are the largest members of each period and then the radii generally decrease to a minimum at the noble gases. Down each family, the atomic radii generally increase.

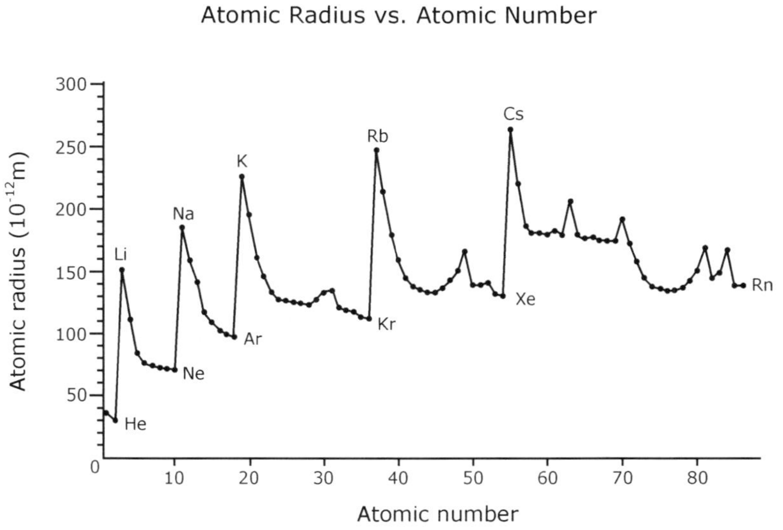

Figure 4.2.3 *Periodic changes in atomic radii as we move from period 1 through period 6*

There are exceptions to the general trends stated above and they can be explained by considering the electron configurations of the atoms and the electron sublevels being filled in each case. For example, as we move across period 4, we start filling the 4th energy level at potassium and the atomic sizes shrink as expected for the first two elements. But when we arrive at the transition elements and begin filling the 3d sublevel, the sizes remain relatively constant as we move across to zinc.

To understand this, remember that $n = 3$ electrons spend most of their time *closer to the nucleus* than those electrons in the $n = 4$ charge cloud. We would therefore expect electrons in the 3d sublevel to be capable of shielding the outer 4s electrons from the increasing nuclear charge as we move across the period. This would reduce Z_{eff}. Consider the elements vanadium and zinc. The electron configuration for V is [Ar]$3d^3 4s^2$ and the electron configuration for Zn is [Ar]$3d^{10} 4s^2$. Even though zinc has a nucleus with 7 more protons than vanadium, the extra shielding provided by zinc's 10 electrons in the 3d sublevel is such that zinc's atomic radius is equal to vanadium's!

This shows how effective inner electrons can be at shielding outer electrons from the "pull" of an increasingly positive nucleus and significantly influence atomic size. A number of other examples can be found throughout the periodic table.

Quick Check

1. Which of the two opposing factors that influence atomic size predominates as we move across a chemical period? What is the general result?

   ____

2. Which of the two opposing factors that influence atomic size predominates as we move down a chemical family? What is the general result?

   ____

3. In general, is "effective shielding" most evident going across a period or down a family? How can you tell?

   ____

Forces Affecting Ion Size

The same forces that influence the sizes of atoms also influence the sizes of ions and in the same way. Let's consider these forces and rank the following species in order of size from largest to smallest: Al^{3+}, F^-, Mg^{2+}, N^{3-}, Na^+, Ne, O^{2-}.

Note that all of the ions have 10 electrons and are therefore isoelectronic with neon. Since each species has the same number of electrons, we can assume that the amount of shielding is also the same for each. This means that the attractive force from each nucleus is the only factor influencing the size of each species. The greater the number of protons present, the stronger the attractive force on the electron cloud and therefore the smaller the atom or ion. This tells us that ranking the species in order of atomic number (positive charge on the nucleus) will also represent the order of decreasing size. Therefore, the answer is:

$N^{3-} > O^{2-} > F^- > Ne > Na^+ > Mg^{2+} > Al^{3+}$

Periodic Trends in Ionization Energy

Ionization energy (*IE*) is defined as the minimum energy required to remove an electron from a gaseous atom or ion. The term is often used to mean the "first" ionization energy (IE_1) whereby a neutral atom becomes a 1^+ cation according to the following equation:

$$\text{atom}\,(g) + IE_1 \rightarrow \text{ion}^+\,(g) + e^-$$

Ionization energy tells us how strongly an atom holds onto its outermost electrons. This is an important property because an element with a low IE_1 will be more likely to lose electrons and form cations during chemical changes. A high IE_1 might signal an element's tendency to gain electrons and form anions or perhaps not forms ions at all.

We might expect that a large atom, whose outer electrons are held less tightly, would have a lower IE_1 than a smaller atom whose outer electrons are held much more strongly. Said another way, as atomic size decreases, ionization energy should increase. This is, in fact, the general trend, as shown in Figure 4.2.4.

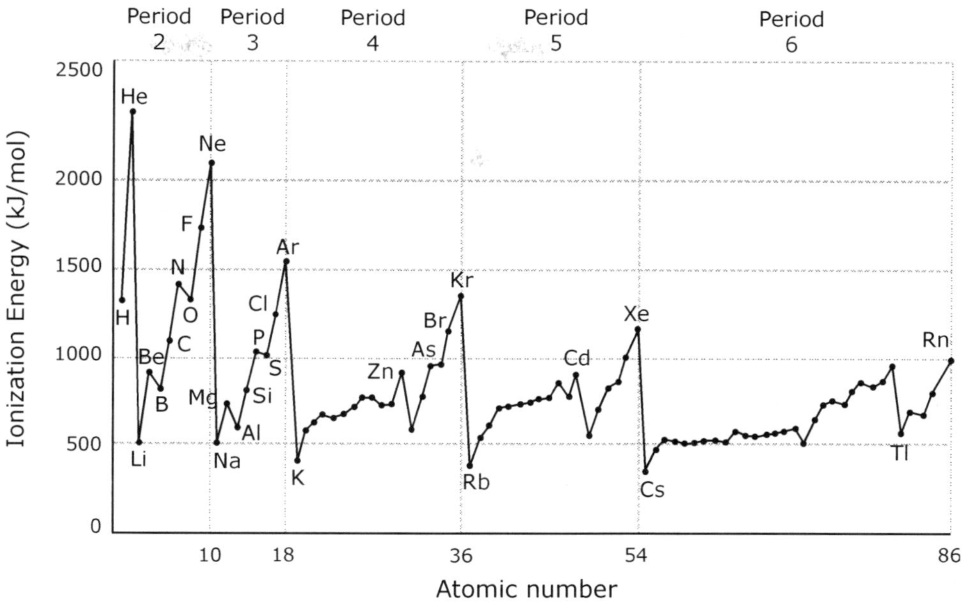

Figure 4.2.4 *As atomic size decreases, ionization energy increases.*

We can see that the lowest IE_1 values are associated with the largest atoms, which are located in the lower left corner of the periodic table. Conversely, the highest IE_1 numbers correspond to the smallest atoms, located in the upper right portion of the table.

At the beginning of each period, the largest atoms are the alkali metals, which have the lowest ionization energies. As we progress across the period and the sizes of the atoms decrease, we see a corresponding general increase in ionization energy until we reach the maximum value at each noble gas. At the beginning of the next period, the dramatic drop in ionization energy reflects the significant increase in size of that next alkali metal. As we move down a chemical family, the increase in atomic size results in a general decrease in ionization energy. The periodic trends are clearly evident up to the end of the 6th period.

The diagram shows that lower ionization energies are associated with elements nearer the left side of the periodic table, namely the metals. This tells us that metals generally tend to lose electrons when they are involved in chemical reactions. Non-metals, on the other hand, with relatively high ionization energies, have a tendency to gain or even share electrons rather than lose them. Of course, noble gases do neither of the above.

Sample Problem – Trends in Ionization Energy

Using only the periodic table, rank each of the following alphabetical lists of elements in order of increasing first ionization energies.

(a) argon chlorine phosphorus sodium silicon
(b) antimony arsenic bismuth nitrogen phosphorus

What to Think about	How to Do It
1. Ionization energy increases left-to-right across a period and moving up a chemical group.	
2. The elements listed in (a) are members of period 3. List the elements in the order they appear from left-to-right in period 3.	Na < Si < P < Cl < Ar
3. The elements listed in (b) belong to group 15 of the periodic table. List the elements in the order they appear from bottom-to-top in group 15.	Bi < Sb < As < P < N

Practice Problems — Trends in Ionization Energy

1. Using only the periodic table, rank the following alphabetical list of elements in order of decreasing first ionization energy.

   aluminum argon cesium magnesium rubidium silicon sodium sulfur

2. Using the periodic table, write the correct number in the space after each statement below:

   Members of this chemical family have the highest IE_1 in their period. ________

   Members of this chemical family have the lowest IE_1 in their period. ________

   Members of this chemical period have the highest IE_1 in their family. ________

   Members of this chemical period have the lowest IE_1 in their family. ________

An Introduction to Electronegativity

Our discussions so far have focused on the electron configurations, properties, and periodic trends associated with *individual atoms* of the elements. This has been directed towards an eventual understanding of how these atoms behave when they form chemical bonds.

Chemical bonding begins when the valence electrons in a region of space between two atoms are attracted by or "shared" between the adjacent nuclei. Each nucleus exerts an influence on those electrons, which ultimately determine the nature of the resulting bond.

To begin to describe this effect and the nature of the resulting bonds, let's look at an elemental property associated with bonded atoms. It is one of the most important properties in chemical bonding.

Electronegativity is defined as the relative ability of a bonded atom to attract shared electrons to itself. Atoms with relatively high electronegativities (EN) tend to pull bonded electrons closer to their nuclei. Atoms with lower EN values have their bonded electrons pulled further away. This will dictate not only the nature of the chemical bonds that form, but also the properties of the compounds containing those bonds.

We might expect that smaller atoms would have higher EN values since their nuclei would be closer to bonded electrons than the nuclei of larger atoms. We might also expect that larger atoms would therefore tend to have lower EN values. This is indeed the case, and because atomic size shows periodic trends, we shouldn't be surprised that electronegativity does as well. In fact, the general trends in electronegativity are similar to those seen in ionization energy.

We can see a clear resemblance to the trends in ionization energy, namely that EN increases going across a period and increases moving up a group (Figure 4.2.6). (The noble gases don't have EN values because they don't generally form chemical bonds.)

Increasing EN

H 2.1																	He
Li 1.0	Be 1.5											B 2.0	C 2.5	N 3.0	O 3.5	F 4.0	Ne
Na 0.9	Mg 1.2											Al 1.5	Si 1.8	P 2.1	S 2.5	Cl 3.0	Ar
K 0.8	Ca 1.0	Sc 1.3	Ti 1.5	V 1.6	Cr 1.6	Mn 1.5	Fe 1.8	Co 1.8	Ni 1.8	Cu 1.9	Zn 1.6	Ga 1.6	Ge 1.8	As 2.0	Se 2.4	Br 2.8	Kr
Rb 0.8	Sr 1.0	Y 1.3	Zr 1.4	Nb 1.6	Mo 1.8	Tc	Ru 2.2	Rh 2.2	Pd 2.2	Ag 1.9	Cd 1.7	In 1.7	Sn 1.8	Sb 1.9	Te 2.1	I 2.5	Xe
Cs 0.7	Ba 0.9	La 1.1	Hf 1.3	Ta 1.5	W 1.7	Re 1.9	Os 2.2	Ir 2.2	Pt 2.2	Au 2.4	Hg 1.9	Tl 1.8	Pb 1.8	Bi 1.9	Po 2.0	At 2.2	Rn
Fr 0.7	Ra 0.9	Ac 1.1															
			Ce 1.1	Pr 1,1	Nd 1.2	Pm	Sm 1.2	Eu 1.2	Gd 1.1	Tb 1.2	Dy 1.2	Ho 1.2	Er 1.2	Tm 1.2	Yb 1.1	Lu 1.2	
			Th 1.3	Pa 1.5	U 1.7												

Increasing EN

Figure 4.2.6 *Periodic table showing trends in electronegativity*

The electronegativity values are numbers ranging from a low of 0.7 for cesium to 4.0 for fluorine (Figure 4.2.7). The values were determined by the great American chemist Linus Pauling. For our purposes, we will only be interested in the relative magnitudes of the numbers.

The trends indicate that metal atoms, which are large with low ionization energies, also have relatively low EN values. Smaller non-metal atoms tend to have higher ionization energies and electronegativities. The consequences of these properties with respect to chemical bonding are coming up in the next section, so stay tuned!

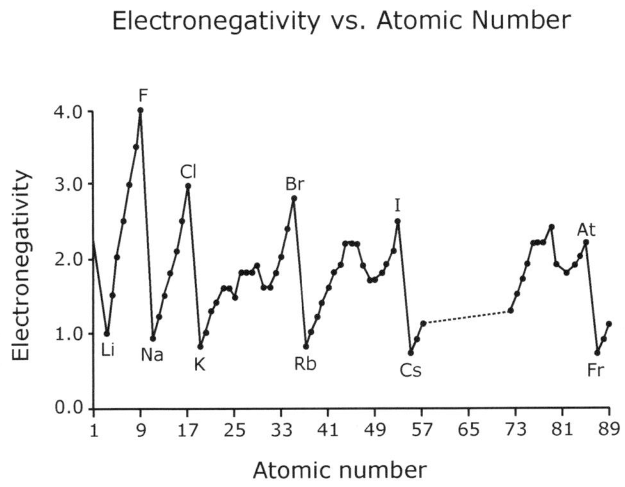

Figure 4.2.7 *Graph showing electronegativity values*

4.1 Activity: A Summary Diagram of Periodic Trends

Question

How can we summarize the three periodic trends discussed in this section using one periodic table?

Materials

Periodic table, a ruler or straight edge

Procedure

1. Consider each of the three periodic trends listed below and complete the following table by writing in either the word "increases" or "decreases" for each of the properties listed in the spaces available.

	Moving Across a Period	Moving Up a Chemical Family
Atomic Size		
Ionization Energy		
Electronegativity		

2. Print a full page version of the periodic table of the elements from whatever website you wish.

3. Using a ruler, draw three parallel vertical arrows facing up on the left margin of the periodic table. Draw three parallel horizontal arrows facing to the right across the top of the table.

4. Label each of the three arrows on the left and across the top with the terms: "Atomic Size," "Ionization Energy," and "Electronegativity." Next to each term, write the appropriate words from the table that you filled in above.

5. Using a ruler, draw a long diagonal arrow beginning at the bottom left corner of the table and extending and pointing to the top right corner. Along the top side of that arrow, write in how each of the three terms listed above changes as you move from the bottom left corner of the periodic table to the top right corner. Save this table because we will refer to it in later sections.

4.1 Review Questions

1. What is meant by the term "periodic trends"?

2. Why is it difficult to measure the sizes of individual atoms?

3. Two of the elemental properties discussed in this section show similar trends when moving across a period and up a chemical family. Identify these and the trend observed.

4. One of the three properties discussed shows periodic trends when moving across a period or up a family opposite to the other two properties. Identify this property and the trend observed.

5. Briefly explain why fluorine is a smaller atom than lithium. Consider which factor is predominating across a period.

6. Where are the largest atoms located on the periodic table? Where are the smallest atoms located on the periodic table?

7. The attraction of electrons to the nucleus and repulsion of the electrons between each other both influence the size of an atom or ion. Use this to complete the following statements.
   (a) A cation will always be ________________ (smaller or larger) than its parent neutral atom because of ________________ (increased or decreased) attraction of the outer electrons for the nucleus and ________________ (increased or decreased) repulsion of the electrons for each other.
   (b) An anion will always be ________________ (smaller or larger) than its parent neutral atom because of ________________ (increased or decreased) attraction of the outer electrons for the nucleus and ________________ (increased or decreased) repulsion of the electrons for each other.

8. What role do inner or core electrons play in determining atomic size and ionization energy?

9. Complete the following table by filling in the words "lower left" or "upper right" in the appropriate spaces.

Where on Periodic Table Elements Show:	
Largest atomic radii	
Smallest atomic radii	
Lowest ionization energy	
Highest ionization energy	
Lowest electronegativity	
Highest electronegativity	

10. Consider the first two ionization energies for lithium:

    IE_1 = 519 kJ/mol IE_2 = 7 285 kJ/mol

    Explain why lithium's second ionization energy is more than 10 times its first.

11. Elements with low ionization energies tend to have relatively low electronegativities. What might this indicate about how they will behave when reacting with high *IE* and EN elements?

12. Elements with high ionization energies tend to have relatively high electronegativities. What might this indicate about how they will behave when reacting with low *IE* and EN elements?

13. What do you think might occur if two non-metal atoms, each with high EN and *IE* values reacted together? (Hint: Will either have a tendency to give away electrons?)

14. Write the electron configuration for nickel and zinc. Use these to explain why an atom of zinc is larger than an atom of nickel.

4.2 Early Models of the Atom

Warm Up

In earlier science classes, you learned that an atom is the smallest part of an element that still has the properties of the element. Recall what you learned about atomic structure to answer the following questions.

1. Complete the following table about the three subatomic particles in an atom.

Subatomic Particle	Relative Charge	Relative Mass	Location in Atom
	1+		
		1 amu	
			outside nucleus

2. The two subatomic particles responsible for almost all of an atom's mass are the ______________ and the ______________.

3. Most of an atom's volume is actually ______________ ______________ (two words).

The Ancient Greeks Had It Right — for Awhile

Think about your favorite detective mystery and why you enjoyed reading it. The most interesting parts of the story were not only the ultimate answer to the mystery, but also how each clue was discovered, processed, and applied to derive that final solution.

The story of our eventual understanding of the building blocks of matter is an equally engaging read because it is like a good mystery novel!

The story begins almost 2500 years ago in ancient Greece with the philosopher Leucippos and his student Democritus. They reasoned that if a sample of solid matter such as gold was repeatedly cut into smaller and smaller pieces, the eventual result would be a particle so small it couldn't be cut into anything smaller. Democritus used the term "atomos" (Greek for "uncuttable") to refer to these smallest particles of matter. He imagined that particles of different sizes and shapes might be components of all the different types of matter.

That sounds like a promising start. However, the ancient philosophers relied largely on intuition rather than experimentation for knowledge, and soon the ideas of another philosopher replaced the idea that matter was composed of tiny particles. Aristotle proposed instead that all types of matter were actually made up of different proportions of four basic elements: earth, air, fire, and water. Unfortunately, this idea and its various incarnations were embraced for almost 2000 years in the practice of alchemy. During the next two millennia, alchemy dominated the chemical landscape (Figure 4.2.1). Many alchemists were searching for a way to change base metals into gold. Although this search was ultimately doomed to failure, some alchemists were actually serious scientists. We owe the discoveries of such useful chemical procedures as distillation, the separation of metals from ores, and the preparation of some acids to alchemy.

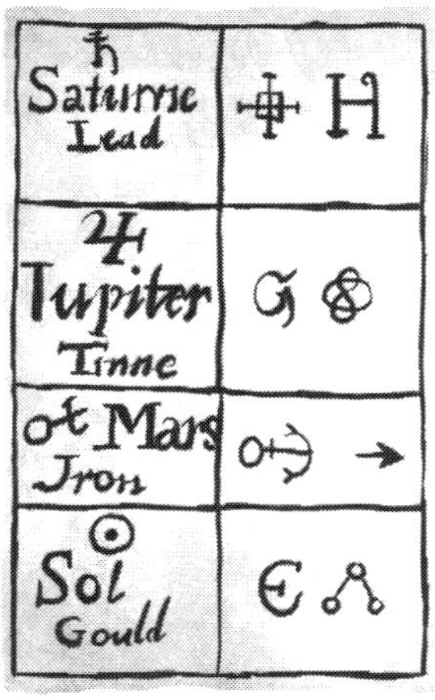

Figure 4.2.1 *Alchemists developed a set of symbols for the elements and linked them to the planets. For example, gold was associated with the Sun and Mars with iron.*

Science Begins and the Atom Returns

Finally, in the last half of the 1600s, the first real scientist emerged. Robert Boyle was the first person to perform and publish the results of true quantitative experiments. All of his observations convinced him that the four-element idea proposed by Aristotle was incorrect. In 1661, Boyle published the *Sceptical Chymist* in which he outlined what we now call the scientific method. He also provided an experimental definition for an element as being an "unmingled body." As this definition and Boyle's insistence on experimentation gained acceptance, more and more elements were discovered, and Aristotle's ideas about matter were eventually discarded.

Further studies over the next 140 years by such scientists as Carl Scheele, Joseph Priestley, Antoine Lavoisier, and Joseph Proust resulted in mass laws governing compound composition and chemical reactions. It was these laws that were used by the English schoolteacher John Dalton to propose a theory about matter first suggested more than 2200 years earlier. In 1808, Dalton published a book called *A New System of Chemical Philosophy* in which he presented his atomic theory. The main points of the theory are shown below.

Dalton's Atomic Theory

1. All matter is composed of extremely small particles called atoms, which cannot be broken into smaller particles, created, or destroyed.
2. The atoms of any given element are all identical to each other and different from the atoms of other elements.
3. Atoms of different elements combine in specific ratios to form compounds.
4. In a chemical reaction, atoms are separated, rearranged, and recombined to form new compounds.

Dalton's theory was a major step forward in our understanding of matter. Experimental evidence had finally led back to an idea that had made sense to some philosophers thousands of years earlier. But there were exciting revelations about the atom soon to be discovered.

Quick Check

1. Suggest a reason why Robert Boyle is often called the first true scientist.

   ____

2. Democritus and Dalton both proposed the existence of atoms. How was the development of their ideas different?

   ____

3. Which part of Dalton's atomic theory is now known to be incorrect?

   ____

Discovering the Subatomic — Thomson's Atomic Model

The relationship between matter and electric charge fascinated scientists in the 1800s. They wondered, for example, how electricity passed through matter and how it might behave in the absence of matter. Between 1859 and 1879, work done by Julius Plücker in Germany and William Crookes in England using special glass tubes soon led to one of the most important discoveries ever made about matter and the nature of the atom.

Gas Discharge Tubes and Strange Green Glows

One such device that Crookes worked with consisted of a sealed glass tube connected to a vacuum pump. (Table 5.1.2). The tube contained a negatively charged electrical terminal (a cathode) embedded in one end, a positive terminal (an anode) located about halfway along the length, and a broad flat cross placed about two-thirds of the way down. When a high voltage was applied across the electrodes as the air was being pumped out, any air remaining in the tube began to glow (by a phenomenon called fluorescence). This glow faded as the air was removed, but close inspection in the darkened laboratory revealed a shadow of the cross surrounded by faint green glow at the end of the tube opposite the cathode and a very faint glow coming from the cathode itself. The location of the shadow and the cathode's glow led Crookes to conclude that something must be travelling from the cathode to the other end of the tube even though all the air was gone.

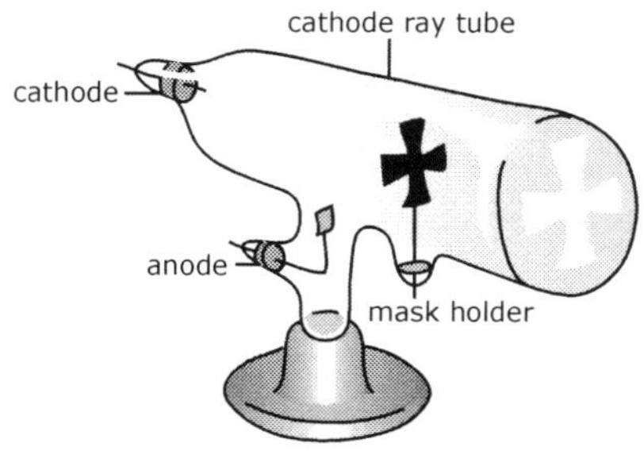

Figure 4.2.2 *Crookes' glass tube*

In Paris, Jean Baptiste Perrin discovered that a magnet placed next to the tube was able to deflect the mysterious beam. Because Perrin knew that only a beam of charged particles can be deflected by a magnetic field, he concluded that the mysterious "cathode ray" must be a stream of charged particles.

Cathode Rays and Subatomic Particles

Many researchers experimented with cathode-ray tubes, as they came to be known. However, it wasn't until the great English physicist Joseph John Thomson ("J.J." to his friends) turned his attention to these mysterious rays that a breakthrough came. In 1897, Thomson set to work to discover the nature of cathode rays. He modified the original Crookes' tube by passing the diffuse cathode ray through a small hole drilled in the centre of an anode and directed that narrow ray onto a fluorescent target. Between the anode and the target he placed an electric field. When the focussed cathode ray was deflected towards the positive plate, Thomson concluded that the charge on these moving particles must be negative (Figure 4.2.3).

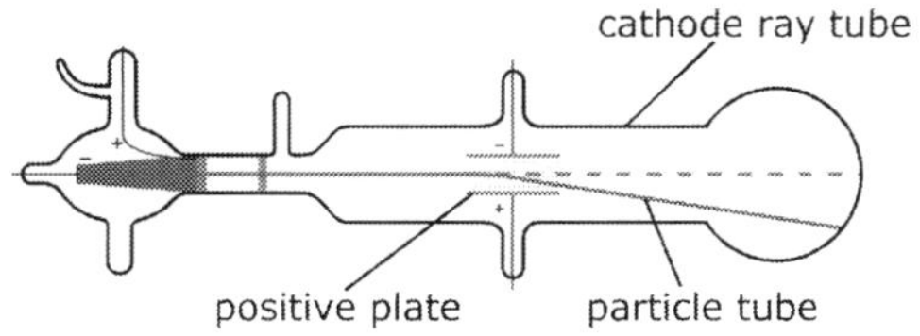

Figure 4.2.3 *The deflection of the particle beam toward the positive electrical plate indicated that the particles had a negative charge.*

Thomson knew that the amount of deflection a charged particle experiences in an electric field depends on the ratio of the particle's charge to its mass. The larger that ratio is (the more charge and the less mass), the greater the deflection. By carefully adjusting the currents in his modified vacuum tube, Thomson was able to calculate the magnitude of the charge-to-mass ratio for the negative particles composing cathode rays. He found that value to be 1.76×10^8 C/g (C stands for coulomb, the SI unit of charge). This was almost 2000 times greater than the charge-to-mass ratio for the hydrogen ion, which was the smallest particle known in 1897. Thomson concluded that the magnitude of charge on these negative particles must equal that of hydrogen ions, but that the mass of the particles was actually 2000 times less than hydrogen ions. This was a revolutionary idea because it meant that Thomson had discovered a particle far smaller than the smallest atom!

The Electronic Nature of the Atom - Thompson's Atomic Model

Thomson repeated the experiments many times with different metals used as the cathode and even different gases inside the tube. Each time the results were the same. This had to mean that these mysterious negative particles were present in atoms of different elements. In a speech given on April 29, 1897, to the Royal Institution, J.J. Thomson told his audience that cathode rays were actually tiny negatively charged "corpuscles" of electricity, each with an identical mass about 2000 times lighter than an atom of hydrogen. The audience was largely sceptical and reluctant to accept Thomson's radical assertion that bits of matter even smaller than atoms existed.

Soon, however, this revolutionary idea was accepted. This tiny "corpuscle" was identified as the **electron** and shown to be a component of every atom. In 1906, Thomson was awarded the Nobel Prize for his work on the conduction of electricity through gases in which he discovered the negative charges that became known as electrons. In an article in England's "Philosophical Magazine" in 1897, Thomson suggested what else might be in an atom. He reasoned that if an intact atom has no charge, then there must be something positive in an atom to balance the negative charge on the electron. He discovered that "something" within a few years.

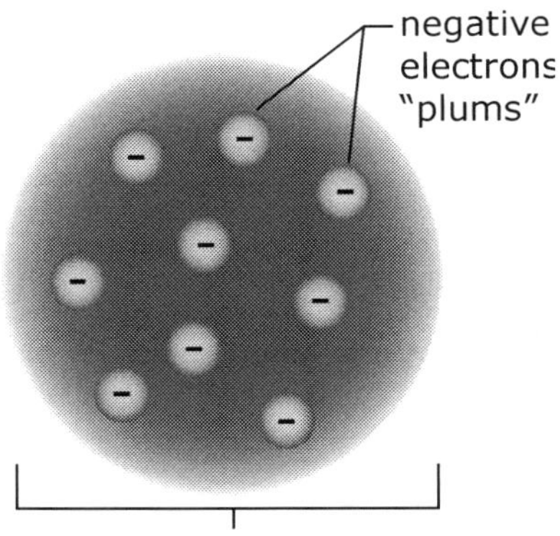

Figure 4.2.4 *Thomson's atomic model (1903)*

At this point, it's valuable to consider the significance of what Thomson discovered. First, he found that atoms were themselves built from even smaller components. Second, and arguably more important, Thomson discovered that these subatomic particles had opposite charges. This meant that the building blocks of matter are essentially electrical entities! Remember that idea, because it will be fundamental to most of the chemistry you will ever learn.

Thomson soon used hydrogen gas in a further modified cathode-ray tube to demonstrate that atoms did indeed have a positively charged component. This led him to propose the first revision to Dalton's 1808 atomic model in almost 100 years. In 1903, Thomson suggested that an atom could be seen as a "spongy ball" or "plum pudding" with negative electrons distributed evenly throughout a positively charged spongy mass, much like bits of fruit in an English pudding or raisins in a muffin. (Figure 4.2.4). Thomson's "plum pudding" atomic model as it became known was soon replaced by other models, but it nonetheless represented a major advance in our understanding of the atom and of matter itself. First, Thomson discovered that atoms were themselves composed of even smaller

Quick Check

1. The electron's charge was determined in 1909 by the American physicist Robert Millikan to be 1.602×10^{-19} C. Use the e/m ratio for the electron (1.76×10^8 C/g) to calculate the electron's mass in grams.
Hint: To determine the mass in grams, begin with the provided value of charge in coulombs and use the e/m ratio as a conversion factor. As the required answer is in grams, the e/m ratio will need to be inverted to allow the coulombs to cancel, providing an answer in grams.

2. What evidence led Crookes to conclude that the unknown ray in his vacuum tube
(a) originated at the cathode?
____
(b) was a beam of charged particles?
____
(c) may be a beam of negatively charged particles?
____

Continued

Quick Check (*Continued*)

3. Identify the two most important components of Thomson's atomic theory.

   (a) ______________________________

   –

   (b) ______________________________

components. Second, and arguably more important, Thomson discovered that these subatomic particles had opposite charges. This meant that the building blocks of matter are electrical entities! The electrical nature of atoms is fundamental to their behavior and thus to most of the chemistry you will ever learn.

Rutherford Changes Things

In 1895, young Ernest Rutherford, working on his father's farm in New Zealand, received the news that he'd won a scholarship to study at the University of Cambridge with J.J. Thomson at the prestigious Cavendish Laboratory. Rutherford arrived at Cambridge in time to work with Thomson during the discovery of negative electric charges. Not surprisingly, therefore, Rutherford fully believed in the "plum pudding" model of the atom.

After training with Thomson, Rutherford went to McGill University in Montreal where he devoted much of his time to studying the nature of the emissions associated with the newly discovered phenomenon of radioactivity. Rutherford's work at McGill would soon give him all the tools he needed to test Thomson's atomic model. Using samples of radioactive elements such as radium provided by Marie and Pierre Curie, Ernest Rutherford and Frederic Soddy discovered three types of emissions associated with radioactivity. They labeled these emissions as alpha particles, beta particles, and gamma rays. Their nature and properties are summarized in Figure 4.2.1.

Table 4.2.1 *Characteristics of Radioactive Emissions*

Emission	Nature of Emission	Penetrating Ability	Emission Speed
Alpha (**α**) particles	helium nuclei	penetrates a few cm of air but stopped by a thin sheet of aluminum foil	~ 16 000 km/s
Beta (**β**) particles	electrons	penetrates a few mm of aluminum but stopped by a thin sheet of lead	~ 200 000 km/s
Gamma (**γ**) rays	high energy waves	penetrates at least 30 cm of lead or 2 km of air	300 000 km/s (speed of light)

By 1909, Rutherford had returned to England and joined the University of Manchester. Working with colleagues Hans Geiger and Ernest Marsden, Rutherford decided to use alpha particles as a type of "probe" to test the makeup of the atom. The experiment involved aiming alpha particles emitted from a radioactive source at very thin (1/2000 mm) sheets of gold foil, and then observing where those alpha particles struck a fluorescent screen after passing through the atoms in the foil.

Recall that Rutherford had been a student of J.J. Thomson and firmly believed that the plum pudding model accurately represented the structure of an atom. Based on that belief, Rutherford fully expected that nothing in Thomson's "spongy" atom was capable of significantly altering the path of alpha particles traveling at 16 000 km/s. All the alpha particles should, therefore, pass through the gold foil without deviating from their original path. If any deflection did occur, it would be minimal at best.

The vast majority of alpha particles behaved exactly as predicted and passed right through the gold foil without deviating (Figure 4.2.5). But (and this is a huge "but") a few particles deviated through large angles and a very few (about 1 in 20 000) didn't go through the foil at all, but rather bounced back! Rutherford wrote in his journal that "it was quite the most incredible event that has ever happened to me in my life. It was almost as incredible as if you had fired a 15-inch shell at a piece of tissue-paper and it came back and hit you." Rutherford was referring to the fact that nothing in Thomson's atomic model was capable of knocking an alpha particle far off its course, let alone turning it around. Clearly, the model of the atom proposed by Thomson needed a major revision and Rutherford was able to do just that.

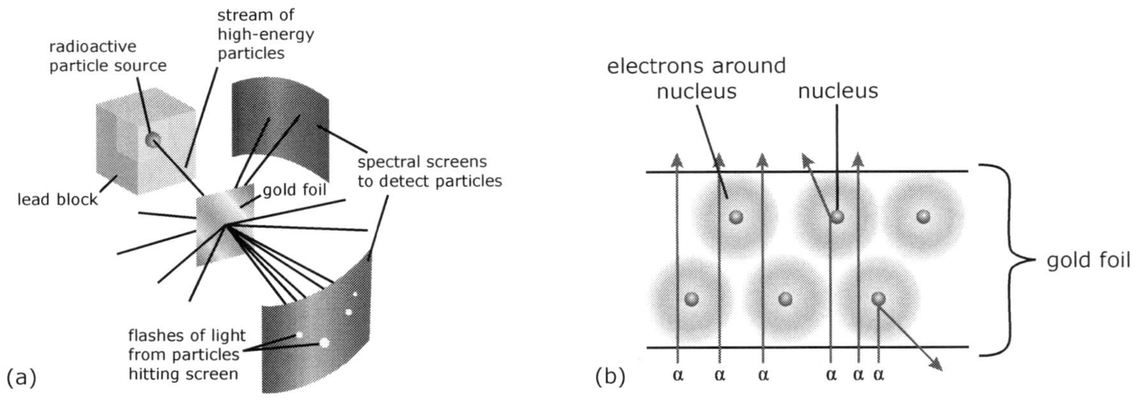

Figure 4.2.5 *(a) Rutherford's gold foil experiment; (b) Rutherford's atomic model explaining the results of the experiment*

Rutherford's Model of the Atom

Rutherford explained the results by suggesting that virtually all the mass of an atom was concentrated in a very tiny, dense, positive structure at the atom's centre he called the **nucleus**. Surrounding this nucleus was a cloud of negatively charged electrons that accounted for all of atom's volume but virtually none of its mass. Rutherford calculated that the nucleus was so small compared to the volume occupied by the surrounding electrons that the vast majority of an atom was actually empty space! Although Rutherford's model for the atom resembled a tiny planetary system with electrons orbiting a nucleus much like planets orbit the sun, Rutherford himself wrote, "The atom has often been likened to a solar system where the sun corresponds to the nucleus and the planets to the electrons....The analogy, however, must not be pressed too far."

Rutherford was responsible for perhaps the most significant contribution ever made to our understanding of atomic structure, and he received the Nobel Prize in chemistry in 1908. Shortly after discovering the nucleus, Rutherford realized that his model explained the charged nature of the atom, but couldn't account for all of its mass. He believed that a neutral particle must also exist in the nucleus that added mass but no charge to the atom. More than 20 years later, James Chadwick discovered that particle, the **neutron**, just as Rutherford had predicted.

Several significant changes to Rutherford's atomic model were still needed to explain electron behavior. However, as Rutherford theorized, the atom is an entity whose tiny positive nucleus accounts for 99.97% of its mass but only about one trillionth of its volume! The negative electrons move rapidly within the available atomic volume held by the attraction of the nucleus. Table 5.1.2 is a simplified summary of the composition of the atom as we view it today.

Table 5.1.2 *The Composition of the Atom*

Subatomic Particle	Relative Charge	Relative Mass	Absolute Mass	Location in Atom
Proton (p^+)	1+	1 amu	1.673×10^{-24} g	inside nucleus
Neutron (n^0)	0	1	1.675×10^{-24} g	inside nucleus
Electron (e^-)	1–	0	9.109×10^{-28} g	outside nucleus

Quick Check

1. Why did Rutherford believe the nucleus was so small compared to the size of the atom itself?

____

2. Why did Rutherford believe that the nucleus had a positive charge?

____

3. To what parts of the gold foil experiment was Rutherford referring when used the following analogies:

   (a) a 15-inch shell ______________________________

   (b) a piece of tissue paper ______________________________

4. Experiments show that the diameter of the nucleus of an atom is about 10^{-14} m and the diameter of an atom itself is about 10^{-10} m. If the diameter of the nucleus was actually 2.0 cm (about the width of your thumb), determine the diameter of the entire atom.

4.2 Activity: Linking the Giants

Question

What were the major scientific achievements of the scientists who contributed to our understanding of the atom?

Procedure

1. Consider the following researchers:

Robert Boyle	Julius Plücker	James Chadwick
Carl Scheele	Jean Baptiste Perrin	Frederick Soddy
Joseph Priestley	William Crookes	Ernest Marsden
Joseph Proust	J.J. Thomson	Hans Geiger
Antoine Lavoisier	Marie and Pierre Curie	Robert Millikan
John Dalton	Ernest Rutherford	

   Construct an "Atomic Theory Timeline" diagram and include all of the names given above including dates and which discovery each individual made that contributed (directly or indirectly) to our understanding of the atom.

2. Write a point-form biography of any one scientist listed above focusing on all of his or her major scientific achievements.

3. Exchange you biography with a classmate or present your biography to the class.

Results and Discussion

1. In looking at your timeline and the discoveries of the different scientists, what can you conclude about the development of scientific knowledge?

2. Why did you choose the scientist whose biography you wrote?

4.3 Quantum Theory and the Bohr Model of the Atom

Warm Up

1. (a) List three properties of waves such as water waves or visible light.

   ____

   (b) What would you expect to happen when two water waves moving in opposite directions met each other?

   ____

2. (a) List three properties of solid objects or particles such as the marbles in a bag.

   ____

   (b) What would you expect to happen when two marbles moving in opposite directions met each other?

   ____

3. Are any of your answers to question 1 identical to question 2? (Stay tuned…)

   ____

Waves Behaving like Particles? Well Hit Me with a Planck!

A serious challenge to Rutherford's atomic model arose almost immediately. A very secure prediction of the physics available at the end of the 1800s was that accelerating charges should radiate energy. Because orbiting electrons are accelerating charges, electrons in atoms should lose energy. That prediction was catastrophic for Rutherford's model. It meant that all atoms, and so also all matter, should collapse in a fraction of a second as their electrons lost energy and spiraled into the nucleus! Obviously, a significant piece of the atomic puzzle was missing and even Rutherford himself was ready to abandon his view of the atom. Yet, his conclusions and his nuclear model were correct. The real problem was that the physics of the day needed to be re-written to explain the behavior of electrons in atoms.

To begin to understand how the solution came about, we must consider the work of German physicist Max Planck. In 1900, this conservative professor began nothing short of a revolution in physics. He proposed that energy, long considered to be strictly a wave phenomenon, could be shown to behave like particles in the form of very tiny, discreet energy packets or bundles he called quanta (plural for quantum). Planck called this the quantum theory and arrived at his conclusions (reluctantly) by studying the energy radiated from heated solids. Planck developed the following equation for the energy associated with each packet or quantum:

$$\boldsymbol{E = hv}$$

where $\boldsymbol{E}$ = energy, $\boldsymbol{v}$ = frequency, $\boldsymbol{h}$ = a very tiny proportionality constant ($h = 6.626 \times 10^{-34}$J·s) called Planck's constant. According to Planck, energy could only be absorbed or emitted in whole numbers of quanta, that is, one quantum of energy ($E = hv$), two quanta ($E = 2hv$), three quanta ($E = 3hv$) and so on, but nowhere in between. Think of each energy quantum as a glass marble in a bag of identical marbles (Figure 4.3.1). In the same way that you could only ever add or remove a specific amount of glass from the bag in the form of a whole number of marbles, so too could amounts of energy only be absorbed or emitted in the form of whole numbers of quanta.

Figure 4.3.1 *Quanta of energy are like marbles in bag. The marbles can only be removed as whole units.*

At the end of the 1800s, the behavior of waves and the behavior of particles were seen as very different and mutually exclusive. Waves were disturbances that moved through space, could pass through and interfere with each other, and could have any value within a range. Particles were objects with definite boundaries that bounced off each other when they collided and could only exist in certain whole-number quantities. A firm experimental and mathematical foundation supported the idea that waves were fundamentally different from particles. To now suggest that waves could behave like particles was almost sacrilegious! Planck himself wrote about his work: "By nature, I am peacefully inclined and reject all doubtful adventures. ...However, a theoretical interpretation had to be found at any cost....I was ready to sacrifice every one of my previous convictions about physical laws."

Planck's theory wasn't taken very seriously at first. But in 1905, a 26-year-old clerk in a Swiss patent office named Albert Einstein wrote five papers that changed the scientific world forever. One of those papers used the quantum theory to explain a phenomenon involving light called the "photoelectric effect" that had baffled physicists until then. According to Einstein, the only way to make sense of the photoelectric effect was to consider light as being composed of tiny discreet packets of energy. (These were later called "photons" by American chemist Gilbert Lewis.) Einstein's paper was the first practical application of the quantum theory and as a result, the theory soon began to gain widespread acceptance. In 1921, Einstein was awarded the Nobel Prize in physics for his explanation of the photoelectric effect.

Quick Check

1. Briefly state what it means for something to be a "quantized."

   ____

2. Give three common examples of things considered to be "quantized."

   ____

   ____

3. According to Planck, could an amount of energy equal to 2.5*hv* be absorbed or emitted by an object? Explain.

   ____

   ____

The Bohr Model

One of the scientists who paid particular attention to the work of Planck and Einstein was a young Danish physicist named Niels Bohr. As a young grad student, Bohr had met Ernest Rutherford at the Cavendish Laboratory in Cambridge and then worked with Rutherford at the University of Manchester. Bohr believed in the nuclear atomic model and started to see a way to "save" it using the quantum theory. If energy was indeed quantized and so could be seen to have only certain values and not others, perhaps the energies associated with electrons orbiting the nucleus had similar restrictions.

Bohr was working on this idea at Rutherford's laboratory in Manchester in 1912. In the middle of his experiments and calculations, he returned to Copenhagen to get married. He was so excited about his work that he managed to convince his new bride to cancel their honeymoon and return to England with him. Soon thereafter, Niels Bohr completed one of the most brilliant papers on atomic structure ever written. In doing so, he managed to rescue Rutherford's nuclear model of the atom.

Scientific theories are carefully constructed on a firm foundation of data gathered from a multitude of meticulously documented, rigorously controlled, and perpetually repeatable experiments. Bohr's theory was no exception. In the previous section, we discussed the conduction of charges through gases in glass discharge tubes. Those experiments in the later years of the 1800s not only led to Thomson's discovery of the electron, but also provided Bohr with valuable data for his ideas about the nature of those electrons in atoms.

Quantum Theory Rescues the Nuclear Model

Bohr knew that when high voltage was applied across the electrodes of a sealed glass tube containing a gas such as hydrogen, the gas was heated and emitted light. As part of his investigations, Bohr looked at this light through a spectroscope. A spectroscope is a device similar to a prism, which separates the light into its component wavelengths. When Bohr viewed the light from the heated hydrogen through the spectroscope, he saw only a series of colored lines against a black background, rather than a continuous rainbow of color. For hydrogen, the same pattern of four colored lines was always seen: a red, blue-green, blue, and violet line (Figure 4.3.2). For each gaseous element used, a bright-line pattern unique to that element called a **bright-line spectrum** always appeared (much like a bar code on a modern grocery item).

The phenomenon had mystified scientists. None could explain why only certain colors of light, each corresponding to specific wavelength, frequency, and energy, were emitted by the heated gases — until Bohr. Bohr realized that by applying quantum principles to the behavior of hydrogen's lone electron, he could not only account for the existence of the bright-line spectrum, but also save Rutherford's nuclear model of the atom.

Figure 4.3.2 *Hydrogen's bright-line spectrum*

Bohr's Postulates

Bohr's postulates for hydrogen are summarized below:

1. The hydrogen atom had only certain **allowed energy levels** or **stationary states.** Each of these states corresponded to a circular electron orbit of a fixed size. The larger the allowed orbit, the greater the energy associated with it. No other orbits existed in the atom. Each allowed energy state was given an integer number "*n*" that Bohr called a **quantum number** with allowed values that ranged from 1 to ∞ (i.e., *n* could equal 1, 2, 3...etc). The lowest energy (smallest) orbit corresponded to the lowest allowed energy state called the **ground state** and was designated as $n = 1$. The larger orbits of greater energy were designated as $n = 2$, $n = 3$, $n = 4$, etc. and were said to be **excited states.**

2. As long as an electron moved in an allowed orbit or stationary state, the electron (and therefore the atom) did not radiate or absorb energy.

3. The electron could only move from one allowed orbit to another if it absorbed or emitted an amount of energy exactly equal to the energy difference between the two orbits, ΔE. This meant that the hydrogen atom could only change from one stationary energy state to another.

Bohr's Postulates — Another Look

Postulate 1 employed Planck's theory by quantizing the energies allowed for the hydrogen atom (and thus the electron). Because only certain-sized orbits were allowed, the atom was restricted to existing in only certain energy states and not others. Think of the electron as a ball on a staircase. Just as the ball can only rest on any particular stair and so have only certain amounts of potential energy and not others, so too is the electron restricted to only specific energies.

Postulate 2 meant that the nuclear model of the atom proposed by Rutherford would not collapse as predicted. Although the postulate violated the laws of classical physics, Bohr insisted that it must be true, even though he didn't know why.

Postulates 1 and 3 explained the origin and nature of hydrogen's bright-line spectrum. An atomic spectrum could not be continuous (i.e., a complete rainbow of colors) because an atom's energy states could only be certain values and not others. When a sample of hydrogen gas is heated in a discharge tube, the electrons in the hydrogen atoms absorb sufficient amounts of energy to "jump" to larger orbits. (In any one hydrogen atom, only one electron is involved, but in a sample of the gas, the electrons of many hydrogen atoms are undergoing many transitions). Once in a higher energy orbit, any electron could then return to a lower energy orbit by emitting a specific amount of energy corresponding exactly to the difference between the higher and lower energy orbits (Figure 4.3.3). If the frequency of that emitted energy corresponds to any part of the visible spectrum, then a bright line of that specific color would be seen. Four of hydrogen's electron transitions emitted energy in the visible spectrum.

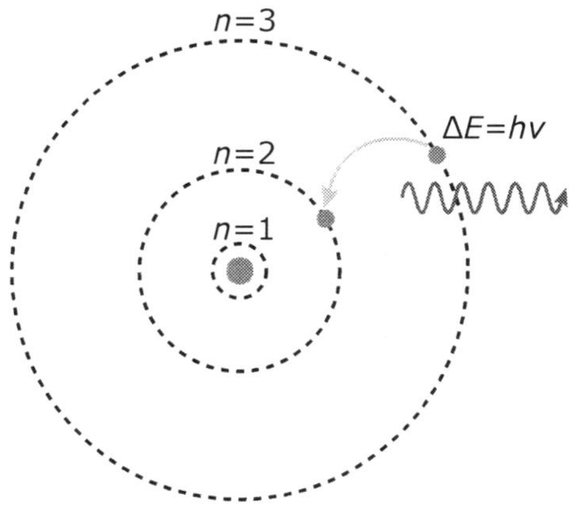

Figure 4.3.3 *When the electron moves to an inner energy level, it emits energy.*

If an excited electron emits energy and drops to $n = 2$ from a higher energy orbit, the wavelength of the emitted energy corresponds to a particular color of visible light. If an electron drops from $n = 3$ to $n = 2$, the energy difference between the two orbits (and therefore the energy emitted) corresponds to that of red light. Hence the red line appears in the emission spectrum. The blue-green line results from an electron transition from $n = 4$ to $n = 2$, the blue line from an electron transition from $n = 5$ to $n = 2$, and the violet line from an electron transition from $n = 6$ to $n = 2$. This series of four bright lines in the visible spectrum is called the Balmer series, named after the Swiss schoolteacher who first derived a mathematical relationship between the lines in hydrogen's visible emission spectrum (Figure 4.3.4).

Bohr's model of the hydrogen atom was successful in explaining the mystery of bright line spectra. His calculations and predictions worked for hydrogen and he even calculated the radius of the orbit for hydrogen's electron in its ground state. In 1922, Niels Bohr was awarded the Nobel Prize in physics.

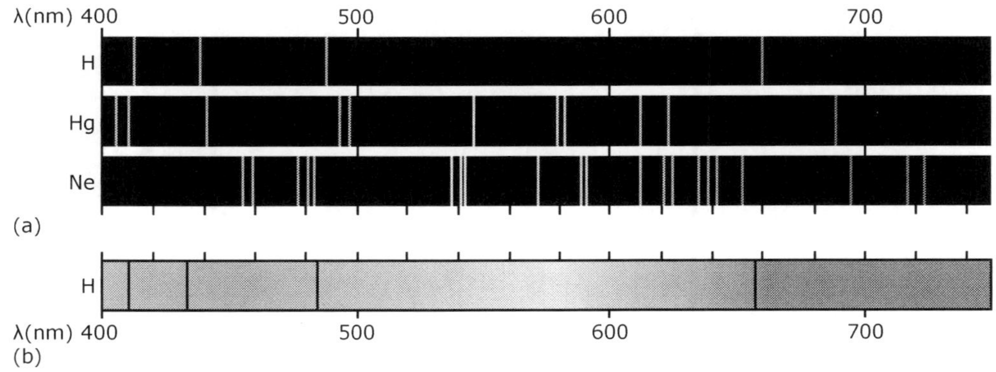

Figure 4.3.4 *(a) The emission spectra of hydrogen, mercury, and neon; (b) The absorption spectrum of hydrogen*

The Emission Spectrum of Hydrogen — Two Views

The diagram on the left in Figure 4.3.5 shows the circular orbits Bohr envisioned for the hydrogen electron and the transitions associated with the Lyman, Balmer, and Paschen emission spectra. The diagram on the right shows that the energy *differences* between various stationary states (n) decrease as the energies of those states increase. The arrows pointing down represent electrons falling to lower energy states and thus emitting energy. Electrons absorbing energy could be indicated by arrows pointing up and would represent absorption spectra.

Any electron transitions from an excited state down to $n = 1$ result in the emission of energy in the ultraviolet region of the electromagnetic spectrum (the Lyman series). Any transitions from excited states down to the third and fourth orbits result in energies in the infrared region being emitted (the Paschen and Brackett series respectively).

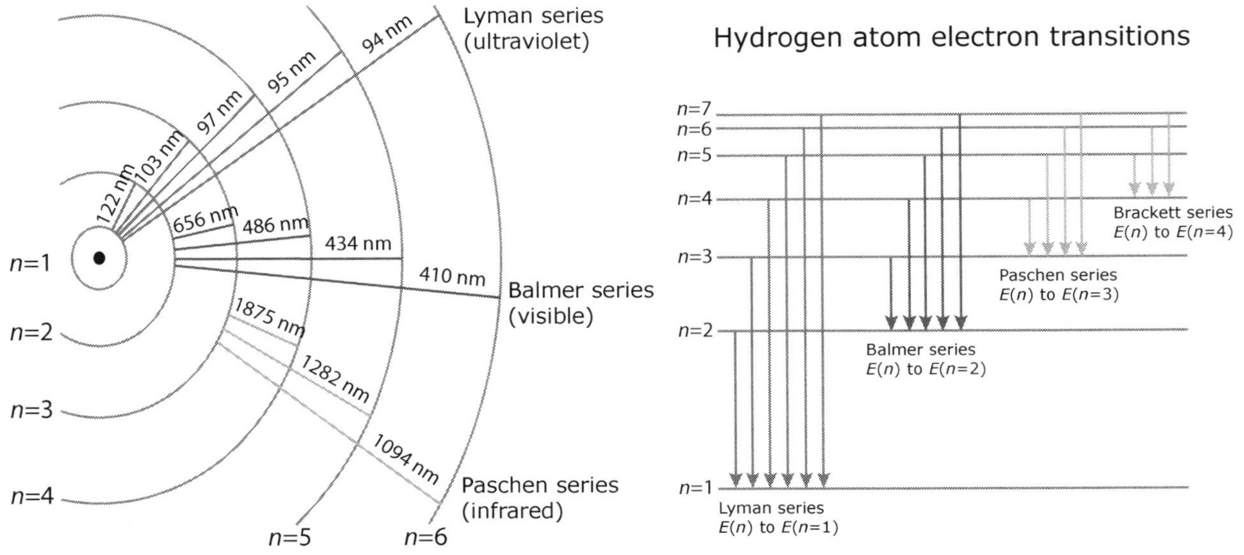

Figure 4.3.5 *The Lyman, Balmer, and Paschen emission series for hydrogen*

Quick Check

1. Describe the appearance of hydrogen's "bright-line" spectrum.

   ____

2. Briefly indicate how electrons generate each visible line in hydrogen's emission spectrum.

   ____

   ____

3. Which electron transitions in the emission spectrum generate lines in the UV region of the electromagnetic spectrum?

   ____

4.3 Review Questions

1. Explain the serious problem initially associated with Rutherford's atomic model.

2. State Planck's quantum theory in your own words.

3. Why was this theory not accepted by most physicists at first?

4. What finally convinced the scientific community that Planck's theory was credible?

5. Explain how the work of Planck and Einstein contributed to Bohr's theory about electron behavior.

6. State how Bohr's theory "saved" Rutherford's nuclear atomic model.

7. Briefly explain why hydrogen's visible emission spectrum does not resemble a continuous spectrum or rainbow

4.4 Beyond Bohr — The Quantum Mechanical Model of the Atom

Warm Up

1. How did Max Planck and Albert Einstein contribute to the development of Niels Bohr's atomic theory?

2. State the main points of Bohr's atomic theory in your own words.

Particles Behaving Like Waves

Niels Bohr's theory firmly established the concept of fixed atomic energy levels. Although there were a few fine details of hydrogen's line spectrum that the theory couldn't account for, his model of the hydrogen atom appeared very promising. Unfortunately, when Bohr's theory was applied to the line spectra of atoms having more than one electron, it didn't work at all. All attempts to modify the theory to make it work were unsuccessful. It soon became clear that the atomic puzzle hadn't yet been solved.

Bohr assumed that an atom had only certain allowable energy levels in order to account for hydrogen's observed line spectrum. However, that assumption was not rooted in any physical theory. In other words, Bohr knew the energy levels had to be there, but not *why* they had to be there. It appeared that a new theory containing some bold ideas about the atom might be needed.

That new theory was eventually called quantum mechanics, and it had its beginnings in 1923 with the ideas of a young French aristocrat. Louis de Broglie had originally earned a degree in history and was trying to decide on a subject for his doctoral thesis in physics. He had just learned that a professor in Missouri named Arthur Compton had proven the existence of the light quanta (later called photons) proposed by Albert Einstein. A fascinating idea occurred to de Broglie: If waves behaved like particles, could it also be possible for particles to have wave properties? By proposing that matter was wavelike, de Broglie was also suggesting a reason, or theoretical foundation, for an electron's fixed energy levels. To understand this reason, we must briefly discuss some aspects of wave behavior.

Applying Quantum Mechanics to Electrons in Atoms

In this section, we will apply the quantum mechanical model of the atom to describing electrons in the atoms of the elements. We will begin with hydrogen and then use that information to expand our discussion to include multi-electron atoms.

A guitar string helped to explain the requirement of standing waves for the allowed energy states of electrons in atoms. If we solve Schrödinger's wave equation for the allowed energy states for hydrogen, we see that each energy state results in different numbers and types of orbitals. The equation shows us that the higher the energy, the greater the number and types of orbitals present.

Quantum Numbers

In an atom, these three-dimensional electron waves or orbitals are more complicated than a standing wave on a guitar string. To describe them, quantum mechanics employs the use of special numbers called **quantum numbers** Each quantum number specifies something different about the orbitals and electrons. We will discuss these numbers as we investigate the orbitals associated with each of allowed energy states for hydrogen.

The Principal Quantum Number (*n*)

The first quantum number is called the **principal quantum number** (*n*). It indicates the relative size of the atomic orbital.

We have already been introduced to this number because it also represents the allowed energy states for the electron. We know that the value of *n* can be a positive integer (1, 2, 3, and so on).

When hydrogen's electron is in the lowest allowed energy state or ground state, then $n = 1$. Schrödinger's equation shows us where an electron possessing that amount of energy will most likely be found. When we represent this pictorially, we see an electron "probability density diagram" resembling a spherical cloud. The cloud is what you might see if you could take many snapshots of the hydrogen electron around the nucleus and then superimpose all of them onto one picture. At the centre of this cloud is the hydrogen nucleus. The cloud's density is not uniform throughout, but is greater near the nucleus and decreases as we move away. This tells us that the probability of locating the electron is higher closer to the nucleus and lower further away from the nucleus.

As we move out from the nucleus, we find that hydrogen's electron in its ground state is likely to spend most of its time a slight distance from the nucleus, rather than at the nucleus itself. This is called the "radial probability." It's interesting to note that the electron's distance from the nucleus to the region of highest probability corresponds exactly to the orbit for this electron that Bohr calculated. Remember, however, that Bohr assumed the electron followed a circular path and would always be found at that distance from the nucleus. Quantum mechanics describes this as the most probable distance from the nucleus for the electron.

When we enclose the cloud in a volume representing about a 90% probability of finding the electron, we call this the 1s orbital. The number "1" represents the principal quantum number, telling us the size of the orbital, and the letter "s" refers to the type or "shape" of the orbital. Figure 4.4.1(a) shows an artistic representation of what a spherical 1s orbital might look like if viewed from the outside. Figure 4.4.1(b) is a cross-sectional view showing radial probability (indicated by greater dot density a slight distance from nucleus).

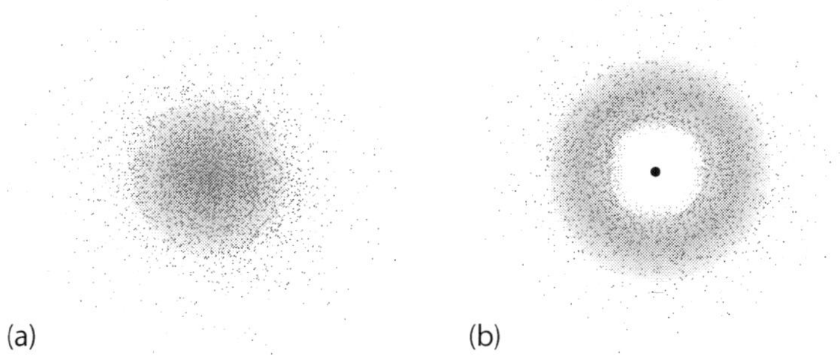

Figure 4.4.1 *(a) A view of a spherical 1s orbital from the outside; (b) A cross-sectional view of a spherical 1s orbital*

The Second Quantum Number (ℓ)

The second quantum number is called the **angular momentum quantum number** (ℓ). It is related to the shape of an atomic orbital.

The different values of ℓ at each energy level represent the number of orbital shapes or sublevels that exist in that energy level. That number equals the energy level itself. So for $n = 1$, there is only one orbital type or shape, namely the s orbital.

Each new energy level has one new orbital shape in addition to those existing in the previous level. So if hydrogen's electron is "excited" and absorbs enough energy to reach the second allowed energy state, then $n = 2$ and two orbital shapes or sublevels exist. There is an s orbital with a shape identical to the 1s, except larger, called the 2s orbital. This means that the electron with this greater amount of energy will spend more of its time farther from the nucleus. There is also a new shape: a p orbital. As $n = 2$, we call it a 2p orbital and it resembles a dumbbell or long balloon pinched in the middle (where the nucleus is located).

The Third Quantum Number (m_ℓ)

The third quantum number, called the **magnetic quantum number** (m_ℓ) tells us the orientation in space of a given atomic orbital.

The number of possible different orientations in space for any orbital shape also represents the number of individual orbitals of that particular shape or sublevel.

Only a single s orbital exists in any given energy level because a spherical cloud can only have one orientation in 3D space. However, this new p sublevel includes three separate orbitals, each with a different spatial orientation. If we consider a 3D set of Cartesian coordinates, one is oriented along an imaginary *x*-axis (with the nucleus at the origin) called a $2p_x$ orbital. The other two are oriented along the *y*- and *z*-axes and are called the $2p_y$ and $2p_z$ orbitals respectively. Each of these 2p orbitals is identical in energy to the others. For hydrogen, they are also identical in energy to the 2s orbital. Chemists call orbitals of equal energy "degenerate" orbitals.

In Figure 4.4.2, note that the lobes of each p orbital in the first three diagrams disappear at the origin where the nucleus is located. This means that the amplitude of the electron wave at the nucleus is zero. A wave amplitude of zero is called a node, and it tells us that there is a zero probability of locating the electron here. In the far left diagram in Figure 4.4.2, all three 2p orbitals are shown together. Once again, the nucleus is at the centre or origin.

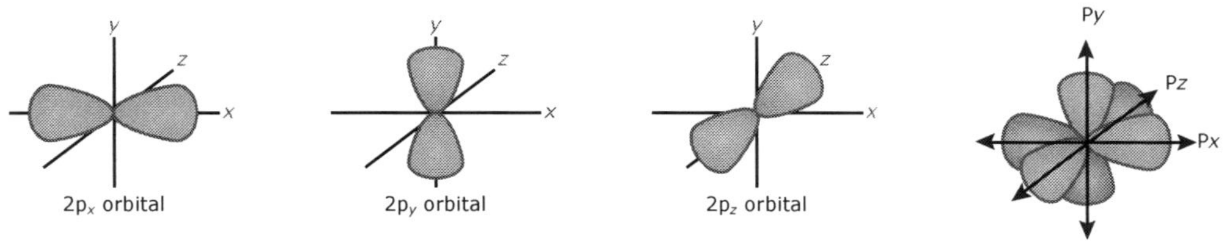

Figure 4.4.2 *The p orbitals are each shown individually in the first three diagrams. The last diagram shows them all together.*

We noted earlier that the number of different sublevels in any energy level equals the value of *n*. We also see here that a total of four orbitals exists in the second energy level. So the value n^2 tells us the number of orbitals existing in the nth energy level. In this case, there are $2^2 = 4$ orbitals: one 2s and three 2p orbitals.

The three quantum numbers, taken together, will always specify a particular atomic orbital because they tell us all we need to know about that orbital: its size, shape, and orientation in space.

If hydrogen's electron absorbs enough energy to reach the third allowed energy state, then *n*

= 3 and three different orbital shapes or sublevels exist. As expected, we see one spherical 3s orbital and three dumbbell-shaped 3p orbitals. But we also discover a third sublevel whose orbitals have a more complicated shape. This is called the 3d sublevel and it contains five different orbitals, each with a different spatial orientation. Orbitals in a given sublevel are equal in energy to each other, and in hydrogen's case, are also equal in energy to all of the other orbitals in the energy level. This means that in a given energy level, hydrogen's electron has an equal likelihood of occupying any of them.

Although the d orbitals are shown in Figure 4.4.3, you may not be required to remember either their shapes or their names. You should, however, know that there are five of them.

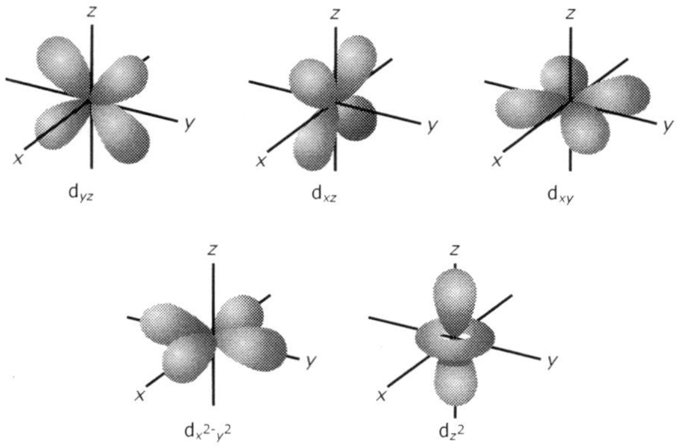

Figure 4.4.3 *The d orbitals*

Notice that as $n = 3$, there are three sublevels: 3s, 3p, and 3d. Also, there are a total of nine orbitals: one 3s orbital, three 3p orbitals, and five 3d orbitals corresponding to 3^2.

Finally, let's elevate hydrogen's electron to the fourth energy level, where $n = 4$. A higher energy level means that the electron will spend more of its time farther from the nucleus than when it possesses energy equal to $n = 1$, 2, or 3. Therefore, the orbitals or "charge clouds" are larger.

In the fourth energy level, we see the expected 4s, three 4p, and five 4d orbitals. As well, because $n = 4$, we also see a fourth shape called the 4f sublevel. Each higher energy level introduces another sublevel with a greater number (by two) of more complicated orbitals than the previous ones, and so there are seven 4f orbitals, each with a more complicated shape than the d orbitals. You should remember the number of f orbitals as well. The fourth energy level results in $4^2 = 16$ orbitals: one 4s, three 4p, five 4d, and seven 4f orbitals, all of which are equal in energy in the case of hydrogen.

Let's summarize what we have learned about energy levels and orbitals using a table and a diagram. Table 4.4.1 shows the sublevels and orbitals for the first four energy levels. Figure 4.4.4 is the energy diagram for hydrogen showing the sublevels and orbitals present from $n = 1$ through $n = 4$. Each circle represents an orbital. Note that all the sublevels are of equal energy in each allowed energy state.

Table 4.4.1 *Sublevels and orbitals for the first four energy levels*

Principal Quantum Number or Energy Level (n)	Number of Orbital Shapes or Sublevels per Energy Level (n)	Total Number of Orbitals per Energy Level (n^2)
1	**1** – 1s sublevel	**1** – the 1s orbital
2	**2** – 2s sublevel 2p sublevel	**4** – one 2s orbital three 2p orbitals
3	**3** – 3s sublevel 3p sublevel 3d sublevel	**9** – one 3s orbital three 3p orbitals five 3d orbitals

4	**4** – 4s sublevel 4p sublevel 4d sublevel 4f sublevel	**16** – one 4s orbital three 4p orbitals five 4d orbitals seven 4f orbitals

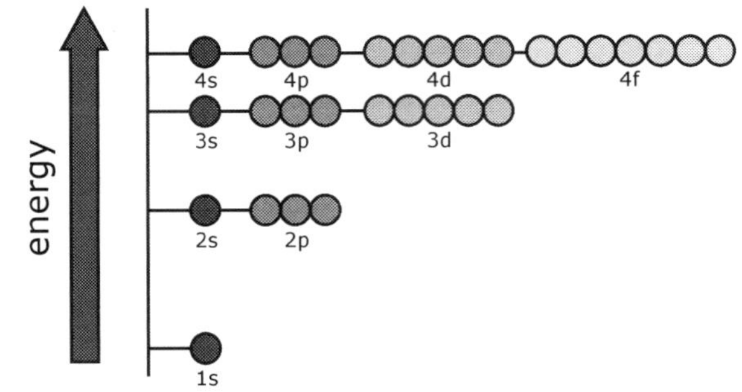

Figure 4.4.4 *Energy diagram for hydrogen. Each circle represents an orbital*

The Orbitals of Multi-Electron Atoms

Hydrogen is the simplest atom with one proton in the nucleus surrounded by one electron in a 1s orbital in its ground state. There are no electron-electron interactions, and in any excited state, all of the atomic orbitals available to that single electron are of equal energy.

We might expect a different situation, however, for multi-electron atoms. Electrons are charged particle-waves. It seems reasonable to conclude that they will affect each other when two or more of them occupy the same region of space around an atom's nucleus — and they do.

To describe those electrons in multi-electron atoms, we must introduce several additional considerations.

Experiments have shown that the single electron in hydrogen generates a tiny magnetic field as if the electron were a spinning charge. Also, in any sample of hydrogen, analyzing the many atoms present shows two opposing magnetic fields. This tells us that in half of the atoms, the electrons seem to spin in one direction and, in the remainder of the atoms, in the other direction. An electron's spin is as fundamental a part of its nature as its charge.

The fourth quantum number is called the **spin quantum number** (m_s). It tells us the two possible electron spins, either +½ or –½.

Quick Check

1. State what each of the three quantum numbers described above tells us about atomic orbitals.

____

____

2. (a) What is the difference between a 1s and a 2s orbital?

____

(b) What is the difference between a $2p_x$ orbital and a $2p_y$ orbital?

____

3. How many different orbitals are available to an excited hydrogen electron in the fourth energy level?

____

The Pauli Exclusion Principle

We already know that we can identify any orbital in an atom by the use of the first three quantum numbers, but we must use all four quantum numbers mentioned to specify any electron in an atom.

This is based on the fact that any atomic orbital can hold a maximum of two electrons. When two electrons are in the same orbital, their spins must be opposite. Originally proposed in 1925 by the Austrian physicist Wolfgang Pauli, this can be viewed as the first rule governing electrons in multi-electron atoms.

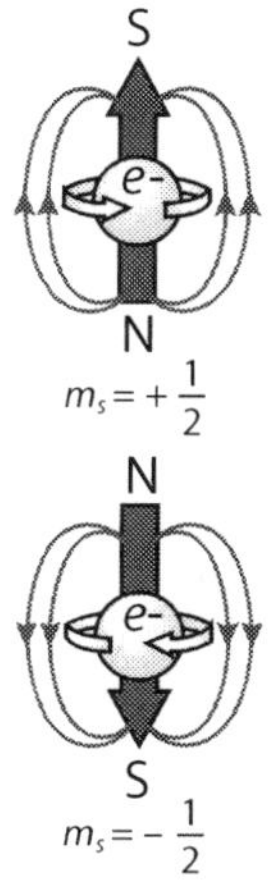

Figure 4.4.5 *The spin quantum number (m_s) identifies which possible spin an electron has.*

1. The **Pauli exclusion principle**: No two electrons in the same atom can be described by the same set of four quantum numbers.

If two electrons are in the same atomic orbital, they therefore have the same first three quantum numbers. Because they then must have opposite spins, their fourth quantum numbers are different.

We noted earlier that the total number of orbitals existing in any level *n* equals n^2.

If two electrons can occupy each orbital, the maximum number of electrons that can exist in any energy level *n* is given by $2n^2$.

A further consideration for multi-electron atoms is the effect of electron-electron repulsions on the relative energies of the sublevels in a given energy level. For hydrogen, where no repulsive forces exist, all of the sublevels in any energy level have identical energies. This is not the case for atoms of other elements. Although the same types of orbitals exist in multi-electron atoms, their relative energies are different. Repulsive forces cause a sublevel with a greater number of orbitals to have a greater energy. Therefore the order of sublevel energies is:

s < p < d < f.

Consider Figure 4.4.6. Compare this energy diagram for a multi-electron atom with Figure 4.4.4 for hydrogen. Note that in several cases energies get closer together as *n* increases. In these cases, repulsive forces are such that some sublevels containing smaller orbitals actually have higher energies than some larger orbitals. For example, observe the relative energy of the 3d compared to the 4s sublevel.

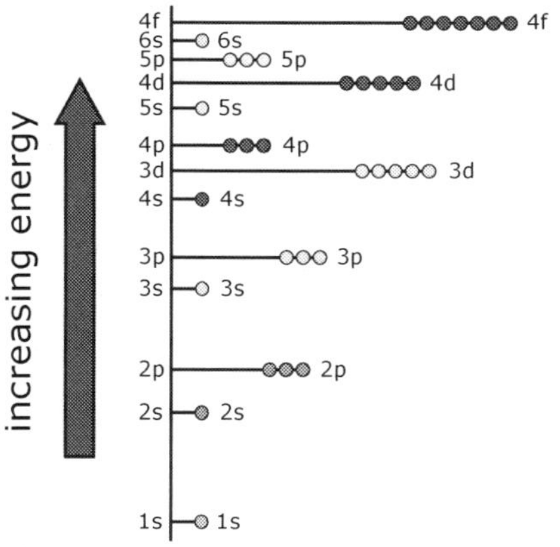

Figure 4.4.6 *Energy diagram for multi-electron atoms*

Electron Configurations and Orbital Diagrams

We are now in a position to organize electrons into orbitals for the atoms of the elements. Understanding this organization will prove to be a powerful tool as we discuss the periodic table and bonding in the next chapter. In beginnning this process, we introduce the second rule associated with describing electrons in multi-electron atoms.

2. The **Aufbau principle**: When filling orbitals, the lowest energy orbitals available are always filled first. ("Aufbau" means a building or a construction in German.)

The order for filling orbitals is given above in Figure 4.4.6, showing sublevel energies. We start at the lowest energy orbitals and move up.

Let's begin with hydrogen. In its lowest energy or ground state, hydrogen's electron exists in the 1s orbital. We can represent this in two ways:

1. We can use a shorthand notation called an **electron configuration,** which is written in the format $n\ell^{\#}$ showing the energy level, sublevel, and number of electrons respectively. Hydrogen's electron configuration is therefore written as: $1s^1$. Read as "one s one," this tells us that hydrogen's one electron resides in the 1s orbital in its ground state.
2. We can construct an **orbital diagram**, which depicts electrons and their spin using arrows facing up and down. The arrows are placed inside boxes or over lines representing individual orbitals in sublevels. Hydrogen's orbital diagram is shown as:

↑

Quick Check

1. What does the fourth quantum number tell us about electrons?

 ____

2. Why can't two electrons in the same atom have the same four quantum numbers?

 ____

3. What is the maximum number of electrons that can exist in the energy levels $n = 1$ through $n = 4$?

 ____

1s

The configuration for the next element, helium, is $1s^2$. This is read "one s two" rather than "one s squared." Following the Pauli exclusion principle, the orbital diagram shows the two electrons with opposite spins in the now full 1s orbital:

↑↓

1s

To indicate increasing sublevel energy, the boxes can be written vertically or also left to right to save space on a page. Let's continue below by moving past helium to the elements in period 2 of the periodic table using horizontally written orbital diagrams. Note that period 2 corresponds to the second energy level, $n = 2$. Following the Aufbau principle:

Electron Configuration	**Orbital Diagram** INCREASING ENERGY		
	1s	**2s**	**2p**

lithium	$1s^2 2s^1$	↑↓	↑			
beryllium	$1s^2 2s^2$	↑↓	↑↓			

For the 2p sublevel:

boron	$1s^2 2s^2 2p^1$	↑↓	↑↓	↑		

Note that the sum of the superscript numbers equals the total number of electrons present. We must now use the third rule governing orbitals in multi-electron atoms:

3. **Hund's rule:** When orbitals of equal energy are being filled, the most stable configuration is the one with the maximum number of unpaired electrons with the same spin.

So carbon and nitrogen's orbital diagrams are:

carbon	$1s^2 2s^2 2p^2$	↑↓	↑↓	↑	↑	
nitrogen	$1s^2 2s^2 2p^3$	↑↓	↑↓	↑	↑	↑

After nitrogen, we must again begin to pair electrons:

oxygen	$1s^2 2s^2 2p^4$	↑↓	↑↓	↑↓	↑	↑
fluorine	$1s^2 2s^2 2p^5$	↑↓	↑↓	↑↓	↑↓	↑
neon	$1s^2 2s^2 2p^6$	↑↓	↑↓	↑↓	↑↓	↑↓

After a noble gas, a new period begins in the periodic table and so too, a new energy level. As we begin period 3, let's represent the elements up to scandium in Table 4.4.2 using electron configurations only. We can condense electron configurations using **core notation**, in which the configuration of the previous noble gas is represented by that noble gas symbol in square brackets as shown in the table. Outer electrons are indicated in **bold** type.

Table 4.4.2 *Electron Configurations of Period 3 Elements up to Scandium*

Element	Full Electron Configuration	Core Notation
sodium	1s^2 2s^2 2p^6 **3s^1**	[Ne] **3s^1**
magnesium	1s^2 2s^2 2p^6 **3s^2**	[Ne] **3s^2**
aluminum	1s^2 2s^2 2p^6 **3s^2 3p^1**	[Ne] **3s^2 3p^1**
silicon	1s^2 2s^2 2p^6 **3s^2 3p^2**	[Ne] **3s^2 3p^2**
phosphorus	1s^2 2s^2 2p^6 **3s^2 3p^3**	[Ne] **3s^2 3p^3**
sulfur	1s^2 2s^2 2p^6 **3s^2 3p^4**	[Ne] **3s^2 3p^4**
chlorine	1s^2 2s^2 2p^6 **3s^2 3p^5**	[Ne] **3s^2 3p^5**
argon	1s^2 2s^2 2p^6 **3s^2 3p^6**	[Ne] **3s^2 3p^6**
potassium	1s^2 2s^2 2p^6 3s^2 3p^6 **4s^1**	[Ar] **4s^1**
calcium	1s^2 2s^2 2p^6 3s^2 3p^6 **4s^2**	[Ar] **4s^2**
scandium	1s^2 2s^2 2p^6 3s^2 3p^6 **4s^2 3d^1**	[Ar] **4s^2 3d^1**

Notice in the table that, as we move from argon to potassium, the 4s sublevel starts to fill before the 3d sublevel. After the 4s sublevel, the 3d sublevel starts to fill, reaching the first transition metal, scandium. Although the 3d sublevel fills after the 4s sublevel, the 3d sublevel still contains electrons that spend most of their time nearer the nucleus and so is inside the 4s sublevel. Some periodic tables indicate the electron configurations in order of sublevel size and so will show scandium's configuration as [Ar] 3d^1 4s^2.

Figure 4.4.7 is a simple way of remembering the order for filling sublevels. We begin at the top with the 1s and fill that sublevel. After reaching the end of each arrow, we then start at the top of the next arrow below it. When using this diagram, you must remember how many electrons each sublevel can hold.

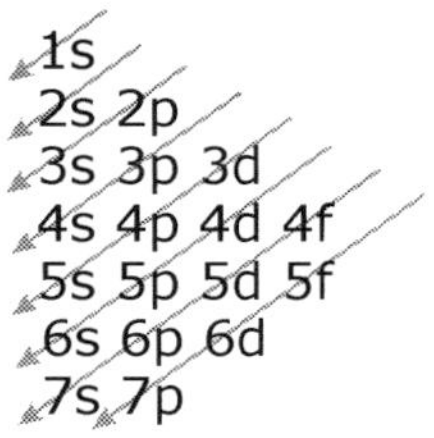

Sample Problem — Drawing an Orbital Diagram

Draw the orbital diagram and write the full electron configuration and the core notation for an atom of cobalt in its ground state.

What to Think about

1. Cobalt's atomic number is 27 and so the orbital diagram must account for 27 electrons. Cobalt is a transition metal in period 4 in the periodic table. We should expect the highest energy electrons to be in the 3d subshell.
2. Remember how many electrons are placed in each subshell as you fill the orbitals and employ Hund's rule as necessary.
3. Sketch the diagonal diagram to help you remember the order that subshells fill.
4. Represent each electron in an orbital using an arrow as in the notation described above.

How to Do It

Orbital diagram for cobalt:

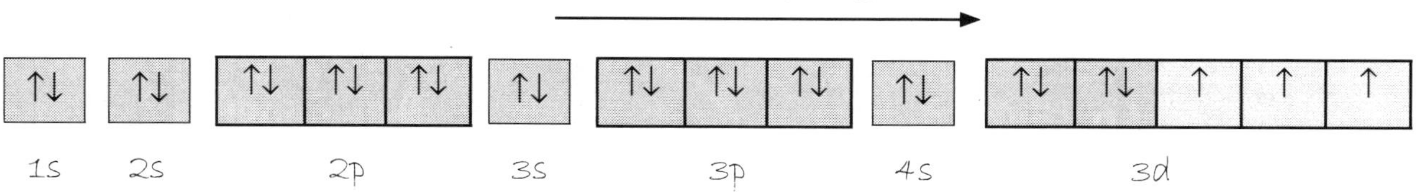

Electron configuration: $1s^2 2s^2 2p^6 3s^2 3p^6 4s^2 3d^7$

Core notation: $[Ar]\ 4s^2 3d^7$ or $[Ar]\ 3d^7 4s^2$

Practice Problem — Drawing an Orbital Diagram

1. Write the full electron configuration and draw the orbital diagram for an atom of titanium in its ground state.

Figure 4.4.7 *This diagram indicates the order for filling sublevels.*

Ions and Other Charged Topics

Recall that a cation has fewer electrons than the original neutral atom and an anion has more. This means that the electron configurations for ions will be different than those for neutral atoms.

The process is easily shown using examples. To write the electron configuration for the S^{2-} anion, we simply need to add two more electrons to the last unfilled sublevel. Thus the configuration: $1s^2\,2s^2\,2p^6\,3s^2\,3p^{\mathbf{4}}$ for the S atom becomes: $1s^2\,2s^2\,2p^6\,3s^2\,3p^{\mathbf{6}}$ for the S^{2-} anion. Notice that the sulphide anion now has the same electron configuration as the nearest noble gas argon. The sulphide ion is therefore considered to be **isoelectronic** with argon because the two species have the same number and configuration of electrons.

To write cation configurations, electrons are always removed *from the outermost orbitals with the highest energy first*. Therefore, it is sometimes worthwhile to first write the neutral atom's configuration in core notation with the final orbitals listed from smallest to largest, rather than in the order the orbitals fill. Then remove the appropriate electrons from the outer orbitals first.

For example, if asked to write the configuration for the Sn^{4+} ion, first write the configuration for a neutral Sn atom as [Kr] $4d^{10}$ $\mathbf{5s^2}$ $\mathbf{5p^2}$ rather than writing [Kr] $\mathbf{5s^2}$ $4d^{10}$ $\mathbf{5p^2}$.

Now remove the four *outermost* electrons to give the configuration for Sn^{4+}: [Kr] $4d^{10}$. This avoids the error of removing two 4d electrons to give [Kr] $\mathbf{5s^2}$ $4d^8$. Note that an Sn^{2+} ion would form by losing the two 5p electrons, as they are at higher energy than the 5s.

As a final note, there are several exceptions to the orbital filling order discussed here. The elements Cr, Cu, Mo, Ag, and Au are examples of such exceptions. Your teacher may choose to discuss these and others and the possible reasons.

We shouldn't be surprised that irregularities exist. We have already seen ample evidence that the quantum world is full of surprises!

4.4 Activity: A Post-it® Periodic Table

Question

Can we organize a series of Post-it® notes on a standard periodic table to represent the order that orbitals are filled according the Aufbau principle?

Materials

- a small pad of each of four different colors of Post-it® or other sticky notes
- transparent tape

Procedure

Refer to the diagonal diagram in Figure 5.4.7 showing the order for filling sublevels.

1. Obtain a pad of small Post-it® or other sticky notes. Choose a separate color for each of the four shapes, s, p, d, and f, and write the symbol for each of the 19 sublevels (1s, 2s, 2p, etc....) on a separate note.

2. Place the notes from left to right on a flat surface in the correct order that each sublevel fills.

3. Obtain a copy of the periodic table from your teacher. Number each horizontal period of the table, beginning with 1 for the top period containing H and He, down to 7 for Fr.

4. Now "read" the periods left-to-right like words on a page, moving down at the end of each. Trim the bottom portion of each Post-it® note to fit, and stick the appropriate sublevel symbol onto each section of each period as you read it.

Results and Discussion

1. Once you're finished, confirm the correct location of each Post-it® note sublevel symbol with your teacher. Then place transparent tape over each to permanently attach it to the periodic table. Save this completed table for the discussion coming up in the next chapter.

THE SUBATOMIC LEVELS

Richard Feynman, a famous American physicist, who won the Nobel Prize for Physics in 1965, worked with Einstein during his career, was a professor of theoretical physics at Caltech and authored several books once said:

> If the human race was about to be wiped out and all scientific knowledge was about to be destroyed and we could pass on one piece of knowledge, the statement that contains the most knowledge in the fewest words is… I believe…all things are made of atoms – little particles that move around in perpetual motion, attracting each other when they are a little distance apart, but repelling upon being squeezed into one another

Quantum mechanics is the study of laws and mathematical equations that describe the motion of subatomic particles.

Who were some of the most influential scientists in the development of the early theory of the atom?

Which subatomic particle plays the most important role in determining the chemistry of an element? Why?

You have already learned to draw and explain the Bohr-Rutherford model of the atom. This model gives a good introductory understanding of how the ___electrons___ are arranged in the atom.

You learned that elements in each period in the periodic table have a certain number of electronic shells on a Bohr-Rutherford diagram e.g. all of the Bohr –Rutherford diagrams for the elements in period 1 have ___1___ electronic shell, all of the elements in period 3 have ___3___ electron shells.

Bohr made some discoveries about the energy that each electron on an atom possesses and from his conclusions he was able to defend a new model of the atom that divided each of these electronic shells into ___sublevels___ and each sublevel into ___orbitals___.

You should not forget all of the information you learned previously because Bohr still used some of the information that could be gathered from the Bohr-Rutherford diagrams. He called each of the electronic shells ___energy levels___ and to each of the energy levels, he assigned a number which he called THE PRINCIPLE QUANTUM NUMBER (symbol "n").

So… all of the electrons that are found on the first electronic shell have a principle quantum number n = 1
All of the electrons in the fourth electronic shell have a principle quantum number n = ___4___

How many energy levels will an atom in the 3rd period have?

3

What would the principal quantum numbers of these energy levels be?
1, 2, 3

In the quantum mechanical model of the atom each energy level (identified by a principle quantum number "n") is divided into sublevels.
There are 4 possible sublevels s, p, d, f

Within any given energy level "n", the sublevels have slightly different energies. The "s" sublevel always has the lowest energy followed by p, then d, and then f.

We also already learned that sublevels are divided into orbitals.

The "s" sublevel has 1 orbital

The "p" sublevel has 3 orbitals

The "d" sublevel has 5 orbitals

The "f" sublevel has 7 orbitals

Each orbital can hold a maximum of 2 electrons.

So in summary draw a flow chart:

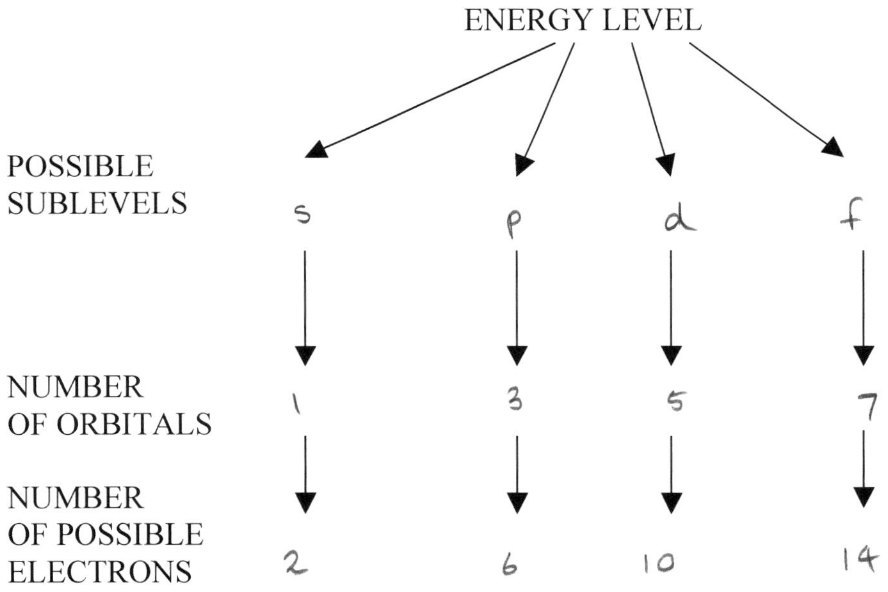

Rules for constructing a model of the atom

1. Electrons always occupy the lowest possible energy level

2. For any energy level "n", there are n^2 actual orbitals and $2n^2$ electrons
Let's see whether this fits in with what we already know:

- The electrons the first energy level have n = 1
- We know that 2 electrons can be placed on the first electronic shell

- If n = 1, then n^2 = __1__ and $2n^2$ = __2__, which means there are __1__ orbitals and __2__ possible electrons in the first energy level

Try the example with the second and third energy level and see whether it agrees with what you learned in grades 9 and 10.

4, 8   9, 18   yes

If we examine the number of orbitals in each energy level we will be able to figure out which sublevels exist at each energy level.

Examples:

n = 1, n^2 = __1__, it would be logical to conclude that because we can only have 1 orbital, the only possible sublevel in the first energy level is the s sublevel

n = 2, n^2 = __4__, there are __4__ orbitals in the second energy level. Which sublevels are part of the second energy level?

1s, 3p

n = 3, n^2 = __9__, there are ______ orbitals in the third energy level. Which sublevels are part of the third energy level?

1s, 3p, 5d

Each energy level and energy sublevel corresponds to the specific quantity of energy that the electrons found in those orbitals have. The energy that an electron has corresponds to the distance that the electron is from the nucleus.

The order in which electrons fill the sublevels depends on the energy of the sublevel. Remember rule # 1 for filling order ⇒ electrons always occupy the __lowest__ possible energy level.

Let's look at some examples of how to write electron configurations of different elements (use your filling order charts to help you)

$_{10}$Ne

$_{18}$Ar

$_{36}$Kr

$_{3}$Li

$_{9}$F

$_{20}$Ca

$_{38}$Sr

Filling order chart

Energy level Diagrams

Oxygen

Copper

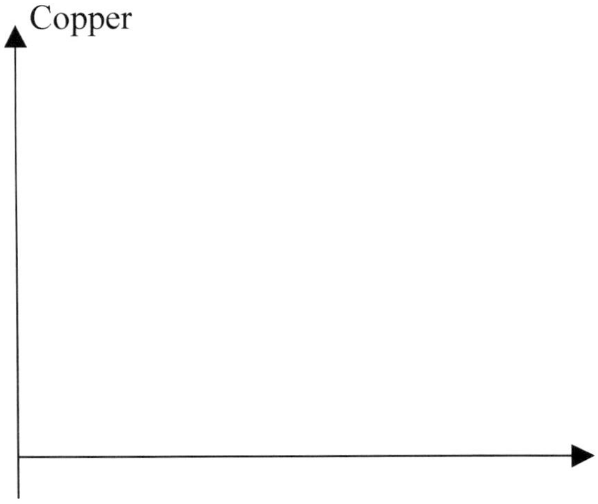

Strontium

Cerium

The Quantum Mechanical Model of the Atom

While Bohr's model described the behaviour of atoms containing a single electron, it failed to explain observations seen with many-electron atoms, or even molecules. Therefore, an alternate model needed to be devised that could explain the spectra of these atoms. In 1926, Erwin Schrödinger developed a theory called wave mechanics. A version of quantum mechanics, wave mechanics uses mathematical expressions, called wave functions, to describe the behaviour of an electron in an atom. Wave functions allow the calculation of probabilities, and in this case the probability of finding an electron in a particular three-dimensional space around the nucleus.

Wave functions are also called orbitals, which define the state of an electron and are identified by the quantum numbers below. No single electron may have the same set of four quantum numbers.

In the quantum mechanical model of the atom we know that electrons move around in______, which are part of_______, which in turn are part of _________. Bohr's model described the energy levels but did not subdivide the energy levels the way ____________ does. We know that orbitals, sublevels and energy levels are not physical entities but rather ______ that define where a particular electron is likely to be found. These spaces are defined by _________________developed by Erwin Schrödinger, who won a Nobel Prize for his work in 1933. Each electron has a wave equation, developed by Schrödinger, that defines the space in which the electron has the greatest ____________of being found. There are ______ quantum numbers that are used in the wave equation that defines the space in which an electron will be found. No two electrons in the same atom will have the same_______ __________ ___________.

What are the quantum numbers?
There is the principal quantum number, symbol "n", the secondary, angular momentum or azimuthal number, symbol " l " , the magnetic quantum number, symbol " m_l" and the spin quantum number, symbol " m_s"

The Principal Quantum Number, *symbol* ____________

- Is identical to the quantum number described by Bohr
- The principal quantum number is often described as the ***shell or energy level***
- *n* can have a value of any ____________ __________ beginning with the value of 1, where the n = 1 shell is closest to the ________________

- The maximum number of electrons that that may be present in a shell is $2n^2$
  - if n = 1 then the maximum number of electrons is ___________
  - if n = 2, then the maximum number of electrons is ___________
  - if n = 3, then the maximum number of electrons is ___________
  - if n = 4, then the maximum number of electrons is ___________

- A maximum of n^2 orbitals may be found in a single shell
  - if n = 1, then the maximum number of orbitals is ___________
  - if n = 2, then the maximum number of orbitals is ___________. Which orbitals are these? One s orbital and 3 p orbitals
  - if n = 3, then the maximum number of orbitals is ___________. Which orbitals are these? _________________________________

- if n = 4, then the maximum number of orbitals is ___________. Which orbitals are these? ____

The Azimuthal Quantum Number (Angular Momentum Quantum Number), ***symbol***

- Determines the **shape** of the orbital in the ______________

- For a give value of n, l has values ranging from 0 to (n - 1)
    - if n = 1, then l will have value(s) of _____, representing the shape of the orbital in the 1s subshell which is _________________
    - if n = 2, then l will have value(s) of _____ and __________
    - if n = 4, then l will have value(s) of

- Within a shell, all orbitals with a given l value are referred to as a ***subshell***
- Each orbital in a subshell may hold a maximum of 2 electrons

***l* value**	0	1	2	3	4	5
Symbol	s	p	d	f	g	h

The Magnetic Quantum Number, ***symbol*** ______________

- Determines the orientation of the orbital in space and also the energy of its electron in a magnetic field
- For a given value of l, m_l will have values ranging from $-l$ to $+l$
- For example if $l = 0$, m_l = ____ so there is __ orientation for an _____ orbital (remember an s orbital is defined by l =0) which makes sense because there is only one orientation for a sphere in 3 dimensional space.
- If l = 1 m_l = ___ , _____, ______
- The number of orbitals in a subshell will always be, $2l + 1$
- How many orbital in an s subshell? __________ In a p subshell? __________ in a d subshell? ________ In an f subshell? __________

Values for the Quantum Numbers *n*, *l* and m_l, from *n*=1 to *n*=4

n	***l***	**Orbital Designation**	m_l	**Number of Orbitals in each Subshell (2*l*+1)**	**Number of Orbitals in each Shell (n^2)**	**Maximum Electrons in Shell ($2n^2$)**
1						
2						
3						
4						

The Spin Quantum Number, *symbol* ________________

- Electrons behave like tiny magnets with their own N and S poles
- The magnetic field of an electron may be oriented in an external magnetic field on only two ways. Therefore, an electron may be found in one of two spins states
- The allowable values of m_s are -$^1/_2$ and +$^1/_2$, and designate equal but opposite spin effects

Example 1: What are the four quantum number corresponding to the final valence electron in a lithium atom?

- The final valence electron is in the 2s subshell, which is part of the second energy level, therefore n = 2
- The final valence electron is in the s subshell defined by $l = 0$
- For the $l = 0$ subshell, there is only one orientation which is $m_l = 0$
- The final valence electron in the orbital is alone (not paired) and the first electron in any particular orbital is always in the up spin, therefore $m_s = +1/2$

Example 2: What are the four quantum numbers corresponding to the final valence electron in a sulfur atom?

- The final valence is in the 3p subshell, which is part of the third energy level so the principal quantum number n = 3
- The final valence electron is in the p subshell defined by $l = 1$
- For the $l = 1$ subshell, there are three orbitals with three different orientations. From the energy level diagram the final valence electron is found in the first orbital designated by $m_l = -1$
- The final valence electron in the orbital is alone paired, therefore $m_s = -1/2$

SUMMARY OF CONCEPTS IN QUANTUM MECHANICS

Aufbau Principle

Hund's Rule

Pauli Exclusion Principle

Heisenberg's Uncertainty Principle

Quantum Mechanics

The Principle Quantum Number

The Secondary Quantum Number

The Magnetic Quantum Number

The Spin Quantum Number

Summary Table

Quantum Number	Name	Values	Meaning

Quantum Numbers and Electron Configurations Practice

1. State the four quantum numbers and the possible values they may have. 1, 2, 3, 4
2. Name the orbitals described by the following quantum numbers.

   a. $n = 3, l = 0$ s
   b. $n = 3, l = 1$ p
   c. $n = 3, l = 2$ d
   d. $n = 5, l = 0$ s

3. Give the n and l values for the following orbitals.

   a. 1s $n=1, l=0$
   b. 3s $n=3, l=0$
   c. 2p $n=2, l=1$
   d. 4d $n=4, l=2$
   e. 5f $n=5, l=3$

4. Place the following orbitals in order of increasing energy: ~~1s~~, ~~3s~~, ~~4s~~, ~~6s~~, ~~3d~~, ~~4f~~, ~~3p~~, ~~7s~~, ~~5d~~, ~~5p~~ 1s, 3s, 3p, 4s, 3d, 5p, 6s, 4f, 5d, 7s

5. What are the possible m_l values for the following types of orbitals?

   a. s 0
   b. p −1, 0, 1
   c. d −2, −1, 0, 1, 2
   d. f −3, −2, −1, 0, 1, 2, 3

6. How many possible orbitals are there for n =

   a. 4 16
   b. 10 100

7. How many electrons can inhabit all of the n=4 orbitals? 32
8. Tabulate all of the possible orbitals (by name, i.e. 4s) for n=4 and give the three quantum numbers which define each orbital.
9. Write the shorthand electron configurations for the following atoms and ions:

   a. H $1s^1$
   b. Kr [Kr]
   c. F $[He]\ 2s^2\ 2p^5$
   d. Br $[Ar]\ 3d^{10}\ 4s^2\ 4p^5$
   e. Ag $[Kr]\ 4d^{10}\ 5s^1$
   f. Cr $[Ar]\ 3d^5\ 4s^1$
   g. La $[Xe]\ 5d^1\ 6s^2$
   h. K $[Ar]\ 4s^1$
   i. Ca^{2+} [Ar] 4s
   j. Pt $[Xe]\ 4f^{14}\ 5d^9\ 6s^1$
   k. P^{3-}
   l. Fe^{3+}
   m. Ag^+
   n. Zn^{2+}

10. Provide the four quantum numbers for the final valence electron in:

    a. Fe b. Pb^{4+} c. He d. U e. Mo f. Au

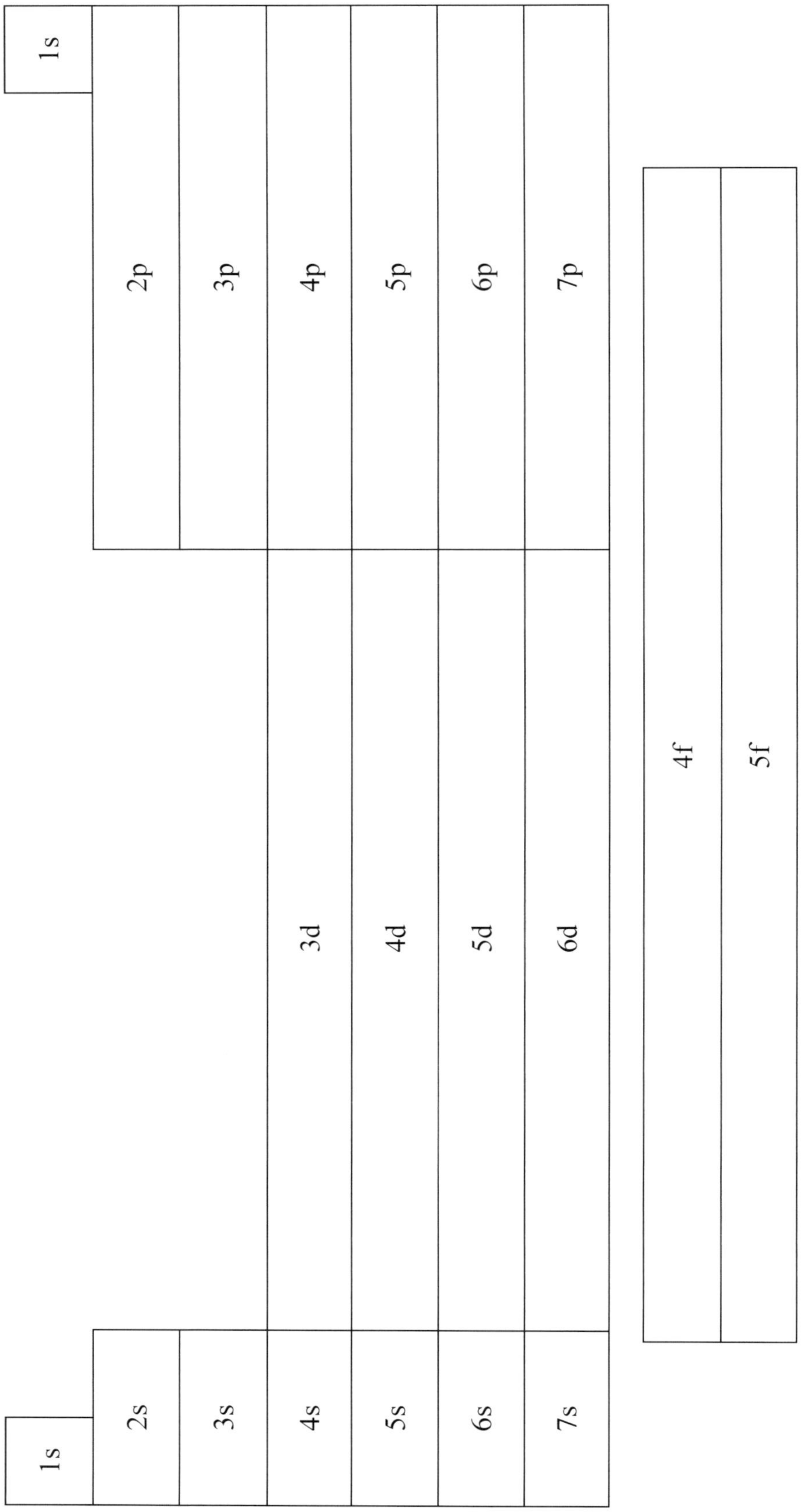
1s
2s
3s
4s
5s
6s
7s
3d
4d
5d
6d
2p
3p
4p
5p
6p
7p
1s
4f
5f

4.4 Review Questions

1. If hydrogen's electron exists in a spherical orbital, why doesn't this mean that the electron moves around the nucleus in a circle?

2. What is the difference between a 1s orbital and a 2s orbital? What does that difference indicate about an electron possessing energy equal to $n = 2$ as compared to $n = 1$?

3. Describe the two differences between a $2p_x$ orbital and a $3p_y$ orbital.

4. The lobes of a p orbital disappear at the nucleus. What does this tell us about electrons in p orbitals?

5. You may have heard in previous science classes that the maximum numbers of electrons that can exist in the first four energy levels are 2, 8, 8, and 18 respectively. Do you agree with those numbers and if not, what should they be?

6. The electron configuration for phosphorus, written in core notation, is [Ne] $3s^2\,3p^3$.
What two things does Hund's rule tell us about the three electrons in the 3p sublevel?

7. Use the periodic table to complete the following table:

Atom or Ion	Full Electron Configuration	Core Notation
Ge		
Zn^{2+}		
Sr		
Br^-		
Sn		
In^{3+}		

8. (a) Use the periodic table to identify the neutral atoms having the following electron configurations:

Electron Configuration	Element Name
[Ne] $3\mathbf{s}^2$	
[Ar] $4s^2\,3\mathbf{d}^5$	
[Kr] $5s^2\,4d^{10}\,5\mathbf{p}^3$	
[Xe] $6s^2\,4\mathbf{f}^7$	

(b) Notice where each of these elements is located on the periodic table. Look at the highest energy sublevel being filled (**bold type**) in each of the atoms in the table, and identify the four different sections of the periodic table associated with each of these four sublevels.

9. Consider the following six stable ions: N^{3-}, O^{2-}, F^-, Na^+, Mg^{2+}, and Al^{3+}.
(a) How many electrons are present in each ion?

(b) Write a single electron configuration representing all of the ions.

(c) Which neutral atom possesses this electron configuration? What does this suggest about a possible reason for some ion formation?

10. (a) Complete the following table for some elements in two families of the periodic table.

Alkali Metals	Core Notation	# Outer Electrons	Halogens	Core Notation	# Outer Electrons
lithium			fluorine		
sodium			chlorine		
potassium			bromine		
rubidium			iodine		

(b) Consider the numbers of outer electrons present and suggest a reason why elements belonging to the same chemical family demonstrate similar chemical behavior.

(c) What change occurs in the atoms as we move down each chemical family?

11. (a) On a separate sheet of paper, draw an orbital diagram for an atom of iron with sublevel energy increasing vertically. Arrange equal energy orbitals in each sublevel horizontally.

(b) Use a highlighter to label the electrons that would be lost when the Fe^{3+} cation forms.

Table 6.1.3 *Electron Configurations of Noble Gases and Nearby Elements*

Element	Electron Configuration for Atom	Nearest Noble Gas	Symbol and Electron Configuration for Stable Ion	
oxygen	$[He]2s^22p^4$	neon	O^{2-}	$[He]2s^22p^6$
calcium	$[Ar]4s^2$	argon	Ca^{2+}	$[Ne]3s^23p^6$
arsenic	$[Ar]4s^23d^{10}4p^3$	krypton	As^{3-}	$[Ar]4s^23d^{10}4p^6$
cesium	$[Xe]6s^1$	xenon	Cs^+	$[Kr]5s^24d^{10}5p^6$

Transition Elements

The **transition elements** include groups 3 through 12 in the periodic table. All are metals and most are hard solids with high melting and boiling points. An explanation of their chemical behavior is beyond the scope of this course, but it differs from the representative elements. For example, the transition elements show similarities within a given period as well as within a group. In addition, many transition elements form cations with multiple charges and those cations often form complex ions. A number of transition metal compounds have distinct and recognizable colors. The differences occur mainly because the last electrons added for transition metals are placed in inner d orbitals. Electrons in these orbitals are usually closer to the nucleus than in the outer s or p orbitals filled for the representative elements.

Quick Check

1. Identify the family number and name to which each of the following properties best apply:

Property	Family Number	Family Name
(a) reactive non-metals possessing seven valence electrons		
(b) reactive solids that form 2+ cations during reactions		
(c) invisible gases that are almost totally unreactive		
(d) soft, very reactive silvery solids with one valence electron		

2. Elements in the same family demonstrate similar chemical behavior. Consider the following chemical formulas: LiBr, K_2O, Sr_3N_2, AlF_3, CaO, H_2S. Write chemical formulas for:

(a) sodium iodide ______________________ (d) rubidium sulfide ______________________

(b) barium sulfide ______________________ (e) magnesium phosphide ______________________

(c) gallium chloride ______________________ (f) hydrogen selenide ______________________

3. Which two families contain the most reactive elements? Can you suggest a possible reason for this given their location on the periodic table?

____

____

4.5 Periodic Trends and the Quantum Mechanical Model

A Quantum Mechanical View of the Periodic Table

Let us look a little more closely at the organization of the periodic table from a quantum mechanics perspective. First we'll look at three different aspects of the elements in the periodic table.

(1) Figure 4.5.3 showing the chemical families separated into the four main blocks of the table. Notice that each block corresponds to one of the four different electron sublevels. Notice also that the number of columns or families in each block exactly matches the number of electrons that occupy that sublevel. (This diagram also includes both the older and newer numbering schemes employed for the chemical families.)

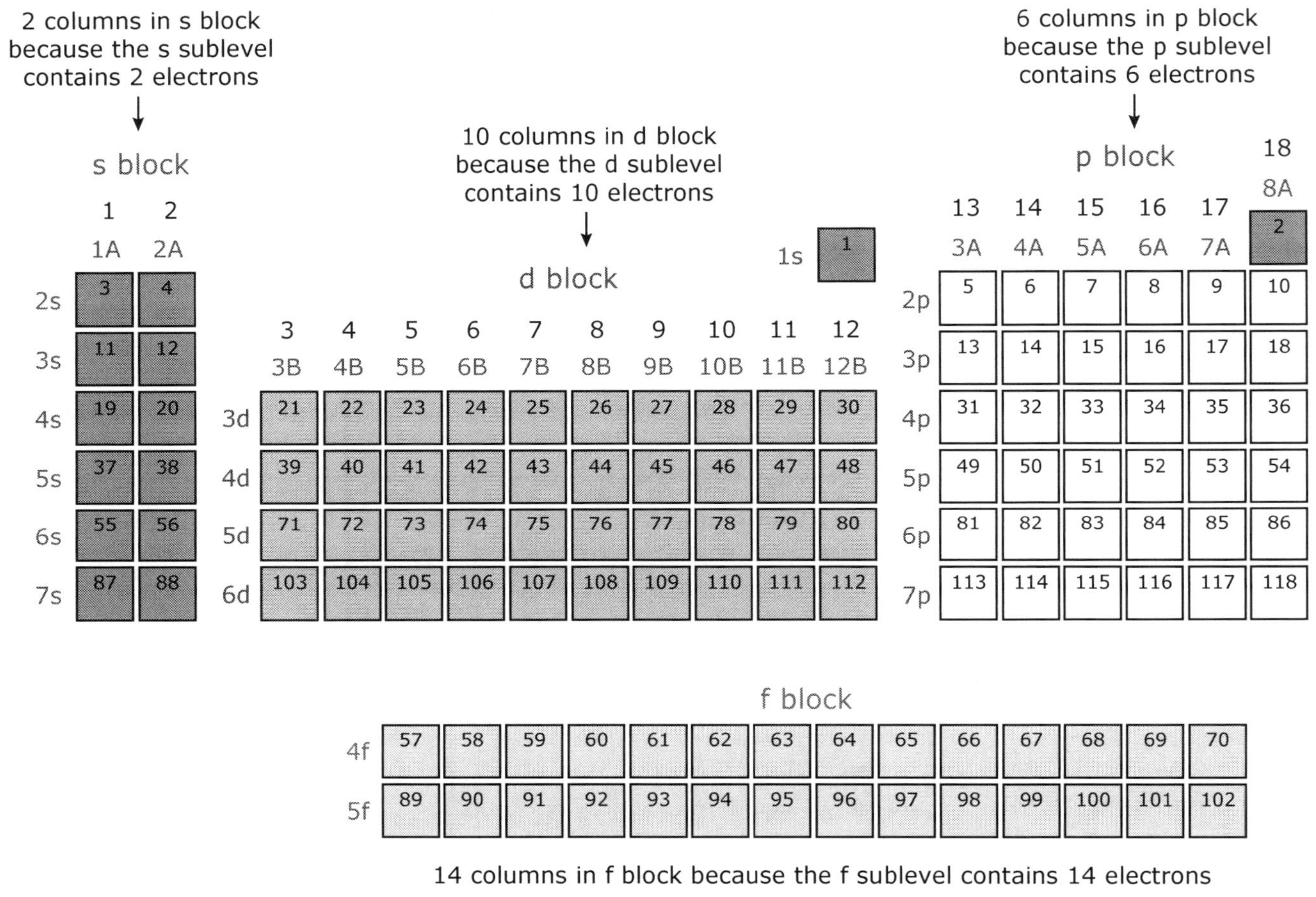

Figure 4.5.3 *The periodic table separated into its four main blocks*

Table 4.5.4 *Order of Filling Sublevels*

1s →			
2s →			2p
3s →			3p
4s	→	3d →	4p
5s	→	4d →	5p
6s →	4f →	5d →	6p
7s →	5f →	6d →	7p

(2) Consider in Figure 4.5.3 the sublevels associated with each of the chemical periods in the table. Notice that as we "read" the sublevels from left to right like the words on a page, we follow exactly the order of filling sublevels specified by the Aufbau principle and summarized by the diagonal diagram in the previous chapter. That order is shown again in Table 4.5.4.
Note also that as we reach each noble gas at the end of a period, we move down and begin a new period. Each new period number specifies the value of the next energy level as we start filling the s orbital for elements on the left side of that period. Thus every new period represents a larger charge cloud or electron "shell" in which electrons spend most of their time farther from the nucleus.

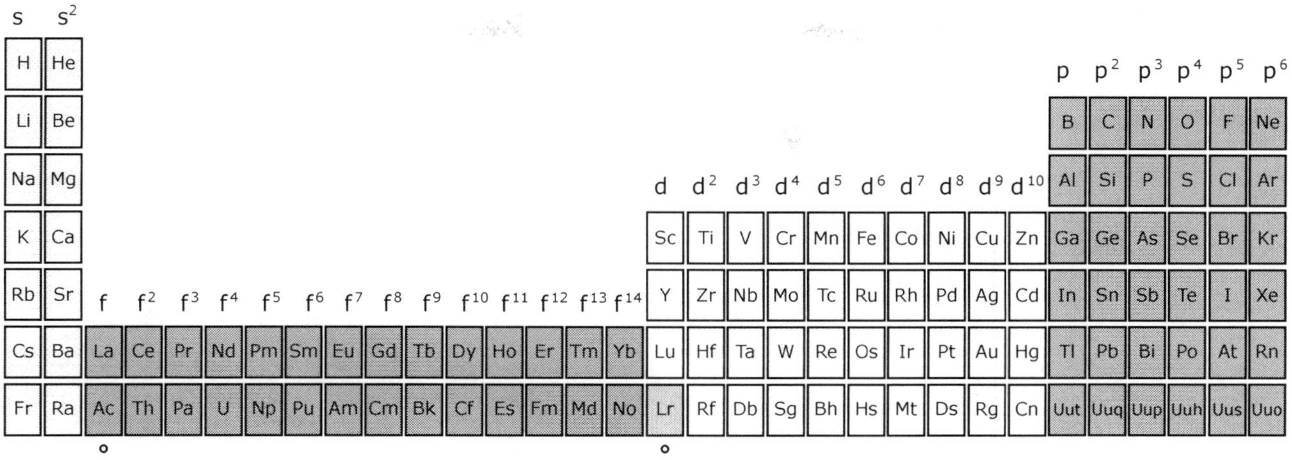

Figure 4.5.4 *Periodic table showing pattern of electron configuration*

(3) Finally, consider Figure 4.5.4, showing the extended form of the periodic table with the f block lanthanides and actinides inserted after barium and radium respectively. Note the consistent order and the obvious connection of electron configuration to element location in the periodic table.

Chemists, like all scientists, don't really believe in coincidences. We have discussed that the structure of the periodic table is based firmly on experimentation. The organization of the periods and chemical families results from and summarizes an enormous amount of empirical data gathered about the elements. It is truly amazing that this arrangement of the elements in the periodic table was essentially in place *before* the development of the quantum mechanical model of the atom! The fact that the electron configurations of the elements specified by quantum mechanics exactly matches their organization in the periodic table is one of the greatest successes in the history of science.

Far from being a coincidence, the exact correlation exists precisely because quantum mechanics provides the theoretical foundation for the experimentally derived periodic table. Stated another way, the quantum mechanical view of the atom is the "why" behind the "what" stated in the periodic law. Of course, it can also be said that the structure of the periodic table is arguably the best piece of supporting evidence for the quantum mechanical model of the atom.

Perhaps John Newlands wasn't far off the mark when he used a musical analogy in referring to elemental properties. Think of the millions of chemical reactions happening around us as symphonies played out by the instruments we call the chemical elements in nature's orchestral arrangement that is the periodic table.

Atomic Size

There are exceptions to the general trends stated above and they can be explained by considering the electron configurations of the atoms and the electron sublevels being filled in each case. For example, as we move across period 4, we start filling the 4th energy level at potassium and the atomic sizes shrink as expected for the first two elements. But when we arrive at the transition elements and begin filling the 3d sublevel, the sizes remain relatively constant as we move across to zinc.

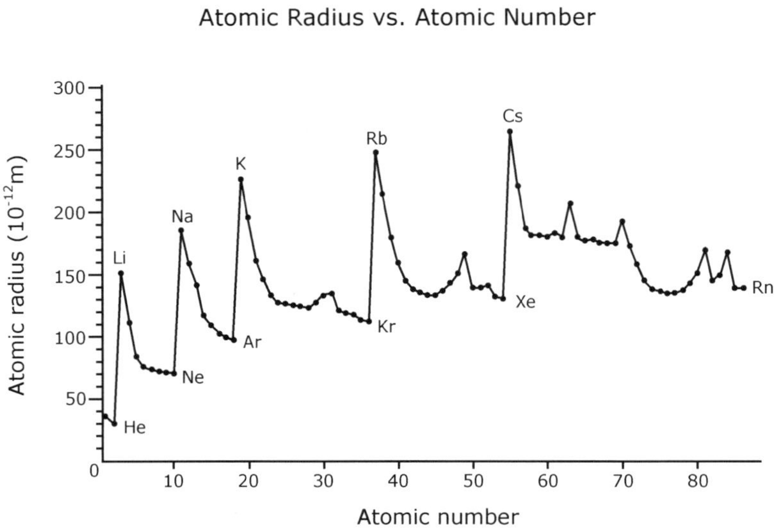

Figure 4.5.3 *Periodic changes in atomic radii as we move from period 1 through period 6*

To understand this, remember that $n = 3$ electrons spend most of their time *closer to the nucleus* than those electrons in the $n = 4$ charge cloud. We would therefore expect electrons in the 3d sublevel to be capable of shielding the outer 4s electrons from the increasing nuclear charge as we move across the period. This would reduce Z_{eff}. Consider the elements vanadium and zinc. The electron configuration for V is $[Ar]3d^34s^2$ and the electron configuration for Zn is $[Ar]3d^{10}4s^2$. Even though zinc has a nucleus with 7 more protons than vanadium, the extra shielding provided by zinc's 10 electrons in the 3d sublevel is such that zinc's atomic radius is equal to vanadium's!

This shows how effective inner electrons can be at shielding outer electrons from the "pull" of an increasingly positive nucleus and significantly influence atomic size. A number of other examples can be found throughout the periodic table.

Ionization Energy

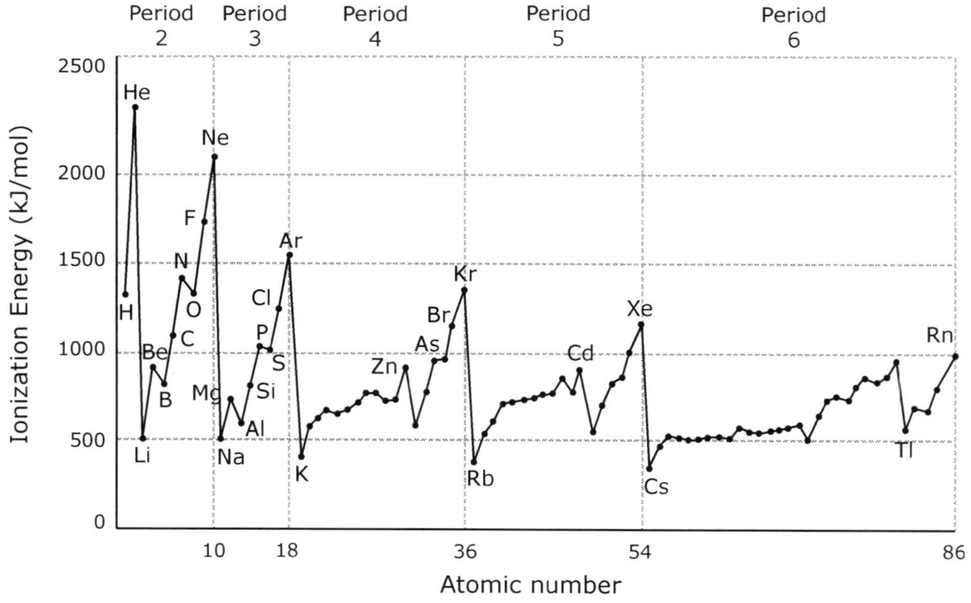

Figure 4.5.4 *As atomic size decreases, ionization energy increases.*

Exceptions to Ionization Energy Trends — One Example

As with atomic radii, there are several exceptions to the general trends in ionization energy, which we can explain by analyzing electron configurations. One example of this occurs with nitrogen and oxygen. Even though oxygen is a smaller atom than nitrogen, oxygen has a lower first ionization energy. Nitrogen has a single electron in each of its three 2p orbitals and a half-filled p sublevel that is quite stable. Oxygen, however, has a pair of electrons in one of its 2p orbitals (Figure 4.5.5). The increased electron-electron repulsion associated with that pairing makes it easier for oxygen to lose one of those electrons when first ionized.

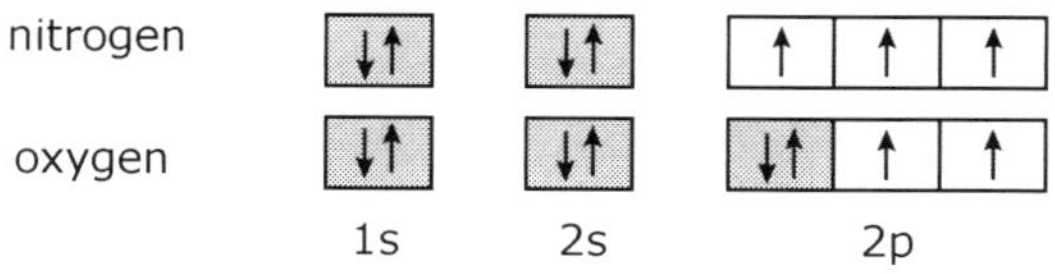

Figure 4.5.5 *Electron configurations in nitrogen and oxygen*

This reminds us that the repulsive forces between electrons, as well as the attractive forces affecting them from the nucleus, have a role to play in determining properties such as size and ionization energy.

Studying ionization energies allows us to do more than predict which elements might tend to lose or gain electrons during chemical changes. Investigating ionization energies also helps us identify which electrons are likely to be associated with those changes.

As we might expect, after removing one electron from an atom, further ionization energies increase. This occurs because each successive electron removed is being separated from an increasingly positive ion. However, those increases are *not regular*. Whenever the last outer or valence electron is removed, the next ionization requires significantly more energy because inner or "core electrons" are now involved. This can be seen using beryllium as an example. The atom has two valence electrons and the electron configuration is $1s^2\,2s^2$. Figure 4.2.4 shows the first three ionization energies for beryllium.

Table 6.2.1 *First Three Ionization Energies of Beryllium*

Species	Electron Configuration	Ionization Energy (kJ/mol)
Be^{o}	$1s^2\,2s^2$	IE_1 = 900
Be^{1+}	$1s^2\,2s^1$	IE_2 = 1 756
Be^{2+}	$1s^2$	IE_3 = 14 860

After the second (and last valence) electron is removed, the dramatic increase in energy required to remove the third electron reflects the fact that it is an inner or "core" electron. This shows us that core electrons are bound much more tightly to the nucleus, and thus do not take part in chemical reactions. This holds true for all of the elements in the periodic table.

Sample Problem – Trends in Ionization Energy

Using only the periodic table, rank each of the following alphabetical lists of elements in order of increasing first ionization energies.

(a) argon chlorine phosphorus sodium silicon
(b) antimony arsenic bismuth nitrogen phosphorus

What to Think about	How to Do It
1. Ionization energy increases left-to-right across a period and moving up a chemical group.	
2. The elements listed in (a) are members of period 3. List the elements in the order they appear from left-to-right in period 3.	Na < Si < P < Cl < Ar
3. The elements listed in (b) belong to group 15 of the periodic table. List the elements in the order they appear from bottom-to-top in group 15.	Bi < Sb < As < P < N

Practice Problems — Trends in Ionization Energy

1. The nature of the 2s sublevel is such that 2s electrons have a higher probability of being found closer to the nucleus than electrons in the 2p sublevel. Consider this and the following electron configurations:

   beryllium: $1s^2 2s^2$ boron: $1s^2 2s^2 2p^1$

   Suggest a reason why boron's first ionization energy is less than beryllium's, even though boron is a smaller atom.

   ____

5 The Mole, Conversions, Empirical and Molecular Formulae

By the end of this chapter, you should be able to do the following:

- Explain the significance and use of the mole
- Perform calculations involving the mole
- Determine relationships between molar quantities of gases at STP
- Perform calculations involving molecular and empirical formulas to identify a substance
- Describe concentration in terms of molarity
- Perform calculations involving molarity

By the end of this chapter you should know the meaning of these **key terms**:

- empirical formula
- molarity
- molar mass
- molar solution
- molar volume
- mole
- molecular formula
- molecular mass
- percentage composition
- relative atomic mass
- standard solution
- stoichiometry
- STP

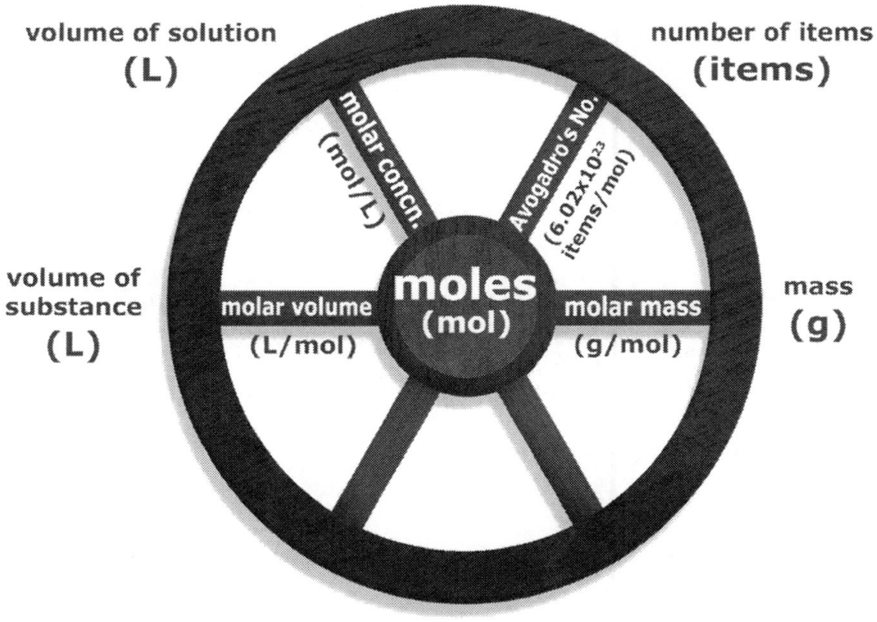

The mole is at the centre of the chemical measurement.

5.1 Scientific Notation and Significant Figures

Using Scientific Notation

Because it deals with atoms, and they are so incredibly small, the study of chemistry is notorious for using very large and very tiny numbers. For example, if you determine the total number of atoms in a sample of matter, the value will be very large. If, on the other hand, you determine an atom's diameter or the mass of an atom, the value will be extremely small. The method of reporting an ordinary, expanded number in scientific notation is very handy for both of these things.

Scientific notation refers to the method of representing numbers in *exponential form*. Exponential numbers have two parts. Consider the following example:

24 500 becomes 2.45×10^4 in scientific notation

Convention states that the first portion of a value in scientific notation should always be expressed as a number **between 1 and 10**. This portion is called the **mantissa** or the **decimal portion**. The second portion is the base 10 raised to some power. It is called the **ordinate** or the **exponential portion**.

mantissa → $\underline{2.45} \times 10^4$ and $2.45 \times \underline{10^4}$ ← ordinate

A positive exponent in the ordinate indicates a *large number* in scientific notation, while a negative exponent indicates a *small number*. In fact the exponent indicates the number of 10s that must be multiplied together to arrive at the number represented by the scientific notation. If the exponents are negative, the exponent indicates the number of tenths that must be multiplied together to arrive at the number. In other words, the exponent indicates the number of places the decimal in the mantissa must be moved to correctly arrive at the **expanded notation** (also called standard notation) version of the number.

A *positive exponent* indicates the number of *places* the decimal must be moved to the *right*, while a *negative exponent* indicates the number of *places* the decimal must be moved to the *left*.

Quick Check

1. Change the following numbers from scientific notation to expanded notation.
   (a) 2.75×10^3 = ______________

   (b) 5.143×10^{-2} = ______________

2. Change the following numbers from expanded notation to scientific notation.
   (a) 69 547 = ______________

   (b) 0.001 68 = ______________

Multiplication and Division in Scientific Notation

To *multiply* two numbers in scientific notation, we *multiply the mantissas* and state their product multiplied by 10, raised to a power that is the *sum of the exponents.*

$$(A \times 10^a) \times (B \times 10^b) = (A \times B) \times 10^{(a+b)}$$

To *divide* two numbers in scientific notation, we divide one mantissa by the other and state their quotient multiplied by 10, raised to a power that is the *difference* between the exponents.

$$(A \times 10^a) \div (B \times 10^b) = (A \div B) \times 10^{(a-b)}$$

Sample Problems — Multiplication and Division Using Scientific Notation

Solve the following problems, expressing the answer in scientific notation.

1. $(2.5 \times 10^3) \times (3.2 \times 10^6) =$
2. $(9.4 \times 10^{-4}) \div (10^{-6}) =$

What to Think about	How to Do It
Question 1	
1. Find the product of the mantissas.	$2.5 \times 3.2 = 8.0$ (the new mantissa)
2. Raise 10 to the sum of the exponents to determine the ordinate.	$10^{(3+6)} = \underline{10^9}$ (the new ordinate)
3. State the answer as the product of the new mantissa and ordinate.	$(2.5 \times 10^3) \times (3.2 \times 10^6) = 8.0 \times 10^9$
Question 2	
1. Find the quotient of the mantissas. When no mantissa is shown, it is assumed that the mantissa is 1.	$9.4 \div 1 = \underline{9.4}$ (the new mantissa)
2. Raise 10 to the difference of the exponents to determine the ordinate.	$10^{(-4-(-6))} = \underline{10^2}$ (the new ordinate)
3. State the answer as the product of the mantissa and ordinate.	$(9.4 \times 10^{-4}) \div (10^{-6}) = 9.4 \times 10^2$

Practice Problems — Multiplication and Division Using Scientific Notation

Solve the following problems, expressing the answer in scientific notation, *without* using a calculator. Repeat the questions using a calculator and compare your answers. Compare your method of solving with a calculator with that of another student.

1. $(4 \times 10^3) \times (2 \times 10^4) =$ ____________
2. $(9.9 \times 10^5) \div (3.3 \times 10^3) =$ ____________
3. $[(3.1 \times 10^{-4}) \times (6.0 \times 10^7)] \div (2.0 \times 10^5) =$ ____________
4. $10^9 \div (5.0 \times 10^6) =$ ____________
5. $[(4.5 \times 10^{12}) \div (1.5 \times 10^4)] \times (2.5 \times 10^{-6}) =$ ____________

Addition and Subtraction in Scientific Notation

Remember that a number in proper scientific notation will always have a mantissa between 1 and 10. Sometimes it becomes necessary to *shift* a decimal in order to express a number in proper scientific notation.

The *number of places* shifted by the decimal is indicated by an *equivalent change* in the *value of the exponent*. If the decimal is shifted *LEFT*, the *exponent* becomes *LARGER*; shifting the decimal to the *RIGHT* causes the *exponent* to become *SMALLER*.

Another way to remember this is if the *mantissa becomes smaller* following a shift, the *exponent becomes larger*. Consequently, if the *exponent becomes larger*, the *mantissa becomes smaller*. Consider AB.C $\times$ 10^x: if the decimal is shifted to change the value of the mantissa by 10^n times, the value of *x* changes $-n$ times.

For example, a number such as 18 235.0 $\times$ 10^2 (1 823 500 in standard notation) requires the decimal to be shifted 4 places to the left to give a mantissa between 1 and 10, that is 1.823 50. A LEFT shift *4* places, means the exponent in the ordinate becomes *4 numbers* LARGER (from 10^2 to 10^6). The correct way to express 18 235.0 $\times$ 10^2 in scientific notation is 1.823 50 $\times$ 10^6. Notice the new mantissa is $10^{\underline{4}}$ *smaller*, so the exponent becomes 4 numbers larger.

Quick Check

Express each of the given values in proper scientific notation in the second column. Now write each of the given values from the *first* column in expanded form in the third column. Then write each of your answers from the *second* column in expanded form. How do the expanded answers compare?

	Given Value	Proper Notation	Expanded Form	Expanded Answer
1.	6 014.51 $\times$ 10^2			
2.	0.001 6 $\times$ 10^7			
3.	38 325.3 $\times$ 10^{-6}			
4.	0.4196 $\times$ 10^{-2}			

When adding or subtracting numbers in scientific notation, it is important to realize that we add or subtract only the mantissa. *Do not add or subtract the exponents!* To begin, it is often necessary to shift the decimal to be sure the value of the exponent is the same for both numbers that will be added or subtracted. Once the arithmetic has been completed, the decimal may be shifted again if required to ensure that the mantissa is, indeed, between 1 and 10.

Shift the decimal to obtain the *same value for the exponent* in the ordinate of both numbers to be added or subtracted. Then simply *sum or take the difference of the mantissas*. Convert back to proper scientific notation when finished.

Sample Problems — Addition and Subtraction in Scientific Notation

Solve the following problems, expressing the answer in proper scientific notation.

1. $(5.19 \times 10^3) - (3.14 \times 10^2) =$
2. $(2.17 \times 10^{-3}) + (6.40 \times 10^{-5}) =$

What to Think about	How to Do It
Question 1	
1. Begin by shifting the decimal of one of the numbers and changing the exponent so that both numbers share the *same exponent*. For consistency, adjust one of the numbers so that *both* numbers have the *larger* of the two ordinates. The goal is for both mantissas to be multiplied by 10^3. This means the exponent in the second number should be increased by one. Increasing the exponent requires the decimal to shift to the left (so the mantissa becomes smaller).	3.14×10^2 becomes 0.314×10^3
2. Once both ordinates are the same, the mantissas are simply subtracted.	5.19×10^3 -0.314×10^3 4.876×10^3
Question 1 — Another Approach	
1. It is interesting to note that we could have altered the first number instead. In that case, 5.19×10^3 would have become 51.9×10^2.	51.9×10^2 -3.14×10^2 48.76×10^2
2. In this case, the difference results in a number that is not in proper scientific notation as the mantissa is greater than 10.	
3. Consequently, a further step is needed to convert the answer back to proper scientific notation. Shifting the decimal one place to the left (mantissa becomes smaller) requires an increase of 1 to the exponent.	48.76×10^2 becomes 4.876×10^3
Question 2	
1. As with differences, begin by shifting the decimal of one of the numbers and changing the exponent so both numbers share the same ordinate. The *larger ordinate* in this case is 10^{-3}.	2.17×10^{-3} will be left as is.
2. Increasing the exponent in the second number from −5 to −3 requires the decimal to be shifted two to the left (make the mantissa smaller).	6.40×10^{-5} becomes 0.0640×10^{-3}
3. Once the exponents agree, the mantissas are simply summed.	2.17×10^{-3} $+\ 0.0640 \times 10^{-3}$ 2.2340×10^{-3}
4. The alternative approach involves one extra step, but gives the same answer.	217×10^{-5} $+\ 6.40 \times 10^{-5}$ 223.40×10^{-5} becomes 2.2340×10^{-3}

Practice Problems — Addition and Subtraction in Scientific Notation

Solve the following problems, expressing the answer in scientific notation, *without* using a calculator. Repeat the questions using a calculator and compare your answers. Compare your use of the exponential function on the calculator with that of a partner.

1. $\begin{array}{r} 8.068 \times 10^{8} \\ -4.14 \times 10^{7} \\ \hline \end{array}$

2. $\begin{array}{r} 6.228 \times 10^{-4} \\ +4.602 \times 10^{-3} \\ \hline \end{array}$

3. $\begin{array}{r} 49.001 \times 10^{1} \\ + \qquad 10^{-1} \\ \hline \end{array}$

Scientific Notation and Exponents

Occasionally a number in scientific notation will be raised to some power. When such a case arises, it's important to remember when one exponent is raised to the power of another, the exponents are multiplied by one another. Consider a problem like $(10^3)^2$. This is really just $(10 \times 10 \times 10)^2$ or $(10 \times 10 \times 10 \times 10 \times 10 \times 10)$. So we see this is the same as $10^{(3 \times 2)}$ or 10^6.

$$(A \times 10^a)^b = A^b \times 10^{(a \times b)}$$

Quick Check

Solve the following problems, expressing the answer in scientific notation, *without* the use of a calculator. Repeat the problems with a calculator and compare your answers.

1. $(10^3)^5$
2. $(2 \times 10^2)^3$
3. $(5 \times 10^4)^2$
4. $(3 \times 10^5)^2 \times (2 \times 10^4)^2$

Pictorial Representation of Data — Graphing

Often in scientific investigations, we are interested in measuring how the value of some property changes as we vary something that affects it. We call the value that responds to the variation the **dependent variable**, while the other value is the **independent variable**. For example, we might want to measure the extension of a spring as we attach different masses to it. In this case, the extension would be the dependent variable, and the mass would be the independent variable. Notice that the amount of extension depends on the mass loaded and not the other way around. The variable "time" is nearly always independent.

The series of paired measurements collected during such an investigation is quantitative data. It is usually arranged in a **data table**. Tables of data should indicate the *unit of measurement* at the top of each column. The information in such a table becomes even more useful if it is presented in the form of a **graph** ("graph" is the Greek word root meaning "picture"). The independent data is plotted on the *x*-axis. A graph reveals many data points not listed in a data table.

Once a graph is drawn, it can be used to find a mathematical **relationship** (equation) that indicates how the variable quantities depend on each other. The first step to determining the relationship is to calculate the **proportionality constant** or **slope** "***m***" for the *line of best fit*. Curved graphs must be manipulated mathematically before a constant can be determined. Such manipulation is beyond the scope of this course. First, the constant is determined by finding the change in y over the change in x ($\Delta y/\Delta x$ or the "rise over the run"). Then substitute the y and x variable names and the calculated value for m, including its units, into the general equation $\mathbf{y = mx + b}$. The result will be an equation that describes the relationship represented by our data.

> $\boldsymbol{y = mx + b}$ is the general form for the equation of a *straight line relationship* where $\boldsymbol{m}$ represents the *slope, determined by* $\mathbf{m = \Delta y/\Delta x}$. In scientific relationships, the slope includes units and represents the constant that relates two variables. For this reason, it is sometimes represented by a $\boldsymbol{K}$.

The three most common types of graphic relationships are shown in Figure 1.2.2.

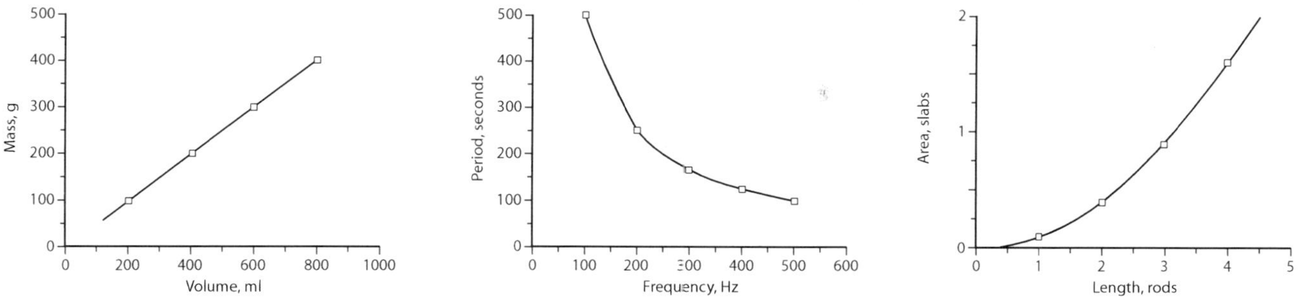

Direct: $y = Kx$	Inverse: $y = K/x$	Exponential: $y = Kx^n$
(y and x increase in direct proportion)	(as x increases, y decreases)	(as x increases, y increases more quickly)

Figure 1.2.2 *Three common types of graphic relationships*

Sample Problem — Determination of a Relationship from Data

Find the relationship for the graphed data below:

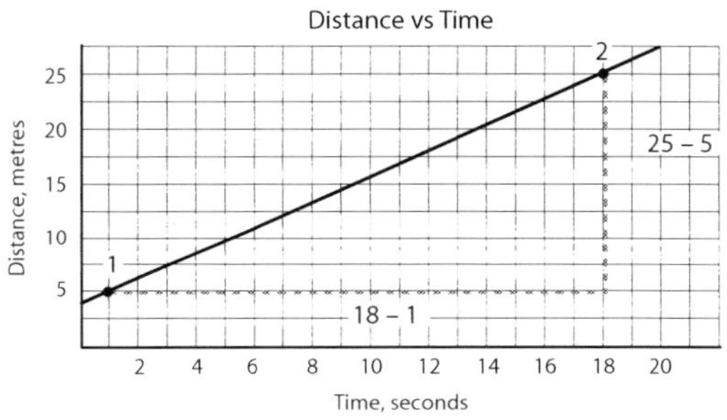

What to Think about	How to Do It
1. Determine the constant of proportionality (the slope) for the straight line. To do this, select two points on the line of best fit. These should be points whose values are easy to determine on both axes. *Do not use data points* to determine the constant. Determine the change in y (Δy) and the change in x (Δx) including the units. The constant is $\Delta y / \Delta x$.	Δy is 25-5 = 20 m Δx is 18 - 1 = 17 s 20 m/17 s = 1.18 m/s
2. The relationship is determined by subbing in the *variable names* and the constant into the general equation, $y = Kx + b$. Often, a straight line graph passes through the origin, in which case, $y = Kx$.	Distance = (1.18 m/s)Time + 4.0 m.

Practice Problem — Determination of a Relationship from Data

Examine the following graphs. What *type of relationship* does each represent? Give the full relationship described by graph (c).

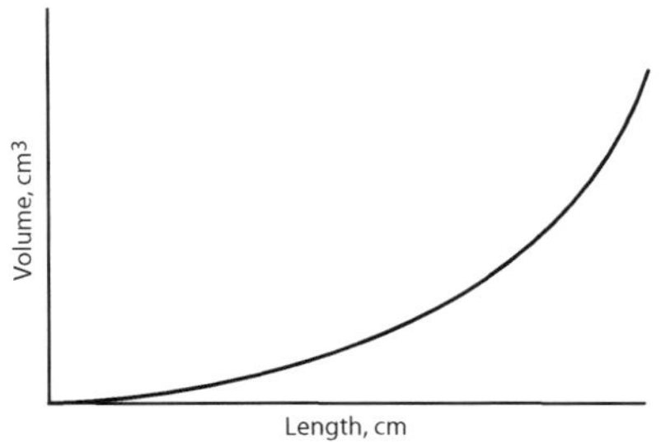

(a)

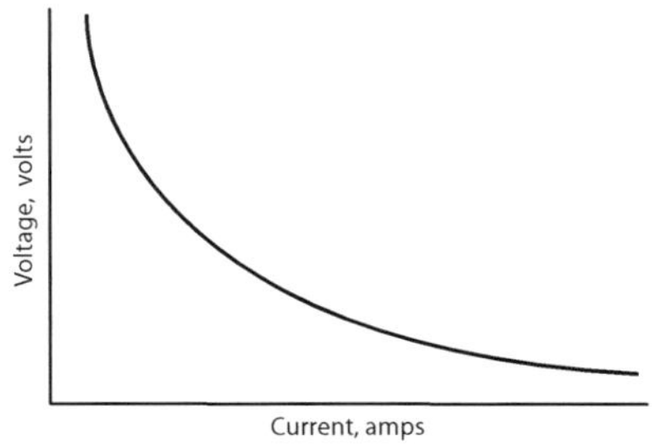

(b)

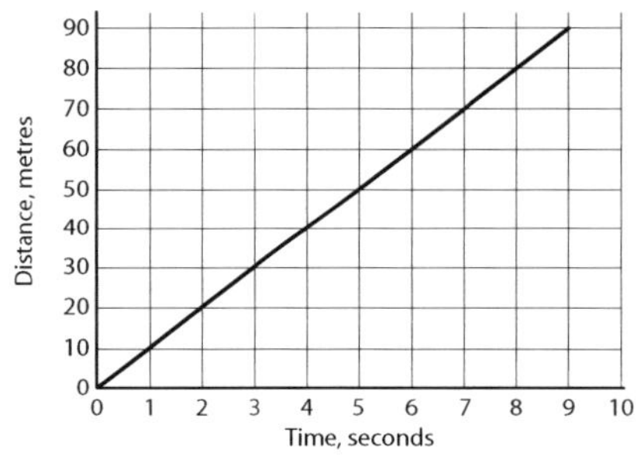

(c)

5.1 Activity: Graphing Relationships

Question

Can you produce a graph given a set of experimental data?

Background

A beaker full of water is placed on a hotplate and heated over a period of time. The temperature is recorded at regular intervals. The following data was collected.

Temperature (°C)	Time (min)
22	0
30	2
38	4
46	6
54	8
62	10
70	12

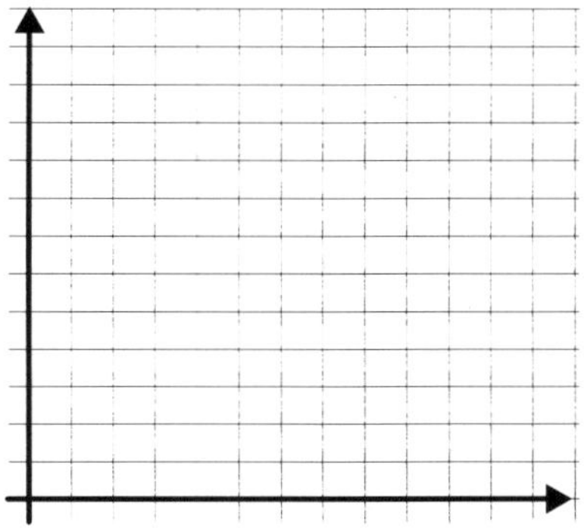

Procedure

1. Use the grid above to plot a graph of temperature against time. (Time goes on the *x*-axis.)

Results and Discussion

1. What type of relationship was studied during this investigation?

2. What is the constant (be sure to include the units)?

3. What temperature was reached at 5 minutes?

4. Use the graph to determine the relationship between temperature and time.

5. How long would it take the temperature to reach 80°C?

6. What does the *y*-intercept represent?

7. Give a source of error that might cause your graph to vary from that expected.

5.1 Review Questions

1. Convert the following numbers from *scientific* notation to *expanded* notation and vice versa (be sure the scientific notation is expressed correctly).

Scientific Notation	Expanded Notation
3.08×10^4	
	960
4.75×10^{-3}	
	0.000 484
0.0062×10^5	

2. Give the product or quotient of each of the following problems (express all answers in proper form scientific notation). Do **not** use a calculator.
(a) $(8.0 \times 10^3) \text{ x } (1.5 \times 10^6) =$
(b) $(1.5 \times 10^4) \div (2.0 \times 10^2) =$
(c) $(3.5 \times 10^{-2}) \times (6.0 \times 10^5) =$
(d) $(2.6 \times 10^7) \div (6.5 \times 10^{-4}) =$
3. Give the product or quotient of each of the following problems (express all answers in proper form scientific notation). Do **not** use a calculator.
(a) $(3.5 \times 10^4) \times (3.0 \times 10^5) =$
(b) $(7.0 \times 10^6) \div (1.75 \times 10^2) =$
(c) $(2.5 \times 10^{-3}) \times (8.5 \times 10^{-5}) =$
(d) $(2.6 \times 10^5) \div (6.5 \times 10^{-2}) =$

4. Solve the following problems, expressing the answer in scientific notation, *without* using a calculator. Repeat the questions using a calculator and compare your answers.
(a) $\begin{array}{r} 4.034 \times 10^5 \\ \underline{-2.12 \times 10^4} \end{array}$
(b) $\begin{array}{r} 3.114 \times 10^{-6} \\ \underline{+2.301 \times 10^{-5}} \end{array}$
(c) $\begin{array}{r} 26.022 \times 10^2 \\ \underline{+7.04 \times 10^{-1}} \end{array}$

5. Solve the following problems, expressing the answer in scientific notation, *without* using a calculator. Repeat the questions using a calculator and compare your answers.
(a) $\begin{array}{r} 2.115 \times 10^8 \\ \underline{-1.11 \times 10^7} \end{array}$
(b) $\begin{array}{r} 9.332 \times 10^{-3} \\ \underline{+6.903 \times 10^{-4}} \end{array}$
(c) $\begin{array}{r} 68.166 \times 10^2 \\ \underline{+ \quad\quad \times 10^{-1}} \end{array}$

6. Solve each of the following problems *without* a calculator. Express your answer in correct form scientific notation. Repeat the questions using a calculator and compare.
(a) $(10^{-4})^3$ (b) $(4 \times 10^5)^3$ (c) $(7 \times 10^9)^2$ d. $(10^2)^2 \times (2 \times 10)^3$

7. Solve each of the following problems *without* a calculator. Express your answer in correct form scientific notation. Repeat the questions using a calculator and compare.

(a) $(6.4 \times 10^{-6} + 2.0 \times 10^{-7}) \div (2 \times 10^{6} + 3.1 \times 10^{7})$

(b) $\dfrac{3.4 \times 10^{-17} \times 1.5 \times 10^{4}}{1.5 \times 10^{-4}}$

(c) $(2 \times 10^{3})^{3} \times [(6.84 \times 10^{3}) \div (3.42 \times 10^{3})]$

(d) $\dfrac{(3 \times 10^{2})^{3} + (4 \times 10^{3})^{2}}{1 \times 10^{4}}$

8. Many science departments use a still to produce their own distilled water. Data representing the volume of distilled water produced over a particular period of time might look like the data shown in the table.

Volume of Distilled Water (L)	Distillation Time (h)
0.8	0.4
1.6	0.8
2.4	1.2
5.0	2.5
7.2	3.6
9.8	4.9

(a) Plot this data on your own piece of graph paper. Where should time be plotted?

(b) Determine the constant for your graph. Show all work on the graph.

(c) Determine the relationship between volume and time.

(d) Assume the still was left on overnight. What volume of water would be collected if a period of 14 h passed?

(e) How long would it take to produce 12.5 L of water with this still?

9. Use the grid provided to plot graphs of mass against volume for a series of metal pieces with the given volumes. Plot all three graphs on the same set of axes with the independent variable (volume in this case) on the *x*-axis. Use a different color for each graph.

Volume (mL)	Copper (g)	Aluminum (g)	Platinum (g)
2.0	17.4	5.4	42.9
8.0	71.7	21.6	171.6
12.0	107.5	32.4	257.4
15.0	134.4	40.5	321.8
19.0	170.2	51.3	407.6

(a) Determine the constant for each metal.

(b) The constant represents each metal's density. Which metal is most dense?

10. Use the grid provided to plot two separate graphs, (a) and (b), for each the following sets of data. Be sure to draw a *smooth curve* through the points. Indicate the type of relationship represented by each graph.

Initial Rate (y) (mol/L/s)	**Concentration** (mol/L)	**Volume** (y) (L)	**Pressure** (kPa)
0.003	0.05	5.0	454
0.012	0.10	10.0	227
0.048	0.20	15.0	151
0.075	0.25	20.0	113
0.108	0.30	25.0	91
0.192	0.40	30.0	76

5.2 Measuring and Recording Significant Data

Warm Up

Draw lines to match the following measured values, stated in SI units (International System of Units), with the appropriate everyday measurement.

SI measured value	Equivalent Everyday Measured Quantity
1 mm	width across a small fingernail
100 kPa	distance from your fingertips to your nose
1 L	pressure exerted by Earth's atmosphere
1 g	one-sixtieth of one minute in time
1 km	thickness of one dime
1 m	length of 10 football fields
1 s	volume of 1000 mL of milk
1 cm	mass of one raisin

SI Units

The **SI system (International System of Units)** is the modern metric system of measurement and the dominant system of international commerce and trade. The abbreviation SI comes from the French, Système international d'unités. The SI system was developed in 1960 and is maintained by the International Bureau of Weights and Measures (BIPM) in France. It is a non-static system devised around the seven base units listed below. Its non-static nature means SI units may be created and definitions may be modified through international agreement as measurement technology progresses and the precision of measuring devices improves. The SI system is the primary system of measurement in all but a small number of countries. The seven fundamental SI units are given in Figure 5.5.3.

The following are some important SI rules or conventions:

- Unit symbols are always lower case letters unless the unit is named after a person. The one exception to this rule is L for liters. The full names of units are always written in lower case with the exception of *degrees Celsius*.
- Unit symbols should never be pluralized.
- Symbols should only be followed by a period at the end of a sentence.
- In general, the term *mass* replaces the term *weight*.
- The symbol cc should not be used in place of mL or cm^3.
- For values less than 1, use a 0 in front of the decimal point (e.g., 0.54 g not .54 g).
- A space rather than a comma should separate sets of three digits to the left *and right* of a decimal point. This practice is optional where there are only four digits involved.
- Use decimal fractions rather than common fractions (0.25 rather than ¼).
- Abbreviations such as sec, cc, or mps are avoided and only standard unit symbols such as s for second, cm^3 for cubic centimeter, and m/s for meter per second should be used.
- There is a space between the numerical value and unit symbol (4.6 g).
- Use the unit symbol in preference to words for units attached to numbers (e.g., 5.0 g/mol rather than 5.0 grams/mole). Note that 5.0 grams per mole is incorrect but five grams per mole is correct.
- A specific temperature and a temperature change both have units of degrees Celsius (°C).

Table 5.2.1 *The Fundamental SI Units*

Name	Unit Symbol	Quantity
meter	m	length
kilogram	kg	mass
second	s	time
ampere	A	electric current
kelvin	K	temperature
candela	cd	luminous intensity
mole	mol	amount of substance

Quick Check

Locate the SI error(s) in each of the following statements and correct them.

1. Ralph bought 6 kilos of potato salad. ______________________________

2. The thickness of the oxide coating on the metal was 1/2 c.m.
____

3. The weight of 1 Ml of water is exactly 1 gms at 4 °c.
____

4. My teacher bought 9.0 liters of gasoline for her 883 c.c. motorcycle.
____

5. Rama's temperature increased by .9 C°. ______________________________

Accuracy and Precision — The Quality of Measurements

Measured values like those listed in the Warm Up at the beginning of this section are determined using a variety of different measuring devices.

There are devices designed to measure all sorts of different quantities. The collection pictured in Figure 5.6.1 measures temperature, length, and volume. In addition, there are a variety of precisions (exactnesses) associated with different devices. The micrometer (also called a caliper) is more precise than the ruler while the burette and pipette are more precise than the graduated cylinder.

Despite the fact that some measuring devices are more precise than others, it is impossible to design a measuring device that gives perfectly exact measurements. All measuring devices have some degree of **uncertainty** associated with them.

The 1-kg mass kept in a helium-filled bell jar at the BIPM in Sèvres, France, is the only exact mass on the planet (Figure 5.6.2). All other masses are measured relative to this and therefore have some degree of associated uncertainty.

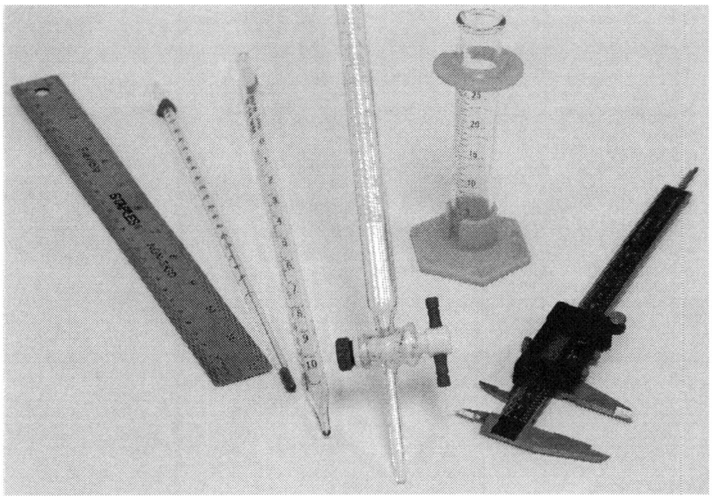

Figure 5.2.1 *A selection of measuring devices with differing levels of precision*

Figure 5.2.2 *This kilogram mass was made in the 1880s and accepted as the international prototype of the kilogram in 1889. (© BIPM — Reproduced with permission)*

Accuracy refers to the *agreement* of a particular value with the *true value.*

Accurate measurements depend on careful design and calibration to ensure a measuring device is in proper working order. The term **precision** can actually have two different meanings.

Precision refers to the reproducibility of a measurement (or the agreement among several measurements of the same quantity).

\- *or* -

Precision refers to the exactness of a measurement. This relates to uncertainty: the lower the uncertainty of a measurement, the higher the precision.

Quick Check

Volumetric devices measure liquids with a wide variety of precisions.

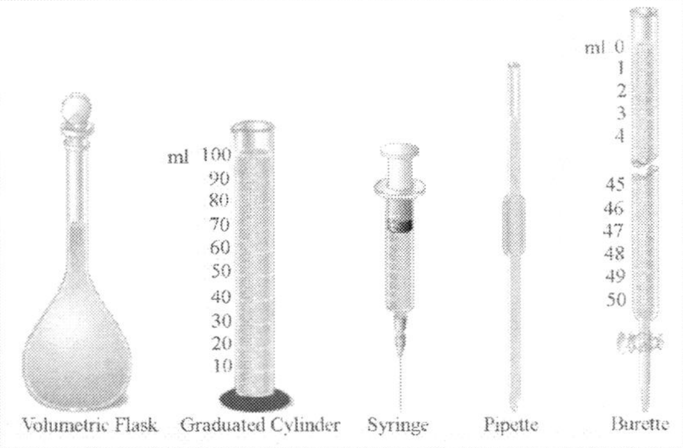

1. Which of these is likely the *most precise*?

   ____

2. Which is likely the *least precise*?

   ____

3. Is the *most precise* device necessarily the *most accurate*?

   ____

   ____

4. Discuss your answers.

   ____

Types of Errors

No measurement can be completely precise. In fact, all measurements must have some degree of uncertainty associated with them, so it must be true that every measurement involves some degree of error. A group of measurements may tend to consistently show error in the same direction. Such a situation is called **systematic error**. When a group of errors occurs equally in high and low directions, it is called **random error**.

Quick Check

Four groups of Earth Science students use their global positioning systems (GPS) to do some geocaching. The diagrams below show the students' results relative to where the actual caches were located.

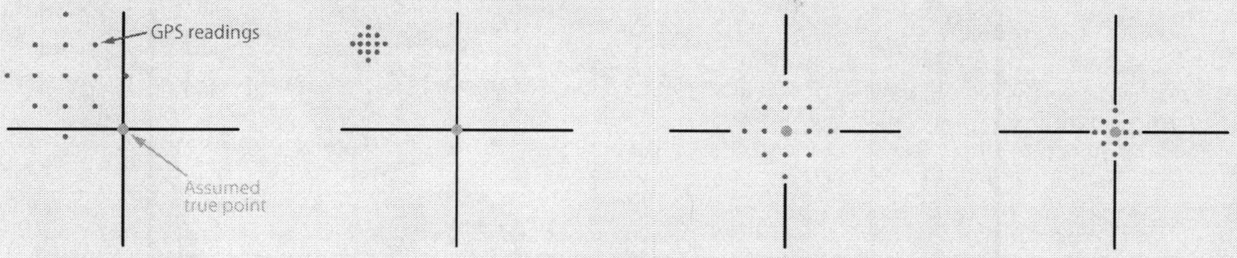

1. Comment on the precision of the students in each of the groups. (In this case, we are using the "reproducibility" definition of precision.)

   ____

2. What about the accuracy of each group?

   ____

3. Which groups were making systematic errors?

   ____

4. Which groups made errors that were more random?

   ____

Uncertainty

Every measurement has some degree of uncertainty associated with it. The uncertainty of a measuring device depends on its precision. The most precise measuring devices have the smallest uncertainties. The most common way to report the uncertainty of a measuring device is as a **range uncertainty.**

The **range uncertainty** is an *acceptable* range of values within which the true value of a measurement falls. This is commonly presented using the *plus* or *minus* notation (shown as +/–).

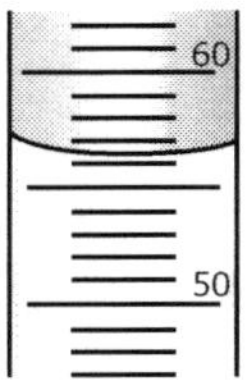

Figure 5.2.3 *A meniscus in a graduated cylinder*

An acceptable range uncertainty is usually considered plus or minus *one-tenth* to *one-half* the smallest division marked on a measuring scale. For the graduated cylinder in 5.6, the smallest division marked on its scale is 1 mL. One-half of this division is 0.5 mL. Therefore, reading the volume from the bottom of the meniscus would give a value of 56.3 mL +/– 0.5 mL. Because it is possible to go down to one-tenth of the smallest division on the scale as a range, the volume could also be reported as 56.3 mL +/– 0.1 mL. Notice that the unit is given twice, before and after the +/– symbol. This is the correct SI convention.

When *two uncertain values* with range uncertainties are *added or subtracted*, their *uncertainties must be added.*

Quick Check

1. Sum the following values:

$$\begin{array}{r} 27.6\text{ mL } +/-\ 0.2\text{ mL} \\ +\ \underline{14.8\text{ mL } +/-\ 0.2\text{ mL}} \end{array}$$

2. Subtract the following values:

$$\begin{array}{r} 19.8\text{ mL } +/-\ 0.2\text{ mL} \\ -\ \underline{7.2\text{ mL } +/-\ 0.2\text{ mL}} \end{array}$$

Compare your answers with your partner. Explain to your partner why the answer to question 1 makes sense. Have your partner explain the answer to question 2.

Absolute uncertainty refers to exactly how much higher or lower a measured value is than an accepted value.

In such a case, an accepted value is the value considered to be the best measurement available. Constants such as the speed of light or the boiling point of water at sea level are accepted values. For absolute uncertainties, a sign should be applied to indicate whether the measured value is above or below the accepted value.

Another common way to indicate an error of measurement is as a percentage of what the value should be.

$$\textbf{percentage error} = \frac{(\text{measured value} - \text{accepted value})}{\text{accepted value}} \times 100\%$$

Quick Check

A student weighs a penny and finds the mass is 2.57 g. Data from the United States Mint indicates a penny from that year should weigh 2.46 g.

1. What is the absolute uncertainty of the penny's mass?
2. What is the percentage error of the penny's mass?
3. Suggest a reasonable source of the error.

   ____

Significant Figures

When determining the correct value indicated by a measuring device, you should always record all of the **significant figures** (sometimes called "sig figs").

> The number of significant figures in a measurement includes *all* of the certain figures *plus* the *first* uncertain (estimated) figure.

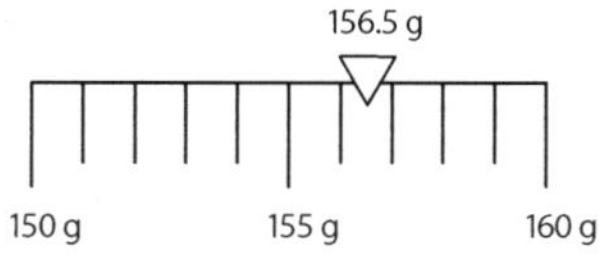

Figure 5.2.4 *Scale on a measuring device*

Say the scale on a measuring device reads as shown in Figure 5.2.4 (Note that *scale* may refer to the numerical increments on any measuring device.) The measured value has *three certain figures* (1, 5, and 6) and *one uncertain* figure (5 or is it 4 or 6?). Hence the measurement has *four significant figures*.

The following rules can be applied to determine how many figures are significant in any measurement.

Counting Significant Figures in a Measured Value

1. All non-zero digits are significant.
2. All zeros between non-zero digits are significant. Such zeros may be called *sandwiched* or *captive* zeros.
3. Leading zeros (zeros to the left of a non-zero digit) are *never* significant.
4. Trailing zeros (zeros to the right of a non-zero digit) are *only* significant if there is a *decimal* in the number.

Another way to determine the number of significant figures in a measured value is to simply express the number in scientific notation and count the digits. This method nicely eliminates the non-significant leading zeros. However, it is only successful if you recognize when to include the trailing (right side) zeros. Remember that trailing zeros are only significant if there is a decimal in the number. If the trailing zeros are significant, they need to be included when the number is written in scientific notation.

Sample Problems — Counting Significant Figures in a Measured Value

Determine the number of significant figures in each example.

1. 0.09204 g
2. 87.050 L

What to Think about	How to Do It
Question 1	
1. To begin with, apply rule 3: leading zeros are never significant. Note that the position of the zero relative to the decimal is irrelevant. These are sometimes referred to as *place holding* zeros. The underlined leading zeros are not significant.	0.09204 g
2. Apply rule 1 next: all non-zero digits are significant. The underlined digits are significant.	0.09204 g
3. Finally, apply rule 2: the captive zero is significant. The underlined zero is sandwiched between two non-zero digits so it is significant.	0.09204 g
4. A check of the number in scientific notation, 9.204×10^{-2} g, also shows four significant figures.	0.09204 g has **four** significant figures.

Continued

Sample Problems — *Continued*

Question 2

1. Apply rule 1: all non-zero digits are significant. All of the underlined digits are significant.	87.050 L
2. Apply rule 2: the captive zero is significant. The underlined zero is between two non-zero digits so it is significant.	87.050 L
3. Finally, consider the trailing or right-side zero. Rule four states that such zeros are only significant if a decimal is present in the number. Note that the position of the zero relative to the decimal is irrelevant.	
As this number does contain a decimal, the underlined trailing zero is significant.	87.050 L
4. Check: 8.7050×10^1 L has five sig figs (note that the right-side zero is retained).	87.050 L has **five** significant figures.

Practice Problems — Counting Significant Figures in a Measured Value

1. How many significant figures are in each of the following measured values?

   (a) 425 mL ___________

   (b) 590.50 g ___________

   (c) 0.00750 s ___________

   (d) 1.50×10^4 L ___________

   (e) 3400 m ___________

2. Round the following measurements to the stated number of significant figures.

   (a) 30.54 s (3 sig figs) _______________

   (b) 0.2895 g (3 sig figs) _______________

   (c) 4.49 m (2 sig figs) _______________

   (d) 100.4°C (2 sig figs) _______________

Significant Figures and Arithmetic — Multiplication and Division

The answer to a multiplication or division problem should have only as many figures as the number having the *least significant digits* in the problem.

Sample Problems — Significant Figures in Multiplication and Division Calculations

Give the answer to each of the following problems with the correct number of significant figures:

1. 8.2 m × 9.47 m =
2. 12 970.0 g ÷ 530.8 mL =

What to Think about	How to Do It
Question 1	
1. Begin by applying rules 1 to 4 to determine the number of significant figures contained in each number in the problem.	8.2 m × 9.47 m = 77.654 m^2 2 sig figs) (3 sig figs)
2. Express the answer should be expressed to *two* significant figures.	77.654 rounds to 78 m^2
Question 2	
1. The second example involves more difficult numbers. Apply rules 1 to 4 to quickly determine the number of sig figs in each value.	12 970.0 g ÷ 530.8 mL = 24.434815... g/mL (6 sig figs) (4 sig figs)
2. Express the answer to *four* significant figures.	24.434815... rounds to 24.43 g/mL

Quick Check

Give the answer to each of the following problems with the appropriate unit and the correct number of significant figures:

1. 0.14 m × 14.00 m = ________________
2. 940 g ÷ 0.850 mL = ________________
3. 0.054 g ÷ 1.10 s = ________________

Significant Figures and Arithmetic – Addition and Subtraction

The answer to an addition or subtraction problem should have only as many figures as the *least precise* (least exact) number in the problem. The number of significant figures in the answer is determined by considering the *place value* of the last significant figure in each number in the problem. (If both measurements include numbers to the right of a decimal, this means you simply round to the smallest number of decimal places.)

Sample Problems — Significant Figures in Addition and Subtraction Calculations

Give the answer to each of the following problems with the correct number of significant figures:

1. 246.812 cm + 1.3 cm =
2. 25 510 km – 7 000 km =

What to Think about	How to Do It
Question 1	
1. In addition and subtraction problems, the most important thing is to determine the *place value* of the last significant figure in each number. 246.812 contains non-zero digits only, so the last significant figure is the last 2, which occupies the thousandths place. The 3 in 1.3 is the last significant figure and occupies the tenths place.	246.812 + 1.3 = 248.112 cm
2. When these two place values are compared, the tenths is *less precise*; that is, it is *less exact* than the thousandths place. Round the final answer to the tenths place, resulting in a number with **four** significant figures. Notice that this rounded to one decimal place.	248.112 rounds to 248.1 cm
Question 2	
1. The problem involves adding and subtracting. Determine the place value of the last significant figure in each number. The last significant figure in 25 510 is the 1. It is in the tens place. The 7 is the last significant figure in 7000. It is in the thousands place.	25 510 – 7 000 = 18 510 km
2. Thousands are far less exact than tens so round the final answer to the thousands place resulting in an answer with two significant figures. Notice that the decimal place simplification does not apply in this example.	18 510 km rounds to → 19 000 km

Practice Problems— Significant Figures in Addition and Subtraction Calculations

Give the answer to each of the following problems with the correct number of significant figures:

1. 16.407 mL + 5.70 mL = ______________
2. 0.32 g + 0.009 g = ______________
3. 750 m + 8.001 m = ______________

Significant Figures — Summary

- When there are a series of arithmetic functions to be performed with measurements, always remember to apply the correct order of operations.
- Use the proper rules for determining the number of significant figures *in each step.*
- Remember that significant figures apply to measured values only.
- They do *not* apply to counted values or values that are defined.

Quick Check

Answer each of the following with the correct number of significant figures.

1. $\frac{9.825\text{g} - 9.804\text{ g}}{9.825\text{ g}} \times 100\% = \frac{0.021\text{ g}}{9.825\text{ g}} \times 100\% =$
2. $804.08\text{ g} \div (424.4\text{ mL} + 42.8\text{ mL}) =$
3. $(3.202\text{ m} \times 4.80\text{ m}) / (26.4\text{ min} - 17.3\text{ min}) =$
4. $7.0 \times 10^2\text{ s} + 6.010 \times 10^3\text{ s} =$

5.2 Activity: Connecting Significant Figures with Uncertainty

Question
What is the uncertainty in an area calculation?

Background
A student was assigned the task of determining the area of a small Post-It® note. She was instructed to use a low-precision plastic ruler, marked in increments of centimeters. Knowing it is acceptable to use between one-tenth and one-half the smallest increments on the ruler, the student decided on a range uncertainty of +/– 0.2 cm.

Dimensions	Measurements
Height	4.6 cm +/– 0.2 cm
Width	5.5 cm +/– 0.2 cm

Procedure
1. Calculate the smallest possible area of the Post-It® (keep **all digits**).

2. Calculate the largest possible area of the Post-It® (again, keep all digits).

3. Determine the area as the average of the values calculated in one and two (keep all figures in your calculation).

Results and Discussion
1. Determine an uncertainty that will include the smallest and largest possible areas (note that uncertainty may be expressed *in one place value only).*

2. The uncertain place will determine what place your area should be rounded to. Now express the area of the Post-It™ including the range uncertainty.

3. How does the number of significant figures in your answer compare with what you would have expected based on what you've learned about calculating with significant figures in this section?

5.2 Review Questions

1. Determine the errors and correct them according to the SI system:

   (a) The package contained 750 Gm of linguine.

   (b) The car accelerated to 90 km per hour in 10 sec.

   (c) The recipe called for 1 ML of vanilla and 250 cc of milk.

   (d) Jordan put 250 gms of mushrooms on his 12 inch pizza.

2. A zinc slug comes from a science supply company with a stated mass of 5.000 g. A student weighs the slug three times, collecting the following values: 4.891 g, 4.901 g, and 4.890 g. Are the student's values accurate? Are they precise (consider both meanings)?

3. A student doing experimental work finds the density of a liquid to be 0.1679 g/cm^3. The known density of the liquid is 0.1733 g/cm^3. What is the absolute uncertainty of the student's work? What is the percent error?

4. Two students weigh the same object with a known mass of 0.68 g. One student obtains a mass of 0.72 g, while the other gets a mass of 0.64 g. How do their percent errors compare? How do their absolute errors compare?

5. In an experiment to determine the density of a liquid, a maximum error of 5.00% is permitted. If the true density is 1.44 g/cm^3, what are the maximum and minimum values within which a student's answer may fall into the acceptable range?

6. What is the mass, including uncertainty, arrived at as the result of summing 45.04 g +/– 0.03 g, and 39.04 g +/– 0.02 g?

7. What is the smallest number that could result from subtracting 22 m +/– 2 m from 38 m +/– 3 m?

8. The dimensions of a rectangle are measured to be 19.9 cm +/– 0.1 cm and 2.4 +/– 0.1 cm. What is the area of the rectangle, including the range uncertainty?

9. Read each of the following devices, including a reasonable range uncertainty:

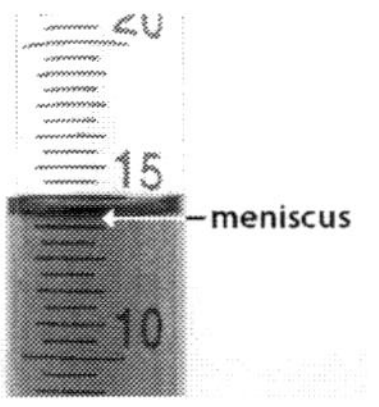

(a)

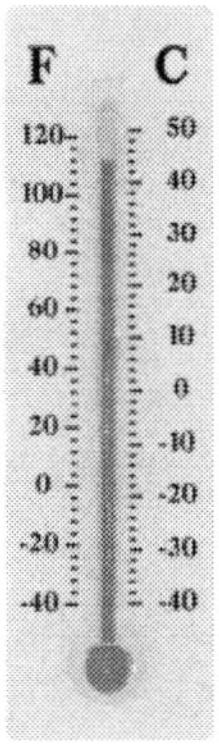

(b)

10. Determine the number of significant figures in each of the following measurements:
    (a) 0.1407 m _______________

    (b) 21.05 mg _______________

    (c) 570.00 km _______________

    (d) 0.0030 cm _______________

    (e) 250 m _______________

    (f) 10 035.00 cm^3 _______________

    (g) 2800 g _______________

    (h) 5000°C _______________

    (i) 1.1×10^2 kPa _______________

    (j) 5.35×10^{-2} m/h _______________

11. Express the following in proper form scientific notation. Then indicate the correct number of significant figures in the value.

(a) 4907 L ______________________

(b) 0.000 052 m ______________________

(c) 7900 g ______________________

(d) 0.060 30 ft ______________________

(e) 790.0 lb ______________________

12. Carry out the following operations and give the answers with the correct number of significant figures. Pay close attention to the units.

(a) 14.6 cm × 12.2 cm × 9.3 cm

(b) 28.0 m × 16.0 m × 7.0 m

13. A chunk of nickel has a mass of 9.0 g and a volume of 1.01 mL. What is its density?

14. The density of copper is 8.9 g/mL. What is the mass of a 10.8 mL piece of copper?

15. Carry out the following operations and give the answer with the correct number of significant figures.

(a) 608 g + 7 g + 0.05 g

(b) 481.33 mL − 37.1 mL

(c) 6620 s + 35.7 s + 1.00 s

(d) 0.007 m + 0.100 m + 0.020 m

16. Determine the answer with the correct number of significant figures:

$$\frac{1.415\ \text{g}}{1.6\ \text{mL}} + \frac{0.240\ \text{g}}{0.311\ \text{mL}} + \frac{40.304\ \text{g}}{0.2113\ \text{mL}}$$

17. Determine the answer to each the following with the correct number of significant figures:

(a) $\dfrac{8.4\ \text{g} + 3.0\ \text{g} + 4.175\ \text{g}}{3}$

(b) $\dfrac{9.00 \times 10^{-23}\ \text{units} \times 2.9900 \times 10^{-25}\ \text{units}}{2.9 \times 10^{-9}\ \text{units}}$

(c) $\dfrac{(5.9 \times 10^{-12}\ \text{u} + 7.80 \times 10^{-13}\ \text{u})}{(4 \times 10^{12}\ \text{u} + 6.700 \times 10^{13}\ \text{u})}$

18. The label on a bottle of mood-elevating medication states that each tablet contains 25.0 mg of imipramine. A test conducted by the bureau of standards shows a tablet to contain 28.0 mg. Legally, drug companies are allowed to be within plus or minus 5% of their labelled quantities.

(a) Give the *percentage* uncertainty for the imipramine tablets:

(b) Is the drug company within the legally allowed limits for their tablets?

5.3 Analysis of Units and Conversions in Chemistry

Warm Up

Place a check by the larger quantity in each row of the table.

Metric Quantity		Imperial Quantity	
A kilogram of butter		A pound of butter	
A five-kilometer hiking trail		A five-mile mountain bike trail	
One liter of milk		One quart of milk	
A twelve-centimeter ruler		A twelve-inch ruler	
A fifteen-gram piece of chocolate		A fifteen-ounce chocolate bar	
A temperature of 22°C		A temperature of 22°F	

Measurement Through History

Units of measurement were originally based on nature and everyday activities. The grain was derived from the mass of one grain of wheat or barley a farmer produced. The fathom was the distance between the tips of a sailor's fingers when his arms were extended on either side. The origin of units of length like the foot and the hand leave little to the imagination.

The inconvenient aspect of units such as these was, of course, their glaring lack of consistency. One "Viking's embrace" might produce a fathom much shorter than another. These inconsistencies were so important to traders and travellers that over the years most of the commonly used units were standardized. Eventually, they were incorporated into what was known as the English units of measurement. Following the Battle of Hastings in 1066, Roman measures were added to the primarily Anglo-Saxon ones that made up this system. These units were standardized by the Magna Carta of 1215 and were studied and updated periodically until the UK *Weights and Measures Act* of 1824 resulted in a major review and a renaming to the **Imperial system of measurement**. It is interesting to note that the United States had become independent prior to this and did not adopt the Imperial system, but continued to use the older English units of measure.

Despite the standardization, its development from ancient agriculture and trade has led to a rather vast set of units that are quite complicated. For example, there are eight different definitions for the amount of matter in a ton. The need for a simpler system, a system based on decimals, or multiples of 10, was recognized as early 1585 when Dutch mathematician, Simon Stevin published a book called *The Tenth*. However, most authorities credit Gabriel Mouton of Lyon, France, as the originator of the metric system nearly 100 years later. Another 100 years would pass before the final development and adoption of the metric system in France in 1795.

Recall the International Bureau of Weights and Measures (BIPM) was established in Sévres, France, in 1825. The BIPM has governed the metric system ever since. Since 1960, the metric system has become the SI system. Its use and acceptance has grown to the point that only three countries in the entire world have not adopted it: Burma, Liberia, and the United States (Figure 5.3.1).

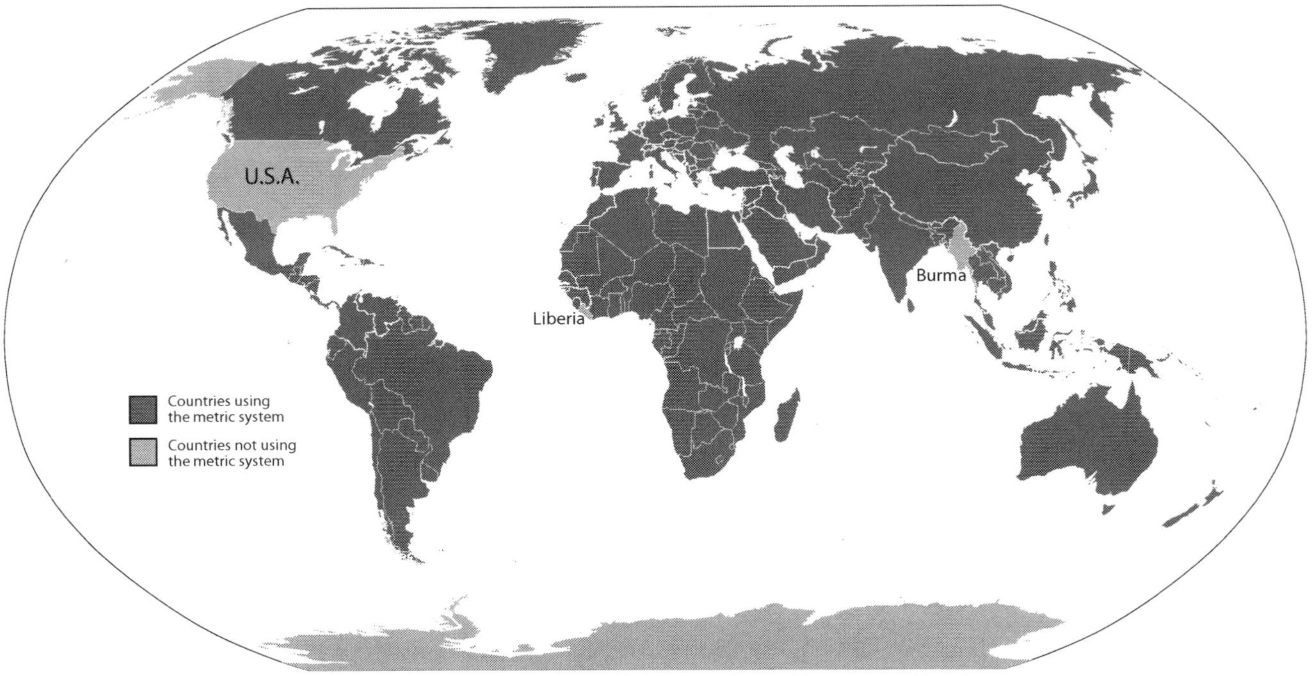

Figure 5.3.1 *Map of the world showing countries that have adopted the SI/metric system*

Dimensional Analysis

Dimensional analysis is a method that allows you to easily solve problems by converting from one unit to another through the use of conversion factors. The dimensional analysis method is sometimes called the *factor label method*. It may occasionally be referred to as the use of *unitary rates*.

A **conversion factor** is a *fraction* or factor written so that the denominator and numerator are *equivalent values* with *different units*.

One of the most useful conversion factors allows the user to convert from the metric to the imperial system and vice versa. Since 1 inch is exactly the same length as 2.54 cm, the factor may be expressed as:

$$\frac{1\ \text{inch}}{2.54\ \text{cm}} \text{ or } \frac{2.54\ \text{cm}}{1\ \text{inch}}$$

These two lengths are identical so multiplication of a given length by the conversion factor will not change the length. It will simply express it in a different unit.

Now if you wish to determine how many centimeters are in a yard, you have two things to consider. First, which of the two forms of the conversion factor will allow you to *cancel* the imperial unit, converting it to a metric unit? Second, what other conversion factors will you need to complete the task? Assuming you know, or can access, these equivalencies: 1 yard = 3 feet and 1 foot = 12 inches, your approach would be as follows:

$$1.00\ \cancel{\text{yards}} \times \frac{3\ \cancel{\text{feet}}}{1\ \cancel{\text{yard}}} \times \frac{12\ \cancel{\text{inches}}}{1\ \cancel{\text{foot}}} \times \frac{2.54\ \text{cm}}{1\ \cancel{\text{inch}}} = 91.4\ \text{cm}$$

Notice that as with the multiplication of any fractions, it is possible to cancel anything that appears in both the numerator and the denominator. We've simply followed a numerator-to-denominator pattern to convert yards to feet to inches to cm.

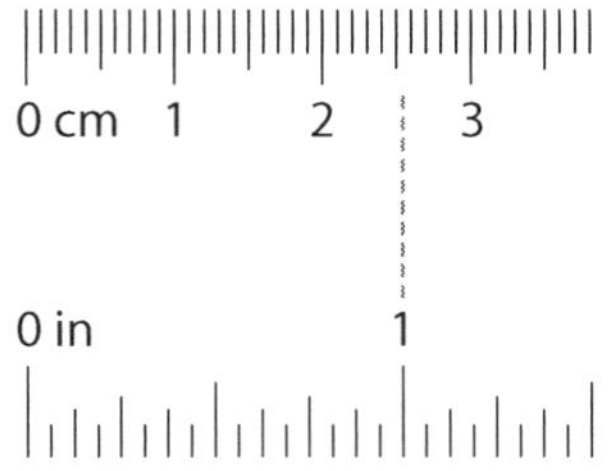

Figure 5.3.2 *A ruler with both imperial and metric scales shows that 1 inch = 2.54 cm.*

The number of feet in a yard and inches in a foot are *defined values*. They are not things we measured. Thus they do not affect the number of significant figures in our answer. This will be the case for any conversion factor in which the numerator and denominator are in the same system (both metric or both imperial). Interestingly enough, the BIPM has indicated that 2.54 cm will be *exactly* 1 inch. So it is the only multiple-system conversion factor that will not influence the number of significant figures in the answer to a calculation. As all three of the conversion factors we used are defined, only the original value of 1.00 yards influences the significant figures in our answer. Hence we round the answer to three sig figs.

Converting Within the Metric System

The metric system is based on powers of 10. The power of 10 is indicated by a simple prefix. 5 is a list of SI prefixes. Your teacher will indicate those that you need to commit to memory. You may wish to highlight them.

Metric conversions require either one or two steps. You will recognize a one-step metric conversion by the presence of a *base unit* in the question. The common base units in the metric system include:

Measures	Unit Name	Symbol
length	meter	m
mass	gram	g
volume	liter	L
time	second	s

One-step metric conversions involve a *base unit* (meters, liters, grams, or seconds) being converted to a *prefixed unit* or a prefixed unit being converted to a base unit.

Two-step metric conversions require the use of two conversion factors. Two factors will be required any time there are two prefixed units in the question. In a two-step metric conversion, you must always *convert to the base unit first*.

Table 5.3.1 *SI Prefixes*

Prefix	Symbol	10^n
yotta	Y	10^{24}
zetta	Z	10^{21}
exa	E	10^{18}
peta	P	10^{15}
tera	T	10^{12}
giga	G	10^{9}
mega	M	10^{6}
kilo	k	10^{3}
hecto	h	10^{2}
deca	da	10^{1}
deci	d	10^{-1}
centi	c	10^{-2}
milli	m	10^{-3}
micro	μ	10^{-6}
nano	n	10^{-9}
pico	p	10^{-12}
femto	f	10^{-15}
atto	a	10^{-18}
zepto	z	10^{-21}
yocto	y	10^{-24}

Sample Problems — One- and Two-Step Metric Conversions

1. Convert 9.4 nm into m.
2. Convert 6.32 μm into km.

What to Think about	How to Do It
Question 1	
1. In any metric conversion, you must decide whether you need one step or two. There is a base unit in the question and only one prefix. This problem requires only one step. Set the units up to convert nm into m. Let the units lead you through the problem. You are given 9.4 nm, so the conversion factor must have nm in the denominator so it will cancel.	$9.4\text{ nm} \times \frac{\text{m}}{\text{nm}} = \quad \text{m}$
2. Now determine the value of nano and fill it in appropriately. **1** nm = **10^{-9}** m Give the answer with the appropriate number of significant figures and the correct unit. Because the conversion factor is a defined equality, only the given value affects the number of sig figs in the answer.	$9.4\text{ nm} \times \frac{10^{-9}\text{ m}}{1\text{ nm}} = 9.4 \times 10^{-9}\text{ m}$
Question 2	
1. This problem presents with two prefixes so there must be two steps. The first step in such a problem is always to convert to the base unit. Set up the units to convert from μm to m and then to km.	$6.32\ \mu\text{m} \times \frac{\text{m}}{\mu\text{m}} \times \frac{\text{km}}{\text{m}} = \quad \text{km}$
2. Insert the values for 1 μm and 1 km. 1 μm = 10^{-6} m 1 km = 10^{3} m	
3. Give the answer with the correct number of significant figures and the correct unit.	$6.32\ \mu\text{m} \times \frac{10^{-6}\text{ m}}{1\ \mu\text{m}} \times \frac{1\text{ km}}{10^{3}\text{ m}} = 6.32 \times 10^{-9}\text{ km}$

Practice Problems — One- and Two-Step Metric Conversions

1. Convert 16 s into ks.

2. Convert 75 000 mL into L.

3. Convert 457 ks into ms.

4. Convert 5.6×10^{-4} Mm into dm.

Derived Unit Conversions

A **derived unit** is composed of more than one unit.

Units like those used to express rate (km/h) or density (g/mL) are good examples of derived units.

Derived unit conversions require *cancellations in two directions* (from numerator to denominator as usual AND from denominator to numerator).

Sample Problem — Derived Unit Conversions

Convert 55.0 km/h into m/s

What to Think about	How to Do It
1. The numerator requires conversion of a prefixed metric unit to a base metric unit. This portion involves one step only and is similar to sample problem one above.	$\frac{55.0\ \text{km}}{\text{h}} \times \frac{\text{m}}{\text{km}} \times \frac{\text{h}}{\text{min}} \times \frac{\text{min}}{\text{s}}$
2. The denominator involves a time conversion from hours to minutes to seconds. The denominator conversion usually follows the numerator. Always begin by putting all conversion factors in place using *units only*. Now that this has been done, insert the appropriate numerical values for each conversion factor.	$= \frac{\text{m}}{\text{s}}$ $\frac{55.0\ \cancel{\text{km}}}{\cancel{\text{h}}} \times \frac{10^3\ \text{m}}{1\ \cancel{\text{km}}} \times \frac{1\ \cancel{\text{h}}}{60\ \cancel{\text{min}}} \times \frac{1\ \cancel{\text{min}}}{60\ \text{s}}$
3. As always, state the answer with units and round to the correct number of significant figures (in this case, three).	$= \frac{15.3\ \text{m}}{\text{s}}$

Practice Problems — Derived Unit Conversions

1. Convert 2.67 g/mL into kg/L. Why has the numerical value remained unchanged?

2. Convert the density of neon gas from 8.9994×10^{-4} mg/mL into kg/L.

3. Convert 35 mi/h (just over the speed limit in a U.S. city) into m/s. (Given: 5280 feet = 1 mile)

Use of a Value with a Derived Unit as a Conversion Factor

A quantity expressed with a derived unit may be used to convert a unit that measures one thing into a unit that measures something else completely. The most common examples are the use of rate to convert between distance and time and the use of density to convert between mass and volume. These are challenging! The keys to this type of problem are determining which form of the conversion factor to use and where to start.

Suppose we wish to use the speed of sound (330 m/s) to determine the time (in hours) required for an explosion to be heard 5.0 km away. It is always a good idea to begin any conversion problem by considering what we are trying to find. Begin with the end in mind. This allows us to decide where to begin. Do we start with 5.0 km or 330 m/s?

First, consider: are you attempting to convert a unit → unit, or a $\frac{\text{unit}}{\text{unit}} \rightarrow \frac{\text{unit}}{\text{unit}}$?

As the answer is unit → unit, begin with the single unit: km. The derived unit will serve as the conversion factor.

Second, which of the two possible forms of the conversion factor will allow conversion of a distance in km into a time in h? Do we require $\frac{330\text{ m}}{1\text{ s}}$ or $\frac{1\text{ s}}{330\text{ m}}$? As the distance unit must cancel, the second form is the one we require. Hence, the correct approach is

$$5.0\,\cancel{\text{km}} \times \frac{10^3\,\cancel{\text{m}}}{1\,\cancel{\text{km}}} \times \frac{1\text{s}}{330\,\cancel{\text{m}}} \times \frac{1\,\cancel{\text{min}}}{60\text{ s}} \times \frac{1\text{ h}}{60\,\cancel{\text{min}}} = 4.2 \times 10^{-3}\text{ h}$$

Sample Problem — Use of Density as a Conversion Factor

What is the volume in L of a 15.0 kg piece of zinc metal? (Density of Zn = 7.13 g/mL)

What to Think about	How to Do It
1. Decide what form of the conversion factor to use: g/mL or the reciprocal, mL/g. Always begin by arranging the factors using *units* only. As the answer will contain one unit, begin with one unit, in this case, kg.	$15.0\text{ kg} \times \frac{\text{g}}{\text{kg}} \times \frac{\text{mL}}{\text{g}} \times \frac{\text{L}}{\text{mL}} = \text{L}$
2. Insert the appropriate numerical values for each conversion factor. In order to cancel a mass and convert to a volume, use the reciprocal of the density: $\frac{1\text{mL}}{7.13\text{ g}}$	$15.0\,\cancel{\text{kg}} \times \frac{10^3\,\cancel{\text{g}}}{1\,\cancel{\text{kg}}} \times \frac{1\,\cancel{\text{mL}}}{7.13\,\cancel{\text{g}}} \times \frac{10^{-3}\text{ L}}{1\,\cancel{\text{mL}}} = 2.10\text{ L}$
3. Calculate the answer with correct unit and number of significant digits.	

Practice Problems — Use of Rate and Density as Conversion Factors

1. The density of mercury metal is 13.6 g/mL. What is the mass of 2.5 L?

2. The density of lead is 11.2 g/cm³. The volumes 1 cm³ and 1 mL are exactly equivalent. What is the volume in L of a 16.5 kg piece of lead?

3. The speed of light is 3.0×10^{10} cm/s. Sunlight takes 8.29 min to travel from the photosphere (light-producing region) of the Sun to Earth. How many kilometers is Earth from the Sun?

Conversions Involving Units with Exponents (Another Kind of Derived Unit)

If a unit is squared or cubed, it may be cancelled in one of two ways. It may be written more than once to convey that it is being multiplied by itself *or* it may be placed in brackets with the exponent applied to the *number* inside the brackets as well as to the *unit*. Hence, the use of the equivalency 1 L = 1 dm³ to convert 1 m³ to L might appear in either of these formats:

$$1\ \text{m}^3 \times \frac{1\ \text{dm}}{10^{-1}\ \text{m}} \times \frac{1\ \text{dm}}{10^{-1}\ \text{m}} \times \frac{1\ \text{dm}}{10^{-1}\ \text{m}} \times \frac{1\ \text{L}}{1\ \text{dm}^3} = 1\ \text{m}^3 \times \left(\frac{1\ \text{dm}}{10^{-1}\ \text{m}}\right)^3 \times \frac{1\ \text{L}}{1\ \text{dm}^3} = 1000\ \text{L}$$

Sample Problem – Use of Conversion Factors Containing Exponents

Convert 0.35 m³ (cubic meters) into mL. (1 mL = 1 cm³)

What to Think about

1. The unit cm must be cancelled three times. Do this by multiplying the conversion factor by itself three times or through the use of brackets.
2. Once the units have been aligned correctly, insert the appropriate numerical values.
3. Calculate the answer with the correct unit and number of significant figures.

How to Do It

$$0.35\ \text{m}^3 \times \frac{\text{cm}}{\text{m}} \times \frac{\text{cm}}{\text{m}} \times \frac{\text{cm}}{\text{m}} \times \frac{\text{mL}}{\text{cm}^3} = \text{mL}$$

or $0.35\ \text{m}^3 \times \left(\frac{\text{cm}}{\text{m}}\right)^3 \times \frac{\text{mL}}{\text{cm}^3} = \text{mL}$

$$0.35\ \text{m}^3 \times \frac{1\ \text{cm}}{10^{-2}\ \text{m}} \times \frac{1\ \text{cm}}{10^{-2}\ \text{m}} \times \frac{1\ \text{cm}}{10^{-2}\ \text{m}} \times \frac{1\ \text{mL}}{1\ \text{cm}^3}$$

$= 3.5 \times 10^5\ \text{mL}$

or $0.35\ \text{m}^3 \times \left(\frac{1\ \text{cm}}{10^{-2}\ \text{m}}\right)^3 \times \frac{1\ \text{mL}}{1\ \text{cm}^3} = 3.5 \times 10^5\ \text{mL}$

Practice Problems — Use of Conversion Factors Containing Exponents

1. Convert 4.3 dm³ into cm³.

2. Atmospheric pressure is 14.7 lb/in². Convert this to the metric unit, g/cm². (Given 454 g = 1.00 lb)

3. Convert a density of 8.2 kg/m³ to lb/ft³ using factors provided in this section.

Measurement of Temperature

Temperature is a measure of the intensity of heat. It is the average kinetic energy of the particles is sample of matter. Heat is the energy transferred between two objects in contact with one another at different temperatures. There are several different scales for measuring temperature. Three of these scales are commonly used, two in physical sciences and one in engineering. The earliest instrument for measuring the intensity of heat involved measuring the expansion and contraction of water and was called a *thermoscope*. This device was invented by an Italian, named Santorio in the late 1500's. The thermoscope, later called the thermometer, was refined around the same time by Galileo Galilei.

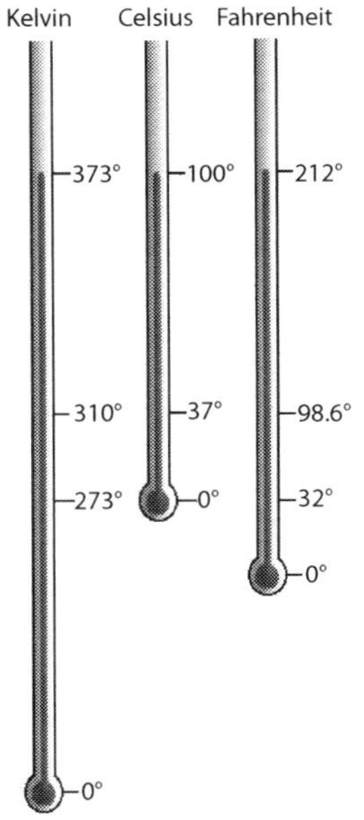

Figure 5.3.3 *The three commonly used temperature scales*

It wasn't until the early 1700s that the Swede Andres Celsius and the German Daniel Gabriel Fahrenheit applied measured scales of temperature to tubes containing alcohol and later, for more precision, mercury. Celsius devised a scale of temperature giving the value of 0°C to the temperature at which water freezes and 100°C to the temperature at which water boils. Fahrenheit, apparently in an attempt to avoid the use of negative numbers on really cold German days, used the coldest temperature he could produce with rock salt and ice as his zero point. His original scale was later adjusted so that the freezing point of water was 32°F and the boiling point of water was 212°F.

In the mid 1800s, Lord William Thomson Kelvin of Scotland, a student at Cambridge University who eventually became a professor at the University of Glasgow, developed the idea of an absolute temperature scale. His theory was that there was an absolute coldest temperature that could ever be attained. This temperature was called **absolute zero** and would be 273.15°C colder than the freezing point of water. The boiling point of water on the absolute scale would be 100°C *and* 100 Kelvin units hotter than the freezing point.

Comparison of these scales helps you see how to convert from one scale to another (Figure 1.4.3). Not only are the conversion factors of 100°C/180°F and 100°C/100 K degrees, which result in 1°C /1.8°F and 1 °C/1 K important, but the difference at the freezing point of water is also important. This requires the addition or subtraction of 32°F and 273.15 K (or slightly less precisely, 273 K) as well.

Consequently, you could simply memorize the following equations for conversion:

$$T_F = \frac{1.8°F}{1°C}(T_C) + 32\,°F \quad \text{and} \quad T_C = (T_F - 32°F) \times \frac{1°C}{1.8°F}$$

Or, even easier (your teacher may elect to use 273 exactly as the addition/subtraction factor):

$$T_K = T_C\frac{(1\text{ K})}{(1°C)} + 273.15\text{ K} \quad \text{and} \quad T_c = (T_k - 273.15\text{ K}) \times \frac{1°C}{1\text{ K}}$$

The number of significant figures in a temperature is generally determined by using the rule of precision**.** That is, if the given temperature is good to the *tenths*, the temperature in the new units is good to the *tenths*. Similarly, if the given temperature was a whole number (good to the ones place), the new temperature should also be stated to the ones place. It is interesting to note by convention there is no degree symbol (°) placed before K.

Some people prefer to memorize formulas and apply them. However, it is nearly always easier to apply logic to derive a method for converting from one unit to another. Notice this method of derivation in the next sample problem.

Sample Problem — Conversion of the Celsius to Fahrenheit Temperature Scale

Convert a warm day temperature from 25.2°C to °F.

What to Think about

1. Is the Fahrenheit temperature bigger or smaller than 25.2°C?
   Based on our common sense understanding, °F should be larger. This means the difference of 32°F should be added to the 25.2°C.
2. Should the 32°F be added to 25.2°C *now*, or following a conversion to °F?
   Units of different types *cannot* be added to one another, so the conversion *must* be completed first.
3. The conversion to °F must occur first and then 32°F should be added on. There are 1.8 F degrees for each 1 C degree.
   Needless to say, the answer is calculated to the *tenths place* as that is the precision of the original temperature given in the problem!
   The final temperature is rounded to the *TENTHS* of a degree.

How to Do It

$25.2°C \times \frac{°F}{°C}$

$25.2°C \times \frac{1.8\ °F}{1°C}\ (+\ 32°F) = 77.4\ °C$

Practice Problems — Conversion Between Units of Temperature

1. Cesium metal is very soft. It has a melting point below body temperature. Convert cesium's melting point of 28.4°C to °F.
2. Air can be liquefied at a temperature of –319°F. Convert this to °C.
3. Convert absolute zero (the coldest possible temperature) from 0 K to °F. Hint: convert to °C first.

5.3 Activity: Our Life in the Metric System

Question

How does our everyday life measure up in the metric system?

Background

Use a measuring tape, a bathroom scale, an odometer on the family car (or an estimate of the distance to school), and be aware of the number of students in your school.

Procedure

1. Measure your height in inches and record it in the table below.
2. Measure the width of your classroom in feet. Convert a fraction of a foot to tenths of a foot. For example, 6 inches or ½ of a foot would be 0.5 ft, 3 inches would be 0.25 foot, etc.
3. Measure the weight of your body in pounds (lb) on a bathroom scale.
4. Determine the distance from your house to your school in miles. If you have to estimate, assume 10 blocks equals 1 mile. Convert fractions of a block to decimals as suggested in procedure two above.

Results and Discussion

Using the space below, calculate the missing distances in the following table. Compare the distances with the units you are familiar with. Show the conversions required.

Measurement	Imperial Measurement	Metric Measurement
Your height	in	cm
Room width	ft	m
Body weight	lb	kg
Home distance	mi	km

5.3 Review Questions

1. Show your work and the result for each of the following conversions.

Measurement	Given Unit	Calculation	Required Unit
Grain of salt's mass	415 μg		g
Earth to the Moon's distance	384.4 Mm		m
Mass of a nickel	3.976 g		μg
Volumetric pipette length	4.5 dm		m
Smoke particle's mass	1.05×10^{-12} g		ng
Distance from home to work	24.99 km		m

2. Show your work and the result for each of the following conversions.

Measurement	Given Unit	Calculation	Required Unit
Energy to heat a grande latte to 65°C	83.60 kJ		MJ
Mass of a college chemistry text	2.54 kg		cg
Average light bulb wattage	600.0 dW		nW
Volume of a can of soda	355 mL		cL
Average time to send one text message	185 das		ms
Distance from Detroit to Boston	987 km		dm

3. The official Mini web site states that the Mini Cooper gets 14.25 km/L fuel economy. Express this value in miles per gallon. (Given 1.609 = 1 mile, 1 gal = 4.546 L)

4. The maximum highway speed limit in some States is 110 km/h. Express this speed in units of meters per second.

5. The density of tantalum (a heavy metal used in cell phone production) is 16.7 g/mL. What is this value in units of lb/L? (Given 1.00 kg = 2.21 lb)

6. The average energy consumption for a new Samsung refrigerator is 5.47×10^2 kWh/year. What is the average energy consumption of this refrigerator in gigajoules per day? (Given 1 GJ = 277.8 kWh, 1year = 365 days)

7. The density of pure iridium metal is 22.68 kg/dm^3. Express this density in units of g/cm^3.

8. The density of mercury metal is 13.6 g/mL. What is the mass of 1.00 L of mercury? Express your answer in kg.

9. Use the Mini Cooper mileage rate in question 3 above to determine how many meters a Mini could travel if its tank contained 120 dL of fuel.

10. Silver has a density of 10.5 g/cm^3. If you have a pure silver coin with a mass of 6.00 g (about the same as a quarter), what is the volume of silver in the coin? Express your answer in units of mL. (1 mL = 1 cm^3)

11. Isopropyl alcohol (also called rubbing alcohol) has a density of 8.34 lb/gal. A large jug of rubbing alcohol weighs 2.3 kg. Determine the volume of this jug in mL. (Given 454 g = 1 pound. Check question 3.)

12. The planet of Bark is fond of dogs of all types. The inhabitants trade the animals much as art collectors on Earth trade sculptures and paintings: 1 pit bull is worth 3 collies; 2 collies are worth 5 poodles; 3 poodles are worth 7 dobermans; 1 doberman is worth 9 german sheep dogs. An inhabitant of Bark (often called a "Bow-wow") owns 4 pit bulls. How many German sheep dogs may she obtain?

13. The planet of Purr is fond of cats of all types. The inhabitants trade the animals with one another: 1 calico is worth 5 Siamese; 2 Siamese are worth 7 Persians; 3 Persians are worth 8 tabbies; 1 tabby is worth 6 Heinz Fifty-Sevens. An inhabitant of Purr (often called a "Purrsian") owns 2 calico cats. How many Heinz Fifty-Sevens may she obtain?

14. What is the engine piston displacement in liters of an engine whose displacement is listed at 325 in^3? (Given: 1 L = 1dm^3)

15. Standard atmospheric pressure on a cold day (0°C) at sea level is 14.7 lb/in^2 (this unit is sometimes written as psi). Determine this atmospheric pressure in units of kg/cm^2. (Given: 1.00 lb = 454 g)

16. If a gallon of paint can cover 400. square feet what is this paint coverage expressed in square meters per liter (1 gal = 4.546 L)?

17. The ignition temperature is the temperature at which something catches fire and burns on its own. The ignition temperature of paper is 451°F. What is this value in °C?

18. In Geneva, on the April 10, 2007, the first sector of CERN's Large Hadron Collider (LHC) was cooled to reach a temperature of 1.9 K. That is colder than deep outer space! What was the temperature of this sector of the LHC expressed in °F?

19. The coldest temperature recorded in Antarctica, the home of the Emperor penguin, was recorded to be –89°C at the Voskok Station on July 21, 1983. An American scientist converted –89°C to °F for the benefit the media. What temperature did the media report to the public expressed in °F?

20. A springlike day in Denver Colorado in February may register a temperature of 9.0°C. Convert to °F.

5.4 Relative Atomic Mass

Warm Up

We express amounts of materials in different ways.

1. Complete the grocery list by filling in the missing units (Figure 3.1a).
   One __________ eggs, Two __________ milk, Three __________ flour
2. From your answer to #1, what are the three ways that we typically express amounts of materials?
   (a) number of items (b) ____________________ (c) ____________________

Relative Mass

Experimental chemistry is essentially figuring out things about matter that cannot be observed directly. The joy of experimental chemistry lies in figuring out how to figure it out. Consider the following ingenious method for determining the relative masses of objects without needing to know their actual masses. **Mass** is the amount of matter. When you say that one object has twice as much mass as another you are expressing the object's **relative mass**. You are comparing one object's mass to the other's.

Suppose you wanted to determine the relative mass of a staple and a grain of rice, each of which is too small to register a mass on your balance (Figure 5.4.1). Why not weigh 100 of each? If 100 identical staples weigh twice as much as 100 identical grains of rice then one staple will weigh twice as much as one grain of rice. The nifty aspect of this technique is that we don't even need to know how many objects we are weighing: we just need to know that we're weighing the same number of each. If some number of staples weighs twice as much as the same number of rice grains then any number of staples will weigh twice as much as that number of rice grains.

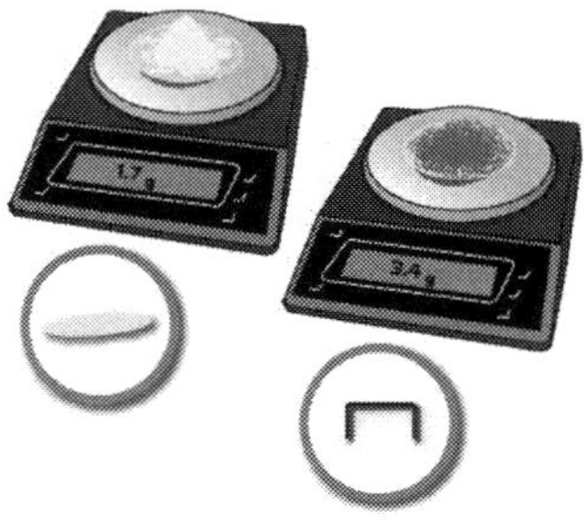

Figure 5.4.1 *One hundred staples and one hundred grains of rice have the same mass ratio as one staple and one grain of rice, 2:1.*

This technique for determining relative mass still works even if the items being weighed are not identical. If the items being weighed for comparison are not identical, then the ratio provided is that of their average masses rather than the ratio of the masses of the individual items since this would depend on which individual items. For example, if a variety of pens weighs 1.52 times as much as the same number of a variety of pencils then the average mass of these pens is 1.52 times the average mass of these pencils.

> The mass ratio of any equal number of items equals the average mass ratio of those individual items.

While you should never confuse the terms "weight" and "mass," the word "weigh" serves double duty. To **weigh** is to find the weight or compare the weights of. Since scales work by comparing weights, you are by definition "weighing" objects and materials with a scale. In fact, a **weighing scale** is a measuring instrument for determining the mass or weight of an object.

Quick Check

1. What does "relative mass" mean? ____
2. You have two bags of candy from a bulk food store: a bag of gumdrops and a bag of jujubes. You intend to determine the relative masses of a jujube and a gumdrop by weighing the contents of each bag. What condition is necessary for this to work? ____

Law of Constant Composition

In this book, as in most chemistry textbooks, much of our current chemical knowledge will be presented in historical context. Instead of just telling you what we know (or think we know), we'll tell you how chemists came to this understanding. This is because chemistry is more than just an accumulated list of facts about matter: it is also the processes that lead us to such information. By learning and assessing these processes, as well as the facts, some of you will decide to continue this quest. In addition, people often acquire a better understanding of a concept by learning the concept in the same manner that it was originally developed.

To use the technique just described to determine the relative masses of different types of atoms, chemists needed to be able to weigh an equal number of different types of atoms. In the early 1800s, chemists discovered that all samples of a given compound have the same mass ratio of their constituent elements. For example, there are 8 g of oxygen for every 1 g of hydrogen in every sample of water. This is called the **law of constant composition**. In 1804, John Dalton, a scientist in England, argued that the law of constant composition not only supported the concept of atoms but also provided their relative masses. He reasoned that the mass ratios in which different elements combine are the mass ratios of their individual atoms or a simple multiple thereof. If one atom of magnesium weighs 1.5 times as much as one atom of oxygen then any number of magnesium atoms would weigh 1.5 times as much as the same number of oxygen atoms. Dalton argued that this was the reason all samples of a compound contained the same mass ratio of its elements.

Sample Problem — Determining Relative Atomic Mass

A chemist carefully heats 0.350 g of magnesium powder in a crucible. The magnesium reacts with atmospheric oxygen to produce 0.580 g of magnesium oxide (MgO). What is the mass of a magnesium atom relative to the mass of an oxygen atom?

What to Think about	How to Do It
1. 0.350 g Mg must have combined with 0.230 g O to produce 0.580 g MgO.	0.580 g MgO − 0.350 g Mg = 0.230 g O
2. Since magnesium oxide has the formula MgO, 0.350 g of magnesium and 0.230 g of oxygen contain equal numbers of atoms.	$\frac{\text{mass of Mg atoms}}{\text{mass of O atoms}} = \frac{0.350\text{ g}}{0.230\text{ g}} = 1.52$
3. If some number of Mg atoms weighs 1.52 times as much as the same number of O atoms then any number of Mg atoms weighs 1.52 times as much as the same number of O atoms, even one of each.	A Mg atom weighs 1.52 times as much as an O atom.

Practice Problems — Determining Relative Atomic Mass

1. A dozen identical AA batteries have a mass of 276 g and a dozen identical watch batteries have a mass of only 26.4 g. The mass of an AA battery is ______ times the mass of a watch battery.

2. A sample of strontium oxide (SrO) is found to contain 2.683 g Sr and 0.490 g O. What is the mass of a strontium atom relative to that of an oxygen atom?

3. A 4.218 g sample of daltonium bromide (DBr) is decomposed and 0.337 g of D is recovered.
   (a) What is the atomic mass of daltonium given that the atomic mass of bromine is 79.9 u?

   ____

   (b) This question uses the fictitious element, daltonium, so you can't just look up the element's atomic mass.

   What element does daltonium represent? ______________________________

Relative Masses of Atoms

According to the sample problem, if all the atoms of an element are identical then the mass of a magnesium atom is 1.52 times the mass of an oxygen atom. If all the atoms of an element do not have the same mass then the average mass of a magnesium atom is 1.52 times the average mass of an oxygen atom. The issue of whether all the atoms of an element are identical wasn't resolved for another century but, as described, we need only insert the word, "average" if they are not.

The element hydrogen was discovered to have the least massive atoms so its atoms were originally assigned an atomic mass of 1 u (atomic mass unit) and the mass of all the other types of atoms were expressed relative to this. The discussion of atomic mass and atomic mass units will continue in chapter 5. Oxygen's atomic mass of 16 u means that the mass of an oxygen atom is 16 times the mass of a hydrogen atom (or that the average mass of an oxygen atom is 16 times the average mass of a hydrogen atom) (Figure 5.4.2). If the mass of a magnesium atom is 1.52 times the mass of an oxygen atom then the mass of a magnesium atom is 1.52 × 16.0 u = 24.3 u. The periodic table of the elements confirms that magnesium has a relative atomic mass of 24.3 u.

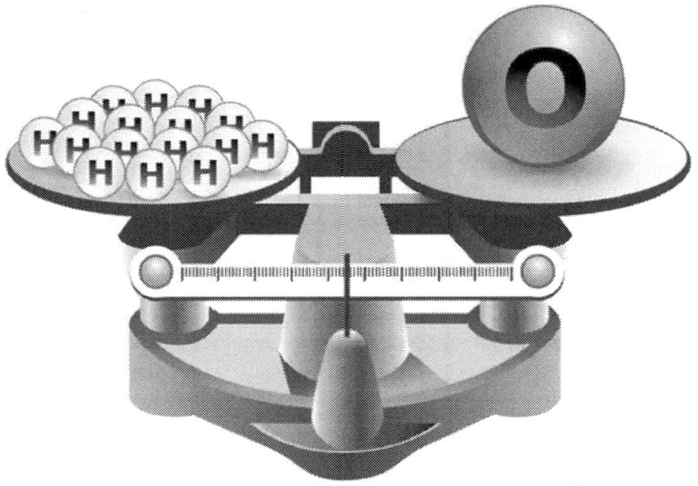

Figure 5.4.2 *The mass of an oxygen atom is equal to the mass of 16 hydrogen atoms.*

Determining the relative masses of the basic units of matter was a remarkable feat. Dalton bridged the gap between the world we experience and the invisible world of atoms by deriving the relative masses of atoms from laboratory observations. But how did Dalton know that the formula of magnesium oxide was MgO? Recall Dalton's important qualification: "or a simple multiple thereof." If the formula of magnesium oxide is MgO_2 then the mass ratio of Mg to O in the compound would need to be doubled to determine their atomic mass ratio. This is necessary because we are weighing half as many magnesium atoms. Therefore, the same number of magnesium atoms would weigh twice as much. Similar adaptations would be required for other possible formulas.

Sample Problem — Determining Relative Atomic Mass (Non 1:1 Formulas)

Barium chloride has a mass ratio of 1.934 g Ba:1.000 g Cl. Chlorine has an atomic mass of 35.5 u. What is the atomic mass of barium if the formula of barium chloride is $BaCl_2$?

What to Think about	How to Do It
If the formula is $BaCl_2$ then we need to double the mass of barium so that we can compare the masses of equal numbers of atoms.	$2(1.934) \times 35.5\ u = 137.3\ u$

Practice Problems — Determining Relative Atomic Mass (Non 1:1 Formulas)

Aluminum iodide has a mass ratio of 1.000 g Al: 14.100 g I. Given that the atomic mass of iodine is 126.9 u, what is the atomic mass of aluminum if the formula of aluminum iodide is:

1. Al I_3? ______________________ 2. Al_2I_3? ______________________

Cannizzaro's Paper

Dalton assumed that atoms combined in the simplest manner possible. He believed that if a pair of elements (A + B) formed only one compound, the formula for the compound would be AB. If they formed a second compound, its formula would be either A_2B or AB_2. Dalton was well aware that he had no evidence for his "rules of simplicity." He conceded that some of his formulas and resulting atomic mass determinations might be incorrect. As you may recall from earlier science classes, the formulas of ionic compounds are simple ratios, but not quite as simple as Dalton supposed.

On September 3, 1860, many of Europe's leading chemists met in Karlsruhe, Germany. At this meeting, the Italian chemist Stanislao Cannizzaro presented a remarkable paper in which he solved the mystery of atomic masses. For example, Dalton hadn't understood how two particles of hydrogen gas could react with one particle of oxygen gas to produce two particles of water vapor. He thought that couldn't happen because it would require splitting the oxygen particle, which he thought was an atom. Cannizzaro showed that Dalton's atomic model was still valid if the hydrogen and oxygen gas particles were made up of pairs of atoms. Hydrogen and oxygen molecules are called **diatomic molecules** because they are formed of two atoms of the same element ("di" means 2).

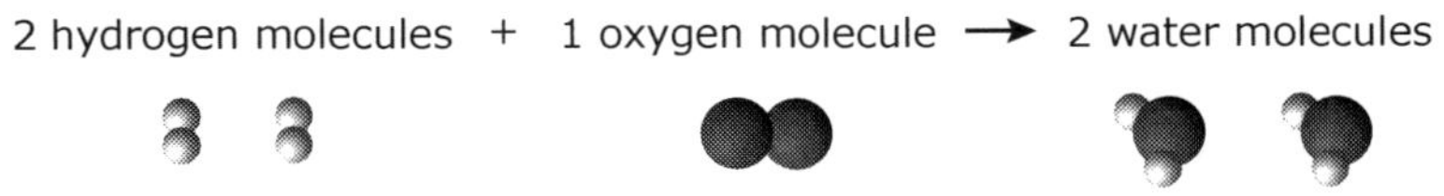

Figure 5.4.3 *Diatomic molecules of hydrogen and oxygen combine to form water molecules.*

Cannizzaro's paper went on to describe and explain three other techniques for determining atomic mass: one for metals, one for liquid or gaseous non-metals, and one for solid non-metals.

Dalton is called the father of the atomic theory because he explained how the law of constant composition provided support for the concept of atoms. However, additional methods were required to determine the relative atomic masses. These atomic masses were, in turn, used to determine the correct formulas of compounds. Dmitri Mendeleev, who published his first periodic table of the elements in 1869, was at Karlsruhe. The correct atomic masses were a prerequisite to Mendeleev's famous table.

5.4 Activity: The Relative Mass of Paper Clips

Question

What is the mass of a large paper clip relative to that of a small paper clip?
(We'll answer this question without weighing only one paper clip of either type.)

Background

If some number of large paper clips weighs twice as much as the same number of small paper clips then any number of large paper clips will weigh twice as much as the same number of small paper clips, including one of each. Remember we don't need to know how many paper clips we are weighing; we just need to know that we're weighing the same number of each. The mass ratio of any equal number of identical items equals the mass ratio of the individual items.

Procedure

1. Weigh a pile of small paper clips. Record this mass in the table provided below.
2. Attach a large paper clip to each small paper clip and measure the total mass of these coupled clips. Record this mass in the table provided below.
3. Calculate the total mass of the attached large paper clips and record this mass in the table below.

Results and Discussion

Objects	Mass (g)
Small paper clips	
Coupled paper clips	
Large paper clips	

1. $\dfrac{\text{mass of some number of large paper clips}}{\text{mass of the same number of small paper clips}} = \dfrac{\underline{\qquad\qquad} \text{ g}}{\underline{\qquad\qquad} \text{ g}} = \underline{\qquad\qquad}$

   The mass of a large paper clip is _______ times the mass of a small paper clip.

2. If we assign a small paper clip a mass of 1.00 smu (stationary mass unit), what is the mass of a large paper clip?

3. Let's check this result by weighing one small paper clip and one large paper clip.

   $\dfrac{\text{mass of one large paper clip}}{\text{mass of one small paper clip}} = \dfrac{\underline{\qquad\qquad} \text{ g}}{\underline{\qquad\qquad} \text{ g}} = \underline{\qquad\qquad}$

4. Why might the ratios calculated in steps 1 and 3 be slightly different?

5.4 Review Questions

1. A certain number of identical glass marbles has a mass of 825 g. The same number of identical steel marbles has a mass of 2245 g.
   (a) Assigning a glass marble a mass of 1.00 mmu (marble mass unit), calculate the mass of a steel marble.

   (b) Why don't you need to know the number of marbles that were weighed?

2. 1.965 g of sodium is placed in a flask containing chlorine gas. 5.000 g of NaCl is produced in the resulting reaction.
   (a) A sodium atom's mass is ______ times a chlorine atom's mass.

   (b) Chlorine has an atomic mass of 35.5 u. What is the atomic mass of sodium?

3. A 10.000 g sample of zubenium fluoride (ZuF) is decomposed and 8.503 g of Zu is recovered.
   (a) What is the atomic mass of zubenium?

   (b) This question uses the fictitious element zubenium so you can't just look up the element's atomic mass. What element does zubenium represent?

4. Zinc sulfide has a mass ratio of 2.037 g Zn: 1.000 g S. Given that the atomic mass of sulfur is 32.1 u, what is the atomic mass of zinc if the formula of zinc sulfide is:
   (a) ZnS?

   (b) ZnS_2?

   (c) Zn_3S_2?

5. A compound of copper and oxygen contains 13.073 g Cu and 1.647 g O. Oxygen has an atomic mass of 16.0 u.
   (a) What is the atomic mass of copper if the formula of the above compound is CuO?

   (b) What is the atomic mass of copper if the formula of the above compound is Cu_2O?

   (c) What is the atomic mass of copper if the formula of the above compound is CuO_2?

6. In 1819, Dulong and Petit noted a relationship between the presumed atomic mass of most metals and their specific heats. The specific heat of a metal divided into 25.0 provides the approximate atomic mass of the metal. The specific heat of a substance is the amount of heat required to raise 1 g of the substance by 1°C. The specific heat of copper is 0.3864 J/g°C.
   (a) Calculate the approximate atomic mass of copper using Dulong and Petit's method.

   (b) Knowing the approximate atomic mass of the metal allowed chemists to determine which of the more accurate atomic masses derived by composition analysis was correct. Which of the atomic masses and corresponding formulas calculated in question 5 is correct for the compound that was analyzed?

7. Determine the percent error of Dulong and Petit's method of approximating a metal's atomic mass for aluminum (0.903 J/g°C), magnesium (1.05 J/g°C) and silver (0.23772 J/g°C).

8. In 1811 Amedeo Avogadro proposed that equal volumes of any gas at the same temperature and pressure contain *the same number of particles*. Cannizzaro realized this allows scientists to weigh equal numbers of atoms of different gaseous elements and determine their relative atomic masses. Complete the following data table showing the mass of equal volumes of two different gases at the same temperature and pressure.

Element	Mass of Gas (g)	Relative Atomic Mass (u)
H	0.210	1.0
	7.455	

9. Potassium has an atomic mass of 39.1 u. What does this mean?

10. Look up the following elements in the periodic table and report each element's atomic mass.

(a) P ____________

(b) Ca ____________

(c) U ____________

11. Eight identical forks have a mass of 213.1 g. Eight identical knives have a mass of 628.2 g.

(a) What is the mass of a knife relative to that of a fork?

(b) Why did you not need to divide the supplied masses by 8 to answer 11(a)?

(c) What could you conclude from this data if the utensils of each type were not identical?

12. A mint is advertising a special set of silver coins containing a 10 g coin, a 20 g coin and a 30 g coin. One of these coins is accidentally being made 1 g lighter than its advertised mass. You have two sets of these coins and have been challenged to identify the undersized coin by weighing only one pile of coins. The single pile may include any combination of the coins that you wish. What combination of the coins would you weigh? How can you use that mass to identify the undersized coin?

5.5 Introducing the Mole — The Central Unit of Chemistry

Warm Up

1. It takes 15 gulps to drink a bottle of water. What information would allow you to calculate how many *slurps* it would take to drink an identical bottle of water?

   ____

2. If 4 slurps = 1 gulp, how many slurps would it take to consume a 15-gulp drink?

   ____

3. If 5 slurps equal 1 gulp, how many gulps would it take to consume a 20-slurp drink? ____________

The Mole Concept

What mass of oxygen has the same number of atoms as 1 g of hydrogen? An oxygen atom (16 u) weighs 16 times as much as a hydrogen atom (1 u). Therefore, it would require 16 g of oxygen to have the same number of atoms as 1 g of hydrogen. Chemists extended this reasoning to all the elements. For example, 55.8 g Fe, 35.5 g Cl, 23.0 g Na, and 12.0 g C all contain the same number of atoms since these masses are in the same ratios as their individual atomic masses. How many atoms are there in the atomic mass of any element expressed in grams? Originally chemists didn't know and even now they only have a very rough estimate but they nevertheless gave a name to that number. They called this number a "mole."

> A **mole** is a quantity equal to the number of atoms in the atomic mass of any element expressed in grams (e.g., the number of atoms in 1.0 g H, 16.0 g O, 63.5 g Cu).

The definition of the mole is under continuous review. It is "fine-tuned" periodically in response to new information about atomic structure and to changes in the definition of the atomic mass unit on which the definition of the mole is based.

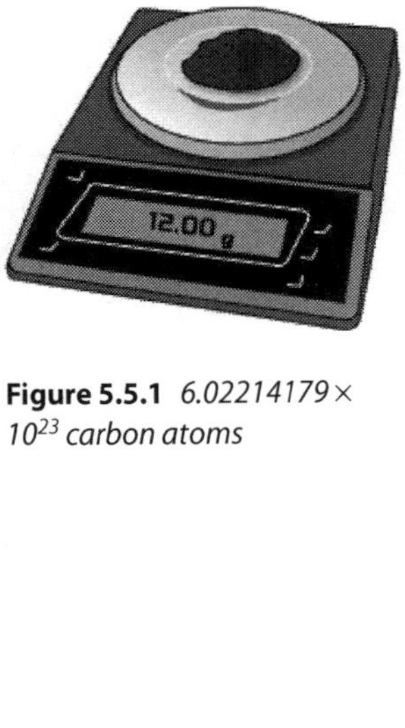

Figure 5.5.1 *6.02214179 × 10^{23} carbon atoms*

The number of things in a mole is also referred to as **Avogadro's number** in honor of the Italian scientist whose insight regarding gases led to a technique for determining the relative atomic masses of non-metals. Just as the word "dozen" refers to a number of something, so does the word "mole." The chief difference is that we know that a dozen is 12 of something but we only have a rough estimate of how many things are in a mole of something. There have been many independent derivations of the number of items in a mole. Chemists currently estimate that a mole is $6.02214179 \times 10^{23}$ give or take a few million billion (Figure 5.5.1). The actual number isn't important unless you're working at the atomic level because whatever the number is, it's the same for a mole of anything.

Just as a dozen is 12 of anything, a mole is approximately 6.02×10^{23} of anything. While a dozen is a fairly small number, a mole is an absurdly large number. A mole of peas would cover the entire Earth's surface with a layer over 200 m deep. Atoms are so small however that you can hold a mole of atoms in the palm of your hand. Just as a dozen is a convenient unit of quantity for a baker to group buns and doughnuts, a mole is a convenient unit of quantity for a chemist to group atoms and molecules. The number of items is one way to express the amount of a material so chemists often refer to a mole of a substance rather than a mole of the substance's particles (e.g., a mole of copper instead of a mole of copper atoms).

The mole was introduced in the early 1900s by Wilhelm Ostwald. Ironically, Ostwald developed the mole concept as an alternative to the atomic theory, which he did not accept. Today, the mole is used throughout modern chemistry as the central unit through which all other quantities of materials are related, but it was not common before the mid-1950s, just two generations of chemists ago. Before that, chemists related quantities of chemicals through their atomic masses without reference to the mole.

Quick Check

1. (a) How is a mole like a dozen?

   ____

   (b) How is a mole different than a dozen?

   ____

2. What does a mole of chlorine atoms weigh? ____________
3. What mass of sulfur has the same number of atoms that are in 1.0 g H? ____________

Conversions Using Avogadro's Number

Many chemistry problems can be solved by examining the units of the values provided and considering the units that the answer must have. This technique of manipulating units is called "dimensional analysis." While it's important to understand the mathematical operation you're performing, it's reassuring to see that the units work out (i.e., that the answer has the appropriate units).

Most chemical conversions involve the mole. The key to conversion is the conversion factor. Chemists know or know where to find the conversion factors they need. At this point in the course, we'll use only two conversion factors: Avogadro's number (the number of items per mole) and molar mass (the number of grams per mole). The items that a chemist would normally be concerned about are chemical species such as atoms, molecules, ions, and formula units. The abbreviation for the unit mole is mol (Figure 5.5.2).

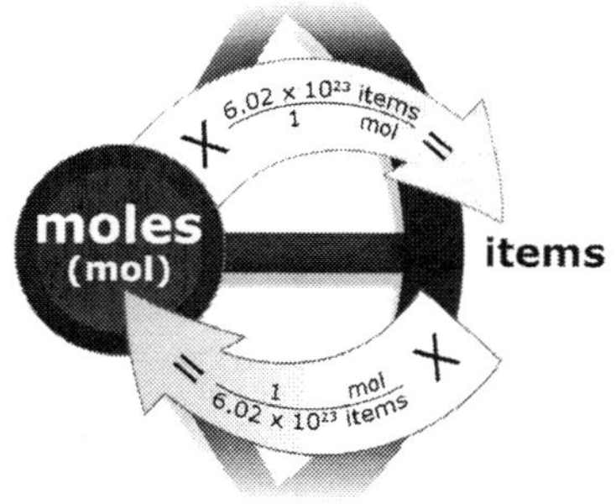

Figure 5.5.2 *Converting the moles and the number of items of a substance*

Name	Equivalence Statement	Conversion Factors	
Avogadro's number	1 mol = 6.02×10^{23} items	$\frac{6.02 \times 10^{23} \text{ items}}{1 \text{ mol}}$	$\frac{1 \text{ mol}}{6.02 \times 10^{23} \text{ items}}$

Sample Problem—Converting Moles to Number of Items

How many oxygen atoms are in 3.2 mol of oxygen atoms?

What to Think about	How to Do It
1. Convert: mol O ⟶ atoms O 2. Setup: $3.2 \text{ mol O} \times \frac{? \text{ atoms O}}{1 \text{ mol O}}$ 3. Conversion factor: 6.02×10^{23} atoms O per 1 mol O	$3.2 \cancel{\text{mol O}} \times \frac{6.02 \times 10^{23} \text{ atoms O}}{1 \cancel{\text{mol O}}} = 1.9 \times 10^{24}$ atoms O
4. Count the number of significant figures of each value in the operation and then round the answer to the least of these.	Note: There is no uncertainty in the 1 mol O. The uncertainty of the conversion factor is expressed in the 6.02×10^{23} atoms O.

Practice Problems—Converting Moles to Number of Items

1. Chromium ions are responsible for the beautiful colors of rubies and emeralds. How many chromium ions (Cr^{3+}) are in 3.5 mol of chromium ions?

2. 30.0 mol H_2O = __________ molecules H_2O

3. How many atoms of sodium are in 0.023 mol Na?

Sample Problem—Converting Number of Items to Moles

7.3×10^{24} carbon monoxide molecules (CO) represent how many moles of carbon monoxide?

What to Think about	How to Do It
1. Convert: molecules CO → mol CO	
2. Setup: $(7.3 \times 10^{24} \text{ molecules CO}) \times \frac{1 \text{ mol CO}}{? \text{ molecules CO}}$	$(7.3 \times 10^{24} \text{ ~~molecules CO~~}) \times \frac{1 \text{ mol CO}}{6.02 \times 10^{23} \text{ ~~molecules CO~~}}$
3. Conversion factor: 1 mol CO per 6.02×10^{23} molecules CO	= 12 mol CO

Practice Problems — Converting Number of Items to Moles

1. Incandescent lights are filled with argon to prevent the glowing filament from burning up. How many moles of argon do 1.81×10^{22} atoms of argon represent?

2. 2.25×10^{24} molecules CO_2 = __________ mol CO_2?

3. A 1-L intravenous bag of saline solution contains 9.27×10^{22} formula units of NaCl. How many moles of NaCl is this?

Molar Mass

The mass of one mole of an element's atoms is called that element's **molar mass** (Figure 5.5.3). It follows from simply restating the definition of a mole that the molar mass of an element is its atomic mass expressed in grams. For example, "one mole is the number of atoms in 16 g of oxygen" can be restated as "one mole of oxygen atoms weighs 16 g." The atomic masses of the elements can be found in the periodic table. The atomic mass of oxygen is 16 u and thus the molar mass of oxygen is 16 g. This is better expressed as a conversion factor for calculation purposes: 16 g per mole of oxygen or 16 g/mol O.

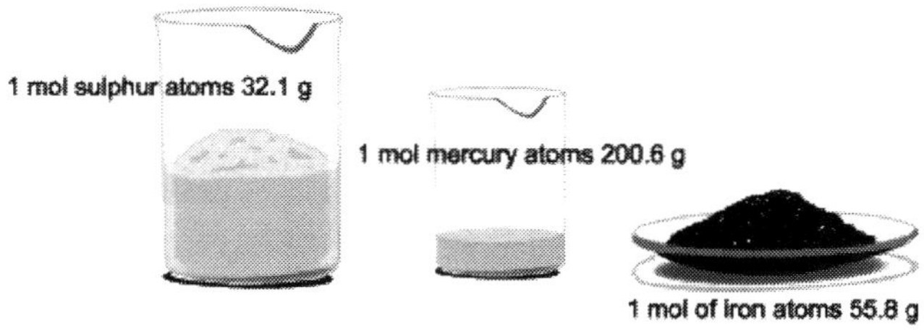

Figure 5.5.3 *The mass of 1 mol of a chemical depends on the atoms that make it up.*

The **molecular mass** or **formula mass** of a compound is the sum of its constituent atomic masses (e.g., H_2O: 2(1 u) + 16 u = 18 u). One mole of water molecules consists of 1 mol of oxygen atoms (16 g) and 2 mol of hydrogen atoms (2 g) and therefore weighs 18 g. Similarly, 1 mol of NaCl formula units consists of 1 mol of sodium atoms (23 g) and 1 mol of chlorine atoms (35.5 g) for a total mass of 58.5 g (Figure 5.5.4).

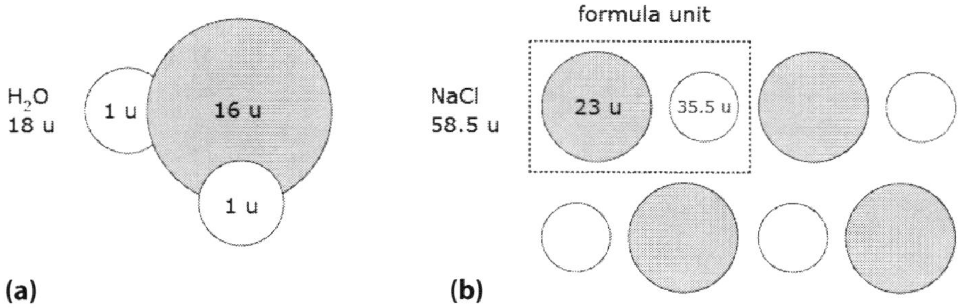

Figure 5.5.4 *(a) The molecular mass of water is the sum of the masses of the oxygen and hydrogen atoms. (b) The formula mass of NaCl is the sum of the masses of sodium and chlorine atoms.*

Just as the molar mass of an element is simply its atomic mass expressed in grams, the **molar mass** of a compound is simply its molecular or formula mass expressed in grams.

The molar mass of a substance is its atomic, molecular, or formula mass expressed in grams.

Sample Problem — Determining a Compound's Formula Mass and/or Molar Mass

What are the formula mass and molar mass of $Al_2(SO_4)_3$?

What to Think About	How to Do It
1. 1 $Al_2(SO_4)_3$ consists of 2 Al's, 3 S's, and 12 O's.	Formula Mass = 2(27.0 u) + 3(32.1 u) + 12(16.0 u) = 342.3 u
2. 1 mol $Al_2(SO_4)_3$ consists of 2 mol Al, 3 mol S and 12 mol O.	Molar Mass = 2(27.0 g) + 3(32.1 g) + 12(16.0 g) = 342.3 g Expressed as a conversion factor, it is 342.3 g/mol.

Practice Problems — Determining a Compound's Formula Mass and/or Molar Mass

1. What is the molecular mass of nitrogen dioxide?

2. What is the molar mass of $Na_2Cr_2O_7$?

3. What is the molar mass of iron(III) sulfide?

Conversions Using Molar Mass

Name	Equivalence Statement	Conversion Factors	
Molar mass	1 mol = ? g	$\frac{?\text{ g}}{1\text{ mol}}$	$\frac{1\text{ mol}}{?\text{ g}}$
Example: H_2O	1 mol = 18.0 g	$\frac{18.0\text{ g}}{1\text{ mol}}$	$\frac{1\text{ mol}}{18.0\text{ g}}$

Sample Problem — Converting Moles to Mass

What is the mass of 3.2 mol of oxygen atoms?

What to Think about

1. Convert: mol O → g O
2. Setup:
   $3.2\text{ mol O} \times \frac{?\text{ g O}}{1\text{ mol O}}$
3. Conversion factor:
   16.0 g O per 1 mol O

How to Do It

$$3.2\text{ }\cancel{\text{mol O}} \times \frac{16.0\text{ g O}}{1\text{ }\cancel{\text{mol O}}} = 51\text{ g O}$$

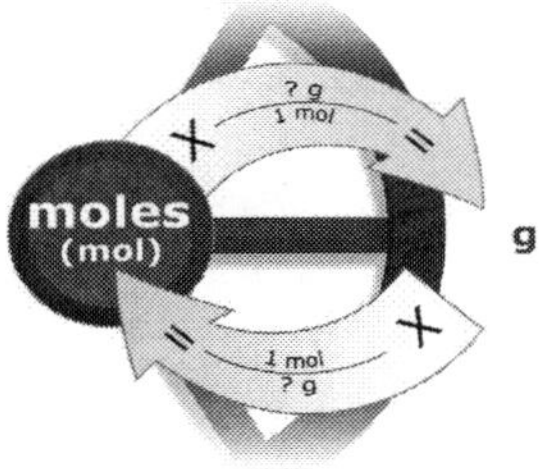

Practice Problems — Converting Moles to Mass

1. What does 2.65 mol of table salt (NaCl) weigh?

2. 0.87 mol NH_3 = ________ g NH_3?

3. Very large quantities of chemicals are produced in the chemical industry. Worldwide production of sulfuric acid (H_2SO_4) is estimated at two trillion (2.0×10^{12}) moles annually. How many tonnes of H_2SO_4 is this? (1 tonne = 1000 kg)

Sample Problem — Converting Mass to Moles

How many moles of water are in 1.8 g of water?

What to Think about	How to Do It
1. Convert: g $H_2O \rightarrow$ mol H_2O 2. Setup: $1.8\ g\ H_2O \times \frac{1\ mol\ H_2O}{?\ g\ H_2O}$ 3. Conversion factor. 1 mol H_2O per 18 g H_2O	$1.8\ \cancel{g\ H_2O} \times \frac{1\ mol\ H_2O}{18.0\ \cancel{g\ H_2O}} = 0.10\ mol\ H_2O$

Practice Problems — Converting Mass to Moles

1. Gold is the most malleable metal. It can be hammered into sheets that are only several hundred atoms thick. In 2010, Vancouver's Science World covered an entire billboard with just two troy ounces (62.2 g) of gold to dramatize this fact. How many moles of gold is this?

2. 3.88 g CO_2 = __________ mol CO_2

3. Smelling salts are used to revive an unconscious athlete. A capsule of smelling salts contains 500.0 mg $(NH_4)_2CO_3$. How many moles of $(NH_4)_2CO_3$ is this?

5.5 Activity: A Mole of Pennies

Question

How long and massive would a stack of 1 mol of pennies be?

Background

The mole is a convenient and useful term for counting very large quantities of things. You know that 1 mol of pennies is approximately 6.02×10^{23} pennies but can you picture just how many that really is? Suppose you stacked 1 mol of pennies. How tall do you think that stack would be? How much would it weigh? Just for fun, try guessing by completing the tables below in pencil before you do the necessary calculations.

Procedure

1. Make a stack of 10 pennies.
2. Measure and record the stack's height in centimeters. ______________
3. Measure and record the stack's mass in grams. ________________

Results and Discussion

1. Calculate the height in kilometers of a stack of 1 mol of pennies.

2.

Would the stack reach...	Distance (km)	✔ or ✗
Moon?	3.9×10^5	
Pluto?	5.9×10^9	
Proxima Centauri (the nearest star)?	4.1×10^{13}	
Andromeda (the nearest galaxy)?	1.9×10^{19}	

3. Calculate the mass in kilograms of 1 mol of pennies.

4.

Would the stack weigh as much as...	Mass (kg)	✔ or ✗
the U.S.S. *Ronald Reagan* (the world's heaviest aircraft carrier)?	2.1×10^7	
the total of all living things on Earth?	2×10^{15}	
Moon?	7.4×10^{22}	
Earth?	6.0×10^{24}	

5.5 Review Questions

1. (a) What is the definition of a mole?

   (b) What is our best estimate of the number of things in a mole?

   (c) What do chemists call this number?

2. (a) What mass of carbon would have the same number of atoms as 1.0 g H?

   (b) What mass of carbon would have the same number of atoms as 3.0 g H?

   (c) What mass of sulfur would have the same number of atoms as 32.0 g O?

3. (a) What does a mole of iron weigh?

   (b) Chemists call this value the ______________________ of iron.

4. (a) What is the molecular mass of propane, C_3H_8?

   (b) What is the formula mass of calcium hydroxide, $Ca(OH)_2$?

   (c) What is the molar mass of carbon tetrachloride, CCl_4?

5. 3.2 mol C = ____________________ atoms C

6. How many molecules are in 0.0085 mol of C_2H_6?

7. 1.4×10^{18} Ag atoms represent how many moles of atoms?

8. 2.99 g Na = ___________ mol Na

9. What is the mass of 5.2 mol of fluorine?

10. Airline regulations prohibit lithium metal batteries that contain over 2.0 g of lithium on passenger aircraft. How many moles of lithium are in 2.0 g Li?

11. What is the mass of 0.32 mol of sodium nitrite?

12. A can of cola contains 58 mg of caffeine, $C_8H_{10}N_4O_2$. How many moles of caffeine are in a can of cola?

13. Carbon dioxide, produced by respiration in plants and animals, causes the slightly acidic nature of normal rain. How many molecules of CO_2 are in 0.725 mol CO_2?

14. The male luna moth can detect specialized chemicals known as pheromones in order to locate a mate. A moth can detect 1.70×10^9 molecules of the pheromone. How many moles of the pheromone is this?

15. Cycling enthusiasts often prefer bicycles made with titanium frames. Titanium is resistant to corrosion and fatigue, has a significantly lower density than steel, and seems to have a natural shock absorbing ability. Suppose a high-quality titanium frame contains 1300 g of titanium. How many moles of titanium does this frame contain?

16. Bluestone is an attractive mineral with the chemical name copper(II) sulfate pentahydrate. What is the mass of a 1.75-mol sample of bluestone?

17. An environmental assessment predicts that a coal plant would emit 8.18×10^6 mol of ammonia into the atmosphere annually. How many tonnes of ammonia is this?

18. Ammonium phosphate is a fertilizer containing nitrogen and phosphorus for healthy plant growth. How many moles of ammonium phosphate are in a bag containing 2.640 kg of it?

19. The movie *Erin Brockovich* dramatizes the efforts of the title character (played by Julia Roberts) to prove that the Pacific Gas and Electric Co. contaminated the water supply of Hinkley, California, with hexavalent chromium. Tin(II) dichromate is a hexavalent chromium compound. What is the mass of 5.925 mol of tin(II) dichromate?

5.6 Mole Conversions

Warm Up

1. Which contains more atoms, 30 g Cl or 15 g C? ____________
2. Which weighs more, 1 mol Zn or 3 mol N? ____________
3. Which contains more molecules, 34 g CH_4 or 58 g O_2? ____________

Two-Step Mole Conversions

The mole serves as a link between the invisible world of atoms and observable quantities of chemicals. The mole is to a chemist what the dollar is to an accountant. Just as the dollar is the central unit of commerce and allows us to keep track of money, the mole is the central unit of chemistry and allows us to keep track of atoms and molecules.

A quantity of a substance can only be related to another quantity of the same substance through the mole.

How would you solve the following problem?
How many atoms are in 5.0 g of copper?

You might split the problem into two parts:

1. How many moles of copper are in 5.0 g Cu?
2. How many copper atoms is this?

This is how chemists solve this type of problem. Think of the mole as the hub of a wheel with the spokes leading out to all the other units. In our wheel model, the spokes represent the conversion factors (Figure 5.6.1).

For now, our conversions are limited to those between moles and items and between moles and grams. Mass and the number of items must be related to each other through the mole: grams to moles to items or items to moles to grams. The beauty of the wheel model is that as you learn more chemical quantities they can simply be added to the rim of the wheel. In order to relate or "connect" a new chemical quantity to all of the others you only need to connect it to the mole. In other words, if you wanted to convert grams into sneebugs, you would convert grams into moles and then moles into sneebugs.

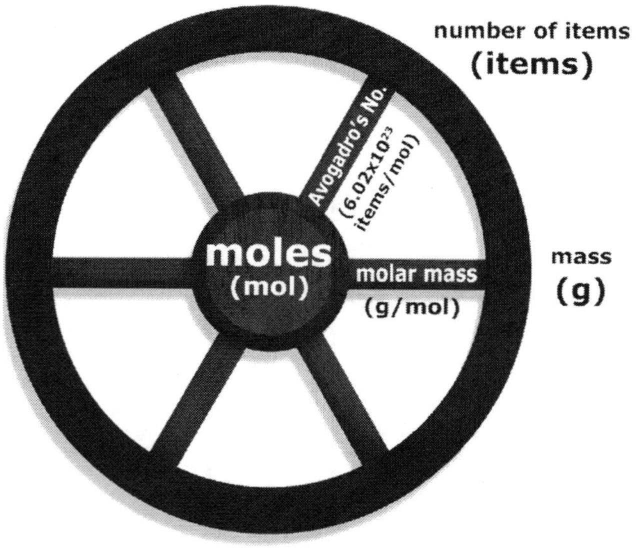

Figure 5.6.1 *The wheel is a useful model for representing conversion factors.*

Sample Problem — Two-Step Conversion: Mass to Number of Items (Atoms)

Chemists count by weighing. How many atoms are in 5.0 g of copper?

What to Think about

1. Plan your route.
   Convert: g Cu → mol Cu → atoms Cu
   Chemists usually perform these two calculations in one continuous sequence.
2. Setup: $5.0 \text{ g Cu} \times \frac{1 \text{ mol Cu}}{? \text{ g Cu}} \times \frac{? \text{ atoms Cu}}{1 \text{ mol Cu}}$

   The numerators show the route; in this case, grams to moles to atoms.
   Each numerator's unit is cancelled by the next denominator's unit until you arrive at your answer.
3. Conversion factors:
   1 mol Cu per 63.5 g Cu
   6.02×10^{23} atoms Cu per 1 mol Cu

How to Do It

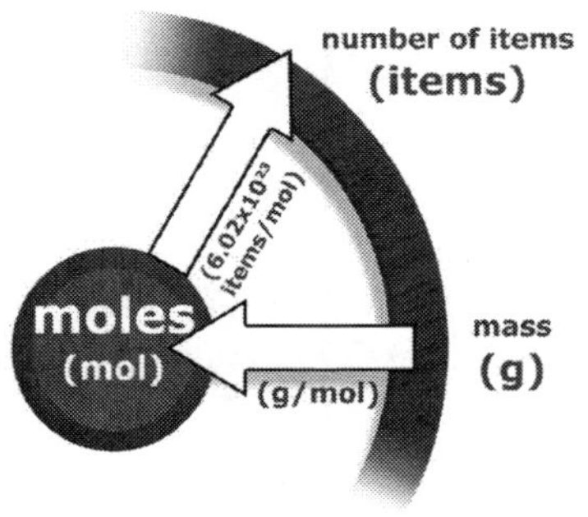

$$5.0 \text{ g Cu} \times \frac{1 \text{ mol Cu}}{63.5 \text{ g Cu}} \times \frac{6.02 \times 10^{23} \text{ atoms Cu}}{1 \text{ mol Cu}}$$
$$= 4.7 \times 10^{22} \text{ atoms Cu}$$

As Avogadro's number is an estimate, so is the above answer. Nevertheless, being able to estimate the number of atoms in any sample of a substance is remarkable. This is perhaps even more evident for the reverse conversion, which allows us to estimate the mass of a single atom in grams.

Sample Problem — Two-Step Conversion: Number of Items (Atoms) to Mass

What is the mass of an oxygen atom in grams?

What to Think about

1. Convert: atom O → mol O → g O
2. Setup: $1 \text{ atom O} \times \frac{1 \text{ mol O}}{? \text{ atoms O}} \times \frac{? \text{ g O}}{1 \text{ mol O}}$
3. Conversion factors:
   1 mol O per 6.02×10^{23} atoms O
   16.0 g per 1 mol O
4. All that we've done here is divide the mass of a mole of oxygen atoms by the number of atoms in a mole to determine the mass of each atom.
   Always check to make sure that your answer is reasonable. 2.66×10^{-23} g is a reasonable answer because an atom would have a very small mass.

How to Do It

$$1 \text{ atom O} \times \frac{1 \text{ mol O}}{6.02 \times 10^{23} \text{ atoms O}} \times \frac{16.0 \text{ g O}}{1 \text{ mol O}}$$
$$= 2.66 \times 10^{-23} \text{ g O}$$

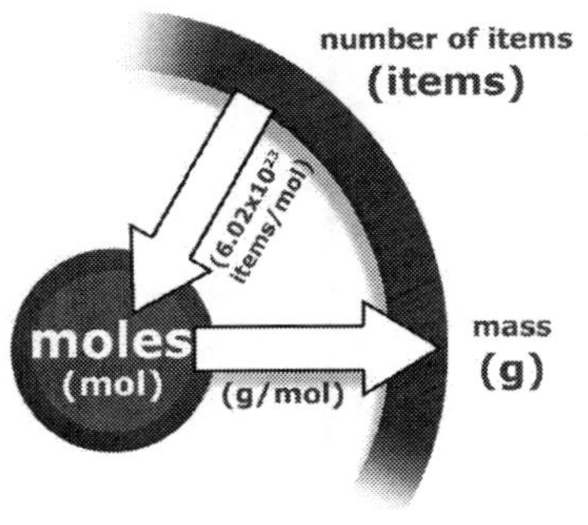

Practice Problems — Two-Step Conversions

1. Fill in the missing entries to determine the mass in grams of a billion billion (1×10^{18}) sulfur dioxide molecules.

$$(1 \times 10^{18} \text{ molecules } SO_2) \times \frac{1 \text{ mol } SO_2}{\_\_\_\_\_\_ \text{ molecules } SO_2} \times \frac{\_\_\_\_\_\_ \text{ g } SO_2}{1 \text{ mol } SO_2} = \_\_\_\_\_\_ \text{ g } SO_2$$

2. How many atoms are in 2.1 g Br?

3. What is the mass in grams of one atom of Ag?

Two Wheel Conversions (Composition Stoichiometry)

Chemists often relate a quantity of one chemical substance to a quantity of another. **Stoichiometry** is the branch of chemistry that deals with the quantitative relationships between elements in a compound (composition stoichiometry) and between the reactants and products in a chemical reaction (reaction stoichiometry). ("Stoichiometry" is from the Greek words *stoicheion* meaning "element" and *metron* meaning "measure.") Our presentation here is limited to composition stoichiometry. To accommodate such conversions, we simply add another wheel to our model. Each wheel in our model represents a different substance or species and, of course, the only functional way to connect two wheels is with an axle. An axle runs between the hubs of wheels and in our model, connects moles of one substance or species to moles of another (Figure 5.6.2).

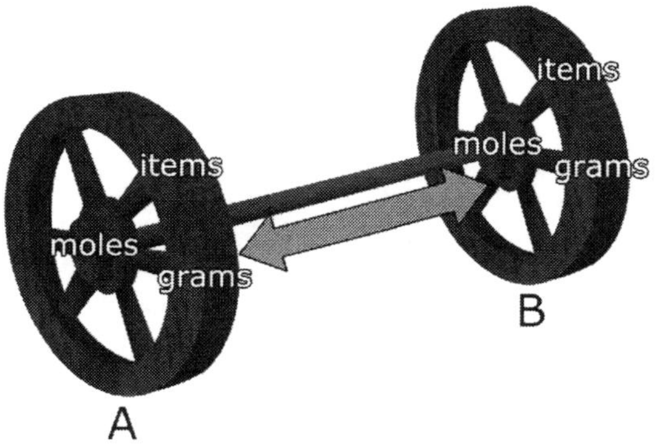

Figure 5.6.2 *The two-wheel-and-axle model for converting between species*

A quantity of a substance or species can only be related to a quantity of another substance or species through the mole.

We already know how to move about (convert units) using single wheels. The only new step added here is represented by the axle, which helps you to convert moles of one substance into moles of another. The conversion factor is found in the compound's formula. There are two oxygen atoms in a CO_2 molecule, so there are two dozen oxygen atoms in a dozen CO_2 molecules and there are… *wait for it*… 2 mol of oxygen atoms in 1 mol of CO_2 molecules.

Name	Equivalence Statement	Conversion Factors	
Chemical Formula	1 molecule A = ? atoms B ∴ 1 mol A = ? mol B	$\frac{1 \text{ mol A}}{? \text{ mol B}}$	$\frac{? \text{ mol B}}{1 \text{ mol A}}$
Example: CO_2	1 molecule CO_2 = 2 atoms O ∴ 1 mol CO_2 = 2 mol O	$\frac{1 \text{ mol } CO_2}{2 \text{ mol O}}$	$\frac{2 \text{ mol O}}{1 \text{ mol } CO_2}$

Sample Problem — One-Step Conversion: Moles of A to Moles of B

How many moles of hydrogen are in 6.0 mol of water?

What to Think about

1. Convert: mol $H_2O \rightarrow$ mol H
2. Setup: $6.0 \text{ mol } H_2O \times \frac{? \text{ mol H}}{1 \text{ mol } H_2O}$
3. Conversion factor:
   There are 2 H's in an H_2O;
   therefore there are
   2 mol of H in 1 mol of H_2O.
4. The values in the conversion factor (2 mol H per 1 mol H_2O) do not limit the significant figures in the answer as these values have no uncertainty. There are exactly 2 H's in an H_2O.

How to Do It

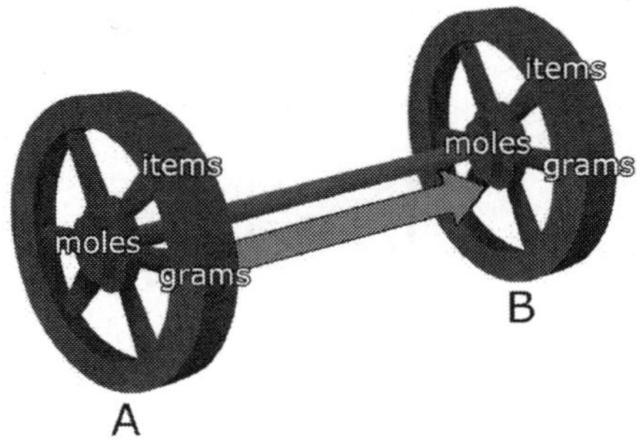

$$6.0 \cancel{\text{mol } H_2O} \times \frac{2 \text{ mol H}}{1 \cancel{\text{mol } H_2O}} = 12 \text{ mol H}$$

Sample Problem — Two-Step Conversion: Mass of A to Moles of B

Hydrogen fuel cells are batteries that are continually supplied or "fuelled" with reactants. Their hydrogen sometimes comes from a process that "scrubs" it off methane molecules. How many moles of methane (CH_4) are required to get 0.860 g of hydrogen?

What to Think about

1. Convert: g H $\rightarrow$ mol H $\rightarrow$ mol CH_4
2. Setup: $0.860 \text{ g H} \times \frac{1 \text{ mol H}}{? \text{ g H}} \times \frac{1 \text{ mol } CH_4}{? \text{ mol H}}$
3. Insert the conversion factors:
   1 mol H per 1.0 g H
   1 mol CH_4 per 4 mol H (given by the formula, CH_4)

How to Do It

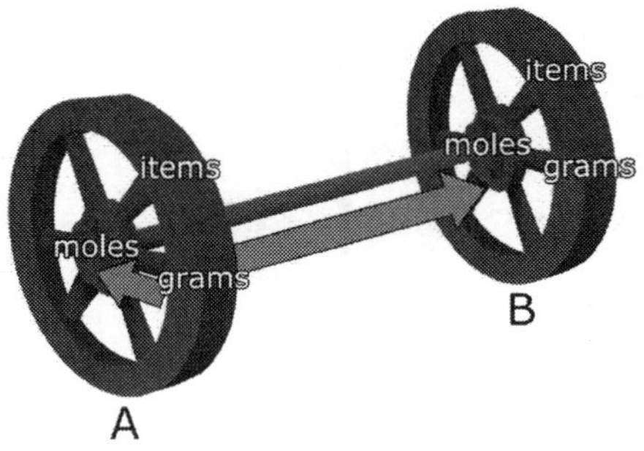

$$0.860 \cancel{\text{g H}} \times \frac{1 \cancel{\text{mol H}}}{1.0 \cancel{\text{g H}}} \times \frac{1 \text{ mol } CH_4}{4 \cancel{\text{mol H}}} = 0.22 \text{ mol } CH_4$$

Sample Problem — Three-Step Conversion: Mass of A to Mass of B

How many grams of oxygen are in 14.6 g CO_2?

What to Think about

1. Convert: g CO_2 → mol CO_2 → mol O → g O
2. Setup:

$$14.6 \text{ g } CO_2 \times \frac{1 \text{ mol } CO_2}{? \text{ g } CO_2} \times \frac{? \text{ mol O}}{1 \text{ mol } CO_2} \times \frac{? \text{ g O}}{1 \text{ mol O}}$$

3. Insert the conversion factors:
   1 mol CO_2 per 44.0 g CO_2
   2 mol O per 1 mol CO_2
   16.0 g O per 1 mol O

How to Do It

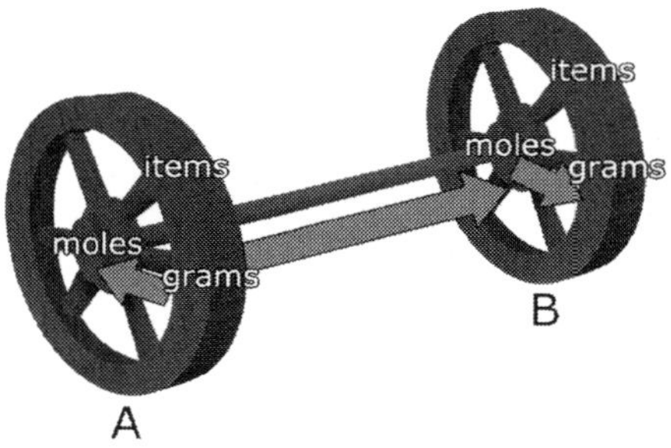

$$14.6 \text{ g } CO_2 \times \frac{1 \text{ mol } CO_2}{44.0 \text{ g } CO_2} \times \frac{2 \text{ mol O}}{1 \text{ mol } CO_2} \times \frac{16.0 \text{ g O}}{1 \text{ mol O}}$$

$= 10.6$ g O

Practice Problems — One-, Two-, and Three-Step Conversions

1. Fill in the missing entries in these "axle" conversion factors.

   (a) $\frac{\_\_\_\_\_ \text{ mol O}}{\_\_\_\_\_ \text{ mol } SO_2}$ (b) $\frac{\_\_\_\_\_ \text{ mol } C_2H_4}{\_\_\_\_\_ \text{ mol H}}$

2. How many moles of KNO_3 contain 14 g of oxygen? ____________________

3. Fill in the missing entry in each conversion factor to determine how many oxygen atoms are in 2.5 g $K_2Cr_2O_7$.

$$2.5 \text{ g } K_2Cr_2O_7 \times \frac{1 \text{ mol } K_2Cr_2O_7}{\_\_\_\_\_ \text{ g } K_2Cr_2O_7} \times \frac{\_\_\_\_\_ \text{ mol O}}{1 \text{ mol } K_2Cr_2O_7} \times \frac{\_\_\_\_\_\_\_\_\_\_\_\_ \text{ atoms O}}{1 \text{ mol O}} =$$

4. What mass of sodium ions is contained in 1.23×10^{24} formula units of sodium sulfide?

5.6 Activity: The Evaporation Rate of Water

Question

What is the evaporation rate of water in molecules per second?

Background

Evaporation occurs when a molecule on the surface of a liquid is struck with enough force by neighboring molecules to break away from its attractions to those around it and enter the gas phase. Evaporation is often depicted like popcorn being popped. Pop…pop, pop, pop…pop, pop, etc. Let's use the mole concept to calculate the actual rate at which water molecules evaporate.

Procedure

1. Half-fill a small beaker with water and weigh it. Record its mass and the time of day.
2. Put the beaker in a place where it won't be disturbed.
3. In about 30 min, weigh the beaker and its contents again, once more recording its mass and the time of day.

Results and Discussion

	Mass of Beaker and H_2O (g)	Time of Day
Initial		
Final		
Change		min

1. Calculate the number of water molecules evaporated during the trial.

2. Calculate the duration of the trial in seconds.

3. Calculate the water's average evaporation rate during the trial in molecules per second.

4. Be suitably amazed. Oh come on, more amazed than that!

5.6 Review Questions

1. Acticoat dressings, developed in 1995 by Robert Burrell of the University of Alberta, are impregnated with crystals of silver that are only 15 nm (nanometers) in size. These nanocrystals are remarkably more effective at healing burns and other severe wounds than any treatment previously available. Acticoat bandages are credited with saving the lives and limbs of many victims in various accidents. What is the mass of a crystal containing 1.0×10^3 silver atoms?

2. Diamond is one way of arranging carbon atoms. The "Star of Africa" diamond, displayed with the crown jewels in the Tower of London, weighs 106.0 g and has an estimated value of over $400 million. How many carbon atoms compose the "Star of Africa" diamond?

3. What is the mass in grams of a chlorine atom?

4. How many propane molecules are in 72.6 g propane, C_3H_8?

5. On a particular day, 31.1 g (1 troy ounce) of gold cost $1300.
   (a) 31 g Au = ______________atoms of Au

   (b) How many atoms of gold could you buy for 1 cent on that day?

6. Complete the following "axle" conversion factors by filling in the appropriate numbers:

   (a) $\dfrac{\_\_\_\_\_\text{ mol O}}{\_\_\_\_\_\text{ mol } N_2O_4}$

   (b) $\dfrac{\_\_\_\_\_\text{ mol } NO_2}{\_\_\_\_\_\text{ mol N}}$

7. 2.3 mol CO_2 = ____________ mol O

8. Calcium oxalate is a poisonous compound found in rhubarb leaves. How many moles of carbon are in 52.4 mg of calcium oxalate?

9. Sodium phosphate is sold as a cleaner at most hardware stores. How many moles of sodium ions are there in 6.80×10^{24} formula units of Na_3PO_4?

10. Sulfuric acid is used to produce a tremendous number and variety of materials including fertilizers, pigments, textiles, plastics, and explosives. What mass of sulfuric acid, H_2SO_4, contains 1.4 mol O?

11. How many carbon atoms are in 0.85 mol of the "pain-killer" acetaminophen, $C_8H_9NO_2$?

12. How many mercury(II) ions are in 100.0 g $HgCl_2$?

13. How many grams of chloride ions are in 8.3 g of copper(II) chloride?

14. What mass of carbon is present in 4.8×10^{26} molecules of ethanol, C_2H_5OH?

15. Hydrogen fluoride, HF, can be used to etch glass. The white lines on the glassware in your lab may have been made by this acidic gas. Determine the mass in kilograms of 3.9×10^{27} molecules of HF.

16. Up to 1.44×10^5 kg of various oxides of nitrogen are emitted by a gas-burning electrical plant in one year. Assuming this entire mass to be nitrogen dioxide, how many oxygen atoms would be present in this gas sample?

17. How many molecules are in 1.000 mg of the organic solvent, carbon tetrachloride?

18. Glycerol, $C_3H_5(OH)_3$, is a viscous, colorless liquid found in cough syrup, toothpaste, soaps, and many other household products. Calculate the number of hydrogen atoms in 4.5 mol of glycerol.

19. How many atoms are in 14.56 g of sodium hydrogen sulfate, the active ingredient in some toilet cleaners?

5.7 Composition Analysis — Determining Formulas

Warm Up

Forensic investigators collect samples from crime scenes. How do technicians identify the unknown samples? An instrument called a **mass spectrometer** can identify the vast majority of compounds. Each compound has a unique mass spectrum; much like each person has a unique fingerprint. A mass spectrometer breaks most of the molecules into fragments. In so doing, it creates a variety of particles from individual atoms to the intact molecule itself, and then marks the mass of each of these particles along a graph's horizontal axis. The height of the line in the spectrum indicates the relative abundance of that particle. Below is a simplified mass spectrum of a compound called pentane (C_5H_{12}).

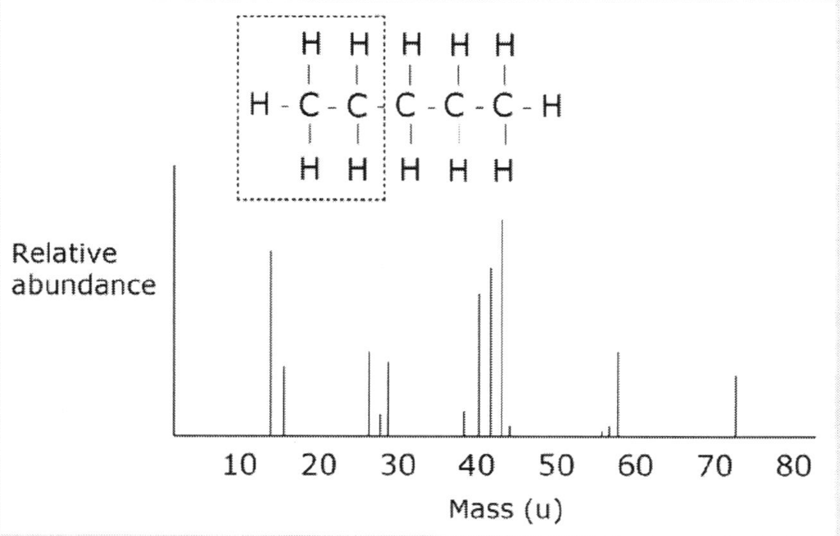

Mass spectrum analysis of pentane

1. The last spectral line represents the intact molecule. What is its molecular mass? ________
2. Draw an arrow to point to the spectral line that represents the mass of the outlined fragment.
3. Why do you think there are more of some fragments than others?

____

____

The important point here is that one of the most sophisticated tools in a chemist's arsenal identifies compounds solely from their "mass profile". In this section, you'll learn to determine a compound's formula from its composition by mass.

Percentage Composition

Percentage composition is the percent of a compound's mass contributed by each type of atom in the compound.

A compound's percentage composition can be determined theoretically from its formula.

Sample Problem — Determining Percentage Composition

What is the percentage composition of a sugar with the formula $C_{12}H_{22}O_{11}$?

What to Think about

1. Calculate the sugar's molar mass.
2. Thus one mole of this sugar contains 144 g C, 22 g H, and 176 g O.
3. Express each element's percentage of the molar mass.

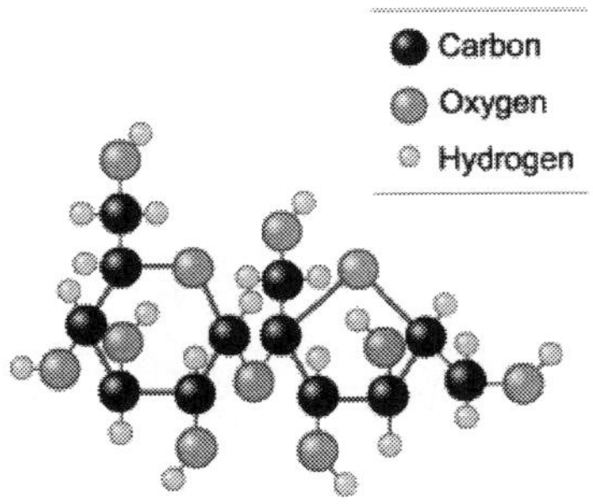

A sugar molecule with 12 carbon atoms, 22 hydrogen atoms, and 11 oxygen atoms.

How to Do It

$$\frac{12 \text{ mol C}}{1 \text{ mol } C_{12}H_{22}O_{11}} \times \frac{12.0 \text{ g C}}{1 \text{ mol C}} = \frac{144.0 \text{ g C}}{1 \text{ mol } C_{12}H_{22}O_{11}}$$

$$\frac{22 \text{ mol H}}{1 \text{ mol } C_{12}H_{22}O_{11}} \times \frac{1.0 \text{ g H}}{1 \text{ mol H}} = \frac{22.0 \text{ g H}}{1 \text{ mol } C_{12}H_{22}O_{11}}$$

$$\frac{11 \text{ mol O}}{1 \text{ mol } C_{12}H_{22}O_{11}} \times \frac{16.0 \text{ g O}}{1 \text{ mol O}} = \frac{176.0 \text{ g O}}{1 \text{ mol } C_{12}H_{22}O_{11}}$$

$$\text{Total} = 342.0 \text{ g/mol } C_{12}H_{22}O_{11}$$

$$\% \text{ C} = \frac{144.0 \text{ g C}}{342.0 \text{ g } C_{12}H_{22}O_{11}} \times 100 = 42.1\ \%$$

$$\% \text{ H} = \frac{22.0 \text{ g H}}{342.0 \text{ g } C_{12}H_{22}O_{11}} \times 100 = 6.4\ \%$$

$$\% \text{ O} = \frac{176.0 \text{ g O}}{342.0 \text{ g } C_{12}H_{22}O_{11}} \times 100 = 51.5\ \%$$

Practice Problems — Determining Percentage Composition

1. Ibuprofen is a common pain reliever and anti-inflammatory. Its formula is $C_{13}H_{18}O_2$. What is its percentage composition?

2. Ammonium sulfate, $(NH_4)_2SO_4$, is a common fertilizer used to lower the pH of soil. Calculate its percentage composition.

3. Many salts are hydrated, which means they have water molecules incorporated into their ionic crystal lattice in a fixed ratio. Magnesium sulfate heptahydrate, $MgSO_4 \cdot 7\ H_2O$, has seven water molecules incorporated into the crystal lattice for each magnesium ion and sulfate ion. Calculate the percentage of water by mass in $MgSO_4 \cdot 7\ H_2O$.

Empirical, Molecular, and Structural Formulas

Every molecular compound has three formulas; an empirical formula, a molecular formula, and a structural formula. They become more specific in that order.

- The **empirical formula** is the simplest integral ratio of the different types of atoms in the compound.
- The **molecular formula** is the actual number of each type of atom in each molecule of the compound.
- The **structural formula** shows how the atoms in a molecule are arranged. It is a diagram that shows the pattern of the atoms' connections.

Organic chemistry is the study of compounds and reactions involving carbon. There are millions of organic compounds. Glucose is an organic compound with a molecular formula of $C_6H_{12}O_6$. The subscripts 6, 12, 6 can be reduced or simplified to 1, 2, 1. We don't show the number 1 as a subscript in a formula so the empirical formula of glucose is CH_2O.

Many compounds have the same empirical formula but different molecular formulas. Their molecular formulas all reduce to the same ratio. For example, all alkenes such as ethene (C_2H_4), propene (C_3H_6), and butene (C_4H_8), have an empirical formula of CH_2 because each of their molecular formulas can be reduced to a 1 to 2 ratio.

Compounds with the same molecular formula but with different structural formulas, i.e. the same atoms are put together differently, are called structural isomers. For example, C_4H_{10} has two structural isomers. You will learn more about structural isomers in chapter 9.

Quick Check

1. Complete the following table.

Structural Formula	Molecular Formula	Empirical Formula
H O I II H - C - C - O - H I H		
O O II II H - O - C - C - O - H		

Determining an Empirical Formula from Percent Composition

In a previous section you learned how to determine an element's relative atomic mass from a compound's percent composition and formula. Earlier in this section, you learned how to determine the percent composition of a compound from its formula and the atomic masses of its component elements. There's only one more arrangement of these variables to learn. That's how to determine the formula of a compound from its percent composition and the atomic masses of its component elements.

The word "empirical" is an adjective meaning that something is based on observation or experiment. Empirical formulas are determined from the mass ratios of a compound's component elements; in other words, from its percent composition. The most direct, but not always easiest, way to experimentally determine a compound's percent composition is to decompose a sample of the compound into its component elements.

Sample Problem — Determining an Empirical Formula

Determine the empirical formula of a compound that is 48.65% carbon, 8.11% hydrogen, and 43.24% oxygen.

What to Think about

1. In 100.0 g of the substance, there would be 48.65 g C, 8.11 g H, and 43.24 g O. Convert these amounts into moles.
2. Divide each molar quantity by the smallest one and then multiply by whatever factor is necessary to find their integral ratio (as shown in a conventional formula).

   The mole ratio and the individual atom ratio are of course the same. This means the subscripts in a formula can be read either as mole ratios or as individual atom ratios. If this compound has 3 mol of carbon atoms for every 2 mol of oxygen atoms then it has 3 dozen carbon atoms for every 2 dozen oxygen atoms, and 3 carbon atoms for every 2 oxygen atoms.

How to Do It

$$48.65 \text{ g C} \times \frac{1 \text{ mol C}}{12.0 \text{ g C}} = 4.0542 \text{ mol C}$$

$$8.11 \text{ g H} \times \frac{1 \text{ mol H}}{1.0 \text{ g H}} = 8.1100 \text{ mol H}$$

$$43.24 \text{ g O} \times \frac{1 \text{ mol O}}{16.0 \text{ g O}} = 2.7025 \text{ mol O}$$

$$\frac{C_{4.0542}H_{8.1100}O_{2.7025}}{2.7025} = C_{1.5}H_3O$$

$$2\,(C_{1.5}H_3O) = C_3H_6O_2$$

Practice Problems — Determining an Empirical Formula

1. A compound is 18.7% Li, 16.3% C, and 65.5% O. Determine its empirical formula.

2. A compound is 9.93% C, 58.6% Cl, and 31.4% F. Determine its empirical formula.

3. A sample of a compound contains 5.723 g Ag, 0.852 g S, and 1.695 g O. Determine its empirical formula.

Determining the Molecular Formula of a Compound

Recall the difference between the empirical formula and the molecular formula of a compound. The empirical formula is the simplest integral ratio of the different types of atoms in the compound. The molecular formula is the actual number of each type of atom in each molecule. A compound's molecular formula is an integral multiple of its empirical formula. Its molecular formula's molar mass is that same integral multiple of its empirical formula's molar mass. For example, butane has an empirical formula of C_2H_5 (29 g/mol) and a molecular formula of C_4H_{10} (58 g/mol).

The "molecular formula's molar mass" is just another way of saying "the compound's molar mass." Therefore, we can determine the compound's molecular formula from its empirical formula and its molar mass.

$$\text{molecular formula} = \text{empirical formula} \times \frac{\text{compound's molar mass}}{\text{molar mass of empirical formula}}$$

There are many ways to experimentally derive a compound's molar mass. If the compound is volatile, meaning it is easily evaporated, then you know from the previous section that 1 mol of any gas occupies 22.4 L at STP. The mass of 22.4 L at STP thus provides the compound's molar mass.

Sample Problem — Determining a Molecular Formula

A compound has an empirical formula of CH_2 and a molar mass of 42.0 g/mol. Determine its molecular formula.

What to Think about	How to Do It
1. Calculate the molar mass of the empirical formula.	$\frac{1 \text{ mol C}}{1 \text{ mol CH}_2} \times \frac{12.0 \text{ g C}}{1 \text{ mol C}} = \frac{12.0 \text{ g C}}{1 \text{ mol CH}_2}$ $\frac{2 \text{ mol H}}{1 \text{ mol CH}_2} \times \frac{1.0 \text{ g H}}{1 \text{ mol H}} = \frac{2.0 \text{ g H}}{1 \text{ mol CH}_2}$ Total $= 14.0 \text{ g/mol CH}_2$
2. Divide the molar mass of the molecular formula by the molar mass of the empirical formula.	$\frac{42.0 \text{ g/mol}}{14.0 \text{ g/mol}} = 3.00$
3. Multiply the empirical formula itself by this factor.	$3\ CH_2 = C_3H_6$

Practice Problems — Determining a Molecular Formula

1. Vinegar is a dilute solution of acetic acid. The molar mass of acetic acid is 60.0 g/mol and it has an empirical formula of CH_2O. What is the molecular formula of acetic acid?

2. A compound has an empirical formula of C_3H_4. Which of the following are possible molar masses of the compound: 20 g/mol, 55 g/mol, 80 g/mol, 120 g/mol?

3. A small sample of antifreeze was analyzed. It contained 4.51 g C, 1.13 g H, and 6.01 g O. From the elevation of water's boiling point, it was determined that the antifreeze's molar mass is 62.0 g/mol. What is the molecular formula of antifreeze?

5.7 Activity: Determining the Empirical Formula of Butane from the Percentage Composition of Its Model

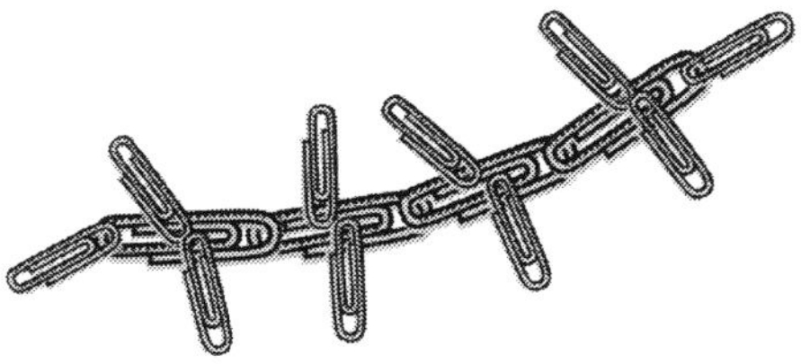

Question

What is the empirical formula of butane?

Background

Recall that "empirical" is an adjective meaning "based on observation or experiment." Empirical formulas are determined from the mass ratios of a compound's component elements (i.e., from its percent composition as determined by analysis). The empirical formula is the simplest integral ratio of the different types of atoms in the compound.

Procedure

1. Use #1 (regular sized) paper clips to represent hydrogen atoms. Jumbo paper clips represent carbon atoms. As a prelude to this exercise, someone must weigh 48 of each type of paperclip and divide by 4 to obtain the mass per dozen. Provide these values to the students to enter in column 3.
2. Form a group of two to five students.
3. Each student links 4 jumbo paper clips together with 10 regular paper clips.
4. Unlink all the clips and weigh all your group's jumbo clips together. Record the mass of your group's jumbo clips as the mass of carbon in the table below.
5. Weigh all your group's regular sized clips together. Record the mass of your group's regular clips as the mass of hydrogen in the table below.

Results and Discussion

Element	Mass (g)	Mass per Dozen (g/doz)	Number (doz)	Dozen Ratio	Empirical Formula
carbon				1.0	
hydrogen					

1. Calculate how many dozens of each type of paper clip are in your group's sample.

2. Calculate the dozen ratio to find out how many dozens of hydrogen atoms there are for each dozen carbon atoms.

3. By what integer do you need to multiply this ratio in order to obtain an integral dozen ratio? ____________

4. What is the empirical formula of butane? ______________________________

5. Given the molecular models you made, what is the molecular formula of butane?

5.7 Review Questions

1. Menthol is a strong-smelling compound that is used in cough drops. It has a formula of $C_{10}H_{20}O$. Calculate its percentage composition.

2. Sodium acetate trihydrate ($NaCH_3COO \cdot 3H_2O$) is a salt commonly used in pickling foods. Calculate the percentage of water by mass in this compound.

3. Trinitrotoluene ($C_7H_5O_6N_3$) is an explosive commonly referred to as TNT. Calculate the percentage of nitrogen by mass in this compound.

4. Complete the following table.

Structural Formula	Molecular Formula	Empirical Formula
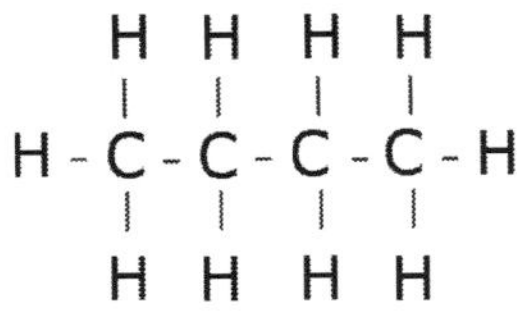		
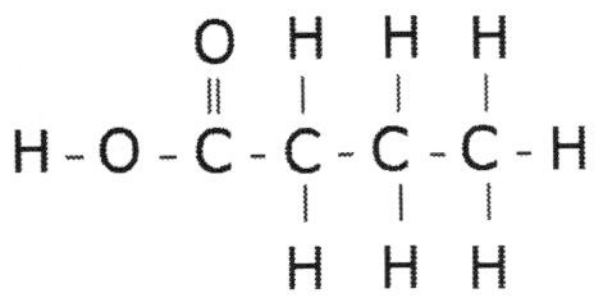		

5. (a) Explain why the empirical formula alone is not enough to identify a compound.

   (b) What other piece of information will allow you to determine its molecular formula?

6. A pigment on a suspected forgery is analyzed using X-ray fluorescence and found to contain 0.5068 mol Ba, 0.5075 mol C, and 1.520 mol O. Determine its empirical formula.

7. A sample of caffeine is analyzed and found to contain 1.4844 g C, 0.1545 g H, 0.4947 g O and 0.8661 g N. Determine the empirical formula of caffeine.

8. (a) In a TV series, a forensic anthropologist uses X-ray fluorescence to analyze a dental filling found in skeletal remains. The results of the analysis are provided as *atomic* percentages: 2.85% Al, 87.4% Si, and 9.75% Yb. Convert these results into mass percentages.

(b) These results identified the filling as a commercial restorative material called Heliomolar. How might identifying the material be useful in helping to identify the remains?

9. A compound has an empirical formula of NH_2 and a molar mass of 32.1 g/mol. What is the compound's molecular formula?

10. A sample of ascorbic acid, also known as vitamin C, was analyzed and found to contain 1.080 g C, 0.121 g H, and 1.439 g O. Ascorbic acid has a molar mass of 176.1 g/mol. Determine the molecular formula of ascorbic acid.

11. A hydrocarbon is a compound containing only carbon and hydrogen. One particular hydrocarbon is 92.29% carbon by mass. If the compound's molar mass is 78.0 g/mol then what is its molecular formula?

12. Cannizzaro determined that a certain compound of carbon and oxygen had a molecular mass of 44.0 u. This meant that a certain volume of this gaseous compound weighed 44.0 times as much as the same volume of hydrogen gas at the same temperature and pressure. This compound was analyzed and found to be 27.3% carbon by mass.

(a) What is the total mass of carbon in a molecule of this compound?

(b) Cannizzaro repeated this experiment on many carbon compounds. Because he never found a molecule with less carbon than this one, Cannizzaro assumed that this molecule had only one carbon atom. Was this assumption correct?

6 Stoichiometry

By the end of this chapter, you should be able to do the following:

- Explain chemical reactions in terms of the rearrangement of the atoms as bonds are broken and new bonds are formed
- Apply the law of conservation of mass to balance formula equations
- Devise balanced equations for various chemical reactions
- Describe reactions in terms of energy changes
- Perform stoichiometric calculations involving chemical reactions

---

By the end of this chapter, you should know the meaning of these key terms:

- acid-base neutralization
- chemical reactivity
- coefficient
- combustion reaction
- decomposition reaction
- double displacement reaction
- endothermic
- exothermic
- formula equation
- limiting reagent
- precipitate
- product
- reactant
- single displacement reaction
- stoichiometry
- synthesis reaction
- thermochemical equation

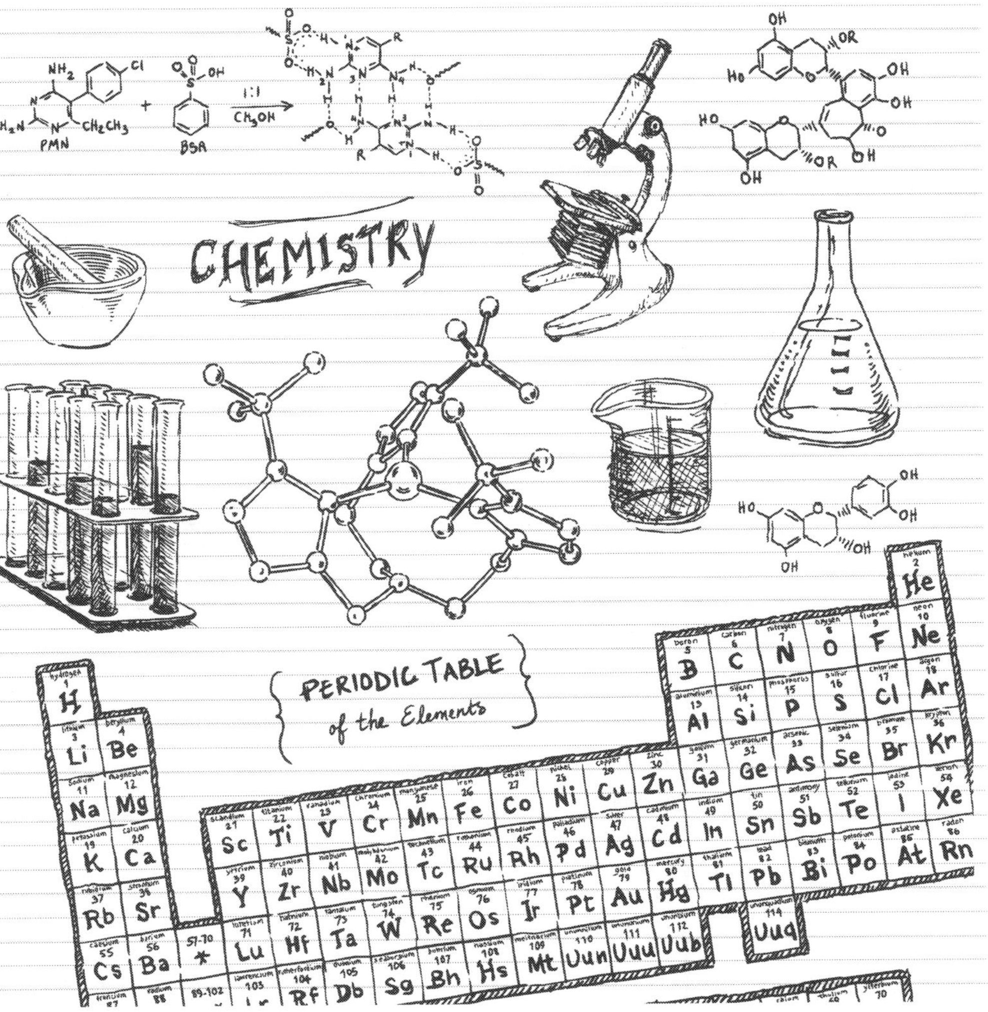

6.1 Stoichiometry

Warm Up

1. Write a balanced equation for the reaction between chromium metal and hydrochloric acid to form chromium(III) chloride and a reactive gas.

2. If 2 mol of chromium metal completely reacted in an excess quantity of hydrochloric acid, how many moles of hydrogen gas would be formed?

3. How many moles of hydrogen gas would form if 4 mol of chromium metal were completely reacted in excess hydrochloric acid?

Moles to Moles — Application of the Mole Ratio

In mole, chapter stoichiometry was introduced through the quantitative relationships between the elements in a chemical compound. It is far more common to use stoichiometry to study the relationships between the various elements and compounds involved in chemical reactions. The key to doing stoichiometric calculations is an understanding of the information provided by a balanced chemical equation.

A balanced chemical equation indicates the relative amounts of the chemicals involved in the reaction. (Recall that the SI unit for amount is the mole.)

Thus for any chemical reaction, the balanced equation may be used to convert moles of reactants to moles of products or vice versa. It may also be used to convert moles of one reactant into another or of one product into another. The key to these conversions is always the *mole ratio*, which is determined from the coefficients in the balanced equation. You may find it helpful to review two-wheel conversions introduced in hte mole chapter and shown in Figure 6.1.1 below.

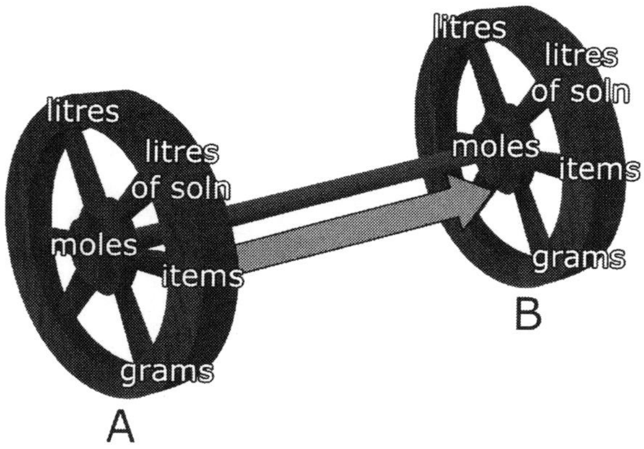

Figure 6.1.1 *The mole ratio is represented by a move across the axle in our wheel model.*

Sample Problem — Moles of One Species ←→ Moles of Another Species

A student places 7.50 mol of chromium metal in an excess of concentrated hydrochloric acid.
How many moles of hydrogen gas are formed?

What to Think about	How to Do It
1. This single replacement reaction will form the most common chloride of chromium, chromium(III). Determine the balanced chemical equation.	$2\,Cr(s) + 6\,HCl(aq) \rightarrow 2\,CrCl_3(aq) + 3\,H_2(g)$
2. As is usual with conversion factors, begin with the end in mind. You are attempting to determine the moles of hydrogen gas. As you are provided with moles of chromium metal, you must begin with this and set up a conversion factor to convert this value into moles of hydrogen gas. As the mole ratio involves whole counting numbers, the significant figures in the answer are *only determined* by the *measured value given in the question*.	$7.50\ \text{mol Cr} \times \frac{\_\_\_\ \text{mol}\ H_2(g)}{\_\_\_\ \text{mol Cr}} = \_\_\_\ \text{mol}\ H_2(g)$ $7.50\ \text{mol Cr} \times \frac{3\ \text{mol}\ H_2(g)}{2\ \text{mol Cr}} = \_\_\_\ \text{mol}\ H_2(g)$ $7.50\ \text{mol Cr} \times \frac{3\ \text{mol}\ H_2(g)}{2\ \text{mol Cr}} = 11.3\ \text{mol}\ H_2(g)$
3. Notice that as long as there is enough HCl to react with all the Cr, we don't need to concern ourselves with the HCl.	

Conversion from one species to another in a chemical reactions is accomplished by using the *mole ratio* between two species in a balanced chemical equation.

Practice Problems — Moles of One Species ←→ Moles of Another Species

Calculate the moles of the requested species given the following information. Be sure to begin with a balanced chemical equation.

1. How many moles of ammonia ($NH_3(g)$) would be formed by the combination of 15.75 mol of nitrogen gas ($N_2(g)$) with a large excess of hydrogen gas ($H_2(g)$)?

2. How many moles of water must be decomposed to form 9.45×10^{-5} mol of $O_2(g)$?

3. How many moles of calcium metal would be required to replace 1.86 mol of silver from a solution of silver nitrate?

Mass to Mass — The Molar Mass Revisited

In the mole chapter, we learned to use the molar mass to convert the mass of a chemical substance to moles. We can now use the mole ratio to take such a conversion one step further. The mole ratio will allow us to convert the moles of one substance in a chemical reaction into moles of another substance. If we wish, we can then convert the moles of the new substance into its mass using an appropriate molar mass. This three-step process was introduced in the mole chapter and is shown again in Figure 6.1.2 below.

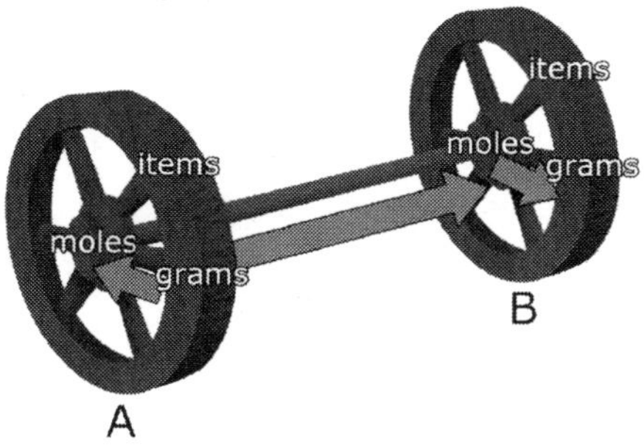

Figure 6.1.2 *Steps for converting mass of substance A to mass of substance B*

Sample Calculation: Mass of One Species ←→ Mass of Another Species

3.50 g of silver nitrate are stirred into a solution containing excess calcium chloride. How many grams of precipitate are formed?

What to think about

1. Write a balanced equation.
   The reaction is a double replacement. Nitrate compounds are always soluble hence the precipitate must be the silver chloride.
2. Begin with the given 3.50 g of $AgNO_3$. Align the conversion factors to convert
   - mass $AgNO_3$ to moles $AgNO_3$
   - moles $AgNO_3$ to moles AgCl
   - moles AgCl to mass AgCl

   Be sure to include the formula as part of the unit.
3. Insert the appropriate molar masses for *1 mol* of the appropriate species and the mole ratio (from the balanced chemical equation).
4. Notice the molar masses are given to one decimal place. The mole ratio is *not reduced*. Be sure to express the answer to the correct number of significant figures. Consider the mass of reactant used and the mole ratio, then ask yourself, does the answer seem reasonable?

How to Do It

$$2\,AgNO_3(aq) + CaCl_2(aq) \rightarrow 2\,AgCl(s) + Ca(NO_3)_2(aq)$$

$$3.50\text{ g }AgNO_3 \times \frac{\text{mol }AgNO_3}{\_\_\_\text{ g }AgNO_3} \times \frac{\text{mol AgCl}}{\_\_\_\text{ mol }AgNO_3} \times \frac{\text{g AgCl}}{\_\_\_\text{ mol AgCl}} = \_\_\_\text{ g AgCl}$$

$$3.50\text{ g }\cancel{AgNO_3} \times \frac{1\text{ }\cancel{\text{mol }AgNO_3}}{169.9\text{ }\cancel{\text{g }AgNO_3}} \times \frac{2\text{ }\cancel{\text{mol AgCl}}}{2\text{ }\cancel{\text{mol }AgNO_3}} \times \frac{143.4\text{ g AgCl}}{1\text{ }\cancel{\text{mol AgCl}}} = 2.95\text{ g AgCl}$$

Practice Problems — Mass of One Species ←→ Mass of Another Species

Show all work for each of the following questions. Begin with a balanced chemical equation if one is not provided. Be sure to include the formulas as part of your units in each step. Give your final answer with the correct number of significant figures.

1. The following reaction is exceptional in that a single reactant species is both oxidized and reduced:
   $2\ KClO_3(s) \rightarrow 2\ KCl(s) + 3\ O_2(g)$.
   What mass of oxygen gas would be formed by the decomposition of 45.65 g of $KClO_3$? (How should your answer compare to the mass of reactant? Does your answer make sense?)

2. This *unbalanced* equation shows one possible set of products for the reaction of aluminum and nitric acid:
   $Al(s) + HNO_3(aq) \rightarrow Al(NO_3)_3(aq) + H_2(g)$.
   Use the balanced version of this equation to determine the mass of nitric acid required to form 170 kg of hydrogen gas.

3. Hydrogen gas can be used as a reducing agent in the production of pure boron from boron trichloride. How many moles of boron would form from the reduction of 500.0 g of boron trichloride with excess hydrogen gas?

   Equation:

4. Write a balanced chemical equation for the reaction between sodium metal and water.
   How many moles of hydrogen gas would form if 2 mol of sodium reacted with excess water? What volume would this gas occupy at STP conditions?

Solutions — Using Molarity in Volume Conversions

One of the best ways to make two chemicals react with one another, particularly ionic compounds, is to dissolve each of them in a suitable solvent and mix the resulting solutions. The conversion factor that is specific to the stoichiometry of reactions in solution is the one that equates the amount of solute in a solution to its volume. This is the molarity. You have learned to calculate molarity and use it to convert between the volume of a solution and the amount of dissolved solute (moles) in that solution. Molarity can be used in combination with a mole ratio and an additional factor involving moles to perform a variety of stoichiometric conversions involving solutions.

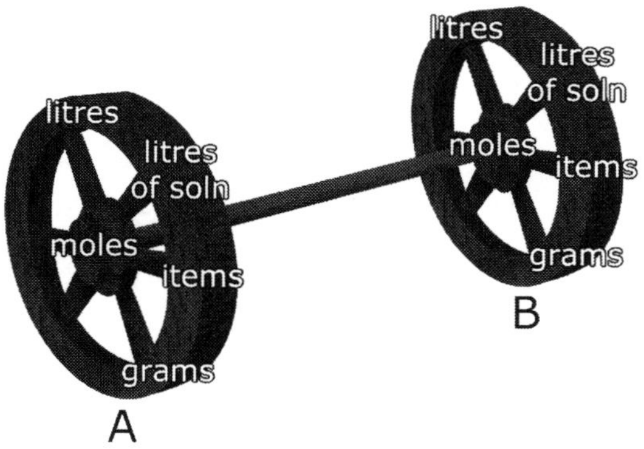

Figure 6.1.3 *This diagram illustrates the application of molar mass, molar volume, molarity, and even Avogadro's number in a variety of stoichiometric calculations.*

Quick Check

1. What is the concentration of a solution made by dissolving 117 g of sodium chloride in water to make a total volume of 1.5 L?

2. Use the molarity of the solution from question 1 to determine the mass of NaCl in 250 mL.

3. What volume of a solution of this same molarity would contain 39.0 g of sodium chloride?

Sample Problem — Calculations Involving Solution Volumes

What mass of nickel wire reacts with all the silver nitrate in 1.25 L of a 0.15 mol/L solution?

What to Think about

1. Write a balanced equation.
2. Begin with the end in mind.
   - As the answer to the problem will be in grams, a single unit, we should start the calculation with 1.25 L, also a single unit.
   - Remember the problem does *not* involve gas so 22.4 L/mol is not appropriate. In this case, we are dealing with 0.15 mol/1 L.
   - The molarity, derived from two units, will be used second, as the first *conversion factor*.
   - As liters will be cancelled, the molarity unit is not inverted. This is followed by the mole ratio and the molar mass.
3. Insert appropriate numerical values and calculate an answer.
   Notice this series converts
   - volume $AgNO_3$ to moles $AgNO_3$
   - moles $AgNO_3$ to moles Ni
   - moles Ni to mass Ni

As the molarity is a measured value, it limits the answer to two significant figures. The answer appears to be reasonable.

How to Do It

$$Ni(s) + 2\,AgNO_3(aq) \rightarrow Ni(NO_3)_2(aq) + 2\,Ag(s)$$

$$1.25\ L \times \frac{\_\_\_\ mol\ AgNO_3}{\_\_\_\ L} \times \frac{\_\_\_\ mol\ Ni}{\_\_\_\ mol\ AgNO_3} \times \frac{\_\_\_\ g\ Ni}{\_\_\_\ mol\ Ni} = \_\_\_\ g\ Ni$$

$$1.25\ \cancel{L} \times \frac{0.15\ \cancel{mol\ AgNO_3}}{1\ \cancel{L}} \times \frac{1\ \cancel{mol\ Ni}}{2\ \cancel{mol\ AgNO_3}} \times \frac{58.7\ g\ Ni}{1\ \cancel{mol\ Ni}} = 5.5\ g\ Ni$$

Practice Problems — Calculations Involving Solution Volumes

Show all work for each of the following questions. Begin with a balanced chemical equation if one is not provided. Be sure to include the formulas as part of your units in each step. Give your final answer with the correct number of significant figures.

1. The exothermic reaction $2\ K(s) + 2\ H_2O(l) \rightarrow 2\ KOH(aq) + H_2(g)$ often releases enough heat to ignite the hydrogen gas it produces. What mass of potassium metal would be required to produce 250 mL of a 0.45 mol/L solution of potassium hydroxide?

2. What volume of 0.80 mol/L sodium iodide solution would completely react with 2.4×10^{24} molecules of chlorine gas?

   Equation:

3. How many liters of carbon dioxide gas would be formed at STP if 1.5 L of 1.75 M phosphoric acid were reacted with excess potassium carbonate solution? Be cautious, as this question requires the use of both molar volume and molarity as conversion factors.

   Equation:

6.1 Activity: Stoichiometric Relationships of Hydrochloric Acid

Question

How can you measure the products of a reaction?

Background

Hydrochloric acid is the most commonly used acid in secondary school chemistry. It can be reacted with a variety of substances in several different types of chemical reactions. The products of such reactions may be separated and measured to study stoichiometric relationships in a variety of ways.

Procedure

1. Use the theoretical information provided in the "Background" above to design two different experiments to isolate and measure a product of two different reactions, each consuming 750 mL of 1.0 M HCl. You must use a single and a double replacement reaction.
   - Describe each design in point-form.
   - Provide a labelled diagram of each design.
2. Compare your designs with those of a classmate. Use your comparison to improve your designs.

Results and Discussion

1. Write a balanced chemical equation for each reaction you selected.

2. Calculate the quantity of product you would expect to measure in each experiment.

3. Exchange your answers to questions 1 and 2 with the same classmate with whom you compared experimental designs. Beginning with the classmate's answers to question 2, calculate the volume of 1.0 mol/L HCl required to form the quantity of product he or she determined for each experiment. Your classmate should perform the same calculations with your question 2 answers.

4. What answer should all students get for question 3?

6.1 Review Questions

1. Malachite is a beautiful green mineral often sculpted into jewellery. It decomposes as follows:

   $Cu(OH)_2 \cdot CuCO_3(s) \rightarrow 2\ CuO(s) + CO_2(g) + H_2O(l)$

   (a) How many moles of CuO are formed from the decomposition of 1.26 mol of malachite?

   (b) If a 1.5 kg piece of malachite is completely decomposed, how many grams of copper(II) oxide are formed?

2. What mass of zinc would completely react with 10.0 mL of 0.45 M hydrochloric acid solution?

   $Zn(s) + 2\ HCl(aq) \rightarrow ZnCl_2(aq) + H_2(g)$

3. How much energy will be required to complete the reaction of 12.2 g of sodium to produce sodium oxide?

   $4\ Na(s) + O_2(g) + 124.7\ kJ \rightarrow 2\ Na_2O(s)$

4. Potassium permanganate reacts with oxalic acid in aqueous sulfuric acid according to the equation:

   $2\ KMnO_4 + 5\ H_2C_2O_4 + 3\ H_2SO_4 \rightarrow 2\ MnSO_4 + 10\ CO_2 + 8\ H_2O + K_2SO_4$

   How many milliliters of a 0.250 M $KMnO_4$ solution are needed to react with 3.225 g of oxalic acid?

Begin the following calculations with a balanced equation.

5. The reaction of scrap aluminum with chlorine gas forms aluminum chloride. What mass of chlorine in the presence of excess aluminum is required to make 4.56 kg of aluminum chloride?

6. How many moles of sulfuric acid could neutralize 0.034 mol of potassium hydroxide solution?

7. What mass of water vapor would be formed from the complete combustion of 35.00 g of ethanol ($C_2H_5OH(l)$)?

8. $PbI_2(s) \rightarrow Pb^{2+}(aq) + 2\,I^-(aq)$ $\Delta H = 46.5$ kJ/mol
How much energy would be required to dissolve 5.00 g of lead (II) iodide?

9. A piece of zinc metal was dropped into a solution of tin(IV) nitrate. If 27.5 g of tin metal was displaced, how many grams of reducing agent were used?

10. Solutions of barium nitrate and potassium sulfate were poured together. If this reaction required 6.5 mol of barium nitrate, how many grams of precipitate were formed?

11. When dinitrogen tetroxide decomposes into nitrogen dioxide, 56 kJ of energy is required for each mole of reactant decomposed. How much heat is absorbed if 1.25 g of product is formed?

12. A flask containing 450 mL of 0.500 M HBr was accidentally knocked to the floor. How many grams of K_2CO_3 would you need to put on the spill to completely neutralize the acid?

13. The acetic acid in a 2.5 mol/L sample of a solution of a kettle scale remover is reacted with an excess of a lead(II) nitrate solution to form a precipitate, which is then filtered and dried. The mass of the precipitate is 8.64 g. What volume of the solution was required to produce that mass?

14. How many milliliters of a 0.610 M NaOH solution are needed to completely neutralize 25.0 mL of a 0.356 M phosphoric acid solution?

6.2 Excess/Limiting Amounts, Percentage Yield, and Impurities

Warm Up

Suppose you are working in an ice cream shop. A group of customers come in and they would like to order ice cream sundaes. The shop's computer page reads as follows for ice cream sundaes:

Sundae Ingredients in Stock	Number of Items	Sundae Recipe
Scoops vanilla ice cream	six scoops	one scoop vanilla ice cream
Chocolate syrup	200 mL	50 ml chocolate syrup
Super sweet red cherries	475 cherries	one cherry on top
		(Do NOT change the recipe)

1. What is the maximum number of sundaes you can make for customers?
2. What item *limits* the number of sundaes you can make?
3. How much of each of the *excess* items will still be left as sundae stock?

Excess and Limiting — Another Issue to Consider

So far, we have made several assumptions about the chemical reactions we've been studying. Given a balanced chemical equation and the quantity of one of the reactants, we've assumed:

- The reactant provided is completely pure.
- The reactant will be totally consumed in the reaction as the reaction proceeds entirely to completion.
- No alternate or side reactions will occur.
- All reactants are consumed completely in **stoichiometric quantities**, that is, in a molar ratio identical to that predicted by the balanced equation.

For example, consider the reaction between carbon monoxide and oxygen gas. Any of the following ratios may be indicated by the balanced chemical equation.

$2\,CO(g)$	+	$O_2(g)$	→	$2\,CO_2(g)$
2 molecules	:	1 molecule	:	2 molecules
2 mol	:	1 mol	:	2 mol
2 L	:	1 L	:	2 L
2(28.0 g) = 56.0g	:	32.0 g	:	2(44.0 g) = 88.0 g

Stoichiometric quantities would be present if the amounts or volumes of $CO:O_2$ reduced to 2:1. Notice the total mass of reactants consumed exactly equals the total mass of products formed. In the real world, however, this is rarely the case. It is more likely that the number of reactant particles will not be present in stoichiometric quantities. Rather one or the other reactant is likely to be **in excess**. That is, there will be more than enough of one reactant to completely react with the other.

Quick Check

Consider the following situation:

$$2\ CO(g) + O_2(g) \longrightarrow 2\ CO_2(g)$$

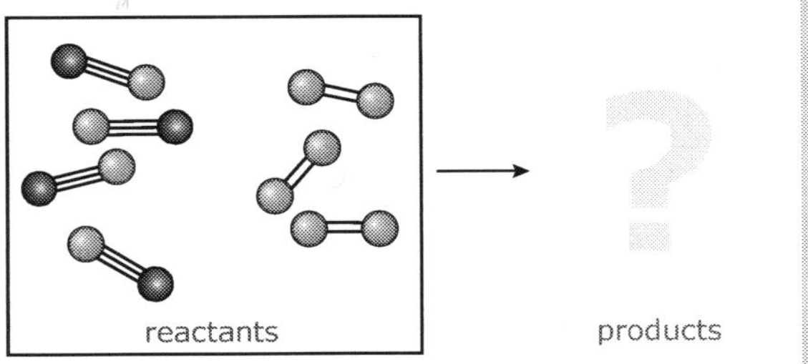

1. Which of the reactants is in excess?
2. Sketch any remaining reactants and products to show what will be present once the reaction is complete.
3. How many CO_2 particles are formed?
4. How many excess reactant particles remain?

The reactant that is totally consumed when a reaction is completed is called the **limiting reactant** (or **reagent**). This species limits the amount of product that can be formed. The reactant that remains once the limiting reactant is completely consumed is called the **excess reactant** (or **reagent**).

In the previous section, you were always told which reactant species was in excess. In limiting and excess problems, you will be given the mass of all of the reactant species and you must determine which of these are in excess and, more importantly, which species limits the amount of product that can form. You may also have to determine how much of the excess species remains once the reaction is complete.

Sample Problem — Limiting and Excess Stoichiometry

What volume of hydrogen gas, measured at STP, is produced when 8.0 g of lithium metal is reacted with 10.0 g of water? What mass of the excess reactant remains once the reaction is completed?

What to Think about	How to Do It
1. As with any stoichiometry problem, begin by determining the balanced equation. 2. This is a single replacement reaction. Thinking of water as HOH, we replace the hydrogen with lithium and form a base.	$2\ Li(s) + 2\ H_2O(l) \rightarrow 2\ LiOH(aq) + H_2(g)$
3. As the mole ratio of reactants is 2:2 (which reduces to 1:1), it is easy to simply compare the moles of $Li:H_2O$ available.	
4. Begin the stoichiometric portion of the problem by determining which reactant is in excess (and which one limits the quantity of product that can be formed). In some cases, it may only be necessary to determine the moles of each reactant and compare.	$8.0\ \cancel{g\ Li} \times \frac{1\ mol\ Li}{6.9\ \cancel{g\ Li}} = 1.2\ mol\ Li$ $10.0\ \cancel{g\ H_2O} \times \frac{1\ mol\ H_2O}{18.0\ \cancel{g\ H_2O}} = 0.556\ mol\ H_2O$

Continued

Sample Problem — *Continued*

What to Think about

5. There are more than twice as many moles of lithium as there are of water. The equation shows that 1.2 mol of Li would require 1.2 mol of H_2O to completely react. Clearly there is insufficient H_2O to use up all the Li.
6. Frequently the reactants do not react in a 1:1 ratio hence each reactant must be converted completely to one product. The reactant that forms the greater quantity of product is in excess. The smaller amount of product will be the correct answer.
   Both methods (comparing moles of reactants *and* comparing the quantity of product) indicate the same species is limiting.
7. To determine the amount of excess reactant left, begin by determining the amount of excess reactant consumed.
   - Begin this calculation with the limiting reagent.
   - Apply stoichiometry to the limiting reagent to determine the amount consumed.
   - Subtract the amount used from the amount of excess present to start.
   - Notice significant figures are determined by place value as subtraction is employed in the last step.
   - Do not use the product to determine the amount consumed, as it is itself a calculated value and thus subject to error.

How to Do It

Lithium is in excess. Water is limiting.

$$8.0\ \cancel{g\ Li} \times \frac{1\ mol\ Li}{6.9\ \cancel{g\ Li}} \times \frac{1\ \cancel{mol\ H_2}}{2\ \cancel{mol\ Li}} \times \frac{22.4\ L\ H_2}{1\ \cancel{mol\ H_2}}$$

$= 13\ L\ H_2$ gas

$$10.0\ \cancel{g\ H_2O} \times \frac{1\ mol\ H_2O}{18.0\ \cancel{g\ H_2O}} \times \frac{1\ \cancel{mol\ H_2}}{2\ \cancel{mol\ H_2O}} \times \frac{22.4\ L\ H_2}{1\ \cancel{mol\ H_2}} = 6.22\ L\ H_2\ gas$$

The limiting reagent is the water. The lithium is in excess.
The correct amount of product is 6.22 L.

$$10.0\ \cancel{g\ H_2O} \times \frac{1\ \cancel{mol\ H_2O}}{18.0\ \cancel{g\ H_2O}} \times \frac{2\ \cancel{mol\ Li}}{2\ \cancel{mol\ H_2O}} \times \frac{6.9\ g\ Li}{1\ \cancel{mol\ Li}} = 3.83\ g\ Li\ used\ up$$

Remaining excess lithium $= 8.0 - 3.83$
$= 4.2$ g

Practice Problems — Limiting and Excess Stoichiometry

1. 25.0 g each of zinc metal and HCl dissolved in aqueous solution are reacted together. What volume of hydrogen gas, measured at STP, is formed and what mass of excess reactant is left over?

2. An acid spill containing 12.0 g of pure sulfuric acid is neutralized by 80.0 g of sodium bicarbonate (baking soda). What volume of water is formed? What mass of excess reactant is left over? (Reminder: density of water = 1.00 g/mL)

Continued

Practice Problems — *Continued*

3. When ammonia is passed over hot calcium, calcium hydride and nitrogen gas are formed. What mass of calcium hydride results when 20.0 L of ammonia measured at STP and 150 g of calcium are reacted? What quantity of excess reactant remains?

Percentage Purity — Impure Reactants

Throughout this chapter, we've treated all of the chemicals involved in stoichiometric calculations as if they were completely pure. In reality, it is virtually impossible to obtain a chemical in a pure form. Even the purest chemicals purchased from chemical supply companies contain impurities. The purity of a chemical is commonly indicated as the percentage purity.

$$\textbf{Percentage purity} \text{ (by mass)} = \frac{\text{mass of pure chemical}}{\text{mass of impure sample}} \times 100\%$$

There are several types of stoichiometric calculations involving impurities. The most common begin with an impure reactant. The more difficult type gives a quantity of product and requires the use of this value to determine the percentage purity of a reactant.

Quick Check

1. Determine the percentage purity of the following:
   (a) A 4.5 g piece of calcium contains only 3.8 g of pure calcium metal.

   (b) Pure phosphorus makes up 17.5 g of a sample of white phosphorus weighing 20.0 g.

2. What mass of pure potassium is contained in a 0.90 g piece of 90.0% pure potassium?

Sample Problems — Percentage Purity

1. What mass of sodium hydride can be formed from the combination of 15.0 g of 80.0% pure sodium with excess hydrogen gas?
2. What is the percentage purity of a 7.5 g sample of sodium metal that formed 7.0 g of sodium hydride when reacted with an excess of hydrogen gas?

What to Think about

Question 1

1. As with any stoichiometry problem, begin by determining the balanced equation.
   There are two elements forming one product so this is a synthesis reaction.
   Remember that hydrogen is a diatomic element.
2. Before beginning the stoichiometric portion of the problem, determine the mass of *pure* sodium available to react.
3. Now simply perform the stoichiometric conversions in the usual way.
   Note that the entire calculation may be done in one combined line of conversions.
   All measured values (including the percentage) indicate an answer with three significant figures.

Question 2

1. Fortunately, the balanced equation for the second problem is the same one.
2. Determining the percentage purity of the 7.5 g sample of sodium requires the mass of pure sodium in the sample.
   This is where stoichiometry is required.
   As the 7.0 g of NaH must be pure, we can use it to determine what mass of pure Na was in the reactant used to form it.
3. Finally, this value may be used to calculate the purity of the sodium.
   The final answer should be expressed to two significant figures

How to Do It

$$2\,Na(s) + H_2(g) \rightarrow 2\,NaH(s)$$

$$15.0\text{ g Na} \times \frac{80}{100} = 12.0\text{ g pure Na}$$

Therefore

$$12.0\text{ g Na} \times \frac{1\text{ mol Na}}{23.0\text{ g Na}} \times \frac{2\text{ mol NaH}}{2\text{ mol Na}} \times \frac{24\text{ g NaH}}{1\text{ mol NaH}}$$

or...

$$15.0\text{ g impure Na} \times \frac{80.0\text{ g pure Na}}{100\text{ g impure Na}} \times \frac{1\text{ mol Na}}{23.0\text{ g Na}} \times \frac{2\text{ mol NaH}}{2\text{ mol Na}} \times \frac{24\text{ g NaH}}{1\text{ mol NaH}} = 12.5\text{ g NaH}$$

$$2\,Na(s) + H_2(g) \rightarrow 2\,NaH(s)$$

$$7.0\text{ g NaH} \times \frac{1\text{ mol NaH}}{24.0\text{ g NaH}} \times \frac{2\text{ mol Na}}{2\text{ mol NaH}} \times \frac{23.0\text{ g Na}}{1\text{ mol Na}} = 6.7\text{ g pure Na}$$

$$\%\text{ purity} = \frac{6.7\text{ g pure Na}}{7.5\text{ g impure Na}} \times 100\% = 89\%$$

The percentage purity of the sodium = 89%

Practice Problems — Percentage Purity

1. The thermite reaction is extremely exothermic, producing temperatures in excess of 2500°C. These high temperatures were used to weld iron tracks together during the early days of the railway. Thermite is a mixture of powdered aluminum and iron(III) oxide (rust) reacting as follows: $2\ Al(s) + Fe_2O_3(s) \rightarrow Al_2O_3(s) + 2\ Fe(s)$. If 2.44 g of 95% pure aluminum is reacted, how many grams of aluminum oxide can be produced?

2. How many grams of 73.0% pure iron(III) oxide are required to form 24.5 g of pure white hot iron metal in the thermite reaction? (Hint: Begin by determining the mass of *pure* oxide required.)

3. When hydrochloric acid is added to 5.73 g of contaminated calcium carbonate, 2.49 g of carbon dioxide is obtained. Write a balanced equation and find the percentage purity of the calcium carbonate.

Percentage Yield — Incomplete Reactions

Every summer, hundreds of students make money planting trees in the reforestation of various States. Imagine you've joined some friends as tree planters and your group has planted 5015 Douglas fir saplings on a mountainside on the Olympic Peninsula located in Washington State. Five years later, a group of forestry surveyors checking for survival find that 4655 of these saplings have taken root and are growing into healthy young trees. The percentage yield of your group's effort would be 93%.

Another of the assumptions we've been making so far is that reactions always go entirely to completion. "Completion" means that all of the limiting reactant has been converted into product, leaving only the excess reactant with none of the limiting reactant remaining at all. In real life, this is not always the case. Some reactions complete themselves only partially. As a result, much like the tree-planting example, such chemical reactions give only a partial percentage yield: less than 100% of the reactants are converted into products.

$$\textbf{Percentage yield} = \frac{\text{amount of product obtained}}{\text{amount of product expected}} \times 100\%$$

The amount of product expected is commonly referred to as the **theoretical yield**.

Sample Problem — Percentage Yield

One of the primary reasons for reforestation is the great loss of forests to fire each summer. The pithy cente of Douglas fir trees consists of cellulose, a starchy material made up of cross-connected molecules of glucose, $C_6H_{12}O_6$. During a small forest fire, the combustion of 8944 kg of $C_6H_{12}O_6$ molecules results in the formation of 5.75×10^6 L of carbon dioxide gas (measured at STP). What is the percentage yield?

What to Think about	How to Do It
1. Once again, in a stoichiometry problem, begin with a balanced equation. This is clearly a combustion reaction with a carbohydrate being combusted. The products are carbon dioxide and water vapour. Oxygen is a diatomic molecule.	$C_6H_{12}O_6(s) + 6\,O_2(g) \rightarrow 6\,CO_2(g) + 6\,H_2O(g)$
2. Using standard stoichiometry, convert the given mass of reactant to product. This is the volume of product formed if the reaction were to proceed 100% to completion (and the gas were measured under STP conditions). In other words, it is the *theoretical yield.* There is a metric conversion required in this problem. "Kilo" means 1000.	$8944\ \text{kg} \times \frac{1000\ \text{g}\ C_6H_{12}O_6}{1\ \text{kg}\ C_6H_{12}O_6} \times \frac{1\ \text{mol}\ C_6H_{12}O_6}{180.0\ \text{g}\ C_6H_{12}O_6} \times \frac{6\ \text{mol}\ CO_2}{1\ \text{mol}\ C_6H_{12}O_6} \times \frac{22.4\ \text{L}\ CO_2}{1\ \text{mol}\ CO_2}$ $= 6.68 \times 10^6\ \text{L}\ CO_2$ The theoretical yield is 6.68×10^6 L CO_2.
3. Calculate the percentage yield as the quotient of the actual yield to the theoretical yield multiplied by 100%. The *entire* theoretical yield should be kept in the calculator throughout the calculation to avoid rounding errors.	Thus the percentage yield is: $\frac{5.75 \times 10^6\ \text{L}}{6.68 \times 10^6\ \text{L}} \times 100\% = 86.1\%$ yield

Practice Problems — Percentage Yield

1. A chunk of zinc metal reacts with an excess of hydrochloric acid solution. What is the percentage yield if a 7.23 g piece of zinc produces 2.16 L of hydrogen gas at STP? Begin with a balanced equation.

2. A solution containing 15.2 g of barium bromide is reacted with a solution containing excess sodium phosphate to form 9.5 g of precipitate. What is the percentage yield of the reaction? Begin with a balanced equation.

3. Copper(II) oxide reacts with hydrogen gas to form water and copper metal. From this reaction, 3.6 g of copper metal was obtained with a yield of 32.5%. What mass of copper(II) oxide was reacted with the excess hydrogen gas? Begin with a balanced equation.

6.2 Activity: Charting and Graphing Stoichiometry

Question

What are some different ways to represent stoichiometric data?

Background

A student performs a single replacement reaction between pure magnesium metal and hydrochloric acid under two different conditions. The quantities involved are measured and recorded in tabular and graphic forms.

The reactions are performed in 250.0 mL of HCl(*aq*). The magnesium is weighed before and after the reactions are completed. The reactions are allowed to proceed for the same period of time in both trials. In both cases, once the reaction is completed, the volume of gas is measured under STP conditions.

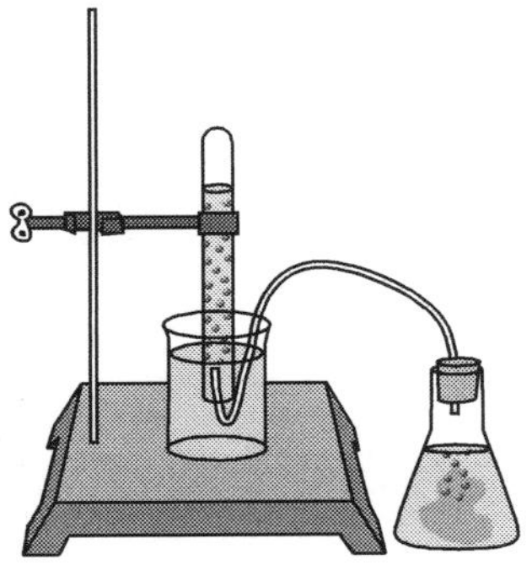

Measured Items	Very Hot	Very Cold
Initial mass of Mg(*s*)	1.00 g	1.00 g
Final mass of Mg(*s*)	0.00 g	0.75 g
Volume of $H_2(g)$	? mL	? mL
Volume of HCl(*aq*)	250.0 mL	250.0 mL
Initial Concentration of HCl(*aq*)	1.00 mol/L	1.00 mol/L

Procedure

1. Complete the following tables for the reaction under very hot and very cold conditions. Include signs in the "change in number of moles row" to indicate an increase or decrease in the number of moles.

Very Hot: $Mg(s) + 2\ HCl(aq) \rightarrow MgCl_2(aq) + H_2(g)$

Reaction species	Mg(*s*)	HCl(*aq*)	$MgCl_2(aq)$	$H_2(g)$
Initial number of moles				
Change in number of moles				
Final number of moles				

Very Cold: $Mg(s) + 2\ HCl(aq) \rightarrow MgCl_2(aq) + H_2(g)$

Reaction species	Mg(*s*)	HCl(*aq*)	$MgCl_2(aq)$	$H_2(g)$
Initial number of moles				
Change in number of moles				
Final number of moles				

Results and Discussion

1. What is the limiting reagent in the reaction under both conditions?

2. What conditions are required to complete the reaction?

3. What volume of hydrogen gas (measured at STP) is formed under very hot conditions? Under very cold conditions?

4. What is the percentage yield under very cold conditions?

5. What is the final concentration of magnesium chloride solution under very hot conditions? Under very cold conditions?

6. Using the graph "paper" below, sketch a graph to show the change in the number of moles of each species as the reaction proceeds under very hot and very cold conditions. Think of the *x*-axis as similar to that in the potential energy diagrams. Compare your graphs with those of a classmate.

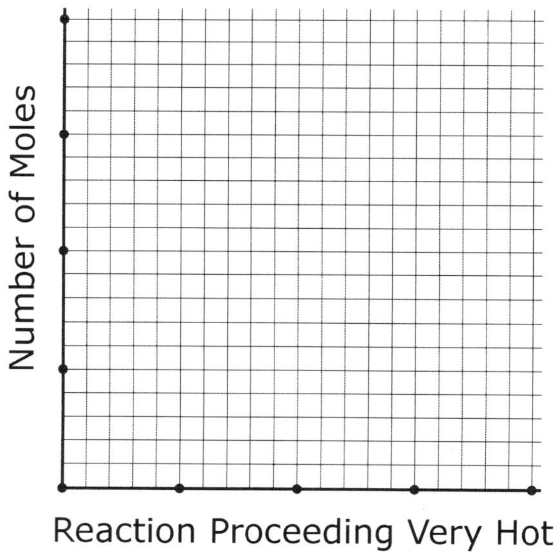

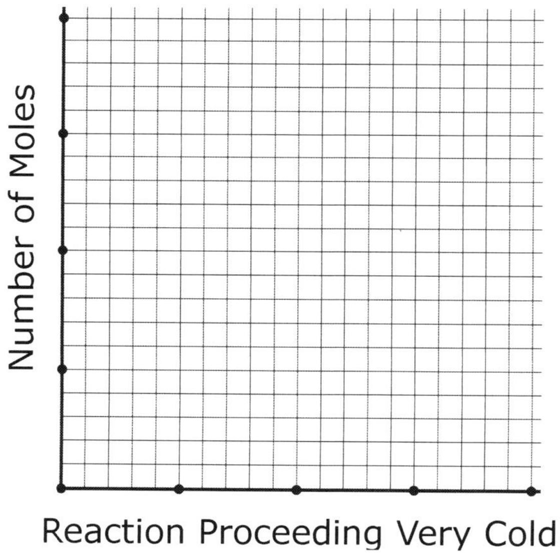

6.2 Review Questions

1. Do all reactions between two chemicals result in a complete reaction in such a way that all the reactants are consumed and turn in to products? Explain.

2. What do we call the chemicals that remain unreacted following a chemical change?

3. What is the percentage yield of a reaction?

4. Are all reactants in a chemical reaction completely pure? How might this affect a stoichiometry calculation?

5. A saturated solution of lithium fluoride, which is sometimes used as a rinse to prevent tooth decay, contains 0.132 g of LiF in 100.0 g of water. Calculate the percentage purity by mass of the LiF.

6. Automotive air bags inflate when solid sodium azide (NaN_3) decomposes explosively into its constituent elements. What volume of nitrogen gas is formed if 120 g of 85% pure sodium azide decomposes? Assume STP conditions.

7. Silver nitrate and aluminum chloride react with each other by exchanging anions:

   $3\ AgNO_3(aq) + AlCl_3(aq) \rightarrow Al(NO_3)_3(aq) + 3\ AgCl(s)$

   What mass of precipitate is produced when 4.22 g of silver nitrate react with 7.73 g of aluminum chloride in solution?

8. GeF_3H is synthesized in the reaction: $GeH_4 + 3\ GeF_4 \rightarrow 4\ GeF_3H$. If the reaction yield is 91.5%, how many moles of GeH_4 are needed to produce 8.00 mol of GeF_3H?

9. What is the maximum mass of sulfur trioxide gas that can be formed from the combination of 5.00 g each of S_8 solid with O_2 gas? Begin with a balanced equation.

10. In the reaction in question 9, 63.2 g of sulfur trioxide are produced using 40.0 g of oxygen and 48.0 g of sulfur. What is the percentage yield?

11. What volume of 0.105 mol/ L silver nitrate solution would be required to react completely with an excess of magnesium chloride solution to produce 8.95 g of precipitate? Assume the precipitate is only 75.0% pure, as it is still damp following filtration. Begin with a balanced equation.

12. What mass of silver could be formed if a large zinc wire is placed in a beaker containing 145.0 mL of 0.095 mol/L silver nitrate and allowed to react overnight? Assume the reaction has a 97% yield.

13. 8.92 g of indium oxide is reacted with an excess of water and forms 10.1 g of base. What is the percent yield?

14. What volume of chlorine gas could be produced under STP conditions if 39.8 g of 84.0% pure potassium chloride were reacted with an excess of fluorine gas?

15. An aqueous solution containing 46.7 g of copper(I) nitrate is placed into an aqueous solution containing 30.8 g of strontium bromide. The resulting mixture was filtered to remove the copper(I) bromide precipitate. Assuming a 100% yield:
(a) What is the mass of solid collected on the filter paper?

(b) Which reactant is in excess?

(c) How many grams of the excess reactant remains when the reaction has gone to completion?

16. A 20.0 g piece of calcium metal reacts with 18.0 mL of water over time. If 10.0 L of hydrogen gas is formed under STP conditions, what is the percentage yield of the reaction? (Recall the density of water is 1.00 g/mL.)

17. Excess silver nitrate is dissolved in a total volume of 250 mL of 0.103 mol/L calcium chloride solution. The resulting reaction produces 4.41 g of silver chloride precipitate. What was the percentage purity of the calcium chloride?

18. A sample of impure silver with a mass of 0.7294 g was dissolved in excess concentrated nitric acid according to the following *unbalanced* equation:
$Ag(s) + HNO_3(aq) \rightarrow AgNO_3(aq) + NO(g) + H_2O(l)$
Once the nitrogen monoxide gas was vented off in a fume hood, the resulting silver nitrate solution was reacted with a slight excess of hydrochloric acid to form a precipitate of silver chloride. The dried precipitate's mass was 0.3295 g. What was the percentage purity of the silver sample?

Reaction Stoichiometry

1. Calculate the number of moles of carbon dioxide formed when 40.0 mol of oxygen are consumed in the burning of propane (C_3H_8).
2. Cassiterite, SnO_2, is the major ore of tin. How many kilograms of carbon are needed to convert 50.0 kg of cassiterite to metallic tin according to the equation below:

   $$SnO_2(s) + 2C(s) \rightarrow Sn(l) + 2CO(g)$$

3. How many grams of magnesium will completely react with 2.25 mol of hydrochloric acid?
4. If a 0.50 mol sample of $KClO_3$ decomposes, how many moles of each product will be produced? How many grams of oxygen will be produced?
5. When heated with oxygen, bismuth metal reacts to form bismuth (III) oxide. How many grams of oxygen will combine with 30.0 g of bismuth?
6. How many grams of oxygen are required to burn 75.0 g of ammonia? (The products are nitrogen monoxide and water)
7. When chlorine gas is bubbled into hot potassium hydroxide solution, potassium chloride, potassium chlorate and water are produced.
   a. How many grams of potassium hydroxide are required to produce 50.0 g of potassium chlorate?
   b. How many grams of chlorine will be consumed in the reaction?
8. How many grams of oxygen are needed to convert 500 g of sulfur dioxide to sulfur trioxide?
9. How many grams of ammonia will be produced when 2.5 g of hydrogen gas reacts in excess nitrogen?
10. How many grams of calcium chloride will be produced if 40.0 g of calcium carbonate reacts with a stoichiometrically equivalent amount of hydrochloric acid?
11. Hydrogen sulfide burns in oxygen to form sulfur dioxide and water. If 17.0 g of hydrogen sulfide are mixed with excess oxygen, what mass of sulfur dioxide will be produced?
12. How many grams of phosphoric acid will be produced if 30.0 g of tetraphosphorus decoxide reacts completely with a stoichiometrically equivalent amount of water?

Answers

1. 24.0 mol
2. 7.97 kg
3. 27.2 g
4. 0.50 mol KCl, 0.75 mol O_2, 24.0 g
5. 3.45 g
6. 176 g
7. (a) 137 g (b) 86.8 g
8. 125 g
9. 14.1 g
10. 44.4 g
11. 32.0 g
12. 41.4 g

More Stoichiometry Problems
Theoretical, Actual and Percent Yield

1. The equation for the synthesis of bromobenzene from bromine and benzene is

   $$C_6H_6\,(l) + Br_2(l) \rightarrow C_6H_5Br(l) + HBr(g)$$

   A 12.85 g yield of bromobenzene was obtained when 8.00 g of benzene and excess bromine were combined. What is the theoretical yield for this reaction? What is the percent yield?

2. Copper (I) sulfide forms when copper is heated in excess sulfur. If 99.8 g of copper was heated in excess sulfur, and 50.0 g of copper (I) sulfide was obtained, what is the percent yield for this reaction?

3. Lye, or caustic soda, (NaOH) is prepared commercially by passing an electric current through a concentrated solution of sodium chloride and water. The other products of the reaction are hydrogen and chlorine gas. Calculate the theoretical yield of lye if 125 kg of sodium chloride is electrolyzed. If 55.4 kg of lye is produced, what it the percent yield for the reaction?

4. Chlorobenzene is a starting material for the production of aspirin and other related compounds and is prepared by reacting benzene with chlorine gas. The other product of the reaction is hydrogen chloride gas. If a 10.0 kg sample of benzene is treated with excess chlorine and yields 10.4 kg of chlorobenzene, what is the percent yield?

5. Freon-12 (CCl_2F_2) is a gas that has been used as a refrigerant. It is prepared by the reaction between carbon tetrachloride and antimony trifluoride. Antimony trichloride is the other product of the reaction. If the percent yield of this reaction is 72.0%, how many grams of antimony trifluoride must be combined in excess carbon tetrachloride to obtain a yield of 25.0 g of Freon-12?

6. Acetic acid can be prepared by heating methanol with carbon monoxide in the presences of a catalyst. If a mixture containing 105 g of methanol and 75.0 g of carbon monoxide is allowed to react, (a) calculate the theoretical yield of acetic acid and (b) the actual yield if the percent yield for the reaction is 85.0%

7. Titanium, an important metal used in the aircraft industry, can be prepared by reacting titanium tetrachloride with magnesium metal. When 180 kg of $TiCl_4$ is mixed with 55.0 kg of molten magnesium, 40.4 kg of titanium is produced. Calculate (a) the theoretical yield for the reaction and (b) the percent yield of titanium

Answers

1. 16.1 g
2. 40.0%
3. 8.56×10^4 g, 64.8%
4. 71.5%
5. 34.7 g
6. 161 g, 137 g
7. 45.4 kg, 88.9%

7 Solutions

This chapter focuses on the following AP Big Ideas from the College Board:

Big Idea 1: The chemical elements are fundamental building materials of matter, and all matter can be understood in terms of arrangements of atoms. These atoms retain their identity in chemical reactions.
Big Idea 2: Chemical and physical properties of materials can be explained by the structure and the arrangement of atoms, ions, or molecules and the forces between them.

By the end of this chapter, you should be able to do the following:

- Distinguish between a solution and a pure substance
- Predict the relative solubility of a solute in a solvent, based on its polarity
- Relate ion formation to electrical conductivity in aqueous solutions
- Calculate the concentration of ions in solution

By the end of this chapter you should know the meaning of these **key terms**:

- acid-base neutralization
- dissociation equation
- electrical conductivity
- ion charge
- ionization equation
- molarity
- molar solution
- mole
- non-polar
- polar
- solute
- solution
- solvent

The interactions of solutes and solvents create solutions with a wide range of useful properties.

7.1 The Nature of Solutions

Warm Up

Below is a list of common substances. Classify each as a pure substance or mixture by placing a checkmark in the appropriate column:

	Pure Substance	Mixture
Car exhaust		
Tap water		
Carbon dioxide		
Freshly squeezed orange juice		
Stainless steel		
Tea		
Diamond		
Cigarette smoke		

Solutions

In the Warm Up above, most of the substances are mixtures. You have learned to classify matter as a pure substance or mixture. Pure substances are either elements or compounds. You can write a chemical formula for a pure substance. A mixture contains two or more components mixed in a variety of proportions. The components can be separated by physical means. There are many types of mixtures: suspensions, colloids, and mechanical mixtures. In this chapter, we will be looking more closely at a specific type of mixture: a solution.

A **solution** is a homogeneous mixture that exists in one phase. It has a uniform composition throughout the sample on a macroscopic level and retains some of the properties of its components. For example, a sample of ocean water is a mixture of water, salts, and other dissolved substances. It looks the same throughout and has some properties of its components such as a salty taste.

A solution is made up of a solute and a solvent. The **solute** is the substance that is dissolved in the solvent. The **solvent** is the substance that dissolves one or more solutes in a solution. More than one type of solute can be dissolved in the solvent. In a solution of salt water, the salts are the solutes and the water is the solvent. Typically the solvent is the substance in the mixture in the greatest quantity, and the solute is the component in the solution in the lesser quantity.

For some solutions, the components can be mixed in any proportion to give a homogeneous mixture. In this case, we say that the components are **miscible**. This means they are soluble in any proportion. For example, we can mix water and alcohol in any proportion to form a solution. Alcohol and water are miscible. When we mix corn oil and water together, they do not mix in any proportion. We say that vegetable oil and water are **immiscible** (Figure 7.1.1).

Figure 7.1.1 *Immiscible liquids do not mix. The liquids are corn oil (above) and water (below).*

A solution can exist in any of the three phases: solid, liquid, or gas. The table below summarizes examples of solutions:

State of Solute	State of Solvent	State of Solution	Example
gas	gas	gas	air
gas	liquid	liquid	carbonated water
gas	solid	solid	hydrogen in palladium
liquid	liquid	liquid	alcohol in water
liquid	solid	solid	mercury in silver amalgam
solid	liquid	liquid	sugar in water
solid	solid	solid	alloys such as brass, a solution of copper and zinc

Quick Check

In the warm up activity, you classified the substances as pure substances or mixtures. For the substances that you classified as mixtures, list the ones that are solutions.

____

Water: The Most Common Solvent

Many chemical reactions occur in solutions. If the solvent is water, we call it an **aqueous** solution. Important reactions happening in your body and many reactions used in your everyday life are aqueous reactions.

A solute that dissolves in a solvent is said to be **soluble.** For example, NaCl is soluble in water.

The **solubility** of a substance is the maximum amount of solute that will dissolve in a given amount of solvent at a particular temperature.

There are many units of solubility including:

- molarity (M): moles of solute/liters of solution
- grams of solute/mL of solution
- grams of solute/100 g water
- ppm: parts per million

When the solubility is given as a molarity, we call it the **molar solubility**.

Sample Problem — Converting Between Units of Solubility

The solubility of $CaSO_4$ is 1.1 g/L at 25°C. Calculate its molar solubility.

What to Think about	How to Do It
1. We need to convert between mass and moles of solute. To do this, use the molar mass of $CaSO_4$.	The molar mass of $CaSO_4$ is 136.1 g/mol.
2. The molar solubility is measured using units mol/L or M.	$M = \frac{1.1\ \text{g}}{1\ \text{L}} \times \frac{1\ \text{mol}}{136.1\ \text{g}} = 8.1 \times 10^{-3}\ \text{M}$ The molar solubility is 8.1×10^{-3} M.

Practice Problems — Converting Between Units of Solubility

1. The molar solubility of $SrCO_3$ is 2.4×10^{-5} M at 25°C. What is its solubility in g/L?

2. The solubility of Ag_3AsO_4 is 1.4×10^{-6} M at 25°C. What is its solubility in g/mL?

3. If 500 mL of a saturated solution of AgCl contains 9.3×10^{-4} g AgCl, what is its molar solubility?

4. The solubility of $Cu(IO_3)_2$ is 2.6×10^{-3} M at 25°C. What mass of dissolved solute is present in 250 mL of solution?

Determining Whether or Not a Solute will Dissolve in Water

Recall that a salt is an ionic compound made up of a cation and anion. Substances that do not dissolve in a given solvent are **insoluble**. For example, carbon is insoluble in water.

Some salts dissolve better in water than others. To predict the solubility of some salts, we can use a solubility table like Table 7.1.1. As you examine this table, note the following:

- The word "soluble" means that more than 0.1 mol of solute will dissolve in 1.0 L of solution at 25°C.
- "Low solubility" means that less than 0.1 mol of solute will dissolve in 1.0 L of solution at 25°C. This does not mean that this substance is insoluble; just that very little can dissolve.
- The alkali ions are listed individually at the top of the table in the first row. Farther down the table, they are simply referred to as "alkali ions."

Table 7.1.1 *Solubility of Common Compounds in Water*

Note: *In this table, soluble means* > 0.1 mol/L at 25°C.

Negative Ions (Anions)	Positive Ions (Cations)	Solubility of Compounds
All	Alkali ions: Li^+, Na^+, K^+, Rb^+, Cs^+, Fr^+	Soluble
All	Hydrogen ion: H^+	Soluble
All	Ammonium ion: NH_4^+	Soluble
Nitrate: NO_3^-	All	Soluble
Chloride: Cl^- Or Bromide: Br^- Or Iodide: I^-	All others	Soluble
	Ag^+, Pb^{2+}, Cu^+, Hg^{2+}	Low solubility
Sulfate: SO_4^{2-}	All others	Soluble
	Ag^+, Ca^{2+}, Sr^{2+}, Ba^{2+}, Pb^{2+}	Low solubility
Sulfide: S^{2-}	Alkali ions, H^+, NH_4^+, Be^{2+}, Mg^{2+}, Ca^{2+}, Sr^{2+}, Ba^{2+}	Soluble
	All others	Low solubility
Hydroxide: OH^-	Alkali ions, H^+, NH_4^+, Sr^{2+}	Soluble
	All others	Low solubility
Phosphate: PO_4^{3-} Or Carbonate: CO_3^{2-} Or Sulfite: SO_3^{2-}	Alkali ions, H^+, NH_4^+	Soluble
	All others	Low solubility

Quick Check

1. What is an anion? A cation?

   ____

2. Salts containing which cations are always soluble? ____________________
3. Salts containing which anion are always soluble? ____________________
4. Salts containing which anions have a low solubility most often? ____________________

Sample Problem — Predicting the Relative Solubility of Salts in Water

According to the solubility table (Table 7.1.1), is AgCl soluble in water, or does it have a low solubility?

What to Think about	How to Do It
1. Identify the anion in the salt.	The anion is chloride: Cl^-
2. On the table, find the anion, then read across from that anion and find the cation in the salt.	The cation is Ag^+
3. If it is soluble, then the salt has a solubility greater than 0.1 M. If it has a low solubility, then its solubility is less than 0.1 M.	AgCl has a low solubility in water.

Practice Problems — Predicting the Relative Solubility of Salts in Water

For the following salts, use the solubility table (Table 7.1.1) to predict whether they are soluble (S), or have a low solubility (LS):

1. NaCl	______	6. zinc sulfite	______
2. $CaCO_3$	______	7. ammonium hydroxide	______
3. $CuCl_2$	______	8. cesium phosphate	______
4. $Al_2(SO_4)_3$	______	9. copper(I) chloride	______
5. BaS	______	10. chromium(III) nitrate	______

Saturated and Unsaturated Solutions

A solution is **unsaturated** when the solute is completely dissolved in the solvent. Consider making a solution of NaCl in water. At the beginning, you add a small amount of NaCl to the water, and the NaCl completely dissolves. The solution is unsaturated. As you add more NaCl, it continues to dissolve. At a certain point, as you add NaCl, no more will dissolve. A **saturated** solution is one in which no more solid will dissolve. For the solution to be saturated, there must be undissolved solid in the solution. Some solutions can be **supersaturated**. In these solutions, there is more dissolved solute than there would normally be. Supersaturated solutions are very unstable. They can be made by preparing a more concentrated solution at a higher temperature, then slowly cooling the solution (Figure 7.1.2).

Figure 7.1.2 *As the supersaturated solution of sodium acetate trihydrate is slowly poured onto a plate, it immediately crystallizes as the solid solute reforms*

7.1 Activity: Change in Solubility with Temperature

Question

How does the solubility of different salts change with temperature?

Background

You have probably observed that you can dissolve more salt in hot water than in cold water because the solubility of a substance changes with temperature. The solubility of some salts in water as a function of temperature is shown in the graph below. Each line on the graph represents a different salt.

From the graph, you can see that different salts have very different solubilities in water. For example, at 100°C, the solubility of NaCl in water is 6.7 M while for AgCl it is 1.4×10^{-4} M. In the example above, AgCl has a low solubility compared to NaCl.

Procedure

1. Use this graph to answer the questions below. The graph represents the solubility of a number of different salts in water. Note the units of solubility given on the *y*-axis.

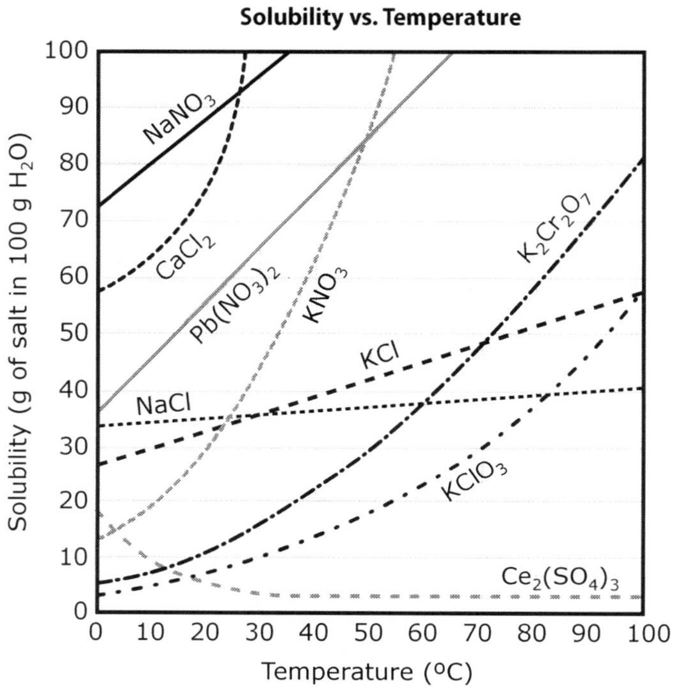

Results and Discussion

1. Which salt has the highest solubility at 5°C? At 28°C?

____

2. Does the salt with the lowest solubility at 0°C have the lowest solubility at 90°C?

____

3. Complete this sentence:
   As the temperature increases, the solubility of most salts ____________. (increases or decreases)

4. For which salt does the amount of solute dissolved decrease as temperature increase?

7.1 Review Questions

1. Define homogeneous, heterogeneous, pure substance, and mixture. Give an example for each.

2. Classify the following as a pure substance or a mixture. If it is a mixture, then state whether or not it is a solution.

   (a) distilled water

   (b) 9 carat gold

   (c) gasoline

   (d) wood

   (e) bronze

   (f) chocolate chip ice cream

   (g) coffee

   (h) coal

3. Complete the following sentences using the terms solute, solvent, miscible, and immiscible.
   A solution is composed of a __________ and __________.
   The ____________ is the substance that makes up the larger part of the solution. If two components can be mixed in any proportions to make a homogeneous mixture, they are _______________.

4. Give an example of two substances that are immiscible when mixed. Describe what you would see if you mixed them together.

5. When the solubility of a substance is given, what information must be specified?

6. The molar solubility of lead(II) bromide is 2.6×10^{-3} M. What is its solubility in g/ml?

7. A saturated solution contains 0.0015g CaC_2O_4 dissolved in 250 mL solution. What is the molar solubility of CaC_2O_4?

8. The molar solubility of $AgIO_3$ is 1.8×10^{-4} M. Express its solubility in g $AgIO_3$ /mL water. Assume that the volume of solvent = volume of solution.

9. What does the term aqueous mean?

10. Using Table 7.1.1, list three salts containing the sulfide anion that would have a low solubility in water at 25°C.

11. Using Table 7.1.1, list three salts containing the anion carbonate that would be soluble at 25°C.

12. List the cations in a salt that are soluble when paired with any anion.

13. Classify each of the following compounds as soluble or low solubility according to Table 7.1.1.

(a) H_2SO_4 ____________________

(b) MgS ____________________

(c) $(NH_4)_2SO_3$ ____________________

(d) RbOH ____________________

(e) $PbSO_4$ ____________________

(f) $CuBr_2$ ____________________

(g) $Zn(NO_3)_2$ ____________________

(h) $FeSO_4$ ____________________

14. A student dissolves 0.53g of $LiCH_3COO$ in water at 25°C to make 100 mL of solution. Is the solution formed saturated or unsaturated? Justify your answer with calculations and by referring to Table 7.1.1.

7.2 What Dissolves and What Doesn't — "Like Dissolves Like"

Warm Up

Chemical bonds *between atoms* in a molecule can be classified as ionic, polar covalent, and nonpolar covalent. These are intramolecular forces. However, there are also attractive forces *between molecules* that are called intermolecular forces. For each of the following substances, list all of the intermolecular forces present.

Substance	Intermolecular Forces Present
Example: H_2O	hydrogen bonding, dipole-dipole, dispersion forces
I_2	
HF	
PCl_3	
CH_3CH_2OH	

Like Dissolves Like

Many people take vitamins to supplement their diet. Two commonly used vitamins are vitamins A and C. Vitamin A plays an important role in maintaining vision, bone growth, and a properly functioning immune system. The most common form of vitamin A is called retinol and is found in foods from animals. Your body can store vitamin A because it is fat-soluble. This vitamin is not soluble in water so it is called "hydrophobic," which means "water hating."

Vitamin C, called ascorbic acid, is also important for your immune system and is a powerful anti-oxidant. Because your body cannot store vitamin C in your fat cells, you must get an adequate amount from your daily diet. A deficiency of vitamin C leads to a disease called scurvy. Historically, sailors on long sea voyages would get scurvy because they didn't have fresh fruit to eat. The link between scurvy and vitamin C was not made until 1932. However, sailors were treated for scurvy earlier than this with citrus fruits. Britain's Royal Navy used limes to prevent scurvy, so British sailors were called "limeys." Vitamin C is water-soluble so is called "hydrophilic," which means "water loving."

In this section we will explore why certain substances dissolve in a particular solvent. Why does vitamin C dissolve in water but not in fat? The answer lies in the structure and intermolecular forces present in the vitamins, fat, and water.

"Like dissolves like" means that a solute will dissolve in a solvent if both contain similar types of intermolecular forces and these forces are of similar magnitude.

There are three important criteria for a substance to dissolve:

1. The particles in the solute must be separated from each other to go into the solvent. The attraction between solute particles must be overcome or replaced.
2. The particles in the solvent must be separated from each other to allow space for the solute particles. The attraction between solvent particles must be overcome or replaced.
3. The solute and solvent particles must interact with each other.

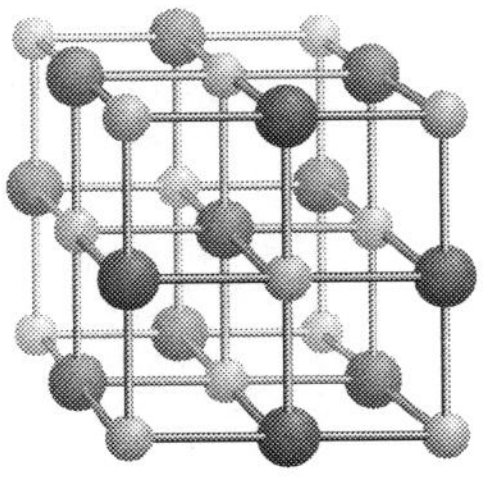

Figure 7.2.1 *NaCl crystal*

An Ionic Solute in a Polar Solvent: NaCl(*s*) in water

- The solute is held together by the attraction of the positive Na+ ions to the negative Cl^- ions (Figure 7.2.1). For this solute to dissolve, the attraction between these two ions must be overcome.

- The water molecules in the solvent are attracted to each other by hydrogen bonding. Each water molecule has a positive end and a negative end. The molecules line up and hydrogen bonds form between water molecules.

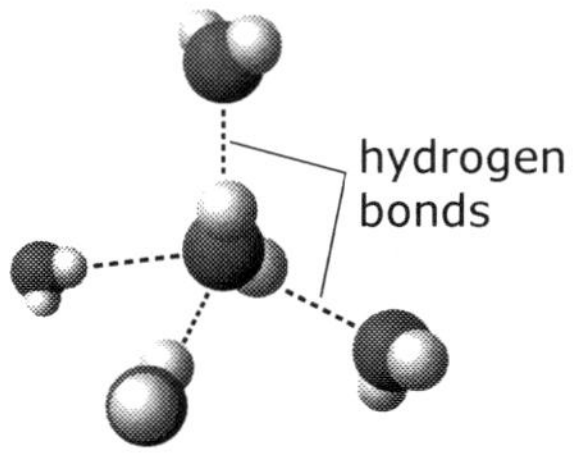

Figure 7.2.2 *Hydrogen bonding in water*

- As water molecules bump into the solid solute, the negative dipoles on the oxygen atoms are attracted to the positive ions in the solute. Likewise, the positive dipoles on the hydrogen atoms are attracted to the negative ions in the solute. Both ions become hydrated, which means they are surrounded by water molecules. The water molecules' attraction for each other and the attraction of the ions for each other are now replaced by the water molecules' attraction for each ion. Notice how the water molecules align themselves around each ion (Figure 7.2.3).

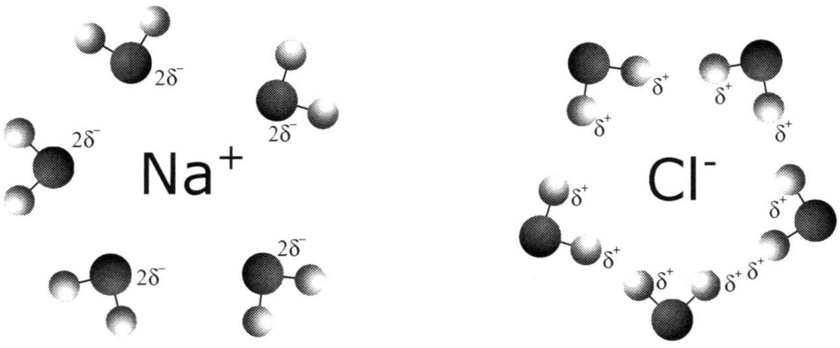

Negative poles on the oxygen atoms are attracted to the positive sodium ions.

Positive poles on the hydrogen atoms are attracted to the negative chloride ions.

Figure 7.2.3 *Water molecules surround the ions from NaCl.*

The strong attraction of water molecules for each ion is called the **ion-dipole force**. This force is similar in size and type to the ionic attractions in the solute and the hydrogen bonds in the solvent.

Not all ionic salts are soluble in water. The detailed explanation of why salts such as AgCl are *not* able to dissolve well in water is beyond the scope of this course. Simply put, the attraction of the Ag^+ ion to the Cl^- ion is too large for the ion-dipole forces to overcome.

Quick Check

1. What is "like" between NaCl and H_2O? Why do they interact as they do?

____

____

2. Explain why water molecules will not surround I_2 molecules? What forces must be overcome between each water molecule?

____

3. Would you expect NaCl to dissolve in oil, which is a non-polar solvent? Explain.

____

4. Predict whether NaCl would dissolve in NH_3 liquid. Draw a diagram to show the forces acting within the solute, the solvent, and the resulting mixture.

____

A Polar Solute in a Polar Solvent: Ethanol in Water

- Ethanol contains an oxygen atom bonded to a hydrogen atom on the end of a hydrocarbon chain (Figure 7.2.4). In an ionic compound, the –OH group is called hydroxide and helps us identify the substance as a base. In an organic molecule such as ethanol, the –OH group is called a hydroxyl group and is associated with an alcohol. The –OH group at the end of the alcohol is polar and forms hydrogen bonds with nearby ethanol molecules. The hydrocarbon chain acts as a non-polar section, but in ethanol it is quite small.

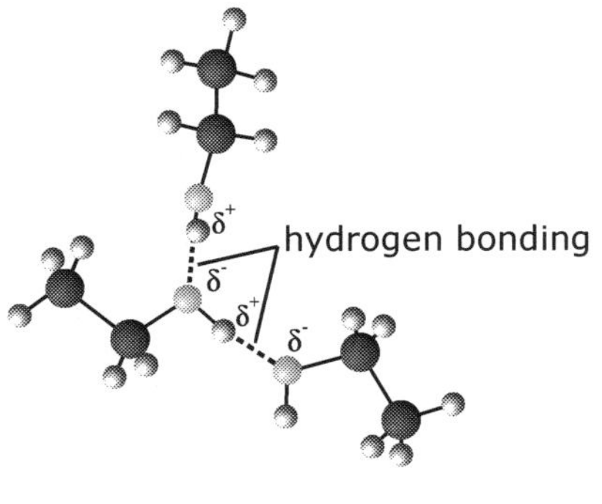

Figure 7.2.4 *Hydrogen bonding in ethanol,* C_2H_5OH

- Water is polar. Water molecules are strongly attracted to each other by hydrogen bonds.
- When ethanol and water are combined, the hydrogen bonding between water and ethanol molecules is similar in strength to the hydrogen bonds in the ethanol solute and water solvent individually. Therefore, water and ethanol are miscible.

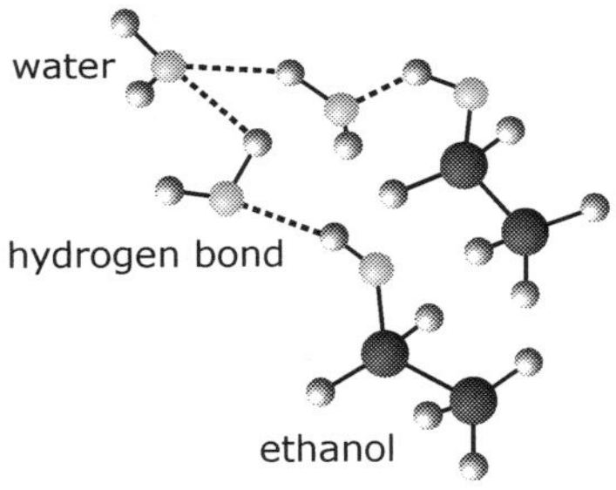

Figure 7.2.5 *Ethanol-water hydrogen bonding*

As the hydrocarbon chain part of an alcohol gets larger, the molecule becomes more non-polar. The hydrogen bonds between the larger alcohols are much weaker so the water molecules are not as attracted to the alcohol molecule. It becomes more difficult for the larger hydrocarbon chain on the alcohol to fit between water molecules. For this reason, butanol and pentanol are only partially soluble in water, and larger alcohols are almost insoluble in water.

Similarly, other organic compounds containing an –OH group are soluble in water. As you know, sugar is highly soluble in water. In fact, sugar has a higher solubility in water than NaCl does.

Each sugar molecule has five –OH groups on it (Figure 7.2.6). Each is available to make hydrogen bonds with water. Generally speaking, the more –OH groups on a hydrocarbon, the more soluble it will be in water.

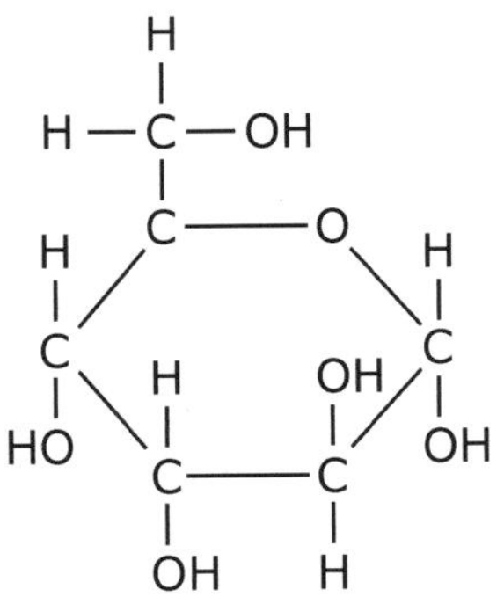

Figure 7.2.6 *Glucose molecule*

Formaldehyde in Chloroform

- Formaldehyde is a polar covalent compound. Molecules of formaldehyde are attracted to each other through **dipole-dipole forces**. In this type of force, the positive pole of one molecule is next to and attracts the negative pole of an adjacent molecule. In formaldehyde, the negative dipole on the oxygen atom in one molecule is attracted to the positive dipole on the carbon atom in the other molecule as shown by the dotted lines in Figure 7.2.7.

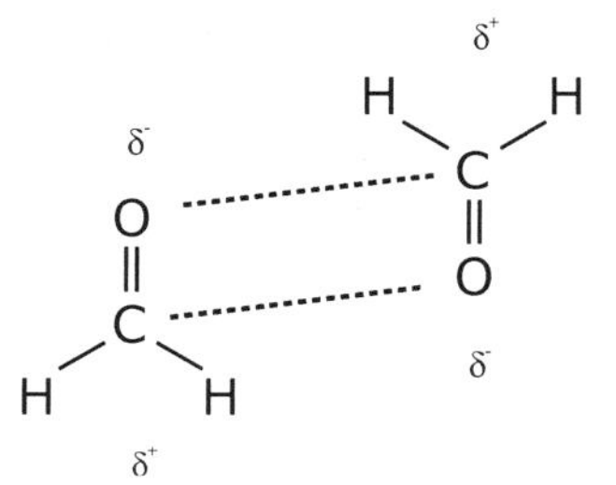

Figure 7.2.7 *Dipole-dipole attraction between formaldehyde molecules*

- Chloroform is also a polar covalent compound containing dipole-dipole forces (Figure 7.2.8).

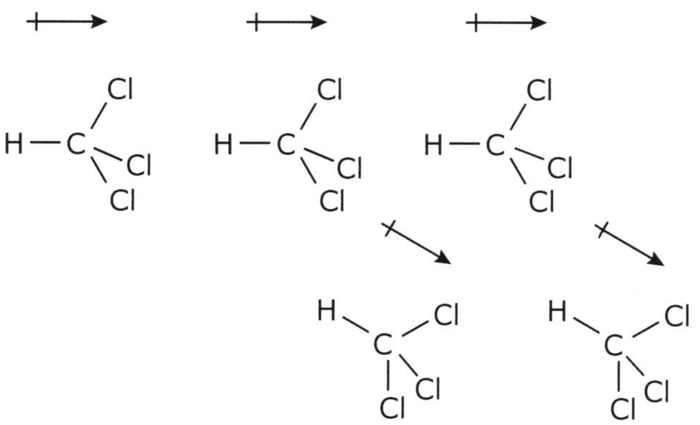

Figure 7.2.8 *Dipole-dipole attraction between chloroform molecules. The arrows point from positive to negative.*

- Formaldehyde is soluble in chloroform because the dipole-dipole interaction between formaldehyde and chloroform molecules in the solution is similar in strength to the dipole-dipole interactions in the solute and solvent individually.

Ionic and polar covalent solutes dissolve in polar covalent solvents.

Quick Check

1. Will ammonia dissolve in water? Explain.

   ____

2. Is ethanol soluble in hexane, C_6H_{14}? Explain.

   ____

3. Which is more soluble in water: C_2H_6 or CH_3OH? Explain.

   ____

4. Octanol has the formula $C_8H_{17}OH$. Explain why octanol does not dissolve in water.

   ____

A Non-polar Solute in a Non-polar Solvent: Iodine in Carbon Tetrachloride

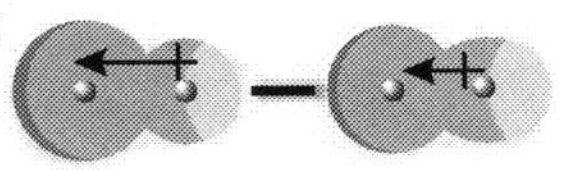

Figure 7.2.9 *Momentary dipoles or dispersion forces between I_2 molecules*

- Iodine, I_2, is a non-polar substance. The only interactions between I_2 molecules are very weak **London dispersion forces**. These forces occur when electrons on the atom of one molecule repel the nearby electrons on the atom of the other molecule. This creates a momentary and very weak positive dipole on the second molecule and the two molecules are weakly attracted to each other (Figure 7.2.9).
- Carbon tetrachloride, CCl_4, is also non-polar and interactions between molecules are limited to dispersion forces only.

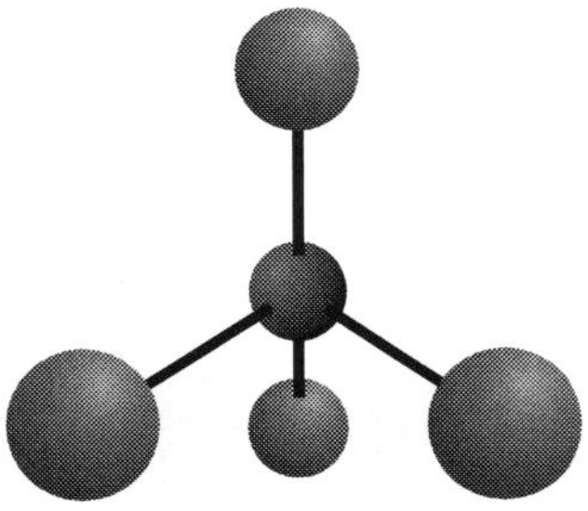

Figure 7.2.10 *Carbon tetrachloride*

- The dispersion forces acting between a molecule of I_2 and a molecule of CCl_4 are similar to the dispersion forces in each solute and solvent.

Non-polar covalent solutes are only soluble in non-polar solvents.

Quick Check

1. Paint thinner is a non-polar covalent solvent. Is iodine soluble in paint thinner? Explain.

   ____

2. Mothballs are made of naphthalene, $C_{10}H_8$. Will a mothball dissolve better in water or paint thinner? Explain.

   ____

3. A student places 10 mL of water and 10 mL of CCl_4 into a beaker. Solid iodine is added to the beaker. Explain what you would see and sketch a diagram of it.

   ____

4. Why can a molecule of CCl_4 not come between water molecules?

   ____

Fat and Water Soluble Vitamins

At the beginning of this section, you learned about the importance of vitamins A and C and their solubility in fat. The fat in your body is made up of non-polar molecules weakly attracted to each other by dispersion forces. By looking at the structure of vitamin A, you can see that it is a long hydrocarbon chain with a polar end on it (Figure 7.2.11). The length of the long hydrocarbon chain makes it essentially non-polar despite the presence of the hydroxyl group, so the forces between the vitamin A molecules are only weak dispersion forces. The fat molecules can dissolve with the vitamin A molecules because the dispersion forces in the fat and vitamin A molecules before they are mixed are replaced by the dispersion forces between the fat and vitamin A molecules in the resulting mixture.

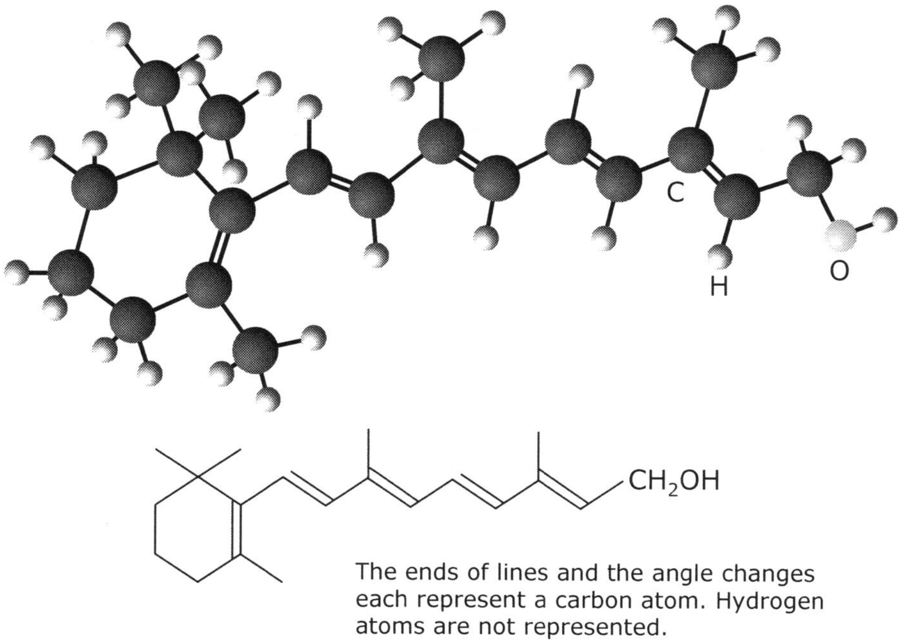

Figure 7.2.11 *Vitamin A*

Vitamin A is not water-soluble because the non-polar vitamin A molecules cannot get between the water molecules. The water molecules are attracted to each other through hydrogen bonds. This attraction cannot be overcome with a non-polar molecule. Vitamin C, however, contains many –OH groups, which makes it polar (Figure 7.2.12). The attraction between water molecules can be overcome by the attraction of water molecules for vitamin C molecules.

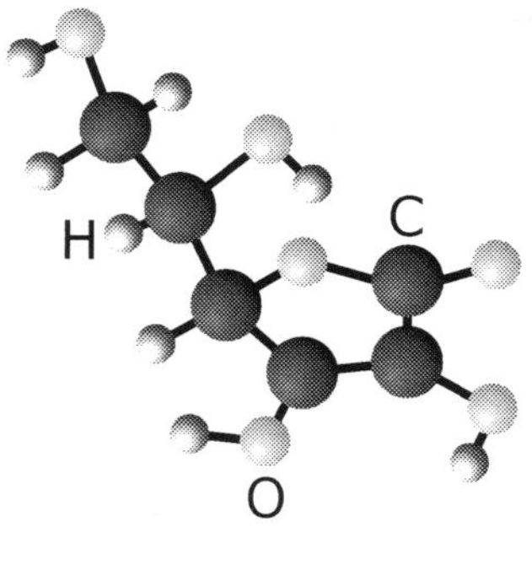

Figure 7.2.12 *Vitamin C*

Soaps

Soaps are an application of the like-dissolves-like principle. They are formulated to use organic molecules that contain positive and negative ions. Each negative ion has a long hydrocarbon "tail" that is non-polar and a "head" that is polar (Figure 7.2.13).

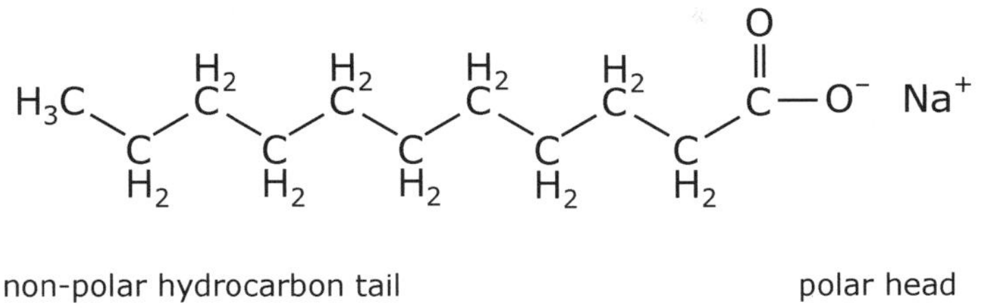

Figure 7.2.13 *A soap ion showing the non-polar "tail" and the polar "head"*

A molecule like this acts as an emulsifying agent, which allows immiscible liquids to become suspended in each other. The head is typically a $-COO^-$ group attached to a long chain made up of carbon and hydrogen. The $-COO^-$ group is polar and carries a negative charge. It interacts with the water molecules via ion-dipole forces and hydrogen bonding. The tail section is largely non-polar and will dissolve other non-polar grease and oil particles.

The soap molecules clump together with the hydrophilic heads pointing out, and the hydrophobic tails pointing in. These clumps are called "micelles" (Figure 7.2.14). The micelles trap the oil and grease in the centre. When you rinse off with water, the hydrophilic outside of the micelle rinses out with the water, taking the hydrophobic greasy centre with it.

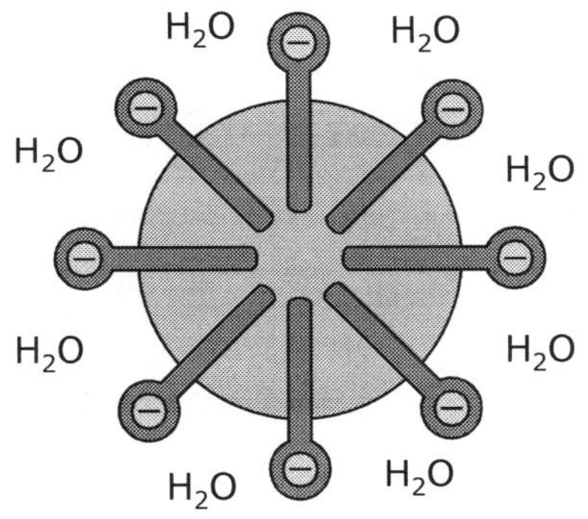

Figure 7.2.14 *A micelle*

7.2 Activity: Determining the Bond Type of a Solute

Question

What type of intramolecular bonds are present in an unknown solute?

Background

Stains on clothing may be thought of as a solute. In order to clean out a stain, it must be dissolved by a solvent. The type of solvent that successfully dissolves the stain identifies the type of stain on the clothing. Remember that "like dissolves like."

Procedure

1. A dry cleaner observes that a stain on a piece of clothing dissolves in water but not in tetrachloroethene. Look at the diagram of the structure of tetrachloroethene and answer the questions below.

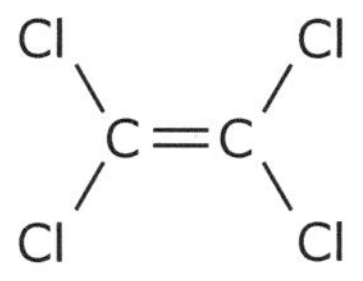

Tetrachloroethene

Results and Discussion

1. What types of intermolecular forces exist in water? In tetrachloroethene?

___

___

2. State the two possible bond types or intramolecular bonds present in the solute.

___

3. Explain why the stain did not dissolve in tetrachloroethene.

___

___

4. Explain why you cannot narrow down the solute bond type to just one type.

___

___

5. Compare your answers to those of another group. How do they compare?

___

___

7.2 Review Questions

1. Explain the phrase "like dissolves like" in your own words.

2. Is ethanol hydrophilic or hydrophobic? Explain using a diagram.

3. Is $Br_2(l)$ more soluble in $CS_2(l)$ or $NH_3(l)$? Explain.

4. Explain why NH_3 is very soluble in water, but NCl_3 is not.

5. When I_2 is added to water, it does not dissolve. However, if I_2 is added to an aqueous solution of KI, it will dissolve. Use the following reaction, and your understanding of intermolecular forces to explain the above observations.
   $I_2(s) + I^-(aq) \rightarrow I_3^-(aq)$

6. Which is more soluble in water? Explain.
   (a) C_4H_{10} or C_3H_6OH

   (b) $MgCl_2$ or toluene (C_7H_8)

7. Glycerin is a common solvent and is found in many skin care products. A student mixed 10 mL of water, 10 mL of glycerin and 10 mL of carbon tetrachloride together. A small amount of $CuCl_2$ was added to the mixture. Explain what you would see.

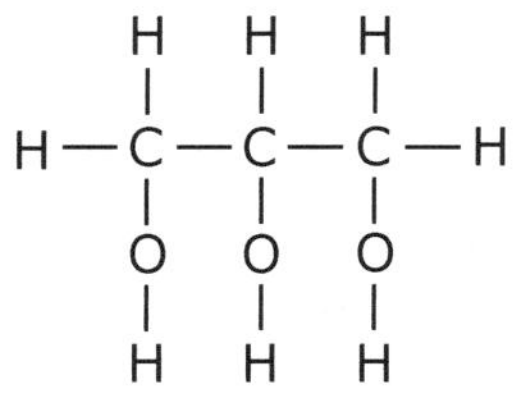

Glycerin

8. Ethylene glycol is commonly used as antifreeze. Underline the solvent in which it would be most soluble in each pair below.

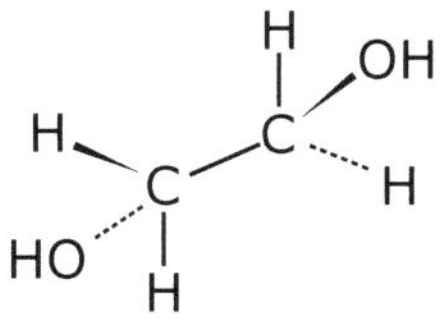

Ethylene glycol

(a) water or paint thinner (a non-polar covalent solvent)

(b) ammonia or carbon tetrachloride

(c) hexene (C_6H_{12}) or glycerin (a polar covalent solvent)

9. List the intermolecular forces present between the following solutes and solvents:

(a) CsCl in H_2O

(b) CH_3OH in glycerin

(c) N_2 in C_8H_{18}

(d) acetone in ammonia

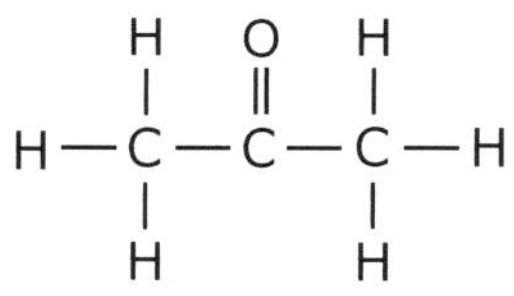

Acetone

7.3 Concentration

Concentration

The concentration of a solution is the amount of solute dissolved in a given amount of solvent.

Concentration can be measured in many ways including percent mass of solute by unit volume of solution (% m/v), percent mass of solute by mass of the solution (% m/m), percent volume of solute by volume tof solution (% v/v) and molar concentration, which is a measure of the number of moles of solute per Litre of solution. The following are the formulae for concentration calculations:

Mass/ Volume Percent concentration

$$\text{Mass/Volume Percent} = \frac{\text{Mass of Solute (g)}}{\text{Volume of Solution (mL)}} \times 100\%$$

Mass/ Mass Percent concentration

$$\text{Mass Percent} = \frac{\text{Mass of Solute}}{\text{Mass of Solution}} \times 100\%$$

Volume/Volume Percent concentration

$$\text{Volume Percent} = \frac{\text{Volume of Solute}}{\text{Volume of Solution}} \times 100\%$$

Molar Concentration

$$M = \frac{\text{Moles of Solute}}{\text{Liters of Solution}}$$

The concentration expression that is used most frequently by chemists is called the **molar concentration or molarity** of the solution. The molarity of a solution is the number of moles of a ______________ dissolved per litre of ______________. The molarity of a solution which contains one mole of solute dissolved in enough solvent to give one litre of solution would be a 1 molar solution. The units of molarity are mol L^{-1} which is often expressed as M.

If you were asked to make up one litre of 1.00 mol/L NaCl, what would you do?

If you were asked to make up one litre of 2.00 M NaCl, what would you do?

Practice problems

Example 1: How many grams of sugar $C_{12}H_{22}O_{11}$ are contained in 50 mL of a 0.40 mol L^{-1} solution of sugar in water?

Example 2: What is the concentration in moles per litre of a solution that contains 49.0 g of sulfuric acid in 3.0 L of solution?

Example 3: Vinegar is a 3.00% solution of acetic acid. How much pure acetic acid does a 2.50×10^2 mL solution of vinegar contain?

Example 4: A sterling silver ring has a mass of 12.0 g and contains 11.1 g of pure silver. What is the percentage concentration of silver in the ring?

Very Low Concentrations

Many concentrations are very low and cannot be reasonable expressed using the concentration units previously described. However, even really low concentrations can have quite a significant impact. For example, the *Guidelines for Canadian Drinking Water Quality* indicate potable water has a maximum limit of 0.0000010% m/m of lead in an aqueous solution of lead and water. These measures are better expressed in parts per million (ppm) or parts per billion (ppb). In this case 0.010 ppm or 10 ppb of lead is the acceptable limit for lead in drinking water according to the guidelines.

1 ppm	=	1g/ 10^6 mL
		1 g/ 1000L
		1 mg/L
		1 mg/kg
		1 µg/g

Practice Problems

Example 5: Dissolved oxygen in natural water is an important measure of the health of the ecosystem. In a chemical analysis of 250 mL of water at SATP, 2.2 mg of oxygen was measured. What is the concentration of oxygen in parts per million?

Example 6: In A sample of well water contains 0.24 ppm of dissolved iron (III) sulfate from the surrounding rocks. What mass of iron (III) sulfate is present in 1.2 L of water in a kettle?

Example 7: Here is a table of v/v concentrations of different gases in air. Calculate the ppm of each gas in air

Gas	v/v %	ppm concentration of the gas
Nitrogen	78.084	
Oxygen	20.945	
Argon	0.934	
Carbon dioxide	0.0350	
Neon	0.001818	
Helium	0.000524	
Methane	0.00017	

Concentration Problems

1. A solution contains 25 g of solute per 100 g of water. What is its percent composition? How much solute is contained in 20g of the solution?
2. What mass of hydrogen chloride is present in 250 mL of a 20% solution of hydrochloric acid whose density is 1.10 g/mL?
3. The density of 20% sulfuric acid is 1.14 g/mL. What mass of hydrogen sulfate is present in 1 L of solution?
4. How many moles of hydrogen nitrate are present in 1 L of a 20% solution of nitric acid and the density of which is 1.12 g/mL?
5. The density of a 14.0% solution of sodium carbonate in water is 1.15 g/mL. What mass of sodium carbonate would be obtained by evaporation of 200 mL of this solution? How many moles of sodium carbonate?
6. Calculate the molarity of a 21.8% solution of ammonia in water. The density of the solution is 0.920 g/mL.
7. A solution was prepared by dissolving 70.0 g of silver nitrate in water in a 1 L volumetric flask. What is the molarity of the solution?
8. How many grams of solute are present in 25.0 mL of a 2.00 M solution of potassium chloride?
9. Calculate the molarity of concentrated nitric acid from the information that it contains 70% HNO_3 by mass and has a density of 1.42 g/mL
10. What mass of iron (III) chloride would be required to prepare 80.0 mL of a 2.0 M solution?
11. What mass of copper (II) sulfate pentahydrate is required to prepare 18 L of a 1.5 M solution?
12. What mass of silver nitrate is required to prepare 100 mL of a 0.250 M solution?
13. A concentrated nitric acid solution has a density of 1.41 g/mL at 20°C, and is 69.0% hydrogen nitrate. What volume of it should be used in preparing 2.00 L of a 3.00 M nitric acid solution?
14. What volume of a 0.5 M oxalic acid solution can be prepared from 500 g of oxalic acid dihydrate ($H_2C_2O_4 \cdot 2H_2O$)?
15. Glacial acetic acid is supplied in about 98% concentration in bottles containing 2.5 L. What volume of 0.1 M acetic acid solution would you be able to prepare from the contents of one bottle? (density of glacial acetic acid = 1.056 g/mL)
16. What volume of 6.0 M hydrochloric acid should be diluted with water to prepare 1 L of a 1.2 M hydrochloric acid solution?
17. What volume of concentrated aqueous ammonia solution, which is 14 M when fresh, should be measured out and diluted with water to make 5.0 L of a 0.1 M solution?
18. Concentrated phosphoric acid is supplied in 85% solution, having a density of 1.44 g/mL. How much of this acid will be required to make 10 L of a 0.1 M solution?
19. The label on a bottle of perchloric acid indicates that it is a solution of 70% concentration and has a density of 1.17 g/mL. Calculate how much of this concentrated acid is needed to prepare 500 mL of a 0.15 M solution.

Answers

1. 20% solute, 4.0 g
2. 55 g
3. 228 g
4. 3.56 mol
5. 32.2 g, 0.304 mol
6. 11.8 M
7. 0.412 M
8. 3.73 g
9. 15.8 M
10. 26.0 g
11. 6.75 x 10^3 g
12. 4.25 g
13. 387 mL
14. 7.94 L
15. 431 L
16. 200 mL
17. 36 mL
18. 80 mL
19. 9.2 mL

Warm Up

1. List three products in your refrigerator that are solutions.

____

2. Name some substances that are dissolved in these solutions.

____

3. Where else in your home are solutions kept?

____

Examples of common household liquids

Molarity — A Useful Unit of Concentration

Many chemicals are dispensed in solution and most chemical reactions occur in solution. Recall that a solution is a type of mixture in which the chemical species are completely mixed. A solute is a minor component of the mixture, generally what has been dissolved. The solvent is the major component of the mixture, generally what the solute was dissolved in.

Concentration is any expression of the proportion of a chemical in a solution. Chemists need to know the amount of solute present in any volume of solution they might dispense. Therefore, concentration is most usefully expressed as an amount of solute per volume of solution rather than per volume of solvent. There are many units of concentration. Common units of concentration express the amount of solute in grams. These include grams per liter of solution, percent m/v, which is the number of grams (mass) per 100 mL (volume) of solution, and parts per million (ppm), when expressed as the number of grams per million grams of solution. A useful unit of concentration for chemists expresses the quantity of solute in moles.

Molarity (M) is the number of moles of the chemical per liter of solution.

For example, 1.8 M HCl means 1.8 mol HCl per liter of solution. Molar concentrations allow chemists to directly compare the number of particles in the same volume of different solutions. For example, 10 mL of 2 M Li^+ contains twice as many ions as 10 mL of 1 M Na^+.

Name	Equivalence Statement	Conversion Factors	
Molar concentration	1 L solution = ? mol solute	$\frac{\text{? mol solute}}{\text{1 L solution}}$	$\frac{\text{1 L solution}}{\text{? mol solute}}$
Example: 3 M HCN	1 L solution = 3 mol HCN	$\frac{\text{3 mol HCN}}{\text{1 L solution}}$	$\frac{\text{1 L solution}}{\text{3 mol HCN}}$

Quick Check

1. Give one reason why solutions are important in chemistry.

 ____

2. What does 2 M NaOH mean?

 ____

3. Why is molarity a useful unit of concentration?

 ____

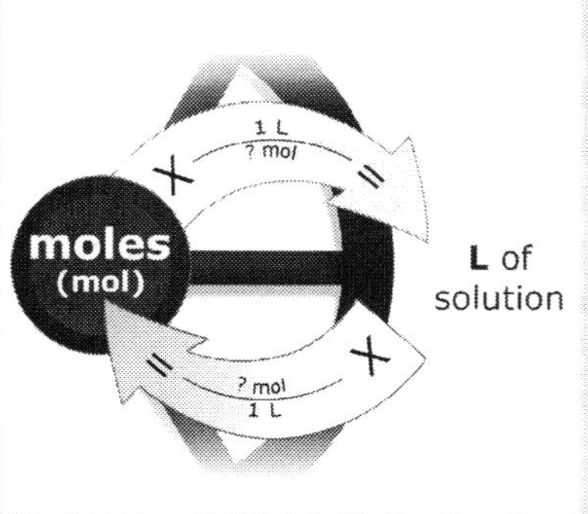

Sample Problem — Converting Volume of Solution into Moles of Solute	
The average salinity (total salt concentration) of seawater is 0.60 M. How many moles of salt are in a toy bucket containing 435 mL of seawater?	
What to Think about	**How to Do It**
1. Convert: mL → L 2. Convert: L soln → mol salt 3. Setup: $0.435 \text{ L soln} \times \frac{\text{? mol salt}}{1 \text{ L soln}}$ 4. Conversion factor: 0.60 mol salt per 1 L soln	$435 \text{ mL} \times \frac{1.0 \text{ L}}{1000 \text{ mL}} = 0.435 \text{ L}$ $0.435 \cancel{\text{L soln}} \times \frac{0.60 \text{ mol salt}}{1 \cancel{\text{L soln}}} = 0.26 \text{ mol salt}$ Note: There is no conventional abbreviation for "solution" but we will use "soln" in our calculations.

Sample Problem — Converting Moles of Solute into Volume of Solution	
What volume of 3.0 M HCl should a chemist dispense to obtain 0.25 mol HCl?	
What to Think about	**How to Do It**
1. Convert: mol HCl → L soln 2. Setup: $0.25 \text{ mol HCl} \times \frac{1 \text{ L soln}}{\text{? mol HCl}}$ 3. Conversion factor: 1 L soln per 3.0 mol HCl	$0.25 \cancel{\text{mol HCl}} \times \frac{1 \text{ L soln}}{3.0 \cancel{\text{mol HCl}}} = 0.083 \text{ L soln}$

Practice Problems — Converting Moles of Solute to/from Volume of Solution

1. 0.72 L of 2.5 M NaOH = _________ mol NaOH

2. An intravenous bag of saline solution contains 0.154 M NaCl. How many moles of NaCl does a 500.0 mL bag contain?

3. 3.0 mol HCl = _________ L of 0.60 M HCl

4. A person's urine may have a distinct odor as soon as 15 min after eating asparagus. Methanethiol, one of the metabolic products responsible for this odor, can be detected by some people in concentrations as low as 4.0×10^{-8} M. At this concentration, what volume of urine contains 1.0 mmol of methanethiol?

Preparing a Standard Solution from a Solid

A solution of known concentration is called a **standard solution**. To prepare a 1 M NaCl(*aq*) solution, you could measure out 1 mol (58.5 g) of NaCl and then add water up to 1 L of solution so that the 1 mol NaCl is dissolved in the resulting 1 L solution. Note that you "add water up to 1 L" not "add up to 1 L of water," which means something entirely different. Adding water *up to* 1 L of solution won't quite require 1 L of water because the solute will displace a small amount of water. You won't always want 1 L of solution, however. To prepare a particular volume and concentration of solution requires calculating the mass of solute to weigh out. Chemists generally memorize the formula for this calculation through countless repetitions in the lab.

Sample Problem — Converting Volume of Solution into Mass of Solute

Describe how to prepare 0.055 L of 0.20 M KCl from the solid.

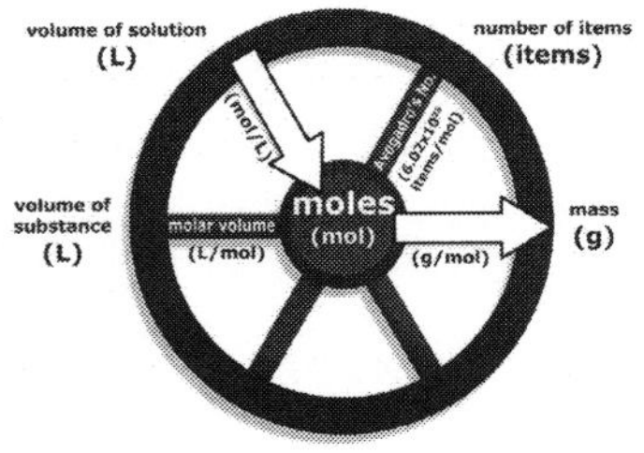

What to Think about	How to Do It
1. Convert: L soln → mol KCl → g KCl	
2. Setup: $0.055 \text{ L soln} \times \frac{? \text{ mol KCl}}{1 \text{ L soln}} \times \frac{? \text{ g KCl}}{1 \text{ mol KCl}}$	$0.055 \text{ ~~L soln~~} \times \frac{0.20 \text{ ~~mol KCl~~}}{1 \text{ ~~L soln~~}} \times \frac{74.6 \text{ g KCl}}{1 \text{ ~~mol KCl~~}} = 0.82 \text{ g KCl}$
3. Conversion factors: 0.20 mol KCl per 1 L soln 74.6 g KCl per 1 mol KCl	Measure out 0.82 g KCl and add water up to 55 mL (0.055 L) of solution.

Sample Problem — Determining Molar Concentration

What molar concentration of KCl is produced by measuring out 1.0 g KCl and adding water up to 0.350 L of solution?

What to Think about	How to Do It
1. Convert: g KCl $\rightarrow$ mol KCl 2. Setup: $1.0 \text{ g KCl} \times \frac{1 \text{ mol KCl}}{? \text{ g KCl}}$ 3. Conversion factor: 1 mol KCl per 74.6 g KCl 4. Molarity is moles per liter meaning the number of moles divided by the number of liters.	$1.0 \text{ g KCl} \times \frac{1 \text{ mol KCl}}{74.6 \text{ g KCl}} = 0.013 \text{ mol KCl}$ Molar Concentration $KCl = \frac{0.013 \text{ mol KCl}}{0.350 \text{ L soln}} = 0.038M \text{ KCl}$

Practice Problems — Converting Volume of Solution into Mass of Solute and Determining Molar Concentration

1. Describe how to prepare 500.0 mL of 1.5 M $CaCl_2$ from $CaCl_2(s)$.

2. What mass of KCl would be recovered if 55 mL of 0.20 M KCl were "evaporated to dryness"? [Hint: this is the same as asking how many grams of KCl are in 55 mL of 0.20 M KCl.]

3. What molar concentration of silver nitrate is produced by measuring out 1.8 g and then adding water to make 75 mL of solution?

Ions in Solution

Recall that ionic compounds have no net charge. The ions associate together in the ratio that results in their charges cancelling. For example:

$2Al^{3+}(aq) + 3SO_4^{2-}(aq) \longrightarrow Al_2(SO_4)_3(s)$

The ionic compound is neutral because the ions have a net charge of zero: 2(3+) + 3(2–) = 0. The ions, however, remain unchanged in the crystal. By convention, chemists don't show the charges of the ions in the formulas of ionic compounds. The charges are implicit (implied) rather than explicit (shown). When an ionic compound dissolves, the same ions that associated together to form the compound now **dissociate** (dis-associate) and travel independently through the solution. For example,

$Al_2(SO_4)_3(s) \longrightarrow 2Al^{3+}(aq) + 3SO_4^{2-}(aq)$

Sample Problem — Two-Step Conversion: Volume of Solution to Number of Ions

Some communities fluoridate their water to reduce tooth decay. Medical authorities report that the most effective F^- concentration for water supplies is between 0.042 M and 0.053 M. How many fluoride ions would a person ingest by drinking 2.0 L of 0.047 M F^-?

What to Think about

1. Convert: L soln $\rightarrow$ mol F^- $\rightarrow$ ions F^-
2. Setup:
$$2.0 \text{ L soln} \times \frac{? \text{ mol } F^-}{1 \text{ L soln}} \times \frac{? \text{ ions } F^-}{1 \text{ mol } F^-}$$
3. Conversion factors:
0.047 mol F^- per 1 L soln
6.02×10^{23} ions F^- per 1 mol F^-

How to Do It

$$2.0 \text{ L soln} \times \frac{0.047 \text{ mol } F^-}{1 \text{ L soln}} \times \frac{6.02 \times 10^{23} \text{ ions } F^-}{1 \text{ mol } F^-}$$

$$= 5.7 \times 10^{22} \text{ ions } F^-$$

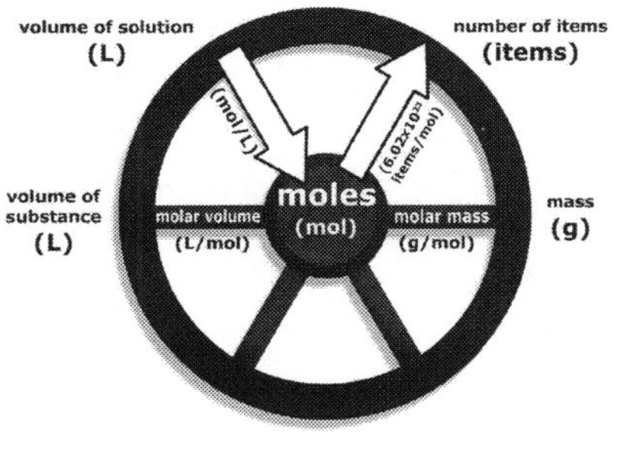

Being able to relate the concentration of dissolved ions to the concentration of their parent compound is extremely important in chemistry. Although it may be misleading, a label is not necessarily intended to indicate what is actually present in the solution. Some knowledge of chemistry is required to realize how a solute behaves in solution. 1 M $Al_2(SO_4)_3$ means that 1 mol of $Al_2(SO_4)_3$ was dissolved per liter of solution. There is no such thing as an $Al_2(SO_4)_3$ particle. The dissociation equation provides the ratio of the released ions to each other and to their parent compound; thus 1 M $Al_2(SO_4)_3$ actually contains 2 M Al^{3+} and 3 M SO_4^{2-}.

Sample Problem — Relating the Concentration of Dissolved Ions to the Concentration of Their Parent Compound

What concentrations of ions are present in 3.0 M $CaCl_2(aq)$?

What to Think about

The ratios in the dissociation equation show that 1 mol Ca^{2+} and 2 mol Cl^- are formed for each mole of $CaCl_2$ dissolved.

How to Do It

$CaCl_2(s)$	$\rightarrow$	$Ca^{2+}(aq)$ +	$2Cl^-(aq)$
3.0 mol/L	dissolves to form	?	?
3.0 mol/L	dissolves to form	3.0 M	6.0 M

This table is shown for teaching purposes only — you don't need to show it in your work.

> The molar concentration of a chemical is indicated by putting square brackets [ ] around the chemical's formula.

For example, [Na^+] means the molar concentration of Na^+. A couple of precautions:

- "M" already means "mol per L" therefore *don't write* "M per L" because that would mean "moles per liter per liter," which doesn't make sense.

- You can write "2 M Na^+" or "$[Na^+]$ = 2 M" but *don't write* "2 M $[Na^+]$" because that would mean "two molar the molar concentration of Na^+," which doesn't make sense.

The dissociation equation provides the conversion factor represented by the axle in our wheel model.

Sample Problem — Three-Step Conversion: Volume of Solution to Number of Ions

Aluminum chloride can be used to produce aluminum chlorohydrate, an active ingredient in antiperspirants. How many chloride ions are in 0.025 L of 0.30 M $AlCl_3$?

What to Think about

1. Convert:
   L soln → mol $AlCl_3$ → mol Cl^- → ions Cl^-
2. Setup: $0.025\text{ L soln} \times \frac{?\text{ mol AlCl}_3}{1\text{ L soln}} \times \frac{?\text{ mol Cl}^-}{1\text{ mol AlCl}_3} \times \frac{?\text{ ions Cl}^-}{1\text{ mol Cl}^-}$
3. Conversion factors:
   0.30 mol $AlCl_3$ per 1 L soln
   3 mol Cl^- per 1 mol $AlCl_3$
   6.02×10^{23} Cl^- ions per 1 mol Cl^-

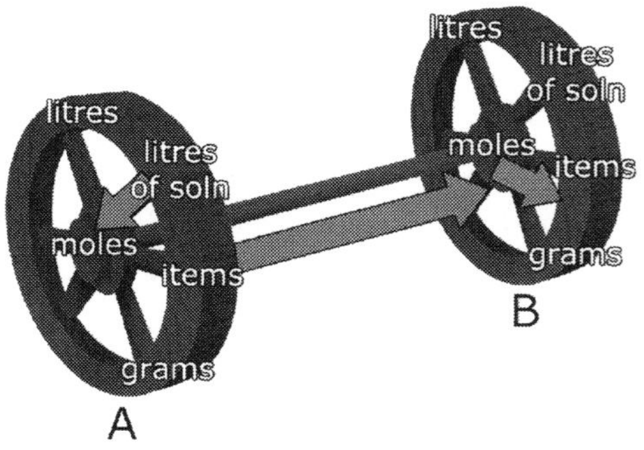

How to Do It

$$0.025\text{ L soln} \times \frac{0.30\text{ mol AlCl}_3}{1\text{ L soln}} \times \frac{3\text{ mol Cl}^-}{1\text{ mol AlCl}_3} \times \frac{6.02 \times 10^{23}\text{ ions Cl}^-}{1\text{ mol Cl}^-} = 1.4 \times 10^{22}\text{ ions Cl}^-$$

Practice Problems — Three-Step Conversion: Volume of Solution to Number of Ions

1. What concentrations of ions are present in 1.5 M $CaCl_2(aq)$?

2. What concentration of sodium phosphate contains 0.60 M Na^+?

3. Write the relationship between the concentrations of the ions present in a solution of lithium phosphate. (Careful; this is tricky. In a $CaCl_2$ solution, $[Cl^-] = 2\,[Ca^{2+}]$).

4. What mass of potassium ions is in 0.75 L of 2.8 M K^+?

5. Iron(III) nitrate solutions are used by jewellers to etch silver. How many NO_3^- ions are dissolved in a 525 mL bath of 3.0 M iron(III) nitrate?

7.3 Activity: Building a Scale Model of a Solution

Question

What is the ratio of solute ions to water molecules in a solution of 1 M NaCl(*aq*)?

Background

Models are very important in science. A model, scientific or otherwise, is anything that represents something else. Chemists can use models to explain and predict the behavior of matter. The American chemist, Linus Pauling, figured out the spiral structure of proteins using paper cut-outs as models. He was awarded the 1954 Nobel Prize in chemistry partly for this accomplishment. In this activity, you will construct a scale model of a solution.

Procedure

1. Calculate how many moles of H_2O molecules occupy one L. (Density of H_2O = 1000 g/L)

$$\frac{\_\_\_\_\_\ \text{g } H_2O}{1 \text{ L } H_2O} \times \frac{1 \text{ mol } H_2O}{\text{g } H_2O} = \_\_\_\_\_\_\_\_\_\_\_\_ \text{ mol } H_2O/\text{l } H_2O$$

   Although its units are moles per liter this value is not a concentration; it is not molarity. It does not describe the proportion of a chemical in a mixture. It describes the number of moles of water in 1 L of the substance and is simply the inverse of water's molar volume.

2. Determine the ion concentrations in 1.0 M NaCl(*aq*).

NaCl	→	**Na^+** +	**Cl^-**
1.0 M	dissolves to form		

3. For simplicity, let's assume that each mole of ions displaces a mole of water molecules. State the ratio of water molecules: sodium ions: chloride ions in 1 M NaCl (*aq*).

   ________ H_2O: ________ Na^+: ________ Cl^-

4. As a class, decide which kind or color of bead will represent each chemical species.

   H_2O molecules ____________________ Na^+ ions ______________________

   Cl^- ions ______________________

5. Count out the beads in the ratio shown in step 3 and pour them into the 500-mL graduated cylinder provided by your teacher for the class.

Results and Discussion

6. State three ways your model differs from an actual 1 M NaCl solution.

7.3 Review Questions

1. What does 1.5 M HCl mean?

2. A cough syrup contains 0.011 M dextromethorphan. How many moles of the cough suppressant are in one teaspoon (5.0 mL) of the cough syrup?

3. 75.0 mmol Ca^{2+} = ________ L of 0.20 M Ca^{2+}

4. The fluid inside living cells is called cytosol. A human hepatocyte (a type of liver cell) with a volume of 500 fL (1 fL (femtoliter) = 10^{-15} L) contains 12 mM Na^+. How many sodium ions are in the cytosol of this cell?

5. Consumer products express concentrations in mg/volume or g/volume because the general public isn't familiar with molarity.
   (a) A medium-sized (296 mL) cup of coffee contains 0.10 g caffeine, $C_8H_{10}N_4O_2$. Express this concentration in molarity.

   (b) A 355 mL can of pop contains 42.6 g sugar, $C_6H_{12}O_6$. What is the sugar's molar concentration?

6. Humans have an average blood volume of 5.0 L with an average blood sugar ($C_6H_{12}O_6$) concentration of 4.0 mM. What is the average mass of glucose coursing through the human bloodstream?

7. Describe how to prepare 250 mL of 0.50 M sodium nitrate. Be sure to answer in a complete sentence.

8. As a glass of cold tap water warms up, small air bubbles will come out of solution on the inner wall of the glass. A glass of cold water contains 0.45 mM O_2. How many milliliters of oxygen gas at STP are dissolved in 300.0 mL of this water?

9. What concentrations of ions are present in:
   (a) 0.35 M $Fe_2(Cr_2O_7)_3$?

   (b) 1.6 mol/L strontium cyanide?

10. In reflected light, iron(III) chloride crystals appear dark green but in transmitted light they appear maroon. What concentration of iron(III) chloride contains 0.038 M Cl^-?

11. In a solution of $Fe_2(SO_4)_3$:
(a) if the $[Fe^{3+}]$ = 1.5 M then what is the $[SO_4^{2-}]$?

(b) if the $[SO_4^{2-}]$ = 3.0 M then what is the $[Fe^{3+}]$?

12. Write the relationship between the concentrations of the ions in a solution of:
(a) zinc chromate

(b) strontium hydroxide

13. Milk has a $[Ca^{2+}]$ of about 31.4 mM. What mass of Ca^{2+} ions are in a 250 mL serving of milk?

14. How many Na^+ ions are dissolved in 1.5 L of 3.0 M Na_2CO_3?

15. It takes 145 drops from a pipette to reach the 5.0 mL mark on a graduated cylinder. How many grams of bromide ions are in one such drop of 0.10 M iron(III) bromide?

16. Phosphoric acid, H_3PO_4, is added to soft drinks to increase their tartness and to act as a preservative. The concentration of H_3PO_4 in Pepsi is proprietary (a company secret) but can be determined from its phosphorus content since H_3PO_4 is the only source of phosphorus in the beverage. There are 49 mg of phosphorus in a 355 mL can of Pepsi. What is the $[H_3PO_4]$ in Pepsi?

17. Draw the plot representing a 1.5 M NaCl solution on the graph provided.

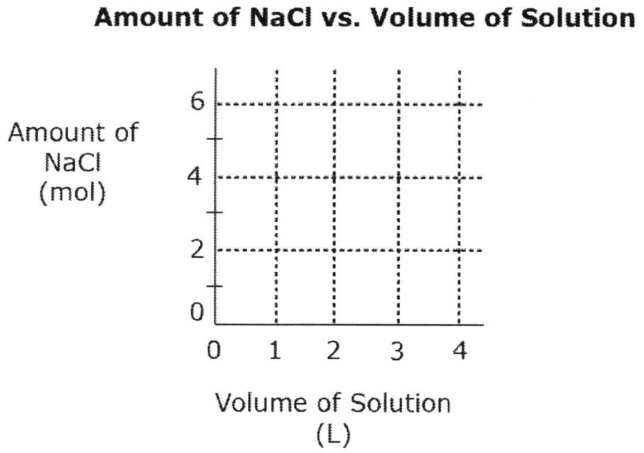

7.4 Dissociation Equations and Solution Chemistry

Warm Up

If you are a coffee drinker, you have experienced the effects of dilution and concentration. Assume you were making yourself a cup of coffee.

1. Describe how you would make a strong cup of coffee. Think about the amounts of water and coffee required.

   ____

2. If you wanted to dilute the coffee in your cup, what would you do?

   ____

3. When you dilute the coffee, have you changed the amount of caffeine present in the cup? Explain.

   ____

Diluting Solutions

You have learned that a solution's concentration can be represented by molarity. The **molarity** of a solution is a measure of the amount of solute in moles in a given volume of solution. When we add water to a solution, its concentration decreases. We say the solution is diluted. The opposite of diluted is concentrated. To make a solution more concentrated, we could evaporate or remove some of the solvent from the solution. We could also add more solute to the solution. The symbol [ ] around a formula indicates molar concentration and is measured in mol/L. For example, in the sample problem below, the question asks "What is the new [HCl]?" This means "What is the new molar concentration of HCl?"

Sample Problem — Dilution Calculation

A 15.0 mL sample of 3.0 M HCl was diluted by adding 10.0 mL of water. What is the new [HCl] ?

What to Think about

1. We have increased the volume of the final solution by adding water. The amount or moles of HCl has not changed.
2. The final volume of solution is 0.0250 L. Use this amount to calculate the new molar concentration.
3. This answer makes sense because the final concentration is less than the original concentration.

This two-step calculation is usually shown as one longer calculation. Notice that the units of L HCl cancel.

How to Do It

$$\text{mol HCl} = \frac{3.0 \text{ mol HCl}}{1 \cancel{\text{L HCl}}} \times 0.015 \cancel{\text{L HCl}}$$
$$= 0.045 \text{ mol HCl}$$

$$15.0 \text{ mL} + 10.0 \text{ mL} = 25.0 \text{ mL.} = 0.0250 \text{ L}$$

$$[\text{HCl}] = \frac{0.045 \text{ mol HCl}}{0.0250 \text{ L solution}}$$
$$= \frac{1.8 \text{ mol HCl}}{1 \text{ L}}$$
$$= 1.8 \text{ M}$$

$$[\text{HCl}] = \frac{3.0 \text{ mol HCl}}{1 \cancel{\text{L HCl}}} \times \frac{0.0150 \cancel{\text{L HCl}}}{0.0250 \text{ L solution}}$$
$$= \frac{1.8 \text{ mol HCl}}{1 \text{ L}}$$
$$= 1.8 \text{ M}$$

Practice Problems — Dilution Calculations

1. A 50.0 mL sample of 0.100 M NaOH was diluted by adding 30.0 mL of water. What was the resulting [NaOH]?

2. A 35.0 mL sample of 1.5 M H_2SO_4 was diluted to 50.0 mL. What was the final [H_2SO_4]? (Note: The wording in this problem is different. What is the final volume?)

3. A student dissolved 0.25 g of calcium nitrate in 100.0 mL water. A 50.0 mL sample of this solution was diluted to 75.0 mL. What was the final concentration?

4. Calculate the concentration that results when 18.0 mL of 0.40 M K_2CrO_4 is added to 20.0 mL of water.

Ions in Solution

Most people are familiar with what happens when table salt is added to water; the salt dissolves. To understand how this happens, we must look at the interactions between the ions in the solid table salt and the water molecules.

In the solid NaCl sample, positively charged Na^+ ions are attracted to negatively charged Cl^- ions. They are arranged in a crystal lattice as shown in Figure 7.4.1. Water molecules are polar. A negative pole exists on the oxygen atom and a positive pole exists on the hydrogen atoms. The oxygen atoms of the water molecules are attracted to the sodium ions in the solid. In the same way, the hydrogen atoms of the water molecules are attracted to the chloride ions in the solid. The solid dissolves as the water molecules separate the ions from the solid NaCl structure. **Solvation** is the process of solvent molecules surrounding solute particles. When the solvent is water, it can also be called **hydration**.

We can write an equation called a dissociation equation to represent the process of the positive and negative ions in the salt being separated by the solvent. An ionization equation is similar to a dissociation equation. Ionization occurs when a molecule is induced by a solvent to form ions which are then separated by the solvent into solution. An ionization equation thus represents the formation and breaking apart of ions from a molecule. Chemists use the term, "percent ionization" to describe the extent to which a given acid's molecules are ionized. When the acid, HCl, dissolves in water, the ionization equation is:

HCl(aq) → H+(aq) + Cl–(aq)

When the salt, CaCl2, dissolves in water, the dissociation equation is:

CaCl2(aq) → Ca2+(aq) + 2 Cl–(aq)

Notice in the balanced equation that two chloride ions are produced for every one calcium ion. It is important to balance these equations for both number of atoms and charge.

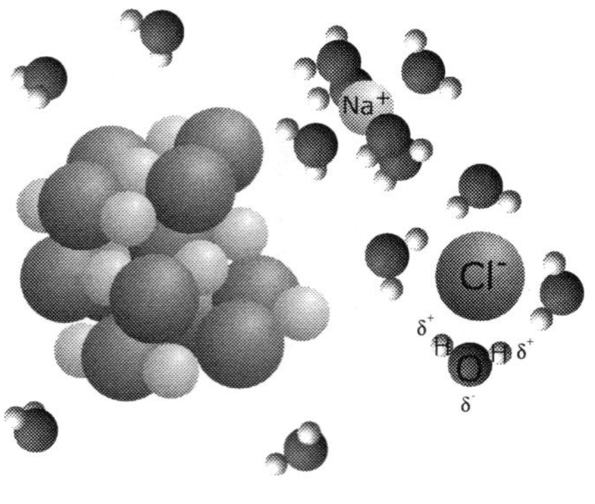

Figure 7.4.1 *NaCl dissolving in water*

Quick Check

Write balanced dissociation equations for each salt when it is dissolved in water.

1. $Al(NO_3)_3$
2. $(NH_4)_2SO_4$
3. potassium chromate
4. zinc phosphate

Calculating Concentration

From the dissociation equations, you can see that the mole ratios represent the relative amounts of ions in solution. If we know the concentration of the solution, we can then calculate the concentration of each individual ion present as well.

Consider a 1.0 M solution of NaCl. According to the dissociation equation, when 1 mol of NaCl dissolves, it produces 1 mol of Na^+ ions and 1 mol of Cl^- ions. So in 1.0 M NaCl: $[Na^+]$ = 1.0 M and $[Cl^-]$ = 1.0 M

$$NaCl(aq) \rightarrow Na^+(aq) + Cl^-(aq)$$
1.0 M　　1.0 M　　1.0 M

If instead we had a 1.0 M solution of $CaCl_2$, according to the dissociation equation: $[Ca^{2+}]$ = 1.0 M but $[Cl^-]$ = 2.0 M

$$CaCl_2(aq) \rightarrow Ca^{2+}(aq) + 2\ Cl^-(aq)$$
1.0 M　　1.0 M　　2(1.0 M) = 2.0 M

Quick Check

Calculate the concentration of all ions in each of the following. Begin by writing the balanced dissociation equation for each.

1. 3.0 M $Zn(NO_3)_2$
2. 0.50 M Na_2CO_3
3. 1.5 M ammonium oxalate
4. 3.2×10^{-3} M calcium phosphate

Dissociation and Dilution

Another example of dilution is when two solutions are mixed together. The resulting solution has a larger volume than the original solutions. The following sample problem combines an understanding of dissociation and dilution concepts.

Sample Problem — Dilution Calculation for Mixed Solutions

A 15.0 mL sample of 3.0 M HCl was added to 10.0 mL of 2.0 M $CaCl_2$. Calculate the concentration of each ion in solution. Assume no reaction occurs.

What to Think about

1. Calculate the concentration in mol/L.
2. Each solution was diluted when mixed, so first calculate the new concentration of each solution.
3. Next, each solution contains ions so we write dissociation equations for each salt.
4. Under each dissociation equation, use the mole ratio to calculate the concentration of each ion.
5. Notice that there are chloride ions from both original solutions, so we add their concentrations together.

How to Do It

$$[HCl] = \frac{3.0 \text{ mol HCl}}{1 \text{ L HCl}} \times \frac{0.0150 \text{ L HCl}}{0.0250 \text{ L solution}} = \frac{1.8 \text{ mol HCl}}{1 \text{ L}} = 1.8 \text{ M}$$

Final volume of solution:
15.0 + 10.0 = 25.0 mL

$$[CaCl_2] = \frac{2.0 \text{ mol } CaCl_2}{1 \text{ L } CaCl_2} \times \frac{0.0100 \text{ L } CaCl_2}{0.0250 \text{ L solution}} = 0.80 \text{ M } CaCl_2$$

$HCl(aq) \rightarrow H^+(aq) + Cl^-(aq)$
1.8 M 1.8 M 1.8 M

$CaCl_2(aq) \rightarrow Ca^{2+}(aq) + 2\,Cl^-(aq)$
0.80 M 0.80 M 2(0.80 M) = 1.6 M

$[H^+] = 1.8$ M
$[Cl^-] = 1.8$ M + 1.6 M = 3.4 M
$[Ca^{2+}] = 0.80$ M

Practice Problems — Calculating the Concentrations of Ions in Solution

Calculate the concentration of each ion in the following solutions. Assume no reactions occur.

1. A 35.0 mL sample of 0.20 M HNO_3 was added to 75.0 mL of 0.15 M $Al(NO_3)_3$.

2. A 22.6 mL sample of 0.85 M H_2SO_4 was added to 35.4 mL of 1.3 M Na_2SO_4.

3. A 50.0 mL sample of 0.10 M potassium phosphate was added to 40.0 mL of 0.20 M potassium oxalate.

4. A 100.0 mL sample of 2.3×10^{-3} M ammonium phosphate was added to 40.0 mL of 4.5×10^{-2} M ammonium sulfide.

Electrical Conductivity of Solutions

Have you ever been in an outdoor swimming pool during an electrical storm? Is a swimming pool a safe place to be in this case? When electric charge is carried through a solution, we say that the solution conducts electricity. If a compound's aqueous solution conducts electricity then that compound is called an electrolyte. If the compound's aqueous solution is a 'good' conductor then the compound is a strong electrolyte. If the compound's aqueous solution is a 'poor' conductor then the compound is a weak electrolyte. If the compound's aqueous solution does not conduct electricity at all then the compound is a nonelectrolyte.

Electric charge is carried through a solution by the movement of ions. The charged ions must be free to move in the solution. The positive ions will move toward the negative electrode, and the negative ions will move toward the positive electrode. The movement of these ions completes the electrical circuit. The more ions present, the greater the conductivity.

A light bulb apparatus is a simple piece of equipment used to test for electrical conductivity (Figure 7.4.2). Your teacher may demonstrate this to you. The light bulb is plugged in, and the electrodes are placed into the solution. The brighter the bulb glows, the stronger the electrolyte is.

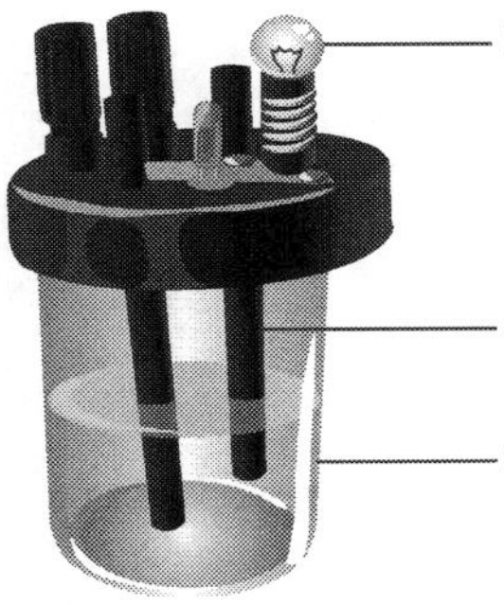

Figure 7.4.2 *Apparatus for testing for electrical conductivity*

In a nonelectrolyte solution, there are no ions to carry the electric charge across the space so no electricity flows. The space between the electrodes acts as an open switch in a circuit. Many covalent or molecular substances are nonelectrolytes. Some covalent substances however, do form ions in solution, so are strong or weak electrolytes. There are a some important exceptions noted below.

All salts are ionic and so they are electrolytes. An ionic solid that has a low solubility in water will produce few free moving ions in solution, so will have low conductivity. A melted liquid of an ionic salt will also conduct electricity; however an ionic solid will not. In a solid, the ions are locked in place and cannot move to carry electric charge.

Electrical Conductivity of Acids and Bases

Acids and bases conduct electricity as well. The formulas of most acids contain only nonmetals. They do not appear to be ionic. However, acids act by releasing an H+ ion. Some acids will dissociate completely in solution. We call these strong acids. Other acids contain molecules that remain mostly intact, with only a small percentage being dissociated. These are called weak acids because they do not form many ions. Water is another example of a molecular or covalent compound that dissociates to a small extent as follows:

$H_2O(l) \rightarrow H^+(aq) + OH^-(aq)$

The concentration of H^+ and OH^- ions in water is only 1.0×10^{-7} M each so water is a poor electrical conductor. Organic acids are compounds containing carbon, hydrogen, and oxygen. They contain the carboxyl group so their formulas end in –COOH. These substances are not ionic, but a few of the molecules in a sample will release the H^+ ion from this group. You should be familiar with vinegar, which is acetic acid, CH_3COOH. It dissociates as follows:

$CH_3COOH(aq) \rightarrow CH_3COO^-(aq) + H^+(aq)$

In a solution of vinegar, there will be only a few ions of H^+ and CH_3COO^- present to carry electrical charge. Therefore vinegar is a weak electrolyte. Table 7.3.1 summarizes some common acids and bases and their relative ability to dissociate into ions.

Table 7.3.1 *Ability of Common Acids and Bases to Dissociate*

Substance	Classification	Extent of Dissociation
HCl, HBr, HI, HNO_3, H_2SO_4, $HClO_4$	strong acid	dissociate 100%
NaOH, KOH, $Ca(OH)_2$	strong base	dissociate 100%
CH_3COOH, C_6H_5COOH	weak acid	very little
NH_3	weak base	very little

Quick Check

1. How can you tell from a substance's formula if it is ionic or molecular? Give two examples of an ionic compound.

____

____

2. Sugar has the formula $C_{12}H_{22}O_{11}$. Will a sugar solution conduct electricity? Explain.

____

____

3. Explain why a 1.0 M solution of HCl will be a stronger electrolyte than a 1.0 M solution of CH_3COOH.

____

____

Key Points about Electrical Conductivity of Solutions

Here are the key points to remember about electrical conductivity of solutions:

- Electric current is carried through a solution by ions. The more ions there are, the higher the solution's conductivity.
- Soluble salts and soluble hydroxides dissolve in water to make aqueous solutions with high ion concentrations and consequently high conductivity. Salts with low solubility and hydroxides with low solubility form solutions with low ion concentrations and therefore low conductivity.
- Molecular compounds do not form ions in aqueous solution so their solutions do not conduct electricity. Exceptions are acids and bases.
- Strong acids and bases ionize completely in solution
- Weak acids and bases ionize very little in solution

One of the most important applications of electrical conductivity of solutions is happening in your body right now. Your brain sends messages to the cells in your body by sending electrical impulses down your nerve cells. The electrical signal is carried along the nerve cell by concentration differences of Na^+ and K^+ ions both inside and outside the cell. The electrical signal must move through the solutions in your tissues. For example, if you do not have enough sodium and potassium ions present, you may experience muscle cramps. Many chemical reactions in your body rely on the fact that ions in solutions conduct electricity.

So, do you stay in the swimming pool during an electrical storm, or do you get out? Since there are salts dissolved in the pool water, it will conduct electricity. You need to get out!

7.4 Activity: Investigating Electrical Conductivity

Question

Which types of solutions are good electrical conductors?

Background

In order for a solution to conduct electricity, it must contain mobile ions. The more ions there are in solution, the stronger the electrolyte.

Procedure

1. A student has a light bulb conductivity apparatus and 100.0 mL of each of the following solutions in a beaker:
   - 4.0 M $C_{12}H_{22}O_{11}$
   - 1.0 M $NaCl$
   - 0.8 M Na_2CO_3
   - 2.0 M CH_3COOH
   - 3.0 M C_2H_5OH (ethanol, an alcohol)
   - 0.8 M HCl
   - 2.0 M NH_3

   Make a sketch of each solution containing a conductivity apparatus. Label each beaker's contents. Use a colored pencil to show the relative brightness of the light bulb in each.

2. Compare your answers to those of another group. Did you agree?

Results and Discussion

1. Which solutions were ionic? Covalent?

2. For each ionic solution, write a dissociation equation for the solute, and calculate the concentration of each ion present.

3. Calculate the total ion concentration of each ionic solution by adding all of the ion concentrations together. Write this value under its corresponding diagram.

4. Rank the solutions in order from highest conductivity to lowest conductivity. List the nonelectrolytes last. Use an equal sign (=) for solutions that are about equally conductive.

5. Summarize the rules for determining if a solute will make a solution that is a good electrical conductor.

7.4 Review Questions

1. Calculate the concentration of the following solutions when:
   (a) 175 mL of 0.55 M HCl is added to 25 mL of water

   (b) 45.0 mL of 0.035 M $Na_2Cr_2O_7$ is diluted to 100.0 mL

   (c) a 100.0 mL sample of 2.0 M NaOH is evaporated until the resulting volume of solution is 75.0 mL

2. Hydrochloric acid can be purchased as a 6.0 M solution. What volume of this stock solution must be used to prepare 250.0 mL of 2.5 M HCl?

3. Explain how the terms "solvation" and "hydration" are different.

4. Explain why the cation in a solute will be attracted to a solvent water molecule.

5. The solute KI is dissolved in water. Sketch a diagram showing the ions present in this solute surrounded by water molecules. Assume six water molecules surround each ion. Be sure to draw the water molecules aligned appropriately around the ion with respect to dipoles.

6. Write balanced dissociation equations to represent the dissolving of the following solutes in water:
   (a) $FeCl_3$

   (b) $MnHPO_4$

   (c) $Zn(SCN)_2$

   (d) $Al_2(Cr_2O_7)_3$

   (e) silver oxalate

   (f) iron(III) sulfite

   (g) chromium(II) chromate

   (h) ammonium hydrogen oxalate

7. A student adds 250.0 mL of 0.60M HCl to 300.0 mL of 1.0 M HCl. What is the final [HCl]?

8. Calculate the concentration of each ion in the following:
(a) 0.20 M $CuCl_2$

(b) 1.5 M $Li_2C_2O_4$

(c) 6.0 M nitric acid

(d) 1.4×10^{-3} M magnesium permanganate

(e) the resulting solution when 18.5 mL of 0.25 M $Al(NO_3)_3$ is mixed with 22.4 mL of 0.50 M $Cu(NO_3)_2$

9. A solution is made by dissolving some solid $(NH_4)_2CrO_4$ in water. If the $[NH_4^+] = 0.60$ M, what is the $[CrO_4^{2-}]$?

10. Sketch a light bulb apparatus in a solution of KNO_3. Show which ions move to the positive and negative electrodes. Is KNO_3 a strong electrolyte? Explain.

11. List the acids that are strong electrolytes. Explain why they are considered strong.

12. You are given two beakers, one containing 3.0 M HNO_3 and one containing 6.0 M $C_{12}H_{22}O_{11}$. Explain how you could use a light bulb apparatus to distinguish between the two solutions.

13. Classify the following as being strong electrolyte, weak electrolyte, or nonelectrolyte, solutions.
(a) 0.1 M $HClO_4$

(b) distilled H_2O

(c) 1.0 M CH_3COOH

(d) 0.1 M $ZnSO_4$

(e) $C_8H_{18}(l)$

(f) 6.0 M NH_3

14. Consider the following statement: "If a solution has a high concentration, it will conduct electricity well." Do you agree or disagree? Explain.

QUANTITATIVE ANALYSIS - Additional Questions

1. The mass of $BaSO_4$ formed when excess 0.200 M Na_2SO_4 solution is added to 0.500 L of 0.500 M $BaCl_2$ solution

b) The minimum volume of the Na_2SO_4 solution needed to precipitate the Ba^{2+} ions from the $BaCl_2$ solution.

2. A sample of impure sodium chloride weighing 1.00 grams dissolved in water and completely reacted with a silver nitrate solution. The dried precipitate of AgCl has a mass of 1.48 g. Calculate the percentage of NaCl in the original impure sample.

3. Solid sodium bicarbonate was used to neutralize 10.0 mL of 18.0 M H_2SO_4 that was accidentally spilled on a laboratory bench top. The container of sodium bicarbonate weighed 155.0 g before the neutralization and 144.5 g afterwards. Was sufficient sodium bicarbonate used? Calculate the limiting reagent and the maximum yield in grams of sodium sulfate.

4. How many mL of 0.400 M $Ba(NO_3)_2$ solution are required to completely precipitate the sulfate ions in 25.0 mL of a 0.800 M K_2SO_4 solution?

5. What mass of silver chloride can be precipitated from a silver nitrate solution by 200.0 mL of a solution of 0.500 M $CaCl_2$?

6. Many popular chemical fertilizers include ammonium dihydrogen phosphate. This compound is made commercially by reacting concentrated aqueous solutions of ammonia and phosphoric acid. What volume of 14.8 mol L^{-1} NH_3 (aq) would be needed to react completely with each 1.00 kL of 12.9 mol L^{-1} H_3PO_4 (aq) to produce fertilizer in a commercial operation?

7. A chemical technologist is monitoring the concentration of solutions in the process stream. Sulfuric acid is a reactant used in the production of sulfates (e.g for fertilizers). In the experiment, a 10.00 mL sample of sulfuric acid reacts completely with 15.9 mL of 0.150 mol L^{-1} potassium hydroxide solution. Calculate the molar concentration of the sulfuric acid.

8. Two students wish to precipitate all of the lead (II) ions from 2.00 L of solution containing, among other substances, 0.34 M of lead nitrate. The purpose of this reaction is to make the filtrate solution non-toxic. If the students intend to precipitate lead (II) sulfate, suggest an appropriate solute and calculate the appropriate concentration and volume of the reacting solution.

9. What is the percent yield of the precipitate if 20.0 mL of 0.210 M sodium sulfide are placed in the same beaker as an excess quantity of aluminium nitrate and 0.190 g of precipitate are measured? Suggest some reasons why 100% recovery of the precipitate might not be achieved.

7.5 Qualitative Analysis — Identifying Unknown Ions

Warm Up

1. The solubility of silver chloride is 1.4×10^{-3} g/L at room temperature. Calculate its molar solubility.

2. The solubility of sodium chloride is 359 g/L at room temperature. Calculate its molar solubility.

3. We define a salt as soluble if its solubility is greater than 0.1 M. Classify NaCl and AgCl as being soluble or having low solubility.

   NaCl ______________________ AgCl ______________________

Precipitate Formation

Salts have different abilities to dissolve in water. When a salt is added to water, it will dissolve if the attraction of the cation and anion to each other is overcome or replaced by an attraction of the ions to a polar water molecule. For example, when NaCl is placed in water, the attraction of the Na^+ cation to the Cl^- anion is replaced. The cation is attracted to the negative dipole on the oxygen atom of the water molecule. The anion is attracted to the positive dipole on the hydrogen atoms of water. Because the ions are attracted to the solvent, dissociation occurs. However, when a salt such as AgCl is placed in water, the Ag^+ cation is more strongly attracted to the Cl^- anion. That attraction can only be slightly overcome by an attraction to water molecules, so most of the AgCl solute remains undissociated. When only a small amount of solute dissolves, we say the solute has *low solubility*. Note that AgCl is not *insoluble*; a small amount of AgCl will dissolve.

A solubility table like Figure 7.2.1 on the next page can be used to help predict which salts will be soluble or have a low solubility in water.

How to Use a Solubility Table

Make note of the following points related to Figure 7.2.1:

- The term *soluble* means that more than 0.1 mol of salt will dissolve in 1.0 L of solution. *Low solubility* means that less than 0.1 mol of salt will dissolve in 1.0 L of solution. It does **not** mean that the salt does not dissolve.
- Because the solubility of a salt changes with temperature, the terms *soluble* and *low solubility* refer to amounts of solute that dissolve at room temperature.
- Alkali metal ions are listed at the top of the table, and are simply referred to as "alkali ions" farther down the table.
- Salts with alkali ions or ammonium ion are soluble.
- Acids are soluble.
- Salts with nitrate ion are soluble.
- Salts containing phosphates, sulfites, and carbonates usually have low solubility (except for alkali and ammonium salts)

To use this table, simply find the anion present in the salt and then read across to identify the cation with which it is *soluble* or has *low solubility*.

Table 7.5.1 *Solubility of Common Compounds in Water*

Note: In this table, soluble means > 0.1 mol/L at 25°C.

Negative Ions (Anions)	Positive Ions (Cations)	Solubility of Compounds
All	Alkali ions: Li^+, Na^+, K^+, Rb^+, Cs^+, Fr^+	Soluble
All	Hydrogen ion: H^+	Soluble
All	Ammonium ion: NH_4^+	Soluble
Nitrate: NO_3^-	All	Soluble
Chloride: Cl^- Or Bromide: Br^- Or Iodide: I^-	All others	Soluble
	Ag^+, Pb^{2+}, Cu^+	Low solubility
Sulfate: SO_4^{2-}	All others	Soluble
	Ag^+, Ca^{2+}, Sr^{2+}, Ba^{2+}, Pb^{2+}	Low solubility
Sulfide: S^{2-}	Alkali ions, H^+, NH_4^+, Be^{2+}, Mg^{2+}, Ca^{2+}, Sr^{2+}, Ba^{2+}	Soluble
	All others	Low solubility
Hydroxide: OH^-	Alkali ions, H^+, NH_4^+, Sr^{2+}	Soluble
	All others	Low solubility
Phosphate: PO_4^{3-} Or Carbonate: CO_3^{2-} Or Sulfite: SO_3^{2-}	Alkali ions, H^+, NH_4^+	Soluble
	All others	Low solubility

Sample Problem — Predicting the Solubility of Salts Using the Solubility Table

Classify the following salts as being "soluble" or having "low solubility."

1. copper(II) chloride
2. aluminum hydroxide
3. sodium phosphate

What to Think About

1. Identify the formula as $CuCl_2$. The anion is Cl^-. The cation is Cu^{2+}. From the table, Cl^- is soluble with Cu^{2+}. (Be careful to note which copper ion you have, as Cl^- has a low solubility with Cu^+.)
2. Identify the formula as $Al(OH)_3$. The anion is OH^-. The cation is Al^{3+}, which falls into the "all others" category on the table. OH^- has low solubility with Al^{3+}.
3. Identify the formula as Na_3PO_4. The anion is PO_4^{3-}. The cation is Na^+. From the table, PO_4^{3-} is soluble with Na^+. (A sodium ion is an alkali ion.)

How to Do It

Copper(II) chloride is soluble.

Aluminum hydroxide has low solubility.

Sodium phosphate is soluble.

Practice Problems — Predicting the Solubility of Salts Using the Solubility Table

1. Classify the following salts as being soluble or having low solubility in water:

   (a) calcium sulfate ____________________

   (b) iron(II) sulfide ____________________

   (c) strontium hydroxide ____________________

   (d) zinc bromide ____________________

   (e) cesium sulfite ____________________

   (f) potassium chromate ____________________

2. Write the formula for the following:

   (a) a salt containing carbonate that is soluble

   (b) a salt containing sulfate with low solubility

   (c) a cation that forms a salt with low solubility with both chloride and sulfate ions

   (d) an anion that forms soluble salts with all cations

3. A student is given a sample of a solution that is either magnesium nitrate or strontium nitrate. When a few drops of a solution of sodium hydroxide is added to the sample, no precipitate forms. Does the sample contain magnesium nitrate or strontium nitrate? Explain your reasoning.

Equations Representing Precipitate Reactions

Three types of chemical equations are used to represent a double replacement or metathesis reaction. Let's use the reaction between solutions of potassium iodide and lead(II) nitrate to illustrate the three types of equations.

A **formula equation** shows the chemical formulas of the compounds and their states. You would use the solubility table to identify the product with the low solubility.

$$2\ KI(aq) + Pb(NO_3)_2(aq) \rightarrow 2\ KNO_3(aq) + PbI_2(s)$$

When writing ionic equations, you must carefully identify all soluble ionic compounds and any strong acids. These species must be shown in their dissociated or ionized forms. All other substances appear in an ionic equation in the same format as they do in a formula equation.

In a **complete ionic equation**, the soluble salts are represented in their dissociated form. Because the precipitate has low solubility, it is not shown dissociated. This makes sense when you consider that the precipitate forms very few ions in solution.

$$2\ K^+(aq) + 2\ I^-(aq) + Pb^{2+}(aq) + 2\ NO_3^-(aq) \rightarrow 2\ K^+(aq) + 2\ NO_3^-(aq) + PbI_2(s)$$

In a **net ionic equation**, only the ions that take part in the reaction appear. Ions that are the same on both sides of the equation are called **spectator ions**. Spectator ions are much like spectators at a sports event. They only watch the event; they do not take part in its outcome. Spectator ions are not included in a net ionic equation.

$$Pb^{2+}(aq) + 2\ I^-(aq) \rightarrow PbI_2(s)$$

Quick Check

1. Write the formula for the precipitate that forms when the following solutions are mixed.
   (a) BaS and $MgSO_4$
   (b) NH_4OH and $FeBr_2$
   (c) H_3PO_4 and $ZnCl_2$
   (d) K_2CO_3 and $CrSO_4$
   (e) MnI_2 and $Sr(OH)_2$
2. Write a formula equation, complete ionic equation, and net ionic equation for the following reactions.
   (a) Solutions of strontium hydroxide and silver nitrate are mixed.
   (b) Solutions of magnesium sulfide and zinc chloride are mixed.
   (c) Solutions of sodium carbonate and barium sulfide are mixed.

Qualitative Analysis

Qualitative analysis refers to any procedure that can be used to help identify unknown ions in solution. There are many different qualitative analysis methods. Simply looking at a colored solution can help identify ions present. For example, solutions containing copper(II) ions are blue. Chromates can be yellow, and dichromates are orange. Permanganate is a deep purple color, and nickel(II) is light green.

Flame tests are another method to identify ions. A sample of the solution is placed in a flame. Depending on the ions present, the flame may change color. Copper(II) ions turn the flame a blue-green, whereas lithium ions turn the flame red and barium ions make it green. Atomic absorption spectroscopy makes use of this property. Samples are vaporized and passed through a flame. The instrument records the quantity of energy or wavelength that is absorbed by the atoms to give off particular spectra.

One important method of testing a sample for the presence of unknown ions involves adding a reagent to the sample to selectively precipitate ions. The color of the precipitate is often indicative of the ion present. For example, you have probably seen the bright yellow precipitate $PbI_2(s)$. Additionally, the amount of precipitate formed or the speed at which the precipitate forms can also help identify ions. By applying the solubility rules you have learned, you can develop a qualitative analysis scheme to determine the identity of ions in a solution. Your scheme should list steps, including the compounds that you are adding to precipitate one ion at a time and how you will remove the precipitate from the solution.

Sample Problem — Selective Precipitation

A solution may contain the ions Ca^{2+}, Sr^{2+}, and Zn^{2+}. How would you precipitate the ions out of solution individually?

What to Think About	How to Do It
1. Since these are all cations, add an anion that will only precipitate one of these cations. Add compounds containing the anion of choice. Moving down the anions on the solubility table, NO_3^- and Cl^- will not precipitate any of the ions. SO_4^{2-} will precipitate both Ca^{2+} and Sr^{2+}. You need an anion that only precipitates one of the cations, so SO_4^{2-} won't work. S^{2-} will precipitate only the Zn^{2+}, so this is a good place to start. Remove the *least* soluble ion first.	S^{2-} precipitates only the Zn^{2+}.
2. To add S^{2-} ions, choose a soluble compound that will contain a significant amount of ions. Compounds containing alkali ions are soluble. The formation of a precipitate when Na_2S is added confirms the presence of Zn^{2+}.	A good source of S^{2-} ions would be Na_2S. First add a solution of Na_2S to the sample.
3. Remove the precipitate.	Remove the precipitate of ZnS by filtration or centrifugation.
4. Only Ca^{2+} and Sr^{2+} remain in solution. OH^- ions will precipitate Ca^{2+} but not Sr^{2+}. Choose a source of OH^- ions.	NaOH is a good source of OH^- ions. Add a solution of NaOH.
5. Remove the precipitate.	Filter out the precipitate of $Ca(OH)_2$.
6. Only Sr^{2+} ions remain in solution. Precipitate this by adding CO_3^{2-}, SO_4^{2-}, or PO_4^{3-}.	Na_2SO_4 is a good source of SO_4^{2-} ions. Finally add a solution of Na_2SO_4. Filter out the precipitate of $SrSO_4$.

Using Tables and Flow Charts

It may help you to organize your thoughts by constructing a table similar to the one below. Use an X to show no precipitate, and a √ to show a precipitate forming. Once the precipitate is formed, consider that cation removed from solution.

	S^{2-}	OH^-	SO_4^{2-}
Zn^{2+}	√	X	X
Ca^{2+}	removed	√	X
Sr^{2+}	removed	removed	√

A flow chart like the one in Figure 7.2.3 can also be used.

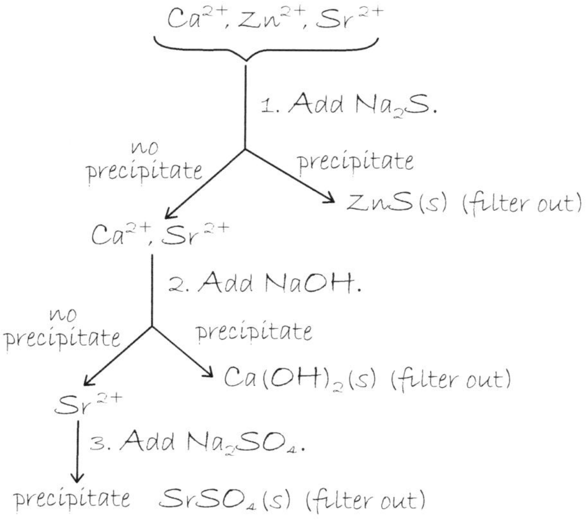

Figure 7.5.1 *A flow chart like this can help you show the process for removing iions from solution.*

Practice Problems — Selective Precipitation

1. Describe a process to individually remove the ions Ag^+, Ba^{2+}, and Be^{2+} from a solution. Be sure to list the compounds that you add in order, and the method of removing the precipitate. You may wish to use a flow chart.

2. Describe a process to individually remove the ions Br^-, SO_4^{2-}, and S^{2-} from a solution. Be sure to list the compounds that you add in order, and the method of removing the precipitate.

3. Describe a process to individually remove the ions OH^-, PO_4^{3-}, and S^{2-} from a solution. Be sure to list the compounds that you add in order, and the method of removing the precipitate.

Identifying Precipitates

While the formation of a precipitate may identify an ion, sometimes the precipitate may have more than one possible identity. There may be more than one ion present in solution that could be responsible for the precipitate. You can see this on the solubility table.

Consider a solution that may contain Cl^- and I^-. From the solubility table, we can see that the addition of Ag^+ ions would precipitate both anions, but due to the similarity in their colors we would be unable to conclude if the precipitate was AgCl, AgI, or both AgCl and AgI. Another part of qualitative analysis involves adding reagents to dissolve precipitates. In our example, if we added a concentrated solution of NH_3 (at least 6 M) to our precipitates, the AgCl would redissolve and the AgI would not. The following equation represents the formation of the silver diammine ion when AgCl dissolves:

$$AgCl(s) + 2\ NH_3(aq) \rightarrow Ag(NH_3)_2^+(aq) + Cl^-(aq)$$

Other common precipitates that can be easily dissolved are carbonates. The addition of a strong acid, such as HCl will cause the carbonate precipitate to dissolve, forming water and carbon dioxide:

$$BaCO_3(s) + 2\ H^+(aq) \rightarrow CO_2(g) + H_2O(l) + Ba^{2+}(aq)$$

Quick Check

1. List three properties that can be used to determine the identity of ions in solution.

   ____

2. Consider a solution that may contain Pb^{2+}, Ag^+, and Cu^{2+}. Devise a qualitative analysis scheme to confirm the presence of each ion in solution. Remove each ion individually from solution.

3. A solution contains carbonate and phosphate ions. How could you remove these two ions individually from solution?

Hard Water

The term *hard water* refers to the presence of Ca^{2+}, Mg^{2+}, and/or Fe^{2+} ions in water at relatively high concentrations. Water without these ions is called *soft water*. There are significant amounts of limestone ($CaCO_3$) and dolomite ($CaMg(CO_3)_2$) in the soil in many parts of the world. When CO_2 from the atmosphere dissolves in water from streams or rain, this solution dissolves limestone:

$$CaCO_3(s) + CO_2(aq) + H_2O(g) \rightarrow Ca^{2+}(aq) + 2\ HCO_3^-(aq)$$

The presence of the Ca^{2+} ions in the water supply poses hazards for municipal water systems and homes. As water is heated, the CO_2 is driven off as a gas, reforming a "scale" of $CaCO_3$ in water heaters, pipes, kettles, and boilers. This results in lowering the efficiency of heating systems and in extreme cases, blocking water pipes.

$$Ca^{2+}(aq) + 2\ HCO_3^-(aq) + \text{heat} \rightarrow \underset{\text{scale}}{CaCO_3(s)} + CO_2(g) + H_2O(g)$$

Soaps also react with Ca^{2+} and Mg^{2+} ions to form soap scum that is commonly visible on bathtubs and laundered clothes. Some laundry detergents contain water softeners to prevent the build up of scum on clothes. Shampoos have lathering agents for producing a rich foam when you wash your hair. Washing your hair in an area with hard water significantly reduces the ability of shampoo to lather.

$$Ca^{2+}(aq) + 2\ \underset{\text{soap}}{NaC_{17}H_{35}COO(aq)} \rightarrow \underset{\text{soap scum}}{Ca(C_{17}H_{35}COO)_2(s)} + 2\ Na^+(aq)$$

Municipal water treatment for hard water often includes the addition of CaO or Na_2CO_3 to underground water reservoirs to precipitate out Ca^{2+} and Mg^{2+} ions. Some home treatment systems use ion exchange resins that attract $Ca^{2+}$and Mg^{2+} to the resin surface and release Na^+ ions (Figure 7.2.4). The system can be "recharged" by flooding it with NaCl to replenish the Na^+ ions on the resin and release the $Ca^{2+}$and Mg^{2+} ions.

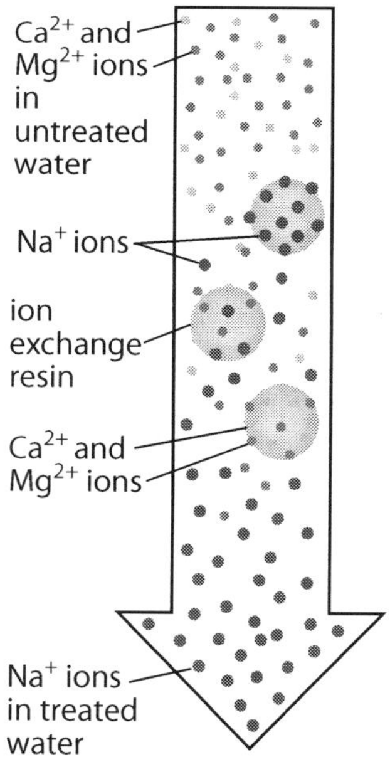

Figure 7.5.2 *Ion exchange treatment for hard water*

7.5 Activity: Using Titration to Calculate the Unknown [Cl^-] In A Sample of Seawater

Question

What is the concentration of Cl^- in seawater?

Background

Titration is an analytical method used to determine the unknown amount of a substance in a sample by reacting it with a measured amount of another substance. You will become more familiar with titration in the acid-base and redox chapters later in this textbook.

Seawater contains a significant amount of salts, largely sodium chloride. In this activity, a sample of seawater is titrated against a standardized solution of silver nitrate. The silver ions cause the chloride ions in the seawater to form a white precipitate. The concentration of chloride ion can be determined by measuring the amount of silver ions required to completely precipitate out the chloride ion. An indicator of potassium chromate is used. When almost all of the chloride ions in the sample have precipitated, any added silver ion will react with the chromate ion, causing a red precipitate to form. The equivalence point is reached once the solution begins to turn reddish.

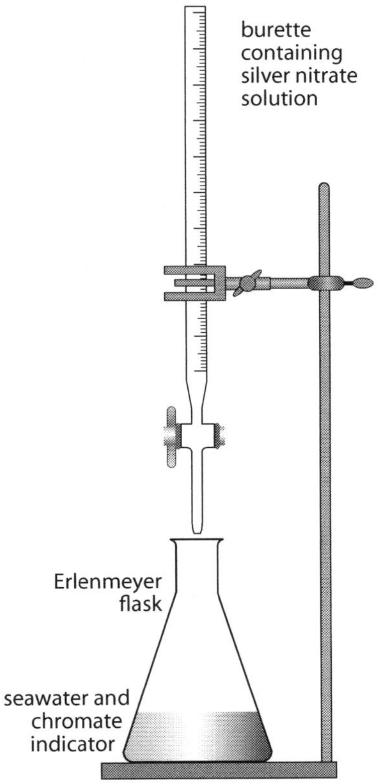

Procedure

1. A 25.0 mL sample of seawater was diluted to 250. mL. From this diluted solution, a 25.0 mL sample was measured out and placed in the Erlenmeyer flask.
2. A few drops of potassium chromate were added to the flask to act as an indicator.
3. A burette was filled with 0.100 M silver nitrate solution. An initial burette reading was taken. The silver nitrate solution was slowly added to the flask. A white precipitate formed. After a few more drops of silver nitrate were added, the precipitate turned a reddish color. At this point, no more silver nitrate was added. A final burette reading was recorded.
4. Procedure steps 1 to 3 were repeated in two more trials, and the data below was recorded.

	Trial 1	Trial 2	Trial 3
Initial burette reading (mL)	0.00	14.70	28.60
Final burette reading (mL)	14.70	28.60	42.35
Volume $AgNO_3$ added (mL)			
Average volume $AgNO_3$ used (mL)			

5. Complete the data table above by subtracting the initial volume from the final volume in each trial to determine the volume of silver nitrate added.
6. The average volume of silver nitrate added is calculated by taking the average of the closest two trials. Calculate the average volume of silver nitrate added, and record it in the data table.

Results and Discussion

1. Write a balanced net ionic equation that represents the reaction between silver ion and chloride ion.

2. Calculate the moles of silver nitrate reacted in the titration using the average volume and concentration of the silver nitrate.

3. Using the mole ratio from the balanced net ionic equation, calculate the moles of chloride ion present in the sample.

4. Using the volume of the *diluted* sample and the moles of chloride calculated above, calculate the concentration of chloride ion in the diluted sample.

5. Calculate the concentration of chloride ion in the original sample of seawater.

6. The level of salt in seawater varies across the planet. The average amount of chloride ion in seawater is 21.2 g/L. How does your sample compare?

7. Silver ions will form a precipitate with both chloride and chromate ions. Use a reference book to look up the solubility of AgCl and Ag_2CrO_4. Calculate the concentration of Ag^+ in a saturated solution of each. Use this information to explain why AgCl precipitates before Ag_2CrO_4.

7.5 Review Questions

1. Classify the following solutes as soluble or low solubility according to the solubility table (Figure 7.2.1):
   (a) Rb_2SO_3

   (b) Al_2S_3

   (c) CuI

   (d) ammonium sulfate

   (e) chromium(III) nitrate

   (f) potassium oxalate

2. According to the solubility table, silver sulfate has a low solubility. In a saturated solution of silver sulfate, are silver and sulfate ions present in solution? Explain.

3. The solubility of silver acetate is 11.1 g/L at 25°C. According to the solubility table, would silver acetate be classified as being soluble or of low solubility?

4. Describe the difference between a formula equation, a complete ionic equation, and a net ionic equation. How are they similar? Different?

5. What is a spectator ion? Give an example of a cation and an anion that are common spectator ions in precipitate reactions.

6. Write a balanced formula equation, complete ionic equation, and net ionic equation for each of the following reactions:

   (a) $(NH_4)_2S(aq) + FeSO_4(aq) \rightarrow$

   (b) $H_2SO_3(aq) + CaCl_2(aq) \rightarrow$

   (c) copper(II) sulfate and calcium sulfide $\rightarrow$

7. Explain why it would be difficult to separate the ions Na^+ and K^+ in solution using precipitation.

8. A solution contains Cr^{3+}, Ca^{2+}, and Mg^{2+} ions. Describe a method to remove each ion individually from solution. Be sure to state the compound you would add and how you would remove the precipitate from solution. For each reaction that occurs, write a net ionic equation.

9. A solution contains PO_4^{3-}, Cl^-, and S^{2-} ions. Describe a method to remove each ion individually from solution. Be sure to state the compound you would add and how you would remove the precipitate from solution. For each reaction that occurs, write a net ionic equation.

10. Why are compounds containing nitrates used to test for anions?

11. Give two examples where re-dissolving is necessary to separate two precipitates.

12. A solution of Na_2CO_3 is added to a solution of $AgNO_3$.
   (a) Write the net ionic equation for this reaction.

   (b) Two different reagents will dissolve the precipitate formed. Write a net ionic equation for each reaction in which the precipitate dissolves.

13. (a) Define *hard water* and *scale*.

   (b) Scale can be removed by adding a solution of HCl to the water. Write a formula equation, complete ionic equation, and net ionic equation for this reaction.

   (c) Suggest a substance that could be added to water to remove both Ca^{2+} and Mg^{2+} from solution.

   (d) Explain why adding a water softener to your washing machine when doing laundry improves the cleaning job on your clothes.

Sequential Qualitative Chemical Analysis

Analytical chemists do not only identify the possible ions in a solution by the colour of the solution or the colour of the flame produced when some of the solution is heated in a Bunsen burner flame. They can also use sequential qualitative chemical analysis which uses the precipitation of low solubility products.

Suppose you were given a solution that might contain either lead(II) ions or strontium ions, or possibly both or neither. How would you determine what is in the solution? You would have to design an experiment. How could you precipitate lead ions out of a solution?

Why can't we simply add only chloride ions?

In order to make sure all of the lead was removed from the solution we would have to add an ______________ of sodium chloride. However, if we add too much sodium chloride we won't be able to tell if we have undissolved sodium chloride or a precipitate in the test tube. What would be the best way to add an excess of sodium chloride?

If there is a precipitate when you add a saturated solution of NaCl to the solution that may contain lead, then we have determined that there is lead in the solution (Note: the lead cations wouldn't be there in isolation either – what is a possible lead compound that may have been dissolved in solution?

Now we need to test our solution for strontium ions. What strontium containing compound would form a precipitate? How would we achieve this precipitate?

In this analysis, what would have happened if you had added the potassium sulfate to the solution first?

Careful planning and experimental design is important for correct qualitative analysis. The flow chart below gives an outline of the analysis. You should draw a similar flow chart when you are analyzing solutions.

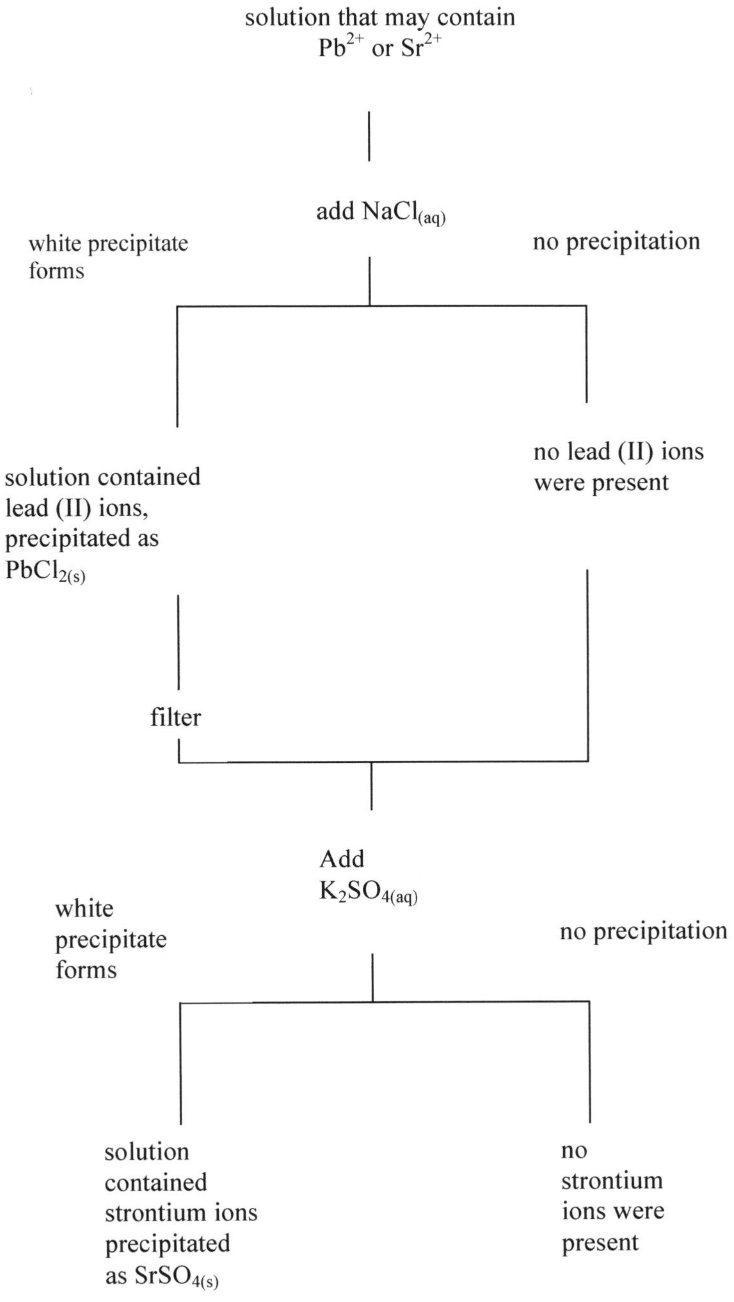

Exercise: Create your own flowchart for a solution that may contain Fe^{3+} and/or Ba^{2+}

7.6 Identifying Acids and Bases

Warm Up

A student tested a number of unknown solutions and recorded the following observations. Based on each observation, place a check mark in the corresponding column that identifies the unknown solution as containing an acid, a base, or either one.

Observation	Acid	Base
Turns phenolphthalein pink		
Feels slippery		
Has pH = 5.0		
Tastes sour		
Conducts electricity		
Reacts with metal to produce a gas		

The Arrhenius Theory of Acids and Bases

In previous years, you learned how to identify an acid or base using a concept developed by a chemist named Svante Arrhenius. According to the Arrhenius theory, acids release H^+ ions in solution, and bases release OH^- ions.

Typically, when an Arrhenius acid and base react together, a salt and water form. A salt is an ionic compound that does not contain H^+ or OH^- ions. The cation from the base and the anion from the acid make up the salt.

Example: $HCl(aq) + NaOH(aq) \rightarrow NaCl(aq) + H_2O(l)$
acid base salt water

Sample Problem — Identifying Arrhenius Acids and Bases

Classify each of the following substances as an Arrhenius acid, an Arrhenius base, a salt or a molecular compound.

(a) HNO_3
(b) $Al(OH)_3$
(c) $Al(NO_3)_3$
(d) NO_2

What to Think About	How to Do It
(a) An acid releases H^+ ions.	HNO_3 is an acid.
(b) A base releases OH^- ions.	$Al(OH)_3$ is a base.
(c) A salt is an ionic compound not containing H^+ or OH^- ions.	$Al(NO_3)_3$ is a salt.
(d) A molecule is not made up of ions.	NO_2 is a molecular compound.

Practice Problems — Identifying Arrhenius Acids and Bases

1. Classify each of the following as an Arrhenius acid, an Arrhenius base, a salt, or a molecular compound.

   (a) H_2SO_4 ____________________

   (b) XeF_6 ____________________

   (c) CH_3COOH ____________________

   (d) $NaCH_3COO$ ____________________

   (e) KOH ____________________

   (f) NH_3 ____________________

2. Complete the following neutralization equations. Make sure each equation is balanced, and circle the salt produced.

   (a) $CH_3COOH + LiOH \rightarrow$

   (b) $HI + Ca(OH)_2 \rightarrow$

   (c) $Mg(OH)_2 + H_3PO_4 \rightarrow$

3. Write the formula of the parent acid and the parent base that react to form each salt listed.

	Parent Acid	Parent Base
(a) KNO_2		
(b) NH_4Cl		
(c) CuC_2O_4		
(d) $NaCH_3COO$		

Brønsted-Lowry Acids and Bases

Arrhenius' definition worked well to classify a number of substances that displayed acidic or basic characteristics. However, some substances that acted like acids or bases could not be classified using this definition. A broader definition of acids and bases was required.

In the practice problem above, you may have classified NH_3 as molecular. While it is molecular, a solution of NH_3 also feels slippery, has a pH greater than 7, and turns phenolphthalein pink. It clearly has basic characteristics, but it is not an Arrhenius base.

Chemists Johannes Brønsted and Thomas Lowry suggested a broader definition of acids and bases:

Brønsted-Lowry acid — a substance or species that donates a hydrogen ion, H^+ (a proton)
Brønsted-Lowry base — a substance or species that accepts a hydrogen ion, H^+

Consider the reaction that occurs in aqueous HCl:

$$\underset{\text{acid}}{HCl(aq)} + \underset{\text{base}}{H_2O(l)} \rightarrow \underset{\text{hydronium}}{H_3O^+(aq)} + Cl^-(aq)$$

In this example, the HCl donates a hydrogen ion (H^+) to the water molecule. The HCl is therefore acting as a Brønsted-Lowry acid. The water accepts the H^+ ion so it is acting as a Brønsted-Lowry base.

The H_3O^+ ion is called a **hydronium ion**. It is simply a water molecule with an extra H^+ ion (Figure 7.1.1). It is also called a protonated water molecule.

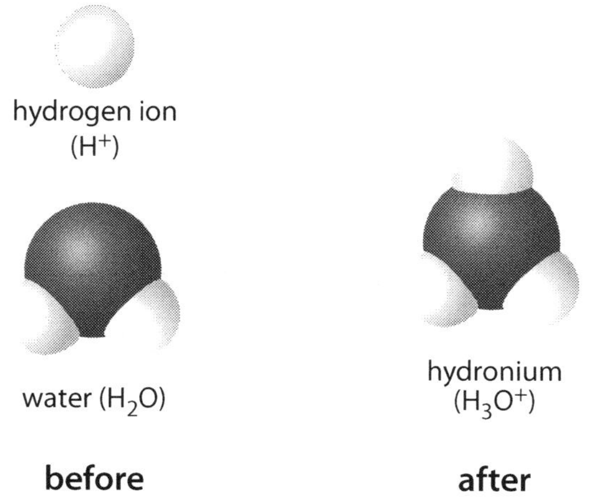

Figure 7.6.1 *A hydronium ion is a water molecule with an extra H+ ion.*

Let's look at NH_3 now. In a solution of ammonia (NH_3) the following reaction occurs:

$$\underset{\text{base}}{NH_3(aq)} + \underset{\text{acid}}{H_2O(l)} \rightleftharpoons NH_4^+(aq) + OH^-(aq)$$

The ammonia molecule accepted a H^+ ion from the water, so NH_3 is acting as a Brønsted-Lowry base, and water is acting as a Brønsted-Lowry acid.

You may notice that in the equation for HCl, a one-way arrow was used, but in the equation for NH_3, an equilibrium arrow was used. The reasons for this will be explained in the next section. Just remember that if you see an equilibrium arrow, then equilibrium is established. More importantly, in an equilibrium, you have both reactants and products present in the system. Both forward and reverse reactions occur. If we look at the reverse reaction for the ammonia system, we can identify Brønsted-Lowry acids and bases:

$$\underset{\text{base}}{NH_3(aq)} + \underset{\text{acid}}{H_2O(l)} \rightleftharpoons \underset{\text{acid}}{NH_4^+(aq)} + \underset{\text{base}}{OH^-(aq)}$$

In the reverse reaction, the NH_4^+ ion donates a proton to the OH^- ion. According to Brønsted-Lowry definitions, the NH_4^+ ion is acting as an acid, and the OH^- ion is acting as a base.

In a Brønsted-Lowry equilibrium, there are two acids and two bases: one for the forward reaction, and one for the reverse reaction. An acid and a base react to form a different acid and base.

Two substances that differ by one H^+ ion are called a **conjugate acid-base pair.**

In the example above, the NH_3 and NH_4^+ together form one conjugate acid-base pair, and the H_2O and OH^- form the other conjugate acid-base pair.

Sample Problems — Identifying Conjugate Acid-Base Pairs

1. In the following equilibrium, identify the acids and bases, and the two conjugate acid-base pairs:

$$HF(aq) + CN^-(aq) \rightleftharpoons HCN(aq) + F^-(aq)$$

2. Complete the following table:

Conjugate Acid	Conjugate Base
$H_2C_2O_4$	
	SO_3^{2-}
HCO_3^-	
	H_2O

3. Complete the following equilibrium, which represents the reaction of a Brønsted-Lowry acid and base. Circle the substances that make up one of the conjugate acid-base pairs.

$$NO_2^-(aq) + H_2CO_3(aq) \rightleftharpoons$$

What to Think About

1. An acid donates a proton and a base accepts a proton.

   In the forward reaction, the HF is the acid and the CN– is the base. In the reverse reaction, the HCN is the acid and the F– is the base.

   The substances in a conjugate acid-base pair differ by one H^+ ion.

2. An acid donates a proton. Find the conjugate base of an acid by removing one H^+. Be careful of your charges on the ions! A base accepts a proton. Find the conjugate acid of a given base by adding one H^+.

3. An acid must be able to donate a H^+ ion. Only the H_2CO_3 has a H^+ to donate. When it donates a H^+ ion, HCO_3^- forms. The NO_2^- ion is forced to accept the H^+, making the NO_2^- a base. When the NO_2^- accepts a proton, it forms HNO_2. The total charge on the reactant side should equal the total charge on the product side. Balance reactions for both.

Note: H_2CO_3 only donates ONE H^+ ion. Substances in a conjugate acid-base pair differ by only ONE H^+ ion. Balance both sides of the equation for number of atoms and charge.

How to Do It

1. The two conjugate acid-base pairs are: HF/F^- and CN^-/HCN.

$$\underset{\text{acid}}{HF(aq)} + \underset{\text{base}}{CN^-(aq)} \rightleftharpoons \underset{\text{acid}}{HCN(aq)} + \underset{\text{base}}{F^-(aq)}$$

2.

Conjugate acid			Conjugate base
$H_2C_2O_4$	→	remove H^+	$HC_2O_4^-$
HSO_3^-	←	add H^+	SO_3^{2-}
HCO_3^-	→	remove H^+	CO_3^{2-}
H_3O^+	←	add H^+	H_2O

3.

$$NO_2^-(aq) + H_2CO_3(aq) \rightleftharpoons HNO_2(aq) + HCO_3^-(aq)$$

Circle around either of the following: NO_2^-/HNO_2 or H_2CO_3/HCO_3^-

Practice Problems — Identifying Conjugate Acid-Base Pairs

1. For the following equilibria, label the acids and bases for the forward and reverse reactions.

   (a) $HIO_3 + NO_2^- \rightleftharpoons HNO_2 + IO_3^-$

   (b) $HF + HC_2O_4^- \rightleftharpoons H_2C_2O_4 + F^-$

   (c) $Al(H_2O)_6^{3+} + SO_3^{2-} \rightleftharpoons HSO_3^- + Al(H_2O)_5OH^{2+}$

2. Complete the following table:

Conjugate Acid	Conjugate Base
H_2O_2	
	$H_2BO_3^-$
HCOOH	
	$C_6H_5O_7^{3-}$

3. Complete the following equilibria. Label the acids and bases for the forward and reverse reactions. Circle one conjugate acid-base pair in each equilibria.

   (a) $HNO_2 + NH_3 \rightleftharpoons$

   (b) $H_3C_6H_5O_7 + CN^- \rightleftharpoons$

   (c) $PO_4^{3-} + H_2S \rightleftharpoons$

Amphiprotic Species

Consider the two equilibria below:

$$\underset{\text{acid}}{NH_3(aq) + H_2O(l)} \rightleftharpoons NH_4^+(aq) + OH^-(aq) \qquad \underset{\text{base}}{HF(aq) + H_2O(l)} \rightleftharpoons H_3O^+(aq) + F^-(aq)$$

In the first reaction, water acts as a Brønsted-Lowry acid. In the second reaction, water acts as a Brønsted-Lowry base. An **amphiprotic** substance has the ability to act as an acid or a base, depending on what it is reacting with. Water is a common amphiprotic substance. Many anions also display amphiprotic tendencies. For a substance to be amphiprotic, it must have a proton to donate and be able to accept a proton. Examples of amphiprotic anions include HCO_3^-, $HC_2O_4^-$, and $H_2PO_4^-$. Uncharged species, with the exception of water, are generally not amphiprotic. For example, HCl will donate one H^+ ion (proton) to form Cl^-, but will not accept a proton to form H_2Cl^+. You should recognize many of the species that form.

Quick Check

1. Write an equation for a reaction between HCO_3^- and CN^- where HCO_3^- acts as an acid.

2. Write an equation for a reaction between HCO_3^- and H_2O where HCO_3^- acts as a base.

3. Circle amphiprotic substances in the following list:

   (a) CH_3COOH (b) $H_2PO_4^-$ (c) PO_4^{3-} (d) $H_2C_2O_4$ (e) $HC_2O_4^-$

7.6 Activity: Conjugate Pairs Memory Game

Question
How many conjugate acid-base pairs can you identify?

Materials
- grid of conjugate pairs, cut into cards
- scissors

Procedure
1. Go to edvantagescience.com for a page of symbols and formulas.
2. Cut along the grid lines to make a set of cards. Each card will have one symbol or formula on it.
3. Place the cards face down on the table in a 6×6 grid.
4. Play in groups of two or three. The first player turns over two cards. If the two substances are a conjugate acid-base pair, the player keeps the two cards and gets one more turn. If they are not a conjugate acid-base pair, the player turns the cards face down again after everyone has seen them.
5. The next player turns over two cards, again looking for a conjugate pair.
6. The play continues until all conjugate acid-base pair cards are collected. The winner is the player with the most cards.

Results and Discussion
1. Define an acid-base conjugate pair.

2. Explain why H_2SO_3 and SO_3^{2-} are not a conjugate pair.

7.6 Review Questions

1. How are the Arrhenius and Brønsted-Lowry definitions of an acid and base similar? How are they different? Use examples.

2. Explain why the H^+ ion is the same as a proton.

3. A hydronium ion is formed when water accepts a proton. Draw a Lewis structure for water, and explain why water will accept a proton. Draw the Lewis structure for a hydronium ion.

4. In the following equations, identify the acids and bases in the forward and reverse reactions. Identify the conjugate acid-base pairs.

   (a) $NH_3 + H_3PO_4 \rightleftharpoons NH_4^+ + H_2PO_4^-$

   (b) $H_2PO_4^- + SO_3^{2-} \rightleftharpoons HSO_3^- + HPO_4^{2-}$

   (c) $CH_3NH_2 + CH_3COOH \rightleftharpoons CH_3COO^- + CH_3NH_3^+$

5. Formic acid, HCOOH, is the substance responsible for the sting in ant bites. Write an equation showing it acting as an acid when reacted with water. Label the acids and bases in the forward and reverse reactions. Identify the two conjugate acid-base pairs.

6. Pyridine, C_5H_5N, is a Brønsted-Lowry base. It is used in the production of many pharmaceuticals. Write an equation showing it acting as a base when reacted with water. Label the acids and bases in the forward and reverse reactions. Identify the two conjugate acid-base pairs.

7. Sodium hypochlorite solution is also known as bleach. It contains the hypochlorite ion ClO^-.
   (a) Write an equation for the reaction between hypochlorite ion and ammonium ion. Label the acids and bases in the forward and reverse reactions. Identify the two conjugate acid-base pairs.

   (b) This equilibrium favors the reactants. Which of the acids is stronger and donates protons more readily?

8. (a) Explain how to write the formula for the conjugate acid of a given base. Use an example.

   (b) Explain how to write the formula for the conjugate base of a given acid. Use an example.

9. (a) Hydrogen peroxide, H_2O_2, is a Brønsted Lowry acid. It is used as an antiseptic and bleaching agent. Write the formula for the conjugate base of hydrogen peroxide.

   (b) Hydrazine, N_2H_4, is a Brønsted-Lowry base used as a rocket fuel. Write the formula for the conjugate acid of hydrazine.

   (c) Phenol, HOC_6H_5, is a Brønsted-Lowry acid used to make plastics, nylon, and slimicides. Write the formula for its conjugate base.

   (d) Aniline, $C_6H_5NH_2$, is a Brønsted-Lowry base used to make polyurethane. Write the formula for its conjugate acid.

10. Define the term *amphiprotic*. List four amphiprotic substances.

11. Baking soda contains sodium bicarbonate.
    (a) Write two equations demonstrating the amphiprotic nature of the bicarbonate ion with water. Describe a test you could perform to identify which equilibrium is more likely to occur.

    (b) Bicarbonate produces CO_2 gas in the batter of cookies or cakes, which makes the batter rise as it bakes. Which of the two equations in (a) represents the action of bicarbonate ion in baking?

12. Water is amphiprotic. Write a reaction showing a water molecule acting as an acid reacting with a water molecule acting as a base. Label the acids and bases for the forward and reverse reactions. Identify the conjugate acid-base pairs.

7.7 pH and pOH

Warm Up

1. Balance the following neutralization equation:
   ___ $H_2SO_4(aq)$ + ___ $NaOH(aq)$ → ___ $H_2O(l)$ + ___ $Na_2SO_4(aq)$

2. Write the balanced equation for the reaction between aluminum hydroxide and hydrobromic acid to form aluminum bromide and water.

3. Complete and balance the following equation:
   $NH_4OH(aq)$ + $H_2SO_4(aq)$ → ____________ + ____________

4. Write the formulas for the acid and base that will react to give the salt K_2CO_3 and water.

The pH Scale

Figure 7.7.1 *A powerful river flows through a narrow valley.*

Look at your answers to question 1 in the Warm Up and consider the magnitude of the difference between the $[H_3O^+]$ and $[OH^-]$ in solution A and solution B — it is 100 trillion times! Consider also that during the neutralization described in question 2, each ion concentration changes instantly by 10 million times to equal the other. Now think about the volume your answer to question 3 actually represents: 10^{14} L of 1.0 M NaOH solution would be required to obtain 1.0 mol of hydronium ions!

Let's try to appreciate how large a volume this is. The average flow rate of large river is approximately 3.5×10^6 L/s (Figure 7.2.12). At this rate, to observe 10^{14} L of water flow by, you would have to watch this mighty river for more than 330 days!

The point behind the above discussion is that a linear arithmetic scale is not only inconvenient, it is cumbersome. It is also often inadequate to use when representing the typically very small hydronium and hydroxide concentrations in most aqueous solutions and the extent to which they can change in a neutralization reaction.

A much more convenient and compact approach was introduced in 1909 by the great Danish chemist S.P. Sorensen. Sorensen's scale is called the **pH** ("potency" or "power" of hydrogen) scale. It is a logarithmic or "power of 10" way to specify the concentration of hydronium ions in a solution.

We define pH as the negative logarithm of the molar concentration of hydronium ions:

$$\mathbf{pH = -log\,[H_3O^+]}$$

The logarithm of a number is the power to which 10 must be raised to obtain that number. For example:

$\log 100 = \log (1 \times 10^2) = 2.0$
$\log 0.01 = \log (1 \times 10^{-2}) = -2.0$

Logarithms and Significant Figures

When we take the logarithm of a number, we must be careful to record the answer to the proper number of significant figures. To understand how to do this, consider the following example:

Determine the pH of a 0.0035 M H_3O^+ solution and record the answer to the proper number of significant figures.

Solution: Note that in the molar concentration, there are two significant figures because the leading zeros are not considered significant. It should make sense to you that any operation done on those zeros yields a value that is also not considered significant. In the solution below, the significant figures are underlined:

$$\begin{aligned} pH &= -\log [H_3O^+] \\ &= -\log (0.00\underline{35}) \text{ (two significant figures)} \\ &= -\log (\underline{3.5} \times 10^{-3}) \end{aligned}$$

(*Note that the log of the product of two numbers equals the sum of the logs of those numbers so that:* $\log (A \times B) = \log A + \log B$)

$$= -\log \underline{3.5} \text{ (significant)} + -\log 10^{-3}$$

(The exponent 3 is not a measured value. Rather, it is an exact number and consequently does not limit the number of significant figures in the answer.)

$$\begin{aligned} &= -0.\underline{54}41 \text{ (significant)} + 3 \\ &= 2.\underline{45}59 \\ &= 2.\underline{46} \text{ (two significant figures)} \end{aligned}$$

We can generalize this into a rule governing logarithms and significant figures:

When taking the logarithm of a number, the result must have the same number of *decimal places* as there are *significant figures* in the original number.

Measuring pH

The pH of a solution is usually determined with an acid-base indicator or, more precisely, by using an instrument called a pH meter (Figure 7.2.13). (Acid-base indicators will be discussed in more detail in Chapter 6.)

A pH meter consists of specially designed electrodes that are sensitive to the concentration of H_3O^+ ions. When the electrodes are dipped into a solution, a voltage between the measuring electrode and a reference electrode is generated that depends on the solution's pH. That voltage is read on a meter which is calibrated in pH units.

Figure 7.7.2 *A pH meter*

Quick Check

1. Convert each of the following hydronium concentrations to pH values. Make sure to record your answers to the proper number of significant figures.

Solution	$[H_3O^+]$	pH
orange juice	3.2×10^{-4} M	
milk of magnesia	2.52×10^{-11} M	
stomach acid	0.031 M	

2. During a titration, if the pH of a solution decreased quickly by 5 units from 8 to 3 at the equivalence point, did the $[H_3O^+]$ increase or decrease and by how much?

____

3. A 100.0 mL sample of an aqueous solution labeled as 0.10 M H_3O^+ is diluted to 1.0 L. Has the pH of the solution increased or decreased and by how much?

____

Antilogarithms

You will be expected to determine the pH of a solution given its hydronium concentration. You must also be able to convert pH values into hydronium concentrations in the reverse process. This is accomplished using the following relationship:

$$[H_3O^+] = 10^{-pH}$$

This is sometimes called taking the antilogarithm, and in this case, we are taking the antilogarithm of the *negative pH value*. It is simply expressing the negative logarithm in its original exponential form. Depending on the type of calculator you use, you should become familiar with the calculation steps to perform this operation. Usually, this requires employing the "10^x," "Y^x," or "inverse" "log" keys.

Sample Problem — Converting pH to $[H_3O^+]$

The pH of a beaker of lemon juice is measured and found to be 2.31. Calculate the concentration of hydronium ions in this solution.

What to Think About	How to Do It
1. Because the pH is well below 7.00, expect the hydronium concentration to be much greater than 1.0×10^{-7} M. The solution is therefore acidic.	$[H_3O^+] = 10^{-pH}$ $[H_3O^+] = 10^{-2.31}$
2. Two decimal places in the pH value will correspond to a molar concentration recorded to two significant figures.	$[H_3O^+] = 4.9 \times 10^{-3}$ M

Practice Problems — Converting pH to $[H_3O^+]$

1. Complete the following table and record your answers to the proper number of significant figures:

$[H_3O^+]$	No. of sig. figures	pH
5.00×10^{-5} M		
		3.34
6.4×10^{-11} M		
		6.055
0.00345 M		

2. During a titration, the pH at the equivalence point changed quickly from 4.35 to 9.65. Calculate the $[H_3O^+]$ just before and just after the equivalence point was reached.

3. A student calculates the pH of a sample of concentrated nitric acid to be –1.20. She thinks she has made a mistake because the value is negative. Calculate the hydronium concentration in this acid solution and decide if an error was made. Why do you think expressing pH values for concentrated strong acid solutions are not really necessary?

Expanding the "p" Concept

The success of the pH concept for representing small hydronium concentrations allowed it to be extended to cover other typically small values. In general:

pX = –log X

Accordingly, we can also represent the hydroxide concentrations in aqueous solutions in a logarithmic way and call that value **pOH**.

pOH = –log [OH⁻]

For example, in a 0.10 M solution of NaOH, we know that the $[OH^-] = 0.10$ M. This allows us to determine the pOH as follows:

$$pOH = -\log 0.10 = -\log (1.0 \times 10^{-1}) = 1.00$$

Recall that the concentrations of hydronium and hydroxide ions in aqueous solutions are inversely related through the equilibrium constant we call K_w. This always equals 1.00×10^{-14} at 25°C as given by: $[H_3O^+][OH^-] = K_w = 1.00 \times 10^{-14}$

We can use this to derive another very useful relationship for any aqueous solution. Begin with:

$$[H_3O^+][OH^-] = K_w$$

Take the negative log of both sides:

$$-\log\left[[H_3O^+][OH^-]\right] = -\log K_w$$

$$= -\log [H_3O^+] + -\log [OH^-] = -\log K_w$$

This is simply:

$pH + pOH = pK_w$

The above relationship is always true for any aqueous solution at any temperature. If we assume a temperature of 25°C, then:

$pH + pOH = 14.00$

In 7.1(a), note the graphical relationship showing the inverse relationship between hydronium and hydroxide concentration in aqueous solutions as given by $[H_3O^+][OH^-] = 10^{-14}$.

Note how the negative logarithm of both sides of the relationship translates to the graphical relationship in (b) as given by pH + pOH = 14.00.

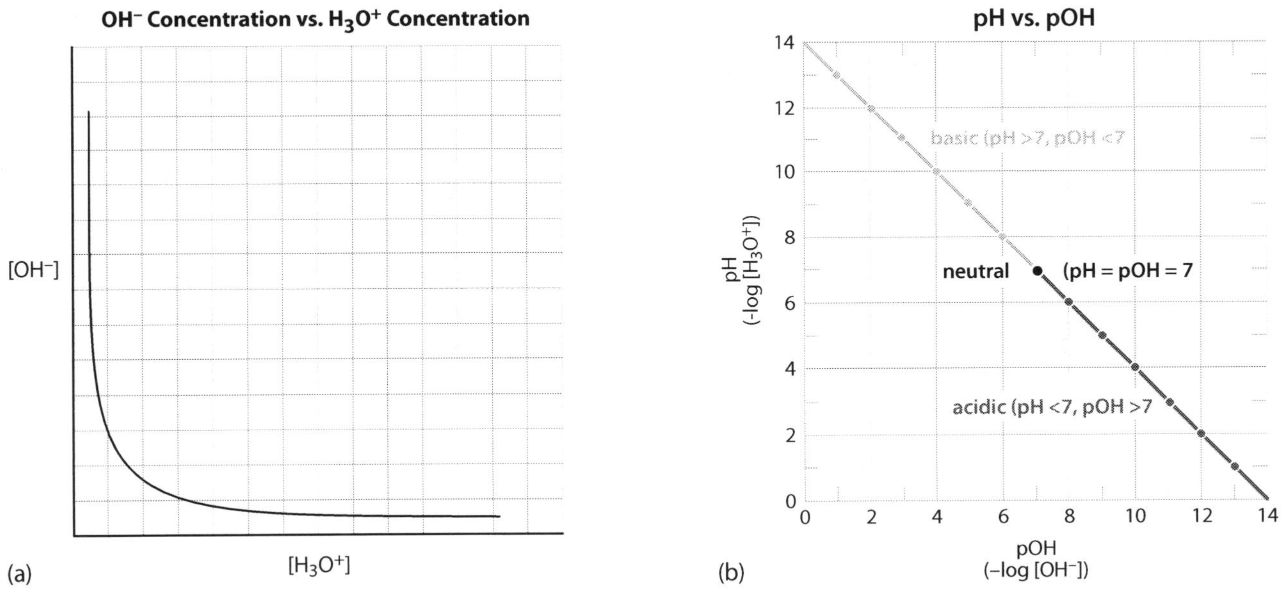

Figure 7.7.3 *(a) The inverse relationship between hydronium and hydroxide concentration in aqueous solutions; (b) This graph uses the negative logs of both sides of the relationship shown in (a).*

This relationship allows us to add to our criteria for designating aqueous solutions as acidic, basic, or neutral by incorporating both pH and pOH (Table 7.7.1).

Table 7.7.1 *pH and pOH Criteria for Designating Aqueous Solutions as Acidic, Basic, or Neutral*

Aqueous Solution at Any Temperature	Aqueous Solution at 25°C	Result
pH = pOH	pH = pOH = 7	Solution is *neutral.*
pH < pOH	pH < 7 and pOH > 7	Solution is *acidic.*
pH > pOH	pH > 7 and pOH < 7	Solution is *basic.*

This relationship also means that for any aqueous solution, if we are given any one of pH, pOH, $[H_3O^+]$, or $[OH^-]$, we can always calculate the remaining three. Consider Figure 7.4.2.

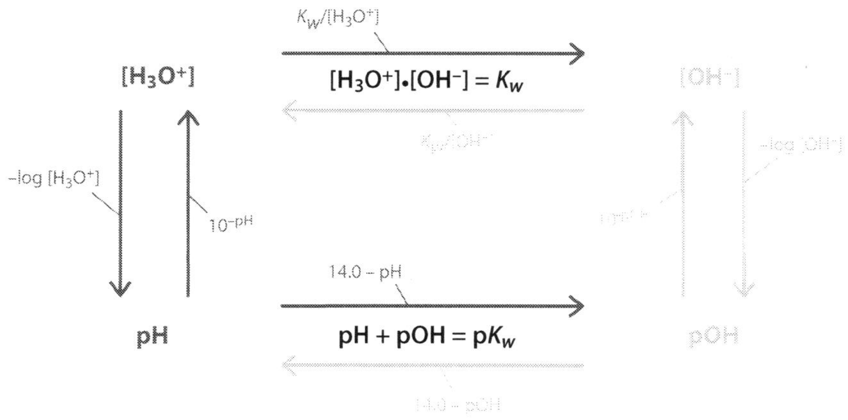

Figure 7.7.4 *This diagram shows how, by knowing one of pH, pOH, $[H_3O^+]$, or $[OH^-]$, we can calculate the other three.*

We can therefore summarize the relationship between pH, pOH, $[H_3O^+]$, and $[OH^-]$ for any aqueous solution at 25°C as shown in Figure 7.7.5. On the chart, consider the "cursor" that sits over the middle of the scale, highlighting a neutral solution. Imagine that this cursor is transparent and movable. It could be moved to the left or the right to identify the conditions associated with increasingly acidic or basic solutions respectively.

Solution becomes more ***acidic.*** ←

→ Solution becomes more ***basic.***

$[H_3O^+]$	1	10^{-1}	10^{-2}	10^{-3}	10^{-4}	10^{-5}	10^{-6}	**10^{-7}**	10^{-8}	10^{-9}	10^{-10}	10^{-11}	10^{-12}	10^{-13}	10^{-14}
pH	0	1	2	3	4	5	6	**7**	8	9	10	11	12	13	14
pOH	14	13	12	11	10	9	8	**7**	6	5	4	3	2	1	0
$[OH^-]$	10^{-14}	10^{-13}	10^{-12}	10^{-11}	10^{-10}	10^{-9}	10^{-8}	**10^{-7}**	10^{-6}	10^{-5}	10^{-4}	10^{-3}	10^{-2}	10^{-1}	1

← **CURSOR** →

↑

Solution is
neutral.

Figure 7.7.5 *The "cursor" on the chart highlights the pH, pOH, $[H_3O^+]$, and $[OH^-]$ for any aqueous solution at 25°C.*

Sample Problem — Calculating pH, pOH, $[H_3O^+]$, and $[OH^-]$

A 0.10 M aqueous solution of Aspirin (acetylsalicylic acid) at 25°C is found to have a pH of 2.27. Determine the $[H_3O^+]$, $[OH^-]$, and pOH for this solution.

What to Think About

1. This solution is acidic so expect the $[H_3O^+]$ to be greater than $[OH^-]$. It is very important to recognize which is the *predominant ion* in a solution such as this. For acids, the $[H_3O^+]$ always predominates. This means it is more prevalent.
2. Two decimal places in the pH correspond to two significant figures in the concentration. Be sure to keep all figures through the entire calculation. Only round to the appropriate number of significant figures at the very end.
3. Consider Figure 5.4.4 and note that there is more than one order in which the calculations can be performed. For example, we could answer the questions in the order they are asked, or we could begin by calculating pOH and then determine $[OH^-]$ and $[H_3O^+]$.

How to Do It

Perform the calculations in the order they are asked. In terms of 7.1, begin in the lower left corner and move around clockwise to answer the questions:

$$[H_3O^+] = 10^{-pH} = 10^{-2.27} = 5.4 \times 10^{-3}\ M$$

$$[OH^-] = K_w/[H_3O^+]$$

$$[OH^-] = \frac{1.0 \times 10^{-14}}{5.4 \times 10^{-3}} = 1.9 \times 10^{-12}\ M$$

$$pOH = -\log(1.86 \times 10^{-12}\ M) = 11.73$$

OR

$$pOH = 14.00 - 2.27 = 11.73$$

$$[OH^-] = 10^{-11.73} = 1.9 \times 10^{-12}\ M$$

$$[H_3O^+] = \frac{1.0 \times 10^{-14}}{1.9 \times 10^{-12}} = 5.4 \times 10^{-3}\ M$$

Practice Problems — pH and pOH

(Unless otherwise indicated, assume all aqueous solutions are at 25°C.)

1. Complete the following table.

Solution	$[H_3O^+]$	$[OH^-]$	pH	pOH	Acidic/Basic/Neutral?
Orange Juice				10.5	
Tears	3.98×10^{-8} M				
Blood			7.40		
Milk		3.16×10^{-8} M			

2. Consider the equations above relating pH, pOH, $[H_3O^+]$, and $[OH^-]$ for an aqueous solution, and complete the following statements:
   (a) As a solution becomes more acidic, both $[H_3O^+]$ and pOH ____________ (increase or decrease) and both $[OH^-]$ and pH ____________ (increase or decrease).
   (b) A basic solution has a pOH value that is ____________ (greater or less) than 7, and $[H_3O^+]$ that is ____________ (greater or less) than 10^{-7} M.
   (c) If the pH of a solution equals 14.0, the $[OH^-]$ equals __________ M.
   (d) If the pOH of a solution decreases by 5, then the $[H_3O^+]$ has ____________ (increased or decreased) by a factor of ____________.
3. For pure water at 10°C, $K_w = 2.55 \times 10^{-15}$. Calculate the pH of water at 10°C and state whether the water is acidic, basic, or neutral.

When Strong Acids and Strong Bases Are Mixed

Look again at your answer to the Warm Up question 2 at the beginning of this section. In this example, hydronium ions from a strong acid reacted with an equal number of moles of hydroxide ions from a strong base. The resulting aqueous solution was neutral because neither ion was in excess following the neutralization reaction. Therefore, the $[H_3O^+]$ and $[OH^-]$ were both 1.0×10^{-7} M, so both the pH and pOH were equal to 7.00.

However, if an excess of either hydronium or hydroxide ions remains in a solution following the reaction of a strong acid with a strong base, the solution will not be neutral. Recall that the net ionic equation for the reaction of a strong acid with a strong base is given by:

$$H_3O^+(aq) + OH^-(aq) \rightarrow 2\,H_2O(l)$$

This allows us to easily determine which ion will be in excess and by how much after a strong acid and a strong base are mixed together. We can then determine pH and/or pOH values.

A convenient approach is to calculate the starting or diluted $[H_3O^+]$ and $[OH^-]$ when the solutions are poured together but *before they react* and then to simply subtract the lesser concentration from the greater concentration to determine the final concentration of the ion in excess. Let us designate those starting concentrations as: $[H_3O^+]_{ST}$ and $[OH^-]_{ST}$. Depending on which of these two concentrations is greater, we use one of the two equations below to calculate the pH or pOH:

If $[H_3O^+]_{ST} > [OH^-]_{ST}$, then we use: $[H_3O^+]_{XS} = [H_3O^+]_{ST} - [OH^-]_{ST}$ to calculate pH or pOH.

If $[OH^-]_{ST} > [H_3O^+]_{ST}$, then we use: $[OH^-]_{XS} = [OH^-]_{ST} - [H_3O^+]_{ST}$ to calculate pH or pOH.

Sample Problem — Mixing Strong Acids and Bases

Calculate the pH of the solution resulting from mixing 30.0 mL of 0.40 M HNO_3 with 70.0 mL of 0.20 M NaOH.

What to Think About

1. Nitric acid is a strong acid and so the concentration of the acid is also the $[H_3O^+]$ in that solution due to 100% ionization.
2. The final volume will be 100.0 mL so each ion concentration will be reduced accordingly upon mixing.

How to Do It

$$[H_3O^+]_{ST} = 0.40\text{ M} \times \frac{30.0\text{ mL}}{100.0\text{ mL}} = 0.12\text{ M}$$

$$[OH^-]_{ST} = 0.20\text{ M} \times \frac{70.0\text{ mL}}{100.0\text{ mL}} = 0.14\text{ M}$$

$$[OH^-]_{XS} = 0.14\text{ M} - 0.12\text{ M} = 0.02\text{ M}$$

$$\text{pOH} = -\log(0.02) = 1.7$$

And so $\text{pH} = 14.0 - 1.7 = 12.3$

An alternative approach would be to calculate the total number of moles of each ion and then subtract the lesser from the greater. Then divide the difference by the final volume to obtain the concentration of the ion is excess.

$$\text{mol } H_3O^+ = 0.0300\text{ L} \times 0.40\,\frac{\text{mol } H_3O^+}{\text{L}} = 0.012\text{ mol } H_3O^+$$

$$\text{mol } OH^- = 0.0700\text{ L} \times 0.20\,\frac{\text{mol } OH^-}{\text{L}} = 0.014\text{ mol } OH^-$$

$$\text{mol } OH^- \text{ in excess} = 0.014\text{ mol} - 0.012\text{ mol} = 0.002\text{ mol } OH^- \text{ in excess}$$

$$\text{The final } [OH^-] = \frac{0.002\text{ mol } OH^-}{0.1000\text{ L}} = 0.02\text{ M}$$

$$\text{pOH} = -\log 0.02 = 1.7 \quad \text{so} \quad \text{pH} = 14.0 - 1.7 = 12.3$$

Sample Problem — Mixing Strong Acids and Bases

Determine the pH of the solution that results when 50.0 mL of 0.200 M H_2SO_4 is mixed with 100.0 mL of 0.400 M NaOH.

What to Think About

1. The final volume will be 150.0 mL and so each ion concentration should be diluted accordingly.
2. H_2SO_4 is a diprotic acid and so the $[H_3O^+]_{ST}$ should be calculated accordingly.
3. The final pH must be recorded to three decimal places.

How to Do It

$$[H_3O^+]_{ST} = 0.200\ \frac{\text{mol } H_2SO_4}{L} \times \frac{2\ \text{mol } H_3O^+}{\text{mol } H_2SO_4} \times \frac{50.0\ \text{mL}}{150.0\ \text{mL}} = 0.1333\ M$$

$$[OH^-]_{ST} = 0.400\ M \times \frac{100.0\ \text{mL}}{150.0\ \text{mL}} = 0.2667\ M$$

$$[OH^-]_{XS} = 0.2667\ M - 0.1333\ M = 0.1333\ M$$

$$pOH = -\log(0.1333) = 0.875$$

$$pH = 14.000 - 0.875 = 13.125$$

Sample Problem — Mixing Strong Acids and Bases

A student adds 35.0 mL of an HCl solution with a pH of 2.00 to 15.0 mL of NaOH solution with a pH of 12.00. Calculate the pH of the final solution.

What to Think A bout

1. The predominant ion in the first solution (with a pH of 2.00) is clearly the hydronium ion, and the predominant ion in the second (pH = 12.00) is hydroxide.
2. Accordingly, determine each ion concentration as shown previously.
3. Record two decimal places in the final pH.

How to Do It

In the acidic solution: $[H_3O^+] = 10^{-2.00} = 0.010\ M$

In the basic solution: $pOH = 14.00 - 12.00 = 2.00$

$$[OH^-] = 10^{-2.00} = 0.010\ M$$

$$[H_3O^+]_{ST} = 0.010\ M \times \frac{35.0\ \text{mL}}{50.0\ \text{mL}} = 0.0070\ M$$

$$[OH^-]_{ST} = 0.010\ M \times \frac{15.0\ \text{mL}}{50.0\ \text{mL}} = 0.0030\ M$$

$$[H_3O^+]_{XS} = 0.0070\ M - 0030\ M = 0.0040\ M$$

$$pH = -\log(0.0040) = 2.40$$

Sample Problem — Mixing Strong Acids and Bases

What mass of NaOH must be added to 500.0 mL of a solution of 0.020 M HI to obtain a solution with a pH of 2.50?

What to think about

1. The final solution still has an excess of H_3O^+ ions so the equation that applies is:

$$[H_3O^+]_{XS} = [H_3O^+]_{ST} - [OH^-]_{ST}$$

2. Solve for $[OH^-]_{ST}$ because both the $[H_3O^+]_{XS}$ and $[H_3O^+]_{ST}$ are provided either directly or indirectly in the question. Therefore manipulate the above equation to give:

$$[OH^-]_{ST} = [H_3O^+]_{ST} - [H_3O^+]_{XS}$$

Then convert your answer from moles per liter to grams required for 0.500 L.

How to Do It

$[H_3O^+]_{ST} = 0.020\ M$

$[H_3O^+]_{XS} = 10^{-2.50} = 0.00316\ M$

$[OH^-]_{ST} = [H_3O^+]_{ST} - [H_3O^+]_{XS}$

$= 0.020\ M - 0.00316\ M$

$= 0.0168\ M\ NaOH$

$0.0168\ \frac{mol}{L} \times 40.0\ \frac{g\ NaOH}{mol} \times 0.500\ L$

$= 0.34\ g\ NaOH$ (2 significant figures)

Practice Problems — Mixing Strong Acids and Bases

1. Calculate the pH of the solution that results from mixing 25.0 mL of 0.40 M HCl with 15.0 mL of 0.30 M KOH.

2. A solution of HCl has a pH of 0.60. A 1.0 g sample of NaOH is dissolved in 250.0 mL of this HCl solution. Calculate the pOH of the resulting solution, assuming no volume change.

3. Calculate the pH of the solution that results when 25.0 mL of a solution with a pOH of 12.00 is mixed with 45.0 mL of a solution with a pH of 11.00.

4. What mass of HCl(*g*) must be dissolved in 1.50 L of a NaOH solution having a pH of 11.176 to produce a solution with a pH of 10.750? (Assume no volume change.)

7.7 Activity: Finding Acidic and Basic Common Solutions

Question

Can you identify a series of common solutions as being acidic, basic, or neutral?

Background

Many common aqueous solutions used around your house are either acidic or basic. Some have pH values that are high or low enough to qualify them as being as hazardous as many chemicals used in the laboratory.

Procedure

1. For each of the common solutions listed below, only one of the four values has been provided. Determine the other three for each solution. (Assume all solutions are at 25°C.)
2. Classify each solution as either acidic, basic, or neutral.

Solution	pH	pOH	$[H_3O^+]$ M	$[OH^-]$ M	Acidic/Basic/Neutral
Unpolluted rainwater	5.5				
Saliva		7.3			
Stomach acid			0.031		
Tears				2.5×10^{-7}	
Vinegar	2.9				
Milk		7.6			
Milk of magnesia			3.2×10^{-11}		
Lemon juice				2.0×10^{-12}	
Tomato juice	4.2				
Orange juice		10.5			
Grapefruit juice			0.0010		
Liquid drain cleaner				1.0	
Black coffee	5.1				
Urine		8.0			
Blood			4.0×10^{-8}		
Laundry bleach				0.010	
Windex	10.7				
Pepto-Bismol		8.2			
Household ammonia			1.3×10^{-12}		
Red wine				3.2×10^{-12}	

Results and Discussion

1. Once you have completed the table, consider the last column. Are many of the solutions listed (or others that you found) actually neutral? Explain.

2. Do the majority of the solutions used for cleaning purposes have a low or a high pH? Try to find them in your home and see how many have a hazardous warning on their label.

3. Are the solutions that you consume generally acidic or basic?

7.7 Review Questions

(Assume all solutions are at 25°C unless otherwise indicated.)

1. Define pH and pOH using a statement and an equation for each.

2. Why do we use Sorensen's pH and pOH scales to express hydronium and hydroxide concentrations in aqueous solutions?

3. Complete the following table, expressing each value to the proper number of significant figures.

$[H_3O^+]$	pH	Acidic/Basic/Neutral
3.50×10^{-6} M	5.46	A
$3.090 \cdot 10^{-12}$ M	11.51	B
0.00550 M	2.2596	A
1.00 M	0.00	A
6.8×10^{-9} M	8.2	B

4. Complete the following table, expressing each value to the proper number of significant figures.

$[OH^-]$	pOH	Acidic/Basic/Neutral
7.2×10^{-9} M	5.1	B
$2.82 \cdot 10^{-10}$ M	9.55	A
4.88×10^{-4} M	3.31	B
$1.000 \cdot 10^{-14}$ M	14.00	A
0.000625 M	3.20412	B

5. Complete the following statements:
   (a) As a solution's pOH value and $[H_3O^+]$ both decrease, the solution becomes more acidic (acidic or basic).

   (b) As a solution's pH value and $[OH^-]$ both decrease, the solution becomes more basic (acidic or basic)

   (c) The ____________ (sum or product) of the $[H_3O^+]$ and $[OH^-]$ equals K_w.

   (d) The ____________ (sum or product) of pH and pOH equals pK_w.

6. Complete the following table, expressing each value to the proper number of significant figures.

$[H_3O^+]$	pOH	Acidic/Basic/Neutral
0.0342 M		
	8.400	
7.2×10^{-12} M		
	3.215	

7. For pure water at 60.0°C, the value of $pK_w = 13.02$. Calculate the pH at this temperature and decide if the water is acidic, basic, or neutral.

8. Calculate the pH of a 0.30 M solution of $Sr(OH)_2$.

9. A 2.00 g sample of pure NaOH is dissolved in water to produce 500.0 mL of solution. Calculate the pH of this solution.

10. A sample of HI is dissolved in water to make 2.0 L of solution. The pH of this solution is found to be 2.50. Calculate the mass of HI dissolved in this solution.

11. Complete the following table, expressing each value to the proper number of significant figures.

$[H_3O^+]$	$[OH^-]$	pOH	pH	Acidic/Basic/Neutral
5.620×10^{-5} M				
	0.000450 M			
		12.50		
			10.5	

12. Calculate the pH resulting from mixing 75.0 mL of 0.50 M HNO_3 with 125.0 mL of a solution containing 0.20 g NaOH.

13. Calculate the pH of the solution that results from mixing 200.0 mL of a solution with a pH of 1.50 with 300.0 mL of a solution having a pOH of 1.50.

14. Calculate the pH of a solution that is produced when 3.2 g of HI is added to 500.0 mL of a solution having a pH of 13.00. Assume no volume change.

15. The following three solutions are mixed together:
25.0 mL of 0.20 M HCl + 35.0 mL of 0.15 M HNO_3 + 40.0 mL of 0.30 M NaOH
Calculate the pH of the final solution.

16. What mass of HCl should be added to 450.0 mL of 0.0350 M KOH to produce a solution with a pH of 11.750? (Assume no volume change.)

17. What mass of LiOH must be added to 500.0 mL of 0.0125 M HCl to produce a solution with a pH of 2.75? (Assume no volume change.)

7.8 An Introduction to Titrations

Warm Up

1. Complete the following table.

Solution	$[H_3O^+]$	$[OH^-]$
A. 1.0 M NaOH		
B. 1.0 M HCl		

2. Determine the $[H_3O^+]$ and $[OH^-]$ in the solution formed when equal volumes of solution A and solution B are combined.

3. Calculate the volume of solution A required to obtain 1.0 mol of H_3O^+ ions.

Titration

A **titration** is a quantitative analysis method used to determine the concentration of an unknown solution by reacting it with another substance of known concentration. The most common types of titrations make use of an acid-base neutralization reaction or a reduction-oxidation reaction. In this section, we will focus on acid-base titrations. In a neutralization reaction, an acid reacts with a base to form a salt and water:

$HCl(aq) + NaOH(aq) \rightarrow NaCl(aq) + H_2O(l)$
acid + base → salt + water

Solving Titration Problems

During this course, you have learned how to perform calculations based on balanced chemical equations. A titration problem is essentially a simple stoichiometric calculation. For any titration, the balanced chemical equation is a good starting point. In a titration, one reactant completely uses up the other reactant. By knowing the amount of one substance used in a reaction, the amount of the unknown substance is calculated by using the mole ratio from the balanced equation.

Sample Problem — Calculating the Unknown Concentration of an Acid

A student completely reacted 10.00 mL of HCl with 18.25 mL of 0.100M NaOH. Calculate the [HCl].

What to Think about	How to Do It
1. Write a balanced chemical equation for the acid-base reaction.	$HCl(aq) + NaOH(aq) \rightarrow NaCl(aq) + H_2O(l)$
2. Calculate the moles of substance that you know.	$\text{moles NaOH} = \frac{0.100 \text{ mol NaOH}}{1 \text{ L NaOH}} \times 0.01825 \text{ L NaOH} = 0.001825 \text{ mol NaOH}$
3. Using the balanced equation, convert the amount of substance you know to the amount of substance you don't know.	$\text{moles HCl} = 0.001825 \text{ mol NaOH} \times \frac{1 \text{ mol HCl}}{1 \text{ mol NaOH}} = 0.001825 \text{ mol HCl}$
4. Calculate the concentration by dividing the moles of HCl by liters of HCl.	
The same type of calculation can be used to calculate the unknown concentration of the base.	$[HCl] = \frac{0.001825 \text{ mol HCl}}{0.01000 \text{ L HCl}} = 0.183 \text{ M}$

Practice Problems — Simple Titration Calculations

1. A student titrated 25.00 mL of HCl with 15.62 mL of 0.30M NaOH. Calculate the [HCl].

2. In a titration, a 10.00 mL sample of NaOH was titrated with 24.25 mL of 0.20M H_2SO_4. Calculate the [NaOH].

3. A student used 22.68 mL of 0.015M $Sr(OH)_2$ to titrate 5.00 mL of HNO_3. Calculate the [HNO_3].

4. What volume of 0.50M $H_2C_2O_4$ is required to titrate 10.00 mL of 0.12M NaOH?

Practical Aspects of Titration

In a titration, there are two solutions. The solution whose concentration is known is called the **standardized solution**. The other solution is of unknown concentration.

Since titration is a quantitative method of analysis, the precision of the measuring tools used will determine how precise your final answer will be. Recording your data to the correct number of significant figures, and paying close attention to significant figures in calculations is very important in a titration. Special glassware enables accurate titration. It is important to know the names of this glassware.

- Burette (Figure 7.8.1): contains the standardized solution. The numbering on the burette allows us to measure the initial volume before the titration and final volume after the titration. Subtracting these two volumes gives us the volume of standardized solution added to the Erlenmeyer flask. Notice the scale reads from 0.00 mL at the top to 50.00 mL at the bottom.

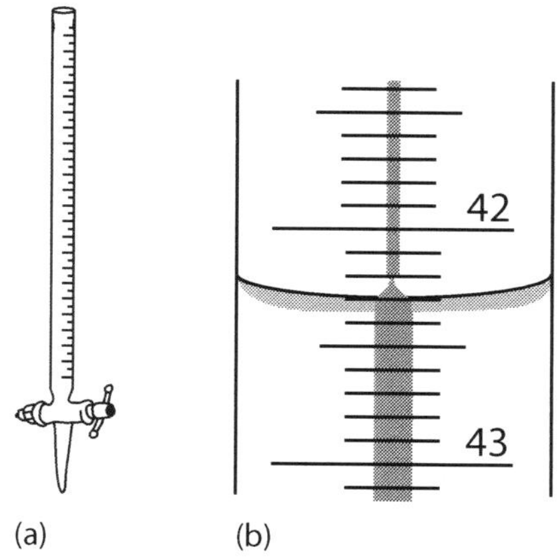

Figure 7.8.1 *(a) A burette (b) The reading on this burette is 42.30 mL.*

- Pipette (Figure 7.8.2): used to measure and deliver a precise volume of the solution of unknown concentration to the Erlenmeyer flask. Pipettes come in a number of sizes: 1.00 mL, 5.00 mL, 10.00mL, 25.00 mL, etc. They may be graduated like a burette, or designed to deliver a specific volume. A pipette bulb is used to suck the solution up into the pipette. Never suction the solution by mouth.

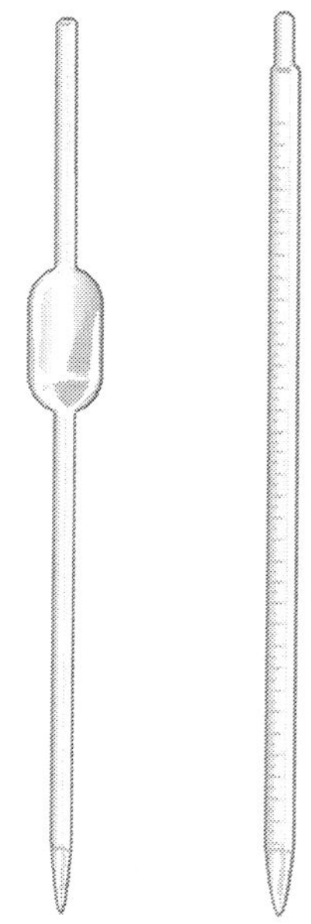

Figure 7.8.2 *Examples of pipettes*

- Erlenmeyer Flask (Figure 7.8.3): contains the measured volume of solution of unknown concentration and a few drops of an indicator at the beginning of the titration. As the titration proceeds, solution from the burette is added drop by drop to the solution in the Erlenmeyer flask where the reaction takes place. The indicator changes color when the reaction between the moles of acid and moles of base is complete.

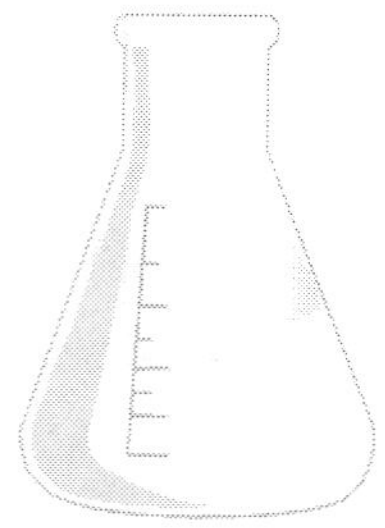

Figure 7.8.3 *An Erlenmeyer flask*

- The **equivalence point** occurs when the moles of H^+ equal the moles of OH^-. When the indicator changes color, the **endpoint** is reached. This is when you record the final burette reading.

When the titration apparatus is put together, it looks like Figure 7.8.4.

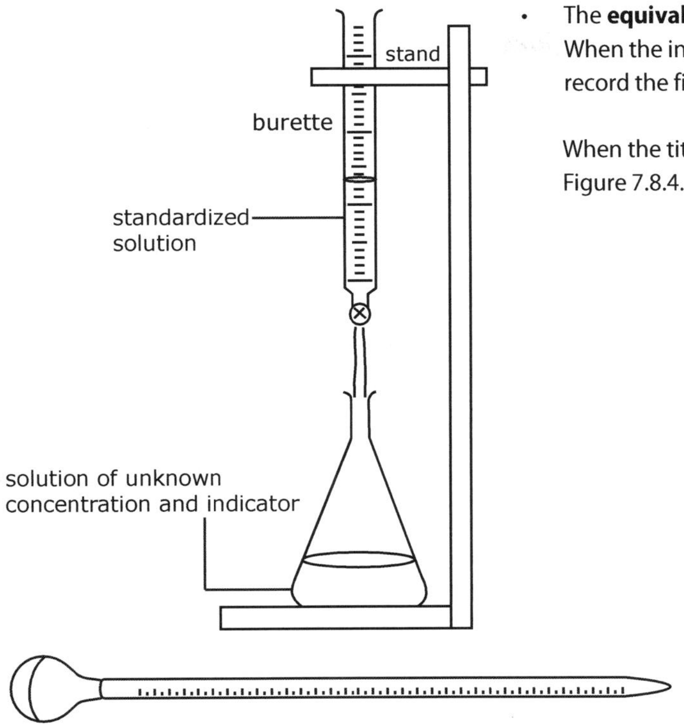

Figure 7.8.4 *A titration apparatus*

Quick Check

1. How is a pipette different from a burette?

   ____

2. What solution goes into the burette?

   ____

3. Which piece of glassware is the indicator added to?

   ____

4. What is "equivalent" at the equivalence point?

   ____

7.8 Activity: Titrating CH_3COOH with NaOH

Question

What is the unknown concentration of a sample of CH_3COOH?

Background

In previous science classes, you learned about chemical indicators and how they are used to test for the presence of acids or bases. An indicator will be one color in the presence of an acid, and a different color in the presence of a base. One such indicator is phenolphthalein. In this activity you will see how phenolphthalein can be used to indicate when an acid has completely reacted with a base. When there is an excess of acid, the phenolphthalein will be colorless. Once the acid has been completely used up and there is an excess of base, the phenolphthalein will turn pink. This color change occurs within one drop of NaOH being added.

Procedure

1. The steps involved in a titration of CH_3COOH using NaOH are described below. Answer the questions following each step to help you to understand what is happening at each part of the titration.
2. Discuss each step with your partner.

Results and Discussion

1. Write a balanced equation for the reaction between $CH_3COOH(aq)$ and $NaOH(aq)$.

2. Consider a solution of CH_3COOH of unknown concentration. It was titrated with a standardized solution of 0.15M NaOH. A student used a pipette to deliver 10.00 mL of CH_3COOH to the Erlenmeyer flask. A few drops of phenolphthalein were added. What would be the color of the solution in the flask? ______________

3. The standardized 0.15 M NaOH was placed in the burette. The initial reading on the burette was 0.50 mL. A few drops of NaOH from the burette were allowed to drip into the flask. The solution in the flask did not change color. Why does the solution in the flask not change color when the NaOH is added?

   ____

4. After adding more NaOH drop by drop, the solution became pink. At this point, no more NaOH was added. The final reading on the burette was 12.30 mL. What volume of NaOH was added to the flask? ____________________

5. When the color of the indicator changed, the endpoint had been reached. Why did the color of the solution become pink?

   ____

6. Once the titration was completed, the contents of the flask were rinsed down the drain, and the flask was rinsed out with

water. To ensure that the data was accurate, a second and third titration was completed. We call these **trials**. An example of the data collected would look like the table shown below.

For each trial, complete the subtraction and calculate the volume of NaOH added. The average volume of NaOH is calculated by averaging the two trials within 0.1 mL. Fill in the table with the appropriate values.

Molarity of NaOH = 0.15 M	Trial #1	Trial #2	Trial #3
Initial burette reading (mL)	0.50	12.31	23.75
Final burette reading (mL)	12.31	23.75	35.22
Volume of NaOH added (mL)			
Average volume NaOH (mL)			

7. Using the concentration of NaOH and average volume of NaOH, calculate the moles of NaOH used in the titration.

8. Use the mole ratio from the balanced equation to calculate the moles of CH_3COOH present in the flask.

9. Calculate the molarity of the CH_3COOH by dividing the moles of CH_3COOH by the volume of CH_3COOH in the flask.

10. Compare your answer to that of another group.

7.8 Review Questions

1. Describe how you can tell from a formula if a substance is an acid or a base. Use examples.

2. Complete and balance the following acid-base neutralization equations:

   (a) $HI(aq) + LiOH(aq) \rightarrow$

   (b) $Ca(OH)_2(aq) + HNO_3(aq) \rightarrow$

   (c) $CH_3COOH(aq) + NH_4OH(aq) \rightarrow$

   (d) $H_2SO_4(aq) + KOH(aq) \rightarrow$

3. A student titrates a standardized solution of $H_2C_2O_4$ to determine the concentration of NaOH. The indicator used was phenolphthalein. Draw an apparatus used for the titration. Label all glassware and their contents. Describe what color the solution would be in the flask at the beginning of the titration and at the end of the titration.

4. Define the terms "standardized," "equivalence point," and "endpoint."

5. A student titrated 10.00 mL HCl with 0.050 M $Sr(OH)_2$. The table below shows the data collected. Calculate the [HCl].

Molarity of $Sr(OH)_2$ = 0.050 M	**Trial #1**	**Trial #2**	**Trial #3**
Initial burette reading (mL)	0.00	16.05	32.93
Final burette reading (mL)	16.05	32.93	49.68
Volume of $Sr(OH)_2$ added (mL)			
Average volume $Sr(OH)_2$ (mL)			

6. A 25.00 mL sample of 0.20 M H_2CO_3 was titrated with 0.50 M NaOH. What volume of NaOH was required to reach the equivalence point?

7. A 10.00 mL sample of vinegar (CH_3COOH) was titrated with 18.20 mL of 0.50 M NaOH. Calculate the [CH_3COOH].

8. In order to standardize a solution of NaOH, 0.18 g of oxalic acid, $H_2C_2O_4 \cdot 2H_2O$, was dissolved to make 250.00 mL of solution. A 25.00 mL sample of this solution was titrated against 15.25 mL NaOH. Calculate the [NaOH].

9. Aspirin has the formula $C_9H_8O_4$. Only one of the H atoms is released when it acts as an acid. An aspirin tablet with a mass of 0.50 g was dissolved in water, and titrated with 18.30 mL of 0.10 M NaOH. Calculate the mass of aspirin in the tablet, and then the percent by mass of aspirin in the tablet.

10. A 250.00 mL sample of $Ca(OH)_2$ was titrated with 7.25 mL 0.10 M HCl. Calculate the mass of $Ca(OH)_2$ present in the solution.

11. A student dissolved 0.1915 g of an unknown acid HA in 10.00 mL of water. This solution was then titrated with 0.100 M NaOH. The table below shows the data collected. Calculate the molar mass of the acid HA.

Molarity of NaOH = 0.100 M	**Trial #1**	**Trial #2**	**Trial #3**
Initial burette reading (mL)	0.00	15.25	30.47
Final burette reading (mL)	15.25	30.47	45.87
Volume of NaOH added (mL)			
Average volume NaOH (mL)			

7.9 Non-metal and Metal Oxides

Warm Up

1. Recall some of the information about chemical bonding that you have studied. Consider the electronegativity values of the main-group elements in groups 1 and 2 and 13 through 17, as shown in the chart below.

Electronegativities of the Elements

H 2.1																	He
Li 1.0	Be 1.5											B 2.0	C 2.5	N 3.0	O 3.5	F 4.0	Ne
Na 0.9	Mg 1.2											Al 1.5	Si 1.8	P 2.1	S 2.5	Cl 3.0	Ar
K 0.8	Ca 1.0	Sc 1.3	Ti 1.5	V 1.6	Cr 1.6	Mn 1.5	Fe 1.8	Co 1.8	Ni 1.8	Cu 1.9	Zn 1.6	Ga 1.6	Ge 1.8	As 2.0	Se 2.4	Br 2.8	Kr
Rb 0.8	Sr 1.0	Y 1.3	Zr 1.4	Nb 1.6	Mo 1.8	Tc	Ru 2.2	Rh 2.2	Pd 2.2	Ag 1.9	Cd 1.7	In 1.7	Sn 1.8	Sb 1.9	Te 2.1	I 2.5	Xe
Cs 0.7	Ba 0.9	La 1.1	Hf 1.3	Ta 1.5	W 1.7	Re 1.9	Os 2.2	Ir 2.2	Pt 2.2	Au 2.4	Hg 1.9	Tl 1.8	Pb 1.8	Bi 1.9	Po 2.0	At 2.2	Rn
Fr 0.7	Ra 0.9	Ac 1.1															

Ce 1.1	Pr 1.1	Nd 1.2	Pm	Sm 1.2	Eu 1.2	Gd 1.1	Tb 1.2	Dy 1.2	Ho 1.2	Er 1.2	Tm 1.2	Yb 1.1	Lu 1.2
Th 1.3	Pa 1.5	U 1.7											

(a) Elements from which two of these seven groups will form the *most ionic* oxides?

____

(b) In which region of the periodic table are elements located that will form the *most covalent* oxides?

____

2. Consider the chemical equations below, representing the typical reaction of two different oxide compounds with water:

$Na_2O(s) + H_2O(l) \rightarrow 2\ NaOH(aq)$

$SO_3(g) + H_2O(l) \rightarrow H_2SO_4(aq)$

Determine the type of chemical bonds in each of the reactant oxide compounds and complete the following *general* statements:

(a) *In general*, the reaction of ____________ (ionic or covalent) oxides with water will produce *basic* solutions.

(b) *In general*, the reaction of ____________ (ionic or covalent) oxides with water will produce *acidic* solutions.

Basic Anhydrides

The periodic table summarizes an enormous amount of empirical data about the elements by classifying them according to their chemical and physical properties. One of the most important of these classifications is the designation of an element as either a metal or a non-metal. Within each of these categories, the elements and the compounds they form often behave in characteristic and predictable ways in several important types of chemical reactions.

One example of such a chemical change is the reaction between two of the most common compounds on our planet — the oxides of the elements and water. *In general,* metal oxides react with water to form bases, and non-metal oxides react with water to form acids.

As with most general statements in chemistry, there are exceptions. For a metal oxide to react with water and produce a *basic* solution, it must be both *highly ionic and soluble*. These criteria are only met by the oxides formed from the group 1 *alkali* metals and all but one of the group 2 *alkaline* earth metals. These families are so-named because their oxides (except for Be) react with water to produce alkaline or basic solutions. Metal oxides that react with water in this way are called *basic anhydrides* ("anhydride" means "without water"). Although the group 2 metal oxides are less soluble than the alkali metal oxides, their aqueous solutions are basic.

Metal oxides formed from the group 1 alkali metals and the group 2 alkaline earth metals (except Be) react with water to produce basic solutions. These oxides are referred to as *basic anhydrides.*

When basic anhydrides react with water, the metal ions are actually spectators. It is really the *dissociated oxide ions that react with water.*

If you locate the oxide ion on the Table of Relative Strengths of Brønsted-Lowry Acids and Bases (Table A5), you will notice that it is found on the bottom right corner of the table where it is identified as a *strong base*. Because of its *enormous affinity for protons*, each oxide ion in water will remove a proton from a water molecule. This converts both itself and the water into hydroxide ions.

We can demonstrate the initial dissociation of a metal oxide and the subsequent reaction of its oxide ion with water (written as "HOH") by using sodium oxide as an example:

Dissociation: $Na_2O(s) \rightarrow 2\,Na^+(aq) + O^{2-}(aq)$

Net ionic equation: $O^{2-}(aq) + HOH(l) \rightarrow OH^-(aq) + OH^-(aq)$

Overall reaction: $Na_2O(s) + H_2O(l) \rightarrow 2\,Na^+(aq) + 2\,OH^-(aq)$

Not all metal oxides are considered to be basic anhydrides. Metal oxides are solid at room temperature, but many are not soluble in water. The oxide ions are locked so tightly in the crystal lattice structure of these compounds that they cannot react with water to generate hydroxide ions.

There are also several metal oxides that are referred to as *amphoteric*. This means that, depending on the reaction conditions, they can behave as either acidic oxides or basic oxides. Some of these compounds include the group 2 metal oxide, BeO, and also Cr_2O_3, Al_2O_3, Ga_2O_3, SnO_2, and PbO_2.

Finally, some transition metal oxides in which the metal has a high oxidation number actually act as *acidic* oxides. (You will learn about oxidation numbers in the next chapter.) For example, manganese(VII) oxide and chromium(VI) oxide both react with water to produce acids:

$$Mn_2O_7(s) + H_2O(l) \rightarrow 2\,HMnO_4(aq)$$
permanganic acid

$$CrO_3(s) + H_2O(l) \rightarrow H_2CrO_4(aq)$$
chromic acid

Quick Check

1. What two criteria must be met for a metal oxide to be considered a basic anhydride?

___

2. Which two families in the periodic table contain elements that satisfy these criteria?

___

3. Calcium oxide, or quicklime, is a component of dry Portland cement, which, when mixed with water, will eventually harden into concrete. Explain why continual contact of your hands with fresh Portland cement can lead to irritation.

___

Acidic Anhydrides

Non-metal oxides that react with water are known as *acidic anhydrides*. In their reactions with water, these molecular or *covalent* oxides produce acids that are also molecular compounds.

In such a reaction, because *no oxide ions are released into water, no hydroxide ions are produced* in the aqueous solution. Instead, the water molecule binds to the molecular oxide, forming a molecular acid. Figure 7.8.3 and Figure 7.9.2 show the Lewis structures of two gaseous non-metal oxides as they react with water to form acids.

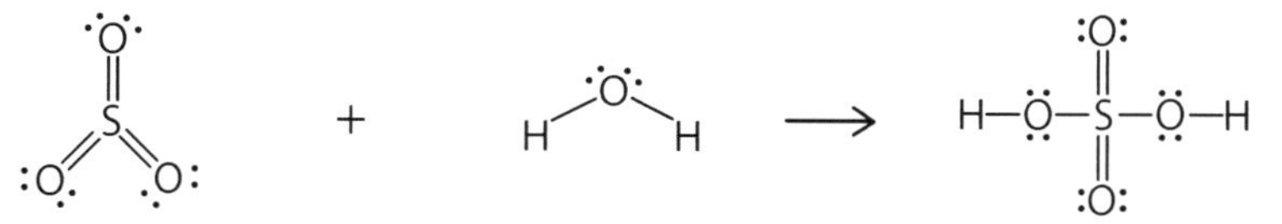

$SO_3(g)$ + $H_2O(l)$ ⟶ $H_2SO_4(aq)$

Figure 7.9.1 *The formation of sulfuric acid from sulfur trioxide and water.*

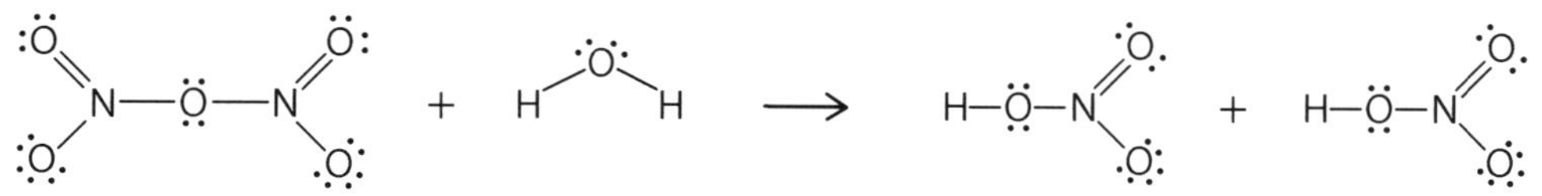

$N_2O_5(g)$ + $H_2O(l)$ ⟶ $HNO_3(aq)$ + $HNO_3(aq)$

Figure 7.9.2 *The formation of two nitric acid molecules from dinitrogen pentaoxide and water*

Acidic anhydrides are normally those containing non-metals with relatively high oxidation states such as SO_3, N_2O_5, and Cl_2O_7. For now, we can interpret that to simply mean molecules containing at least two oxygen atoms per non-metal atom. The "lower" non-metal oxides, such as NO and CO, do *not* react with water to form acids and so are not considered to be acidic anhydrides.

Non-metal oxides that react with water to produce acids are called *acidic anhydrides.*

As we discussed earlier, several metal oxides react with water to produce *acidic* solutions, but *no non-metal oxides that react with water are known to produce basic solutions.*

Although carbon monoxide does not combine with water to form an acid, carbon dioxide does. The reaction of CO_2 and water produces the weak acid carbonic acid, which is too unstable to be isolated in its pure form. Therefore, aqueous solutions of CO_2 contain varying amounts of the bicarbonate and hydronium ions and can be represented as shown below. This reaction explains why pure water will gradually become acidic when exposed to air containing CO_2 and why unpolluted rainwater is slightly acidic with a pH of about 5.6.

$$CO_2(g) + 2\,H_2O(l) \rightleftharpoons H_3O^+(aq) + HCO_3^-(aq)$$

In addition to making general statements about the reactions of metal oxides and non-metal oxides with water, we can also detect a *periodic trend* in the acid-base properties of the element oxides of the main group elements.

In general, as elements become less metallic, their oxides that react with water produce more acidic solutions. This occurs as we move both left to right across a chemical period and bottom to top up a chemical family.

Quick Check

1. A student adds a few drops of universal indicator to a small beaker of pure water and sees the expected pale green color indicating a pH of slightly less than 7. She then repeatedly blows exhaled air through a straw into the solution and notices the green color slowly change to yellow and then to pale orange. Explain these results.

   ____

2. Why are no hydroxide ions formed when covalent oxides react with water?

   ____

Sample Problem — Metal and Non-metal Oxides

Two 500. mL aqueous solutions on a lab bench have had their labels removed. One solution contains 0.50 mol of Li_2O and one solution contains 0.50 mol of SO_3. How could phenolphthalein be used to identify each solution? Include the chemical equations as part of your answer.

What to Think About	How to Do It
1. One of the solutes is an alkali metal oxide. This solution must be basic.	The Li_2O reacts with water to produce a basic solution of LiOH according to the following: $Li_2O(s) + H_2O(l) \rightarrow 2\,LiOH(aq)$
2. One of the solutes is a covalent oxide that reacts with water. This solution must be acidic.	Phenolphthalein will be *pink* in this solution.
3. Phenolphthalein is pink in a basic solution.	The SO_3 reacts with water to form a strong acid according to the following: $SO_3(g) + H_2O(l) \rightarrow H_2SO_4(aq)$ Phenolphthalein will be *colorless* in this solution.

Practice Problems — Metal and Non-metal Oxides

1. Complete and balance the following formula equations:

(a) $K_2O(s) + H_2O(l) \rightarrow$

(b) $MgO(s) + H_2O(l) \rightarrow$

2. (a) Each of the following third period oxides reacts with water to produce acids. Arrange these oxides in order from least acidic to most acidic.

SO_3 Cl_2O_7 SiO_2 P_4O_{10} Al_2O_3

________ < ________ < ________ < ________ < ________

(b) Two of the above oxides react with water to produce strong acids. Write the balanced equations for those reactions below.

3. Complete the following statements using either "ionic" or "molecular" in the blank spaces.

(a) In general, *ionic oxides* react with water to produce ______________ (ionic or molecular) bases.

(b) In general, *molecular oxides* that react with water produce acids. Acids are ______________ (ionic or molecular) compounds.

The Problem of Acid Rain

Many of the advantages we enjoy and often take for granted in our industrialized and mobile society also come with environmental costs. One of the most serious and widespread is the problem of acid precipitation in the form of rain, snow, fog, and even dry deposits on particles.

As noted earlier, normal rainwater has a pH of about 5.6 because of dissolved CO_2. If the pH of rainwater is below 5.3, it is referred to as *acid rain*.

Although natural causes also exist, virtually all of the acid precipitation that humankind is responsible for can ultimately be traced back to the burning of fossil fuels in our homes, vehicles, and power plants, and the processing of mineral ores in industry. The products of such activities and the reactions they undergo are further examples of the important impact chemistry has on our lives.

The Human Causes of Acid Rain

Precipitation in any form is an atmospheric event that involves water. Because our atmosphere is a gaseous solution, it should come as no surprise that the major substances responsible for acid precipitation are themselves gases that react with water. *Each is a non-metal oxide that reacts with water to produce an acid.*

Let's discuss how our modern society produces each of the gaseous substances that cause acids to fall from the sky.

Sources of Sulfur Oxides

Many coal and oil deposits contain sulfur impurities. When electrical power plants burn these fossil fuels to drive steam turbines, the sulfur is oxidized to SO_2. For example, the main sulfur impurity in coal is iron disulfide or *pyrite*, FeS_2. The combustion of the coal also burns the pyrite and produces SO_2 according to the following reaction:

$$4\ FeS_2(s) + 11\ O_2(g) \rightarrow 2\ Fe_2O_3(s) + 8\ SO_2(g)$$

Although the levels of sulfur impurities are often less than 3%, the huge quantities of fossil fuels burned worldwide result in the production of hundreds of millions of tonnes of SO_2.

Another source of SO_2 is the process of *smelting*, which extracts metals from their ores by heating. Several important metals such as copper, lead, and zinc are present in Earth's crust, mainly as sulfides. The first step in the smelting of these minerals usually involves *roasting*, in which the sulfides are heated at high temperatures in air. For example, when ZnS is heated to about 700°C, the following reaction occurs in the roaster:

$$2\ ZnS(s) + 3\ O_2(g) \rightarrow 2\ ZnO(s) + 2\ SO_2(g)$$

Much like carbonic acid, the weak acid produced from the reaction of SO_2 and water, called sulfurous acid, H_2SO_3, is unstable and doesn't exist in its molecular form in water. As a result, we can represent aqueous solutions of sulfur dioxide as follows:

$$SO_2(g) + 2\ H_2O(l) \rightleftharpoons H_3O^+(aq) + HSO_3^-(aq)$$

This means that rainwater falling through gaseous SO_2 will be more acidic than normal when it reaches the ground.

The problem becomes worse in polluted air containing ozone, O_3, and fine dust particles where, especially in the presence of sunlight, oxygen and ozone will oxidize some of the SO_2 to SO_3:

$$2\ SO_2(g) + O_2(g) \rightarrow 2\ SO_3(g)$$

$$SO_2(g) + O_3(g) \rightarrow SO_3(g) + O_2(g)$$

Sulfur trioxide now reacts with water to form the *strong acid* sulfuric acid:

$$SO_3(g) + H_2O(l) \rightarrow H_2SO_4(aq)$$

Because 100% ionization occurs when sulfuric acid reacts with water, rainwater in the presence of this acid is much more acidic. A gaseous mixture of SO_2 and SO_3 is sometimes referred to as SO_x.

Natural processes such as volcanic eruptions also introduce enormous amounts of sulfur oxides into the atmosphere, but they represent only about 5% to 10% of the total released by human activities.

Sources of Nitrogen Oxides

The air we breathe is composed of about 79% nitrogen and 21% oxygen. These two gases will not react with each other under normal conditions of temperature and pressure because the activation energy for the reaction is far too high. However, when air is mixed with fossil fuels and burned in the internal combustion engine of vehicles or in electric power plants, the high temperatures and pressures generated cause the two atmospheric gases to react according to the following reaction:

$$N_2(g) + O_2(g) \rightarrow 2\ NO(g)$$

When the NO gas in a hot exhaust stream encounters cooler outside air, it reacts with oxygen gas to produce NO_2 gas. This gaseous mixture of NO and NO_2 is often referred to as NO_x.

Nitrogen dioxide gas reacts with water in the atmosphere to produce the strong acid HNO_3 and the weak acid HNO_2 as shown below:

$$2\ NO_2(g) + H_2O(l) \rightarrow HNO_3(aq) + HNO_2(aq)$$

As with sulfur oxides, nature also generates a significant amount of nitrogen oxides. Lightning and decaying vegetation are both sources of NO, but we can do nothing to affect those processes.

7.2 summarizes the causes and effects of acid rain.

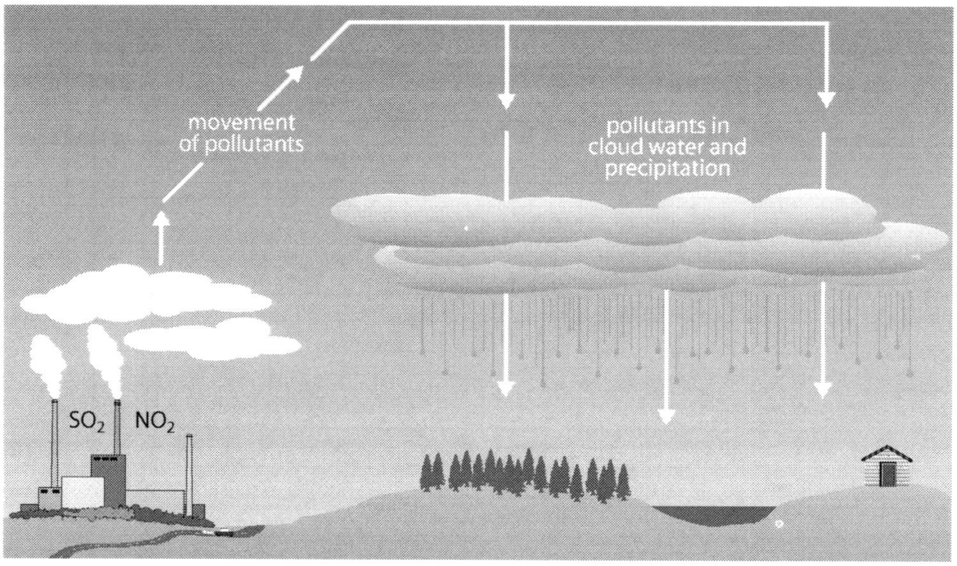

Figure 7.9.3 *Acid rain kills plants, pollutes rivers, lakes, and streams and erodes stone.*

Quick Check

1. Identify the three non-metal oxides that react with water in the atmosphere to produce acid precipitation.

____

2. How do coal-burning electrical power plants produce the sulfur oxide responsible for acid rain?

____

3. Why can the problem of sulfur oxide acid precipitation become worse in polluted air?

____

Consequences of Acid Rain

Acid precipitation in the form of rain, snow, fog, or dry deposits on particles has been recorded on every continent on Earth — even at the north and south poles! Because the oxides of sulfur and nitrogen that cause acid precipitation are gases that are carried into the atmosphere, prevailing winds can potentially push clouds containing these oxides more than 1500 km from their sources. For example, Scandinavia receives acid precipitation from Germany, England, and countries in eastern Europe. Southern Ontario and Quebec can receive the acid precipitation that originated anywhere in the U.S. industrial belt extending from Chicago to Boston.

Measurements taken in Europe and North America confirm how acidic some precipitation can be. Rainwater with a pH of 2.7 (approximately equal to vinegar) has been recorded in Sweden and a pH of 1.8 (almost equal to *stomach acid*) has been recorded for rain in West Virginia.

The effects of acid rain are both serious and widespread. Both aquatic and terrestrial ecosystems can be severely affected when exposed to acidic conditions. Most species of fish die at pH levels below 5, and entire forests have been devastated by acidic precipitation.

Obviously, contaminating the water supplies that our species depends on also has serious direct and indirect consequences. The soils in many areas contain aluminum salts that are nearly insoluble in normal groundwater, but begin to dissolve in more acidic solutions. This dissolving soil not only releases the Al^{3+} ions that are very toxic to fish, but also leaches out many valuable nutrients from the soil, which are lost in the runoff. 7.4 shows some examples of acid rain damage.

Many buildings, monuments, and even cemetery headstones contain $CaCO_3$ in the form of either marble or limestone. Carbonate salts dissolve in acids and long-term exposure to acid rain significantly damages such structures. Although not an environmental consequence, the cost of such damage to our society is significant.

Figure 7.9.4 *Trees, soil, water, and fish can all be damaged or destroyed by acid rain*

Figure 7.9.5 *This statue shows the damage from years of exposure to acid rain.*

Some Reasons for Optimism

Some lakes in regions where acid precipitation occurs are naturally protected because they are bounded by soils rich in limestone. The same reaction that dissolves the calcium carbonate in statues and buildings allows these lakes to resist changes in their pH. As the limestone dissolves, the hydronium ions from acid rain cause more bicarbonate ions to form as shown below.

$$CO_3^{2-}(aq) + H_3O^+(aq) \rightleftharpoons HCO_3^-(aq) + H_2O(l)$$

Over time, as the $[HCO_3^-]$ increases, the lakes become effective bicarbonate/carbonate buffer systems and maintain a relatively constant pH.

If a lake's soil does not contain sufficient limestone, a *temporary* solution is to add $CaCO_3$ or CaO directly to the lake. Over time, however, such lakes will eventually once again suffer the effects of acid rain unless the sources of the SO_2 and NO_2 are controlled.

Growing environmental awareness on a global scale over the past several decades has focused the attention of the public, the politicians who represent them, and the scientific community on attempting to solve the problem of acid precipitation. There is still much work to be done, but there are few disciplines as powerful as chemistry when it comes to solving our problems and so there are reasons for optimism.

Strict government emission standards are forcing automobile manufacturers to produce much cleaner and more efficient vehicles. Modern vehicles are equipped with a catalytic converter, which significantly reduces the levels of carbon monoxide, unburned hydrocarbons, and nitrogen oxides released into the atmosphere. One of the reaction chambers in the converter uses catalytic materials such as transition metal oxides and palladium or platinum metals to convert gaseous nitrogen oxides in the exhaust stream to nitrogen and oxygen gas before it leaves the tailpipe. The catalyzed reaction can be represented as shown below.

$$2\ NO_x(g) \rightarrow x\ O_2(g) + N_2(g)$$

(The value of "*x*" is either 1 or 2.)

Over the past several years, most major car companies have produced "hybrid" vehicles, which normally use two distinct power sources to move the vehicle. The most common hybrid vehicles are hybrid electric vehicles (HEVs), which combine an internal combustion engine with one or more electric motors. In addition, several major car companies including General Motors and Nissan have invested heavily in the production of electric vehicles such as the Volt and the Leaf, which are available to the general public.

Industrial efforts to reduce sulfur and nitrogen oxide emissions have also intensified over the past several decades. One method of removing sulfur dioxide gas from the exhaust stream of a coal-fired power plant or a metal smelter is by a process called *scrubbing*. This involves first blowing powdered limestone ($CaCO_3$) into the combustion chamber where heat decomposes it to CaO and CO_2. The calcium oxide (lime) then combines with the sulfur dioxide gas to produce solid calcium sulfite:

$$CaO(s) + SO_2(g) \rightarrow CaSO_3(s)$$

As a second step, to remove the $CaSO_3$ and any unreacted SO_2, an aqueous suspension of CaO is then sprayed into the exhaust gases before they reach the smokestack to produce a thick suspension of $CaSO_3$ called a slurry. The process is not without its drawbacks, however. First, it is expensive and consumes a great deal of energy. Second, because no use has yet been found for the $CaSO_3$, the great quantities of this compound that are produced by the process are usually buried in landfills.

A recently developed process for removing SO_2 involves using H_2S gas to convert the SO_2 into elemental sulfur according to the following reaction:

$$16\ H_2S(g) + 8\ SO_2(g) \rightarrow 3\ S_8(s) + 16\ H_2O(l)$$

To reduce the nitrogen oxide emissions from power plants, gaseous ammonia is reacted with the hot stack gases to produce nitrogen and water vapor:

$$4\ NO(g) + 4\ NH_3(g) + O_2(g) \rightarrow 4\ N_2(g) + 6\ H_2O(l)$$

The problem of acid precipitation has not yet been solved. A number of major hurdles must still be overcome, particularly as they relate to international agreements and enforcement. Economics, employment, industrial development, political will, environmental protection, and scientific advancement do not always merge harmoniously on our planet.

As you read this, consider the problem a challenge to you and your generation. Although the stakes are very high and the problems are significant, human ingenuity and chemistry have combined to surmount many enormous challenges in our world in the past. Maybe it's your turn to begin such an endeavor now!

Sample Problem — Acid Rain

Lead is most commonly found in Earth's crust as lead(II) sulfide, PbS, a mineral called *galena*. The first step in smelting lead converts the galena to lead(II) oxide by the process of *roasting*.

(a) Write the formula equation for the reaction.
(b) Identify the product of the reaction that contributes to acid precipitation.

What to Think About	How to Do It
1. Roasting reacts oxygen in air with the sulfide mineral.	$2\ PbS(s) + 3\ O_2(g) \rightarrow 2\ PbO(s) + 2\ SO_2(g)$
2. The non-metal oxide product is precursor to acid precipitation.	Both the SO_2 and the SO_3 that it can produce contribute to acid precipitation.

Practice Problems — Acid Rain

1. Write the formula equations for the reactions between each of the three oxides and water that result in the production of the acids responsible for acid precipitation.

2. Explain why the release of Al^{3+} ions into aquatic ecosystems poses a serious threat to the organisms living there

3. How does the process of "scrubbing" remove sulfur dioxide gas from exhaust streams at coal-fired power plants and smelters? Include the relevant chemical equations in your answer.

7.9 Activity: The Canada–United States Air Quality Agreement Then and Now — Some Reasons for Optimism

Question

What can you learn from about efforts to reduce acid rain from the major international agreement between Canada and the United States relating to the control of acid rain?

Background

The *Canada-United States Air Quality Agreement* was signed by Canada and the United States in Ottawa, Ontario, on March 13, 1991, to address trans-boundary air pollution leading to acid rain.

Procedure

Part 1: The Original Document

1. Perform an Internet search using the title: "Canada-U.S. Air Quality Agreement."
2. When you locate the document, scroll down to "Annex 1." Review the document carefully as you answer the following questions about sulfur dioxide and nitrogen oxide emissions for each country.
   (Note that 1 tonne = 1.1 tons)

Sulfur Dioxide

A. For the United States
   What was the target permanent national emissions cap for SO_2 produced by electrical utilities by the year 2010?

B. For Canada
   What was the target total permanent national emissions cap for SO_2 by the year 2000?

Nitrogen Oxides

A. For the United States
   Before the Acid Rain Program (ARP) was implemented, the projected annual NO_x emission levels from stationary sources for the year 2000 were 8.1 million tons. How far below this did the ARP set as a target level for total annual NO_x emissions for the year 2000? (Note that *stationary sources* refers to power plants, major combustion sources, and metal smelting operations, and *mobile sources* refers to all vehicles.)

B. For Canada
   Before the ARP was implemented, the projected annual NO_x emission levels from stationary sources for the year 2000 were 970 000 tonnes. How far below this did the ARP set as a target level for total annual NO_x emissions for the year 2000?

Part 2: The 2010 Progress Report

1. From the original page that loaded for the Air Quality Agreement, select the icon: "Canada-U.S. Air Quality Agreement Progress Report 2010."
2. Load the PDF file and select the "Acid Rain Annex." Review the document carefully as you answer the following questions.

Sulfur Dioxide Emission Reductions

A. For Canada

(a) In 2008, what were Canada's total SO_2 emissions and what percentage of the national cap established by the ARP do these represent?

(b) What continues to be the largest source of SO_2 emissions in Canada?

B. For the United States

(a) Consider the graph labeled "Figure 2. U.S. Emissions from Acid Rain Program Electric Generating Units, 1990–2009." In 2009, what were the total SO_2 emissions from the electric power sector and what percentage of the 2010 cap established by the ARP does this represent?

(b) Note that the ARP for the United States did *not* cover SO_2 emissions from non-electric power generators such as metal smelting. What were the *total* SO_2 emissions from all sources in the U.S. in 1980 and also in 2008? What percentage of that total do the emissions from the electric power sector represent?

Nitrogen Oxide Emission Reductions

A. For Canada

(a) In 2008, what were Canada's total NO_x emissions from stationary sources and what percentage of the original forecast for the year 2000 do they represent?

(b) What percentage of the total NO_x emissions do transportation sources represent?

B. For the United States

(a) In 2009, what were the total NO_x emissions from stationary sources (those covered by the ARP)?

(b) Before the Acid Rain Program (ARP) was implemented, the projected annual NO_x emission levels from stationary sources for the year 2000 were 8.1 million tons. What percentage of this projected amount does your answer to (a) represent?

Results and Discussion

The *Canada–United States Air Quality Agreement* is a large document with many clauses and statistics and many more questions (and discussions) are possible than the few we have mentioned here. Consider these questions to be merely the beginning of a much broader conversation concerning the problem of and potential solutions to acid rain. Your answers to the questions should convince you that there are reasons for optimism, but you should also note the final sentence of the "Overview" at the beginning of the 2010 Progress Report:

"However, despite these achievements, studies in each country indicate that although some damaged ecosystems are showing signs of recovery, further efforts are necessary to restore these ecosystems to their pre-acidified conditions."

Consider that restoration to be one of the challenges to you and your generation.

7.9 Review Questions

1. Complete the following formula equations:

(a)	$Rb_2O(s)$	+	$H_2O(l)$	→
(b)	$SrO(s)$	+	$H_2O(l)$	→
(c)	$SeO_2(s)$	+	$H_2O(l)$	→
(d)	$N_2O_5(g)$	+	$H_2O(l)$	→

2. Calcium oxide (lime) is often added to lawns to *sweeten* the soil and help reduce moss growth. Write the chemical equation for the reaction that occurs in moist soil and indicate what is meant by the term *sweeten*.

3. Tetraphosphorus decaoxide, P_4O_{10}, is a potent dehydrating agent. This acidic anhydride is a white solid that reacts vigorously with water to produce a molecular acid that is listed on the Table of Relative Strengths of Brønsted-Lowry Acids and Bases (Table A5). Write the balanced equation for this reaction below.

4. Even though nitrogen and oxygen account for more than 99% of the gases in our atmosphere, they don't react to produce NO gas as they do when fossil fuels are burned in internal combustion engines. Why not?

5. In point-form below, identify four serious problems associated with acid precipitation.

6. Complete the following equations associated with the formation of acid rain:

(a) $SO_3(g)$ + $H_2O(l)$ →

(b) $NO_2(g)$ + $H_2O(l)$ →

7. Why can acid precipitation occur great distances from where the non-metal oxides causing the problem are actually produced?

8. Why are some lakes naturally protected from acid precipitation and what temporary protection can be employed to help those lakes that aren't?

9. (a) What is the purpose of "scrubbers" in coal-burning electrical power plants and smelters?

(b) What problems are associated with the process of scrubbing?

10. How does the catalytic converter in a vehicle's exhaust system help to reduce the problem of acid rain?

11. What role does ammonia play in the reduction of NO_x emissions from power plants?

8 Gases

By the end of this chapter, you should be able to do the following:

- Use KMT and intermolecular forces to predict the macroscopic properties of real gases
- Use particle representations to explain the effect of changes in the macroscopic properties of gases
- Calculate temperature, pressure, volume, and moles of an ideal gas
- Analyze data for real gases to identify deviations from ideal behavior and explain using molecular interactions

---

By the end of this chapter you should know the meaning of these key terms:

- *a* and *b* factors
- atmospheric pressure
- Avogadro's hypothesis
- barometer
- Boyle's law
- Charles's law
- combined gas law
- Dalton's law of partial pressures
- diffusion
- effusion
- gas
- gas laws
- Guy-Lussac's law
- ideal gas law
- kinetic molecular theory
- manometer
- mean free path
- mole fraction
- partial pressure
- root mean square velocity
- standard atmospheric pressure
- torr
- vapor pressure
- volatile

In a hot air balloon, a gas burner is used to heat air to a temperature of about 212°F (100°C). Since hot air is lighter and less dense than the cool air around the balloon, the heated air causes the whole balloon to rise.

8.1 The Gaseous State

Warm Up

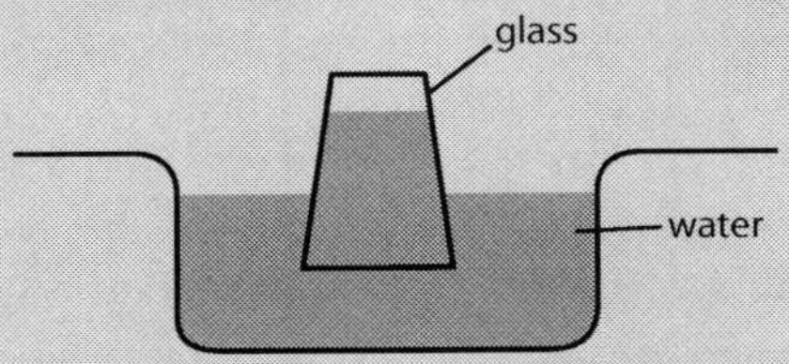

1. No matter how many dishwashers you have in your home (in my home there were three — my brother, my sister, and me), you've likely inverted a glass filled with water in the sink and noted the water didn't run out completely. Why does the water remain in the glass?

2. If you lived in Denver Colorado, often called the "mile high city" due to its elevation of 5280 ft or 1610 m, how would the height of the supported water column compare? Explain your answer.

Introducing Gases

We have occasionally used gases to illustrate some of the topics dealt with in Chemistry so far this year. In this unit, we will study the behavior of gases in detail and examine some of the most frequently encountered properties of gases. We will be discussing the kinetic molecular theory, and we will develop a number of mathematical relationships between pressure, volume, temperature, and the amount of substance present. These relationships are called **gas laws**.

Specific Properties of Gases

The word **gas** comes from *gaos*, a Dutch form of the word *chaos*. Gases were the last set of substances to be understood chemically. Until about 1750, the only gas known was the most familiar one, the air, which lies over Earth in a blanket about 80 km thick. Air is composed of 78% nitrogen and 21% oxygen, with small quantities of argon, carbon dioxide and a variety of other gases.

Most substances can exist as solids, liquids, or gases. The state in which we observe any substance depends on the temperature and pressure. The state in which a particular substance exists at a specific temperature and pressure depends on the attractive forces between particles of that substance. The state affects the physical properties of the substance.

Special Properties of Gases

- Gases, unlike solids and liquids, expand to fill any space available.
- Most gases are colorless and many are odorless.
- All gases have a very low density.
- All gases can be mixed in any proportion to form solutions.
- The volume of a gas changes dramatically with a change in pressure or temperature.
- The three properties of volume, pressure, and temperature are interrelated for a particular mass of gas.

Measurement of Gas Pressure

Pressure is the exertion of a force by one body on another. The forces exerted on your body, and everything else, by the air in the atmosphere is known as **atmospheric pressure**. There are two devices that are commonly used to measure pressure exerted by gases. One is used mainly for the measurement of atmospheric pressure. The other is used to measure the pressure of enclosed gas samples under various conditions.

The Barometer

Like all earthly matter, air is subject to the pull of gravity. Air near Earth's surface is compressed by the mass of air above it. For this reason, the pressure of the atmosphere has its maximum value at sea level. In Denver, Colorado, 1.6 km, or 1 mile, above sea level, the atmospheric pressure has decreased by 20%. Some football enthusiasts feel this is why the Denver Broncos rarely lose when playing at home in the Mile High Stadium. Above 3 km, the low pressure makes breathing uncomfortable for people not used to such altitudes. This is the reason for the breathing apparatus used by mountain climbers, pressurized cabins in commercial airplanes, and pressure control in spacecraft.

The **barometer** is used to measure atmospheric pressure (Figure 8.1.1). Designed by an Italian scientist named Evangelista Torricelli in the early 1600s, it consists of a long glass tube sealed at one end and filled with a liquid. The tube is then inverted and placed in a dish of the same liquid. This causes some of the liquid to flow out of the tube into the dish, creating a vacuum at the sealed end of the tube. Not all of the liquid flows out because the force exerted by the air — the atmospheric pressure — on the surface of the dish supports the column of liquid. The distance or height between the surface of the liquid in the tube and the surface of the liquid in the dish is a measure of the pressure exerted by the atmosphere. The height of the column depends on the liquid used and the elevation of the barometer. The most commonly used liquid in a barometer is mercury. The height of such a mercury column at sea level where the elevation is 0 m is 760 mm. This measurement, 760 mm of mercury, is defined as **standard atmospheric pressure**.

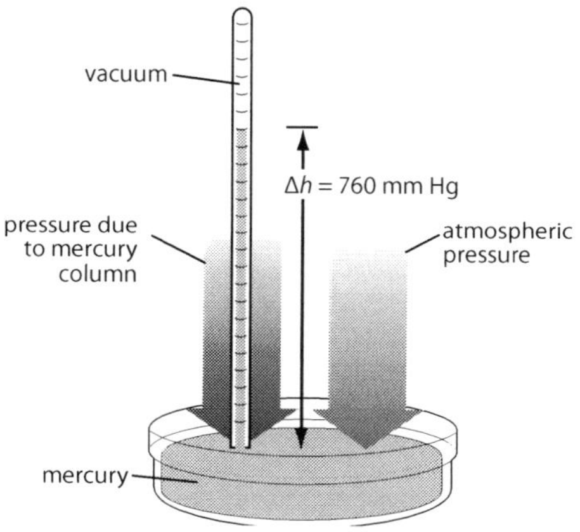

Figure 8.1.1 *A barometer measures atmospheric pressure as a reflection of the height of a column of mercury the pressure can support.*

The Manometer

The pressure exerted by a gas in a closed container can be measured using a **manometer**. The principle involved is the same as that of the barometer. A manometer consists of a U-tube partially filled with mercury. One side of the U-tube is connected to the gas container. The other side is open to a region of known pressure, most often the atmosphere. The gas in the container exerts a force on the mercury that tends to push it down. Atmospheric pressure exerts a force on the mercury at the open end of the tube. The difference between the heights of the two mercury levels is a direct measure of the difference between the two gas pressures. This pressure difference is often referred to as "delta h" or $\boldsymbol{\Delta} h$. Referring to the Figure 8.1.2, we can say that:

$$P_{gas} = (P_{atm} + P \text{ due to } \Delta h) \text{ mm Hg}$$

Knowing the atmospheric pressure as read on a barometer and the value of Δh, we can readily calculate the pressure exerted by the gas in a closed container. All pressures must be in the same units.

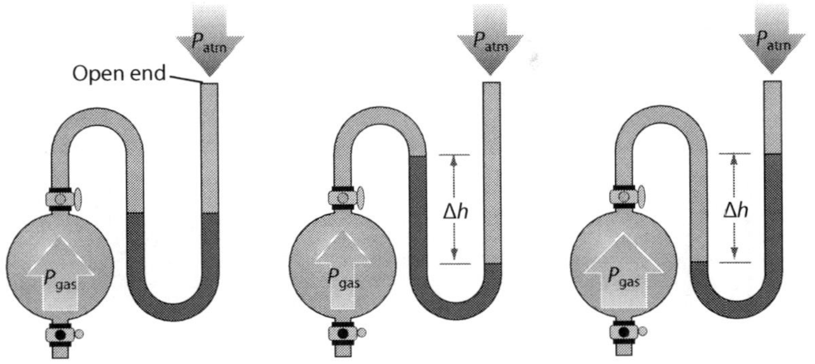

A $P_{gas} = P_{atm}$

A $P_{gas} < P_{atm}$
$P_{gas} = P_{atm} - \Delta h$

A $P_{gas} > P_{atm}$
$P_{gas} = P_{atm} + \Delta h$

Figure 8.1.2 *Manometers measure the pressure exerted by an enclosed sample of gas. Note that Δh may be added or subtracted depending on whether the enclosed gas pressure is greater or less than atmospheric pressure.*

Sample Problem — Measuring Gas Pressure

When a container of gas is connected to a manometer, the mercury in the open end of the U-tube rises until it is 112 mm higher than the mercury in the container side. If the atmospheric pressure, measured with a barometer, is 765 mm Hg, what is the gas pressure in the container?

What to Think About	How To Do It
1. Visualize the manometer.	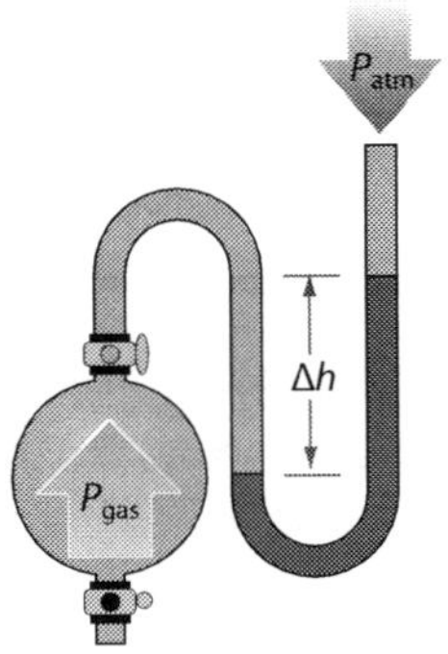
2. Is the contained gas pressure more or less than atmospheric pressure?	
3. In this example, the enclosed gas pressure is 112 mm greater than atmospheric pressure so Δh must be *added* to the atmospheric pressure.	$765 + 112 = 877$ mm Hg

Practice Problems — Measuring Gas Pressure

1. Consider the following two measuring devices found in a chemistry laboratory. What is the pressure of the enclosed gas sample?

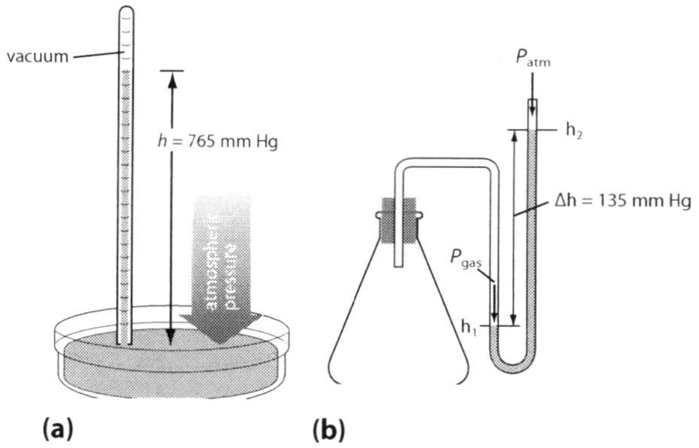

2. Assume the barometer in Practice Problem 1 supports a 72.4 cm column of mercury. Consider this second device found in the lab. What is the pressure of the sealed gas sample?

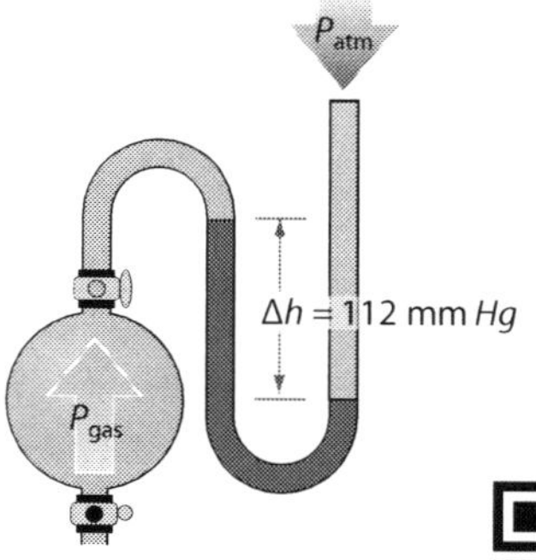

Units of Pressure Measurement

There are several different units that may be used to measure pressure. We encountered some of these at the start of the course while studying conversion factors. Pressure is defined as the force per unit area. In his work with the mercury barometer, Torricelli's use of the height of a mercury column to reflect pressure led to gas pressures being expressed in units of "mm Hg." Because mm Hg is awkward to write, this unit is often called a **torr** in honor of Torricelli. Thus standard atmospheric pressure can be expressed as 760 mm Hg or 760 torr. This equivalence has led to another unit, the atmosphere for pressure. One atmosphere (atm) equals 760 mm Hg or 760 torr. This unit is particularly useful for the measurement of very high pressures.

Another common unit of pressure is "pounds per square inch" or psi. If you remember that pressure is a force per unit area, this unit makes perfect sense. Atmospheric pressure at sea level, or standard atmospheric pressure, is nearly 15 psi. Atmospheric pressure at sea level is also very nearly one bar. This unit comes from the Greek word root *baro*, meaning pressure.

The SI unit for pressure is the pascal (Pa), named after physicist and mathematician, Blaise Pascal. The pascal is defined as a pressure of 1 newton per square meter. The pascal is really a very small unit. For example, a playing card lying flat on a table exerts about 1 pascal of pressure. As a result, it is common to use the kilopascal (kPa) instead.

To summarize, it is possible to express standard atmospheric pressure or pressure at sea level in many different ways. The equivalences between the various units of pressure are very important for use as conversion factors.

1.00 atm = 760. mm Hg = 760. torr = 14.7 psi = 101.3 kPa = 1.01 bar

Sample Problem — Using Pressure Units The city of Denver is commonly referred to as the "Mile High City" due to its elevation in the Rocky Mountains. Assume atmospheric pressure in Denver is only 82.0% of the pressure at sea level. Calculate this pressure. Express your answer in each of the six units defined above.	
What to Think About	**How To Do It**
1. Determine atmospheric pressure in Denver by taking 82.0% of the pressure at sea level.	$\frac{82.0}{100} \times 1.00\ \text{atm} = \mathbf{0.820\ atm}$
2. Use the equivalences in the box above to create appropriate conversion factors to convert 0.820 atm to the required units.	$0.820\ \cancel{\text{atm}} \times \frac{760.\ \text{mm Hg}}{1.00\ \cancel{\text{atm}}} = \mathbf{623\ mm\ Hg}$ $= \mathbf{623\ torr}$ $0.820\ \cancel{\text{atm}} \times \frac{14.7\ \text{psi}}{1.00\ \cancel{\text{atm}}} = \mathbf{12.1\ psi}$ $0.820\ \cancel{\text{atm}} \times \frac{101.3\ \text{kPa}}{1.00\ \cancel{\text{atm}}} = \mathbf{83.1\ kPa}$ $0.820\ \cancel{\text{atm}} \times \frac{1.01\ \text{bar}}{1.00\ \cancel{\text{atm}}} = \mathbf{0.828\ bar}$
3. Ensure that the number of significant figures is correct in each calculation.	All answers should be expressed to three significant figures.

Practice Problems — Using Pressure Units

1. Any pressure measured in a closed container is actually being measured relative to the atmospheric pressure that surrounds it. A common example is tire pressure. The total pressure in a tire is the sum of the pressure read on a tire gauge and atmospheric pressure. Bicycle tires can be inflated to a much higher pressure than automobile tires. The recommended gauge pressure for a mountain bike tire is between 40 and 60 psi. If a tire gauge indicates the pressure in a mountain bike tire is 55.0 psi, what is the overall tire pressure in units of kPa? Assume the atmospheric pressure is "standard" or 14.7 psi.

2. A closed-end manometer has all the gas removed from the U-tube before mercury is added. The result is a vacuum in the sealed end of the U-tube. This produces a device that can measure the total pressure in a closed container directly. With a closed-end manometer there is no need to add atmospheric pressure to determine the total pressure in a container. Consider closed-end manometer (a) below. Determine the total pressure in the flask once it is filled with gas in (b). Express your answer in atm.

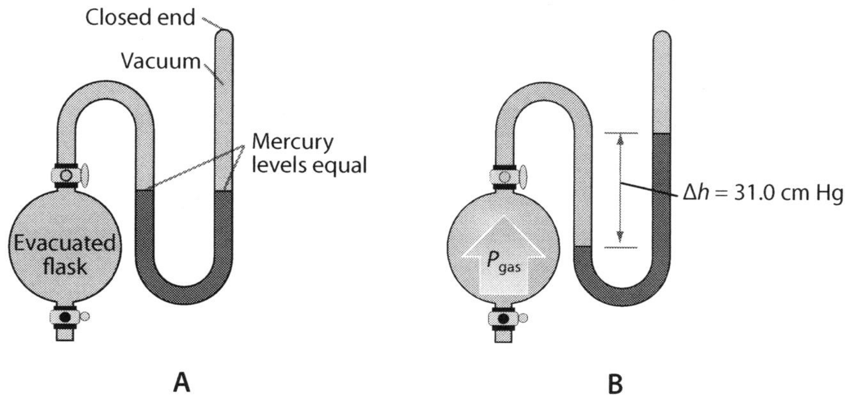

3. The pressure gauge in a full scuba tank in Cuba reads 206 bar. Convert this pressure to units of psi which are standard scuba units in North America.

8.1 Review Questions

A barometer appears as follows at sea level.

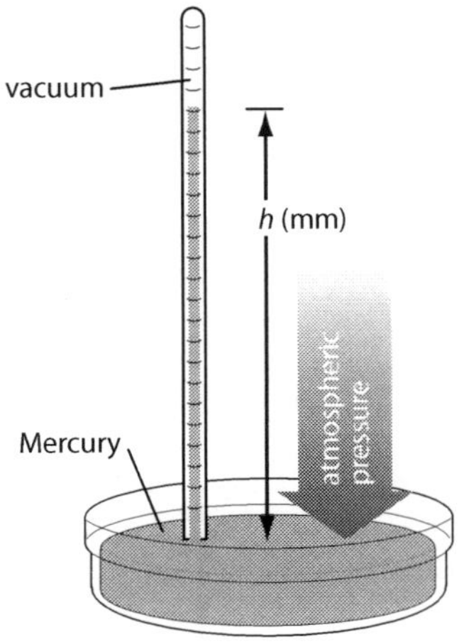

1. Imagine the barometer is placed in a hyperbaric chamber where the pressure is greatly increased. How will this affect the height of the mercury column and therefore the pressure reading? Give a clear explanation.

2. Complete the following table. Support your answers with appropriate calculations.

mm Hg	atm	**kPa**
	9.34 atm	
		555.696 kPa

3. Complete the following table. Be sure to show all work.

mm Hg	atm	**kPa**
	6.375 atm	
		94.8 kPa

4. What is the pressure of the following gas samples attached to U-tube manometers open to an atmospheric pressure of 749.5 mmHg?

   (a) left arm height = 208.6 mm
   Right arm height = 585.9 mm

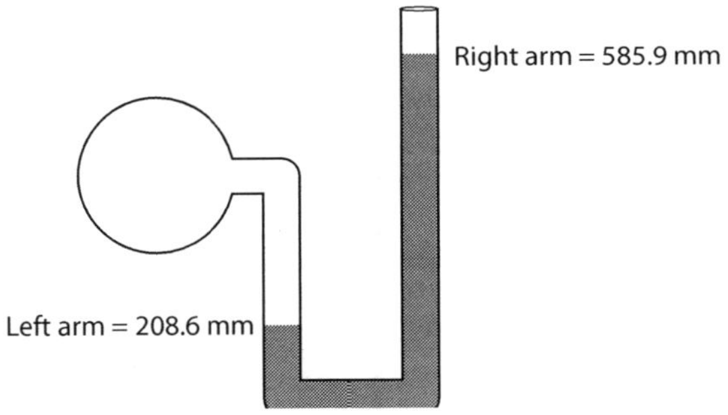

Pressure in bulb: ____________________

(b) Left arm height = 57.2 cm right arm height = 34.6 cm

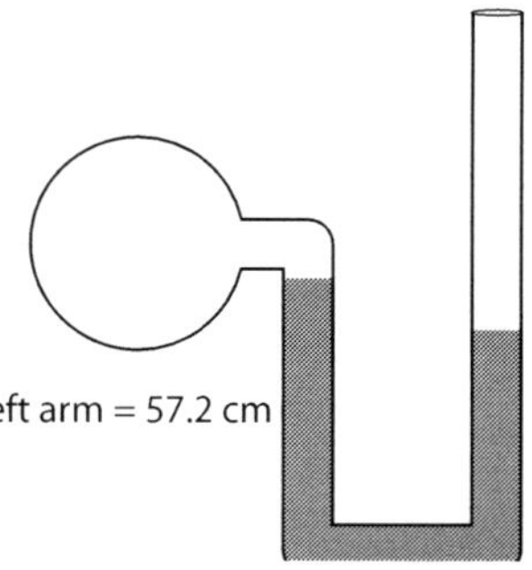

Pressure in bulb: ____________________

5. Racing bicycle tires may be inflated to pressures close to double those of mountain bikes. Additionally, the tires have smooth surfaces and are much thinner than mountain bike tires so that far less surface area is in contact with the pavement. These factors combine to allow racing bikes to ride much faster than mountain bikes. The gauge pressure of a racing bike tire reads 118 psi. What is the total pressure exerted by the air in the racing bike tire? Assume the atmospheric pressure is standard 14.7 psi and express your final answer in units of torr.

6. The atmospheric pressure is 17.4 psi, h_1 is 136.5 mm, and h_2 is 199.8 mm. Calculate the pressure inside the bulb and state in units of kPa.

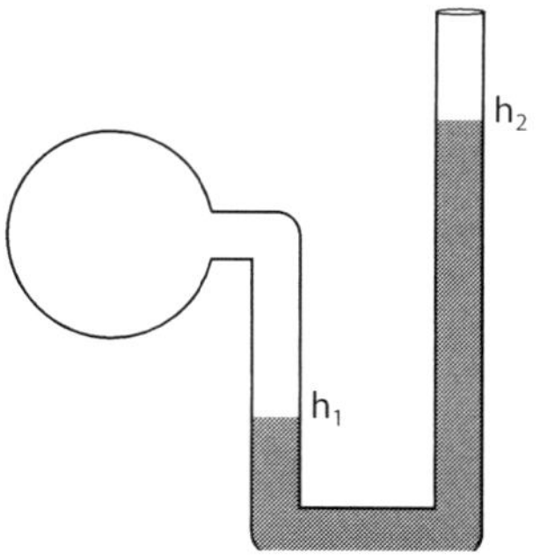

Pressure in bulb: ____________________

7. The pressure in the bulb is 8.03 psi, the h_1 is 46.00 cm, and the h_2 is 16.83 cm. Calculate the atmospheric pressure and state in units of torr.

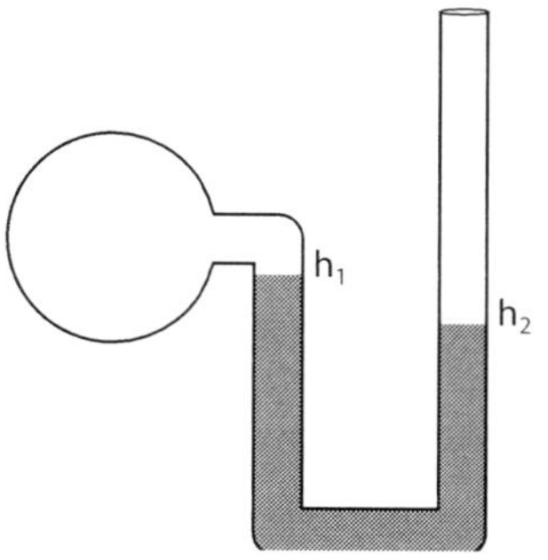

Atmospheric Pressure: ____________________

8.2 The Gas Laws

Warm Up

Consider a sealed glass syringe half filled with gas as shown.

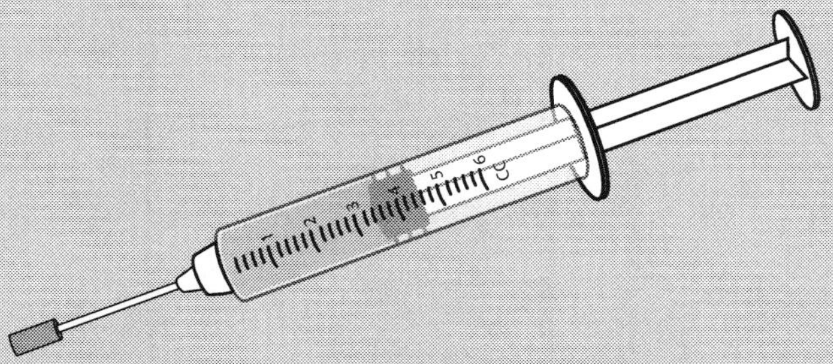

1. Predict what would happen to the volume of the gas sample under each of the following conditions. Give a reason for each of your predictions.

   (a) The syringe is placed into a hyperbaric chamber where the pressure exerted on its exterior (including the plunger) is increased.

   (b) The syringe is dropped into a beaker of boiling water.

2. Assume a nail is driven through the body of the syringe and the shaft of the plunger so the plunger cannot move. Predict what would happen to the pressure exerted by the gas inside the syringe under condition (b) above.

Boyle's Law: Pressure and Volume

Robert Boyle studied the relationship between the volume and the pressure of a sample of a gas in 1662. Boyle was already known for his book *The Skeptical Chemist* in which he refuted the Aristotle's idea that all matter was composed of earth, air, fire and water. He redefined elements as "unmingled bodies." Using a J-tube containing a trapped air sample, Boyle used the multistory entryway of his home to study the effect of altering pressure on the volume of the air. He found that increasing the pressure on a gas sample causes the volume to decrease proportionally. If the pressure is doubled, the volume is cut in half. If the pressure is tripled, the volume becomes one-third of its original value.

An alternative way to perform Boyle's experiment would be to manipulate the volume. If the volume of a container of gas were halved, the same number of gas particles would now strike the sides of the container twice as frequently, effectively doubling the pressure of the gas sample (Figure 8.2.1).

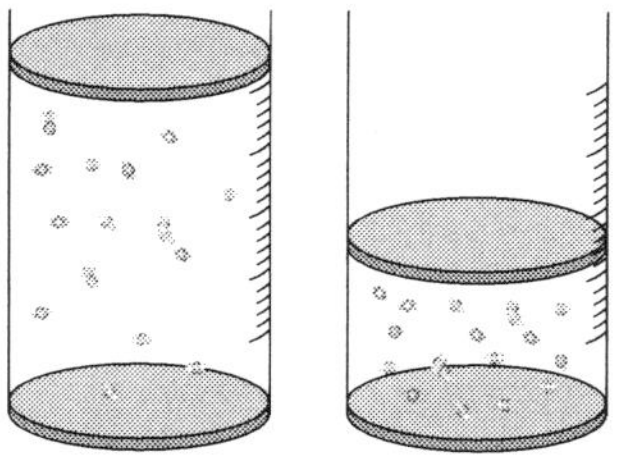

Figure 8.2.1 *Halving the volume of a gas sample results in twice as many collisions with the walls of the container. This causes the pressure to double.*

Fortunately for Boyle, the temperature of his air sample remained relatively constant since a variation in temperature would have affected his results. Boyle plotted his volume data against pressure and obtained the graph in Figure 8.2.2. Manipulation of the data resulted in a straight line being obtained when volume was plotted against the inverse of pressure:

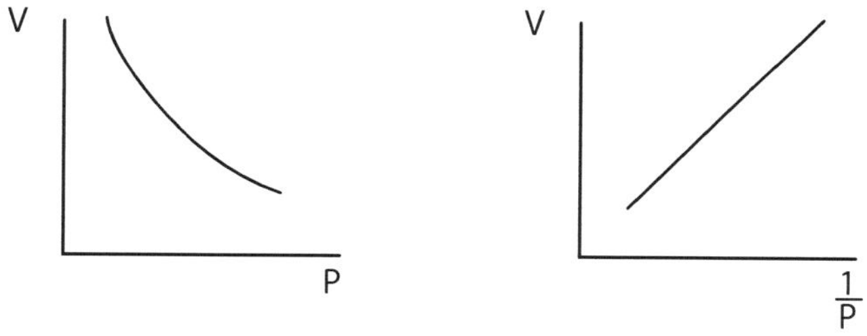

Figure 8.2.2 *A plot of volume versus pressure for a trapped sample of gas with the temperature held constant produces a hyperbola. This is typical of a reciprocal or inverse relationship. Replotting the same volumes against the reciprocal of pressure gives a direct relationship. Note that the line appears to intersect the origin.*

The result of this experiment was **Boyle's law** that states:

At constant temperature, the volume occupied by a fixed mass of gas is inversely proportional to its pressure.

Mathematically speaking, we can say that:

$$V \propto \frac{1}{p}$$

This proportionality can be changed into an equivalency by introducing a constant, *k* so that $y = mx + b$ becomes:

$$V = k\frac{1}{P} + 0 \text{ or } V = \frac{k}{P} \text{ or } PV = k$$

The value of the constant, *k* depends on the size of the sample and the temperature.

This law is commonly used to calculate the new pressure or volume after one of these variables has been changed. As Boyle's law states that the product of pressure and volume will be a constant for a fixed temperature, we can modify our mathematical relationship.

$$P_1V_1 = P_2V_2$$

Note that P_1 and V_1 represent the original pressure and volume of the gas, and P_2 and V_2 represent the pressure and volume after some change.

Sample Problem — Boyle's Law: Pressure and Volume

Zippy decides to go to Colorado for a skiing vacation. He fills his favorite red balloon with air. The volume of the balloon is 5.0 L in Seattle at 101 kPa pressure. He takes the balloon to Steamboat Colorado where the atmospheric pressure is only 91 kPa when he arrives. If the temperature is the same in both places, what is the new volume of the balloon?

What to Think About	How to Do It
1. Since $P_1V_1 = P_2V_2$ this is really just a simple algebra problem. The tricky part is correctly identifying which conditions are initial (P_1 and V_1) and which are final (P_2 and V_2).	Initially the volume of the balloon is 5.0 L. So this is V_1. V_2 is to be determined. The initial pressure is 101 kPa, while the final pressure is 91 kPa.
2. From $P_1V_1 = P_2V_2$, algebra shows us that $V_2 = \frac{P_1V_1}{P_2}$.	So $V_2 = \frac{101 \text{ kPa} \times 5.0 \text{ L}}{91 \text{ kPa}} = \mathbf{5.5\ L}$
3. It is always helpful to consider *what* sort of answer to expect and whether your answer *makes sense*.	The pressure has decreased by a factor of 101/91 or 1.1 (one and one-tenth) times. Thus it makes perfect sense that the volume has increased by one-tenth or 0.5 L.

Practice Problems — Boyle's Law: Pressure and Volume

1. While in Colorado, Zippy decides to take in a football game. At half time. he buys a bag of Cheese Curls. He finds the bag is puffed up because the air sealed inside at sea level has expanded under the lower pressure of the venue formerly known as Mile High Stadium. If 100.0 mL of air was sealed inside the bag at sea level, what volume will the air occupy at the same temperature at Mile High Stadium? Remember the pressure at Mile High Stadium is 83.1 kPa, as determined in the second practice problem in the first section. Assume the bag was so wrinkled when filled that it would not limit gas expansion.

2. Zippy feels like celebrating (the Seahawks beat the Broncos in an away game) and so he takes his red balloon up to his 24th floor hotel room. Remember the balloon's volume was 5.0 L at a pressure of 101 kPa in Seattle. If the balloon's volume is now 5.6 L and the temperature has not changed, what is the pressure in Zippy's hotel room?

Charles's Law: Volume and Temperature

We know that air expands when heated, thereby decreasing its density. On December 1, 1783, the French scientist, Jacques Charles's was on the second balloon ever to lift a human being off the surface of Earth. Heated air with a lowered density was responsible for this amazing feat. This accomplishment so impressed King Louis XVI that Charles was given a laboratory at the Sorbonne. Charles studied the effect of temperature on the volume of gases. Not surprisingly, as temperature increased, so does volume. In fact, the relationship is a direct one (doubling the temperature doubles the volume) *as long as the temperature is in degrees Kelvin.*

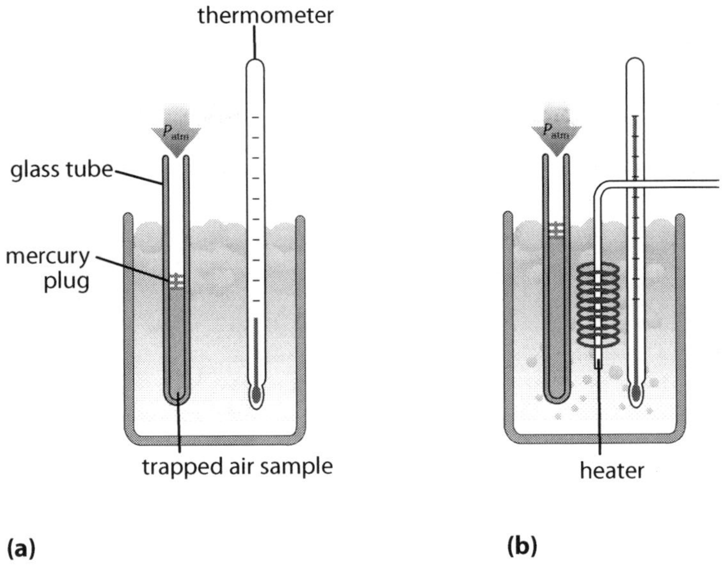

Figure 8.2.3 *Moving a trapped gas sample from an ice bath (a) to a boiling water bath (b) results in a significant increase in the volume of the sample.*

Charles originally plotted his volume data against Celsius temperatures. The result, shown in Figure 8.2.4(a) indicated that a volume of zero would occur at –273°C. At this temperature, there would be a total lack of motion of particles. Later, Lord Kelvin suggested that this represented an absolute minimum of temperature. The result of this finding was the Kelvin temperature scale in which a degree is the same size as a Celsius degree, but 0 K = –273°C. A second plot of volume against temperature in degrees Kelvin shows a straight-line relationship that is easier to work with as it passes through the origin (Figure 8.2.4(b)).

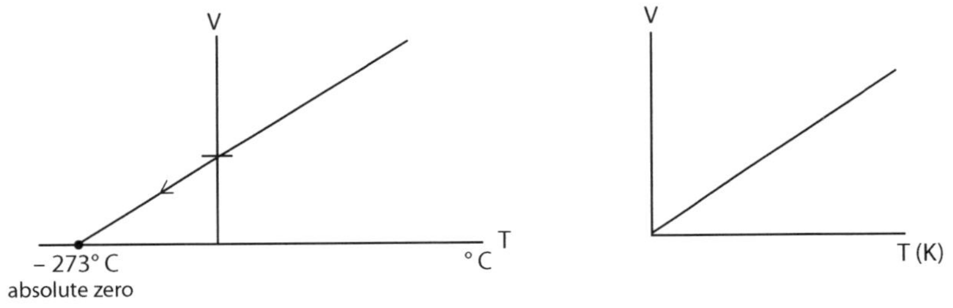

Figure 8.2.4 *Volume versus temperature produces a linear relationship with an x-intercept that represents absolute zero using both Celsius and Kelvin scales.*

The most difficult part of studying this relationship, called Charles's law is the maintenance of a constant pressure. At constant pressure, the volume of a fixed mass of any gas is directly proportional to its Kelvin temperature.

The equation for the graph plotted above shows that: $V = kT$ or $\frac{V}{T} = k$

where V is the volume of a gas at temperature T in Kelvin degrees.

Since we usually wish to relate the volume of a fixed mass of gas at two different temperatures, we rewrite the equation in a more useful form.

$$\frac{V_1}{T_1} = \frac{V_2}{T_2}$$

Much like Boyle's law, V_1 and V_2 are the initial and final volumes, and T_1 and T_2 are the initial and final Kelvin temperatures.

Sample Problem — Charles's Law: Volume and Temperature

When Zippy arrives at the football game, he forgets his red balloon in the rental car. The balloon's volume at this point is 5.5 L and the temperature is 2.0°C. While in the car, the hot sun increases the temperature of the balloon to 26.5°C. Assuming the pressure in the car remains constant, what is the balloon's new volume when Zippy returns?

What to Think About	How to Do It
1. As with Boyle's law, the key is the proper identification of variables. Charles's law has an added twist in that the temperatures must be converted to the Kelvin scale. (Your teacher may wish to convert by adding 273.15 K for a more precise temperature.) It is important to remember that the **precision** of the original temperature will determine the number of **sig figs** in the new temperature.	Initial conditions involve a 5.5 L balloon at 2.0°C. $2.0°\text{C} \times \frac{1\text{ K}}{1°\text{C}} + 273\text{ K} = 275.0\text{ K}$ Thus $V_1 = 5.5$ L and $T_1 = 275.0$ K $26.5°\text{C} \times \frac{1\text{ K}}{1°\text{C}} + 273\text{ K} = 299.5\text{ K}$
2. Charles's law states that $\frac{V_1}{T_1} = \frac{V_2}{T_2}$	Application of algebra shows that $V_2 = \frac{V_1 T_2}{T_1} = \frac{5.5\text{ L} \times 299.5\text{ K}}{275.0\text{ K}}$ $= 6.0$ L
3. As always, it is helpful to consider *what* sort of answer to expect and whether your answer *makes sense*. Notice leaving the temperatures in Celsius would have predicted an increase in volume of over 13X. Definitely not a reasonable prediction.	The Kelvin temperature has increased by a factor of 299.5/275.0 or 1.089 times. This means the new volume should be approximately 1.1 (one and one-tenth) times larger and it is!

Practice Problems — Charles's Law: Volume and Temperature

1. When he leaves for breakfast the next day, Zippy places his Cheese Curls on the windowsill in the sun. Over a period of time, the temperature of the Cheese Curls increases from 19.0°C to 34.5°C. If the volume of the bag is 121.9 mL when they are placed on the windowsill, what will the volume be after warming? (Assume the pressure remains constant.)

2. Alarmed by the increase in volume of his Cheese Curls bag, Zippy decides to place them in the mini-bar in an effort to restore the original volume. Assuming the pressure remains constant, if the volume is reduced from 128.4 mL at the windowsill temperature of 34.5°C to 115.0 mL, what is the temperature of the mini-bar?

Gay-Lussac's Law: Pressure and Temperature

Charles never did publish his work. Rumor has it he was having too much fun riding around in hot air balloons. In the early 1800s, another French scientist names Joseph Gay-Lussac repeated Charles's work and published the results. Like Charles, Gay-Lussac was a hot air balloon fanatic. In 1804, he ascended to a height of 7 km in a hydrogen-filled balloon setting an altitude record that remained unbroken for 50 years.

Gay-Lussac discovered that if a gas is contained in a vessel that cannot expand then as the Kelvin temperature is increases, the pressure increases proportionally (Figure 8.2.5).

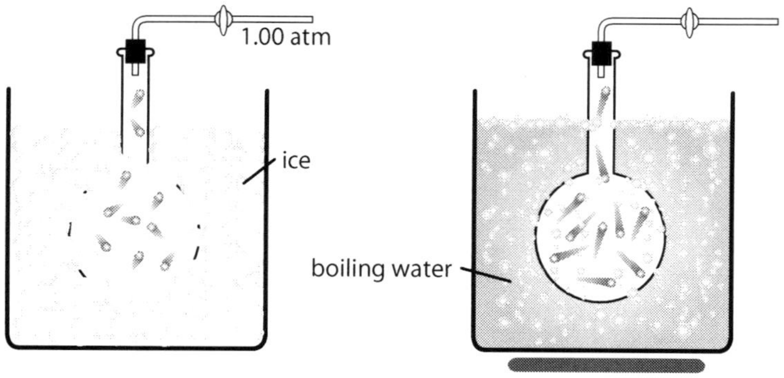

Figure 8.2.5 *The particles of gas in a sealed flask undergo a significant increase in kinetic energy and hence, velocity, when moved from an ice bath (a) to a bath of boiling water (b). The more frequent and more energetic collisions with the walls of the flask produce a significant increase in pressure.*

Gay-Lussac's measurements of pressure related to temperature resulted in the graph in Figure 8.2.6.

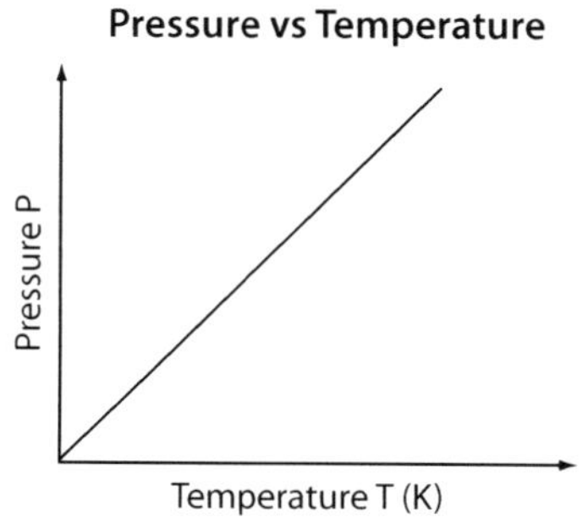

Figure 8.2.6 *A plot of pressure versus Kelvin temperature produces a direct relationship passing through the origin.*

The mathematical relationship is $P = kT + 0$ or $\frac{P}{T} = k$

At constant volume, the pressure of a fixed mass of any gas is directly proportional to its Kelvin temperature.

The most useful mathematical form of Gay-Lussac's law relates pressures at two different temperatures with the volume held constant.

$$\frac{P_1}{T_1} = \frac{P_2}{T_2}$$

where P_1 and P_2 are the initial and final pressures, and T_1 and T_2 are the initial and final Kelvin temperatures.

Sample Problem — Gay-Lussac's Law: Pressure and Temperature

On opening the cupboard that contained the mini-bar, Zippy notices a series of high-priced snacks on a shelf just above the fridge. He is particularly interested in a 255 mL vacuum packed can of Pring-Pong Potato Chips. Assume the Pring-Pong Chips were sealed at a pressure of 505 mm Hg and a temperature of 5.0°C. As Zippy is examining the can in his 19.0°C hotel room, what is the pressure inside the can now?

What to Think About	How To Do It
1. As with Charles's law, we must properly assign the variables. In addition, we must convert both temperatures into degrees Kelvin.	Initial conditions are 505 mm Hg and 5.0°C. These values are P_1 and T_1 and the temperature must be converted to degrees Kelvin. $5.0\text{°C} \times \frac{1\text{ K}}{1\text{°C}} + 273\text{ K} = 278.0\text{ K}$ The final temperature, T_2, will be $19.0\text{°C} \times \frac{1\text{ K}}{1\text{°C}} + 273 = 292.0\text{ K}$
2. Attention must be paid to the algebra. In this case, we are solving for the final pressure (or P_2).	$\frac{P_1}{T_1} = \frac{P_2}{T_2}$, hence, $P_2 = \frac{P_1 T_2}{T_1}$ $= \frac{505\text{ mm Hg} \times 292.0\text{ K}}{278.0\text{ K}}$ $=$ **530. mm Hg**
3. Does the answer make sense or is it … *nonsense?*	An increased temperature should cause the pressure to increase by a factor of 292.0/278.0 or 1.05 times. This is equivalent to an increase of one-half of one-tenth of the total pressure or approximately 25 mm Hg.

Practice Problems — Gay-Lussac's Law: Pressure and Temperature

1. Returning from breakfast, Zippy finds himself hungry again. He decides to finally eat his Cheese Curls. He rather enjoys the cold Curls and decides to try the Pring-Pongs cold as well. He places the can into the mini-bar and leaves it in the 2.4°C environment until it reaches that temperature. Considering the pressure in the can was 530. mm Hg at 19.0°C, what will the pressure be once the can has equilibrated in the mini-bar?

2. Zippy decides he needs a drink to wash down the cold Pring Pongs. There are two 355 mL cans of Kookie Cola in the mini-bar. The Kookie Cola is carbonated and the refrigerated can is under 36.5 psi pressure even at 2.4°C. Zippy drinks one can and accidentally leaves the other one on the dresser. If the pressure in the can rises to 38.9 psi, what is the temperature in Zippy's hotel room at this point? Assume the solubility of the carbon dioxide is not affected by this temperature change.

The Combined Gas Law — Pressure, Volume, and Temperature

In each of the three laws discussed so far, one of the variables important to gases —pressure, volume, or temperature — was held constant. However, in real life, it is much more common that all three variables change. For example, if we consider a weather balloon which is released into the atmosphere. As its altitude increases, the temperature, volume, and pressure of the gas inside the balloon change.

Wouldn't it be great if we could calculate the new value of any one of the three variables when the other two change? The relationship that will allow us to do just that is simply a combination of Boyle's, Charles's, and Guy-Lussac's laws. This relationship is called the **combined gas law.**

$$\frac{P_1V_1}{T_1} = \frac{P_2V_2}{T_2}$$

In order to compare the results obtained in experiments involving gases at various temperatures and pressures, scientists have adopted a set of standard conditions to which such results may be readily converted. These conditions are called standard temperature and pressure. Recall one mole of any gas occupies a volume of 22.4 L under these conditions.

Standard temperature and pressure (STP) refers to a temperature of 273°K (0°C) and a pressure of 101.3 kPa (1 atm)

Normally it is not very convenient to carry out an experiment at STP since the temperature in most laboratories is well above 0°C and the atmospheric pressure is seldom exactly 101.3 kPa. However, as long as we record the temperature and pressure when we make our measurements, we can use the combined gas law equation to convert our data to these standard conditions if required.

Sample Problem — The Combined Gas Law: Pressure, Volume, and Temperature

Zippy's second day of skiing led to a big toe sprain on the rope tow at the bunny hill. Zippy is required to spend 24 hours in a Colorado hospital under observation. He passes the time creating and solving gas law problems much like this one: Once upon a time, the economy size (325 mL) can of Big Brute Aerosol Deodorant contained a propellant gas at 445 kPa and 12°C (which explained why it was so cold under the arms when applied in the morning). What volume would this propellant gas occupy if it were allowed to escape into a 101 kPa and 21°C environment?

What to Think About	How To Do It
1. As with the simple laws, we must properly assign the variables. In addition, we must convert both temperatures into degrees Kelvin.	Initial conditions are 325 mL, 445 kPa and 12°C. These values are V_1, P_1 and T_1. The temperature must be converted to degrees Kelvin. $12 ~~°C~~ \times \frac{1\ K}{1 ~~°C~~} + 273\ K = 285\ K$ The final temperature, T_2, will be $21 ~~°C~~ \times \frac{1\ K}{1 ~~°C~~} + 273 = 294\ K$
2. Attention must be paid to the more complex algebra. In this case, we are solving for the final volume (or V_2).	Since $\frac{P_1V_1}{T_1} = \frac{P_2V_2}{T_2}$ $V_2 = \frac{P_1V_1T_2}{T_1P_2}$ $= \frac{445\ \text{kPa} \times 325\ \text{mL} \times 294\ \text{K}}{285\ \text{K} \times 101\ \text{kPa}}$ $= 1477.150 = \mathbf{1480\ mL}$
3. Does the answer make sense?	There is a small increase in temperature (294/285) and a large pressure decrease (445/101) both of which contribute to an increase in volume.

Practice Problems — The Combined Gas Law: Pressure, Volume, and Temperature

1. To ensure a more comfortable stay at the hospital, Zippy decided to place his rubber air mattress over the hard hospital bed. Noting a gas cylinder chained near the bed, Zippy decided to use this gas source to inflate his air mattress. If the gas cylinder had a volume of 58.0 L of oxygen contained under a pressure of 222 psi and a temperature of 12°C, what volume would the gas occupy if it were released at standard atmospheric pressure (14.7 psi) and a temperature of 22°C? If Zippy's mattress was rated for a volume of 500 L, was this a good idea?

2. While in the hospital, Dr. Bundolo decided to remove a rather bothersome plantar's wart located conveniently near Zippy's big toe. The doctor used a gaseous anesthetic to prepare Zippy for the operation. This gas, a nitrogen compound, occupies a volume of 18.0 L at a pressure of 44.4 kPa and a temperature of 125°C. What would its volume be at STP?

The Ideal Gas Law: Pressure, Volume, Temperature, and Moles

The simple gas law equations are concerned with the relationships between temperature, pressure, and volume. While these equations are very useful, they do not relate temperature, pressure, or volume to the amount of gas that is present. We know, from our study of molar volume, that the amount of gas present is related to the volume of the gas at STP through the molar volume, 22.4 L/mol. The ideal gas equation is an equation that relates the amount of a substance (remember the SI unit for *amount* is the *mole*) to pressure, volume, and temperature, so that if any three of these four parameters are know, the fourth may be readily determined.

ideal gas law: $PV = nRT$

where P = pressure of the gas
V = volume of the gas in liters
n = amount of the gas in moles
R = ideal gas constant
T = temperature of the gas in Kelvin degrees

The Ideal Gas Constant

Recall we learned of **Avogadro's hypothesis** that states that one mole of any gas occupies the same volume as long as the temperature and pressure are held constant (Figure 8.2.7).

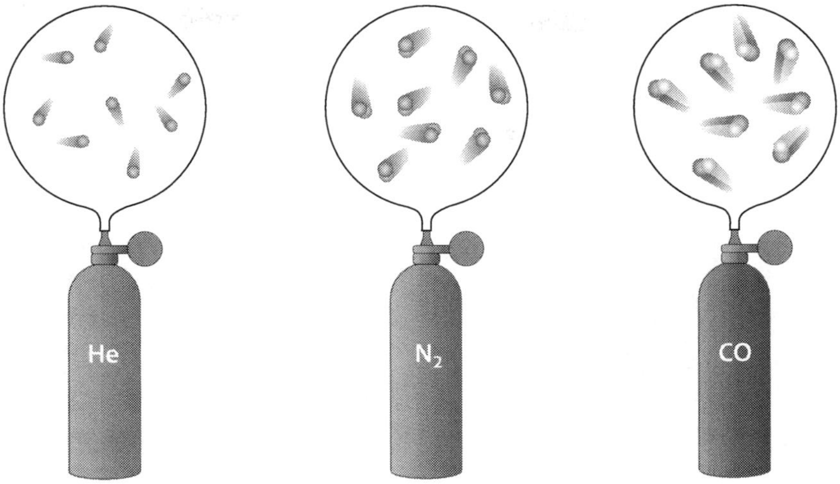

n = 1 mol	n = 1 mol	n = 1 mol
P = 1 atm (760 torr)	P = 1 atm (760 torr)	P = 1 atm (760 torr)
T = 0°C 273 K)	T = 0°C 273 K)	T = 0°C 273 K)
V = 22.4 L	V = 22.4 L	V = 22.4 L
Number of gas particles = 6.02×10^{23}	Number of gas particles = 6.02×10^{23}	Number of gas particles = 6.02×10^{23}
Mass = 4.003 g	Mass = 28.02 g	Mass = 28.01 g

Figure 8.2.7 *Regardless of identity, 22.4 L of gas under STP conditions will always contain the same number of gas particles – 6.02 x 10^{23} or 1 mole.*

This hypothesis is very handy as it allows us to determine the value of the ideal gas constant, *R*, by merely substituting 1 mole of gas at STP conditions into the ideal gas equation.

$$\text{Since } PV = nRT,\ R = \frac{PV}{nT} = \frac{(101.3\text{ kPa}) \times 22.4\text{ L}}{1\text{ mole} \times 273\text{ K}} = 8.31\ \frac{\text{kPa·L}}{\text{mol·K}}$$

Quick Check

Determine other values for the ideal gas constant, *R*, by substituting the following standard atmospheric pressures for *P* into the ideal gas equation. Note that the molar volume 22.4 L is rounded to three significant figures. Consequently, *R* values determined by this method are correct to only three significant figures.

Standard *P*	Substitution Work Shown	*R* Value
1 atm	$\frac{(1\ \text{atm}) \times 22.4\ \text{L}}{1\ \text{mol} \times 273\ \text{K}}$	$0.0821\ \frac{\text{L·atm}}{\text{mol·K}}$
760. mm Hg	$\frac{(\qquad) \times 22.4\ \text{L}}{1\ \text{mol} \times 273\ \text{K}}$	$\frac{\text{mm Hg·L}}{\text{mol·K}}$
14.7 psi		
101.3 kPa		

R values provided in the AP exam table of constants:

$$8.314\ \frac{\text{L·kPa}}{\text{mol·K}} = 0.08206\ \frac{\text{L·atm}}{\text{mol·K}} = 62.36\ \frac{\text{L·torr}}{\text{mol·K}}$$

R is occasionally presented in tables of constants as 8.31 J/mol·K due to the fact that a Pa is really the amount of pressure exerted by a force of 1 newton on an area of 1 m^2 and 1 L is really the same as 1 dm^3. Hence, 1 kPa × 1 L is the same as 1 newton-meter, which you may recall from physics is the same as 1 joule. This *R* value was also used briefly in enthalpy and will be used much more frequently in AP II.

What Is an "Ideal" Gas?

Strictly speaking, the ideal gas equation should only be applied to "*ideal gases,*" that is, gases that conform to the assumptions of the kinetic molecular theory. Two of the assumptions of this theory are that the molecules of a gas possess zero volume (virtually all of the volume of any gas sample is empty space), and that there are no attractive forces between gases (gas collisions are completely elastic — particles lose no momentum following a collision). In fact, the molecules of all gases do possess some, though very little, volume and there is a small attraction between their particles.

However, provided the temperature involved is not too low and the pressure is not too high, most gases behave as if they are ideal, and the ideal gas equation gives us a correct answer to our calculations. Later in this chapter, you will find an equation that takes into account the attractive forces acting between molecules and the actual volume of the molecules themselves. This equation may be used when the ideal gas equation is not applicable.

Sample Problem — The Ideal Gas Law

A 1.45 L container is filled with sulfur dioxide gas at a pressure of 115.0 kPa and a temperature of 28°C.

(i) How many moles of sulfur dioxide gas are in the container?

(ii) Calculate the mass of sulfur dioxide gas in the container.

What to Think About	How To Do It
1. This is a classic substitution into $PV = nRT$ to find the missing variable calculation. 2. As the pressure is provided in units of kPa, be sure to use the appropriate R value of 8.31 kPa/mol·K.	Simply begin with $PV=nRT$ and solve for n using the appropriate values and units for R and T. $28°C \times \frac{1\ K}{1°C} + 273\ K = 301\ K$ $n = \frac{PV}{RT} = \frac{115.0\ kPa \times 1.45\ L}{8.31\ \frac{L \cdot kPa}{mol \cdot K} \times 301\ K}$
3. The second part of the problem would typically not be separated out. You would need to recognize the necessity of finding moles and then simply multiply by the molar mass.	$n = \mathbf{0.0667\ mol}$ $m = 0.0667\ mol \times \frac{64.1\ g\ SO_2}{1\ mol}$ $= \mathbf{4.27\ g\ of\ SO_2\ gas}$

Practice Problems — The Ideal Gas Law

1. Find the volume of 1.00 g of water if it were converted to the gas state at its boiling point of 100.0°C at standard atmospheric pressure.

Continued

Practice Problems — The Ideal Gas Law (continued)

2. At 30.0°C and 98.1 kPa, a 3.26 g sample of an unknown, unreactive gas has a volume of 3.00 L. What is the molar mass of the gas? Assume it is a diatomic gas and identify it. Hint: The first step is to determine the number of moles, then apply the unit g/mol for molar mass to calculate the value.

3. A diatomic gas has a density of 1.95 g/L at 1.50 atm and 27°C. Determine the molar mass of this gas and identify it. Hint: The density tells us that 1.00 L of the gas under the given *T* and *P* has a mass of 1.95 g. Now solve the problem as in number 2.

Derivations Using *PV* = *nRT*

$PV = nRT$ may be used as the genesis of each of the simple gas laws. Of course, each of Boyle's, Charles's, Gay-Lussac's and even the combined gas law is very intuitive and can be easily figured out. However, if there is a short cut available to help verify the validity of our intuition, why not use it? Since *R* is a constant, it stands to reason that

R is the *ratio* of $\frac{PV}{nT} = \frac{PV}{nT}$ now and forever. Hence, $\frac{P_1V_1}{n_1T_1} = \frac{P_2V_2}{n_2T_2}$. Now if we

simply cancel any variables that remain constant, we can derive each of the simple gas laws in turn. Boyle's law for example involves a fixed quantity of gas, at a constant temperature, hence *n* and *T* are constant, leaving: $\frac{P_1V_1}{\cancel{n_1T_1}} = \frac{P_2V_2}{\cancel{n_2T_2}}$ becomes $P_1V_1 = P_2V_2$.

Quick Check

Use the information in the paragraph above as a model to complete the following table.

Simple Law	Constant Variables	Derivation Shown	Final Form of Law
Charles's law	pressure & moles	$\frac{\cancel{P_1}V_1}{\cancel{n_1}T_1}=\frac{\cancel{P_2}V_2}{\cancel{n_2}V_2}$	
Gay-Lussac's law			
Combined gas law			

Molar Mass and Density: Another Ideal Gas Law Derivation

In the mole chapter we discussed a simple method for converting between molar mass, molar volume, and density. These conversions work nicely for any system at STP. We can expand on this relationship for non-STP situations using the ideal gas law.

We know that molar mass $= \frac{\text{mass}}{\text{moles}} = \frac{\text{m}}{\frac{PV}{RT}} = \frac{\text{m}}{} \times \frac{RT}{VP} = \frac{mRT}{VP}$

Since m/*V* is actually density, the equation can be written as $MM = \frac{dRT}{P}$

Some folks prefer to write the equation as the "kitty cat equation."

$$\text{molecular weight} = \text{molar mass} = MW = \frac{dRT}{P}$$

The nickname comes from MeoW for molecular weight. The "*dRT*" is what kitty cats put on the "*P*" in their litter boxes — just a little something to fall back on if your derivation fails you.

Quick Check

1. Solve problems 2 and 3 from the ideal gas law Practice Problems using the "kitty cat equation." Compare your answers.

8.2 Review Problems

1. Consider the following identical containers each filled with 1 mole of helium gas. Container one is rigid and cannot expand. The piston in container two can rise or drop to allow free expansion or contraction of the gas volume.

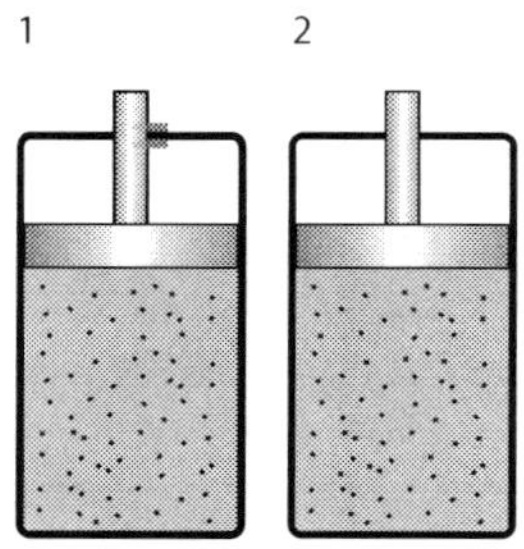

What is the effect on the (i) pressure and (ii) density of each sample if:

(a) The containers are dropped into an ice bath?

(b) Another mole of gas is injected through a rubber portion of the piston?
Be sure to support your answer with an explanation.

2. Consider the following flasks, each containing the same number of particles of the same gas at the same temperature. What simple gas law is depicted? How is the ratio of *PV*/*nT* held constant?

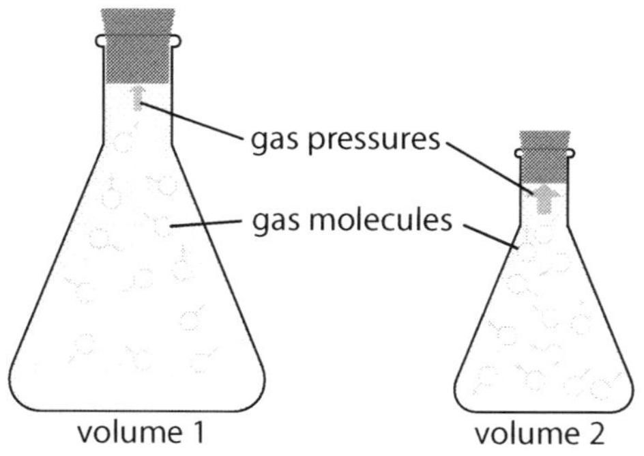

3. Consider the following flexible containers each containing the same number of particles of the same gas at the same pressure. What simple gas law is depicted? How is the ratio of *PV*/*nT* held constant?

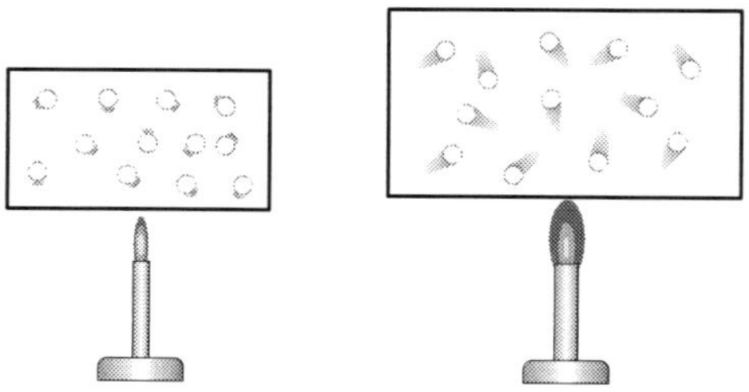

4. Consider the following container under two different conditions. From condition one to two, there are twice as many gas particles and the Kelvin temperature has been doubled. The volume remains constant. How is the ratio *PV*/*nT* maintained?

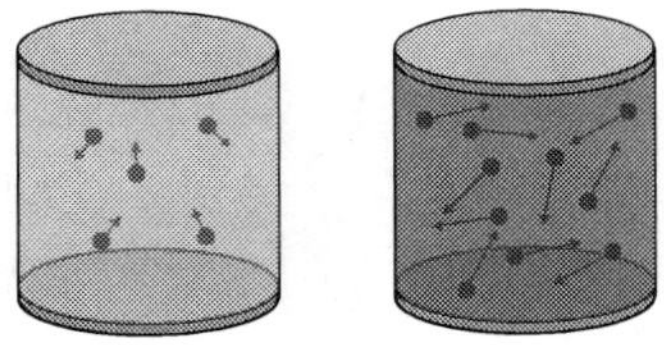

5. At 46°C, a sample of ammonia gas exerts a pressure of 4.8 atm. What is the pressure when the volume of the gas is reduced by 1/10 (0.10) of the original value when the temperature remains constant?

6. A 1.45 L sample of radon gas is kept in a sealed radiation-resistant container at 1.53 atm and 32°C. What will the pressure be if the temperature is lowered to 21.663°C?

7. A sample of polluted air is kept in a sealed container at 34.6°C and 31 psi. During winter, the temperature decreased to –15.672°C. At what temperature did the pressure in the container reach 26.75 psi?

8. A sample of the gas "bozone" occupies a volume of 53.1 L at 52°C and 675 torr. What volume will this gas occupy at STP?

9. A gas lecture cylinder is labeled to deliver 52.3 L of helium gas at room pressure. Assuming room pressure is 101.3 kPa, what is the pressure of the gas inside the cylinder when it arrives from the company fully sealed? The volume of the cylinder is 1.40 L.

10. A racing tire has a pressure of 34.8 psi at 15°C. Assuming the volume remains constant during the race, what is the new tire pressure when the car crosses the finish line and the tire's temperature has increased to 91°C?

11. A standard scuba tank holds a volume of 70.0 ft^3 of air under SATP conditions (25°C and 1.00 atm). What volume would this air occupy if released under the conditions a diver experiences under 20 m of water on the northwest coast while winter diving? This diver would experience temperatures of 6.5°C and a pressure of 315 kPa.

12. Jo Bob collects a sample of gas from the exhaust pipe of his sister's car. The sample contains 1.21×10^{23} molecules of gas at a pressure of 775 mm Hg and a temperature of 38°C. What is the volume of the gas sample?

13. A 44.8 L sample of gas weighs 128.2 g at a temperature of 273 K and a pressure of 760.0 torr. What is the molar mass of this gas?

14. A 7.50 g sample of lithium metal is dropped into 25.0 mL of 1.5 M hydrochloric acid. What volume of hydrogen gas would be evolved once the limiting reactant has been consumed? (The reaction is performed at SATP conditions; hence the temperature is 25.0°C and the pressure is 101.3 kPa.)

15. The propane tank by the science portable near the backfield of a typical school has a volume of 2210 L. Assuming the tank contains 3150 moles of propane gas, what is the pressure inside the tank on a nice warm day of 28°C?

16. Bonzo lives on the planet X, which has an atmospheric pressure of 164 kPa. A nice day on planet X has a temperature of –36°C. If Bonzo exhales 11.0 g of carbon dioxide, what is the volume of gas?

17. For an unknown gaseous *element*, 3.23 g occupy 5.60 L at 153°C and 101.3 kPa.

    (a) What is the molar mass of the element?

    (b) How many *atoms* are contained in 3.23 g of this element?

    (c) What is the identity of the mysterious unknown element?

8.3 Vapor and Partial Pressures

Warm Up

Use the box on the left to sketch a molecular representation of a sample of clean air (remember that air is a roughly 80:20 parts $N_2(g)$:$O_2(g)$ mixture). Use the box on the right to do the same for a sample of moist air. This box will show what happens when the "humidity is high."

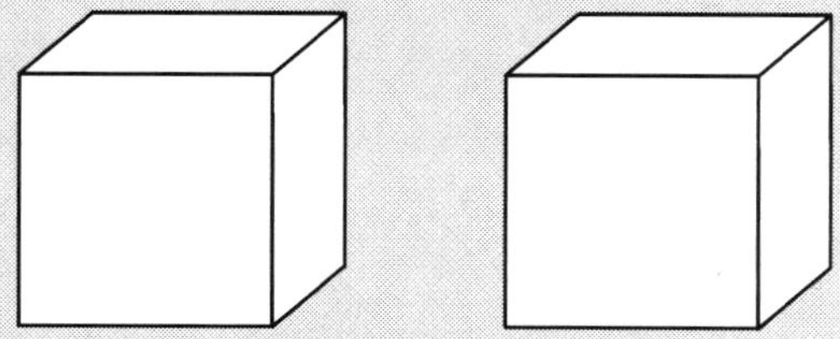

Keep Avogadro's hypothesis in mind as you do this. Equal volumes of gas should contain equal numbers of particles.

(a) Are these accurate representations of what the gas samples actually look like? Explain your answer.

(b) What percent of the pressure exerted by particles colliding with the walls of the box on the left is due to oxygen gas? How does the pressure exerted by oxygen (called the "partial pressure" of oxygen) in the box on the right compare with that in the box on the left? Explain.

(c) Why do meteorologists say the "barometer is falling" when it is about to rain?

Vapor Pressure

We know from everyday experience that puddles of water eventually evaporate after a rain even though the temperature is well below water's boiling point. At room temperature, the average kinetic energy of the water molecules is not sufficient for vaporization to take place, yet some of the molecules have enough energy to escape from the surface of the water and enter the gas phase (Figure 8.3.1). Hence, over a period of time, an entire puddle of water evaporates, even at room temperature.

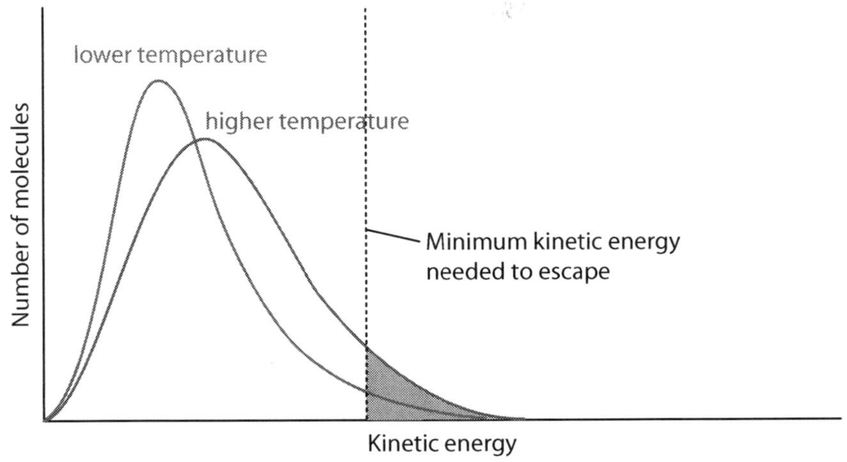

Figure 8.3.1 *There is a distribution of energies in any sample of matter. In the case of a liquid sample, some of the molecules have very little energy and some have enough to actually escape the surface of the liquid and become gaseous. The area under the curve to the right of the minimum "escape KE" represents the particles with enough energy to evaporate. The lower curve, shifted to the right, represents what would happen to the distribution at a higher temperature.*

English chemist and weather aficionado John Dalton found that even when water was placed in a sealed container, some of the liquid evaporated. This gaseous water exerted a pressure on the walls of the container. We now use the term "vapor" for the gaseous portion of a substance present above the liquid phase of that substance (Figure 8.3.2).

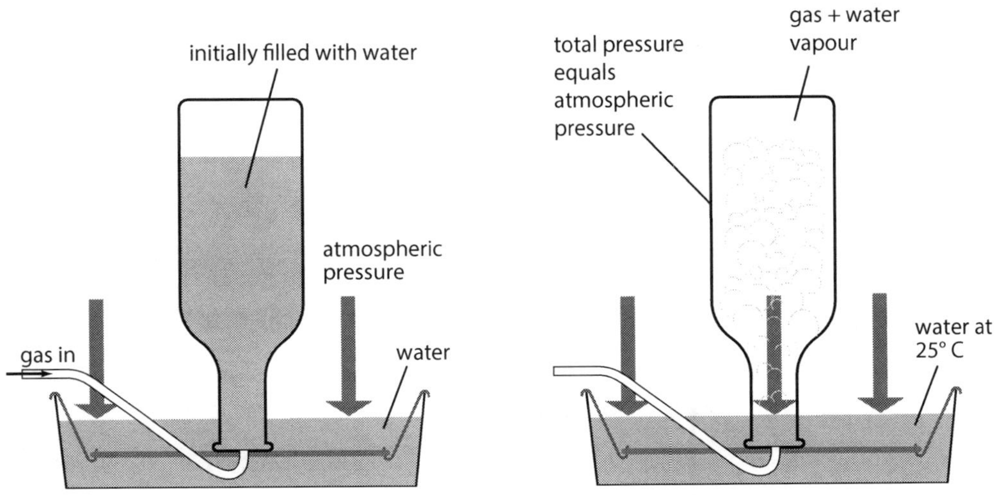

Figure 8.3.2 *Gas collected over water will contain some gaseous water due to water's vapor pressure.*

The pressure exerted by the vapor of a substance is known as the **vapor pressure** of the substance. Vapor pressure explains why we can smell some liquid substances such as nail polish remover and even some solids like black licorice.

The vapor pressure of a substance depends first, on its chemical structure and second, on the temperature of the substance. At a given temperature, there is a maximum value the vapor pressure can reach.

Vapor Pressure and Boiling Point

Every liquid possesses a vapor pressure. As shown in Table 8.3.1, the vapor pressure of a liquid, in this case water, increases with an increase in temperature. When the vapor pressure reaches atmospheric pressure, the liquid begins to boil.

Table 8.3.1 *As water temperature increases, so does vapor pressure.*

Temperature (°C)	Vapor Pressure (kPa)
0	0.61
20	2.34
40	7.37
60	19.9
80	47.3
100	101.3

From this information, we arrive at a definition for the boiling point of a liquid as the temperature at which its vapor pressure equals atmospheric pressure (Figure 8.3.3).

The boiling point of a substance is the temperature at which the substance's vapor pressure reaches atmospheric pressure.

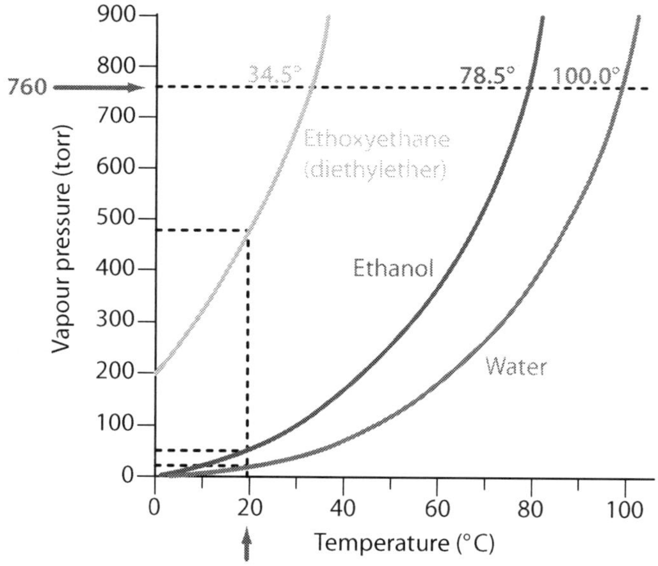

Figure 8.3.3 *The vapor pressure versus temperature graph for three different liquids. The boiling points may be read as the temperatures at which the liquids' vapor pressures reach 760 torr (or 760 mm Hg). This is atmospheric pressure at sea level. The vapor pressures can be read as the values on the y-axis at room temperature.*

Boiling and Atmospheric Pressure

It should follow from the information above that boiling points change with atmospheric pressure. As the atmospheric pressure decreases, boiling points become lower and lower. For example, the boiling point of water in Denver, Colorado, is 94°C. As a consequence, it takes longer to boil an egg at high altitudes, since the water is boiling at a lower temperature (Figure 8.3.4).

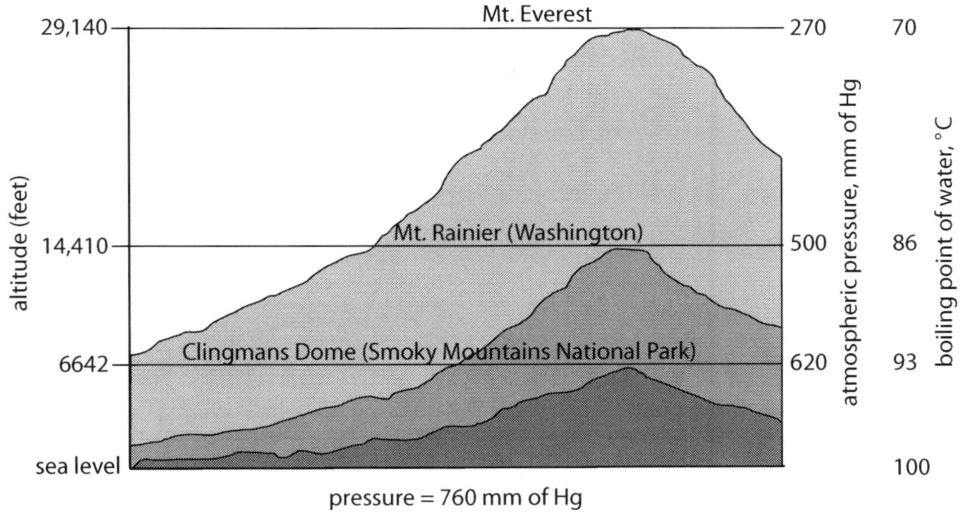

Figure 8.3.4 *The effect of altitude on atmospheric pressure and consequently on the boiling point of water. The boiling point drops 1 °C for every 300 m (or 1,000 ft) of altitude.*

Intermolecular Forces and Boiling Point

The reason different liquids have different boiling points is related to the attractive forces between the particles of different liquids. *Intermolecular forces* (*IMFs*), including *London dispersion forces*, *dipole-dipole forces,* and *hydrogen bonds,* were discussed in previous sections. Stronger IMFs result in fewer molecules (or atoms) having enough energy to overcome the attraction and escape into the gas phase.

Table 8.2.2 *Vapor Pressure (at 25°C) and Boiling Points for Various Liquids*

Liquid	Vapor Pressure (kPa at 25°C)	Boiling Point (°C)
Diethyl ether	57.9	34
Ethanol	5.6	78
Water	2.3	100
Mercury	0.024	357

Diethyl ether's (ethoxyethane's) bent shape gives it a slight polarity that produces dipole-dipole forces that hold its molecules together. Ethanol, like all alcohols, can hydrogen bond to its neighbors, but to a lesser extent than water can. The liquid metal, mercury, bonds to its neighboring atoms using the "sea of electrons" bonding model that holds its atoms tightly together, making its vapor pressure very small.

Liquids that have a high vapor pressure will evaporate very readily and are said to be **volatile**.

Quick Check

1. A "bell jar" is placed over a beaker partially filled with water.

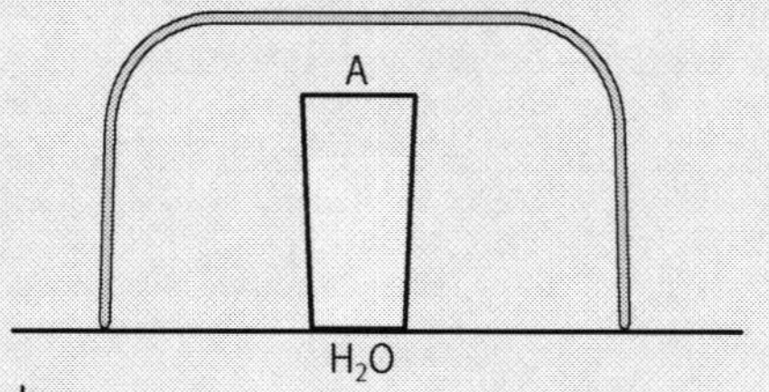

(a) What will happen to the height of the water in the beaker over time? Explain why.

(b) If the temperature of system is increased, how will the answer to part (a) change? Explain clearly.

(c) If the system is transported to the top of Mount Rainier in Washington where the atmospheric pressure is only 500 mm Hg, how will the answer to part (a) change?

2. A "bell jar" is placed over the two beakers shown. Acetone is a low polarity, volatile liquid. How will the vapor pressure of the water inside the bell jar compare with the vapor pressure of the acetone after one hour has passed? Explain your answer.

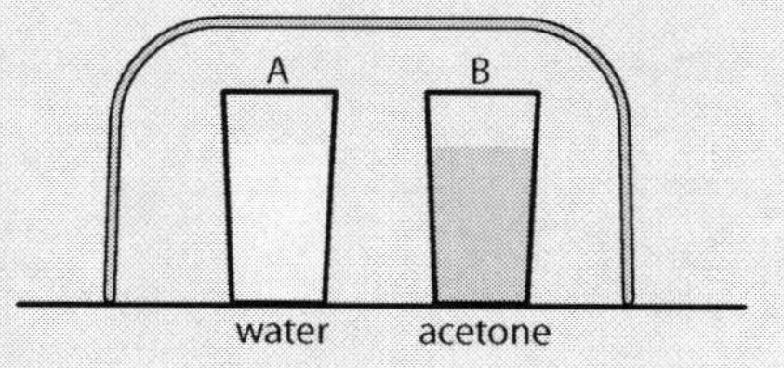

Dalton's Law of Partial Pressures

Dalton did a series of experiments in which he prepared various gases and collected them in a glass collection jar by displacing water from the jar using a pneumatic trough.

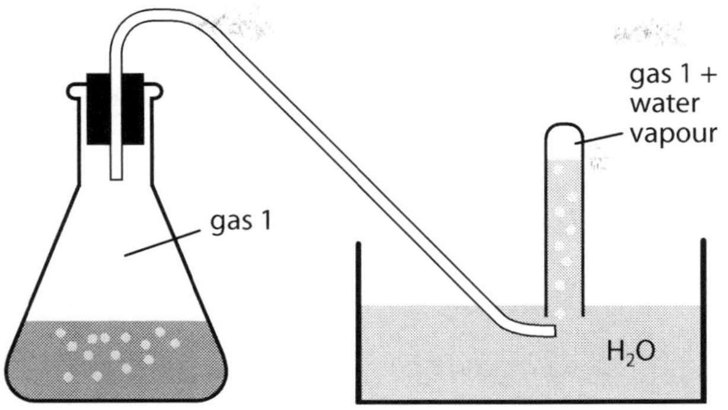

Figure 8.3.5 *Any gas collected over water is actually a mixture of the dry gas and water vapor.*

At first, Dalton assumed that by doing this, he obtained a jar full of the gas he was preparing and nothing else. Later he realized that he was wrong and that the jar must also contain a certain amount of water vapor mixed with the gas (Figure 8.3.5). Dalton realized at this point that each of these gases contributed to the total pressure in the jar. The contribution made by each gas is called its **partial pressure**. The result of these studies was **Dalton's law of partial pressures**.

> The total pressure of a mixture of gases is equal to the sum of the partial pressures of the component gases (Figure 8.3.6).

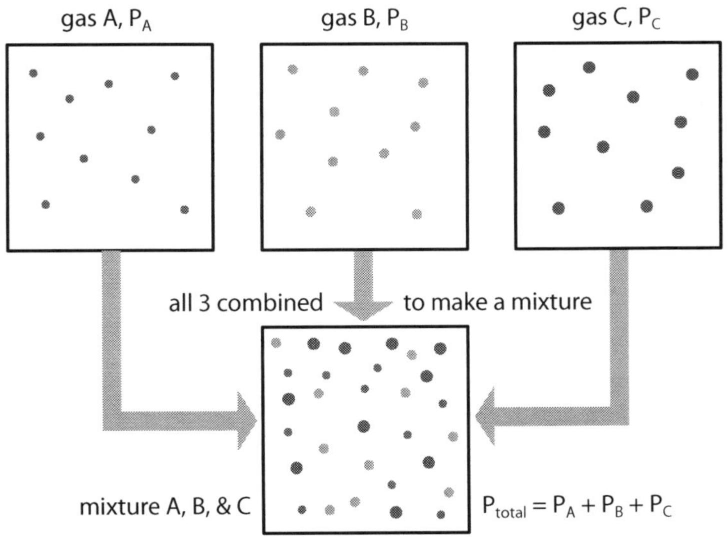

Figure 8.3.6 *When combined each individual gas continues to exert its own partial pressure producing a mixture of gases whose overall pressure is simply the sum of the individual partial pressures.*

Sample Problem — Dalton's Law of Partial Pressures

When a certain amount of nitrogen is introduced into a 1.0 L flask already containing oxygen, the pressure in the flask increases from 35 kPa to 77 kPa. Calculate the partial pressure of each gas in the final mixture.

What to Think About	How To Do It
1. Dalton's law of partial pressures says that the total pressure is the sum of the partial pressures.	The total pressure is 77 kPa and the P_{oxygen} gas was initially 35 kPa.
2. As the given pressure of 35 kPa is for oxygen, the difference must be due to the pressure of nitrogen.	The pressure of oxygen is given as the initial pressure. $P_{oxygen} = 35$ **kPa** The pressure of the nitrogen is the remaining pressure, or $P_{nitrogen} = 77 - 35 = 42$ **kPa**

Practice Problems — Dalton's Law of Partial Pressures

1. Two gases are combined and sealed in a 2.0 L container. The 3.0 L of argon gas and 1.0 L of xenon gas each exert 1.00 atm pressure on the walls of their container.

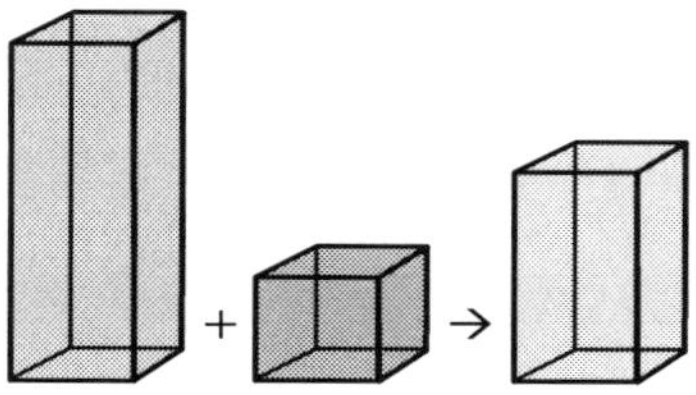

3 L Argon + 1 L Xe → 2 L mixture

   (a) Calculate the partial pressure of each gas in the 2.0 L container.

   (b) What is the total pressure in the 2.0 L container?

2. Examine the labeled system below. Assume all three valves are opened and the gases diffuse throughout the system and equilibrate. What is the total pressure in the system?

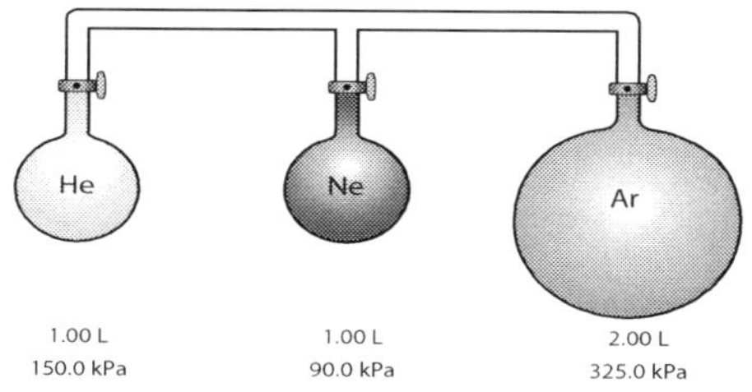

Collecting Gas Over Water: The Partial Pressure of Water Vapour

Returning to the production of gases in the laboratory, if we perform calculations involving the pressure or volume of gas formed in the lab, we must correct for the water vapor present. We do this by subtracting the vapor pressure of water from the pressure of the wet gas. The vapor pressure of water at various temperatures can be found in reference tables.

Sample Problem — The Partial Pressure of Water Vapor

A student performs an experiment in which she prepares hydrogen gas by reacting hydrochloric acid with zinc metal. After collecting 250.0 mL of the gas by displacement of water from a gas collection jar over a pneumatic trough, the student equilibrates the system to an atmospheric pressure of 99.2 kPa and the lab temperature of 24°C. Given that the vapor pressure of water is 2.98 kPa at 24°C, what mass of hydrogen has she collected?

What To Think About	How To Do It
1. The pressure of the *dry* hydrogen must be determined by subtracting the partial pressure of water vapor at the appropriate temperature from the total pressure in the collection jar.	$P_{total} = 99.2$ kPa and $P_{water\ vapor} = 2.98$ kPa, thus $P_{dry\ hydrogen} = 99.2 - 2.98 = 96.22$ kPa
2. As each gas expands individually to fill the entire container, the volume of the dry gas is the same as that of the container. This volume, the dry gas pressure and the temperature can be used to calculate the moles of gas present using the ideal gas law.	$PV = nRT$ and $24°C \times \frac{1\ K}{1°C} + 273\ K = 297\ K$ hence, $n = \frac{PV}{RT} = \frac{96.22\ kPa \times 0.2500\ L}{8.31\ \frac{L \cdot kPa}{mol \cdot K} \times 297\ K}$ $= 0.0097465$ mol
3. The mass of hydrogen can be determined from the moles using the molar mass of diatomic hydrogen gas.	$0.0097465\ mol \times \frac{2.0\ g\ H_2}{mol}$ $= 0.020$ g (2 sig figs)

Practice Problems — The Partial Pressure of Water Vapor

1. A 0.65 g sample of powered zinc metal reacts completely in sulfuric acid to produce zinc sulfate and hydrogen gas. The gas is collected over water as shown in the accompanying diagram. Assuming the pressure in the laboratory is 101.3 kPa and the temperature of the gas sample is 20.0°C, what is the volume of the dry H_2 gas collected?

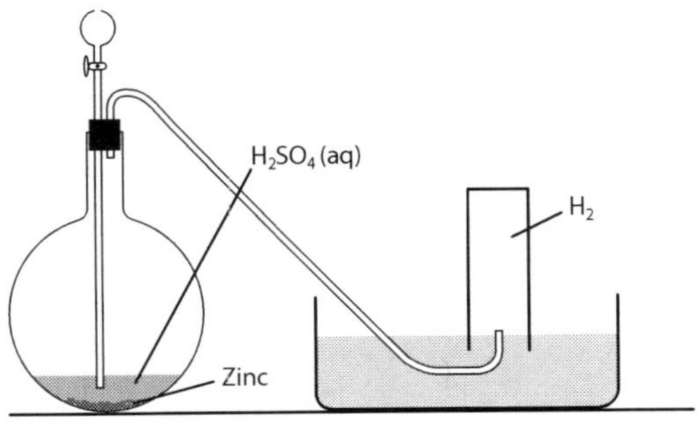

Continued

Practice Problems — Continued

2. Nitrogen gas is collected over water at 25.0°C and 14.7 psi. Given that the vapor pressure of water is 23.8 mm Hg at this temperature, what total volume of gas must be collected to obtain 4.10 g of nitrogen?

The Calculation of Partial Pressures

We can derive a general formula which will allow calculation of the partial pressure of each gas present in a mixture of gases if the total pressure and the composition of the mixture are known. From the ideal gas law:

$P_{total}V = n_{total}RT$, so we can set up the following ratio:

$$\frac{P_{one\ component}V}{P_{total}V} = \frac{n_{one\ component}RT}{n_{total}RT}$$

Now by cancelling the constant values *V*, *R*, and *T*, we obtain:

$$\frac{P_{one\ component}}{P_{total}} = \frac{n_{one\ component}}{n_{total}}$$

Finally, this can be rearranged to give a new expression for the partial pressure of any one component in a mixture of gases:

$$P_{one\ component} = P_{total} \times \frac{n_{one\ component}}{n_{total}}$$

The fraction $\frac{n_{one\ component}}{n_{total}}$ is called the **mole fraction** of the component.

We can always check our answers for the partial pressures of each gas in a mixture by adding them together once they have been calculated. The overall sum should always equal the total pressure of the mixture.

Sample Problem — Calculating Partial Pressures

A technician injects 7.50 g of liquid nitrogen into a sealed glass bulb filled with 12.0 g of neon gas. The nitrogen vaporizes and fills the container to produce a total pressure of 1.40 atm. What is the partial pressure of each of the gases in the container?

What to Think About	How To Do It
1. The mole fraction of each gas is required to calculate its partial pressure. This requires the moles of each gas.	$7.50\text{ g } N_2 \times \frac{1\text{ mol}}{28.0\text{ g}} = 0.268\text{ mol}$ $12.0\text{ g Ne} \times \frac{1\text{ mol}}{20.0\text{ g}} = 0.600\text{ mol}$ $n_{total} = 0.268 + 0.600 = 0.868\text{ mol}$
2. The partial pressure of each gas is determined by multiplying the mole fraction of each gas by the total pressure.	$P_{nitrogen} = \frac{0.268\text{ mol}}{0.868\text{ mol}} \times 1.40\text{ atm}$ $= \mathbf{0.432\text{ atm}}$ $P_{neon} = \frac{0.600\text{ mol}}{0.868\text{ mol}} \times 1.40\text{ atm}$ $= \mathbf{0.968\text{ atm}}$
3. All figures should be carried through the entire calculation and only rounded at the end.	A quick check should show that the sum of each of the partial pressures equals the total pressure: $0.432 + 0.968 = 1.400\text{ atm}$

Practice Problems — Calculating Partial Pressures

1. A mixture of 0.50 mol of hydrogen and 0.25 mol of oxygen in a sealed flask has a total pressure of 6.0×10^1 kPa. Calculate the partial pressure exerted by each of the two gases.

2. A mixture of gases contains 5.00×10^{23} molecules of CO_2, 6.00 g of CH_4, and 0.300 mol of NH_3. The total pressure exerted by the gases is 80.0 kPa. What is the partial pressure of each gas? Hint: First change all the quantities given into moles.

8.3 Review Questions

1. Assume the total pressure of both gases depicted in the sealed container is 760.0 torr. What is the partial pressure of each of the component gases?

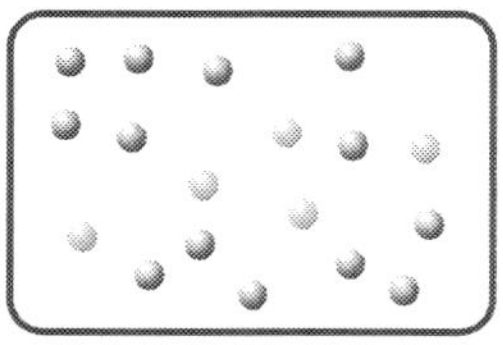

2. (a) Is the vapor pressure of water at 25°C at an altitude of 3000 m in the mountains less than, equal to, or more than the vapor pressure of water at sea level at 25°C?

   (b) The vapor pressure of a liquid, X at 25°C is equal to that of a liquid, Y at 50°C. If the sizes of molecules X and Y are essentially the same, which of the two liquids has the stronger intermolecular forces? Justify your choice.

   (c) Why does the rate of evaporation of a beaker of water inside a larger sealed container at a constant temperature decrease with time?

(3) A pressure cooker is essentially a large pot with a lid that can be sealed air tight.

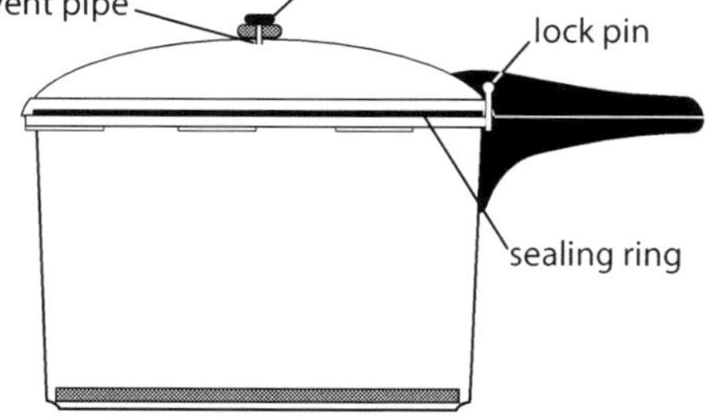

Explain how a pressure cooker is able to cook dried beans in a fraction of the time required to cook them in a normal pot.

4. A steel tank contains 40.0 g of helium, 180.0 g of oxygen, and 50.0 g of nitrogen gas. What is the partial pressure of each gas if the total pressure is 175 kPa?

5. If 2.00 g of carbon dioxide and 4.00 g of argon gas are placed into a 1.25 L container at 75°C, what is the total pressure?

6. A sealed glass bulb contains 20.0 g of oxygen, 30.0 g of nitrogen, and 40.0 g of argon gas. If the partial pressure of the oxygen gas is 66.0 kPa, what is the total pressure in the bulb?

7. Anaerobic bacteria can live without oxygen. A gas mixture designed to support such bacteria contains 3.0% hydrogen and 97.0% carbon dioxide gases by mass. If the total pressure is 1.00 atm, what is the partial pressure of each gas in the mixture?

8. The following system contains 20.0 psi each of gases A and B in the end bulbs with an evacuated bulb in the centre. Both stopcocks are opened at once. What is the new overall pressure in the system?

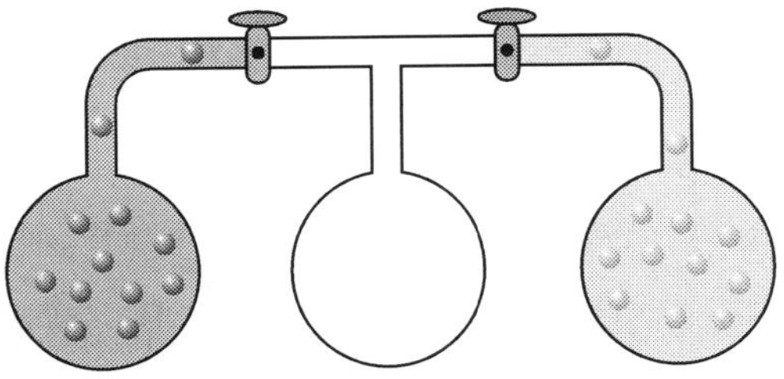

9. The following system is equilibrated with an atmospheric pressure of 1.00 atm in all parts. A thin layer of catalyst near the opened valve causes the gases to react to form ammonia. Give the partial pressures of each gas and the total pressure in the system when the reaction is complete.

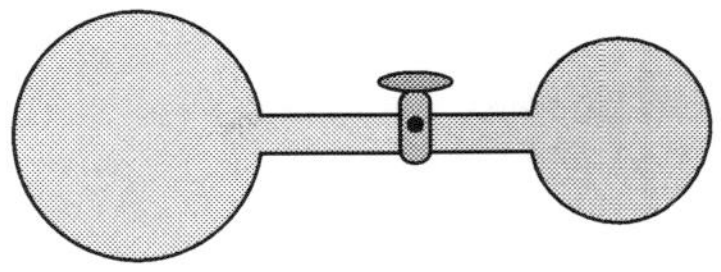

2.00 L H_2 1.00 L N_2

10. The penny coin was removed from circulation in Canada In February of 2014. The United States may soon do the same. The major reason for this move was the rising value of copper metal. When copper's value increased, pennies were produced as a zinc slug with a thin layer of copper plated over top. Zinc reacts readily with hydrochloric acid, while copper does not. A triangular file is used to nick the edge of a penny to expose the zinc slug below the layer of copper. The zinc reacts with the acid releasing bubbles from the nicked area until nothing remains but a thin shell of copper. If 0.948 L of hydrogen gas is collected over water at 20.0°C and a total pressure of 752 mm Hg, determine the percentage by mass of the copper in the 2.586 g penny.

11. A 239.4 mg sample of a drug designed to treat malaria was run through a series of reactions to convert all the nitrogen in the compound into $N_2(g)$. The gas collected over water at 23.8°C and a pressure of 755.5 torr had a volume of 18.66 mL. The vapor pressure of water at this temperature is 22.11 torr.

(a) Calculate the percent by mass of nitrogen in the sample.

(b) A 3.239 mg sample of the drug is combusted in air to produce 8.785 mg of $CO_2(g)$ and 2.160 mg of water vapor. Determine the percent by mass of carbon and hydrogen in the sample. Assume that any remaining element is oxygen and calculate the empirical formula.

(c) If the molar mass of the compound is 324.0 g/mol, what is the actual molecular formula of the drug?

12. Deep sea scuba divers breathe a gas mixture called heliox. Under very high pressures, the nitrogen in air enters the blood stream and causes a drunken type of state called nitrogen narcosis. The lack of nitrogen allows divers to descend to very deep depths without worrying about nitrogen toxicity. A 12.5 L scuba tank contains a helium-oxygen mixture containing 250.0 g of helium and 47.5 g of oxygen at 25°C. Calculate the partial pressure of each of the gases in the tank and determine the total pressure exerted by the heliox.

8.4 The Kinetic Molecular Theory and Real Gas Behavior

Warm Up

Assume the box shown here has a volume of 22.4 L and exists under standard temperature and pressure (STP) conditions. Draw a molecular representation of oxygen gas filling the box. List three ways in which your drawing fails to represent the actual situation.

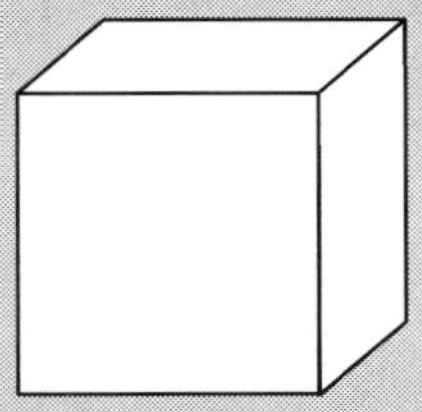

A Model for Gases — The Kinetic Molecular Theory

Your first introduction to chemistry in elementary school may have been a study of the kinetic molecular theory of matter (KMT). This theory states that matter is composed of particles such as molecules, atoms, or ions in continuous motion (Figure 8.4.1). In the solid state, the particles are close together and only vibrate. In a liquid, the particles are farther apart and move around. In a gas, the particles are much farther apart and move around freely in a random fashion. A mole of gas occupies 22.4 L, while a mole of most liquids has a volume of only 18 mL. In this section, we will take a closer look at how this theory applies to gases.

Figure 8.4.1 *The particles of a solid are packed tightly together. Liquid particles are farther apart and can move freely. A gas is virtually impossible to represent because the particles are no more than tiny points in space with less than 0.01% of the volume occupied by the actual gas molecules. There is a regular distribution of speeds for the molecules. Some are hardly moving while others have far more energy and are moving very quickly.*

When we use KMT to explain the behavior of gases, we make a number of assumptions about the size of the molecules, the way they behave, and what does and does not occur during particle collisions. Such assumptions are included in the *postulates* of the kinetic molecular theory.

The Postulates of the Kinetic Molecular Theory

1. The volume of gas particles can be assumed to be negligible relative to the space between them.
2. Gas particles are in constant motion. Gas particles colliding with the walls of their container produce pressure.
3. Gas particles neither attract nor repel one another.
4. The average kinetic energy of a gas sample is directly proportional to the temperature of the gas in Kelvin degrees.

Molecular Size

The size of individual gas particles is so small compared to the distance between them that at room temperature and standard atmospheric pressure more that 99.99% of the volume of any gas is actually empty space. Because of all this empty space, it is easy to compress a gas so that it occupies a smaller volume just by applying an external force.

Continuous Motion of Gas Particles

Individual gas particles are in perpetual, random, straight-line motion. During the course of this motion, they frequently collide with one another and then rebound in a perfectly elastic manner. The continuous random motion of gas particles prevents them from collecting in one area and causes them to be uniformly distributed throughout any container they are placed in. This movement is called "diffusion" and is a property of all gases. Diffusion also allows gases of different types to be mixed together to form solutions of any proportion.

Kinetic Energy of Gas Particles

Kinetic energy is the energy resulting from movement. The value of the kinetic energy of an object depends on its mass and velocity. This may be expressed mathematically as kinetic energy = $\frac{1}{2}mv^2$ where *m* is the mass and *v* is the velocity.

$$KE = 1/2mv^2$$

There is a *normal distribution of energies* in any sample of matter (Figure 8.4.2).

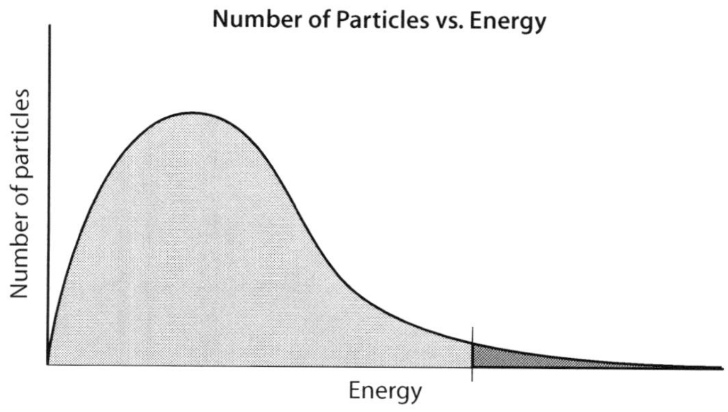

Figure 8.4.2 *Any gas sample contains a normal distribution of energies.*

At any given temperature, however, the molecules in all gases have the same *average* kinetic energy. This average kinetic energy is directly proportional to the Kelvin temperature.

$$KE = 3/2RT$$

Thus, if we have a sample of hydrogen gas and oxygen gas at the same temperature, both gases will have the same average kinetic energy. It follows that the average velocity of an oxygen molecule must be less than that of a hydrogen molecule since the mass of the oxygen is 16 times greater. The relatively high velocities of molecules of hydrogen and atoms of helium account for the fact that Earth's atmosphere contains very little of these two gases. They escaped from Earth's gravitational attraction many millions of years ago.

The Elasticity of Gas Particles

In any sample of gas, the particles are moving very quickly. Gas particles at room temperature or 25°C move at speeds in the order of 200 to 2000 m/s, which convert to 450 to 4500 miles per hour. As explained on the previous page, the speed is related to the mass of the gas particles (Figure 8.4.3).

As a result of this tremendous speed, gas particles collide with one another very frequently. One of the assumptions of the KMT is that no energy is lost during these collisions. In other words, the collisions are perfectly elastic. If this were not the case, the particles would gradually lose their kinetic energy. In fact, particles do transfer kinetic energy from one to another during collisions, but the average kinetic energy of all the particles present in a sample remains constant. Collisions between the gas particles and the walls of their container produce pressure (Figure 8.4.3).

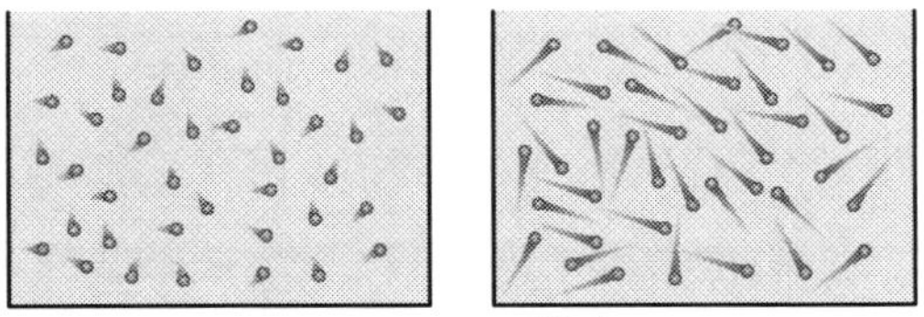

Figure 8.4.3 *The average velocity of gas particles is directly related to the Kelvin temperature of the sample. There is a normal distribution of energies in any gas sample with some particles barely moving while others move extremely quickly. Collisions between the particles are perfectly elastic and collisions with the walls of the container produce pressure. The representations above show the molecules much larger than they actually are. In reality, less than 0.01% of the volume of the container is occupied by gas particles.*

Quick Check

Use the postulates of the kinetic molecular theory to explain each of the following gas laws:

(a) Boyle's law

(b) Charles's law

(c) Gay-Lussac's law

(d) Dalton's law of partial pressures

Root Mean Square Velocity

The Kelvin temperature is a measure of the average kinetic energy (*KE*) of any sample of gas particles.

For a mole of any gas:

$$KE_{avg} = \frac{3}{2}RT \qquad \text{(I)}$$

where $R = 8.31$ J/K·mol

Also,

$$KE_{avg} = N_A(½m\overline{\mu}^2) \qquad \text{(II)}$$

where N_A = the number of particles in a mole (Avogadro's number)
m = the mass of the gas particle
$\overline{\mu}^2$ = average of the squares of the particle velocities

Thus, the average kinetic energy of one gas particle in a sample is equal to $½m\overline{\mu}^2$.

The average velocity of a gas particle is called the root mean square velocity and is written as:
$V_{rms} = \sqrt{\overline{\mu}^2}$

Rearranging equations (I) and (II) from above gives:

$$\frac{3}{2}RT = ½m\overline{\mu}^2$$

$$\mu_{rms} = \sqrt{\frac{3RT}{m}}$$

It is necessary to insert the molar mass in kg to allow proper unit analysis. One joule is equivalent to one $\frac{kg \cdot m^2}{s^2}$. The molar mass in kg cancels, leaving the square root of m^2/s^2, which gives an appropriate unit for velocity of m/s.

Sample Problem — Root Mean Square Velocity and Average Kinetic Energy

Calculate the root mean square velocity and the kinetic energy of carbon monoxide gas at 25°C.

What To Think About

1. The root mean square velocity equals the square root of 3RT/M, where *R* is 8.31 J/mol·K, *T* is in Kelvin degrees and *M* is the molar mass in kg.
2. Be sure to divide *before* taking the square root.
3. Unit analysis requires the substitution of $\frac{\text{kg}\cdot\text{m}^2}{\text{s}^2}$ for J and insertion of the molar mass in kg/mol.
4. The kinetic energy is simply 3/2*RT* where *R* = 8.31 J/mol·K and the temperature is in Kelvin degrees.

How To Do It

$$\mu_{rms} = \sqrt{\frac{3RT}{M}}$$

$$\mu_{rms} = \sqrt{\frac{3(8.31\ \text{J/mol}\cdot\text{K})(298\ \cancel{\text{K}})}{0.0028\ \cancel{\text{kg}}}}$$

$$\mu_{rms} = \sqrt{\frac{3\left(8.31\ \frac{\cancel{\text{kg}}\cdot\text{m}^2/\text{s}^2}{\cancel{\text{mol}\cdot\text{K}}}\right)(298\ \cancel{\text{K}})}{0.028\ \cancel{\text{kg/mol}}}}$$

$$= 515\ \text{m/s}$$

$$KE_{avg} = 3/2RT$$

$$= 3/2 \times 8.31\ \text{J/mol}\ \cancel{\text{K}} \times 298\ \cancel{\text{K}}$$

$$= 3710\ \text{J}$$

Practice Problems — Root Mean Square Velocity & Average Kinetic Energy

1. Calculate the root mean square velocity and the average kinetic energy of atoms of Ar gas at 25°C.

2. Calculate the root mean square velocity and the average kinetic energy of ozone molecules, O_3, high in the stratosphere where the temperature is –83°C.

Range of Velocities in a Gas Sample

In a real gas, there are large numbers of collisions between gas particles. When the lid is removed from a perfume bottle, it takes some time for the odor to move through the air. This is due to collisions occurring between the perfume vapor and the oxygen and nitrogen particles that make up most of the air. The average distance a particle travels between collisions in a sample of gas is called the **mean free path**. This distance is typically very small and in the range of 60 nanometers. The many collisions result in a wide range of velocities as particles collide and exchange kinetic energy. Figure 8.4.4 and Figure 8.4.6 illustrate the velocity distributions for various gases at STP conditions and a particular gas under changing conditions of temperature. The peak of each curve indicates the most common particle velocity.

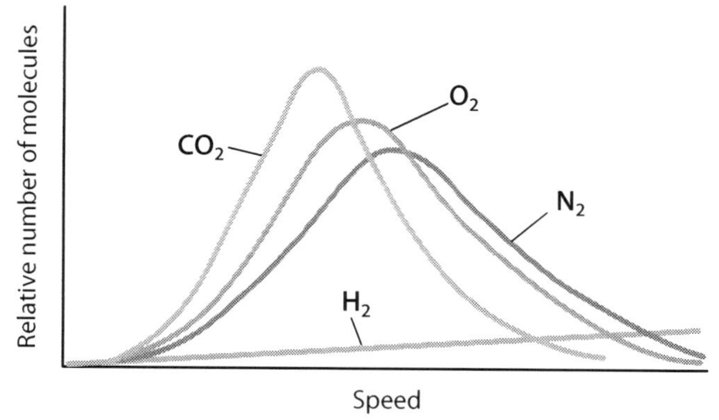

Figure 8.4.4 *The velocity distributions reflect the kinetic energy distribution for all the particles in samples of CO_2, O_2, N_2, and H_2 gas. While the average velocity of an oxygen molecule is 500 m/s, many O_2 particles have other velocities. As the mass of a particle increases, its average velocity decreases.*

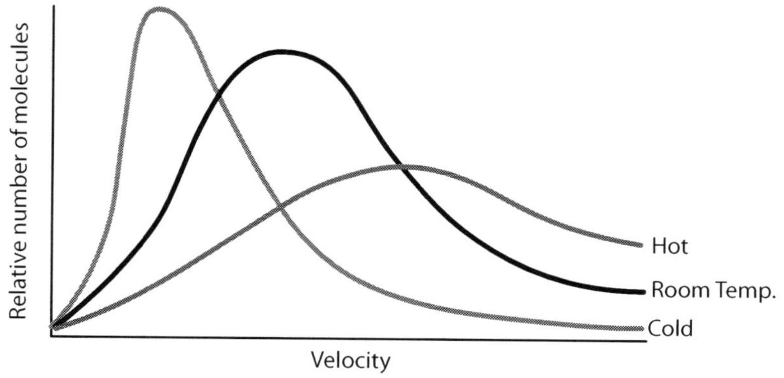

Figure 8.4.5 *Increasing the temperature of a gas sample broadens the entire distribution of velocities, causing the average velocity of a particle to increase.*

Effusion and Diffusion

Two important terms for describing gases are diffusion and effusion. The odor emitted from a perfume bottle takes several moments to permeate an entire room as the vapor bounces off oxygen and nitrogen molecules, zigzagging its way through the air in random straight-line motion. **Diffusion** is the term used to describe the mixing of one gas through another. The rate of diffusion is the rate of this mixing.

The rate of diffusion is calculated by directly relating the relative distance travelled by two types of molecules in the same period of time to their relative velocities. Both of these ratios are inversely related to the square root of the ratio of the molecules' masses.

$$\frac{\text{distance travelled by gas 1}}{\text{distance travelled by gas 2}} = \frac{\mu_{rms}\text{ for gas 1}}{\mu_{rms}\text{ for gas 2}} = \sqrt{\frac{m_2}{m_1}}$$

Effusion is the passage of a gas through a tiny orifice into an evacuated chamber. The rate of effusion measures the speed at which the gas is transferred into the chamber.

Figure 8.4.6 *Lighter gases move more quickly and effuse more rapidly than heavier ones, as predicted by the equation, KE = 1/2mv².*

Scottish chemist Thomas Graham developed Graham's law of effusion. It states the rate of effusion is inversely proportional to the square root of the mass of its particles.

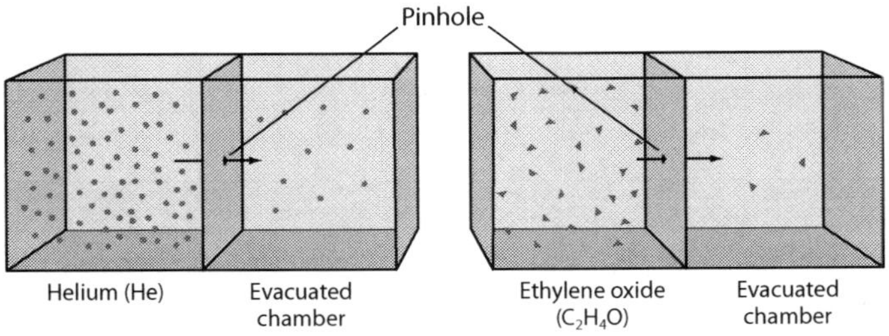

Figure 8.4.7 *The rate of effusion of a light gas such as helium is much faster than that of a more massive gas like ethylene oxide.*

Since the effusion rate for a gas depends directly on the average velocity of its particles, the rates of effusion of two gases at the same temperature may be compared by an equation similar to the one used for diffusion above.

$$\frac{\text{rate of effusion for gas 1}}{\text{rate of effusion for gas 2}} = \frac{\mu_{rms}\text{ for gas 1}}{\mu_{rms}\text{ for gas 2}} = \frac{\sqrt{M_1}}{\sqrt{M_2}} = \sqrt{\frac{M_2}{M_1}}$$

Sample Problem — Graham's Law

Carbon monoxide effuses at a rate that is 2.165 times faster than that of an unknown noble gas. Calculate the molar mass of the unknown gas and determine its identity.

What to Think About	How To Do It
1. Graham's law of effusion is required to solve this problem. 2. Identify the lighter gas as gas 1 so the effusion rate ratio is >1. This makes the algebra a little easier.	$\frac{\text{effusion Rate for gas 1}}{\text{effusion Rate for gas 2}} = \frac{\sqrt{M_2}}{\sqrt{M_1}}$ $\frac{\text{effusion Rate for gas 1}}{\text{effusion Rate for gas 2}} = \frac{\sqrt{M \text{ of X}}}{\sqrt{M \text{ of CO}}}$
3. Substitute 2.165 for the effusion rate ratio. The molar mass of CO may be substituted as 28.0 g/mol. It is not necessary to convert the molar mass to kg as the kilo prefix will cancel in the ratio form of the equation.	$2.165 = \frac{\sqrt{M \text{ of X}}}{\sqrt{28.0 \text{ g/mol}}}$ $\therefore \sqrt{M \text{ of X}} = 2.165(\sqrt{28.0 \text{ g/mol}})$ $= 11.4561 \text{ g/mol}$
4. Determine the identity of the noble gas by comparison of known molar masses of the noble gas family with the calculated molar mass.	$\therefore M \text{ of X} = 11.4561^2 = 131 \text{ g/mol}$ The molar mass matches that of **xenon gas.**

Practice Problems — Graham's Law

1. Calculate the ratio of the effusion rates of H_2 and UF_6. UF_6 is a gas used to produce fuel for nuclear reactors.

2. A popular experiment involves the determination of the distances travelled by NH_3(*g*) and HCl(*g*) from opposite ends of a glass tube. When the two gases, meet they form a visible white ring of NH_4Cl.

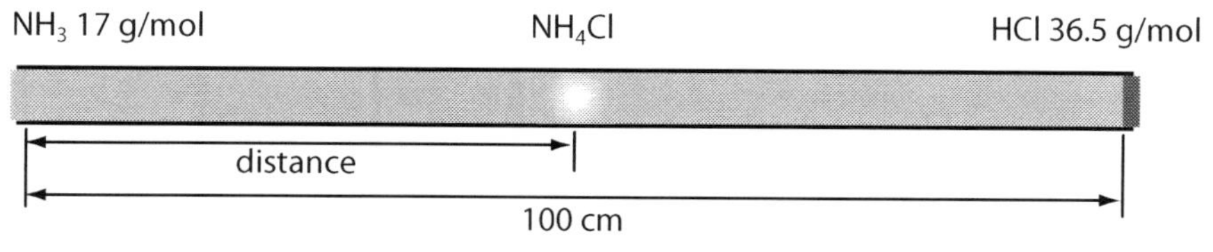

(a) Which end of the tube will be closer to the white ring of ammonium chloride? Justify your answer with an explanation.

Continued

Practice Problems — Continued

2. (b) Calculate the ratio of the distance traveled by $NH_3(g)$ to distance traveled by $HCl(g)$.

   (c) Give two factors that must be carefully controlled to ensure the expected result.

3. If the average velocity of a N_2 molecule is 475 m/s at 25°C, what is the average velocity of a He atom at 25°C?

The Effects of Volume and Intermolecular Forces on Real Gases

Measurement of the volume of one mole of most gases at STP results in a number that is *near, but seldom exactly equal to* 22.4 L. As pressure increases and temperature decreases, the volume of one mole of gas deviates even further from this value. In a previous section it was stated that gases behave most ideally when *pressure is low* and *temperature is high*. The reason for this is two-fold:

1. Real gases *do* have some volume, while ideal gases are assumed to have no volume and to exist as tiny points in space.
2. Real gases *exert some attractive forces* on their neighboring particles, while ideal gases are assumed to be completely independent of the gas particles that surround them.

In 1873, Johannes van der Waals modified the ideal gas law to fit the behavior of real gases. Van der Waals inserted two small correction factors. The first accounts for the *volume* of the gas particles themselves and the second corrects for the *IMFs* existing between gas particles. The Van der Waal's equation is really just a more complex form of the ideal gas law.

actual pressure ↓   **actual volume** ↓

$$\underbrace{P + a\left(\frac{n}{V}\right)^2}_{\text{ideal gas pressure}} \times \underbrace{(V - nb)}_{\text{ideal gas volume}} = nRT$$

The "correction factors" include an ***a* factor** and a ***b* factor**, which account for the attractive forces and the volume that real gases demonstrate. Every gas has its own unique values for *a* and *b*. Note that the units of *a* and *b* allow proper cancellation to produce units of pressure and volume respectively when substituted into the van der Waals equation.

Table 8.4.1 *Van der Waals Constants for Common Gases*

	a atm liters² / mole²	*b* liters/mole
N_2	1.39	0.0391
O_2	1.36	0.0318
CO	1.49	0.0399
CO_2	3.59	0.0427
CCl_4	20.4	0.138
HCl	3.67	0.408
H_2	0.244	0.0266
H_2O	5.64	0.0237
CH_4	2.25	0.0428
He	0.034	0.0237
Ne	0.211	0.0171
Ar	1.35	0.0322
Kr	2.32	0.0398
Xe	4.19	0.0511

The effect of IMF's and gas volume on real gas behavior becomes quite obvious when you examine a graph of *PV/nT* versus *P* for real gases (Figure 8.4.8). Since $PV = nRT$, *PV/nT* should equal *R*.

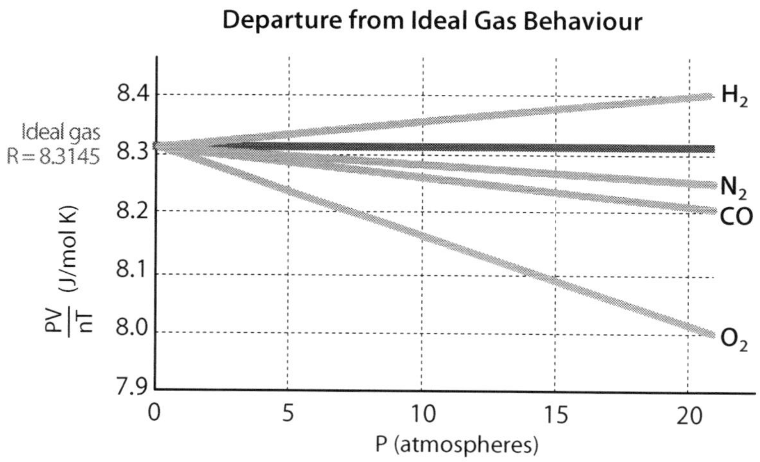

Figure 8.4.8 *As pressure increases, deviation from ideal behavior becomes more pronounced. The deviation is most noticeable for larger gases. This makes sense as larger gases have a greater volume and exert larger London dispersion forces on each other.*

The effect is further demonstrated with examination of a graph of *PV/RT* versus *P* for one mole of a gas at three different temperatures (Figure 8.4.9). Since $PV = nRT$, *PV/RT* should equal 1 for one mole of gas.

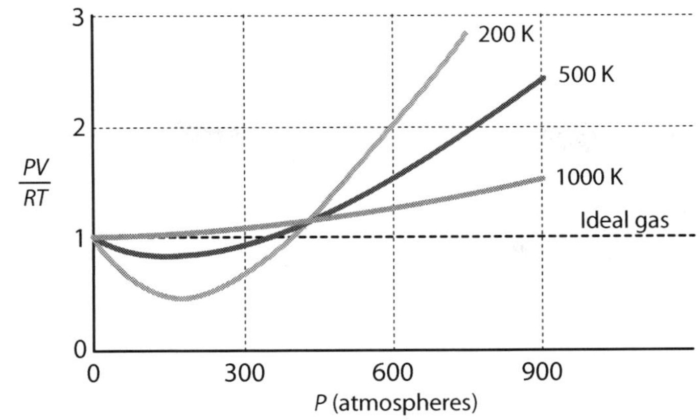

Figure 8.4.9 *As temperature decreases, deviation from ideal behavior becomes more pronounced. Gases behave most ideally when the temperature is high.*

Examination of the data in Table 8.4.1 and the graphs in Figure 8.4.8 and Figure 8.4.9 provides support for the statement that gases behave most ideally when pressure is low and temperature is high. Low pressure and high temperature make real gas volume and real gas attractive forces *less noticeable*.

Quick Check

1. Examine the graphs in Figure 8.4.8 and Figure 8.4.9.
   (a) Which particle deviates the most from ideal behavior? Give two reasons for this behavior.

   (b) What temperature provides the most ideal behavior? Explain.

2. Explain the general pattern for the values of *a* and *b* moving down the noble gas family. (A simple statement of the trend is *not* an adequate answer.)

3. Explain the same pattern moving from N_2 to CO_2 to CCl_4.

4. Explain the same pattern moving from N_2 to CO to HCl to H_2O.

8.4 Review Questions

1. Calculate the average kinetic energies of Ne(*g*) and N_2(*g*) at 298 K and 596 K. What pattern is noticeable between kinetic energy and temperature?

2. Calculate the root mean square velocities of Ne(*g*) and N_2(*g*) at 298 K and 596 K. What pattern is noticeable between root mean square velocities and temperature?

3. At 25°C and 1 atmosphere pressure, which of the following gases shows the greatest deviation from ideal behavior? The least? Give two reasons for your choice.
   CH_4 SO_2 O_2 H_2

4. Consider the van der Waals equation for real gases.
   (a) Which of the two molecules, H_2O or H_2S, has the higher value for *a* and which has the higher value for *b*? Explain.
   (b) One of the van der Waals constants can be correlated with the boiling point of a substance. Specify which constant and how it is related to the boiling point.

5. Five identical balloons are shown below. Each is filled to the same volume with the pure gases indicated at 25°C and 1.0 atmosphere pressure.

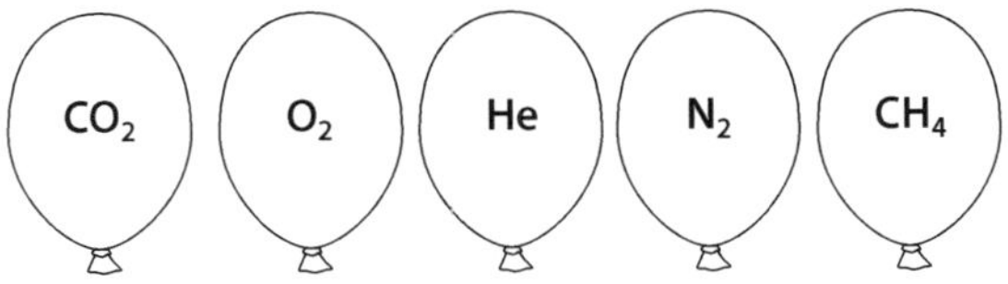

   (a) Which balloon contains the greatest mass of gas? Explain.

(b) Compare the average kinetic energies of the gas molecules in the balloons. Explain.

(c) Which balloon contains the gas that would be expected to deviate most from the behaviour of an ideal gas? Explain.

(d) Twelve hours after being filled, all the balloons have decreased in size. Predict which balloon will be the smallest. Explain your reasoning.

6. Consider a 5.0 L container of helium gas at STP. How will the following be affected by the changes given below?
   (a) kinetic energy

   (b) average velocity

   (c) frequency of collisions

   (i) The Kelvin temperature is increased by 100°C.

   (ii) The volume is halved.

   (iii) The number of moles of gas is doubled.

7. Calculate the root mean square velocity and the average kinetic energy of Br_2, Cl_2, and F_2. Which has the greatest:
   (a) velocity?

   (b) kinetic energy?

   (c) effusion rate?

8. A sample of neon effuses from a container in 38 s. The same amount of an unknown noble gas requires 77.5 s. What is the unknown gas?

9. The rate of effusion of an unknown gas is four times faster than oxygen gas. Calculate the molar mass and identify the gas.

10. A sample of helium takes 9.0 minutes to effuse into a 2.0 L evacuated container. How long would it take for a sample of oxygen gas to effuse into the same container?

11. Calculate the pressure exerted by 0.250 mol of CH_4 gas in a 0.500 L container at 25.0°C.

(a) Using the ideal gas law

(b) Using the van der Waals equation

(c) Explain the difference in the values.

12. (a) Repeat question 11 using a 50.0 L container.

(b) Explain the differences between the answers for the two questions.

Names, Formulas, and Charges of Some Common Ions

** Aqueous solutions are readily oxidized by air.*
*** Not stable in aqueous solution*

Positive Ions (Cations)

Al^{3+}	aluminum	Pb^{4+}	lead(IV), plumbic
NH_4^+	ammonium	Li^+	lithium
Ba^{2+}	barium	Mg^{2+}	magnesium
Ca^{2+}	calcium	Mn^{2+}	manganese(II), manganous
Cr^{2+}	chromium(II), chromous	Mn^{4+}	manganese(IV)
Cr^{3+}	chromium(III), chromic	Hg_2^{2+}	mercury(I)*, mercurous
Cu^+	copper(I)*, cuprous	Hg^{2+}	mercury(II), mercuric
Cu^{2+}	copper(II), cupric	K^+	potassium
H^+	hydrogen	Ag^+	silver
H_3O^+	hydronium	Na^+	sodium
Fe^{2+}	iron(II)*, ferrous	Sn^{2+}	tin(II)*, stannous
Fe^{3+}	iron(III), ferric	Sn^{4+}	tin(IV), stannic
Pb^{2+}	lead(II), plumbous	Zn^{2+}	zinc

Negative Ions (Anions)

Br^-	bromide	OH^-	hydroxide
CO_3^{2-}	carbonate	ClO^-	hypochlorite
ClO_3^-	chlorate	I^-	iodide
Cl^-	chloride	HPO_4^{2-}	monohydrogen phosphate
ClO_2^-	chlorite	NO_3^-	nitrate
CrO_4^{2-}	chromate	NO_2^-	nitrite
CN^-	cyanide	$C_2O_4^{2-}$	oxalate
$Cr_2O_7^{2-}$	dichromate	O^{2-}	oxide**
$H_2PO_4^-$	dihydrogen phosphate	ClO_4^-	perchlorate
CH_3COO^-	ethanoate, acetate	MnO_4^-	permanganate
F^-	fluoride	PO_4^{3-}	phosphate
HCO_3^-	hydrogen carbonate, bicarbonate	SO_4^{2-}	sulfate
$HC_2O_4^-$	hydrogen oxalate, binoxalate	S^{2-}	sulfide
HSO_4^-	hydrogen sulfate, bisulfate	SO_3^{2-}	sulfite
HS^-	hydrogen sulfide, bisulfide	SCN^-	thiocyanate
HSO_3^-	hydrogen sulfite, bisulfite		

Solubility of Common Compounds in Water

Note: *In this table, soluble means* > 0.1 mol/L at 25°C.

Negative Ions (Anions)	Positive Ions (Cations)	Solubility of Compounds
All	Alkali ions: Li^+, Na^+, K^+, Rb^+, Cs^+, Fr^+	Soluble
All	Hydrogen ion: H^+	Soluble
All	Ammonium ion: NH_4^+	Soluble
Nitrate: NO_3^-	All	Soluble
Chloride: Cl^- Or Bromide: Br^- Or Iodide: I^-	All others	Soluble
	Ag^+, Pb^{2+}, Cu^+	Low solubility
Sulfate: SO_4^{2-}	All others	Soluble
	Ag^+, Ca^{2+}, Sr^{2+}, Ba^{2+}, Pb^{2+}	Low solubility
Sulfide: S^{2-}	Alkali ions, H^+, NH_4^+, Be^{2+}, Mg^{2+}, Ca^{2+}, Sr^{2+}, Ba^{2+}	Soluble
	All others	Low solubility
Hydroxide: OH^-	Alkali ions, H^+, NH_4^+, Sr^{2+}	Soluble
	All others	Low solubility
Phosphate: PO_4^{3-} Or Carbonate: CO_3^{2-} Or Sulphite: SO_3^{2-}	Alkali ions, H^+, NH_4^+	Soluble
	All others	Low solubility

Answer Key

For the most current version of the answer key, scan the appropriate QR code with your mobile device. Or, go to edvantagescience.com, login and your course. The answer keys are posted in each chapter.

Chapter 1

Chapter 2

Chapter 3

Chapter 4

Chapter 5

Chapter 6

Chapter 7

Chapter 8

75106534R10242

Made in the USA
Columbia, SC
14 August 2017